THE COMPLETE ECOLOGY FACT BOOK

PHILIP NOBILE is a free lance writer and editor whose work has appeared in *The New York Times Magazine, Esquire, Commonweal, New York Review of Books* and *Book World.* He has edited several books and was formerly an editor of *Commonweal.*

JOHN DEEDY is Managing Editor of *Commonweal,* and, in addition to his published books, he writes for *The New York Times, New Republic, New York, The Critic* and other publications.

The Complete Ecology Fact Book

Edited by
Philip Nobile and John Deedy

ANCHOR BOOKS
Doubleday & Company, Inc.
GARDEN CITY, NEW YORK

The Complete Ecology Fact Book was published originally in a hardcover edition in 1972 by Doubleday & Company, Inc.

Anchor Edition: 1972

ACKNOWLEDGMENTS

The authors are grateful to Wes Barthelmes, a colleague (of J.D.) from *Worcester Telegram* (Mass.) days, who is now Special Assistant to Senator Frank Church of Idaho. Mr. Barthelmes provided invaluable research assistance.

We would also like to acknowledge the consummate latitude our wives and children allowed us during the days of this book.

Grateful acknowledgment is made to the following for permission to reprint their material:

Excerpt from *Murder in the Cathedral* by T. S. Eliot, copyright 1935 by Harcourt Brace Jovanovich, Inc; copyright 1963 by T. S. Eliot. Reprinted by permission of Harcourt Brace Jovanovich, Inc., and Faber and Faber, Ltd.

Charts: "How the American Paper Industry Performed" and "The Paper Industry's Capital Expenditures for Air and Water Pollution Control" reprinted by permission of the American Paper Institute.

"Laws of Ecology" from the Appendix to "Ecological Impact and Human Ecology" by Pierre Dansereau in the book *Future Environments of North America* edited by F. Fraser Darling and John P. Milton, copyright © 1966 by The Conservation Foundation, reprinted by permission of Doubleday & Company, Inc.

Figure 1: from *Population Geography* by E. Clark, 1965, reprinted by permission of Pergamon Press, Ltd., and John Bartholomew & Son, Ltd., Scotland.

Figure 17: from *Too Many* by Georg Borgstrom, copyright © 1969 by Georg Borgstrom, reprinted with permission of The Macmillan Company.

Figure 7: from *The Hungry Planet* by Georg Borgstrom, copyright © 1965 by Georg Borgstrom, reprinted with permission of The Macmillan Company.

Table 3: from "Population: Population Growth" by John V. Grauman. Reprinted with permission of the publisher from *The International Encyclopedia of the Social Sciences,* edited by David L. Sills, Vol. 12, p. 379. Copyright © 1968 by Crowell Collier and Macmillan, Inc.

Table 2-2: from *Principles of Demography* by Bogue, 1969, by permission of John Wiley & Sons, Inc.

"Plastics—Millions of Pounds" chart from 1968 article "Plastics: A 15 Year Outlook" reprinted by permission of *Modern Plastics* magazine, McGraw-Hill, Inc.

"Profile of Mauritius, United Kingdom" from *Population Bulletin,* Vol. 18, No. 5, 1966, and selected Bibliography from *Population Bulletin,* Vol. 25, No. 5, 1969, reprinted with the permission of the Population Reference Bureau, Inc.

Appendix on number of people who have lived on earth, text and illustration from *World Data Sheet,* 1970, reprinted with the permission of the Population Reference Bureau, Inc.

Figure 3-1: from *Uses of the Seas* edited by Edmund A. Gullion, copyright © 1968 by The American Assembly, Columbia University, New York. Reprinted by permission of Prentice-Hall, Inc., Englewood Cliffs, New Jersey.

Tables 57 and 58: from *The Study of Population* by Hauser and Duncan, copyright © 1959 by the University of Chicago Press, reprinted by permission of the publisher.

Excerpts from *NAC News and Pesticide Review,* Vol. 28, No. 3, reprinted by permission of the National Agricultural Chemicals Association.

Table page 13 from *Wildlife in Danger* by Fisher, Simon, Fraser, © IUCN, 1969, published by The Viking Press, Inc. Reprinted by permission of George Rainbird, Ltd.

"Orang Utan" from the *Red Data Book,* Vol. I, reprinted by permission of International Union for Conservation of Nature and Natural Resources.

Excerpt from "More of Less People" by Wayne H. Davis, first published in *The New Republic,* June 20, 1970. Reprinted by permission of Wayne H. Davis.

"World Climate Table" reproduced from *The Times Atlas of the World,* 1967, by kind permission of John Bartholomew & Son, Ltd., and Times Newspapers, Limited.

"Quality Classification of Tilled Land" from Doan's *World Balance Sheet* 1967, reproduced by permission of Harper & Row, Publishers.

"World Food Crop Said to Stagnate," October 3, 1970, dispatch, reprinted by permission of the Associated Press.

Map on World Calories, January 24, 1966, copyright © 1966 by The New York Times Company. Reprinted by permission.

Figures on protein 4-5 and 4-6: from *Population, Resources, Environment: Issues in Human Ecology* by Paul R. Ehrlich and Anne H. Ehrlich. W. H. Freeman & Company, copyright © 1970.

Table: on lifetimes of minerals from "Realities of Mineral Distribution by Preston Cloud, *Texas Quarterly,* 1969, Vol. II. Reprinted by permission of Preston Cloud.

Figure 54: from *Energy Resources,* Publication 1000-D, Committee on Natural Resources, National Academy of Sciences—National Research Council, Washington, D.C., 1962.

Table 2: "Air Pollutants with recognized or potential long-term effects on health at usual air-pollution levels" from *World Health Organization Technical Report Ser.* 1968, No. 406.

"Polluted Waters" EQ Index 1970, courtesy of *National Wildlife Magazine,* October-November 1970.

Excerpts by Shirley A. Briggs from the Appendix of *Since Silent Spring* by Frank Graham, first published in the *Atlantic Naturalist,* copyright © 1967 by Shirley A. Briggs. Used by permission of the author.

Lists of endangered forms from the *Red Data Book* and the list of extinct birds are used with permission of the International Union for Conservation of Nature and Natural Resources and the Rainbird Publishing Group, Ltd.

TO

Daniel and Philip Berrigan

Ecologists of a different sort

Contents

HOW TO READ THIS BOOK

Ecology is a science of myriad data. Unfortunately most of this data, scattered throughout hundreds of thousands of books, papers and official reports, remains unknown and unavailable to the nonspecialist. THE COMPLETE ECOLOGY FACT BOOK attempts to bring together such hard-to-find information in a simple, comprehensive compilation of ecology statistics. From population to pesticides, from endangered animals to solid-waste disposal, the editors have culled the most recent and pertinent ecological facts from United Nations, United States Government, private industry, foundation and individual sources.

Why an ecology fact book? Precisely because this is the one area that seems to have been missed in the present upsurge of ecological interest. We know the ecosystem is in jeopardy, but it is not so simple to lay one's hands on the proof. Thus we concentrated on the statistic—with just enough explanatory text to make the statistic meaningful.

The ecosystem and the stresses upon it are, of course, changing faster than man's ability to measure. Yesterday's fact may very well be out-of-date tomorrow. We have spent great effort, therefore, to obtain the latest counts. Since many statistics in the ecological sciences take years to gather, there should be no fear about the relevance of the data herein.

Despite the title of our book, we urge readers to return to the original sources cited if more information on a particular subject is desired. We hope we have at least provided an instant retrieval system of ecological data that narrows the gap between research and researcher.

Foreword

CONSERVATION—AN AMERICAN TRAGEDY

If earth is the same age as the oldest meteorites to be measured by radioactive methods, it is at least 4.5 billion years old. Man, in turn, has inhabited earth since the Pleistocene period, 500,000 to 1,000,000 years ago. It is a long relationship—and a one-sided one. Man has used the earth, exploited it, despoiled it. Now he is on the verge of overcrowding, exhausting, and rendering it unlivable, if not uninhabitable.

Until very recently it was only the rare individual, a Malthus, who worried about the earth and who sensed that earth—the good earth—could not endlessly yield up space, resources, riches, blessings without losing something of its own precious balances. It was only the rare individual, a Sanger, who worried that man would ever run out of room or the means with which to provide for the mouths which must be fed. And rarer still were those who foresaw that man, under the massive pressures of his own technological capabilities and his demands of comfort and affluence, might succeed in making earth a Gehenna rather than an Eden.

Yet precisely that is happening, and man has awakened from his centuries-long reverie to appreciate the fact. It is a slow and tardy awakening, however, for not all or even most of the damage done earth by man can ever be undone. On the other hand, it is not too late to reverse some trends and to head off greater and more calamitous damage. It is this prospect that gives encouragement to ecologists (too few yet in number) and impetus to the conservation movement.

No nation or people has abused its measure of earth more thoroughly than have Americans. In less than 200 years of nationhood, Americans have succeeded in doing to their land, air, and water what Europeans, barring serious but isolated examples, still have not done to theirs, despite Europe's larger population developments, tighter clusters, and infinitely longer use of its natural resources. This is not to say that Europe's ecological sensitivities are historically keener than those of America; it is just that Europeans have been slower to make of Europe, for whatever reasons, accidental or otherwise, the wasteland that Americans have made, almost systematically, of their geography. It is not to say, either, that Europeans will not eventually do to Europe what Americans have done to America. There is strong evidence that the former are already about this perverse task—in the Rhineland, in Italy and other places.

Americans have made America—the major part, at least—a jungle of waste, a sea of pollution; they have dirtied the air and denuded the forests; they have exterminated animal and plant species by the score. And until a relatively few years ago, until the administration of Theodore Roosevelt in fact, hardly anyone gave it a second thought. America was used as if its resources were a bottomless lode. They are not, and the fact that they are not has proved a sobering experience.

But the sobering-up process has been fuzzy and jumbled. Theodore Roosevelt, for instance, wrung his hands in the last years of the last century over the lot of the buffalo, but it was not always clear whether his concern derived from the fact that another great sport and test of man's skill—the buffalo hunt—was gone, or whether his was a more fundamental concern that man was wiping out another animal species. In the 1930s, there was some worry over land abuse; in the '40s over water availability; in the late '40s and '50s, over air pollution; and in the '60s, over chemical pesticides and solid wastes. But no one ever tied it all together. There was no focus, no overriding feeling of emergency, no awareness that the isolated abuses of the past decades could ever mass themselves into one giant threat to man and his environment.

Even in the '60s, the focus was slow in sharpening—primarily because vision was lacking at the highest levels. Arthur M. Schlesinger, Jr., crystallized a condition that was historic when he wrote of President John F. Kennedy: he "cared deeply about the loveliness of lakes and woods and mountains and detested the clutter and blight which increasingly defaced the landscape. But in the pressures of presidential life in the sixties, conservation had a rather low priority."[1] It seemed to be ever so. Presidents—e.g., the two Roosevelts, Lyndon Johnson, even Kennedy himself—could set aside natural-beauty areas for park lands, nature reservations, and national shrines, but no chief executive, at least through the Johnson Administration, made a point of marshaling interest in earth and nature into a comprehensive program on behalf of the environment.

It was a writer's document rather than any single ecological incident or governmental initiative that finally ignited American interest in ecology and propelled ecology-as-issue into the national consciousness. A large part of the credit for the interest that developed can be claimed by *The New Yorker* magazine, which, on May 16, 1959, inaugurated a feature aimed at alerting readers to the problems of the environment. The feature was in the form of bulletins tracing man's "progress" in

[1]*A Thousand Days,* Houghton Mifflin, Boston, 1965; p. 659.

making the planet uninhabitable. They were written by E. B. White and appeared under the heading, "These Precious Days." The historic importance of the feature, as it turned out, was in a response which it evoked from one individual: Rachel Carson. Miss Carson wrote to Mr. White suggesting that he do an extended article, not just bulletins, on environmental pollution. Mr. White responded by inviting Miss Carson to write the article herself. The result was three long essays that appeared in *The New Yorker* in 1962 and a best-selling book *Silent Spring,*[2] which hit the nation like a bombshell and at last started Americans thinking seriously about what was happening to the environment. "Rachel Carson pointed the way," *Newsweek* was to say in a cover story several years later.[3] "Rachel Carson started a revolution," stated the Washington Post.[4]

Like most revolutions, this one had its false starts, its detractors, its minimizers. Senator Gaylord Nelson (D.-Wis.) recalled some of this when eulogizing Miss Carson and her book before the Senate on April 14, 1969, the fifth anniversary of her death. As Senator Nelson made clear, her enormous sensitivities and research notwithstanding, Rachel Carson, if anything, understated the case; environmental pollution could not get any worse without putting man in the grips of a major catastrophe.

The thoughts planted by Rachel Carson matured slowly at first. Lyndon Johnson seemed to have strong conservation instincts (see Appendix F), but he was too tied down with the war in Vietnam to bring them effectively into play. Lady Bird Johnson took some initiative and helped promote a nationwide "Keep America Beautiful" campaign. This did not save the country from another Disneyland in Florida, however. Nor did it prevent the Disney people from pressing ahead with plans for a pseudo-Alpine resort, the ultimate in absurdities, in the Sierra Nevadas, near Sequoia National Park.[5] Congress did pass the Highway Beautification Act in 1965, making many roadside billboards illegal, but five years later only 334 had come down. There were still 800,000 billboards all over the American landscape, and Department of Transportation staffers were calculating that at the 1965–70 rate of removal, the department would be in the billboard removal business for 11,000 years.[6]

[2]Houghton Mifflin, Boston, 1962.

[3]"The Ravaged Environment," *Newsweek,* January 27, 1970.

[4]February 22, 1970.

[5]Conservationists fought the Alpine village scheme to the Supreme Court, and on February 22, 1971, the high court agreed to hear the case. Institutor of the action was the Sierra Club. On April 19, 1972, the court ruled 4-to-3 against the club.

[6]*Conservation News,* Vol. 35, No. 18, September 15, 1970, p. 2.

Yet unsatisfactory as these limited governmental programs may have been in terms of purpose and tangible results, they did help nourish a new American consciousness of the environment—our nation's, certainly, and, to an extent, the world's. It was a consciousness that became pronounced, then so insistent as to draw some landmark commitments from President Johnson's successor, Richard M. Nixon. The most important of these was the dedication, on paper at least, of the 1970s as the decade in which "America pays its debt to the past by reclaiming the purity of its air, its waters and our living environment."[7] Mr. Nixon articulated a philosophy and policy for a new ecological value system in his State of the Union Address of January 22, 1970 (see Appendix G), and in a special Message on the Environment, February 10, 1970 (see Appendix H). The latter was the most comprehensive statement ever made by an American President on the subject. More concretely, Mr. Nixon established the Environmental Protection Agency to co-ordinate the environmental interests of the government; he named a Council on Environmental Quality to advise and assist the White House on conservation questions; he signed a number of bills to control pollution and improve the ecological quality of life in America.

The impetus for this activity was external—from the public, directly and indirectly—fully as much as it was derived from the inner idealism of Richard Nixon and his administration. To put it another way, the Nixon Administration occupied the seat of authority at the time when public opinion on conservation coalesced, when concern for the environment had so altered that what was hitherto an avocation of elitists or "quirky" nature lovers had become a cause popular enough to include all classes and ages and groups, especially the young. To its credit, the Nixon Administration responded on the issue. Some critics tended to downgrade this response, holding that the Nixon Administration embraced ecology as a convenient defuser of protest and deflector of attention from the war in Indochina. This proposition can be defended, but the fact cannot be denied that the Nixon Administration did institute vital organizational steps for combating pollution and exploitation of the environment. Further, Mr. Nixon raised concern for world as well as national environmental problems. In his State of the World Message of February 25, 1971, he called for broad international controls over pollution, and insured American cooperation in the 1972 United Nations Stockholm Conference which met toward that end.

At the same time, however, the Nixon Administration's commitment has never seemed unequivocal. Time and again Mr. Nixon backed

[7] *The New York Times,* January 2, 1970, p. 1.

away from pollution-control deadlines which industry opposed. And on no less an occasion than the first observance of Earth Day—April 22, 1970—Mr. Nixon's then Secretary of the Interior, Walter J. Hickel, informed the public of Interior Department willingness to issue a right-of-way permit to a consortium of companies anxious to build an 800-mile oil pipeline across Alaska, a project strenuously opposed by conservationists. Then, early in 1971, after sending to the Congress a far-reaching program to regulate noise, surface and underground mining, power plant sites, ocean dumping and pesticides, Mr. Nixon turned around and "assured" officers of more than 200 major corporations that industry would not be made "scapegoats" in the drive for an improved environment. "The Government—this Administration, I can assure you—is not here to beat industry over the head," President Nixon told members of the National Industrial Pollution Control Council at a White House reception.[8] He was even more emphatic some months later. "I have been in countries that have no industrialization," Mr. Nixon said in a talk before members of the Economic Club of Detroit. "I have been in countries that have very few automobiles, and let me say I would rather live in the United States of America . . . . We are committed to cleaning up the air and cleaning up the water, but we are also committed to a strong economy and we are not going to allow the environmental issue to be [used] sometimes falsely and sometimes in a demagogic way basically to destroy the industrial system that made this country the great country that it is."[9] To many, notes such as these signaled that ecology was still mistress, not spouse, of government, that government's heart will be with ecology when ecology is as profitable as business.

The judgment may be tendentious—time will tell—but given the history of ecology, the pessimism is not out of place. The best intentions seem forever giving way to the pragmatics of profit and consumer demand when conservation enters the equation. Business and industry are the generators of the economy, and in a society like the United States which measures the "good life" in terms of the GNP, conservation has built-in disadvantages. Mr. Nixon's administrator of the Environmental Protection Agency, William D. Ruckelshaus, urges on business and industry the necessity of developing a new "environmental ethic."[10] It could help, of course, and business and industry are beginning to pay lip service to the idea. But their primary duties and obligations are still formed by responsibility to the stockholder. Until this changes, not much more is likely to change environmentally—at least not for the better in the United States.

[8]James M. Naughton in *The New York Times,* February 11, 1971, p. 1.

[9]Robert B. Semple, Jr., in *The New York Times,* September 24, 1971, p. 1.

[10]E. W. Kenworthy in *The New York Times, Week in Review,* February 14, 1971.

THE LAWS OF ECOLOGY

Twenty-seven basic propositions may be said to cover ecological formulae and comprise the body of the so-called Laws of Ecology. The propositions have taken shape over a number of years, and have been collated by Pierre Dansereau, head of the Department of Ecology at the New York Botanical Garden and Adjunct Professor of Botany at Columbia University.[1] Mr. Dansereau is credited with the authorship of several of the propositions and with the reformulation of others. Mr. Dansereau's compendium follows:

A. PHYSIOLOGY OF ECOTOPIC FITNESS (1–9)

1. *Law of the inoptimum.* No species encounters in any given habitat the optimum conditions for all of its functions.
2. *Law of aphasy.* "Organic evolution is slower than environmental change on the average, and hence migration occurs."
3. *Law of tolerance.* A species is confined, ecologically and geographically, by the extremes of environmental adversities that it can withstand.
4. *Law of valence.* In each part of its area, a given species shows a greater or lesser amplitude in ranging through various habitats (or communities); this is conditioned by its requirements and tolerances being satisfied or nearly overcome.
5. *Law of competition-cooperation.* Organisms of one or more species occupying the same site over a given period of time, use (and frequently reuse) the same resources through various sharing processes which allow a greater portion to the most efficient.
6. *Law of the continuum.* The gamut of ecological niches, in a regional unit, permits a gradual shift in the qualitative and quantitative composition and structure of communities.
7. *Law of cornering.* The environmental gradients upon which species and communities are ordained either steepen or smoothen at various times and places, thereby reducing utterly or broadening greatly that part of the ecological spectrum which offers the best opportunity to organisms of adequate valence.
8. *Law of persistence.* Many species, especially dominants of a community, are capable of surviving and maintaining their spatial position after their habitat and even the climate itself have ceased to favor full vitality.
9. *Law of evolutionary opportunity.* The present ecological success of a species is compounded of its geographical and ecological breadth, its population structure, and the nature of its harboring communities.

[1]Collated as an Appendix to an article, "Ecological Impact and Human Ecology," by Pierre Dansereau in the book *Future Environments of North America,* edited by F. Fraser Darling and John P. Milton; The Natural History Press, division of Doubleday & Company; New York, 1966, 1970.

B. STRATEGY OF COMMUNITY ADJUSTMENT (10–14)

10. *Law of ecesis.* The resources of an unoccupied environment will first be exploited by organisms with high tolerance and generally with low requirements.

11. *Law of succession.* The same site will not be indefinitely held by the same plant community, because the physiographic agents and the plants themselves induce changes in the whole environment, and these allow other plants heretofore unable to invade, but now more efficient, to displace the present occupants.

12. *Law of regional climax.* The processes of succession go through a shift of controls but are not indefinite, for they tend to an equilibrium that allows no further relay; the climatic-topographic-edaphic-biological balance of forces results in an ultimate pattern which shifts from region to region.

13. *Law of factorial control.* Although living beings react holocenotically (to all factors of the environment in their peculiar conjunction), there frequently occurs a discrepant factor which has controlling power through its excess or deficiency.

14. *Law of association segregation.* Associations of reduced composition and simplified structure have arisen during physiographic or climatic change and migration through the elimination of some species and the loss of ecological status of others.

C. REGIONAL CLIMATIC RESPONSE (15–20)

15. *Law of geoecological distribution.* "The specific topographical distribution (microdistribution) of an ecotypic plant species or of a plant community is a parallel function of its general geographical distribution (macrodistribution), since both are determined by the same ecological amplitudes and ultimately by uniform physiological requirements."

16. *Law of climatic stress.* It is at the level of exchange between the organism and the environment (microbiosphere) that the stress is felt which eventually cannot be overcome and which will establish a geographic boundary.

17. *Law of biological spectra.* Life-form distribution is a characteristic of regional floras which can be correlated to climatic conditions of the present as well as of the past.

18. *Law of vegetation regime.* Under a similar climate, in different parts of the world, a similar structural-physiognomic-functional response can be induced in the vegetation, irrespective of floristic affinities and/or historical connections.

19. *Law of zonal equivalence.* Where climatic gradients are essentially similar, the latitudinal and altitudinal zonation and cliseral shifts of plant formations also tend to be; where floristic history is essentially identical, plant communities will also be similar.

20. *Law of irreversibility.* Some resources (mineral, plant, or animal) do not renew themselves, because they are the result of a process (physical or biological) which has ceased to function in a particular habitat or landscape at the present time.

D. GEOGRAPHIC DISTRIBUTION (21–27)

21. *Law of specific integrity.* Since the lower taxa (species and subordinate units) cannot be polyphyletic, their presence in widely separated areas can be explained only by former continuity or by migration.

22. *Law of phylogenetic trends.* The relative geographical positions, within species (but more often genera and families), of primitive and advanced phylogenetic features are good indicators of the trends of migration.

23. *Law of migration.* Geographical migration is determined by population pressure and/or environmental change.

24. *Law of differential evolution.* Geographic and ecological barriers favor independent evolution, but the divergence of vicariant pairs is not necessarily proportionate to the gravity of the barrier or the duration of isolation.

25. *Law of availability.* The geographic distribution of plants and animals is limited in the first instance by their place and time of origin.

26. *Law of geological alternation.* Since the short revolutionary periods have a strong selective force upon the biota, highly differentiated life forms are more likely to develop during those times than during equable normal periods.

27. *Law of domestication.* Plants and animals whose selection has been more or less dominated by man are rarely able to survive without his continued protection.

THE COMPLETE ECOLOGY FACT BOOK

Clear the air! clean the sky! wash the wind! take stone from stone and wash them.
The land is foul, the water is foul . . .
I wander in a land of barren boughs

T. S. Eliot, *Murder in the Cathedral*

I Population

1. HISTORY

It is estimated that between 60 and 100 billion people have come into this world in the past 600,000 or more years (Box 1-1). Until very modern times, owing to the occupational hazards of keeping body and soul together in the hostile environment of pre-technological society, human population neither increased nor multiplied in startling fashion. If 200 to 300 million individuals were alive in A.D. 1 (as is commonly reckoned), there were only 500 million in 1650 and only one billion as late as 1850. Thus it took 18½ centuries to reach the billion mark in population. The next billion, however, was only eighty years away, for by 1930 the inhabitants of planet earth numbered two billion. In 1975, a mere forty-five years later, mankind will have doubled again to four billion (Figure 1-1). Plausible projections for the year 2000 point toward a population figure of at least 5½ billion and go as high as seven billion (see Part 5). What accounts for this runaway and perhaps, as some think, doomsday arithmetic?

The elementary explanation is a declining death rate. Prey to a thousand forms of fatality, from appendicitis to famine, from breach births to plagues, the life expectancy of earlier men was not a long one. Periodic depopulation was common. The Black Death (1348–50) probably wiped out a quarter of Europe. Natural disasters like floods, droughts and blights, and man-made disasters like war often destroyed, in addition to their primary victims, the delicate balance between food supply and demand. The casualties of war have been legion. But the rape of the Indians in Mexico and Peru after the European conquest, the way in which the American West was won and the forty million dead in World War II are special examples of the demographic evil that men do.

Prior to the eighteenth century, fantastically high infant mortality rates and all the rest kept the normal life span down to thirty years. But change was now just around the corner. The average rate of world population increase, less than .1 percent in ancient and medieval times, crept up to .3 percent by the beginning of the 1700s. Halfway through the nineteenth century the average annual increase was .6 percent and rose steadily, except for the disruptions of the two world wars, to the 2 percent rate of 1970 (Table 1-1).

BOX 1-1. The Number of People Who Have Lived on Earth

The statistical and general demographic assumptions used to determine the number of people who have ever been born were provided the Population Reference Bureau by J. Fletcher Wellemeyer, an independent manpower consultant, Washington, D.C., in consultation with Frank Lorimer, American University, Washington, D.C.

The estimate was made on the basis of three time periods:

Period	Number of years in period	Number of births per year at beginning of period	Number of births per year at end of period	Number of births in period
I. 600,000-6000 B.C.	594,000	"1"	250,000	12 billion
II. 6000 B.C.-A.D. 1650	7,650	250,000	25,000,000	42 billion
III. A.D. 1650-1962	312	25,000,000	110,000,000	23 billion
			Total	77 billion

To obtain the number of births at the beginning and end of these periods, certain assumptions were made regarding birth rates and the size of populations. It was assumed that at the beginning of the Neolithic era the population was five million and that the annual birth rate was 50 per thousand. The procedure assumes a smooth increase. The growth was undoubtedly irregular, but the estimates may fairly represent the net effect of the ups and downs.

By 1650, the annual number of births was estimated at 25 million, corresponding to a population of about 500 million. The 1962 world population of 3.05 billion, the number of births and birth rate of 36 per thousand are based on United Nations estimates.

The 600,000 years' duration of the Paleolithic era is based on the assumption that man-like types were then in existence but in very small numbers. Earlier dates have been given a few species by certain authorities, but some of these dates are questionable, and the earlier species may have been considerably less than man-like. The 600,000-year period seems a reasonable compromise between extreme possibilities.

Once the number of births at the dates indicated was determined, the total number of births for each period was calculated at a constant rate of increase for the period.

The estimated rates of increase differ sharply. For the long Paleolithic period, the average annual rate of increase was only 0.02 per thousand; during 6000 B.C. to A.D. 1650, it rose to 0.06; and during 1650-1962, it reached 4.35.

For the figures derived here, the following equation was used: $\Sigma B_t = \frac{B_o e^{rt}}{r}$

B_o is the number of births per year at the beginning of the period; t is the number of years in the period; e is the base of natural logarithms; and r is the annual rate of increase during the period.

The value of r is obtained by solving for r the equation $\frac{B_t}{B_o} = e^{rt}$

where B_o is the number of births the first year of the period, and B_t is the number of births the final year of the period.

Source: Population Bulletin, Vol. 18, No. 1.

NOTE: Nathan Keyfitz corrects the 77 billion sum to 69 billion in his article "How Many People Have Lived on the Earth," in Demography, Vol. III, pp. 581-82.

FIGURE 1-1. The Growth of Human Numbers

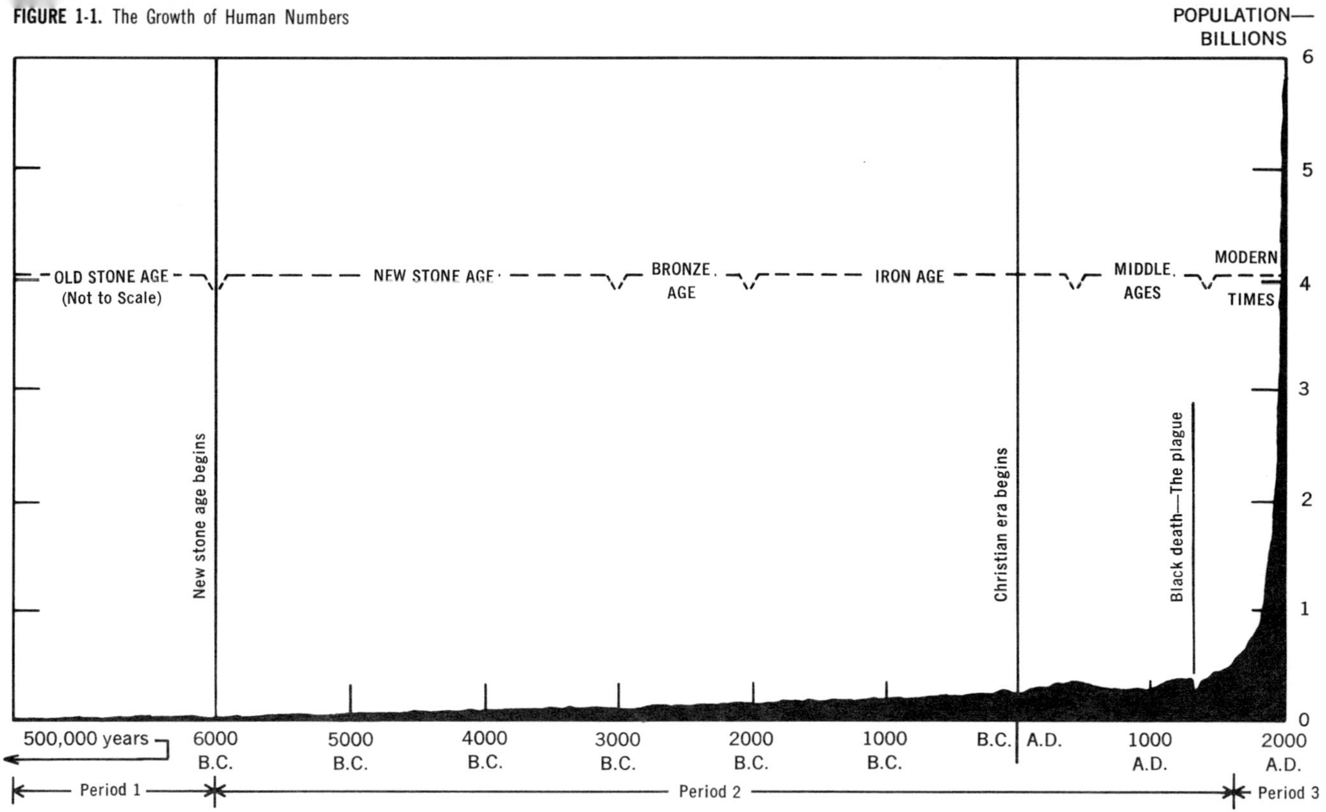

The major part of man's history has been spent in a slow unspectacular horizontal growth in population. Only in relatively recent times, as this chart illustrates, has population growth speeded up and become vertical in its direction. If the plotting of population growth appears out of proportion, it should be pointed out that a rendition to scale would extend the Old Stone Age baseline thirty five feet to the left. So the modern leap in population growth is actually several times more precipitous than it seems here

Source: Population Bulletin, Vol. 18, No. 1

TABLE 1-1. Average Annual Rates of World Population Growth (Percent), for Selected Periods, 1750-1960

	Asia[a]	Europe[a]	Africa	North America[b]	Latin America[c]	Oceania[d]	World total
1750-1800	0.5	0.6	–	3.0	1.1	–	0.4
1800-1850	0.4	0.7	–	3.1	1.1	–	0.5
1850-1900	0.4	0.8	0.5	2.3	1.3	2.2	0.6
1900-1950	0.8	0.6	1.2	1.4	1.9	1.6	0.9
1900-1910[e]	0.8	1.2	1.2	2.1	1.8	2.3	1.0
1910-1920[e]	0.3	0.2	0.6	1.4	1.8	1.6	0.4
1920-1930	1.0	0.9	1.4	1.5	1.8	1.7	1.1
1930-1940	1.1	0.7	1.5	0.7	2.0	1.0	1.1
1940-1950	1.0	−0.1[f]	1.5	1.4	2.2	1.4	0.9
1950-1960	1.9	1.0	2.1	1.8	2.7	2.1	1.8

[a] Includes portions of Soviet Union and Turkey, as traditionally assigned to Asia and Europe respectively.
[b] United States, Canada, Greenland, and minor areas.
[c] Caribbean, Middle and South America.
[d] Includes Hawaii.
[e] Author's rough conjecture.
[f] Net decrease due to heavy war losses.
Sources: Adapted from Carr-Saunders 1936 (estimates for 1750-1900); United Nations 1966 (estimates for 1920-1960); figures for 1910 are author's rough conjectures.
Source: Grauman, "Population Growth," in The International Encyclopedia of the Social Sciences, Vol. 12.

In the West, this advance can be traced to a confluence of factors. Agricultural output increased dramatically with the discovery of clover as a nitrogen-restoring agent for farm soil. Fields no longer had to lie fallow every third year. Large-scale farming and improvement of farming techniques also contributed to the lessening of food scarcities. Public and private efforts regarding sanitation reduced the occurrence of disease, especially those sicknesses carried by insects. Despite the human rigors of the Industrial Revolution, its effect on mortality was generally beneficent. Medicine was also on the verge of several major breakthroughs. At the dawn of the twentieth century, it seemed that the growth rate in the West had no place to go but up.

Curiously, it did not. Population rose, of course. Sinking death rates took care of that. But the 1970 growth rates of Europe and North America, as opposed to the 1900–10 rates, dropped from 1.2 to .8 percent in Europe and from 2.1 percent to 1.1 percent in North America. Why did this happen? Why should the beneficial effects of the industrial and technological revolutions reduce the birth, and hence the growth, rates of Western countries?

There is no scientific answer. In the absence of hard evidence, we must suppose that modern technology makes large families obsolete.

Removed from the land and the industries of the hearth, we no longer need to depend on the sweat of our children's brows. Our children, instead, depend upon us. In the new technocracy the young are, economically speaking, liabilities rather than assets. Thus Western growth rates have reverted to pre-1900 levels.

This demographic transition (from rising to falling growth rates) has rarely been repeated in other parts of the globe. While the death rates in the underdeveloped countries plummeted in the '20s and '30s following the introduction of DDT, modern drugs and various public health measures (thereby taming the scourges of malaria, yellow fever, smallpox, cholera, and other diseases), birth rates remained constant. This combination of circumstances (low death rates and high birth rates) is the reason for the ever expanding growth rates in Latin America, Asia and Africa—each of whose population rates have practically doubled since 1900. In fact, these last three continents taken together presently have a growth rate more than twice that of Europe, North America and the U.S.S.R. (2.4 to 1).

Translating these percentages into the index of doubling times, we learn that the average time it will take Latin America, Asia and Africa to double their populations is only twenty-eight years (as opposed to a seventy-year average for Europe, North America and the U.S.S.R.).

Consider what an alarming development this is. India, which can now scarcely cope with a population of a half billion or so, will have to contend with a billion in just twenty-seven years. In twenty-five years there will be twice as many Brazilians; in twenty-eight years twice as many Nigerians; in fifty years twice as many Chinese. Few non-Western cultures, Japan being the glaring exception, have achieved the demographic transition from high to low death rates with a concomitant reduction in birth rates. And given the age structure imbalance of the underdeveloped world (42 percent of its peoples under the age of fifteen) and the meager investments of funds and energy in birth control programs, nothing short of catastrophe will stay population growth before the year 2000.

2. POPULATION CHARACTERISTICS

Birth Rates

The birth rate is calculated according to the number of births per 1,000 inhabitants. The number of births in a given year is divided by the estimated population of the territory in question at the mid-point of that year. The result of this division is the *crude* birth rate, that is, a raw rate figure without reference to age, sex, and other relevant data concerning the composition of the population. Thus the crude rate, without proper interpretation, can be deceptive.

For example, the fact that Jordan has a birth rate of 47 per 100 and Denmark 15.8 as of 1970 does not mean that on the average every Jordanian couple is having three times as many children as their Danish counterpart. It may well mean, as is the case here, that Jordan has significantly more people in the childbearing years vis-à-vis the rest of its population than does Denmark. Therefore, Jordan's birth rate will be higher than Denmark's without indicating that the average young Jordanian family is necessarily larger than the average Danish family. There are just proportionally more young childbearing Jordanian families around.

The ratio between the sexes is an important factor in comparing the birth rates of different countries. Whenever the balance is seriously tipped toward either sex, there will be fewer marriages and hence fewer births.

War and migration are further deflections from the birth continuum. War disrupts normal domestic life, and the influx of, say, middle-aged immigrants into a country naturally drives down the crude birth rate.

A more accurate assessment of the true birth rate of a country can be had from the fertility rate—the number of live births per 1,000 women in their childbearing years (15–44). By eliminating the deviations of sex and age structure, the fertility rate is a more specific estimate of a country's birth situation than crude birth statistics.

Most developed countries have birth rates under 20. Ireland, Spain, Portugal, Iceland, Yugoslavia, New Zealand, Chile, Paraguay and Uruguay are the only exceptions, and none of these are over 30 save Uruguay (43), Paraguay (52) and Chile (100). The high rates of 30 and above, excepting the nations previously mentioned, are confined exclusively to the underdeveloped countries. This difference is illustrated in Map 1-1.

Death Rates

The death rate is computed in the same manner as the birth rate: the number of deaths in a year divided by the total population. The crude death rate is also subject to misunderstanding if taken at face value. It is important to remember that high and low death rates need not have any direct connection with existing conditions. A high death rate in one country does not automatically denote a less healthy environment than that of another country with a low death rate. Once again the age structure of the population must be figured into the equation. A wave of middle-aged immigrants could give a developed country a higher death rate than that of an underdeveloped country whose over-all health conditions are much worse.

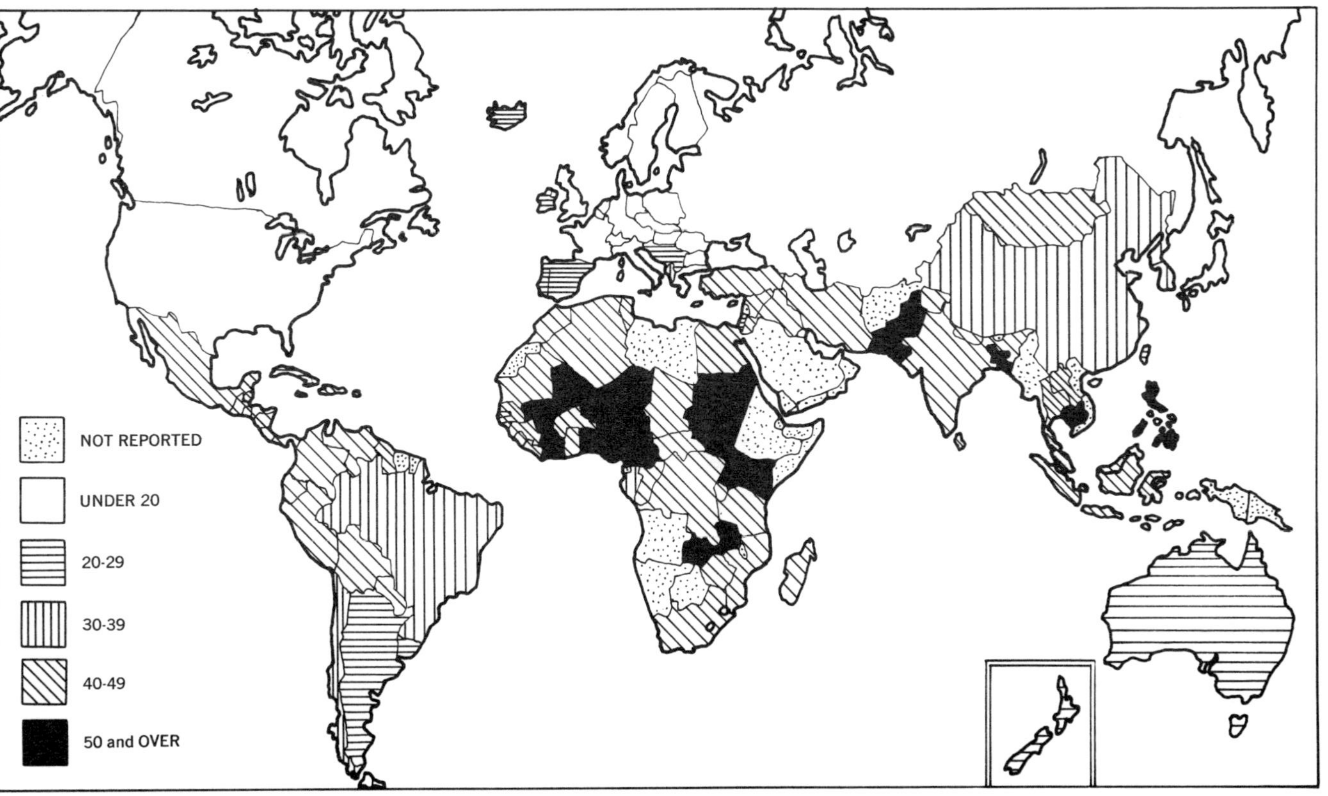

MAP 1-1. Major Areas and Regions by Birth Rate

In 1970, Costa Rica had a lower death rate (8 percent) than the United States (9 percent). But this anomaly persists only because Costa Rica's population contains so many young people—48 percent under the age of 15 as compared to a U.S. figure of 30 percent under 15.

Thus death rates, like birth rates, demand the qualification of additional data before their real meaning is understood.

Growth Rates

The growth rate of a population is expressed in terms of the percent of annual increase. This percentage is arrived at by the simple subtraction of the death rate from the birth rate (or vice versa to compute the rate of decline). The estimated world birth rate in 1970 was 34. The death rate 14. Therefore the growth rate equals

$$\frac{(34 - 14 = 20)}{1{,}000} \text{ or 2 percent.}$$

This 2 percent annual growth rate is considered "explosive" by demographers. The largest eruptions occur in the underdeveloped regions: Asia's average growth rate is 2.3, Africa's is 2.7 and Latin America's is 2.9. These high rates contrast with the relatively low rates of the industrialized West: North America grows at 1.2 percent, the U.S.S.R. at 1 and Europe at .8 percent. (See Table 1-2 for a scale of growth rates according to relative speed and doubling time.)

TABLE 1-2. Rating of the Levels of Population Growth and the Number of Years Required for the Population to Double in Size

Rating	Annual rate of growth	Number of years required for the population to double in size
Stationary population	No growth	....
Slow growth	less than 0.5 percent	more than 139 years
Moderate growth	0.5 to 1.0 percent	139 to 70 years
Rapid growth	1.0 to 1.5 percent	70 to 47 years
Very rapid growth	1.5 to 2.0 percent	47 to 35 years
"Explosive" growth	2.0 to 2.5 percent	35 to 28 years
"Explosive" growth	2.5 to 3.0 percent	28 to 23 years
"Explosive" growth	3.0 to 3.5 percent	23 to 20 years
"Explosive" growth	3.5 to 4.0 percent	20 to 18 years

Source: Bogue, Principles of Demography, John Wiley and Sons, 1969.

Doubling Time

Doubling time is an arbitrary but simplified means of fathoming population growth. The 2 percent annual growth rate for 1970 seems

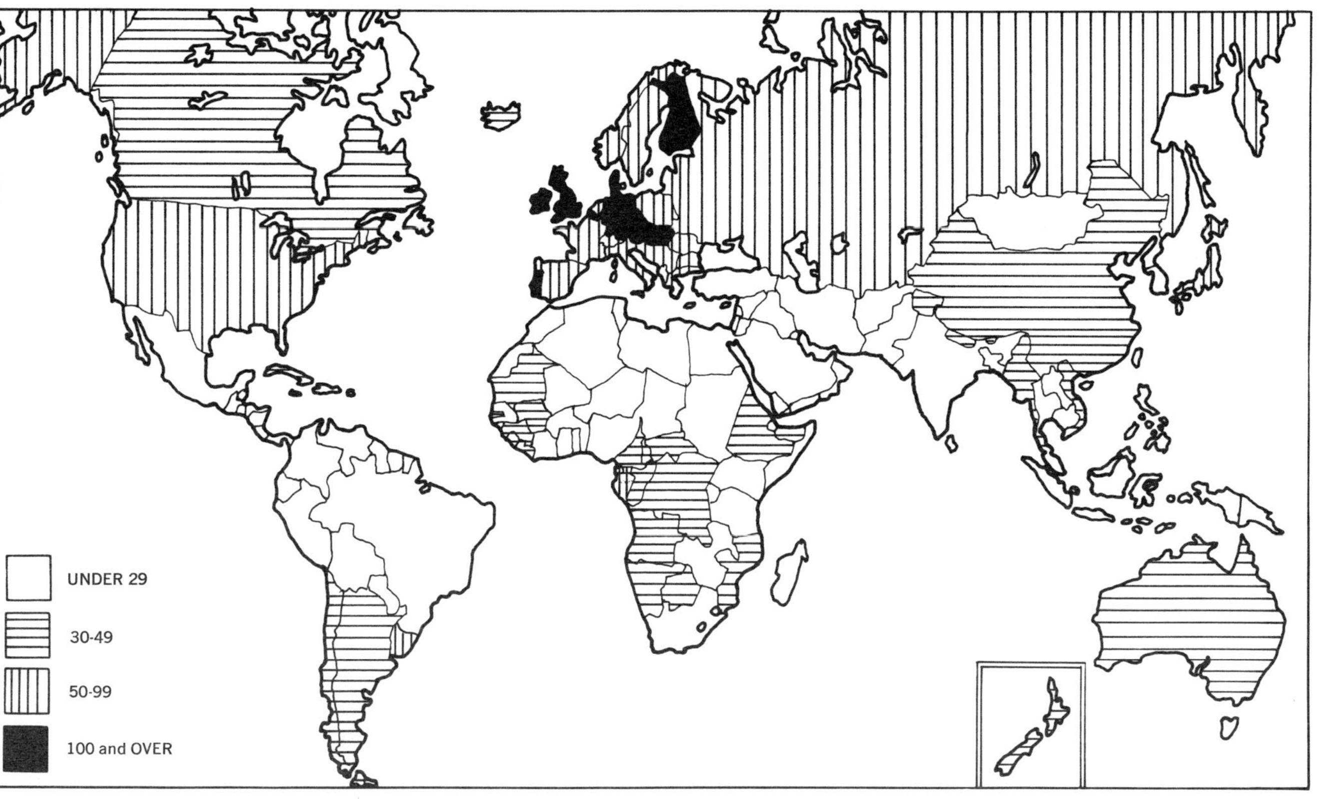

MAP 1-2. Major Areas and Regions by Doubling Time

quite within reason until you realize that this apparently innocuous increment carried on each year for the next thirty-five years spells a doubling of our present population. People, like money, increase at compound interest rates. The children of parents have their own children just as the interest on principle earns its own interest when compounded. Thus a population of 1,000 (or $1,000) which grows annually at 2 percent compound interest will double in thirty-five years.

TABLE 1-3. Doubling Times

Date	Estimated world population	Time for population to double
A.D. 1	200-300 million	1,650 years
A.D. 1650	500 million	200 years
A.D. 1850	1,000 million (1 billion)	80 years
A.D. 1930	2,000 million (2 billion)	45 years
A.D. 1975	4,000 million (4 billion)	35-37 years

Infant Mortality Rates

The infant mortality rate is calculated according to the number of deaths per 1,000 live births of children under one year. Since infants are an especially isolated and stable sample of the population, their mortality rate is an excellent gauge of comparative health conditions. An international breakdown shows a wide discrepancy between developed and underdeveloped nations. While no Western European country (Portugal excepted) has an infant mortality rate of over 35 per 1,000 (the majority has a rate of under 20), not a single major African country has a rate of less than 100. Asian statistics are scanty, but Turkey, India, Pakistan, Indonesia and Cambodia record infant mortality rates of over 100. And so do Brazil and Chile in South America. Of all the underdeveloped nations, only Formosa (21), Singapore (25), Jamaica (30) and Kuwait (31), none of whom are underdeveloped in the typical fashion and all of whom have benefited from unusual amounts of Western aid, have infant mortality rates comparable to those in highly developed countries.

That the populations of Asia, Africa and South America can still grow at twice the rate of Europe, the U.S. and the U.S.S.R. despite such staggering infant mortality rates is a sobering demographic fact.

Population Structure

National populations are not just indiscriminate conglomerations of people. Rather each population exhibits a unique demographic profile. The age structure tells what percentage of a population belongs to different age groups. Since this structure depends on an interaction between birth and death rates, we can categorize certain countries according to basic structure types.

Those underdeveloped countries like Mauritius (Figure 1-2) with high birth rates and declining death rates will have a large percentage of youthful population. Owing to this increasing body of potential child producers, such profiles tend to be self-perpetuating. Barring instant and miraculously effective birth control programs or natural calamities, a proportionally young population is a rapidly expanding population.

A developed Western nation like Britain (Figure 1-3), which has had low birth and death rates for many generations, will display an evenly distributed age pattern resembling a rectangle rather than a triangle.

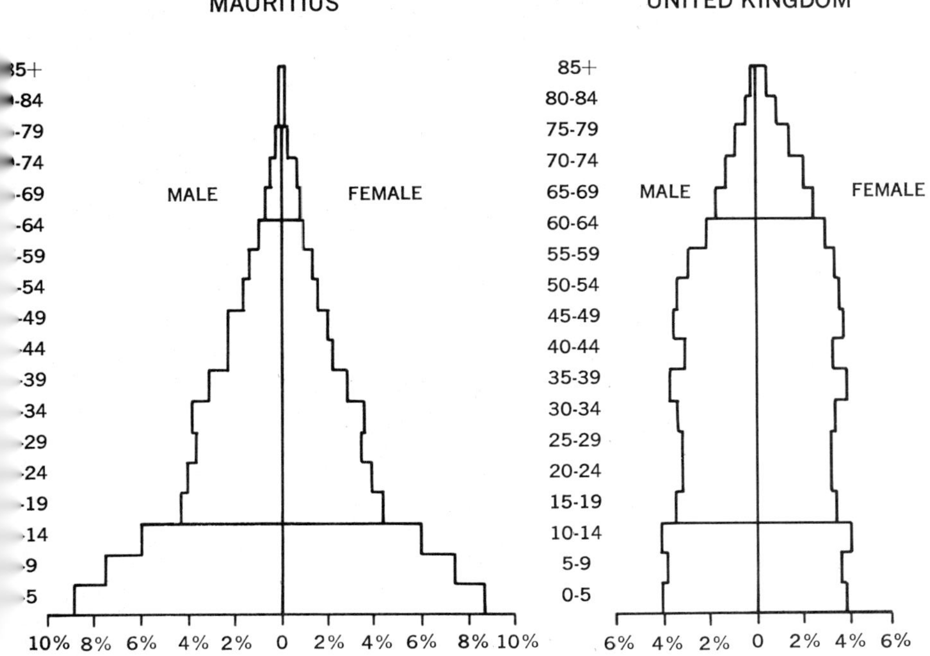

FIGURE 1-2. Age Structure of Mauritius in 1959

Source: Population Bulletin, Vol. 18, No. 5, 1966

FIGURE 1-3. Age Structure of the United Kingdom in 1960

Source: Population Bulletin, Vol. 18, No. 5, 1966

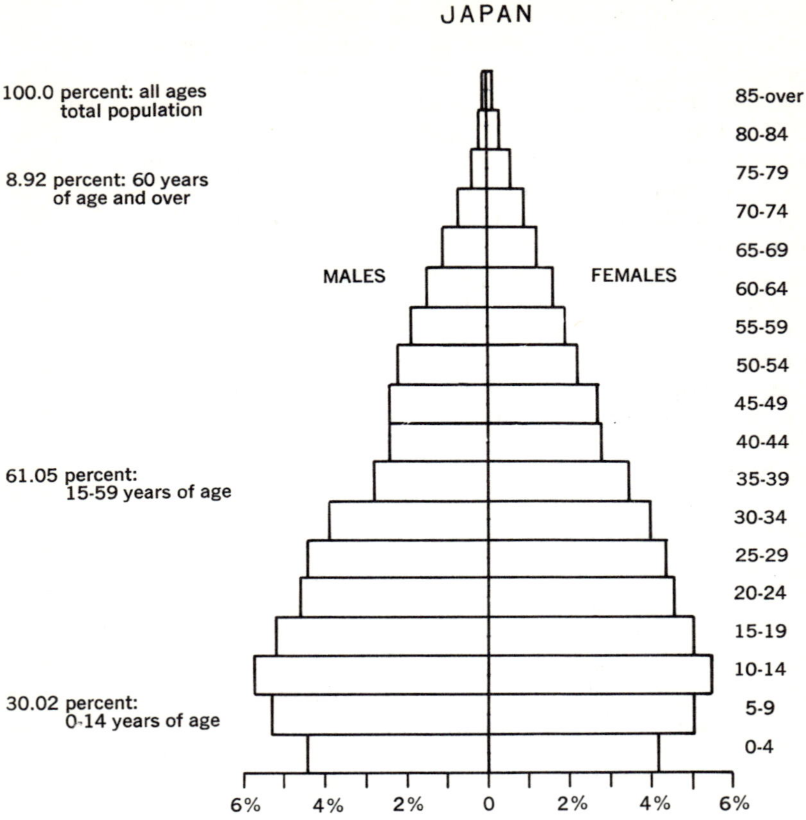

FIGURE 1-4. Population Structure of Japan in 1960

Source: Thompson and Lewis, Population Problems, 5th Ed., McGraw-Hill, 1965

The 1960 profile of Japan (Figure 1-4), a country which emphatically reversed its high birth rates after World War II, shows a steadily rising population base (like that of Mauritius) until the advent of the 10–14 age group, when the birth rates suddenly dropped and continued to drop in succeeding years. Observe how the base of the profile has narrowed accordingly.

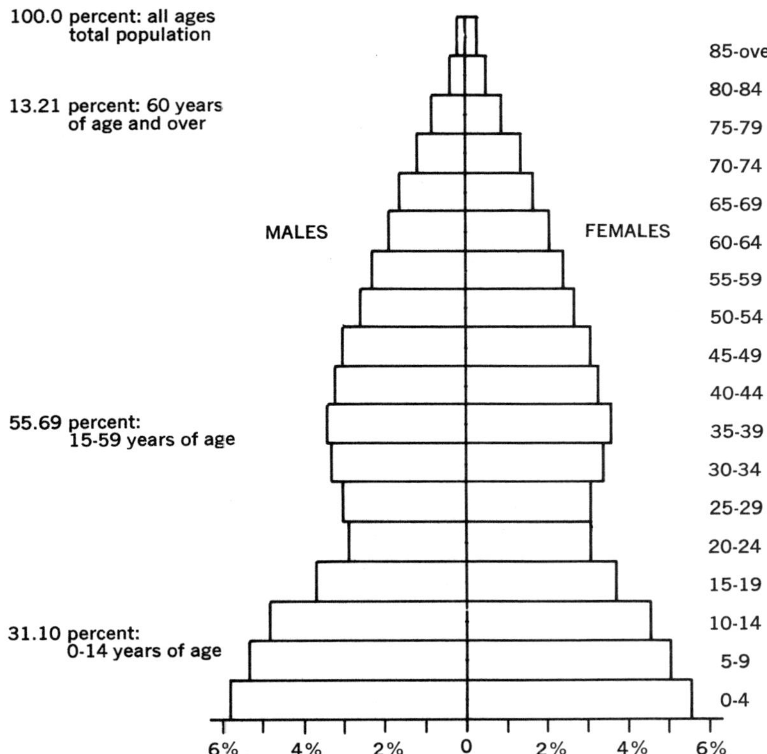

FIGURE 1-5. Population Structure of the United States in 1960

Source: Thompson and Lewis, Population Problems, 5th Ed., McGraw-Hill, 1965

The U.S. profile (Figure 1-5), much like that of England's until the post-World War II avalanche of babies, shows what happens when a population, long subject to low birth and death rates, experiences a swift surge in birth rates.

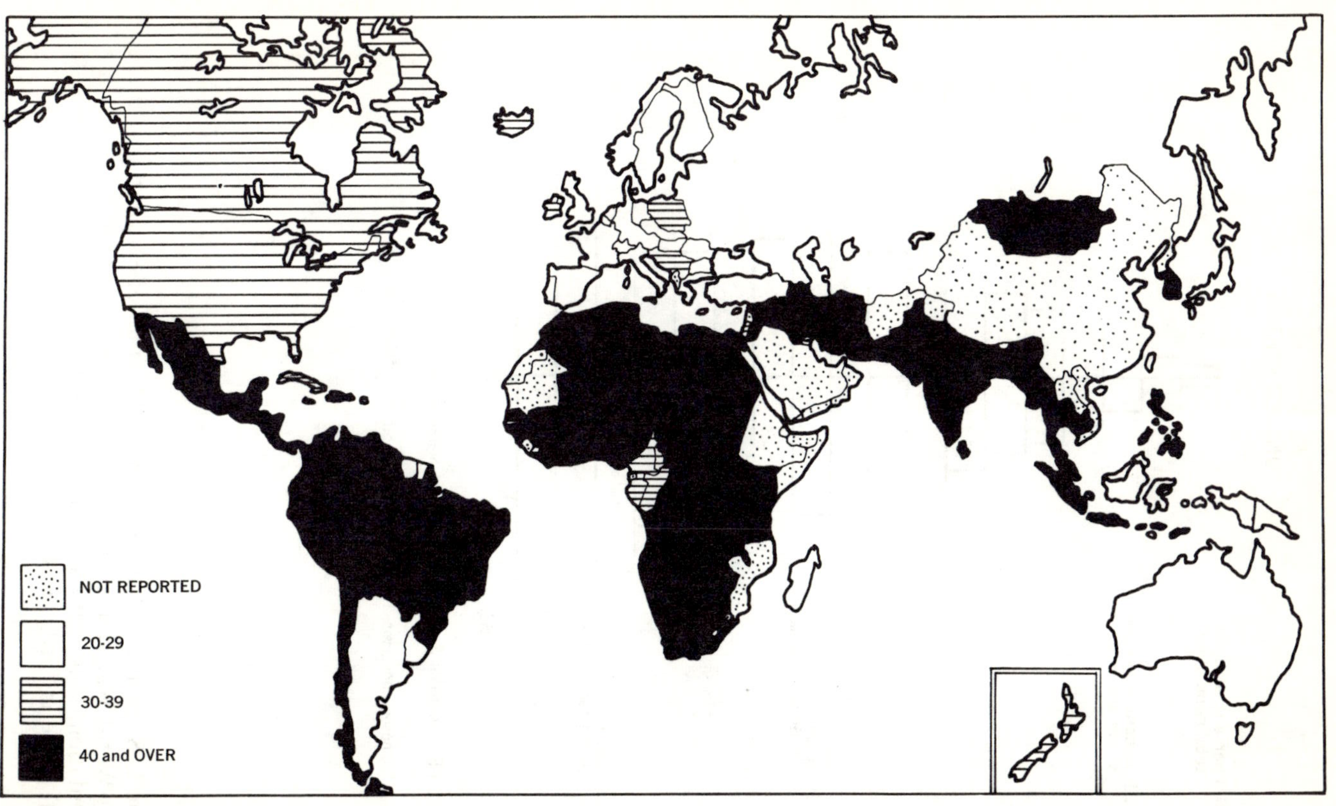

MAP 1-3. Major Areas and Regions by Population Under Fifteen Years (Percentage)

The World Population Data Sheet *is compiled every year by the Population Reference Bureau in Washington D.C. Since censuses are not taken every year in every country, its figures are based on reasonable projections. As an annual report, the sheet is the most up-to-the-minute guide on world demographic data. The previous sections in this chapter have attempted to interpret the meaning of its data.*

Region or Country	Population estimates mid-1970 (millions)†	Births per 1,000 population‡	Deaths per 1,000 population‡	Current rate of population growth (percent)	Number of years to double population □	Infant mortality rate (deaths under one year per 1,000 live births)‡	Population under 15 years (percent) ▲	Population illiterate 15 years and over (percent) ○	Per capita gross national product (US $)§	Population increase 1965-1970 (millions)†
WORLD	**3,706**[1]	**34**	**14**	**2.0**	**35**	–	**37**	**39**	–	**343**
AFRICA	**354**[2]	**47**	**20**	**2.7**	**26**	–	**44**	**82**	–	**41**
NORTHERN AFRICA	**89**	**47**	**16**	**3.1**	**23**	–	**45**	–	–	**12.1**
Algeria	14.5	50	17	3.3	21	86	47	75-85	220	2.1
Libya	1.9	46	16	3.1	23	–	44	80-87	1,020	0.3
Morocco	16.3	50	15	3.3	21	149	46	80-90	190	2.4
Sudan	16.3	49	18	3.2	22	–	47	80-88	100	2.2
Tunisia	5.3	45	14	3.1	23	74	44	75-85	220	0.7
UAR	34.9	44	15	2.8	25	118	43	75-80	170	4.4
WESTERN AFRICA	**104**	**49**	**23**	**2.6**	**27**	–	**44**	–	–	**11.7**
Dahomey	2.8	51	26	2.6	27	110	46	90-95	80	0.3
Gambia	0.4	42	23	1.9	37	–	38	90-95	100	0.03
Ghana	9.3[4]	48	18	3.0	24	156	45	70-75	170	1.3
Guinea	4.0	47	25	2.3	31	216	44	80-90	90	0.4
Ivory Coast	4.4	46	23	2.4	29	138	43	85-92	260	0.5
Liberia	1.2	41	23	1.9	37	188	37	90-95	210	0.1
Mali	5.2	50	25	2.4	29	120	46	85-95	90	0.6
Mauritania	1.2	45	23	2.2	32	187	–	90-97	180	0.1
Niger	4.0	52	23	2.9	24	200	46	95-99	70	0.5
Nigeria	56.5	50	25	2.6	27	–	43	80-88	70	6.4
Senegal	4.0	46	22	2.4	29	–	42	90-95	170	0.4
Sierra Leone	2.7	45	22	2.3	31	136	–	80-90	150	0.3
Togo	1.9	51	24	2.6	27	127	48	80-90	100	0.2
Upper Volta	5.5	49	28	2.1	33	182	42	85-92	50	0.5

1971 WORLD POPULATION DATA SHEET (cont.)

Region or Country	Population estimates mid-1970 (millions)†	Births per 1,000 population‡	Deaths per 1,000 population‡	Current rate of population growth	Number of years to double population □	Infant mortality rate (deaths under one year per 1,000 live births)‡	Population under 15 years (percent) ▲	Population illiterate 15 years and over (percent) ○	Per capita gross national product (US $)§	Population increase 1965-1970 (millions)†
EASTERN AFRICA	**100**	**47**	**21**	**2.6**	**27**	–	**44**	–	–	**11.4**
Burundi	3.7	48	25	2.3	31	150	47	85-92	50	0.4
Ethiopia	25.6	46	25	2.1	33	–	–	90-95	70	2.4
Kenya	11.2	50	20	3.1	23	–	46	70-75	130	1.5
Malagasy Republic	7.1	46	22	2.7	26	102	46	60-67	100	0.9
Malawi	4.6	49	25	2.5	28	148	45	85-93	50	0.5
Mauritius	0.9	27	8	1.9	37	72	41	35-40	230	0.1
Mozambique*	7.9	43	23	2.1	33	–	–	90-95	200	0.7
Reunion*	0.5	37	9	3.1	23	–	–	–	610	0.1
Rwanda	3.7	52	23	2.9	24	137	–	85-90	70	0.5
Somalia	2.9	46	24	2.4	29	–	–	90-95	60	0.3
Southern Rhodesia	5.2	48	14	3.4	21	122	47	70-75	220	0.8
Tanzania (United Republic of)	13.6	47	22	2.6	27	162	42	80-90	80	1.6
Uganda	8.8[4]	43	18	2.6	27	160	41	65-75	110	1.0
Zambia	4.4	50	20	3.0	24	259	45	55-60	220	0.6
MIDDLE AFRICA	**37**	**46**	**23**	**2.2**	**32**	–	**42**	–	–	**3.6**
Angola*	5.8	50	30	2.1	33	–	42	90-97	190	0.5
Cameroon (West)	5.9	43	21	2.2	32	137	39	80-90	140	0.6
Central African Republic	1.6	48	26	2.2	32	190	42	70-77	120	0.2
Chad	3.8	48	23	2.4	29	160	46	75-82	60	0.4
Congo (Dem. Republic)- Zaire (Rep. of) △	17.8	44	21	2.3	31	104	42	50-55	90	0.1
Congo (Republic of)	1.0	44	23	2.3	31	180	–	80-85	230	1.8
Equatorial Guinea	0.3	35	22	1.4	50	–	–	–	260	0.02
	[illegible]	[illegible]	[illegible]	0.9	78	229	36	85-90	310	0.02

[illegible]	23	41	17	2.4	29	–	40	–	–	2.5
Botswana	0.6	44	23	2.2	32	–	43	70–80	100	0.1
Lesotho	1.1	40	23	1.8	39	181	43	–	80	0.1
South Africa	20.6	40	16	2.4	29	–	40	65–70	}650	2.2
Namibia (Southwest Africa)*	0.6	44	25	2.0	35	–	40	60–70		0.1
Swaziland	0.4	52	22	3.0	24	–	–	–	200	0.1
ASIA	**2,104**[2]	**38**	**15**	**2.3**	**31**	–	**40**	**54**	–	**223**
SOUTHWEST ASIA	**79**	**44**	**15**	**2.9**	**24**	–	**43**	–	–	**10.3**
Cyprus	0.6	23	8	0.9	78	27	35	20–25	830	0.02
Iraq	10.0	49	15	3.4	21	–	45	75–85	260	1.5
Israel	3.0	26	7	2.4	29	23	33	10–15	1,360	0.3
Jordan	2.4	48	16	3.3	21	–	46	60–70	260	0.3
Kuwait	0.8	43	7	8.2	9	36	38	50–55	3,540	0.2
Lebanon	2.9	–	–	3.0	24	–	–	40–50	560	0.4
Muscat and Oman	0.7	42	11	3.1	23	–	–	–	250	–
Saudi Arabia	8.0	50	23	2.8	25	–	–	85–95	360	1.0
Southern Yemen	1.3	–	–	2.8	25	–	–	–	120	0.2
Syria	6.4	47	15	3.3	21	–	46	65–70	210	0.9
Turkey	36.5	43	16	2.7	26	155	44	60–65	310	4.4
Yemen (Arab Republic)	5.9	50	23	2.8	25	–	–	90–95	70	0.7
MIDDLE SOUTH ASIA	**783**	**44**	**16**	**2.7**	**26**	–	**43**	–	–	**96.9**
Afghanistan	17.4	50	26	2.5	28	–	–	85–95	80	1.9
Bhutan	0.9	–	–	2.2	32	–	–	–	60	0.1
Ceylon	12.9	32	8	2.4	29	48	41	25–30	180	1.4
India	569.5[4]	42	17	2.6	27	139	41	70–75	100	67.9
Iran	29.2	48	18	3.0	24	–	46	75–85	310	3.8
Nepal	11.5	45	23	2.2	32	–	40	85–95	80	1.2
Pakistan (inc. Bangladesh)△△	141.6	50	18	3.3	21	142	45	75–85	100	20.6
SOUTHEAST ASIA	**295**	**43**	**15**	**2.8**	**25**	–	**44**	–	–	**37.6**
Burma	28.4	40	17	2.3	31	–	40	30–40	70	3.0
Cambodia	7.3	45	16	3.0	24	127	44	60–70	120	1.0
Indonesia	124.9	47	19	2.9	24	125	42	55–60	100	16.3
Laos	3.1	42	17	2.5	28	–	–	70–80	100	0.4
Malaysia	11.1	37	8	2.8	25	–	44	70–80	330	1.4

1971 WORLD POPULATION DATA SHEET (cont.)

Region or Country	Population estimates mid-1970 (millions)†	Births per 1,000 population‡	Deaths per 1,000 population‡	Current rate of population growth	Number of years to double population □	Infant mortality rate (deaths under one year per 1,000 live births)‡	Population under 15 years (percent) ▲	Population illiterate 15 years and over (percent) ■	Per capita gross national product (US $)§	Population increase 1965–1970 (millions)†●
Philippines	39.4	46	12	3.4	21	72	47	25-30	180	5.8
Singapore	2.2	25	5	2.4	29	–	43	40-50	700	0.2
Thailand	37.4	42	10	3.3	21	–	43	30-35	150	5.4
Vietnam (Dem. Republic of)	21.6	–	–	2.1	33	–	–	–	90	2.2
Vietnam (Republic of)	18.3	–	–	2.1	33	–	–	–	130	1.8
EAST ASIA	**946**	**30**	**13**	**1.8**	**39**	**–**	**36**	**–**	**–**	**78.1**
China (Mainland)	772.9	33	15	1.8	39	–	–	40-50	90	64.6
China (Taiwan)	14.3	26	5	2.3	31	19	44	35-45	270	1.6
Hong Kong*	4.3	21	5	2.5	28	21	40	25-30	710	0.5
Japan	104.7	18	7	1.1	63	15	25	0-2	1,190	5.5
Korea (Dem. People's Rep. of)	14.3	39	11	2.8	25	–	–	–	250	1.8
Korea (Republic of)	32.9	36	11	2.5	28	–	42	–	180	3.7
Mongolia	1.3	42	10	3.1	23	–	44	5	430	0.2
Ryukyu Islands*	1.0	22	5	1.7	41	11	39	–	580	0.1
NORTHERN AMERICA	**229**[2]	**18**	**9**	**1.2**	**58**	**–**	**30**	**2**	**–**	**13.2**
Canada	21.8	17.6	7.3	1.7	41	20.8	33	0-3	2,460	1.8
United States[3]	207.1	18.2	9.3	1.1	63	19.8	30	0-3	3,980	11.4
LATIN AMERICA	**291**[2]	**38**	**9**	**2.9**	**24**	**–**	**42**	**34**	**–**	**37**
MIDDLE AMERICA	**70**	**43**	**9**	**3.4**	**21**	**–**	**46**	**–**	**–**	**10.5**
Costa Rica	1.9	45	8	3.8	19	60	48	10-20	450	0.3
El Salvador	3.6	47	13	3.4	21	63	45	45-50	280	0.5
Guatemala	5.3	42	13	2.9	24	94	46	60-70	320	0.7
Honduras	2.8	49	16	3.4	21	–	51	50-60	260	0.4
Mexico	52.5[4]	42	9	3.4	21	66	46	30-35	530	8.0

Nicaragua	2.1	[illegible]	[illegible]	3.0	24	–	48	45-50	370	0.3
Panama	1.5	41	8	3.3	21	41	43	20-30	580	0.2
CARIBBEAN	**26**	**34**	**10**	**2.2**	**32**	**–**	**40**	**–**	**–**	**2.7**
Barbados	0.3	21	8	0.8	88	42	38	0-10	440	0.01
Cuba	8.6	27	8	1.9	37	40	37	15-25	310	0.8
Dominican Republic	4.4[4]	48	15	3.4	21	64	47	40	290	0.7
Guadeloupe*	0.4	32	8	2.4	29	35	42	–	510	0.04
Haiti	5.4	44	20	2.5	28	–	42	80-90	70	0.6
Jamaica	2.0	33	8	2.1	33	39	41	15-20	460	0.2
Martinique*	0.4	30	8	1.9	37	34	42	–	610	0.03
Puerto Rico*	2.9	24	6	1.4	50	29	39	15-20	1,340	0.2
Trinidad & Tobago	1.1	30	7	1.8	39	37	43	15-25	870	0.1
TROPICAL SOUTH AMERICA	**155**	**39**	**9**	**3.0**	**24**	**–**	**43**	**–**	**–**	**20.8**
Bolivia	4.8	44	19	2.4	29	–	44	55-65	150	0.5
Brazil	95.7	38	10	2.8	25	170	43	30-35	250	12.3
Colombia	22.1	44	11	3.4	21	78	47	30-40	310	3.3
Ecuador	6.3	45	11	3.4	21	86	48	30-35	220	1.0
Guyana	0.8	37	8	2.9	24	40	46	15-25	340	0.1
Peru	14.0	43	11	3.1	23	62	45	35-40	380	1.9
Surinam*	0.4	41	7	3.2	22	30	46	–	430	–
Venezuela	11.1	41	8	3.4	21	46	46	30-35	950	1.6
TEMPERATE SOUTH AMERICA	**40**	**26**	**9**	**1.8**	**39**	**–**	**33**	**–**	**–**	**3.4**
Argentina	24.7	22	9	1.5	47	58	29	5-8	820	1.7
Chile	10.0[4]	34	11	2.3	31	92	40	13-16	480	1.1
Paraguay	2.5	45	11	3.4	21	52	45	20-25	230	0.4
Uruguay	2.9	21	9	1.2	58	50	28	8-10	520	0.2
EUROPE	**466[2]**	**18**	**10**	**0.8**	**88**	**–**	**25**	**5**	**–**	**18**
NORTHERN EUROPE	**81**	**16**	**11**	**0.6**	**117**	**–**	**24**	**–**	**–**	**2.3**
Denmark	5.0	14.6	9.8	0.5	140	14.8	24	0-1	2,070	0.2
Finland	4.7	14.5	9.8	0.4	175	13.9	27	0-1	1,720	0.1
Iceland	0.2	20.7	7.2	1.2	58	11.7	34	0-1	1,680	0.02
Ireland	3.0	21.5	11.5	0.7	100	20.6	31	0-1	980	0.1
Norway	3.9	17.6	9.9	0.9	78	13.7	25	0-1	2,000	0.2

1971 WORLD POPULATION DATA SHEET (cont.)

Region or Country	Population estimates mid-1970 (millions)†	Births per 1,000 population‡	Deaths per 1,000 population‡	Current rate of population growth	Number of years to double population □	Infant mortality rate (deaths under one year per 1,000 live births)‡	Population under 15 years (percent) ▲	Population illiterate 15 years and over (percent) ■	Per capita gross national product (US $)§	Population increase 1965-1970 (millions)† ●
Sweden	8.1	13.5	10.4	0.5	140	13.0	21	0-1	2,620	0.3
United Kingdom	56.3	16.6	11.9	0.5	140	18.6	23	0-1	1,790	1.4
WESTERN EUROPE	**150**	**16**	**11**	**0.6**	**117**	–	**24**	–	–	**5.5**
Austria	7.5	16.5	13.4	0.4	175	25.4	24	0-1	1,320	0.2
Belgium	9.7	14.6	12.4	0.4	175	21.8	24	0-3	1,810	0.2
France	51.5	16.7	11.3	0.7	100	16.4	25	0-3	2,130	2.4
Germany (Federal Republic of)	58.9	15.0	12.0	0.4	175	23.3	23	0-1	1,970	1.7
Luxembourg	0.4	13.5	12.6	1.0	70	16.7	22	0-3	2,170	0.02
Netherlands	13.1	19.2	8.4	1.1	63	13.2	28	0-1	1,620	0.7
Switzerland	6.4	16.5	9.3	1.1	63	15.4	23	0-1	2,490	0.3
EASTERN EUROPE	**105**	**17**	**10**	**0.8**	**88**	–	**25**	–	–	**4.0**
Bulgaria	8.6	17.0	9.5	0.7	100	30.5	24	10-15	770	0.3
Czechoslovakia	14.8	15.5	11.2	0.5	140	22.9	25	0-5	1,240	0.5
Germany (Dem. Republic)	16.2	14.0	14.3	0.1	700	20.1	22	0-1	1,430	0.2
Hungary	10.3	15.0	11.3	0.4	175	35.7	23	0-5	980	0.1
Poland	33.3	16.3	8.1	0.9	78	34.3	30	0-5	880	1.5
Romania	20.6	23.3	10.1	1.3	54	54.9	26	5-15	780	1.3
SOUTHERN EUROPE	**130**	**19**	**9**	**0.9**	**78**	–	**27**	–	–	**5.7**
Albania	2.2	35.6	8.0	2.7	26	86.8	–	20-30	400	0.3
Greece	9.0	17.4	8.2	0.8	88	31.9	25	15-20	740	0.3
Italy	54.1	17.6	10.1	0.8	88	30.3	24	5-10	1,230	2.1
Malta	0.3	15.8	9.4	−0.8	–	24.3	32	35-45	640	−0.01
Portugal	9.6	19.8	10.6	0.7	100	56.8	29	35-40	460	0.3
Spain	33.6	20.2	9.2	1.0	70	29.8	27	10-20	730	1.6
Yugoslavia	20.8	18.8	9.2	1.0	70	56.3	30	15-25	510	1.1

USSR	**245**	**17.0**	**8.1**	**1.0**	**70**	**25.7**	**28**	**12**	**1,110**	**12.1**
OCEANIA	**20[2]**	**25**	**10**	**2.0**	**35**	**–**	**32**	**0-2**	**–**	**2.0**
Australia	12.8	20.0	9.1	1.9	37	17.7	29	0-1	2,070	1.1
Fiji	0.5	29	5	2.7	26	22	45	–	330	–
New Zealand	2.9	22.5	8.7	1.7	41	16.9	33	0-1	2,000	0.2

FOOTNOTES

† Estimates from United Nations, "Total Population Estimates for World, Regions and Countries, Each Year, 1950–1985," Population Division Working Paper No. 34, October 1970.

‡ Latest available year. Except for Northern American rates, estimates are essentially those available as of January 1971 in UN Population and Vital Statistics Report. Series A, Vol. XXIII, No. 1, with adjustments as deemed necessary in view of deficiency of registration in some countries.

► Latest available year. Derived from UN World Population Prospects, 1965–85, As Assessed in 1968, Population Division Working Paper No. 30, December 1969 and UN Demographic Yearbook, 1967.

§ 1968 data supplied by the International Bank for Reconstruction and Development.

○ Annual rate of population growth (composed of the rate of natural increase modified by the net rate of in- or out-migration) is derived from the latest available published estimates by the United Nations, except where substantiated changes have occurred in birth rates, death rates or migration streams.

□ Assuming no change in growth rate.

* Nonsovereign country.

△ Congo (Dem. Republic of), also referred to as Congo-Kinkasha in this book changed its name to Zaire (Republic of) in 1971. The original designations have been kept throughout.

△△ Bangladesh, formerly known as East Pakistan, is subsumed under the name of Pakistan throughout.

[1] Total reflects UN adjustments for discrepancies in international migration data.

[2] Regional population totals take into account small areas not listed on the Data Sheet.

[3] US figures are based on Series D projections of the 1970 census and vital statistics data available as of April 1971.

[4] In these countries, the UN estimates show a variation of more than 3 percent from recent census figures. Because of uncertainty as to the completeness or accuracy of census data, the UN estimates are used.

NOTE: The completeness and accuracy of data in many developing countries are subject to deficiencies of varying degree. In some cases, the data shown are estimates prepared by the United Nations.

■ Assuming continued growth at current annual rate; figures are from the 1968 Data Sheet of the Population Reference Bureau.

● Estimates from the United Nations. World Population Prospects, 1965–1985, As Assessed in 1968, United Nations Population Division Working Paper No. 30, December. 1969. Figures are from the 1970 Data Sheet of the Population Reference Bureau.

3. POPULATION DENSITY

WORLD AND REGIONAL POPULATION (millions)

	World	Asia	Europe	USSR	Africa	North America	Latin America	Oceania
Mid-1971	3706	2104	466	245	354	299	291	20
UN MEDIUM ESTIMATE, 2000	6494	3777	568	330	818	333	652	35

The world is not densely populated. Bracket out all other measures except that of people per square kilometer and you get the feeling that the population crisis is a terrible hoax. If the total land area of the earth contains a mere twenty-six persons per square kilometer, then the population density of the world is only slightly higher than the United States' density (22 per sq. km.). And who can say that the United States, where approximately 70 percent of the people live on 3 percent of the land, is crowded?

Actually, the United States has a very reasonable distribution, with less population per square kilometer than any European country (excepting the quasi-Arctic nations of Norway, Sweden, Finland and Iceland). Even Ireland, which is considered relatively empty, has almost double the U.S. density, at 42 per square kilometer. Conversely, it is interesting to note that only one Latin-American nation—Equador with 21 per square kilometer—comes close to the U.S. figure. Yet despite these sharp density contrasts, we have come to regard Latin America as overpopulated and Europe as not.

What is missing in the analysis? Everything. Space vis-à-vis people is a neutral ratio signifying next to nothing. It's what goes on within that space that is important. Climate, tillable land, agricultural yield, resources and energy supplies are some of the natural factors that must be fed into the equation. Another crucial element is the level of a nation's or region's economic development. Is the technology of the given country sufficient to maximize the native potential and bring to its population the basic goods and services of modern industrial society? Because Europe is handicapped in neither of these regards, while Latin America is wanting in both to a greater or lesser degree, Europe's density of 93 per square kilometer does not compare in demographic seriousness with Latin America's lesser density of 13 per square kilometer.

Mainland China, after all, has an unspectacular density of 77 per square kilometer, which is less than that of France, Austria and Denmark. The densities of West Germany, Italy and England still beat India's density of 164 per square kilometer. Here we have, then, two of the most overpopulated countries in the world with relatively unalarming over-all population densities. Thus overpopulation is not automatically associated with high density or high density with overpopulation.

Density figures can mislead in another way. A crude population density statistic for a very large country violently distorts the distribution distinctions within the interior. The average density for the U.S.S.R., for example, is 11. But this general figure hardly reflects the density differences between European Russia (33 per sq. km.) and Asian Russia (4 per sq. km.), nor does it do justice to the higher densities of Byelorussia (43 per sq. km.) or the Ukraine (78 per sq. km.).

World density is subject to the same numerical distortion. Since roughly two-thirds of the world's population lives on just one-seventh of the land, dividing all the people of the earth by all the square kilometers on earth does not by any means accurately portray the density picture. If you look at a map plotting population distribution (Map 1-4), you will see that vast tracts of land are uninhabited and/or uninhabitable for reasons of extreme cold, severe aridity, high mountains or equatorial forest. Arctic Canada and Asiatic Russia, the heartlands of Latin America and China and the Sahara, Kalahari and Australian deserts have environments excruciatingly hostile to human settlement.

The highest and most extended concentrations of people are in the urban centers of the United States, Europe and Japan, and in the rural regions of India, China and other South East Asian countries.

When is density a problem? The answer would seem to be whenever an area cannot adequately support its population. A thousand people per square kilometer would be the upper limit in rural parts where survival depends on agriculture. This maximum is exceeded only in Java, which is blessed with uncommonly rich soil. In the Szechwan district of China densities of over 700 per square kilometer are known. The fertility of the Nile Valley likewise admits of large densities between 400 and 600 per square kilometer.

Cities are in a league of their own so far as density is concerned. Paris, one of the West's more crowded cities at over 34,000 per square kilometer, has only one-half the density of London and one-fifth that of Manhattan.

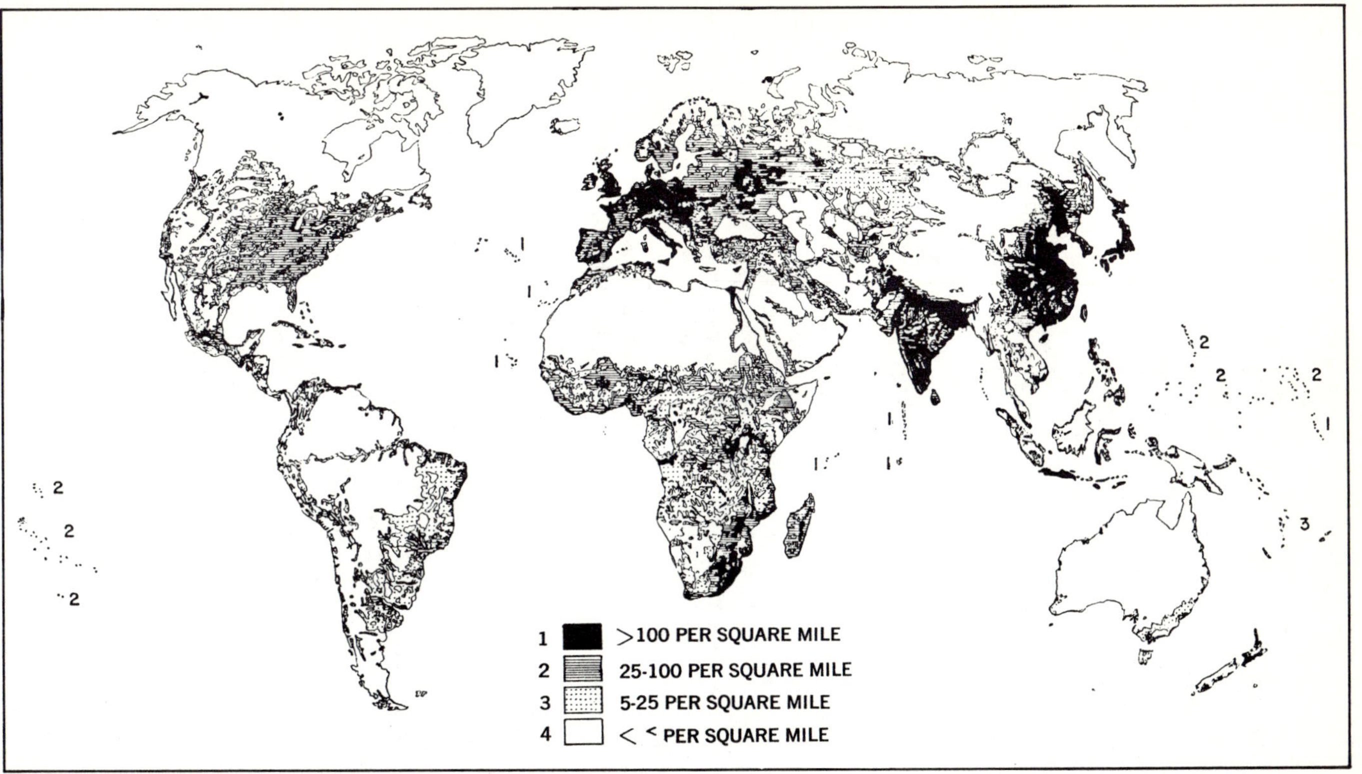

MAP 1-4. The World Distribution and Density of Population. Simplified from The Times Atlas of the World. Vol. 1, 1958

Source: Clarke, Population Geography, Pergamon Press, 1965

POPULATION DENSITY BY COUNTRY

from the United Nations Demographic Yearbook, 1969

Major areas and regions	Area in square kilometers (000's)	Density[1] 1969
WORLD TOTAL	135,772	26
AFRICA	30,313	11
Western Africa	6,143	18
Eastern Africa	6,331	15
Northern Africa	8,525	10
Middle Africa	6,613	5
Southern Africa	2,701	8
AMERICA[2]	42,080	12
Northern America[2]	21,515	10
Latin America	20,565	13
Tropical South America	13,699	11
Central America (mainland)	2,496	26
Temperate South America	4,134	9
Caribbean	236	105
ASIA[5]	27,532	72
East Asia[6]	11,757	77
Mainland Region	11,129	67
Japan	370	277
Other East Asia	258	230
South Asia[7]	15,775	69
Middle South Asia	6,771	109
South East Asia	4,498	62
South West Asia	4,506	16
EUROPE[8]	4,934	93
Western Europe	993	149
Southern Europe	1,315	98
Eastern Europe	990	104
Northern Europe	1,636	49
OCEANIA[2]	8,511	2
Australia and New Zealand	7,956	2
Melanesia	525	5
Polynesia and Micronesia	30	38
U.S.S.R.	22,402	11

FOOTNOTES

[1] Population per square kilometer of area based on the United Nations Demographic Yearbook, 1969, mid-year estimates.

[2] Hawaii, a state of the United States of America, is included in Northern America rather than Oceania.

[3] Rate reflects combined effect of natural increase and migration.

[4] Weighted average of recorded rates.

[5] Excluding the U.S.S.R., shown separately, but including both the Asian and European portions of Turkey.

[6] Excluding the U.S.S.R., shown separately below.

[7] Including both the Asian and European portions of Turkey.

[8] Excluding the U.S.S.R., shown separately below, and the European portion of Turkey, which is included in South Asia.

POPULATION DENSITY BY COUNTRY

from The United Nations Demographic Yearbook, 1969

Continent and country	Area in square kilometers	Density 1969[1]
AFRICA		
Algeria	2,381,741	6
Angola[2]	1,246,700	4
Botswana[3]	600,372	1
British Indian Ocean Territory[4]	78	26
Burundi	27,834	125
Cameroon	475,442	12
Cape Verde Islands	4,033	62
Central African Republic	622,984	2
Chad	1,284,000	3
Comoro Islands	2,171	124
Congo (Brazzaville)	342,000	3
Congo (Democratic Republic of)	2,345,409	7
Dahomey	112,622	23
Equatorial Guinea[5]	28,051	10
Fernando Poo	2,034	39
Rio Muni	26,017	8
Ethiopia	1,221,900	20
French Southern and Antarctic Territories[6]	7,557	0
French Territory of the Afars and the Issacs	22,000	4
Gabon	267,667	2
Gambia	11,295	32
Ghana	238,537	36
Guinea	245,857	16
Ifni[7]	–	–
Ivory Coast	322,463	13
Kenya'	582,644	18
Lesotho	30,355	31
Liberia	111,369	10
Libya[8]	1,759,540	1
Madagascar	587,041	11
Malawi	118,484	37
Mali	1,240,000	4
Mauritania	1,030,700	1
Mauritius	2,045	402
Island of Mauritius	1,865	428
Rodrigues	109	211
Others	71	14
Morocco[9]	445,050	34
Ifni	1,500	37
Mozambique[8]	783,030	9
Namibia[10]	824,292	1
Niger	1,267,000	3
Nigeria	923,768	69
Portuguese Guinea	36,125	15
Réunion	2,510	174
Rwanda	26,338	133

POPULATION DENSITY BY COUNTRY (cont.)

Continent and country	Area in square kilometers	Density 1969
St. Helena[11]	122	41
Ascension	88	5
Tristan da Cunha	104	3
São Tomé and Principe	964	68
Senegal	196,192	19
Seychelles	376	136
Sierra Leone	71,740	35
Somalia	637,657	4
South Africa[12,13]	1,221,037	16
Southern Rhodesia[14]	389,361	13
Spanish North Africa	32	5,125
Ceuta	19	4,564
Melilla	12	6,441
Others[15]	1	530[16]
Spanish Sahara[17]	266,000	0
Sudan[8]	2,505,813	6
Swaziland	17,363	24
Togo	56,000	32
Tunisia	164,150	31
Uganda	236,036	40
United Arab Republic	181,001,449	32
United Republic of Tanzania	939,703	14
Tanganyika	937,063	13
Zanzibar	2,640	140
Upper Volta	274,200	19
Zambia	752,614	6
NORTH AMERICA		
Antigua	442	143
Bahamas	11,405	17
Barbados	430	591
Bermuda[19]	53	990
British Honduras	22,965	5
British Virgin Islands	153	59
Canada[8]	9,976,139	2
Cayman Islands	259	46
Costa Rica[8]	50,700	33
Cuba[8]	114,524	72
Dominica	751	99
Dominican Republic	48,734	86
El Salvador	21,393	158
Greenland	2,175,600	200
Grenada[21]	344	305
Guadeloupe[22]	1,779	181
Guatemala	108,889	46
Haiti	27,750	172
Honduras	112,088	22
Jamaica[8]	10,962	179
Leeward Islands[23]	1,102	302
Martinique	1,102	302

POPULATION DENSITY BY COUNTRY (cont.)

Continent and country	Area in square kilometers	Density 1969
Mexico	1,972,546	25
Montserrat	98	149
Netherlands Antilles[8]	961	227
Aruba[8], Bonaire[8], Curaçao[8]	873	242
Others[8,24]	88	80
Nicaragua[8]	130,000	15
Panama[25]	75,650	19
Canal Zone[26]	1,432	40
Puerto Rico[26]	8,897	310
St. Kitts-Nevis-Anguilla	357	157
St. Lucia	616	179
St. Pierre and Miquelon	242	21
St. Vincent[27]	388	245
Trinidad and Tobago	5,128	203
Turks and Caicos Islands	430	14
United States of America[28]	9,363,353	22
United States Virgin Islands[26]	344	174
St. Croix	207[29]	135
St. John	52[29]	19
St. Thomas	83[29]	373
Windward Islands[30]		
SOUTH AMERICA		
Argentina	2,776,889	9
Bolivia	1,098,581	4
Brazil[31]	8,511,965	11
British Antarctic Territory[32]		
Chile	756,945	13
Colombia	1,138,914	18
Ecuador[33]	283,561	21
Falkland Islands (Malvinas)[34,35]	11,961	0
French Guiana	91,000	0
Guyana	214,969	3
Paraguay	406,752	6
Peru	1,285,216	10
Surinam	163,265	2
Uruguay	177,508	16
Venezuela[36]	912,050	11
ASIA		
Afghanistan	647,497	26
Bahrain	598	346
Bhutan	47,000	16
Brunei[37]	5,765	20
Burma	678,033	40
Cambodia[38]	181,035	37
Ceylon	65,610	187

POPULATION DENSITY BY COUNTRY (cont.)

Continent and country	Area in square kilometers	Density 1969
China (mainland)	9,561,000	77
China (Taiwan)	35,961	384
Cyprus	9,251	68
Hong Kong[40]	1,034[41]	3,859
India[42]	3,268,090	164
Indonesia[43]	1,491,564	78
West Irian[44]	412,781	2
Iran	1,648,000	17
Iraq	434,294	20
Israel	20,700	136
Japan[45]	369,881	277
Jordan[46]	97,740	22
Korea	220,231[47]	202
North Korea	120,538	110
Republic of Korea[48]	198,477	316
Kuwait	16,000	36
Laos	236,800	12
Lebanon[49]	10,400	254
Macau[8,50]	16	16,250
Malaysia		
East Malaysia[37]	201,320	8
Sabah[37]	76,115	8
Sarawak[37]	125,205	8
West Malaysia[37]	131,313	69
Maldives	298	362
Mongolia	1,565,000	1
Muscat and Oman	212,457[51]	3
Nepal	140,797	77
Pakistan (including Bangladesh)[52]	946,716	118
Palestine[53]	27,090	–
Gaza Strip[54]	378	1,370
Philippines	300,000	124
Portuguese Timor	14,925	40
Qatar	22,014	5
Ryukyu Islands[55,56]	2,196	447
Saudi Arabia	2,149,690	3
Sikkim	7,107	27
Singapore[57]	581	3,471
Southern Yemen[58]	287,683	4
Syria[59]	185,180	32
Thailand	514,000	68
Trucial Oman[60]	83,600	2
Turkey	780,576	44
in Asia	756,953	41
in Europe	23,623	126
Vietnam	329,556	119
North Vietnam	158,750	134
Republic of Vietnam	173,809	103
Yemen	195,000	26

POPULATION DENSITY BY COUNTRY (cont.)

Continent and country	Area in square kilometers	Density 1969
EUROPE		
Albania	28,748	72
Andorra	453	41
Austria[8]	83,849	88
Belgium[8]	30,513	316
Bulgaria	110,912[61]	76
Channel Islands	195	600
Guernsey[62]	78	628
Jersey	116	586
Czechoslovakia	127,869	113
Denmark[8,63]	43,069	114
Faeroe Islands[8]	1,399	27
Finland[8]	337,009	14
France[64,65]	547,026	92
Germany		
Eastern Germany[8]	107,771	149
Federal Republic of Germany	247,973	237
East Berlin[8]	403	2,695
West Berlin[8]	481	4,439
Gibraltar[66]	6	4,500
Greece	131,944	67
Holy See	0[67]	2,273
Hungary	93,030	111
Iceland	103,000	2
Ireland	70,283	42
Isle of Man	588	85
Italy	301,225	177
Liechtenstein	157	134
Luxembourg[8]	2,586	130
Malta[68]	316	1,022
Monaco	1[69]	15,436
Netherlands[8]	40,844[70]	315
Norway[8]	324,219	12
Poland[71]	312,677	104
Portugal[72]	92,082	104
Romania	237,500	84
San Marino	61	307
Spain[73]	504,750	65
Svalbard and Jan Mayen Islands[74]	62,422	–
Sweden[8]	449,750	18
Switzerland[8]	41,288	151
United Kingdom of		
Great Britain and Northern Ireland[75]	244,013	228
England and Wales	151,126	323
Northern Ireland	14,146	107
Scotland	78,772	66
Yugoslavia	255,804	80

POPULATION DENSITY BY COUNTRY (cont.)

Continent and country	Area in square kilometers	Density 1969
OCEANIA		
American Samoa	197	162
Australia[76]	7,686,810	2
British Solomon Islands[77]	29,785	5
Canton and Enderbury Islands[78]	70	5[16]
Christmas Island	135	25
Cocos (Keeling) Islands	14	43
Cook Islands[79]	234	85
Fiji	18,272	28
French Polynesia[80]	4,000	26
Gilbert and Ellice Islands[81]	886	61
Guam[82]	549	186
Johnston Island	1	156[16]
Midway Islands	5	400
Nauru	21	310
New Caledonia[83]	19,000	5
New Guinea[84]	238,693[85]	7
New Hebrides[86]	14,763	5
New Zealand[87]	268,675	10
Niué Island	259	21
Norfolk Island	36	38
Pacific Islands[88]	1,779	55
Papua[89]	222,998	3
Pitcairn Island	5	18
Tokelau Islands	10	200
Tongo	699	119
Wake Island	8	125
Wallis and Futuna Islands	200	45
Western Samoa	2,842	50
UNION OF SOVIET SOCIALIST REPUBLICS		
Union of Soviet Socialist Republics	22,402,200	11
in Asia	16,831,000	4
In Europe	5,571,000	33
Byelorussian Soviet Socialist Republic	207,600	43
Ukrainian Soviet Socialist Republic	603,700	78

FOOTNOTES

[1] Population per square kilometre of area in 1969.

[2] Including the enclave of Cabinda.

[3] Population is de jure and includes nomads estimated at 14,150 at 1964 census.

[4] Created 8 November 1965 and comprising Chagos Archipelago (formerly dependency of Mauritius) and the islands of Aldabra, Farquhar and Des Roches (formerly dependencies of Seychelles).

[5] Comprising Fernando Póo (which includes Annobón) and Río Muni (which includes Corisco and Elobeys).

[6] Comprising the islands of St. Paul and Amsterdam, the Kerguelen and Crozet Archipelagos and Adélie Coast.

[7] See under Morocco.

[8] Population is de jure.

[9] Excluding data for Ifni, shown separately hereunder.

[10] Including data for Walvis Bay, which is an integral part of South Africa but is administered as if it were part of Namibia (area 1,124 km², population 12,648 in 1960).

[11] Excluding data for dependencies, two of which are shown separately hereunder; the other dependencies, Gough, Inaccessible and Nightingale Islands (total area 105 km²), are presumed to be uninhabited.

[12] Excluding data for Walvis Bay, which is an integral part of South Africa but is administered as if it were part of Namibia (area 1,124 km², population 12,648 in 1960).

[13] "Type" of estimates for Asiatic, Coloured and White segments of population is A_9b_1.

[14] "Type" of estimates for Asiatic and White segments of population is A_7b_1.

[15] Comprising Alhucemas, Chafarinas and Peñón de Vélez de la Gomera.

[16] For 1960.

[17] Comprising the Northern Region (former Saguia el Hamra) and the Southern Region (former Río de Oro).

[18] Inhabited and cultivated territory accounts for 35,580 km²; corresponding density is 913.

[19] Population excludes tourists and members of United Kingdom and United States armed forces and their dependants stationed in the area.

[20] Area of ice-free portion is 341,700 km²; corresponding density is 0.1.

[21] Including data for Carriacou and other dependencies in the Grenadines.

[22] Including data for dependencies: Marie-Galante, la Désirade, les Saintes, Petite-Terre, St. Barthélemy and French part of St. Martin.

[23] See Antigua, British Virgin Islands, Montserrat and St. Kitts-Nevis-Anguilla.

[24] Comprising Saba, St. Eustatius and Dutch part of St. Martin.

[25] Excluding data for Canal Zone, shown separately hereunder.

[26] Population is de jure, but includes armed forces stationed in the area.

[27] Including data for Bequia and other dependencies in the Grenadines.

[28] Shown elsewhere as "United States." Population is de jure but excludes civilian citizens absent from country for extended period of time, estimated at 764,701 at time of 1960 census.

[29] Excludes inland water.

[30] See Dominica, Grenada, St. Lucia and St. Vincent.

[31] Population excludes Indian jungle inhabitants, numbering 45,429 at 1950 census and estimated at 150,000 in 1956.

[32] Created 3 March 1962 and comprising former dependencies of Falkland (Malvinas) Islands south of 60° latitude, i.e. the South Orkney Islands (area 622 km²), South Shetland Islands (area 4,622 km²), Graham Land and the sector of Antarctic Continent between longitudes 20°W and 80°W.

[33] Population excludes nomadic Indian tribes.

[34] Excluding data for dependencies, of which South Georgia (area 3,755 km²) had an estimated population of 499 in 1964 (494 males, 5 females). The other dependencies, i.e. the South Sandwich group (area 337 km²) and a number of smaller islands, are presumed to be uninhabited.

[35] A dispute exists between the governments of Argentina and the United Kingdom of Great Britain and Northern Ireland concerning sovereignty over the Falkland Islands (Malvinas).

[36] Population excludes Indian jungle inhabitants estimated at 31,800 in 1961.

[37] Population excludes transients afloat.

[38] Population excludes foreign diplomatic personnel and their dependants.

[39] Excludes Quemoy and Matsu Islands.

[40] Comprising Hong Kong Island, Kowloon and the New (leased) Territories.

[41] Land area only. Total, including ocean area within administrative boundaries, is 2,916 km². Increase due to land reclamation presumably in Victoria on Hong Kong Island.

[42] Including Andaman, Nicobar, Laccadive, Minicoy and Amindivi Islands; excluding Sikkim shown separately on page 120; except for census figures, also including Jammu and Kashmir, the final status of which has not yet been determined (area 222,800 km²), population of the Indian-held part of this territory numbered 3,560,976 at 1961 census and was estimated at 3,678,000 at midyear 1963 and 3,729,000 at midyear 1964.

[43] Excluding West Irian, shown separately hereunder.

[44] Western part of island of New Guinea.

[45] Comprising Hokkaido, Honshu, Shikoku, Kyushu, the Amami Islands, and the Tokara Archipelago. Population excludes diplomatic personnel outside the country and foreign military and civilian personnel and their dependants stationed in the area.

[46] Including military and diplomatic personnel and their families abroad numbering 933 for both sexes at 1961 census, excluding foreign military and diplomatic personnel and their families in the country, numbering 389 for both sexes at 1961 census. Also including registered Palestinian refugees, numbering 654,092 and 722,687 at 30 June 1963 and 31 May 1967, respectively.

[47] Includes the area of the demilitarized zone (1,262 km^2).

[48] Population excludes alien armed forces, civilian aliens employed by armed forces, and foreign diplomatic personnel and their dependants.

[49] Excluding registered Palestinian refugees, numbering 149,983 on 30 June 1963 and 171,517 on 30 June 1969.

[50] Comprising Macau City and islands of Taipa and Coloane.

[51] Includes 78 km^2 for Kuria Muria Islands ceded to Muscat and Oman on 30 November 1967.

[52] Data are for territory excluding Jammu and Kashmir, the final status of which has not yet been determined (area 222,800 km^2, population of the Indian-held part of the territory, numbered 3,560,976 at 1961 census and was estimated at 3,678,000 at midyear 1963 and 3,729,000 at midyear 1964); data also exclude Junagardh, Manavadar, Gilgit and Baltistan, and census data probably also exclude a considerable number of nomads.

[53] Former mandated territory administered by the United Kingdom, until Armistice of 1949.

[54] Comprising that part of Palestine under Egyptian (United Arab Republic) administration following the Armistice of 1949 until June 1967, when it was occupied by Israeli military forces.

[55] Comprising those islands of the Ryukyu group south of the 28th degree of North Latitude, except the Amami Islands which reverted to Japan on 25 December 1951 and 25 December 1953. Administered under military government by the United States.

[56] Population excludes United States military and civilian personnel and their dependants stationed in the area.

[57] Population excludes transients afloat and non-locally domiciled military and civilian personnel and their dependants, numbering 3,466 and 27,299, respectively at 1957 census.

[58] Excluding data for islands of Perim (area 13 km^2) and Kamaran (area 57 km^2).

[59] Population includes Palestinian refugees numbering 141,028 on 31 December 1963 and 163,041 on 31 December 1967.

[60] Comprising 7 sheikdoms of Abu Dhabi, Dubai, Sharjah, Ajman, Umm al Qaiwain, Ras al Khaimah and Fujairah, and the area lying within the modified Riyadh line as announced in October 1955.

[61] Excludes area of frontier rivers.

[62] Including data for dependencies: Alderney, Brechou, Herm, Jethou, Lihou and Sark Islands.

[63] Excluding Faeroe Islands and Greenland, shown separately.

[64] Excluding Overseas Departments, namely French Guiana, Guadeloupe, Martinique and Réunion, shown separately.

[65] Population is de jure, but excludes diplomatic personnel outside the country and includes foreign diplomatic personnel not living in embassies or consulates.

[66] Population excludes armed forces.

[67] Area is 0.44 km^2.

[68] Including data for Gozo and Comino Islands. Population excludes non-Maltese armed forces stationed in the area and includes civilian nationals temporarily outside the country.

[69] Area is 1.49 km^2.

[70] Area of 33,612 km^2 previously shown, excluded inland waters.

[71] Population excludes civilian aliens within the country but includes civilian nationals temporarily outside the country.

[72] Continental Portugal, which includes the Azores and Madeira Islands.

[73] Continental Spain which includes the Balearic and Canary Islands.

[74] Inhabited only during winter season. Census data are for total population while estimates refer to Norwegian population only, included also in the de jure population of Norway.

[75] Shown elsewhere as "United Kingdom" and excluding Channel Islands and Isle of Man, shown separately.

[76] Population excludes armed forces stationed outside the country, numbering 48,106 in May 1959.

[77] Comprising the Solomon Islands group (except Bougainville and Buka which are included with New Guinea below), Ontong, Java, Rennel and Santa Cruz Islands.

[78] Part of Phoenix Islands group (see also Gilbert and Ellice Islands shown below). Jointly administered as a condominium, by United Kingdom and United States.

[79] Excluding Niue, shown separately, which is part of Cook Islands, but, because of remoteness, is administered separately.

[80] Comprising Austral, Gambier, Marquesas, Rapa, Society and Tuamotu Islands.

[81] Including also data for Christmas, Fanning, Ocean and Washington Islands, and the Phoenix Islands group except Canton and Enderbury Islands which are shown separately above.

[82] Population includes United States military personnel, their dependants and contract employees.

[83] Including the islands of Huon, Chesterfield, Loyalty and Walpole Islands and Belep Archipelago.

[84] Comprising north-eastern part of New Guinea, the Bismarck Archipelago, Bougainville and Buka of Solomon Islands group and about 600 smaller islands. United Nations Trust Territory administered by Australia.

[85] Land area only; total including ocean area within administrative boundaries, is approximately 2,589,988 km^2.

[86] Jointly administered, as a condominium, by United Kingdom and France.

[87] Including Campbell and Kermadec Islands (population 20 in 1961, area 148 km^2) as well as Antipodes, Auckland, Bounty, Snares, Solander and Three Kings Islands, all of which are uninhabited. Population includes diplomatic personnel and armed forces stationed outside the country, the latter numbering 1,936 at 1966 census; population also excludes alien armed forces within the country.

[88] Comprising the Caroline, Mariana and Marshall Islands except Guam, shown separately. United Nations Trust Territory administered by the United States.

[89] South-eastern part of the island of New Guinea.

4. LIFE EXPECTANCY

Life expectancy refers to the expectation of life at birth. Since the risk of death at birth is particularly great, those nations with high infant mortality rates have proportionally lower life expectancy. Likewise, those nations deficient in the control of infectious diseases whose primary victims are infants and children also suffer a reduction in total life expectancy.

The gap between developed and underdeveloped countries, quite broad at the beginning of this century, has considerably narrowed because of advances in medicine and hygiene. The life expectation gap between male and female in all countries, however, continues to spread.

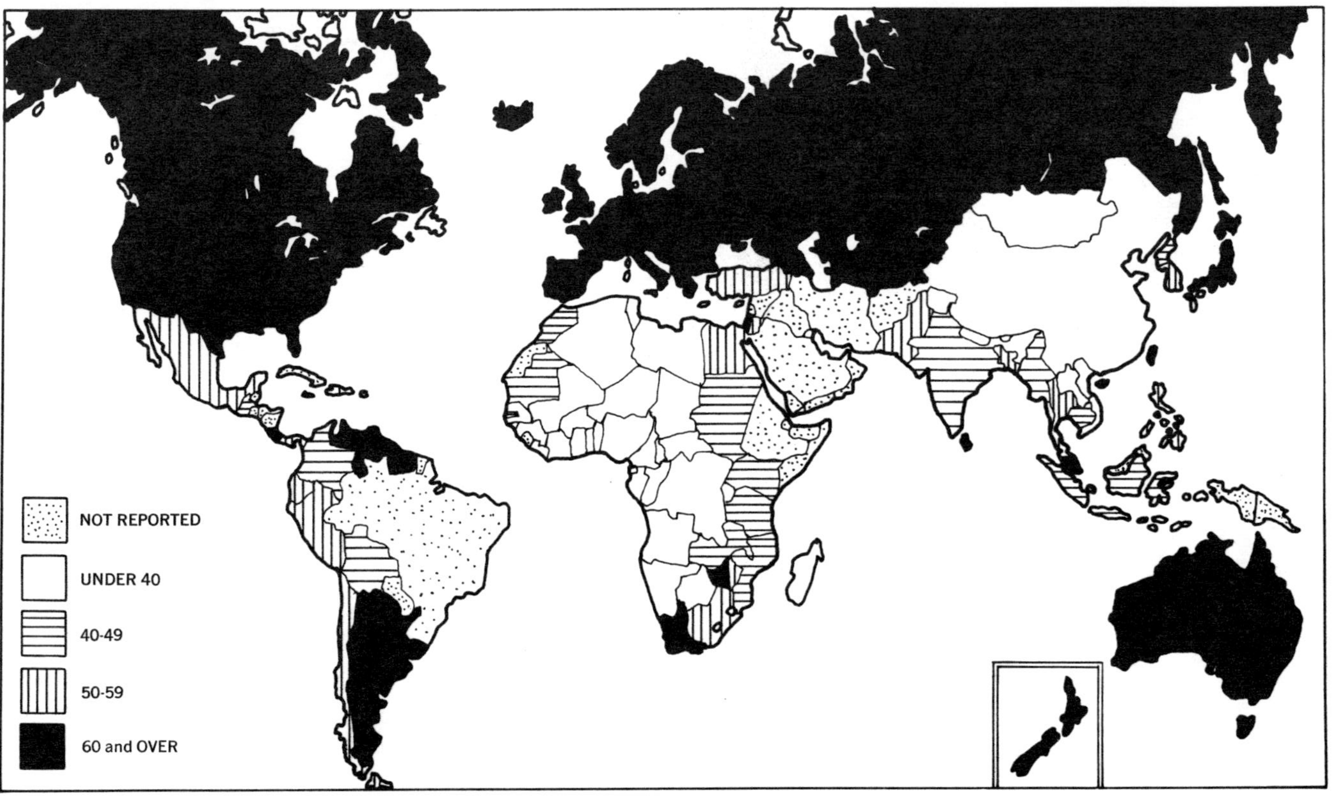

MAP 1-5. Major Areas and Regions by Life Expectancy

LIFE EXPECTANCY

from The United Nations Demographic Yearbook, 1969

AFRICA

Country / population	Year	Sex	Life expectancy
Algeria			
Algerian population	1948	Both sexes	[1]35
Non-Algerian population	1954	Both sexes	[1]63
Angola			
African population	1940	Both sexes	35
Burundi[2]	1965	Male	35.0
		Female	38.5
Cameroon			
West Cameroon[3]			
African population	1964-1965	Male	34.3
		Female	37.2
Central African Republic[2]			
African population	1959-1960	Male	33
		Female	36
Chad[2]			
African population	1963-1964	Male	29
		Female	35
Congo (Brazzaville)[2]			
African population	1960-1961	Both sexes	*37
Congo (Democratic Republic of)[4]			
African population	1950-1952	Male	37.64
		Female	40.00
Dahomey[2]			
African population	1961	Both sexes	37.3
Gabon[5]	1960-1961	Male	25
		Female	45
Gambia	1962-1963	Both sexes	[1]43
Ghana			
African population	1960	Male	37.08
Guinea[2]			
African population	1955	Male	26
		Female	28
Ivory Coast[6]			
African population	1957-1958	Both sexes	35
Kenya			
African population	1962	Both sexes	[7]40-45
Liberia	1962	Male	[1]36.1
		Female	[1]38.6
Madagascar[2]	1966	Male	37.5
		Female	38.3
Mali[2]	1960	Both sexes	35
Mauritania	1961-1962	Both sexes	[8]40
Mauritius			
Island of Mauritius	1961-1963	Male	58.66
		Female	61.86
Morocco	1962.	Both sexes	47
Mozambique			
African population	1940	Both sexes	45
Niger[2]	1959-1960	Both sexes	37
Nigeria	1965-1966[9]	Male	37.2
		Female	36.7
Réunion	1959-1963	Male	54.10
		Female	60.60
Senegal	1957	Both sexes	[10]37
Seychelles	1960[11]	Male	60.8
		Female	65.9
South Africa			
Asiatic population	1959-1961	Male	57.70
		Female	59.57
Coloured population	1959-1961	Male	49.62
		Female	54.28
White population	1959-1961	Male	64.73
		Female	71.67

LIFE EXPECTANCY (cont.)

Southern Rhodesia		
African population		
1962	Both sexes	[12]50
European population		
1961-1963	Male	66.9
	Female	74.0
Sudan		
1950	Both sexes	40
Swaziland		
African population		
1966	Both sexes	44
Togo		
1961[13]	Male	31.6
	Female	38.5
United Arab Republic		
1960	Male	51.6
	Female	53.8
United Republic of Tanzania		
1967	Both sexes	[1]40-41
Tanganyika		
1957	Both sexes	35-40
Zanzibar		
1958	Both sexes	[14]42.8
Upper Volta[2]		
1960-1961	Male	32.1
	Female	31.1
Zambia		
African population		
1963	Both sexes	[15]40

NORTH AMERICA

Antigua		
1959-1961	Male	60.48
	Female	64.32
Barbados		
1959-1961	Male	62.74
	Female	67.43
Bermuda		
1965-1966	Male	65.61
	Female	72.35
British Honduras		
1944-1948[16]	Male	44.99
	Female	48.97
British Virgin Islands[17]		
Canada		
1960-1962	Male	68.35
	Female	74.17
Costa Rica		
1962-1964	Male	61.87
	Female	64.83
Dominica		
1958-1962	Male	56.97
	Female	59.18
Dominican Republic		
1959-1961	Male	57.15
	Female	58.59
El Salvador		
1960-1961	Male	56.56
	Female	60.42
Greenland		
1952-1959	*Male	51.4
	Female	53.6
Grenada		
1959-1961	Male	60.14
	Female	65.60
Guadeloupe and Martinique[18]		
1959-1963	Male	62.5
	Female	66.5
Guatemala		
1963-1965	Male	48.29
	Female	49.74
Haiti		
1950[19]	Both sexes	32.61
Jamaica		
1959-1961	Male	62.65
	Female	66.63
Leeward Islands[20]		
1946	Male	49.53
	Female	54.76
Martinique and Guadeloupe[21]		
Mexico		
1959-1961	Male	57.61
	Female	60.32
Montserrat[17]		
Panama[22]		
1960-1961	Male	57.62
	Female	60.88
Puerto Rico[23]		
1959-1961	Male	67.14
	Female	71.88
St. Kitts-Nevis-Anguilla		
1959-1961	Male	57.97
	Female	61.90
St. Lucia		
1959-1961	Male	55.13
	Female	58.47

LIFE EXPECTANCY (cont.)

Country / Year	Sex	Years
St. Vincent		
1959-1961	Male	58.46
	Female	59.67
Trinidad and Tobago		
1959-1961	Male	62.15
	Female	66.33
United States		
1967	Male	67.0
	Female	74.2
SOUTH AMERICA		
Argentina		
1959-1961	Male	63.13
	Female	68.87
Bolivia		
1949-1951	Male	49.71
	Female	49.71
Chile		
1960-1961	Male	54.4
	Female	59.9
Colombia		
1950-1952	Male	44.18
	Female	45.95
Ecuador[24]		
1961-1963	Male	51.04
	Female	53.67
Guyana[25]		
1959-1961	Male	59.03
	Female	63.01
Peru		
1960-1965	Male	52.59
	Female	55.48
Surinam		
1963	Male	62.5
	Female	66.7
Uruguay		
1963-1964	Male	65.51
	Female	71.56
Venezuela		
1961	Both sexes	66.41
ASIA		
Burma		
1954[26]	Male	40.8
	Female	43.8
Cambodia		
1958-1959[27]	Male	44.2
	Female	43.3
Ceylon		
1962	Male	61.9
	Female	61.4
China (Taiwan)		
1965	Male	65.84
	Female	70.44
Cyprus		
1948-1950	Male	63.6
	Female	68.8
Hong Kong		
1968[28]	Male	66.74
	Female	73.29
India		
1951-1960	Male	41.89
	Female	40.55
Indonesia		
1960	Male	47.5
	Female	47.5
Israel		
1968	Male	69.32
	Female	72.88
Japan		
1967[29]	Male	68.91
	Female	74.15
Jordan		
1959-1963[30]	Male	52.6
	Female	52.0
Korea		
1938[31]	Male	47.20
	Female	50.59
Republic of Korea		
1955-1960	Male	51.12
	Female	53.73
Malaysia		
West Malaysia		
1966	Male	63.13
	Female	66.04
Pakistan		
1962*[32]	Male	53.72
	Female	48.80
Philippines		
1946-1949	Male	48.81
	Female	53.36
Ryukyu Islands		
1960	Male	68.02
	Female	74.65

LIFE EXPECTANCY (cont.)

Thailand		
1960	Male	53.6
	Female	58.7
Turkey		
1966	Both sexes	[33]53.7
EUROPE		
Albania		
1965-1966	Male	64.9
	Female	67.0
Austria		
1968	Male	66.73
	Female	73.50
Belgium		
1959-1963	Male	67.73
	Female	73.51
Bulgaria		
1965-1967	Male	68.81
	Female	72.67
Czechoslovakia		
1966	Male	67.33
	Female	73.57
Denmark[34]		
1965-1966	Male	70.1
	Female	74.7
Finland		
1961-1965	Male	65.4
	Female	72.6
France		
1966	Male	68.2
	Female	75.4
Germany		
Eastern Germany[35]		
1965-1966	Male	68.72
	Female	73.66
Federal Republic of Germany		
1965-1967	*Male	67.62
	Female	73.57
West Berlin		
1949-1951	Male	63.70
	Female	68.39
Greece		
1960-1962	Male	67.46
	Female	70.70
Hungary		
1964	Male	67.00
	Female	71.83
Iceland		
1961-1965	Male	70.8
	Female	76.2
Ireland		
1960-1962	Male	68.13
	Female	71.86
Italy		
1960-1962	Male	67.24
	Female	72.27
Luxembourg		
1946-1948	Male	61.69
	Female	65.75
Malta		
1965-1967	Male	67.53
	Female	71.64
Netherlands		
1967	Male	71.0
	Female	76.5
Norway		
1961-1965	Male	71.03
	Female	75.97
Poland		
1965-1966	Male	66.85
	Female	72.83
Portugal		
1959-1962	Male	60.73
	Female	66.35
Romania		
1963	Male	65.35
	Female	70.25
Spain		
1960*	Male	67.32
	Female	71.90
Sweden		
1967	Male	71.85
	Female	76.54
Switzerland		
1958-1963	Male	68.72
	Female	74.13
United Kingdom		
England and Wales		
1965-1967	Male	68.7
	Female	74.9
Northern Ireland		
1966-1968	Male	68.19
	Female	73.45
Scotland		
1968	Male	66.92
	Female	73.05
Yugoslavia		
1961-1962	Male	62.41
	Female	65.58

LIFE EXPECTANCY (cont.)

OCEANIA		
Australia[36]		
1960-1962	Male	67.92
	Female	74.18
Fiji		
Fijian Population		
1966	Male	66.99
	Female	72.05
Indian Population		
1966	Male	65.00
	Female	67.05
Gilbert and Ellice Islands		
1958-1962	Male	56.9
	Female	59.0
New Zealand		
1960-1962	Male	68.44
	Female	73.75
UNION OF SOVIET SOCIALIST REPUBLICS		
USSR		
1967-1968	Both sexes	70
Ukrainian SSR		
1966-1967	Both sexes	72
	Male	68
	Female	75

FOOTNOTES

*Provisional.

[1]Source: United Nations Economic Commission for Africa.

[2]Data based on results of sample survey described in Table 2.

[3]Data based on results of January 1964-January 1965 sample survey.

[4]Data based on results of a sample survey of mortality of about 3.6 per cent of the population, except for ages 70 and over, which are estimated.

[5]Data based on results of sample survey of mortality conducted at time of October 1960-May 1961 census.

[6]Data based on results of sample survey of mortality conducted between October 1957 and April 1958 in 69 villages.

[7]Based on analysis of data from 1962 post-censal sample survey.

[8]For 27 urban centres, based on analysis of data from November 1961-August 1962 urban census.

[9]Data are for rural areas only and were obtained from the Rural Demographic Sample Survey conducted in 1965-1966.

[10]For Basse Vallée (population estimated at 270,000), based on results of 1957-1958 sample of 77 rural villages and 5 urban centres.

[11]Data are estimates, based on results of 1960 population census.

[12]Based on results of 1962 population census.

[13]Data based on results of 1961 sample survey of mortality.

[14]For Afro-Arab population for the island of Zanzibar only; expectation of life at birth for island of Pemba is 40.3 for both sexes; based on results of 1958 population census.

[15]Based on results of 1963 population census.

[16]Data for age 1, 2, 3 and 4 years based on mortality rates computed on population assumed to have same age distribution as Jamaica, 1946.

[17]See Leeward Islands.

[18]Similarity in mortality and advantages of greater stability in larger numbers led to decision to compile life tables on combined experience.

[19]Data based on mortality rates implied from apparent survivorship rates between census of 1950 and an estimate for 1951 which was constructed on an assumed rate of growth.

[20]Comprising Antigua, Montserrat, St. Kitts-Nevis-Anguilla and British Virgin Islands.

[21]See Guadeloupe and Martinique.

[22]Excluding data for Canal Zone; also excluding tribal Indian population numbering 62, 187 in 1960.

[23]Data published by Department of Preventive Medicine and Public Health, School of Medicine, University of Puerto Rico, San Juan.

[24]Excluding nomadic Indian tribes.
[25]Excluding Amerindians.
[26]Data are for 46 municipal towns and are based on the 1953 census of population and the vital statistics returns for 1954.
[27]Data based on results of April 1959 sample survey of mortality in 345 villages.
[28]Data are based on the results of the sample survey taken on 2 August 1966.
[29]Data are for Japanese nationals only.
[30]Data are estimates based on analysis of 1961 population census results and annual average of reported deaths during 1959 to 1963.
[31]Including data for North Korea and the Republic of Korea.
[32]Data based on mortality rates estimated during 1962 according to Pakistan's Population Growth Estimation Project (PGE).
[33]Based on incomplete returns of Turkish Demographic Survey.
[34]Excluding data for Faeroe Islands and Greenland.
[35]Including data for East Berlin, not available separately.
[36]Excluding full-blooded aborigines, estimated at 40,081 in June 1961.

5. URBANIZATION

The continuum of urbanization has proceeded without interruption in modern times. As progress in agricultural methods gradually freed large numbers of laborers from work on the land and new industries provided the technological knowledge to support big clusters of dense population, cities began to grow and have never ceased growing.

In the urbanized West, where birth rates are relatively low, the urban population appears to increase at the expense of the rural population. In the United States, for example, the percentage of people living in rural areas has been cut in half since 1900 (Table 1-4). Whereas 60 percent of all Americans made their homes in small towns and in the country at the turn of the century, only 30 percent do so now. This means that in 1970, 70 percent or more Americans live in big cities or their suburban environs.

In the less urbanized regions of the world—on the continents of Asia, Africa and South America where urbanization increases at a rate almost double that of the West—high and rising birth rates still keep the rural populations expanding almost five times faster than their Western counterparts. Thus, while urbanization is undeniably a world-wide trend, it is not the only trend, especially in the underdeveloped regions.

For purposes of comparison, we refer to cities as "agglomerated" population limited to localities of 20,000 or more. This nomenclature and minimum population figure were adopted by the United Nations' study—*Growth of the World's Urban and Rural Population, 1920–2000,* from which all the data in this section is drawn—in order to eliminate many local peculiarities in urban-rural distinctions.

"Agglomerated" populations can be divided into cities of five sizes.

"Agglomerated" or "city and big-town":

(*a*) Super-conurbation: 12,500,000 or more inhabitants;
(*b*) Multimillion cities: 2,500,000 or more inhabitants;
(*c*) Big-city population: 500,000 or more inhabitants;
(*d*) City population: 100,000 or more inhabitants;
(*e*) Agglomerated population: 20,000 or more inhabitants;

Rural populations fall into two categories.

"Rural and small-town" population:

(*a*) Small-town population: towns smaller than 20,000 inhabitants but included among "urban" according to national definitions;
(*b*) Rural population: population not classified as "urban" in national definitions.

Now that our terms are straight we can discuss some of the more remarkable happenings in recent world urbanization. The story begins with an over-all picture of the agglomerated-rural division in the forty years between 1920 and 1960. In 1920 there was roughly a quarter of a billion people (266.4 million) living in agglomerations—29 percent (197.7 million) of the population in the more developed regions and 6 percent (68.7 million) of the population in less developed regions.

But by 1960, the agglomerations counted a little less than three quarters of a billion (760.3 billion) with 46 percent (449.6 million) of the population in the more developed regions and 15 percent (310 million) of the population in the less developed regions. These 1960 figures represent a 227 percent increase in the agglomerated population of the more developed regions and a 452 percent increase in the same population of the less developed regions.

While 14 percent of the world population resided in agglomerations in 1920, 25 percent lived in cities by 1960. Statistically then, the urbanization index is steadily on the ascent.

What obtained in the rural and small-town populations during this same period? They grew too—from a worldwide number of 1.6 billion in 1920 to more than 2.2 billion in 1960, an increment of 38 percent. As noted above, the fact of high birth rates in the less developed regions explains the concurrent climb in both their agglomerated and rural populations. In the less developed regions, the rural population rose 52 percent as opposed to 11 percent in the more developed regions. In 1960, despite the long-standing trend toward urbanization, 75 percent of the world population still lived in rural areas, in localities of less than 20,000—85 percent of the people in the less developed countries and 54 percent in the more developed.

TABLE 1-4. The Urbanizing United States, 1800-1968

Year	Urban population (thousands)	%	Rural population (thousands)	%	Total resident population
1800	322	6	4,986	94	5,308
1830	1,127	9	11,739	91	12,866
1860	6,217	20	25,227	80	31,444
1890	22,106	35	40,841	65	62,947
1920	54,158	51	51,552	49	105,710
1950	96,847	64	54,479	36	151,326
1968	146,225	73	53,621*	27	199,846

*Estimate based on extrapolation from the 1950-1960 period.
Source: Historical Statistics of the United States, Colonial Times to 1957, U. S. Bureau of the Census.

BOX 1-2. Composition of Major Areas by Regions and Countries according to Growth of the World's Urban and Rural Population, 1920-1960

The basic scheme of geographical classification used in this report refers to eight major areas that do not conform entirely to the conventional definitions of the continents, and are so drawn as to obtain somewhat greater homogeneity in sizes of population, types of demographic circumstances and accuracy of demographic statistics. Six of the major areas were further subdivided into regions.

Because countries such as the Soviet Union, Turkey and the United States of America overlap the traditional boundaries of continents, the major areas could not be defined to coincide with continents, with the exception of Africa. In view of its size, the Soviet Union is considered as a major area by itself, hence the areas designated here as Europe or Asia include no part of the Soviet Union. The distinction of East Asia and South Asia as separate major areas was dictated largely by the size of their population. Northern America and Latin America were distinguished as major areas, rather than the conventional distinction being made between the continents of North America and South America, because population trends in the middle American mainland and the Caribbean region more closely resemble those of South America than those of America north of Mexico. Latin America as defined here has somewhat wider limits than the twenty American republics of Spanish, Portuguese and French speech which constitute Latin America in a stricter sense.

The scheme of major areas and component regions followed in this report was first used in a recent United Nations publication entitled World Population Prospects as Assessed in 1963.[a] The following modifications of the previous scheme have been observed in this report:

(a) To permit allocation of population figures for the previously undivided city of Berlin, West Berlin has been included with the region of eastern Europe;

(b) The regions of western, eastern and middle Africa, of the previous report, have been combined into one region, namely, Tropical Africa; and

(c) The regions of Melanesia, Polynesia and Micronesia have been combined into one, namely Other Oceania, i.e., other than Australia and New Zealand, and not including Hawaii which is included with the United States.

The outlines of each region are illustrated in map 1-6. Map 1-6 also indicates the current levels of urbanization in each region (as defined by the percentage of total population in cities of 20,000 or more inhabitants in 1960).

For present purposes—as also in the previous report on World Population Prospects as Assessed in 1963—the major areas have been divided into two categories of regions, considering the levels of economic, social and demographic indicators by which they can be distinguished. In these respects, however, some heterogeneity is noted among regions constituting the same major areas. Japan and Temperate South America are among the more developed regions but they are situated in the major areas of East Asia and Latin America, respectively, the greater part of which are less developed. Oceania, in its majority a more developed major area, comprises the less developed region of Other Oceania (other than Australia and New Zealand, i.e., Melanesia, Polynesia and Micronesia). Consequently, the grouping of more developed, or less developed, major areas does not coincide with the grouping of more developed, or less developed, regions.

In the list which follows, countries are listed under the regions in which they have been grouped, and the regions according to the major areas of which they form part. The list follows the order of size of urban population in 1960 and includes all countries with a population larger than 5,000 inhabitants.

[a] The purpose of this report is to describe world population on the basis of urban and rural geographic definitions rather than political definitions. For this reason, the entire city of Berlin has been included in eastern Europe.

Major area	Region	Countries
I. More developed major areas		
Europe	Western Europe	Federal Republic of Germany, France, Netherlands, Belgium, Austria, Switzerland, Luxembourg, Monaco, Liechtenstein
	Southern Europe	Italy, Spain, Yugoslavia, Portugal, Greece, Albania, Malta, Gibraltar, San Marino, Andorra
	Eastern Europe[a]	Poland, Romania, Eastern Germany, Czechoslovakia, Hungary, Berlin, Bulgaria
	Northern Europe	United Kingdom of Great Britain and Northern Ireland, Sweden, Denmark, Finland, Norway, Ireland, Iceland, Channel Islands, Isle of Man, Faeroe Islands
Northern America	Northern America	United States of America (including Alaska and Hawaii), Canada, Bermuda, Greenland, St. Pierre and Miquelon
Soviet Union	Soviet Union	Union of Soviet Socialist Republics
Oceania	Australia and New Zealand	Australia, New Zealand
	Other Oceania	Melanesia (including New Guinea, Papua, British Solomon Islands, New Caledonia, New Hebrides, and Norfolk Island), Polynesia and Micronesia (including Fiji Islands, Western Samoa, Pacific Islands under United States administration, French Polynesia, Guam, Tonga, Gilbert and Ellice Islands, American Samoa, Cook Islands and smaller islands with fewer than 5,000 inhabitants)
II. Less developed major areas		
East Asia	Mainland region	Mainland China, Hong Kong, Mongolia, Macau
	Japan	Japan
	Other East Asia	Korea, China (Taiwan), Ryukyu Islands
South Asia	Middle South Asia	India, Pakistan, Iran, Afghanistan, Ceylon, Nepal, Bhutan, Sikkim, Maldive Islands
	South-East Asia	Indonesia, Viet-Nam, Philippines, Thailand, Burma, Malaysia, Cambodia, Laos, Singapore, Portuguese Timor, Brunei
	South-West Asia	Turkey, Iraq, Saudi Arabia, Syria, Yemen, Israel, Jordan, Lebanon, Southern Yemen, Cyprus, Muscat and Oman, Palestine (Gaza Strip), Kuwait, Bahrain, Trucial Oman, Qatar
Latin America	Tropical South America	Brazil, Colombia, Peru, Venezuela, Ecuador, Bolivia, Guyana, Surinam, French Guiana
	Middle America (mainland)	Mexico, Guatemala, El Salvador, Honduras, Nicaragua, Costa Rica, Panama, British Honduras, Canal Zone
	Temperate South America	Argentina, Chile, Uruguay, Paraguay, Falkland Islands
Africa	Northern Africa	United Arab Republic, Sudan, Morocco, Algeria, Tunisia, Libya, Spanish North Africa, Ifni, Spanish Sahara
	Tropical Africa	Western Africa (including Nigeria, Ghana, Upper Volta, Mali, Ivory Coast, Senegal, Guinea, Niger, Sierra Leone, Dahomey, Togo, Liberia, Mauritania, Portuguese Guinea, Gambia, Cape Verde Islands and St. Helena); Eastern Africa (including Ethiopia, Tanzania, Kenya, Uganda, Mozambique, Madagascar, Rhodesia, Malawi, Zambia, Rwanda, Burundi, Somalia, Mauritius, Rèunion, Comoro Islands, French Somaliland and Seychelles); Middle Africa (including Democratic Republic of the Congo, Angola, Cameroon, Chad, Central African Republic, Congo (Brazzaville), Gabon, Equatorial Guinea and São Tomé and Principe)
	Southern Africa	South Africa, Lesotho, Namibia, Botswana and Swaziland

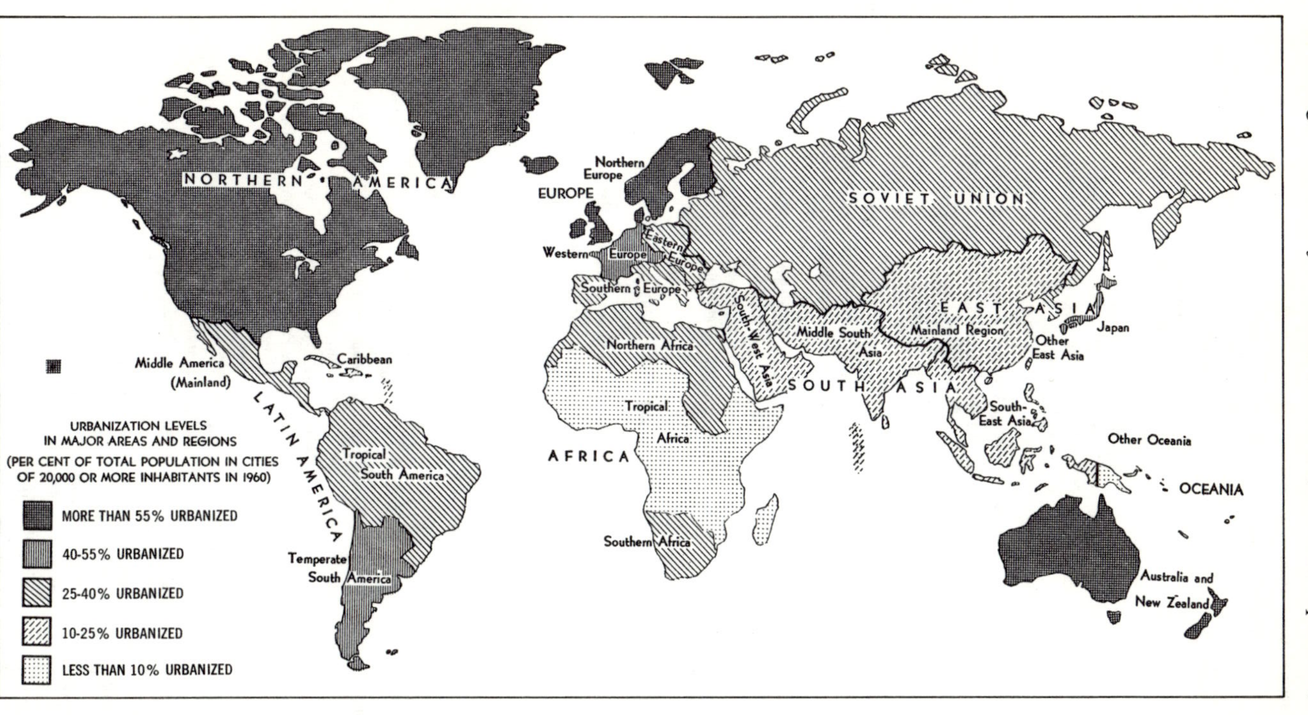

MAP 1-6. Urbanization Levels in Major Areas and Regions of the World (Percentage of Total Population in Cities of 20,000 or More Inhabitants in 1960)

The boundaries shown on this map do not imply official endorsement or acceptance by the United Nations. (Map No. 1819. United Nations)

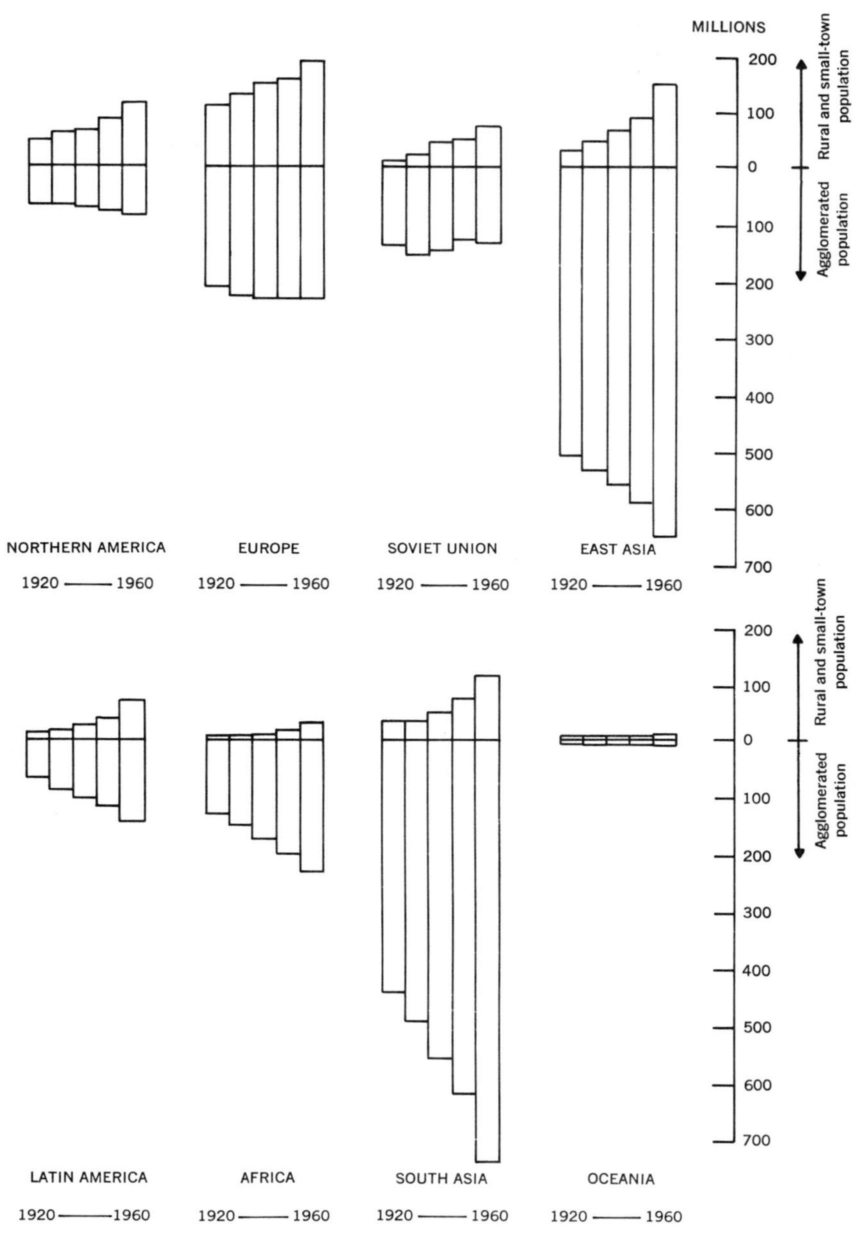

FIGURE 1-6. Agglomerated and Rural and Small-town Population in Eight Major Areas of the World, 1920–60

TABLE 1-5. Total Agglomerated and Rural and Small-Town Population in the World and Major Areas, 1920–1960, and 1960 Population Relative to 1920 Population

Major area	1920	1930	1940 (Millions)	1950	1960	Index, 1960 (1920 = 100)
Total population						
World total	1,860.0	2,068.6	2,295.1	2,515.5	2,990.8	161
More developed major areas	604.4	677.1	729.2	750.6	853.5	141
Europe	324.9	353.9	378.9	391.8	424.7	131
Northern America	115.7	134.2	144.3	166.1	198.7	172
Soviet Union	155.3	179.0	195.0	180.0	214.4	138
Oceania	8.5	10.0	11.0	12.7	15.7	184
Less developed major areas	1,255.6	1,391.5	1,565.9	1,764.9	2,137.3	170
East Asia	553.4	591.2	634.4	684.3	794.1	144
South Asia	469.8	529.0	610.1	696.7	857.9	183
Latin America	89.5	107.5	129.9	162.4	212.4	237
Africa	142.9	163.8	191.5	221.5	272.9	191
More developed regions	672.7	757.9	820.6	857.8	976.5	145
Less developed regions	1,187.3	1,310.7	1,474.5	1,657.7	2,014.1	170
Agglomerated population (localities of 20,000 or more inhabitants)						
World total	266.4	338.2	431.5	533.0	760.3	285
More developed major areas	179.9	222.0	267.9	299.6	389.5	217
Europe	112.9	131.8	149.8	159.5	187.9	166
Northern America	47.9	62.4	66.6	84.3	115.3	241
Soviet Union	16.0	24.0	47.0	50.0	78.0	488
Oceania	3.1	3.8	4.5	5.8	8.3	266
Less developed major areas	86.5	116.2	163.6	233.4	370.8	429
East Asia	39.8	53.9	73.7	94.1	147.1	370
South Asia	26.9	34.5	50.6	77.1	117.5	437
Latin America	12.9	18.1	25.5	40.7	69.7	540
Africa	6.9	9.7	13.8	21.5	36.5	535
More developed regions	197.7	247.1	303.9	343.2	449.6	227
Less developed regions	68.7	91.1	127.6	189.8	310.7	452
Rural and small-town population (localities smaller than 20,000)						
World total	1,593.6	1,730.4	1,863.6	1,982.5	2,230.5	140
More developed major areas	424.5	455.1	461.3	451.0	464.0	109
Europe	212.0	222.1	229.1	232.3	236.8	112
Northern America	67.8	71.8	77.7	81.8	83.4	123
Soviet Union	139.3	155.0	148.0	130.0	136.4	98
Oceania	5.4	6.2	6.5	6.9	7.4	137
Less developed major areas	1,169.1	1,275.3	1,402.3	1,531.5	1,766.5	151
East Asia	513.6	537.3	560.7	590.2	647.0	126
South Asia	442.9	494.5	559.5	619.6	740.4	167
Latin America	76.6	89.4	104.4	121.7	142.7	186
Africa	136.0	154.1	177.7	200.0	236.4	174
More developed regions	475.0	510.8	516.7	514.6	526.9	111
Less developed regions	1,118.6	1,219.6	1,346.9	1,467.9	1,703.4	152

TABLE 1-6. Percentages of World's Total, Agglomerated and Rural and Small-Town Population in Each of the Major Areas, 1920–1960

Major area	1920	1930	1940	1950	1960
Total population					
World total	100.0	100.0	100.0	100.0	100.0
More developed major areas	32.5	32.8	31.8	29.9	28.5
Europe	17.5	17.1	16.5	15.6	14.2
Northern America	6.2	6.5	6.3	6.6	6.6
Soviet Union	8.3	8.7	8.5	7.2	7.2
Oceania	0.5	0.5	0.5	0.5	0.5
Less developed major areas	67.5	67.2	68.2	70.1	71.5
East Asia	29.7	28.7	27.6	27.1	26.6
South Asia	25.3	25.6	26.6	27.7	28.7
Latin America	4.8	5.2	5.7	6.5	7.1
Africa	7.7	7.9	8.3	8.8	9.1
More developed regions	36.2	36.6	35.8	34.1	32.7
Less developed regions	63.8	63.4	64.2	65.9	67.3
Agglomerated population					
World total	100.0	100.0	100.0	100.0	100.0
More developed major areas	67.6	65.7	62.0	56.4	51.3
Europe	42.4	39.0	34.7	30.1	24.7
Northern America	18.0	18.5	15.4	15.8	15.2
Soviet Union	6.0	7.1	10.9	9.4	10.3
Oceania	1.2	1.1	1.0	1.1	1.1
Less developed major areas	32.4	34.3	38.0	43.6	48.7
East Asia	15.0	15.8	17.2	17.5	19.2
South Asia	10.0	10.2	11.7	14.5	15.5
Latin America	4.8	5.4	5.9	7.6	9.2
Africa	2.6	2.9	3.2	4.0	4.8
More developed regions	74.2	73.1	70.4	64.4	59.1
Less developed regions	25.8	26.9	29.6	35.6	40.9
Rural and small-town population					
World total	100.0	100.0	100.0	100.0	100.0
More developed major areas	26.6	26.3	24.7	22.7	20.7
Europe	13.3	12.8	12.3	11.7	10.6
Northern America	4.3	4.1	4.2	4.1	3.7
Soviet Union	8.7	9.0	7.9	6.6	6.1
Oceania	0.3	0.4	0.3	0.3	0.3
Less developed major areas	73.4	73.7	75.3	77.3	79.3
East Asia	32.3	31.0	30.2	29.8	29.1
South Asia	27.8	28.6	30.0	31.3	33.2
Latin America	4.8	5.2	5.6	6.1	6.4
Africa	8.5	8.9	9.5	10.1	10.6
More developed regions	29.8	29.5	27.7	26.0	23.6
Less developed regions	70.2	70.5	72.3	74.0	76.4

TABLE 1-7. Amounts of Increase in Total, Agglomerated and Rural and Small-Town Population, 1920–1960 and Each Decade, in the World and Major Areas

(Millions)

Major areas	1920-1960	1920-1930	1930-1940	1940-1950	1950-1960
Total population					
World total	1,130.8	208.6	226.5	220.4	475.3'
More developed major areas	249.1	72.7	52.1	21.4	102.9
Europe	99.8	29.0	25.0	12.9	32.9
Northern America	83.0	18.5	10.1	21.8	32.6
Soviet Union	59.1	23.7	16.0	−15.0	34.4
Oceania	7.2	1.5	1.0	1.7	3.0
Less developed major areas	881.7	135.9	174.4	199.0	372.4
East Asia	240.7	37.8	43.2	39.9	109.8
South Asia	388.1	59.2	81.1	86.6	161.2
Latin America	122.9	18.0	22.4	32.5	50.0
Africa	130.0	20.9	27.7	30.0	51.4
More developed regions	303.8	85.2	62.7	37.2	118.7
Less developed regions	826.8	123.4	163.8	183.2	356.4
Agglomerated population					
World total	493.9	71.8	93.3	101.5	227.3
More developed major areas	209.6	42.1	45.9	31.7	89.9
Europe	75.0	18.9	18.0	9.7	28.4
Northern America	67.4	14.5	4.2	17.7	31.0
Soviet Union	62.0	8.0	23.0	3.0	28.0
Oceania	5.2	0.7	0.7	1.3	2.5
Less developed major areas	284.3	29.7	47.4	69.8	137.4
East Asia	107.3	14.1	19.8	20.4	53.0
South Asia	90.6	7.6	16.1	26.5	40.4
Latin America	56.8	5.2	7.4	15.2	29.0
Africa	29.6	2.8	4.1	7.7	15.0
More developed regions	251.9	49.4	56.8	39.3	106.4
Less developed regions	242.0	22.4	36.5	62.2	120.9
Rural and small-town population					
World total	636.9	136.8	133.2	118.9	248.0
More developed major areas	39.5	30.6	6.2	−9.7	13.0
Europe	24.8	10.1	7.0	3.2	4.5
Northern America	15.6	4.0	5.9	4.1	1.6
Soviet Union	−2.9	15.7	−7.0	−18.0	6.4
Oceania	2.0	0.8	0.3	0.4	0.5
Less developed major areas	597.4	106.2	127.0	129.2	235.0
East Asia	133.4	23.7	23.4	29.5	56.8
South Asia	297.5	51.6	65.0	60.1	120.8
Latin America	66.1	12.8	15.0	17.3	21.0
Africa	100.4	18.1	23.6	22.3	36.4
More developed regions	51.9	35.8	5.9	−2.1	12.3
Less Developed regions	584.8	101.0	127.3	123.0	235.5

TABLE 1-8. Estimated Average Rates of Growth in Total Agglomerated and Rural and Small-Town Population in the World and Major Areas, 1920–1960

(Percentage)

Major area	1920-1930	1930-1940	1940-1950	1950-1960
Total population				
World total	1.1	1.1	0.9	1.7
More developed major areas	1.1	0.7	0.3	1.3
Europe	0.9	0.7	0.3	0.8
Northern America	1.5	0.7	1.4	1.8
Soviet Union	1.4	0.9	−0.8	1.8
Oceania	1.7	1.0	1.4	2.3
Less developed major areas	1.0	1.2	1.2	1.9
East Asia	0.7	0.7	0.8	1.5
South Asia	1.2	1.4	1.3	2.1
Latin America	1.8	1.9	2.3	2.8
Africa	1.4	1.6	1.5	2.1
More developed regions	1.2	0.8	0.4	1.3
Less developed regions	1.0	1.2	1.2	2.0
Agglomerated population (20,000 and over)				
World total	2.4	2.5	2.1	3.6
More developed major areas	2.1	1.9	1.1	2.7
Europe	1.6	1.3	0.6	1.7
Northern America	2.7	0.7	2.4	3.2
Soviet Union	4.1	7.0	0.6	4.5
Oceania	2.0	1.8	2.6	3.5
Less developed major areas	3.0	3.5	3.6	4.7
East Asia	3.1	3.2	2.5	4.6
South Asia	2.5	3.9	4.3	4.3
Latin America	3.4	3.5	4.8	5.5
Africa	3.6	3.6	4.5	5.4
More developed regions	2.3	2.1	1.2	2.7
Less developed regions	2.9	3.4	4.1	5.1
Rural and small-town population (localities up to 20,000)				
World total	0.8	0.7	0.6	1.2
More developed major areas	0.7	0.1	−0.2	0.3
Europe	0.5	0.3	0.1	0.2
Northern America	0.6	0.8	0.5	0.2
Soviet Union	1.1	−0.5	−1.3	0.5
Oceania	1.5	0.4	0.4	0.9
Less developed major areas	0.9	1.0	0.9	1.4
East Asia	0.5	0.4	0.6	0.9
South Asia	1.1	1.2	1.0	1.8
Latin America	1.5	1.6	1.5	1.6
Africa	1.3	1.4	1.2	1.7
More developed regions	0.7	0.1	0.0	0.2
Less developed regions	0.9	1.0	0.9	1.5

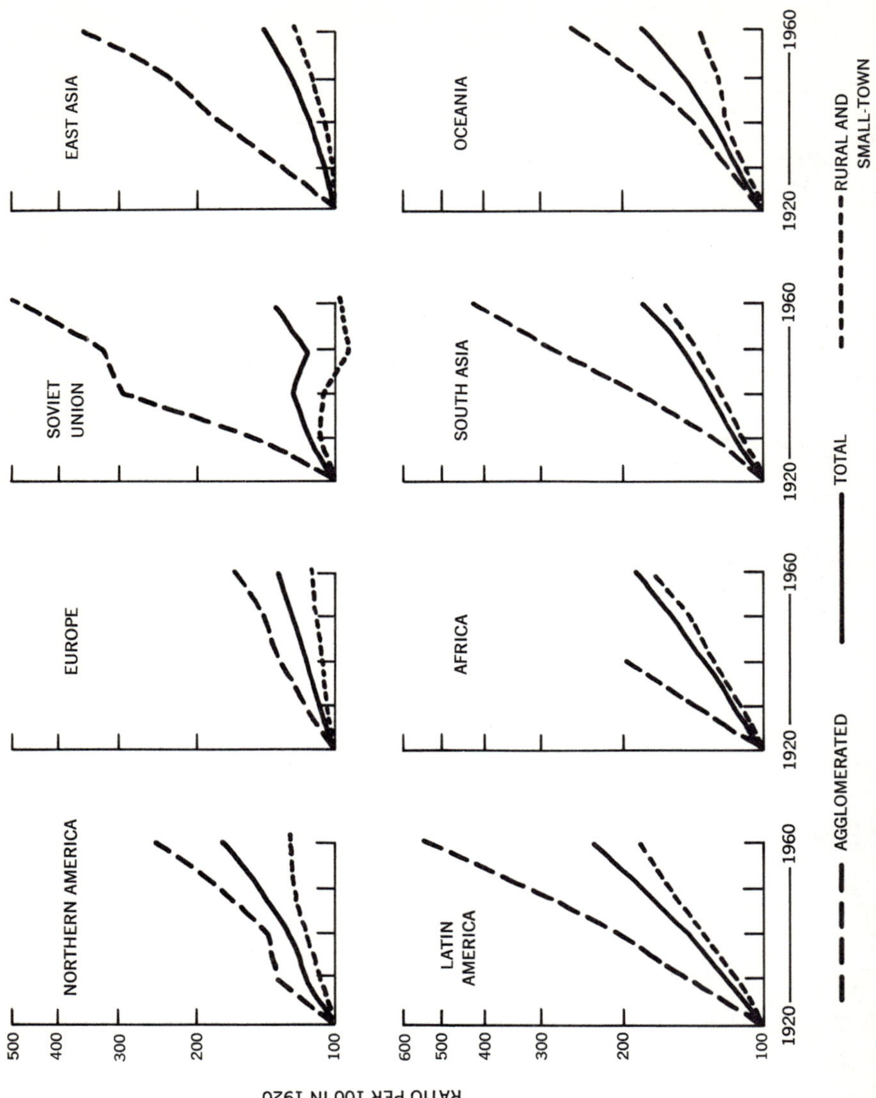

FIGURE 1-7. Ratio of Population in 1930, 1940, 1950 and 1960 relative to 100 Population in 1920, in Eight Major Areas of the World (Total, Agglomerated and Rural and Small-town)

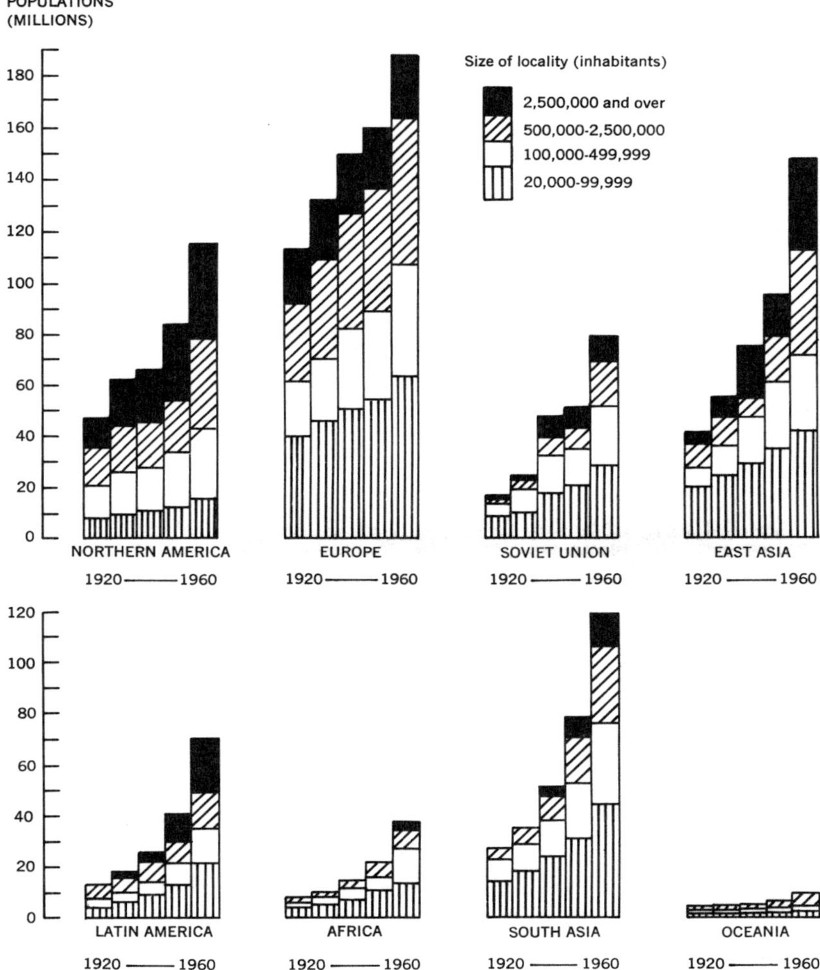

FIGURE 1-8. Agglomerated Population by Size of Locality, 1920–60

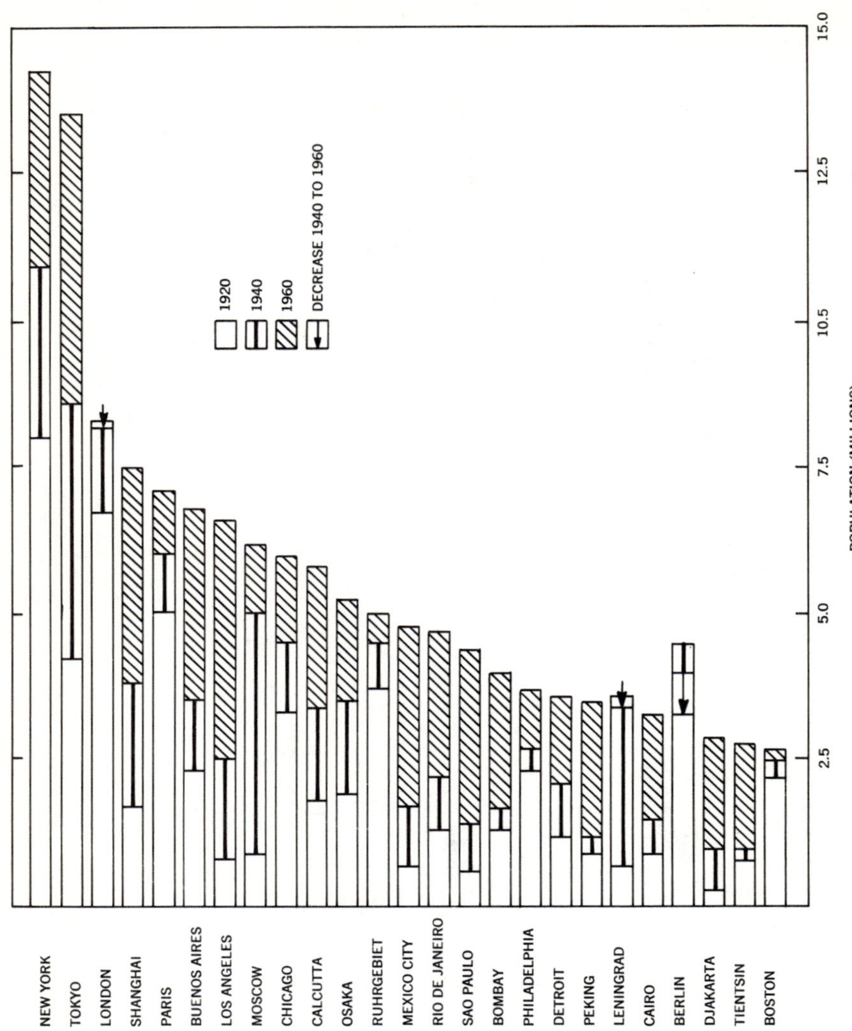

FIGURE 1-9. Population of the World's Twenty-five Largest Cities, 1920–60

TABLE 1-9. Percentage of Total Population in Localities with 20,000 or More Inhabitants in the World and Major Areas, 1920–1960

Major area	1920	1930	1940	1950	1960
World total	14	16	19	21	25
More developed major areas	30	33	37	40	46
Europe	35	37	40	41	44
Northern America	41	46	46	51	58
Soviet Union	10	13	24	28	36
Oceania	37	38	41	46	53
Less developed major areas	7	8	10	13	17
East Asia	7	9	12	14	19
South Asia	6	7	8	11	14
Latin America	14	17	20	25	33
Africa	5	6	7	10	13
More developed regions[a]	29	33	37	40	46
Less developed regions[b]	6	7	9	11	15

[a] Europe, Northern America, Soviet Union, Japan, Temperate South America and Australia and New Zealand.

[b] East Asia without Japan, South Asia, Latin America without Temperate South America, Africa and Oceania without Australia and New Zealand.

Big Cities

Urbanization has had a direct effect on the size of cities. There were only eighty-three big cities (pop. 500,000 or more) in 1920–1969 in the more developed regions and only fourteen in the less developed. By 1960, big cities in the more developed regions had increased to 139 (a 60 percent leap) and 95 in the less developed (an increase of almost 700 percent).

TABLES and MAPS on BIG CITIES

According to *Growth of the World's Urban and Rural Population, 1820–1960*

TABLE 1-10. Number of Big Cities and Multimillion Cities in the World and Major Areas, 1920-1960

Major area	1920	1930	1940	1950	1960
Big cities (500,000 inhabitants and over)					
World total	83	102	126	158	234
More developed major areas	62	73	85	97	126
Europe	40	47	50	52	56
Northern America	18	20	21	29	41
Soviet Union	2	4	12	14	25
Oceania	2	2	2	2	4
Less developed major areas	21	29	41	61	108
East Asia	11	13	16	22	50
South Asia	4	7	14	22	29
Latin America	5	7	8	11	19
Africa	1	2	3	6	10
More developed regions	69	81	94	105	139
Europe	40	47	50	52	56
Other[a]	29	34	44	53	83
Less developed regions	14	21	32	53	95
Multimillion cities (2,500,000 inhabitants and over)					
World total	7	11	15	20	26
More developed major areas	6	8	10	12	12
Europe	4	4	4	4	4
Northern America	2	3	4	6	6
Soviet Union	–	1	2	2	2
Oceania	–	–	–	–	–
Less developed major areas	1	3	5	8	14
East Asia	1	2	3	3	6
South Asia	–	–	1	2	3
Latin America	–	1	1	3	4
Africa	–	–	–	–	1
More developed regions	7	11	13	15	15
Europe	4	4	4	4	4
Other[a]	3	7	9	11	11
Less developed regions	–	–	2	5	11

[a] Northern America, Soviet Union, Japan, Temperate South America, Australia and New Zealand.

TABLE 1-11. Population of Big Cities and Multimillion Cities in the World and Major Areas, 1920–1960 (Millions)

Major area	1920	1930	1940	1950	1960
Big cities (500,000 inhabitants and over)					
World total	106.6	142.3	181.1	227.4	352.2
More developed major areas	82.1	106.4	125.2	140.7	186.0
Europe	51.7	62.4	68.4	70.5	81.4
Northern America	27.0	36.1	39.0	51.0	72.5
Soviet Union	1.7	5.8	15.4	16.2	26.9
Oceania	1.7	2.1	2.4	3.0	5.2
Less developed major areas	24.5	35.9	55.9	86.7	166.2
East Asia	13.6	19.5	27.8	35.0	77.8
South Asia	4.6	6.3	13.4	26.1	42.4
Latin America	5.4	8.4	11.8	19.6	35.2
Africa	0.9	1.7	2.9	6.0	10.8
More developed regions	92.9	121.7	145.7	162.0	221.6
Europe	51.7	62.4	68.4	70.5	81.4
Other[a]	41.2	59.3	77.3	91.5	140.2
Less developed regions	13.7	20.6	35.4	65.4	130.6
Multimillion cities (2,500,000 inhabitants and over)					
World total	35.5	53.8	74.8	95.4	141.5
More developed major areas	31.3	42.3	52.1	59.9	69.8
Europe	19.9	22.4	22.8	22.1	23.6
Northern America	11.4	17.3	20.7	29.5	36.6
Soviet Union	–	2.6	8.6	8.3	9.6
Oceania	–	–	–	–	–
Less developed major areas	4.2	11.5	22.7	35.5	71.7
East Asia	4.2	8.7	15.8	16.3	35.1
South Asia	–	–	3.4	7.2	12.6
Latin America	–	2.8	3.5	12.0	20.7
Africa	–	–	–	–	3.3
More developed regions	36.5	53.8	67.6	76.4	97.6
Europe	19.9	22.4	22.8	22.1	23.6
Other[a]	15.6	31.4	44.8	54.3	74.0
Less developed regions	–	–	7.2	19.0	43.9

[a] Northern America, Soviet Union, Japan, Temperate South America, Australia and New Zealand.

TABLE 1-12. Population of Big Cities (500,000 Inhabitants or Over) in the World and Three Selected Regions 1920–1960, According to Their Sizes in 1920

(Millions)

Selected region	1920	1930	1940	1950	1960	Increase, 1920–1960
All big cities (500,000 inhabitants or over at any given date)						
World total	106.6	143.3	181.1	228.2[a]	353.6[b]	247.0[b]
Europe	51.7	62.4	68.4	71.3[a]	82.8[b]	31.1[b]
Other more developed regions	41.2	60.3	77.3	101.5	140.2	99.0
Less developed regions	13.7	20.6	35.4	55.4	130.6	116.9
Cities of one million or more inhabitants in 1920						
World total	67.7	80.3	90.2	97.5	121.0	53.3
Europe[c]	33.9	37.6	38.6	37.9	40.1	6.2
Other more developed regions[d]	26.6	34.8	39.8	43.4	57.4	30.8
Less developed regions[e]	7.2	7.9	11.8	16.2	23.5	16.3
Cities of 500,000–999,999 inhabitants in 1920						
World total	38.9	50.9	62.0	72.8[a]	99.1[b]	60.2[b]
Europe[f]	17.8	20.5	22.9	24.0[a]	29.7[b]	11.9[b]
Other more developed regions[g]	14.6	21.8	28.1	32.2	42.6	28.0
Less developed regions[h]	6.5	8.6	11.0	16.2	26.8	20.3
Entry of "new big cities" (cumulative)[i]						
World total	–	9.5	21.5	37.5	74.5	74.5
Europe[j]	–	3.5	5.0	6.0	8.0	8.0
Other more developed regions[k]	–	2.5	7.5	12.0	26.5	26.5
Less developed regions[l]	–	3.5	9.0	19.5	40.0	40.0
Gorwth of "new big cities" entered[m]						
World total	–	2.6	7.4	22.4	59.0	59.0
Europe[j]	–	0.8	1.9	3.0	5.0	5.0
Other more developed regions[k]	–	1.2	1.9	3.9	13.7	13.7
Less developed regions[l]	–	0.6	3.6	13.5	40.3	40.3

[a] Including Dresden and Wroclaw, though their populations had fallen below 500,000 in 1950.
[b] Including Dresden Wroclaw and Sheffield, though their populations had fallen below 500,000 in 1960.
[c] London, Paris, Berlin, the Ruhrgebiet, Manchester, Vienna, Birmingham, Glasgow, Hamburg, Leeds, Budapest, Liverpool and Brussels.
[d] New York, Tokyo, Chicago, Philadelphia, Boston, Buenos Aires, Osaka, Pittsburgh and Detroit.
[e] Calcutta, Shanghai, Rio de Janeiro, Bombay and Istanbul.
[f] Twenty-seven cities.
[g] Twenty cities.
[h] Peking, Cairo, Tientsin, Canton, Wuhan, Mexico City, Sao Paulo, Hong Kong and Madras.
[i] Arithmetic result of attainment of 500,000 by each of the cities having attained such size since 1920.
[j] Seven cities by 1930, 10 by 1940, 12 by 1950 and 16 by 1960.
[k] Five cities by 1930, 15 by 1940, 24 by 1950 and 53 by 1960.
[l] Seven cities by 1930, 18 by 1940, 39 by 1950 and 80 by 1960.
[m] Cumulative result of growth beyond 500,000 of cities having attained such size since 1920.

TABLE 1-13. Estimated Annual Rates of Growth in Total, Agglomerated and Rural and Small-Town Population, 1920–1940, 1940–1960, 1960–1980 and 1980–2000

Major areas	1920–1940	1940–1960	1960–1980	1980–2000
Total population				
World total	1.1	1.3	1.9	1.7
More developed major areas	0.9	0.8	1.0	1.0
Europe	0.8	0.6	0.6	0.5
North America	1.1	1.6	1.5	1.5
Soviet Union	1.1	0.5	1.3	1.2
Oceania	1.3	1.8	1.8	1.7
Less developed major areas	1.1	1.6	2.2	2.0
East Asia	0.7	1.1	1.4	1.1
South Asia	1.3	1.7	2.5	2.1
Latin America	1.9	2.5	2.9	2.6
Africa	1.5	1.8	2.5	2.7
More developed regions	1.0	0.9	1.0	0.9
Less developed regions	1.1	1.6	2.2	2.0
Agglomerated population				
World total	2.4	2.9	2.9	2.8
More developed major areas	2.0	1.9	1.9	1.6
Europe	1.4	1.1	1.2	1.0
Northern America	1.7	2.8	2.2	1.8
Soviet Union	5.5	2.6	3.0	2.3
Oceania	1.9	3.1	2.3	1.8
Less developed major areas	3.2	4.2	3.9	3.5
East Asia	3.1	3.5	3.0	2.4
South Asia	3.2	4.3	4.1	3.9
Latin America	3.5	5.2	4.4	3.8
Africa	3.5	5.0	4.6	4.5
More developed regions	2.2	2.0	1.9	1.6
Less developed regions	3.1	4.5	4.1	3.7
Rural and small-town population				
World total	0.8	0.9	1.4	1.2
More developed major areas	0.4	0.0	0.1	0.1
Europe	0.4	0.2	0.1	−0.1
Northern America	0.7	0.4	0.7	0.9
Soviet Union	0.3	−0.4	0.0	−0.2
Oceania	0.9	0.7	1.3	1.6
Less developed major areas	0.9	1.2	1.7	1.4
East Asia	0.5	0.7	0.9	0.5
South Asia	1.2	1.4	2.2	1.7
Latin America	1.6	1.6	2.1	1.4
Africa	1.3	1.4	2.1	2.2
More developed regions	0.4	1.0	0.1	0.1
Less developed regions	0.9	1.2	1.8	1.4

MAP 1-7. Big Cities (500,000 or More Inhabitants) and Multimillion Cities (2,500,000 or more inhabitants) in 1920

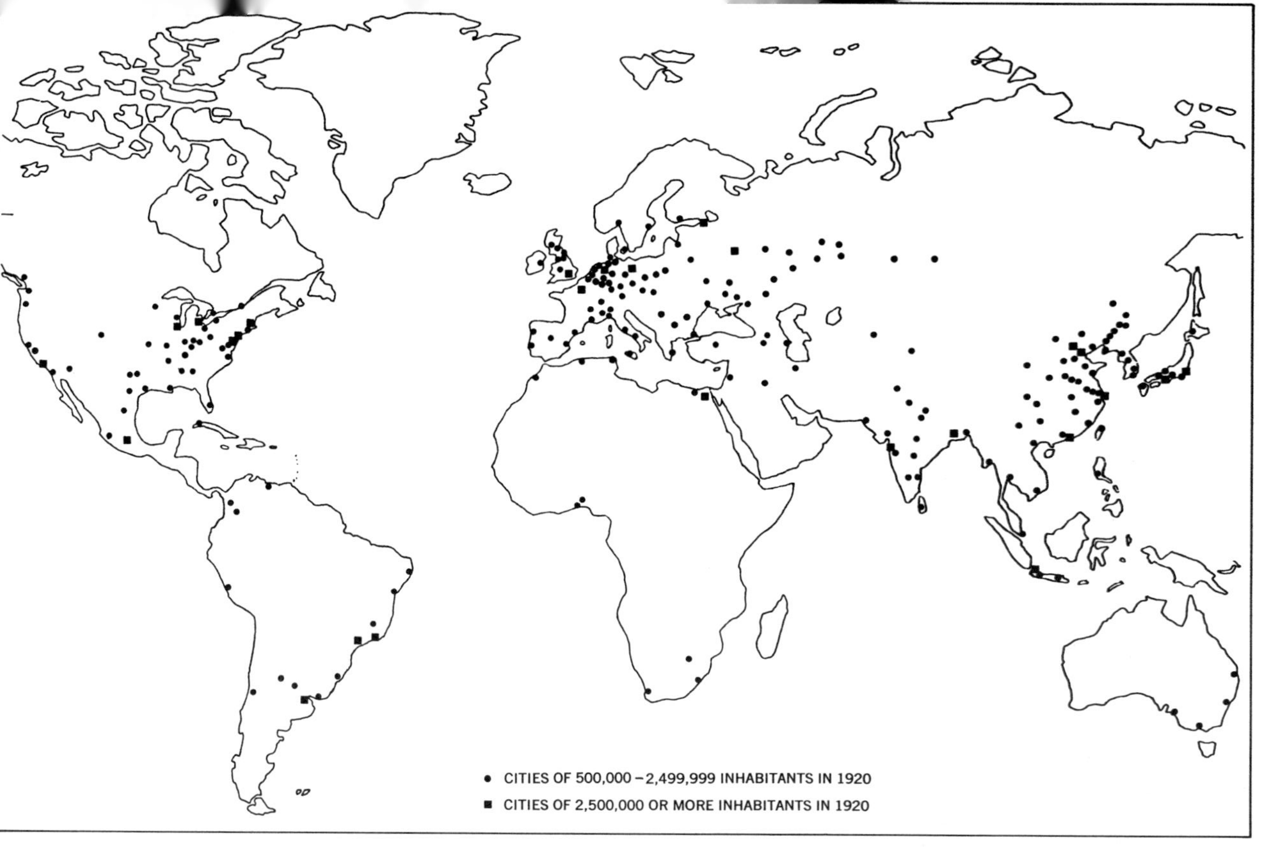

MAP 1-8. Big Cities (500,000 or More Inhabitants) and Multimillion Cities (2,500,000 or More Inhabitants) in 1960

Map No. 1821 United Nations. September 1968

The Future of Urbanization

Incorporating the data from another UN study which projects world population into the year 2000,[1] *Growth of the World's Urban and Rural Population, 1920–1960,* spends a chapter on the future of urbanization. Its assessment is based on the "medium" variant[2] projection from the aforesaid study.

The agglomerated population in the more developed regions has more than doubled in the forty years between 1920 and 1960 (197.7 to 449.6 million). It could double again to 900 million by the year 2000.

Between 1920 and 1960, the agglomerated population in the less developed regions more than quadrupled (68.7 to 310.7 million). This population could repeat its own history and quadruple again: the "medium" variant estimate for 2,000—1,436 million—is close to five times the 1960 figure.

The rural and small-town population in the more developed regions, which showed a gain of 11 percent in the 1920–1960 period, is expected to gain less than 3 percent in the forty years thereafter. If so, the 1960 rural population of 526 million will grow to only 540 million.

In contrast, the same population in the less developed regions, which had a 52 percent increase between 1920 and 1960, may result in more than a 90 percent increase in the next forty years if it is to have a projected population of 3,235 million in the year 2000.

Therefore the 2000 agglomerated-rural population breakdown calculated on the "medium" variant projection looks like this:

TABLE 1-14. Agglomerated-Rural Population in 2000 (according to the "Medium" Variant Projection)

Population	More developed regions	Less developed regions	Combined totals
Agglomerations	901	1,436	2,337
Rural	540	3,235	3,775
Total	1,441	4,671	6,112

These figures indicate that in the year 2000, 38 percent of the world's population will live in agglomerations—up 13 percent from the 1960 statistic of 25 percent. Conversely the rural population of the less developed world will be down the same number of points—from 75 percent in 1960 to 62 percent in 2000.

[1] *World Population Prospects As Assessed in 1963,* United Nations (New York, 1966).

[2] The "medium" variant represents the most plausible projection for a population in a given region. See Part 5 on The Future of Population.

To appreciate the weight of these projections, consider the following real possibilities: if the "medium" estimate is proved correct, in the year 2000 the rural population of the less developed regions will be *greater than the total world population of 1960* and there will be *more people in the agglomerations of these same less developed regions than in all the agglomerations in 1960.*

TABLES and FIGURES on the FUTURE of URBANIZATION

According to *Growth of the World's Urban and Rural Population, 1920–1960*

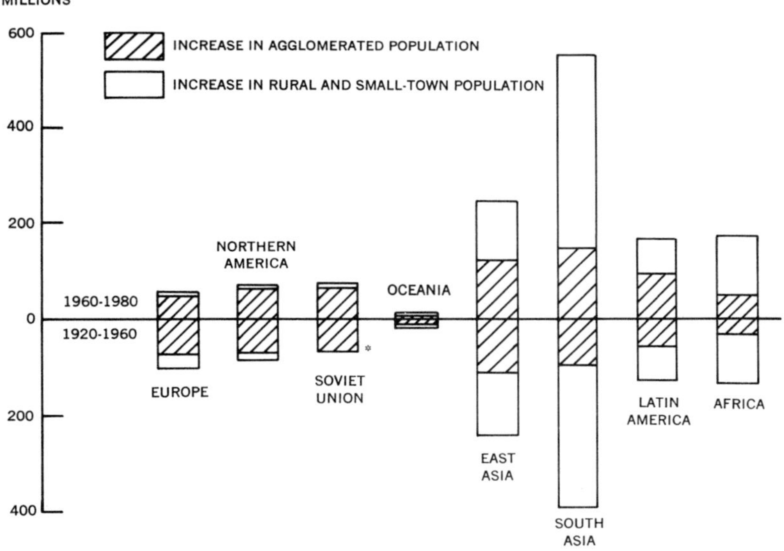

FIGURE 1-10. Increases in Agglomerated and Rural and Small-town Population in Eight Major Areas, 1920–60 and 1960–80

TABLE 1-17. World Population in 2000.

(Population in thousands)

	Medium	High	Low	Constant fertility, no migration
Population in more developed regions	1,441,402	1,574,079	1,293,175	1,580,049
Population in less developed regions	4,668,332	5,419,907	4,155,358	5,942,169
Total population	6,129,734	6,993,986	5,448,533	7,522,218

NOTE: Map 1-6 outlines the major areas and regions that conform to the geographical divisions established in World Population Prospects As Assessed in 1963. These divisions were somewhat streamlined in the later study Growth of the World's Urban and Rural Population (Part 5).

TABLE 1-15. Total, Agglomerated, and Rural and Small-Town Population of the World and Major Areas, as Estimated for 1920, 1940, 1960, 1980 and 2000

(Millions)

Major areas	1920	1940	1960	1980	2000
Total population					
World total	1,860	2,295	2,991	4,318	6,112
More developed major areas	604	729	854	1,042	1,266
Europe	325	379	425	479	527
Northern America	116	144	199	262	354
Soviet Union	155	195	214	278	353
Oceania	8	11	16	23	32
Less developed major areas	1,256	1,566	2,137	3,276	4,846
East Asia	553	634	794	1,041	1,287
South Asia	470	610	858	1,408	2,153
Latin America	90	130	212	378	638
Africa	143	192	273	449	768
More developed regions	673	821	976	1,194	1,441
Less developed regions	1,187	1,474	2,015	3,125	4,671
Agglomerated population (localities of 20,000 inhabitants and over)					
World total	267	432	760	1,354	2,337
More developed major areas	180	268	389	567	784
Europe	113	150	188	237	290
Northern America	48	67	115	177	253
Soviet Union	16	47	78	141	222
Oceania	3	4	8	13	19
Less developed major areas	87	164	371	786	1,553
East Asia	40	74	147	267	425
South Asia	27	51	118	266	568
Latin America	13	25	69	163	342
Africa	7	14	37	90	218
More developed regions	198	304	450	661	901
Less developed regions	69	128	310	693	1,436
Rural and small-town population (localities of less than 20,000 inhabitants)					
World total	1,593	1,862	2,231	2,964	3,775
More developed major areas	424	461	465	474	482
Europe	212	229	237	242	237
Northern America	68	77	84	85	101
Soviet Union	139	148	136	137	131
Oceania	5	7	8	10	13
Less developed major areas	1,169	1,402	1,766	2,490	3,293
East Asia	513	560	647	774	862
South Asia	443	559	740	1,142	1,585
Latin America	77	105	143	215	296
Africa	136	178	236	359	550
More developed regions	475	517	526	533	540
Less developed regions	1,118	1,346	1,705	2,431	3,235

TABLE 1-16. Estimated Annual Rates of Growth in Total, Agglomerated and Rural and Small-Town Population, 1920–1940, 1940–1960, 1960–1980 and 1980–2000

Major areas	1920-1940	1940-1960	1960-1980	1980-2000
Total population				
World total	1.1	1.3	1.9	1.7
More developed major areas	0.9	0.8	1.0	1.0
Europe	0.8	0.6	0.6	0.5
Northern America	1.1	1.6	1.5	1.5
Soviet Union	1.1	0.5	1.3	1.2
Oceania	1.3	1.8	1.8	1.7
Less developed major areas	1.1	1.6	2.2	2.0
East Asia	0.7	1.1	1.4	1.1
South Asia	1.3	1.7	2.5	2.1
Latin America	1.9	2.5	2.9	2.6
Africa	1.5	1.8	2.5	2.7
More developed regions	1.0	0.9	1.0	0.9
Less developed regions	1.1	1.6	2.2	2.0
Agglomerated population				
World total	2.4	2.9	2.9	2.8
More developed major areas	2.0	1.9	1.9	1.6
Europe	1.4	1.1	1.2	1.0
Northern America	1.7	2.8	2.2	1.8
Soviet Union	5.5	2.6	3.0	2.3
Oceania	1.9	3.1	2.3	1.8
Less developed major areas	3.2	4.2	3.9	3.5
East Asia	3.1	3.5	3.0	2.4
South Asia	3.2	4.3	4.1	3.9
Latin America	3.5	5.2	4.4	3.8
Africa	3.5	5.0	4.6	4.5
More developed regions	2.2	2.0	1.9	1.6
Less developed regions	3.1	4.5	4.1	3.7
Rural and small-town population				
World total	0.8	0.9	1.4	1.2
More developed major areas	0.4	0.0	0.1	0.1
Europe	0.4	0.2	0.1	−0.1
Northern America	0.7	0.4	0.7	0.9
Soviet Union	0.3	−0.4	0.0	−0.2
Oceania	0.9	0.7	1.3	1.6
Less developed major areas	0.9	1.2	1.7	1.4
East Asia	0.5	0.7	0.9	0.5
South Asia	1.2	1.4	2.2	1.7
Latin America	1.6	1.6	2.1	1.4
Africa	1.3	1.4	2.1	2.2
More developed regions	0.4	1.0	0.1	0.1
Less developed regions	0.9	1.2	1.8	1.4

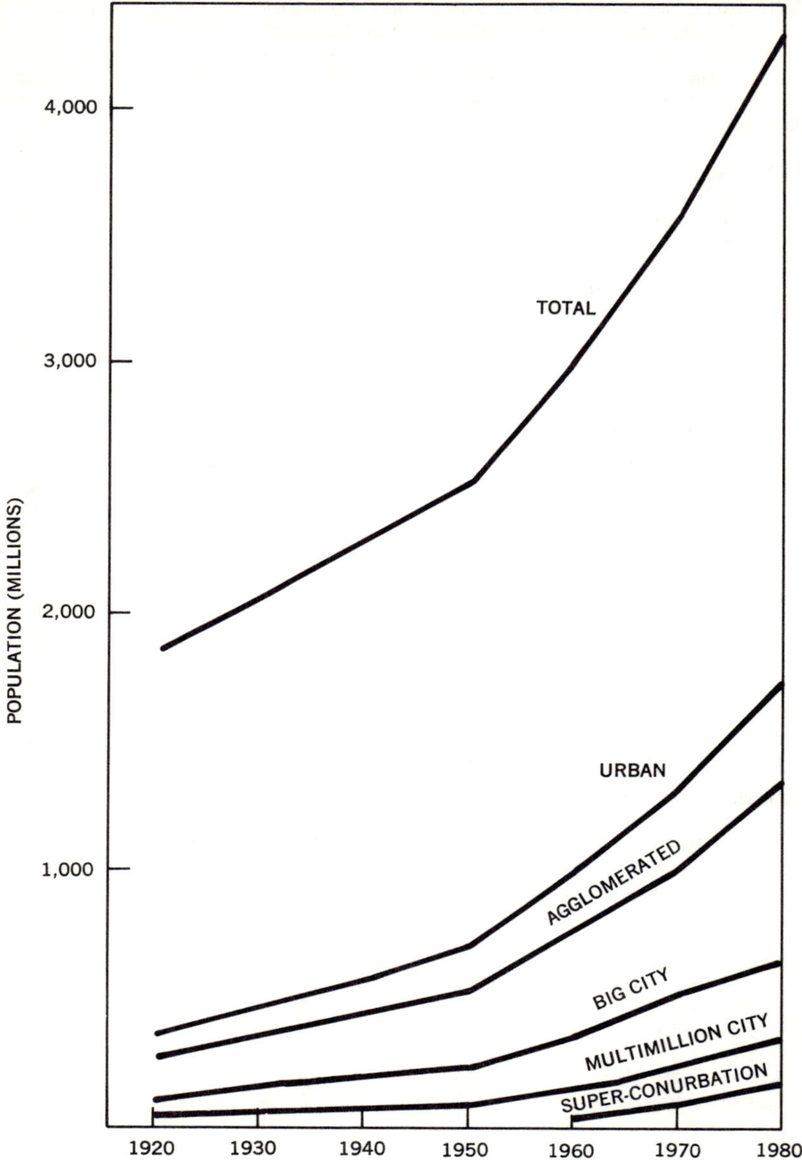

FIGURE 1-11. Growth of World Total Population and Urban Population in Various Categories, 1920–80

6. THE FUTURE OF POPULATION

In 1966, the United Nations published a demographic study entitled *World Population Prospects As Assessed in 1963.* It is a detailed and carefully revised report on the range of possible directions in world population from 1960 through the year 2000. To allow for variables, four sets of estimates were employed:

The "medium" variant represented the most plausible projection, given past experience and the contemporary situation in each region.

The "high" variant represented the upper limits of plausibility.

The "low" variant represented the lower limits of plausibility.

A "constant fertility, no migration" variant was also included for comparative purposes. This variant operated on the assumption that the high birth and declining death rates of the 1950s would remain constant throughout the projection period (a most unlikely occurrence) and that there would be no migration between the regions.

The high variant estimate projects a 6,993,986,000 world population for 2000. To achieve this number, population would have to grow at a 24 percent rate during the 1970s, slowing down only a single point through the 1990s.

The low variant would yield a 5,448,533,000 world population in 2000. A decline in the world growth rate would have already appeared in the 1960s (which did not happen) and continue down through the 1990s. But the low variant's projected 14 percent rate of increase in the 1990s would still be higher than that of any decade prior to the 1950s whose own rate of increase was 19 percent. (The rate for the 1920s and 1930s, for example, was 11 percent.)

The medium variant, using approximately the 19 percent rate of the 1950s, suggests a world population of 6,129,734,000 in 2000.

The constant fertility, no migration variant would have the highest world population of all in 2000—7,522,218,000—by assuming absolutely no decline in birth rates and a constant decline in mortality rates. Until 1980, this variant and the medium variant are not too far apart. But where the medium variant projects plausible future reductions in fertility in the fast growing populations of East and South Asia after 1980, reductions that would make a considerable difference in world totals twenty years hence, the constant fertility, no migration variant indicates nothing but the same constant growth in birth rates and decreases in death rates.

According to the four variants, here is what the world population portends for 2000. A capsule of the totals are presented first in Table 1-17, and then the complete UN statistics are given.

TABLES of POPULATION ESTIMATES and PROJECTIONS

From the United Nation's *World Population Prospects as Assessed in 1963*

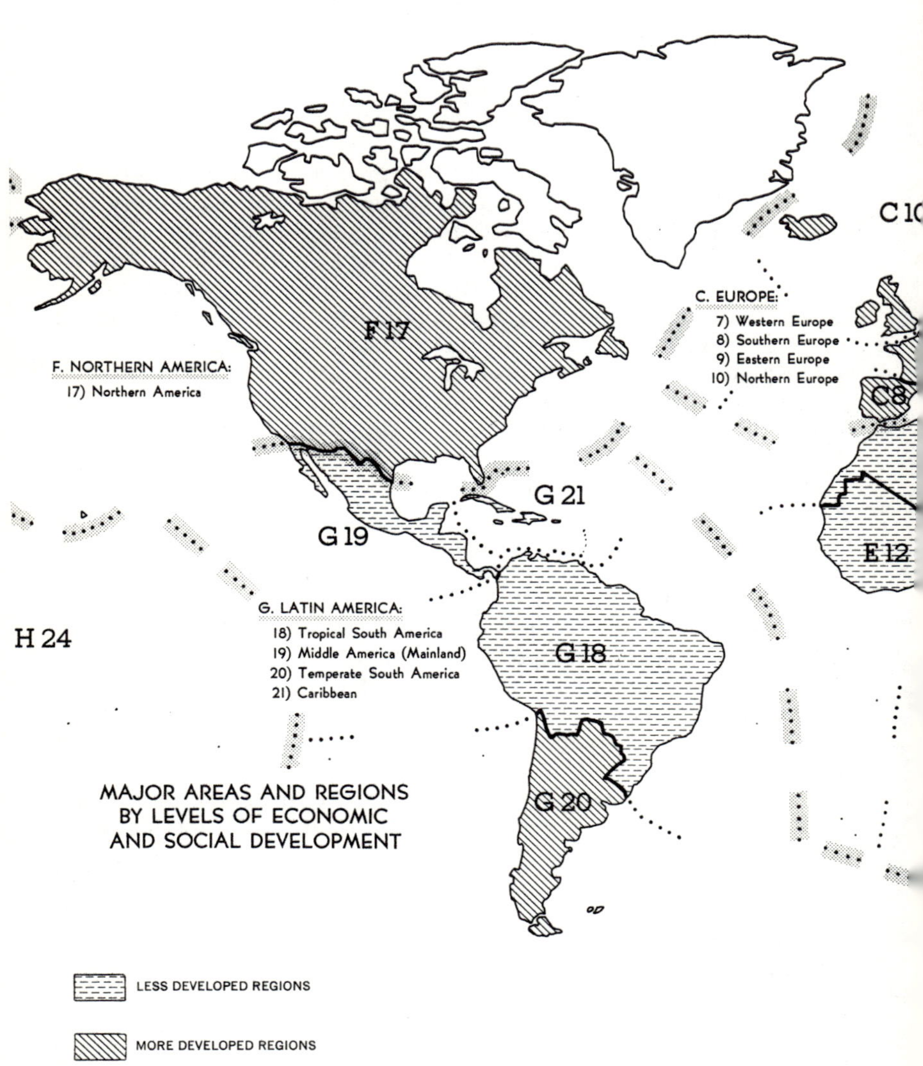

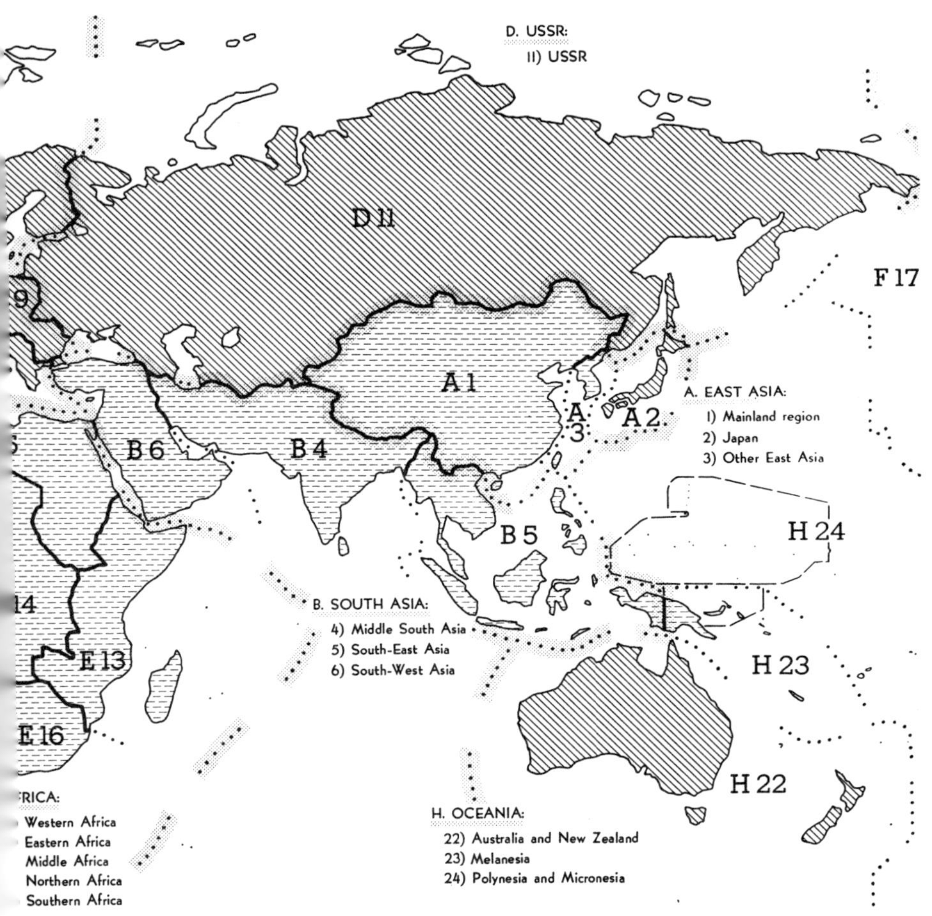

MAP 1-9.

The boundaries shown on this map do not imply official endorsement or acceptance by the United Nations. Map No. 1620. United Nations. October 1965

TABLE 1-18. Population Estimates, 1920–1960, for Major Areas and Regions of the World

(Population in thousands)

Major areas and regions	1920	1930	1940	1950	1960
WORLD TOTAL	1,859,892	2,068,629	2,295,033	2,515,425	2,998,180
More developed regions[a]	672,619	757,856	820,696	857,673	976,414
Less developed regions[b]	1,187,273	1,310,773	1,474,337	1,657,752	2,021,766
A. **East Asia**	553,345	591,244	634,420	684,353	794,144
1. Mainland region	476,382	501,742	532,911	563,228	654,181
2. Japan	55,391	63,872	71,400	82,900	93,210
3. Other East Asia	21,572	25,630	30,109	38,225	46,753
B. **South Asia**	469,770	528,964	609,993	696,722	865,247
4. Middle South Asia	333,100	370,876	422,173	479,039	587,277
5. South-East Asia	107,971	126,711	150,366	172,514	218,866
6. South-West Asia	28,699	31,377	37,454	45,169	59,104
C. **Europe**	324,800	353,947	378,920	391,717	424,657
7. Western Europe	101,351	108,583	113,246	122,437	134,536
8. Southern Europe	82,776	92,624	102,516	108,364	117,488
9. Eastern Europe	78,702	87,745	94,855	88,439	96,852
10. Northern Europe	61,971	64,995	68,303	72,477	75,781
D. 11. **USSR**	155,300	179,000	195,000	180,000	214,400
E. **Africa**	142,921	163,846	191,458	221,538	272,924
12. Western Africa	40,000	48,000	58,000	67,500	85,973
13. Eastern Africa	40,000	46,000	54,000	62,500	75,032
14. Middle Africa	20,000	21,000	23,000	25,000	28,345
15. Northern Africa	35,075	39,119	44,773	52,594	65,955
16. Southern Africa	7,846	9,727	11,685	13,944	17,619

F. 17. **Northern America**	115,661	134,166	144,342	166,073	198,664
G. **Latin America**	89,574	107,418	129,840	162,345	212,431
18. Tropical South America	45,639	54,494	66,767	84,102	112,479
19. Middle America (Mainland)	19,443	22,456	26,863	34,694	46,811
20. Temperate South America	14,826	18,877	22,319	26,856	32,796
21. Caribbean	9,666	11,591	13,891	16,693	20,345
H. **Oceania**	8,521	10,044	11,060	12,677	15,713
22. Australia and New Zealand	6,641	7,994	8,715	10,127	12,687
23. Melanesia	1,500	1,600	1,750	1,900	2,166
24. Polynesia and Micronesia	380	450	595	650	860

[a] Including Europe, the USSR, Northern America, Japan, Temperate South America, Australia and New Zealand.

[b] Including East Asia less Japan, South Asia, Africa, Latin America less Temperate South America and Oceania less Australia and New Zealand.

TABLE 1-19. Population Estimates According to the "Medium" Variant, 1960-2000, for Major Areas and Regions of the World

(Population in thousands)

Major areas and regions	1960	1965	1970	1975	1980	1985	1990	1995	2000
WORLD TOTAL	2,998,180	3,280,522	3,591,773	3,994,137	4,330,037	4,746,409	5,187,929	5,647,923	6,129,734
More developed regions[a]	976,414	1,031,759	1,082,150	1,135,587	1,193,854	1,256,179	1,318,433	1,379,812	1,441,402
Less developed regions[b]	2,021,766	2,248,763	2,509,623	2,808,550	3,136,183	3,490,230	3,869,496	4,268,111	4,688,332
A. **East Asia**	794,144	851,520	910,524	975,935	1,041,097	1,104,903	1,167,882	1,228,006	1,287,270
1. Mainland region	654,181	700,000	748,000	799,000	850,000	900,000	950,000	998,000	1,045,000
2. Japan	93,210	97,523	101,465	106,174	111,064	115,169	118,280	120,561	122,400
3. Other East Asia	46,753	53,997	61,059	70,761	80,033	89,734	99,602	109,445	119,870
B. **South Asia**	865,247	976,341	1,106,905	1,256,352	1,420,258	1,596,329	1,782,525	1,973,889	2,170,648
4. Middle South Asia	587,277	659,977	746,892	846,932	953,709	1,064,374	1,177,133	1,288,246	1,398,810
5. South-East Asia	218,866	249,213	283,035	320,720	364,310	414,686	471,973	535,170	603,272
6. South-West Asia	59,104	67,151	76,978	88,700	102,239	117,269	133,419	150,473	168,566
C. **Europe**	424,657	440,303	453,918	466,772	479,391	491,891	503,858	515,674	526,968
7. Western Europe	134,536	139,456	143,766	147,876	151,845	155,724	159,769	163,635	167,699
8. Southern Europe	117,488	121,831	125,671	129,205	132,569	136,342	139,238	142,539	145,360
9. Eastern Europe	96,852	101,414	105,354	109,341	113,597	117,414	121,601	125,181	128,426
10. Northern Europe	75,781	77,602	79,127	80,350	81,380	82,411	83,250	84,319	85,483
D. 11. **USSR**	214,400	231,000	245,700	260,800	277,800	296,804	316,090	334,845	353,085
E. **Africa**	272,924	306,173	345,949	393,257	448,869	513,026	586,702	671,207	767,779
12. Western Africa	85,973	98,359	112,862	129,851	149,818	173,369	201,832	236,082	277,192
13. Eastern Africa	75,032	81,957	90,397	100,505	112,515	126,518	142,528	161,153	183,119
14. Middle Africa	28,345	30,553	33,299	36,632	40,592	45,225	50,610	56,965	64,519
15. Northern Africa	65,955	75,351	86,712	100,408	116,369	133,920	152,577	172,185	192,148
16. Southern Africa	17,619	19,953	22,679	25,861	29,575	33,994	39,155	44,822	50,801

Region									
F. 17. **Northern America**	198,664	213,150	226,803	242,942	261,629	283,105	305,926	329,186	354,007
G. **Latin America**	212,431	244,880	283,263	327,584	378,437	435,558	497,920	565,681	638,111
18. Tropical South America	112,479	131,334	153,838	179,798	209,506	242,902	279,613	319,463	361,985
19. Middle America (mainland)	46,811	54,844	64,595	76,359	90,433	106,662	124,655	144,469	165,901
20. Temperate South America	32,796	35,966	39,302	42,708	46,221	49,778	53,227	56,771	60,514
21. Caribbean	20,345	22,736	25,528	28,719	32,277	36,216	40,425	44,978	49,711
H. **Oceania**	15,713	17,155	18,711	20,495	22,556	24,793	27,026	29,435	31,866
22. Australia and New Zealand	12,687	13,817	14,962	16,191	17,749	19,432	21,052	22,775	24,428
23. Melanesia	2,166	2,338	2,549	2,804	3,107	3,461	3,874	4,360	4,938
24. Polynesia and Micronesia	860	1,000	1,200	1,500	1,700	1,900	2,100	2,300	2,500

[a] Including Europe, the USSR, Northern America, Japan, Temperate South America, Australia and New Zealand.

[b] Including East Asia less Japan, South Asia, Africa, Latin America less Temperate South America and Oceania less Australia and New Zealand.

TABLE 1-20. Population Estimates According to the "High" Variant, 1960–2000, for Major Areas and Regions of the World

(Population in thousands)

Major areas and regions	1960	1965	1970	1975	1980	1985	1990	1995	2000
WORLD TOTAL	2,998,180	3,305,862	3,659,157	4,070,083	4,550,733	5,096,198	5,689,910	6,325,593	6,993,986
More developed regions[a]	976,414	1,038,410	1,102,074	1,170,451	1,244,728	1,321,537	1,402,019	1,485,660	1,574,079
Less developed regions[b]	2,021,766	2,267,452	2,557,083	2,899,632	3,306,005	3,774,661	4,287,891	4,839,933	5,419,907
A. **East Asia**	794,144	869,950	956,283	1,056,589	1,170,951	1,289,018	1,405,321	1,515,953	1,623,170
1. Mainland region	654,181	718,000	791,000	875,000	971,000	1,070,000	1,167,000	1,258,000	1,345,000
2. Japan	93,210	97,865	102,972	109,536	116,554	122,819	128,216	133,311	138,731
3. Other East Asia	46,753	54,085	62,311	72,053	83,397	96,199	110,105	124,642	139,439
B. **South Asia**	865,247	976,550	1,107,569	1,262,512	1,447,692	1,665,607	1,909,998	2,174,390	2,443,531
4. Middle South Asia	587,277	659,977	746,892	850,684	974,841	1,120,290	1,280,930	1,450,581	1,614,152
5. South-East Asia	218,866	249,422	283,699	322,951	369,613	425,211	489,796	563,154	645,358
6. South-West Asia	59,104	67,151	76,978	88,877	103,238	120,106	139,272	160,655	184,021
C. **Europe**	424,657	441,268	457,850	474,801	491,701	508,703	526,139	544,349	563,159
7. Western Europe	134,536	139,752	144,962	150,299	155,539	160,800	166,407	172,168	178,478
8. Southern Europe	117,488	122,119	126,839	131,573	136,180	141,481	145,770	150,962	155,968
9. Eastern Europe	96,852	101,636	106,270	111,236	116,542	121,175	126,983	132,100	137,151
10. Northern Europe	75,781	77,761	79,779	81,693	83,440	85,247	86,979	89,119	91,562
D. 11. **USSR**	214,400	233,853	253,827	274,157	296,032	319,891	346,010	373,775	402,772
E. **Africa**	272,924	306,563	348,468	399,989	462,886	538,972	629,061	736,266	864,282
12. Western Africa	85,973	98,535	114,007	132,973	156,165	184,631	219,799	263,572	317,915
13. Eastern Africa	75,032	82,120	91,342	102,955	117,330	134,780	155,244	179,841	209,946
14. Middle Africa	28,345	30,559	33,548	37,361	42,104	47,971	54,917	63,402	73,792
15. Northern Africa	65,955	75,351	86,712	100,408	116,884	136,236	157,732	180,749	204,982
16. Southern Africa	17,619	19,998	22,859	26,292	30,403	35,354	41,369	48,702	57,647

F. 17. **Northern America**	198,664	215,513	232,746	252,113	274,818	298,182	323,083	348,542	376,141
G. **Latin America**	212,431	244,935	283,436	328,902	383,243	449,815	521,603	600,624	686,084
18. Tropical South America	112,479	131,334	153,842	180,327	211,871	251,892	294,611	343,866	386,113
19. Middle America (mainland)	46,811	54,845	64,597	76,595	91,522	109,223	128,856	149,725	171,574
20. Temperate South America	32,796	36,020	39,469	43,184	47,236	51,704	56,479	61,542	67,077
21. Caribbean	20,345	22,736	25,528	28,796	32,614	36,996	41,657	46,491	51,320
H. **Oceania**	15,713	17,230	18,978	21,020	23,410	26,010	28,695	31,694	34,847
22. Australia and New Zealand	12,697	13,891	15,210	16,660	18,387	20,238	22,092	24,141	26,199
23. Melanesia	2,166	2,339	2,568	2,860	3,223	3,672	4,203	4,853	5,648
24. Polynesia and Micronesia	860	1,000	1,200	1,500	1,800	2,100	2,400	2,700	3,000

[a] Including Europe, the USSR, Northern America, Japan, Temperate South America, Australia and New Zealand.

[b] Including East Asia less Japan, South Asia, Africa, Latin America less Temperate South America and Oceania less Australia and New Zealand.

TABLE 1-21. Population Estimates According to the "Low" Variant, 1960–2000, for Major Areas and Regions of the World

(Population in thousands)

Major areas and regions	1960	1965	1970	1975	1980	1985	1990	1995	2000
WORLD TOTAL	2,998,180	3,265,555	3,544,781	3,840,439	4,147,337	4,462,720	4,782,859	5,109,362	5,448,533
More developed regions[a]	976,414	1,028,862	1,069,745	1,110,340	1,153,323	1,195,026	1,234,313	1,266,219	1,293,175
Less developed regions[b]	2,021,766	2,236,693	2,475,036	2,730,099	2,994,014	3,267,694	3,549,546	3,843,143	4,155,358
A. **East Asia**	794,144	839,970	883,366	926,689	966,092	1,002,895	1,039,118	1,079,058	1,118,122
1. Mainland region	654,181	689,000	722,000	754,000	782,000	808,000	834,000	864,000	893,000
2. Japan	93,210	97,159	100,328	104,081	107,762	110,750	112,950	114,378	115,326
3. Other East Asia	46,753	53,811	61,038	68,608	76,330	84,145	92,168	100,680	109,796
B. **South Asia**	865,247	975,777	1,101,743	1,237,117	1,378,496	1,526,188	1,675,465	1,825,655	1,984,435
4. Middle South Asia	587,277	659,977	743,752	832,611	922,138	1,012,824	1,101,103	1,188,439	1,283,065
5. South-East Asia	218,866	248,792	281,465	317,082	356,997	401,363	449,372	499,081	549,594
6. South-West Asia	59,104	67,008	76,526	87,424	99,361	112,001	124,990	138,135	151,776
C. **Europe**	424,657	439,340	449,988	458,742	467,081	475,079	481,578	486,999	490,777
7. Western Europe	134,536	139,160	142,570	145,452	148,151	150,648	153,132	155,101	156,920
8. Southern Europe	117,488	121,543	124,503	126,838	128,958	131,203	132,707	134,115	134,753
9. Eastern Europe	96,852	101,193	104,439	107,446	110,651	113,653	116,219	118,263	119,700
10. Northern Europe	75,781	77,444	78,476	79,006	79,321	79,575	79,520	79,520	79,404
D. 11. **USSR**	214,400	230,627	243,486	255,768	268,865	282,387	296,533	307,306	316,464
E. **Africa**	272,924	305,859	343,633	386,653	434,486	486,730	545,614	611,088	684,132
12. Western Africa	85,973	98,269	112,093	127,711	145,401	165,336	189,339	217,461	250,284
13. Eastern Africa	75,032	81,884	89,773	98,847	109,155	120,572	133,531	148,217	164,976
14. Middle Africa	28,345	30,471	32,969	35,816	39,080	42,755	46,990	51,835	57,395
15. Northern Africa	65,955	75,282	86,119	98,418	111,400	124,770	138,452	152,152	165,899
16. Southern Africa	17,619	19,953	22,679	25,861	29,450	33,297	37,302	41,423	45,578

F. 17. **Northern America**	198,664	212,028	222,156	234,102	248,250	261,592	274,207	284,736	294,337
G. **Latin America**	212,431	244,828	281,805	321,313	362,278	404,483	446,466	488,133	532,388
18. Tropical South America	112,479	131,334	153,168	176,533	200,745	225,453	249,924	274,147	299,977
19. Middle America (mainland)	46,811	54,844	64,304	74,908	86,443	98,525	110,699	122,976	136,241
20. Temperate South America	32,796	35,914	38,906	41,633	44,067	46,724	49,463	52,080	54,586
21. Caribbean	20,345	22,736	25,427	28,239	31,023	33,781	36,380	38,930	41,584
H. **Oceania**	15,713	17,126	18,604	20,055	21,789	23,366	24,878	26,387	27,878
22. Australia and New Zealand	12,687	13,794	14,881	16,014	17,298	18,494	19,582	20,720	21,685
23. Melanesia	2,166	2,332	2,523	2,741	2,991	3,272	3,596	3,967	4,393
24. Polynesia and Micronesia	860	1,000	1,200	1,300	1,500	1,600	1,700	1,700	1,800

[a] Including Europe, the USSR, Northern America, Japan, Temperate South America, Australia and New Zealand.

[b] Including East Asia less Japan, South Asia, Africa, Latin America less Temperate South America and Oceania less Australia and New Zealand.

TABLE 1-22. Population Estimates According to "Constant Fertility, No Migration", 1960–2000, in Major Areas and Regions of the World

(Population in thousands)

Major areas and regions	1960	1965	1970	1975	1980	1985	1990	1995	2000
WORLD TOTAL	2,998,180	3,297,482	3,640,970	4,042,761	4,519,146	5,088,112	5,763,577	6,564,584	7,522,218
More developed regions[a]	976,414	1,037,209	1,100,340	1,168,202	1,241,660	1,319,857	1,401,980	1,488,187	1,580,049
Less developed regions[b]	2,021,766	2,260,273	2,540,630	2,874,559	3,277,486	3,768,255	4,361,597	5,076,397	5,942,169
A. **East Asia**	794,144	863,258	942,256	1,034,364	1,142,609	1,272,236	1,424,527	1,601,016	1,810,678
1. Mainland region	654,181	711,000	776,000	852,000	942,000	1,051,000	1,180,000	1,330,000	1,509,000
2. Japan	93,210	98,011	103,341	108,861	114,055	118,457	121,948	124,809	127,160
3. Other East Asia	46,753	54,247	62,915	73,503	86,554	102,779	122,579	146,207	174,518
B. **South Asia**	865,247	975,940	1,105,563	1,259,456	1,446,153	1,674,235	1,952,050	2,290,246	2,701,865
4. Middle South Asia	587,277	660,148	746,062	848,430	972,506	1,123,880	1,308,534	1,534,394	1,811,220
5. South-East Asia	218,866	248,641	282,523	322,149	370,409	430,006	502,966	590,983	696,620
6. South-West Asia	59,104	67,151	76,978	88,877	103,238	120,349	140,550	164,869	194,025
C. **Europe**	424,657	442,416	460,136	478,209	496,448	514,820	533,108	551,655	570,785
7. Western Europe	134,536	139,157	143,583	148,036	152,284	156,621	161,183	166,123	171,520
8. Southern Europe	117,488	123,273	129,224	135,221	141,304	147,498	153,492	159,291	164,962
9. Eastern Europe	96,852	101,654	106,234	111,105	116,313	121,475	126,498	131,411	136,213
10. Northern Europe	75,781	78,332	81,095	83,847	86,547	89,226	91,935	94,830	98,090
D. 11. **USSR**	214,400	233,411	252,498	272,415	294,594	318,896	345,084	372,800	402,077
E. **Africa**	272,924	306,563	347,791	397,830	458,251	531,213	619,748	728,013	860,462
12. Western Africa	85,973	98,535	114,007	132,973	156,165	184,631	219,799	263,572	317,915
13. Eastern Africa	75,032	82,210	90,910	101,579	114,355	129,384	146,976	167,803	192,725
14. Middle Africa	28,345	30,559	33,303	36,578	40,444	45,001	50,389	56,832	64,427
15. Northern Africa	65,955	75,351	86,712	100,408	116,884	136,843	161,215	191,104	227,748
16. Southern Africa	17,619	19,998	22,859	26,292	30,403	35,354	41,369	48,702	57,647

F. 17. **Northern America**	198,664	213,840	230,409	249,840	272,238	297,348	324,955	354,914	388,264
G. **Latin America**	212,431	245,080	283,899	330,488	386,856	455,131	537,450	636,447	755,579
18. Tropical South America	112,479	131,334	153,838	180,933	213,792	253,728	302,118	360,626	431,302
19. Middle America (mainland)	46,811	54,926	64,775	76,878	91,921	110,535	133,312	161,037	194,816
20. Temperate South America	32,796	35,896	39,287	43,018	47,123	51,647	56,587	61,966	67,786
21. Caribbean	20,345	22,924	25,999	29,659	34,020	39,221	45,433	52,818	61,675
H. **Oceania**	15,713	16,974	18,418	20,159	21,997	24,233	26,655	29,493	32,508
22. Australia and New Zealand	12,687	13,635	14,669	15,859	17,202	18,689	20,298	22,043	23,977
23. Melanesia	2,166	2,339	2,549	2,800	3,095	3,444	3,857	4,350	4,931
24. Polynesia and Micronesia	860	1,000	1,200	1,500	1,700	2,100	2,500	3,100	3,600

[a] Including Europe, the USSR, Northern America, Japan, Temperate South America, Australia and New Zealand.

[b] Including East Asia less Japan, South Asia, Africa, Latin America less Temperate South America and Oceania less Australia and New Zealand.

TABLE 1-23. Decennial Rates of Increase of Population, 1920–1960 and 1960–2000 According to "Medium" Estimates, for Major Areas and Regions of the World

(Per cent increase of population during ten-year periods)

Major areas and regions	1920-1930	1930-1940	1940-1950	1950-1960	1960-1970	1970-1980	1980-1990	1990-2000
A. **East Asia**	6.8	7.3	7.9	16.0	14.7	14.3	12.2	10.2
1. Mainland region	5.3	6.2	5.7	16.1	14.3	13.6	11.8	10.0
2. Japan	15.3	11.8	16.1	12.4	8.9	9.5	6.5	3.5
3. Other East Asia	18.8	17.5	27.0	22.3	30.6	31.1	24.5	20.3
B. **South Asia**	12.6	15.3	14.2	24.2	27.9	28.3	24.5	21.8
4. Middle South Asia	11.3	13.8	13.5	22.6	27.2	27.7	23.4	18.8
5. South-East Asia	17.4	18.7	14.7	26.9	29.3	28.7	29.6	27.8
6. South-West Asia	9.3	19.4	20.6	30.9	30.2	32.8	30.5	26.3
C. **Europe**	9.0	7.1	3.4	8.4	6.9	5.6	5.1	4.6
7. Western Europe	7.1	4.3	8.1	9.9	6.9	5.6	5.2	5.0
8. Southern Europe	11.9	10.7	5.7	8.4	7.0	5.5	5.0	4.4
9. Eastern Europe	11.5	8.1	−6.8	9.5	8.8	7.8	7.0	5.6
10. Northern Europe	4.9	5.1	6.1	4.6	4.4	2.8	2.3	2.7
D. 11. **USSR**	15.3	8.9	−7.7	19.1	14.6	13.1	13.8	11.7
E. **Africa**	14.6	16.9	15.7	23.2	26.8	29.8	30.7	30.9
12. Western Africa	20.0	20.8	16.4	27.4	31.3	32.7	34.7	37.3
13. Eastern Africa	15.0	17.4	15.7	20.1	20.5	24.5	26.7	28.5
14. Middle Africa	5.0	9.5	8.7	13.4	17.5	21.9	24.7	27.5
15. Northern Africa	11.5	14.5	17.5	25.4	31.5	34.2	31.1	25.9
16. Southern Africa	24.0	20.1	19.3	26.4	28.7	30.4	32.4	29.7
F. 17. **Northern America**	16.0	7.6	15.1	19.6	14.2	15.4	16.9	15.7
G. **Latin America**	19.9	20.9	25.0	30.9	33.3	33.6	31.6	28.2
18. Tropical South America	19.4	22.5	26.0	33.7	36.8	36.2	33.5	29.5
19. Middle America (mainland)	15.5	19.6	29.2	34.9	38.0	40.0	37.8	33.1

20. Temperate South America	27.3	18.2	20.3	22.1	19.8	17.6	15.2	13.7
21. Caribbean	19.9	19.8	20.2	21.9	25.5	26.4	25.2	23.0
H. **Oceania**	17.9	10.1	14.6	23.1	19.1	20.5	19.8	17.9
22. Australia and New Zealand	20.4	9.0	16.2	25.3	17.9	18.6	18.6	16.0
23. Melanesia	6.7	9.4	8.6	14.0	17.7	21.9	24.7	27.5
24. Polynesia and Micronesia	18.4	32.0	9.2	32.3	(40.0)[a]	(35.0)[a]	(25.0)[a]	(15.0)[a]

[a] Arbitrarily assumed.

TABLE 1-24. Decennial Rates of Increase of Population 1960–2000 According to "High", "Low" and "Constant Fertility, No Migration" Estimates, for Major Areas and Regions of the World

(Per cent increase of population during ten-year periods)

Major areas and regions	"High" variant				"Low" variant				"Constant fertility, no migration" variant			
	1960-1970	1970-1980	1980-1990	1990-2000	1960-1970	1970-1980	1980-1990	1990-2000	1960-1970	1970-1980	1980-1990	1990-2000
A. **East Asia**	20.4	22.5	20.0	15.5	11.2	9.4	7.6	7.6	18.7	21.3	24.7	27.1
1. Mainland region	20.9	22.8	20.2	15.3	10.4	8.3	6.6	7.1	18.6	21.4	25.3	27.9
2. Japan	10.5	13.2	10.0	8.2	7.6	7.4	4.8	2.1	10.9	10.4	6.9	4.3
3. Other East Asia	33.3	33.8	32.0	26.6	30.6	25.1	20.7	19.1	34.6	37.6	41.6	42.4
B. **South Asia**	28.0	30.7	31.9	27.9	27.3	25.1	21.5	18.4	27.8	30.8	35.0	38.4
4. Middle South Asia	27.2	30.5	31.4	26.0	26.6	24.0	19.4	16.5	27.0	30.4	34.6	38.4
5. South-East Asia	29.6	30.3	32.5	31.8	28.6	26.8	25.9	22.3	29.1	31.1	35.8	38.5
6. South-West Asia	30.2	34.1	34.9	32.1	29.5	29.8	25.8	21.4	30.2	34.1	36.1	38.0
C. **Europe**	7.8	7.4	7.0	7.0	6.0	3.8	3.1	1.9	8.4	7.9	7.4	7.1
7. Western Europe	7.7	7.3	7.0	7.3	6.0	3.9	3.4	2.5	6.7	6.1	5.8	6.4
8. Southern Europe	8.0	7.4	7.0	7.0	6.0	3.6	2.9	1.5	10.0	9.3	8.6	7.5
9. Eastern Europe	9.7	9.7	9.0	8.0	7.8	5.9	5.0	3.0	9.7	9.5	8.8	7.7
10. Northern Europe	5.3	4.6	4.2	5.3	3.6	1.1	0.3	0.2	7.0	6.7	6.3	6.7
D. 11. **USSR**	18.4	16.6	16.9	16.4	13.6	10.4	10.3	6.7	17.8	16.7	17.1	16.5
E. **Africa**	27.7	32.8	35.9	37.4	25.9	26.4	25.6	25.4	27.4	31.8	35.2	38.8
12. Western Africa	32.6	37.0	40.7	44.6	30.4	29.7	30.2	32.2	32.6	37.0	40.7	44.6
13. Eastern Africa	21.7	28.5	32.2	35.2	19.6	21.6	22.3	23.5	21.2	25.8	28.5	31.1
14. Middle Africa	18.4	25.5	30.4	34.4	16.3	18.5	20.2	22.1	17.5	21.4	24.6	27.9
15. Northern Africa	31.5	34.8	34.9	30.0	30.6	29.4	24.3	19.8	31.5	34.8	37.9	41.3
16. Southern Africa	29.7	33.0	36.1	39.3	28.7	29.9	26.7	22.2	29.7	33.0	36.1	39.3
F. 17. **Northern America**	17.2	18.1	17.6	16.4	11.8	11.7	10.5	7.3	16.0	18.2	19.4	19.5

G. **Latin America**	33.4	35.2	36.1	31.5	32.7	28.5	23.0	19.5	33.6	36.3	38.9	40.6
18. Tropical South America	36.8	37.7	39.1	34.5	36.2	31.1	24.5	20.0	36.8	38.0	41.3	42.8
19. Middle America (mainland)	38.0	41.7	40.8	33.2	37.4	34.4	28.1	23.1	38.4	41.9	45.0	46.1
20. Temperate South America	20.3	19.7	19.6	18.8	18.6	13.3	12.2	10.4	19.8	19.9	20.1	19.8
21. Caribbean	25.5	27.8	27.7	23.2	25.0	22.0	17.3	14.3	27.8	30.9	33.5	35.7
H. **Oceania**	20.8	23.4	22.6	21.4	18.4	17.1	14.2	12.1	17.2	19.4	21.2	22.0
22. Australia and New Zealand	19.9	20.9	20.2	18.6	17.3	16.2	13.2	10.7	15.6	17.3	18.0	18.1
23. Melanesia	18.6	25.5	30.4	34.4	16.5	18.5	20.2	22.2	17.7	21.4	24.6	27.8
24. Polynesia and Micronesia	(42.0)	(45.0)	(35.0)	(25.0)	(35.0)	(25.0)	(15.0)	(5.0)	40.0[b]	43.0[b]	45.0[b]	46.0[b]

[a] Arbitrarily assumed.

[b] Conforms to a theoretical model.

TABLE 1-25. Population Estimates, 1920-1960, and Projections up to 1980, for Countries in Each Region*

(Population in thousands)

Region and Country		1920	1930	1940	1950	1960	1965	1970	1975	1980
A. **East Asia**										
1. Mainland region	**Total**	**476,382**	**501,742**	**532,911**	**563,228**	**654,181**	**700,000**	**747,780**	**798,585**	**850,365**
Mainland China[a]		475,000	500,000	530,000	560,000	650,000	695,000	742,000	792,000	843,000
Hong Kong		648	821	1,786	2,265	3,075	3,750	4,350	4,950	5,500
Mongolia		650	725	750	775	937	1,075	1,250	1,450	1,675
Macao		84	196	375	188	169	175	180	185	190
2. Japan		**55,391**	**63,872**	**71,400**	**82,900**	**93,210**	**97,523**	**101,465**	**106,174**	**111,064**
3. Other East Asia	**Total**	**21,572**	**25,630**	**30,109**	**38,225**	**46,753**	**53,890**	**61,734**	**70,270**	**79,217**
Korea[b]		17,264	20,438	23,547	29,907	35,265	40,755	46,940	53,718	60,837
Republic of Korea		–	–	–	20,167	24,665	28,648	33,119	38,075	43,364
North Korea		–	–	–	9,740	10,600	12,107	13,821	15,643	17,473
China (Taiwan)		3,736	4,614	5,987	7,619	10,612	12,175	13,754	15,427	17,180
Ryukyu Islands		572	578	575	699	876	960	1,040	1,125	1,200
B. **South Asia**										
4. Middle South Asia	**Total**	**333,100**	**370,876**	**422,173**	**479,039**	**587,277**	**659,566**	**745,918**	**845,855**	**954,222**
India[c]		250,500	278,000	317,000	359,250	432,750	483,500	543,200	611,000	682,300
Pakistan[d]		54,000	60,000	67,500	75,040	99,950	115,000	134,000	157,000	183,000
Iran[e]		11,000	12,400	14,000	16,276	20,182	22,570	25,440	28,900	33,050
Afghanistan[f]		7,000	8,350	10,000	12,000	14,400	15,900	17,600	19,600	22,100
Ceylon		4,486	5,253	5,972	7,678	9,896	11,490	13,370	15,630	18,300
Nepal		5,574	6,250	7,000	8,000	9,180	10,100	11,200	12,500	14,100
Bhutan		390	440	500	575	670	740	820	910	1,030
Sikkim		80	105	120	135	160	175	195	220	245
Maldive Islands		70	78	81	85	89	91	93	95	97

5. South-East Asia	**Total**	**107,971**	**126,711**	**150,366**	**172,514**	**218,866**	**248,503**	**282,641**	**321,965**	**369,190**
Indonesia[g]		52,300	60,750	70,500	76,700	94,250	105,500	118,250	133,500	152,750
Viet-Nam[h]		15,000	17,500	21,000	24,500	30,500	34,400	38,500	42,400	46,400
Philippines		10,600	13,094	16,459	20,316	27,407	32,315	38,432	46,063	55,750
Thailand		9,460	11,838	15,296	19,500	26,438	31,127	36,311	41,731	47,516
Burma		13,100	14,282	16,119	18,489	22,325	24,732	27,584	30,990	35,000
Malaysia and Singapore		3,861	5,032	6,027	7,122	9,742	11,374	13,251	15,470	18,121
(Malaya)		(2,850)	(3,700)	(4,475)	(5,190)	(6,909)	(8,009)	(9,301)	(10,838)	(12,693)
(Singapore)		(391)	(596)	(751)	(1,022)	(1,634)	(1,971)	(2,333)	(2,758)	(3,223)
(Sarawak)		(400)	(440)	(495)	(562)	(745)	(866)	(1,008)	(1,170)	(1,379)
(Sabah)[i]		(220)	(296)	(306)	(348)	(454)	(528)	(609)	(704)	(826)
Cambodia		2,400	2,800	3,400	4,074	5,600	6,390	7,330	8,450	9,810
Laos		800	930	1,075	1,325	1,805	2,000	2,240	2,520	2,870
Portuguese Timor		425	455	451	442	515	565	625	700	800
Brunei		25	30	39	46	84	100	118	141	173

*Unless otherwise indicated, the population estimates, 1920–1960, given in this table are those supplied by official sources, or interpolations and extrapolations thereof. The projections up to 1980 were prepared by the United Nations or derived from official and other projections according to the procedures explained in chapter 9 of World Population Prospects.

[a] See chapter 10 of World Population Prospects for an evaluation of the figures.

[b] The estimates for 1920, 1930, 1940 are census data unadjusted for mid-year. The 1950 estimates for the whole country and the Republic of Korea are actually estimates obtained from Republic of Korea, Economic Planning Board, Korea Statistical Yearbook, Seoul, 1963. The 1950 estimate for North Korea was obtained by subtraction.

[c] Adjusted for each date to include former French and Portuguese possessions, Nagaland, North-East Frontier Agency, and the area of Kashmir-Jammu, the final status of which has not yet been determined.

[d] Adjusted in view of probably incomplete census enumeration in 1931 and excessive enumeration in 1941. The 1960 total was adjusted for under-enumeration as estimated by the Planning Commission's report. No attempt was made to adjust the 1950 total.

[e] Estimates for 1920 to 1940 are derived by applying assumed rates of growth.

[f] Estimates are derived by applying assumed rates of growth.

[g] Including West Irian (former West New Guinea) now administered by Indonesia.

[h] All figures are for the whole country. The 1960 estimate was obtained by adding the official figures of 16,400 for North Viet-Nam and 14,100 for the Republic of Viet-Nam.

[i] Former North Borneo.

TABLE 1-25. Population Estimates, 1920–1960, and Projections up to 1980, for Countries in Each Region (cont.)

Region and country		1920	1930	1940	1950	1960	1965	1970	1975	1980
6. South-West Asia[j]	**Total**	**28,699**	**31,377**	**37,454**	**45,169**	**59,104**	**67,405**	**77,305**	**89,259**	**103,044**
Northern Arab countries[k]		**5,650**	**7,000**	**8,750**	**11,617**	**15,832**	**18,664**	**22,010**	**26,168**	**31,285**
Iraq		–	–	–	–	7,000	8,200	9,700	11,500	13,800
Syria		–	–	–	–	4,682	5,500	6,450	7,700	9,250
Lebanon		–	–	–	–	1,793	2,050	2,350	2,700	3,100
Jordan		–	–	–	–	1,695	2,000	2,350	2,800	3,350
Gaza Strip (Palestine)		–	–	–	–	375	440	500	620	750
Kuwait		–	–	–	–	287	474	660	848	1,035
Southern Arab countries[l]		**7,250**	**8,200**	**9,350**	**10,850**	**12,767**	**14,007**	**15,464**	**17,316**	**19,488**
Saudi Arabia		–	–	–	–	6,150	6,750	7,450	8,350	9,400
Yemen		–	–	–	–	4,500	4,925	5,450	6,100	6,900
Protectorate of Southern Arabia		–	–	–	–	1,000	1,100	1,200	1,350	1,500
Muscat and Oman		–	–	–	–	630	690	760	850	960
Aden		–	–	–	–	200	240	280	320	360
Bahrain		–	–	–	–	147	150	160	170	180
Trucial Oman		–	–	–	–	100	110	120	130	140
Qatar		–	–	–	–	40	42	44	46	48
Turkey[m]		13,000	15,100	17,821	20,947	27,818	31,781	36,602	42,267	48,478
Israel[n]		480	720	1,120	1,258	2,114	2,360	2,615	2,875	3,141
Cyprus		319	357	413	497	573	593	614	633	652
C. **Europe**										
7. Western Europe	**Total**	**101,351**	**108,583**	**113,246**	**122,437**	**134,536**	**140,345**	**144,045**	**147,785**	**151,820**
Germany Federal Republic		35,000	37,500	40,600	47,847	53,224	55,600	56,600	57,300	58,500
France[o]		38,750	41,150	41,300	41,736	45,684	47,800	49,500	51,500	53,250
Netherlands		6,820	7,884	8.879	10,114	11,480	12,150	12,750	13,400	14,050
Belgium		7,552	8,076	8,301	8,639	9,153	9,360	9,580	9,850	10,100

Austria		6,455	6,684	6,705	6,935	7,081	7,160	7,220	7,220	7,275
Switzerland		3,881	4,059	4,234	4,694	5,362	5,760	5,920	6,080	6,250
West Berlin		2,600	2,900	2,900	2,139	2,199	2,150	2,100	2,050	2,000
Luxembourg		261	297	296	297	314	325	333	342	350
Monaco		23	23	20	22	23	24	25	26	27
Liechtenstein		9	10	11	14	16	16	17	17	18
8. Southern Europe	**Total**	**82,776**	**92,624**	**102,516**	**108,364**	**117,488**	**122,415**	**127,520**	**132,560**	**137,827**
Italy[p]		37,006	40,293	43,840	46,603	49,642	51,200	52,900	54,600	56,400
Spain		21,196	23,445	25,757	27,868	30,303	31,700	33,100	34,500	36,000
Yugoslavia[q]		12,450	14,360	16,425	16,346	18,402	19,500	20,650	21,700	22,750
Portugal		6,000	6,804	7,696	8,405	8,826	9,120	9,320	9,520	9,750
Greece		5,078	6,447	7,410	7,566	8,327	8,620	8,920	9,200	9,500
Albania[r]		800	1,003	1,088	1,219	1,607	1,885	2,225	2,625	3,000
Malta and Gozo		210	240	270	312	329	337	350	360	370
Gibraltar		20	16	14	25	26	26	26	26	26
San Marino		10	10	10	13	17	17	18	18	19
Andorra		5	5	5	6	8	9	10	10	11
Holy See		1	1	1	1	1	1	1	1	1

[j] The figure for 1920 includes an allowance of two million as an estimate of deficiency in the 1923 estimate provided by the State Planning Organization of Turkey (see footnote m below). Prior to 1914, the population in the present area of Turkey probably surpassed 15 million, but may not have increased subsequently in view of Turkey's involvement in World War I and ensuing disturbances. A further decrease of population from 1920 to 1923 resulted from continuance of the civil war and from an extensive exchange of ethnic minorities between Turkey, Bulgaria and Greece.

[k] The totals for 1920 to 1950 are the sums of estimates based on fragmentary data, for individual countries. The figures for 1950 and 1960 include Palestinian refugees.

[l] The totals for 1920 to 1950 are the sums of estimates, based on fragmentary data, for individual countries.

[m] The estimate for 1920 is actually the 1923 estimate taken from Turkey, State Planning Organization, First Five-year Plan (1963–1967), vol. I, p. 8. The 1930 estimate was adjusted to include Hatay, then under French administration.

[n] The figures for 1920 to 1940 are estimates of population within the present territory of Israel, derived in part from 1922 and 1931 censuses of Palestine and in part from official population estimates by ethnic group.

[o] Estimate for 1939.

[p] Estimates for 1920 to 1940 are adjusted for the present territory.

[q] Estimates for 1920 to 1940 are adjusted for the present territory.

[r] Estimates for 1920 to 1940 are adjusted to include estimates for Dodecanese Island, not under Greek administration at those dates.

TABLE 1-25. Population Estimates, 1920–1960, and Projections up to 1980, for Countries in Each Region (cont.)

Region and country		1920	1930	1940	1950	1960	1965	1970	1975	1980
9. Eastern Europe	**Total**	**78,702**	**87,745**	**94,855**	**88,437**	**96,852**	**100,600**	**104,875**	**109,350**	**113,625**
Poland[s]		26,000	29,500	31,500	24,977	29,703	31,500	33,600	35,900	38,000
Romania		12,407	14,212	15,901	16,100	18,403	19,325	20,300	21,250	22,250
Eastern Germany[t]		14,300	15,400	16,800	18,388	17,241	17,250	17,400	17,500	17,600
Czechoslovakia		12,979	13,964	14,713	12,389	13,654	14,125	14,675	15,275	15,800
Hungary		7,950	8,649	9,280	9,334	9,984	10,175	10,325	10,500	10,700
Bulgaria[u]		5,066	6,020	6,661	7,251	7,867	8,225	8,575	8,925	9,275
10. Norther Europe	**Total**	**61,971**	**64,995**	**68,303**	**72,477**	**75,781**	**78,008**	**79,880**	**81,787**	**83,620**
United Kingdom		43,718	45,866	48,226	50,616	52,508	54,000	55,100	56,200	57,250
Sweden		5,876	6,131	6,356	7,014	7,480	7,700	7,920	8,150	8,375
Denmark		3,243	3,542	3,832	4,271	4,581	4,730	4,890	5,040	5,200
Finland		3,133	3,449	3,698	4,009	4,430	4,630	4,830	5,050	5,250
Norway		2,635	2,807	2,973	3,265	3,581	3,735	3,900	4,080	4,250
Ireland		3,103	2,927	2,958	2,969	2,834	2,830	2,840	2,850	2,860
Iceland		93	107	121	145	176	190	205	220	235
Channel Islands		90	92	65	104	109				
Isle of Man		60	50	47	53	48	193	195	197	200
Faeroe Islands		20	24	27	31	34				
D. 11. **USSR**[v]		**155,300**	**179,000**	**195,000**	**180,000**	**214,400**	**231,000**	**245,700**	**260,800**	**277,800**
E. **Africa**										
12. Western Africa	**Total**	**40,000**	**48,000**	**58,000**	**67,500**	**85,973**	**97,773**	**111,624**	**128,130**	**147,810**
Nigeria		–	–	–	–	50,000	58,000	67,400	78,400	91,200
Ghana		–	–	–	–	6,777	7,808	9,054	10,500	12,250
Upper Volta		–	–	–	–	4,340	4,685	5,090	5,620	6,285
Mali		–	–	–	–	4,100	4,515	4,990	5,600	6,395
Ivory Coast		–	–	–	–	3,230	3,555	3,925	4,395	4,995

					–	3,110	3,330	3,610	3,970	4,435
Guinea		–	–	–	–	3,072	3,430	3,825	4,320	4,960
Niger		–	–	–	–	2,823	3,120	3,460	3,900	4,460
Sierra Leone		–	–	–	–	2,450	2,710	2,995	3,310	3,660
Dahomey		–	–	–	–	1,921	2,100	2,320	2,615	2,990
Togo		–	–	–	–	1,440	1,580	1,755	1,985	2,285
Liberia		–	–	–	–	980	1,040	1,100	1,160	1,230
Mauritania		–	–	–	–	694	715	740	790	860
Other areas		–	–	–	–	1,036	1,185	1,360	1,565	1,805
13. Eastern Africa[w]	**Total**	**40,000**	**46,000**	**54,000**	**62,500**	**75,032**	**82,768**	**91,760**	**102,745**	**115,410**
Ethiopia		–	–	–	–	20,000	21,750	23,750	26,250	29,000
United Republic of Tanzania										
Tanganyika		–	–	–	–	9,239	10,150	11,260	12,600	14,140
Zanzibar		–	–	–	–	309	335	370	415	465
Kenya		–	–	–	–	8,115	9,150	10,350	11,800	13,600
Uganda		–	–	–	–	6,677	7,350	8,100	9,000	10,000
Mozambique		–	–	–	–	6,482	7,000	7,575	8,275	9,050
Madagascar		–	–	–	–	5,393	5,775	6,235	6,845	7,610
Southern Rhodesia		–	–	–	–	3,640	4,275	5,025	5,970	7,100
Malawi		–	–	–	–	3,500	4,000	4,600	5,300	6,100
Zambia		–	–	–	–	3,210	3,675	4,225	4,900	5,700
Rwanda		–	–	–	–	2,671	2,840	3,025	3,250	3,500
Burundi		–	–	–	–	2,500	2,850	3,250	3,700	4,200
Somalia		–	–	–	–	2,010	2,190	2,400	2,650	2,925
Mauritius		–	–	–	–	658	738	835	950	1,085
Other areas[x]		–	–	–	–	628	690	760	840	935

[s] Estimate for 1939.

[t] Including East Berlin.

[u] Estimates for 1920 to 1940 include adjustment for territory previously part of Romania.

[v] Estimates 1920 and 1930 are based on those of Biraben and adjusted to agree with official estimates for other dates.

[w] Portuguese Guinea, Gambia, Cape Verde Islands and St. Helena; population assumed to increase at same rates as regional "medium" projection.

[x] Réunion, Comoro Islands, French Somaliland and Seychelles, population assumed to increase at same rates as regional "medium" projection.

TABLE 1-25. Population Estimates, 1920–1960, and Projections up to 1980, for Countries in Each Region (cont.)

Region and country		1920	1930	1940	1950	1960	1965	1970	1975	1980
14. Middle Africa	**Total**	**20,000**	**21,000**	**23,000**	**25,000**	**28,345**	**30,315**	**32,715**	**35,985**	**40,275**
Democratic Republic of the Congo		–	–	–	–	14,139	15,285	16,715	18,725	21,480
Angola		–	–	–	–	4,642	4,910	5,200	5,575	5,975
Cameroon		–	–	–	–	4,097	4,320	4,580	4,930	5,370
Chad		–	–	–	–	2,660	2,875	3,115	3,420	3,815
Central African Republic		–	–	–	–	1,210	1,280	1,355	1,455	590
Congo (Brazzaville)		–	–	–	–	850	855	915	995	1,095
Gabon		–	–	–	–	440	455	470	485	510
Other areas[y]		–	–	–	–	307	335	365	400	440
15. Northern Africa	**Total**	**35,075**	**39,119**	**44,773**	**52,594**	**65,955**	**75,357**	**86,740**	**100,400**	**116,460**
United Arab Republic		13,277	14,822	16,942	20,448	25,952	29,800	34,500	40,150	46,750
Sudan		6,750	7,500	8,500	9,750	11,770	13,200	14,900	16,900	19,250
Morocco		6,330	6,980	7,750	8,876	11,626	13,600	16,000	18,900	22,400
Algeria		5,788	6,489	7,628	8,753	11,020	12,600	14,500	16,800	19,500
Tunisia		2,085	2,381	2,877	3,555	4,168	4,600	5,125	5,750	6,450
Libya		725	800	900	1,195	1,325	1,475	1,650	1,650	1,850
Spanish North Africa		85	112	136	141	152	156	160	165	170
Spanish Sahara and Ifni[z]		35	35	40	46	72	76	80	85	90
16. Southern Africa	**Total**	**7,846**	**9,727**	**11,685**	**13,944**	**17,619**	**19,940**	**22,860**	**25,875**	**29,575**
South Africa		6,842	8,541	10,353	12,447	15,822	17,950	20,650	23,400	26,800
Basutoland		494	537	566	596	685	740	800	870	950
South West Africa		225	283	336	405	522	600	690	800	925
Bechuanaland		170	227	276	301	330	350	370	395	420
Swaziland		115	139	154	195	260	300	350	410	480
F. 17. **Northern America**	**Total**	**115,661**	**134,166**	**144,342**	**166,073**	**198,664**	**214,307**	**229,329**	**246,943**	**267,313**
United States[aa]		106,782	123,616	132,594	152,271	180,676	194,406	207,552	223,003	240,893
Canada		8,839	10,498	11,693	13,737	17,909	19,814	21,680	23,832	26,300

Bermuda		22	32	32	37	43	46	50	54	58
Greenland		14	16	19	23	31	36	42	49	57
St. Pierre and Miquelon		4	4	4	5	5	5	5	5	5
G. **Latin America**										
18. Tropical South America[bb]	**Total**	**45,639**	**54,494**	**66,767**	**84,142**	**112,479**	**129,796**	**149,808**	**172,990**	**199,470**
Brazil[cc]		27,554	33,718	41,525	52,328	70,459	81,450	93,902	108,013	123,716
Colombia[dd]		6,089	7,280	9,097	11,679	15,468	17,787	20,514	23,774	27,691
Peru[ee]		5,313	5,752	6,784	8,096	10,199	11,611	13,275	15,238	17,560
Venezuela[ff]		2,438	2,980	3,740	5,004	7,394	8,752	10,429	12,464	14,857
Ecuador[gg]		1,930	2,102	2,546	3,277	4,355	5,013	5,819	6,809	7,981
Bolivia		1,864	2,153	2,508	3,013	3,696	4,136	4,658	5,277	6,000
British Guiana		295	309	344	440	567	654	757	886	1,045
Surinam		130	170	193	235	308	355	411	481	567
French Guiana		26	30	30	30	33	38	43	48	53
19. Middle America (mainland)	**Total**	**19,443**	**22,456**	**26,863**	**34,694**	**46,811**	**55,323**	**65,565**	**77,975**	**93,141**
Mexico		14,500	16,589	19,815	25,826	34,988	41,460	49,282	58,822	70,581
Guatemala		1,450	1,771	2,201	2,805	3,765	4,343	5,033	5,867	6,878
El Salvador		1,168	1,350	1,550	1,868	2,442	2,859	3,346	3,917	4,585
Honduras		783	948	1,146	1,428	1,838	2,182	2,592	3,078	3,656
Nicaragua		600	700	825	1,060	1,403	1,666	1,979	2,350	2,791
Costa Rica		421	499	619	801	1,171	1,424	1,718	2,049	2,419
Panama[hh]		447	523	620	797	1,079	1,249	1,458	1,713	2,023
British Honduras[ii]		44	51	56	67	90	105	122	144	173
Canal Zone[jj]		20	25	31	42	35	35	35	35	35

[y] Spanish Equatorial Region, and São Tomé and Principe; population assumed to increase at same rates as regional "medium" projection.

[z] The 1960 estimates for Ifni and Spanish Sahara are 49,000 and 23,000 respectively.

[aa] Including Alaska and Hawaii and, except in 1920, armed forces abroad.

[bb] Except British Guiana, Surinam and French Guiana, estimates taken from Statistical Bulletin for Latin America, vol. 1, No. 1, March 1964, Economic Commission for Latin America, Santiago, Chile.

[cc] Including jungle inhabitants estimated at the constant figure of 150,000. The estimates for 1950 and 1960 are taken from C. Arretx, Proyeccion de la poblacion del Brazil, Santiago, Chile, 1963.

[dd] Estimates for 1950 and 1960 are adjusted to include allowance for omissions at 1951 census.

[ee] Including jungle inhabitants estimated at the constant figure of 101,000.

[ff] Including jungle inhabitants estimated at the constant figure of 30,000.

[gg] Including jungle inhabitants estimated at the constant figure of 80,000.

[hh] Including tribal Indians, but not including Canal Zone. The figure for 1930 includes an estimate of 52,000 tribal Indians at 1930 census.

[ii] The figure for 1920 is actually for 31 December.

[jj] Civilian population only.

TABLE 1-25. Population Estimates, 1920–1960, and Projections up to 1980, for Countries in Each Region (cont.)

Region and country		1920	1930	1940	1950	1960	1965	1970	1975	1980
20. Temperate South America	**Total**	**14,826**	**18,877**	**22,319**	**26,856**	**32,796**	**36,067**	**39,574**	**43,359**	**47,485**
Argentina		8,861	11,896	14,169	17,189	20,956	22,841	24,784	26,828	28,998
Chile		3,785	4,365	5,063	6,073	7,627	8,625	9,753	10,996	12,378
Uruguay		1,479	1,734	1,974	2,195	2,491	2,647	2,802	2,960	3,126
Paraguay		699	880	1,111	1,397	1,720	1,952	2,233	2,573	2,981
Falkland Islands		2	2	2	2	2	2	2	2	2
21. Caribbean	**Total**	**9,666**	**11,591**	**13,891**	**16,693**	**20,345**	**22,757**	**25,500**	**28,598**	**32,119**
Cuba		2,950	3,837	4,566	5,508	6,797	7,523	8,307	9,146	10,034
Haiti		2,124	2,422	2,827	3,380	4,140	4,645	5,255	6,001	6,912
Dominican Republic[kk]		1,140	1,400	1,759	2,243	3,030	3,588	4,277	5,124	6,174
Puerto Rico		1,312	1,552	1,880	2,218	2,361	2,557	2,754	2,935	3,117
Jamaica		855	1,009	1,212	1,403	1,607	1,720	1,840	1,960	2,080
Trinidad and Tobago		389	405	510	632	844	975	1,120	1,280	1,450
Windward Islands[ll]		200	220	259	277	315	350	395	445	480
Martinique[mm]		165	175	200	222	277	315	358	406	463
Guadeloupe[nn]		150	160	185	206	270	306	347	392	445
Barbados		155	159	179	209	232	255	270	280	285
Netherlands Antilles[oo]		55	72	107	162	190	210	230	245	260
Leeward Islands[pp]		85	86	99	113	130	143	157	170	180
Bahama Islands		55	61	70	79	105	120	135	155	175
Virgin Islands[qq]		20	22	25	27	33	36	40	44	48
Cayman Islands		5	6	7	7	8	8	9	9	10
Turks and Caicos Islands		6	5	6	7	6	6	6	6	6
H. **Oceania**										
22. Australia and New Zealand	**Total**	**6,641**	**7,994**	**8,715**	**10,127**	**12,687**	**14,015**	**15,244**	**16,572**	**18,237**
Australia[rr]		5,400	6,503	7,079	8,219	10,315	11,356	12,300	13,308	14,571
New Zealand		1,241	1,491	1,636	1,908	2,372	2,659	2,944	3,264	3,666

23. Melanesia	**Total**	**1,500**	**1,600**	**1,750**	**1,900**	**2,166**	**2,338**	**2,549**	**2,804**	**3,107**
New Guinea		–	–	–	–	1,402	1,509	1,639	1,799	1,985
Papua		–	–	–	–	503	549	605	672	753
British Solomon Islands		–	–	–	–	124	132	142	151	167
New Caledonia		–	–	–	–	77	83	91	101	112
New Hebrides		–	–	–	–	59	64	71	80	89
Norfolk Island		–	–	–	–	1	1	1	1	1
24. Polynesia and Micronesia	**Total**	**380**	**450**	**595**	**650**	**860**	**1,011**	**1,212**	**1,456**	**1,745**
Polynesia		**268**	**314**	**392**	**511**	**678**	**797**	**956**	**1,147**	**1,376**
Fiji Islands		161	181	218	289	394	463	556	667	800
Western Samoa		35	45	61	79	107	126	151	181	217
French Polynesia		32	39	50	61	76	89	107	128	154
Tonga		23	28	37	48	63	74	89	107	128
American Samoa		8	10	13	19	20	24	28	34	41
Cook Islands		9	11	13	15	18	21	25	30	36
Micronesia		**112**	**136**	**203**	**139**	**182**	**214**	**256**	**309**	**369**
Pacific Islands[ss]		56	70	134	57	76	89	107	129	154
Gilbert and Ellice Islands		30	34	34	38	46	54	65	78	93
Guam[tt]		14	19	22	30	40	47	56	68	81
Other islands[uu]		12	13	13	14	20	24	28	34	41

[kk] Figures for 1920 and 1930 adjusted for probable under-enumeration at 1920 census.

[ll] Dominica, Grenada, St. Lucia and St. Vincent.

[mm] Estimates for 1920 to 1940 were prepared by assuming the population to have been growing similar to Windward Islands.

[nn] Estimates for 1920 to 1940 were prepared by assuming the population to have been growing similar to Windward Islands.

[oo] Curaçao, Aruba, Bonaire, Saba, St. Eustatius, and part of St. Martin.

[pp] Antigua, Montserrat, St. Kitts-Nevis and Anguilla, and Virgin Islands, under United Kingdom administration.

[qq] St. Thomas, St. Croix, and St. John, under United States administration.

[rr] Including full-blooded aborigines estimated at a constant figure of 40,000.

[ss] Under United States administration.

[tt] For indigenous population only. The indigenous populations in 1950 and 1960 have been estimated from fragmentary data, as official population estimates include a relatively large number of United States military personnel and their dependants.

[uu] Islands with population smaller than 5,000 in 1960, namely: Nive, Nauru, Christmas Islands, Midway Islands, Tokelau Islands, Wake Islands, Cocos (Keeling) Islands, Canton and Enderbury Islands, Bonin Islands, Johnston Islands.

7. ZERO POPULATION GROWTH

Zero Population Growth (ZPG) is both a theory and a movement. Theoretically, ZPG means the alignment of birth and death rates, the consequence of which is a zero growth rate. Since death rates can hardly be forced upward to parallel birth rates without intolerable violations of morality, ZPG seeks the solution in birth reductions.

In the United States, for example, each family has an average of approximately 2.3 children. That does not seem like a disproportionate number, but 2.3 children a family gives the United States an annual growth rate of approximately 1 percent. Thus, our corresponding doubling time is thirty-five years. ZPG would be achieved, however, if the average American family had on the average 2.11 children.

This prescription is not really as harsh as it appears. *Average* is the key word. Not every family would be restricted to just two children. Deviations are normal and accounted for in the ZPG scheme. Economist Stephen Enke has figured out a sliding scale that can accommodate idiosyncratic demands to some extent. According to Enke, 50 percent of the families would have two children (always the norm). The remaining 50 percent then could deviate above and below this norm:

30 percent with 3 children
10 percent with 1 child
5 percent childless
5 percent with more than 3 children
with an average of 5

As an organization, Zero Population Growth is dedicated to the proposition that political lobbying is the most effective way of bringing about the ZPG. Founded in 1968 by a group of biologists that included Dr. Paul Ehrlich, ZPG has a membership of approximately 35,000 in roughly 350 chapters across the country. ZPG supports free distribution of birth control pills, legalized abortion, voluntary male sterilization, tax exemptions for no more than two children and ZPG-oriented candidates.

Although many developed and underdeveloped countries have growth rates considerably higher than the United States, ZPG purposely confines its activities within our borders. Why? Because ecologically speaking, America's population problem is the world's worst. Americans do more per capita damage to the ecosystem than any other nationality. To quote Wayne Davis' article "Overpopulated America" from *The New Republic:*

> An American can be expected to destroy a piece of land on which he builds a home, garage and driveway. He will contribute his share to the 142 million

tons of smoke and fumes, seven million junked cars, 20 million tons of paper, 48 billion cans, and 26 billion bottles the overburdened environment must absorb each year. To run his air conditioner we will strip-mine a Kentucky hillside, push the dirt and slate down into the stream, and burn coal in a power generator, whose smokestack contributes to a plume of smoke massive enough to cause cloud seeding and premature precipitation from Gulf winds which should be irrigating the wheat farms of Minnesota.

In his lifetime he will personally pollute three million gallons of water, and industry and agriculture will use ten times this much water in his behalf. To provide these needs the US Army Corps of Engineers will build dams and flood farmland. He will also use 21,000 gallons of leaded gasoline containing boron, drink 28,000 pounds of milk and eat 10,000 pounds of meat. The latter is produced and squandered in a life pattern unknown to Asians. A steer on a Western range eats plants containing minerals necessary for plant life. Some of these are incorporated into the body of the steer which is later shipped for slaughter. After being eaten by man these nutrients are flushed down the toilet into the ocean or buried in the cemetery, the surface of which is cluttered with boulders called tombstones and has been removed from productivity of range land. Add to this the erosion of overgrazed lands, and the effects of the falling water table as we mine Pleistocene deposits of groundwater to irrigate to produce food for more people, and we can see why our land is dying far more rapidly than did the great civilizations of the Middle East, which experienced the same cycle. The average Indian citizen, whose fecal material goes back to the land, has but a minute fraction of the destructive effect on the land that the affluent American does.

Thus I want to introduce a new term, which I suggest be used in future discussions of human population and ecology. We should speak of our numbers in "Indian equivalents." An Indian equivalent I define as the average number of Indian citizens required to have the same detrimental effect on the land's ability to support human life as would the average American. This value is difficult to determine, but let's take an extremely conservative working figure of 25. To see how conservative this is, imagine the addition of 1,000 citizens to your town and 25,000 to an Indian village. Not only would the Americans destroy much more land for homes, highways and a shopping center, but they would contribute far more to environmental deterioration in hundreds of other ways as well. For example, their demand for steel for new autos might increase the daily pollution equivalent of 130,000 junk autos which *Life* tells us that US Steel Corp. dumps into Lake Michigan. Their demand for textiles would help the cotton industry destroy the life in the Black Warrior River in Alabama with endrin. Add they would contribute to the massive industrial pollution of our oceans (we provide one third to one half the world's share) which has caused the precipitous downward trend in our commerical fisheries landings during the past seven years.

The per capita gross national product of the United States is 38 times that of India. Most of our goods and services contribute to the decline in the ability of the environment to support life. Thus it is clear that a figure of 25 for an Indian equivalent is conservative. It has been suggested to me that a more realistic figure would be 500.

In Indian equivalents, therefore, the population of the United States is at least four billion. And the rate of growth is even more alarming. We are growing at one percent per year, a rate which would double our numbers in 70 years. India is growing at 2.5 percent. Using the Indian equivalent of 25, our population growth becomes 10 times as serious as that of India. According to the Reinows in their recent book *Moment in the Sun,* just one year's crop of American babies can be expected to use up 25 billion pounds of beef, 200 million pounds of steel and 9.1 billion gallons of gasoline during their collective lifetime. And the demands on water and land for our growing population are expected to be far greater than the supply available in the year 2000. We are destroying our land at a rate of over a million acres a year. We now have only 2.6 agricultural acres per person. By 1975 this will be cut to 2.2, the critical point for the maintenance of what we consider a decent diet, and by the year 2000 we might expect to have 1.2.

You might object that I am playing with statistics in using the Indian equivalent on the rate of growth. I am making the assumption that today's Indian child will live 35 years (the average Indian life span) at today's level of affluence. If he lives an American 70 years, our rate of population growth would be 20 times as serious as India's.

But the assumption of continued affluence at today's level is unfounded. If our numbers continue to rise, our standard of living will fall so sharply that by the year 2000 any surviving Americans might consider today's average Asian to be well off. Our children's destructive effects on their environment will decline as they sink ever low into poverty.

How would ZPG work in the United States? Enke has written one possible scenario. If, by 1975, American families could be persuaded to abide by the average of two children, it would take seventy-five more years before birth and death rates canceled each other off. (The present age structure of the United States with a heavy concentration of the population under thirty guarantees a continually steady growth rate even at two children a family.)

During the seventy-five years (until 2050) ZPG is gestating, the American population will have grown to 293 million. The difference between inaugurating ZPG in 1975 and letting the 2.3 average go unchecked is illustrated dramatically by Enke's picture of the year 2060. At that point, if successful, ZPG will have so stayed population growth that there will be just three Americans then for every two now. In contrast, an unchallenged maintenance of the 2.3 children average will yield by 2060 seven Americans for every two now living.

SELECTED BIBLIOGRAPHY

The study of population has an enormous literature. The Population Reference Bureau has published in its bi-monthly *Population Bulletin* (Vol. XXV, No. 5, Nov. 1969) an extremely useful annotated bibliography which serves as a general introduction to the most important books in the field. Here we draw on several sections of that well-nuanced bibliography in addition to our own selected insertions.

References

Keyfitz, Nathan, and Flieger, Wilhelm, *World Population: An Analysis of Vital Data,* Chicago, University of Chicago Press, 1968.

Wealth of demographic statistics for different countries over varying periods of time; includes both basic data and refined measures.

Office of Population Research, Princeton University, and Population Association of America, Inc., *Population Index,* (Statistical appendix). Princeton, published quarterly.

Each issue of the *Population Index* has a short section of current intercensal demographic data, such as population estimates for countries throughout the world, annual rates of growth, current fertility and life expectations.

Population Reference Bureau, *World Population Data Sheet,* Washington, D.C., published annually.

In tabular form, a listing of current populations, vital statistics, growth rates, population under 15 and latest per capita Gross National Product figures for over 135 countries.

United Nations, *Demographic Yearbook,* New York, United Nations, published annually since 1949.

Basic demographic statistics for over 200 countries and territories assembled by the Statistical Office of the United Nations from official publications and from data transmitted in monthly and annual questionnaires by national statistical services or similar offices in these countries.

United Nations, *Growth of the World's Urban and Rural Population, 1920–2000,* New York, United Nations, 1969.

United Nations, *Statistical Yearbook,* New York, United Nations, published annually since 1949.

Statistical data for over 200 countries and territories covering a wide range of economic and social subjects.

United Nations, *World Population Prospects,* New York, United Nations, 1966.

Standard Texts

Bogue, Donald J., *Principles of Demography,* New York, John Wiley & Sons, 1969.

Comparative work stressing demography as a unique systematic discipline; in covering the subfields of demography, key data are presented to verify or support the generalizations being made; an extensive bibliography follows each section.

Hauser, Philip M., and Duncan, Otis Dudley, eds., *The Study of Population: An Inventory and Appraisal,* Chicago, University of Chicago Press, 1959.

Investigation of the status of demography as a science with chapters contributed by leading scholars in the field; provides a description and evaluation of the data, theory and methods of demography and an assessment of its relationship to other scientific disciplines.

Heer, David M., *Society and Population,* Englewood Cliffs, N.J., Prentice-Hall, 1968.

Brief text limited to the consideration of population of nation-states and of the world as a whole, rather than to the population of social systems and strata within societies; demonstrates how an understanding of population is important to a proper study of sociology.

Petersen, William, *Population,* 2nd ed., New York, Macmillan Co., 1969.

Standard text for undergraduate study of population.

Sheps, Mindel L., and Ridley, Jeanne Clare, eds., *Public Health and Population Change,* Cambridge, Mass., Schenkman Publishing Co., 1965.

Historical discussion of factors causing accelerated population growth and reduced natality, with attention to current natality and biological aspects of reproduction in the West.

Thomlinson, Ralph, *Population Dynamics: Causes and Consequences of World Demographic Change,* New York, Random House, 1965.
Standard text for undergraduate study of population.

Thompson, Warren S., and Lewis, David T., *Population Problems,* 5th ed., New York, McGraw-Hill Book Co., 1965.
Standard text for undergraduate study of population; the senior author is a pioneer of American demography.

United Nations, *The Determinants and Consequences of Population Trends,* New York, United Nations, 1953.
Summary of then-existing scientific studies of the relationships between population trends and economic and social development.

Readers: Collections of Articles for Use with Texts

Heer, David M., ed, *Readings on Population,* Englewood Cliffs, N.J., Prentice-Hall, 1968.
Supplement to Heer's text, *Society and Population,* with articles chosen because they challenge well-established beliefs, attempt to present all factors bearing on a given problem and are nontechnical.

Kammeyer, Kenneth C., ed., *Population Studies: Selected Essays and Research,* Paperback, Chicago, Rand McNally & Co., 1969.
Selection of papers offering generalizations or syntheses of population theories.

Nam, Charles B., ed., *Population and Society: A Textbook of Selected Readings,* Boston, Houghton Mifflin Co., 1968.
Broad selection of nontechnical writings on the social importance of demographic trends.

Spengler, Joseph J., and Duncan, Otis Dudley, eds., *Demographic Analysis: Selected Readings,* Glencoe, Ill., Free Press, 1956.
Works dealing with concrete demographic problems and their analysis; particularly helpful in showing how demography functions as a science.

Szabady, Egon, ed., *World View of Population Problems,* Tenth Anniversary Publication of the Hungarian quarterly journal *Demografia,* Budapest, Demographic Committee of the Hungarian Academy of Sciences and Demographic Research Institute, 1968.
Papers by prominent demographers from all over the world, covering recent developments and issues in demography.

General Presentations

American Academy of Political and Social Science, "World Population," *The Annals,* Vol. 369, January 1967.
Thirteen papers for the general reader on many aspects of population growth.

Appleman, Philip, *The Silent Explosion,* Boston, Beacon Press, 1965.
Account of the economic and social effects of overpopulation and their implications for the United States.

Cook, Robert C., and Lecht, J. *People!: An Introduction to the Study of Population,* Washington, D.C., Columbia Books, 1968.
Introduction for the general reader to the problems of population growth in the world today, originally prepared for secondary schools but suitable for general readers.

Fisher, Tadd, *Our Overcrowded World,* New York, Parent's Magazine Press, 1969.
World population growth seen in broad perspective; a readable presentation of basic demographic data and their implications.

Hauser, Philip M., ed, *The Population Dilemma,* Englewood Cliffs, N.J.: Prentice-Hall, 1963.
Presentation of demographic facts, problems and policies; includes a section on population and economic development and separate treatments of population control and population policy.

Hauser, Philip M., "World Population Problems," *Headline Series,* No. 174 (December 1965).
Brief description of the problems of population growth and the benefits of controlling this growth.

Kiefer, David M., "Population," *Chemical and Engineering News,* October 14, 1968. Reprint.
Two-part feature article. Part 1 discussess population growth and the inability of technology alone to deal with it. Part 2 documents population trends in the United States.

National Academy of Sciences, *The Growth of World Population,* National Research Council Publication 1091, Washington, D.C., National Academy of Sciences, 1963.
Analysis of the population situation in the world today in a report by a committee under William D. McElroy; deals with social, economic and medical factors and suggests courses of action.

Osborn, Fairfield, ed., *Our Crowded Planet: Essays on the Pressures of Population,* New York, Doubleday & Co., 1962.
Essays by authorities of varied backgrounds on the population question; contributors deal with population and economics, humanities, mores, peace, biological principles and religion.

Sauvy, Alfred, and Lenica, Jan, *Population Explosion: Abundance or Famine,* New York, Dell Publishing Co., 1962. Out of print.
Descriptive text with visual representations of the population explosion—its causes, consequences and possible solutions.

More Detailed Discussions

Borgstrom, Georg, *The Hungry Planet,* New York, Macmillan Co., 1965.
Well-documented presentation of the dilemma posed by increasing human populations and decreasing resources; special emphasis on gap between well-fed and undernourished peoples of the world.

Brown, Harrison, *The Challenge of Man's Future,* New York, Viking Press, 1954.
Call for action to maintain a desirable balance between population and resources as a necessary step toward survival.

Cook, Robert C., *Human Fertility: The Modern Dilemma,* London, Victor Gollancz, 1951. Out of print.
Early discussion of the modern population dilemma, its causes and the policies needed to deal with it; includes a section on problems of eugenics.

Freedman, Ronald, ed., *Population: The Vital Revolution,* Garden City, N.Y.: Doubleday & Co., 1964.
Brief, authoritative essays on major aspects of contemporary population trends, originally prepared for the Voice of America.

Hauser, Philip M., *Population Perspectives,* New Brunswick, N.J., Rutgers University Press, 1961.
Elaboration of three lectures in the Brown and Haley Lecture Series at the University of Puget Sound, March 1960, on changes in population size, composition and distribution; stresses trends in the United States.

Malthus, Thomas; Huxley, Julian; and Osborn, Frederick, *Three Essays on Population,* New York, Mentor Books, 1960.
Three essays—Malthus's classic statement and Huxley's and Osborn's more current discussions, particularly with regard to underdeveloped nations—provide a broad perspective on the population problem.

Mudd, Stuart, ed., *The Population Crisis and the Uses of World Resources,* Bloomington, Ind., Indiana University Press, 1964.
Wide-ranging essays on population growth, its economic, social and political consequences, regional patterns, the role of biology, the consumption of world resources and programs to restrain population increase.

Osborn, Fairfield, *Our Plundered Planet,* New York, Pyramid Books, 1968.
Study of man's conflict with nature and ravaging of natural resources, intensified by his growing numbers. (First published in 1948.)

Sauvy, Alfred, *Fertility and Survival: Population Problems from Malthus to Mao Tse-Tung,* New York, Criterion Books, 1961.
Analyzing some extreme theories of population, Sauvy discusses the problem of supporting a growing population and describes attempts to control fertility.

Thomlinson, Ralph, *Demographic Problems, Controversy over Population Control,* Belmont, Calif., Dickenson Publishing Co., 1967.
Sociological analysis of selected population trends, problems and controversies in the contemporary world, especially the United States.

Udall, Stewart, *The Quiet Crisis.* New York: Holt, Rinehart & Winston, 1963.
Broad account of the destruction of America's natural surroundings by affluent, growing population.

Wrong, Dennis H., *Population and Society,* 3rd ed. New York, Random House, 1967.
Excellent, brief introduction to the main aspects of the population dilemma.

Current Population Problems: General Works Dealing with Present-Day Concerns and Controversies

Brown, Harrison, *et al., The Next Hundred Years,* New York, Viking Press, 1957.
Attempt to assess the future of our scientific, technological and industrial civilization, with reference to demographic trends.

Clark, Colin, *Population Growth and Land Use,* New York, St. Martin's Press, 1967.
Personal, unorthodox approach to selected problems of population growth; the increase of wealth in certain favored regions of increasing population, their attraction of migrants and the unmanageable spread of their cities.

Ehrlich, Paul R., *The Population Bomb,* New York, Ballantine Books, 1968.
Polemical discussion of population problems by a biologist who argues the need for decisive, possibly extreme measures.

Fabre-Luce, Alfred, *Men or Insects?, A Study of Population Problems.* Translated from the French by Robert Baldick. New York, Horizon Press, 1965.
Look at some of the issues involved in population growth, including speculation on the effects of overpopulation on life-styles.

Moran, William E., Jr., ed., *Population Growth—Threat to Peace?* New York, P. J. Kenedy & Sons, 1965.
Papers of the 37th Annual Conference of the Catholic Association for International Peace; a general treatment of the world population problem by Catholic and non-Catholic experts, followed by proposals for an acceptable Catholic course of action.

Paddock, William and Paul, *Famine—1975!,* Boston, Little, Brown & Co., 1967.
Two brothers, one a foreign service officer and the other an agronomist, present an extremely pessimistic view of the problem of overpopulation and the capacity of agriculture to cope with it.

Population Reference Bureau, "Spaceship Earth in Peril," *Population Bulletin,* Vol. XXI, No. 1 (March 1969).
Analysis of the views of British scientist Lord C. P. Snow and Soviet physicist Andrei Sakharov on population, hunger and great-power politics, with a call for Soviet-U.S. cooperation and institutions to deal with the crisis.

Sax, Karl, *Standing Room Only, The Challenge of Overpopulation,* Boston, Beacon Press, 1960.
Early, spirited presentation of the population problem. (First published in 1955.)

U.S. Congress, Senate, Committee on Government Operations, Sub-Committee on Foreign Aid Expenditures, *Population Crisis,* The Gruening Hearings). 14 Vols., Washington, D.C., Government Printing Office, 1965-1968.
Well-indexed views of most present-day authorities on population; an exhaustive compliation with recommendations for policy in a summary volume.

Vogt, William, *People! Challenge to Survival,* New York, William Sloane Associates, 1960.

Discussion of excessive population growth based on the author's travels in more than 25 countries and in 49 U.S. states.

Young, Louise B., ed., *Population in Perspective,* New York, Oxford University Press, 1968.

Sponsored by the American Foundation for Continuing Education, this anthology of short selections presents views on population from writers of many disciplines.

Historical Demography: Population Trends in Earlier Times

Banks, J. A., and Banks, Oliver, *Feminism and Family Planning in Victorian England,* Liverpool, Liverpool University Press, 1964.

Analysis of fertility decline in 19th-century England.

Carr-Saunders, Alexander M., *World Population: Past Growth and Present Trends,* London, Frank Cass & Co., 1964.

General review of world population history during the modern era up to the early 1930s, particularly in Europe and "Europe Overseas"; detailed analysis of migration. (First published in 1936.)

Drake, Michael, *Population and Society in Norway, 1735-1865,* Cambridge, England, Cambridge University Press, 1969.

Discussion of demographic aspects of the population of Norway, with attention to historical trends.

Finch, Bernard E., and Green, Hugh, *Contraception through the Ages,* Springfield, Ill., Charles C. Thomas, 1963.

Historical discussion of contraception and its refinements through the ages.

Glass, David V., *Population—Policies and Movements in Europe,* New York, Augustus M. Kelley, 1967.

Historical background of population dynamics in Europe up to World War II. (First published in 1940.)

Glass, David V., and Eversley, D. C. C., eds, *Population in History—Essays in Historical Demography,* Chicago, Aldine Publishing Co., 1965.

Twenty-seven essays on the history of population of Europe and the United States.

Himes, Norman E., *Medical History of Contraception.* New York: Gamut Press, 1964.

Review of the history of contraception; includes discussion of medical, social and economic implications.

Keyfitz, Nathan, "How Many People Have Ever Lived On Earth?", *Demography,* Vol. 63, pp. 581–582, 1966.

Population Reference Bureau, "How Many People Have Ever Lived On Earth?", *Population Bulletin,* Vol. XVIII, No. 1 (February 1962).

Historical review of population growth from man's beginnings to 1962.

Rossiter, W. S., *A Century of Population Growth: 1790–1900.* Baltimore: Genealogical Publishing Co., 1967.

Historical presentation of U.S. census data from colonial times to 1900.

Russell, J. C., "Late Ancient and Medieval Population," *Transactions of the American Philosophical Society,* Vol. 48, Part 3 (June 1958), Philadelphia, American Philosophical Society, 1958.

Discusses the late Roman Empire and traces the demographic development of Europe and the Mediterranean countries through the Middle Ages.

Spengler, Joseph J., *France Faces Depopulation.,* Durham, N.C., Duke University Press, 1938. Out of print.

Description of the demographic history of France to the mid-1930s, with particular emphasis on fears of depopulation.

Woytinsky, Wladimir S., and Emma S., *World Population and Production,* New York, Twentieth Century Fund, 1953. Out of print.

International demographic trends and their relationships with agriculture, energy, mining, manufacturing and standards of living.

Wrigley, E. A., *Industrial Growth and Population Change,* Cambridge, England, Cambridge University Press, 1961.

Historical review of the relationship between population growth and industrial development, with emphasis on the demographic history of northwest Europe.

Periodicals

Bobbs-Merrill Reprint Series S (Sociology). Bobbs-Merrill Co., Inc., 4300 W. 62nd St., Indianapolis, Ind. 46206. Published at frequent intervals. $.25-$1.00.

Series S offers a broad range of articles on sociology, including many dealing with population.

Conservation Foundation Letter. Conservation Foundation, 1250 Connecticut Ave., N.W., Washington, D.C. 20036. Published 14 times yearly. $6.00/year.

Well-documented short articles on current problems of environmental quality and legislation.

Country Profiles. Population Council and International Institute for the Study of Human Reproduction, Columbia University. Population Council, 245 Park Ave., New York, N.Y. 10017. Price n.a.

Each *Profile* reviews population trends, policies and programs for a given country.

Demography. Population Association of America, P.O. Box 14182, Benjamin Franklin Sta., Washington, D.C. 20044. Quarterly. $10.00/year.

Presents manuscripts on topics of interest to demographers; occasionally includes technical or mathematical works but also presents articles of interest to the general reader.

Environment. Committee for Environmental Information, 438 N. Skinker Blvd., St. Louis, Mo. 63130. Monthly. $6.00/year.

Publishes polemical, well-documented articles on man's disruption of the environment.

Family Planning Perspectives. Center for Family Planning Development. Technical Assistance Division of Planned Parenthood-World Population, 545 Madison Ave., New York, N.Y. 10022. Quarterly. Available on request.

Articles consider many aspects of family planning, with analyses of actual programs and data.

International Migration Review. Center for Migration Studies, 209 Flagg Place, Staten Island, N.Y. 10304. Monthly. $1.75/issue.

Articles on migration trends around the world and reviews of migration literature.

Journal of Marriage and the Family. National Council on Family Relations, Case Western University, Cleveland, Ohio 44106. Quarterly. $12.00/year.

Articles on family size, birth rates, child spacing, attitudes toward fertility and many other factors relating to marriage and the family.

Land Economics. University of Wisconsin Press, Madison, Wis. 53706. Quarterly. $8.00/year.

Studies on both urban and rural land use and resources in relation to an expanding population.

Milbank Memorial Fund Quarterly. Milbank Memorial Fund, 40 Wall St., New York, N.Y. 10005. Quarterly. $2.00/issue.

Scholarly papers analyzing demographic trends and family planning programs.

Natural History. American Museum of Natural History, Central Park West at 79th St., New York, N.Y. 10023. Published monthly October-May; bimonthly June-September. $1.00/copy.

Articles on natural phenomena, ecology, conservation, and, occasionally, population.

Population. L'Institut National d'Etudes Demographiques, 23 Ave. Franklin-Roosevelt, Paris VIIIe. France. Published six times yearly. $3.00/year.

Published in French only, this journal offers scientific articles on all aspects of population dynamics.

Population Bulletin. Population Reference Bureau, 1755 Massachusetts Ave., N.W., Washington, D.C. 20036. Published six times a year. $3.00 for teachers and students, $5.00 for regular members/year.

Issues and interprets well-documented facts about population trends in the United States and abroad, with discussions of the consequences for governments and individuals.

Population Chronicle. Population Council and International Institute for the Study of Human Reproduction, Columbia University. Population Council, 245 Park Ave., New York, N.Y. 10017. Monthly. Free.

A newsletter aimed at informing the general public about demography and family planning.

Population Index. Office of Population Research, Princeton University, and Population Association of America, Inc. Office of Population Research, Princeton University, Princeton, N.J. 08540. Quarterly. $15.00/year.

A technical review providing in-depth articles and comprehensive listings for on-going literature in all phases of population dynamics; useful for the demographer and the student.

Population Review. Indian Institute for Population Studies. Gandhinagan, Madras 20, India. Published twice a year. $4.00/year.

A review of demographic articles presenting scientific studies on population.

Population Studies. Population Investigation Committee, London School of Economics, Houghton St., Aldwych, London W.C.2, England. Published three times a year. $8.50/year.

A demographic journal offering articles by demographic professionals from all over the world.

Social Biology (formerly *Eugenics Quarterly*). American Eugenics Society. University of Chicago Press, 5750 Ellis Ave., Chicago, Ill. 60637. Quarterly. $9.00/year.

Papers consider biological and socio-cultural factors affecting human populations, their structure and composition.

Studies in Family Planning. Population Council, 245 Park Ave., New York, N.Y. 10017. Published irregularly. Free.

Descriptions and analyses of family planning programs around the world.

Population Libraries and Information Centers Offering Services to Qualified Researchers

Bureau of the Census, Washington, D.C. 20233

205,000 book titles, 1,200 periodicals. Area of specialization: Foreign and U.S. censuses; public finance and government functions of states, large cities and countries; statistical methods and techniques.

International Planned Parenthood Federation, Western Hemisphere Region, 51 Ease 42nd St., New York, N.Y. 10017

1,500 book titles, 40 periodicals. Area of specialization: Population and family planning in the Caribbean and Latin America.

National Institute for Child Health and Human Development, Scientific Information Center, Bethesda, Md. 20014

Periodicals, n.a. Area of specialization: Demography; research on new birth control techniques and reproductive physiology; use, acceptance, biomedical and behavioral effects of contraception.

Pan American Sanitary Bureau, 525 23rd St., N.W., Washington, D.C. 20037

40,000 book titles, 1,000 periodicals. Area of specialization: Medicine and public health in Latin America.

Planned Parenthood-World Population, 515 Madison Ave., New York, N.Y. 10017

1,500 book titles, 85 periodicals. Area of specialization: All aspects of family planning research, service and program development.

Population Council, Bio-Medical Division, 2 East 103rd St., New York, N.Y. 10029
6,000 book titles, 40 periodicals. Area of specialization: Sociological and biomedical aspects of fertility control.

Population Reference Bureau, 1755 Massachusetts Ave., N.W., Washington, D.C. 20036
2,000 book titles, 250 periodicals. Area of specialization: International demography, censuses and statistics; social, economic, public health aspects of population; special section on Latin America.

Major Private Organizations in the Field of Population and Family Planning

Ford Foundation:
320 East 43rd St., New York, N.Y. 10017
Population program established in 1952. Activities include support for training and research in reproductive biology, establishment or extension of university population studies centers in the United States, population programs in developing countries. Expenditures: $8,947,567 (1968).

International Planned Parenthood Federation
Regional Offices:
Europe & Near East Region, 64 Sloane St., London, S.W. 1, England
Southeast Asia & Oceania Region, c/o 1st Floor, F.P.A. Bldg., 26 Dunearn Rd., Singapore 11
Indian Ocean Region, I.O.R. Office, 4 Harley St., Rawalpindi, W. Pakistan
Western Hemisphere Region, Inc., 51 East 42nd St., New York, N.Y. 10017
Western Pacific Region, c/o Hoken Kaikan, No. 2, 1-chome, Ichigaya Sadoharacho, Shinjuku-ku, Tokyo, Japan
Africa Region, P.O. Box 30234, Nairobi, Kenya
Established in 1952. Activities include training for physicians, nurses, social workers and public health experts in the administration and creation of family planning associations throughout the world; promotion of research in human reproduction and biological methods of controlling fertility. Expenditures: $6.5 million (1968).

The Pathfinder Fund, 850 Boylston St., Chestnut Hill, Mass. 02167
Established in the United States in 1929, internationally in 1952. Activities include provision of educational materials, support for local physicians interested in establishing contraceptive clinics, support for local studies of effectiveness and acceptability of contraceptive methods, and aid for the development of training programs in demography and family planning. Recent expenditures n.a.

Planned Parenthood-World Population, 515 Madison Ave., New York, N.Y. 10022
Established in 1916 as the Planned Parenthood Federation, merged in 1961 with the World Population Emergency Campaign. Activities in family planning include a public information program, operation of clinics offering instruction in family planning techniques, orientation sessions on family planning programs and contributions to I.P.P.F. Expenditures: $5,983,226 (1968).

The Population Council, 245 Park Ave., New York, N.Y. 10017
Established in 1952. Activities in reproductive biology and family planning include research grants, training programs, technical assistance to family planning programs, development of contraceptive technology, information services, and promotion of public awareness in population matters. Expenditures: over $12 million (1968).

Rockefeller Foundation, 111 West 50th St., New York, N.Y. 10020
Population program established in 1954. Activities include study and research grants, support for training programs, physiological research and action programs in demography and family planning. Expenditures: $5.1 million (1967).

II Endangered Species

1. INTRODUCTION

The most discernible casualties of our ecological Armageddon are the animals of the world. Unable to defend themselves against man-made imbalances of nature, they are all too easy victims of endangerment and extinction.

The faunal body-count is most depressing. According to statistics in *Wildlife in Danger,* a popular guide to endangered species compiled by James Fisher, Noel Simon and Jack Vincent, three researchers attached to the International Union for the Conservation of Nature and Natural Resources (IUCN), animals are in serious trouble. In 1600, for example, there were approximately 4,226 living species of mammals. By 1970, at least 36 (or .85 percent) of these have become extinct. And at least 120 more species (or 2.84 percent) are in danger of extinction.

When the statistics shift to subspecies or geographical races, the necrology grows. Sixty-four subspecies of mammals have died out since 1600 and another 223 find themselves listed in the *Red Data Book*—a late warning system of rare and endangered species published by the IUCN.

Birds share in the jeopardy of their unfeathered friends. Of the 8,684 species of birds extant in 1600, 94 (or 1.09 percent) have disappeared from the face of the earth. At least another 187 species (or 2.16 percent) are today considered likely prospects for extinction.

Regarding subspecies, birds have suffered 164 extinctions and presently have 287 members in the *Red Data Book.*

When all these figures are tallied, we discover that one-hundredth of the higher animals alive in 1600 are no longer with us and one-fortieth, more than double the number of the already deceased, may soon pass in that irreversible direction.

No animal is immortal. Evolutionary senility strikes down every species in its own good time. Two million years is all any form survives. There is irrefutable evidence, however, that man has accelerated the natural aging process in some cases. The authors of *Wildlife in Danger* speculate that three-quarters of the birds and two-thirds of the mammals which have become extinct since 1600 owe their sad state to human causes. Four-sixths of the birds and five-sixths of the mammals

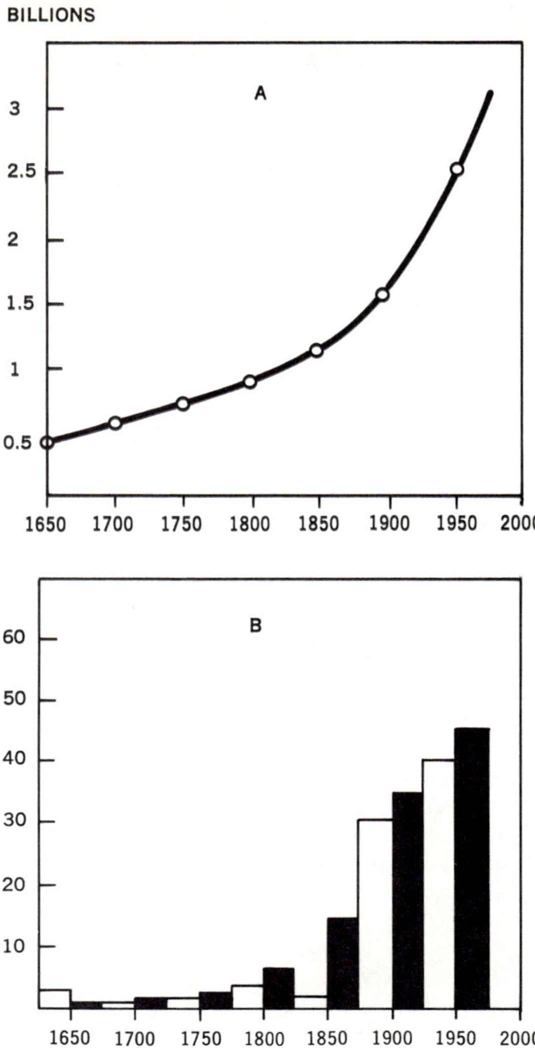

FIGURE 2-1. Correlation Between the Increase in Human Population and the Extinction of Mammals and Birds since 1600

(a) The increase in human population over the last three hundred years. (b) The number of exterminated mammal forms (white bars) and bird forms (black bars) eliminated over the last three hundred years. Each bar represents a fifty-year period

Source: Ziswiler, Extinct and Vanishing Animals, 1967

	BIRDS Non-passerine (large)	BIRDS Passerine (small)	BIRDS Total	MAMMALS
Cause of extinction	*per cent*	*per cent*	*per cent*	*per cent*
Natural	26	20	24	25
Human	74	80	76	67
hunting	54	13	42	33
introduced predators	13	21	15	17
other introductions	–	14	4	6
habitat disruption	7	32	15	19
	100	100	100	100
Cause of present rarity				
Natural	31	32	32	14
Human	69	68	68	86
hunting	32	10	24	43
introduced predators	9	15	11	8
other introductions	2	5	3	6
habitat disruption	26	38	30	29
	100	100	100	100

TABLE 2-2. Comparison Between Natural and Human Causes Regarding the Extinction of Mammals and Birds Since 1600

Source: Fisher et al., Wildlife in Danger, 1969

currently under the sword of extinction likewise find man their potential executioner (Table 2-2).

How does man commit such deadly sins? The most obvious instances have to do with *direct extermination*—hunting and trapping. Principally for reasons of fun and profit, although genuine food need sometimes enters as a factor, hunters have killed off and continue to decimate species. The American bison and passenger pigeon, for example, were gratuitously slaughtered in this country. Valuable hides, furs and feathers make life precarious for several species. The souvenir business threatens walrus and elephants—tusks, you know. Superstitious beliefs also take their toll—the alpine ibex was hunted out of existence in the seventeenth century for the supposed curative powers of its parts. The rhinoceros is similarly threatened in this century—powdered rhino horns are thought to be aphrodisiac by some. Then there is that perennial killer—the trophy hunter who is responsible for, among other atrocities, the depletion of the Indian lion.

Indirect extermination is just as fatal to animals and the cause again is man, even though he may not be found at the scene of the crime. The disruption of habitat is the chief killer in this regard. Animals are always seriously affected when their natural context is tampered with. Deforestation, draining of swamps and wetlands, the destruction of natural vegetation and grazing lands, air and water pollution, predators introduced by man and diseases from introduced animals have disastrous effects on the world's fauna.

For example, the disappearance of forests has depleted the orangutan population; migrating birds are victimized when their breeding and nesting spots give way to land developments; overgrazing by one species reduces the food supply of another; and the importation of aggressive foreign mammals like the mongoose, the rat and feral dogs, cats and pigs can do considerable damage to more tender native species.

The *Red Data Book* published by the IUCN is the most comprehensive international guide to endangered species. Its four loose-leaf volumes—on mammals, birds, amphibians and reptiles, and fishes—are subject to constant revision as naturalists' reports on animal survival come in from five continents. While global in treatment, the *Red Data Book* cannot be described as an up-to-the-minute accounting. Some of its reports are years old; no annual census is taken for rare animals. So some of the species listed in the *Red Data Book,* although identified as in danger of immediate extinction, are probably already extinct. And even that ultimate designation is hard to prove beyond a shadow of a doubt. Some animals have reappeared after lengthy absences.

Despite the good intentions of the *Red Data Book*—to warn the world about its impending faunal doom so that corrective measures will be taken—some conservationists consider the mere mention of a species or subspecies therein a certain kiss of death because animal rarity is such a difficult process to reverse.[1] Although many of these endangered animals can survive in zoos and therefore may never fall into total oblivion, a species extinct in the wild is a species virtually extinct.

2. ANIMALS EXTINCT SINCE 1600

Extinct Mammals

The following list of extinct (since 1600) mammals is taken from *Extinct and Vanishing Animals* by Vincenz Ziswiler. Ziswiler's classification is according to popular and scientific names, location, year or century of extinction and cause of extinction (in letter code). The compilation is digested principally from two classic studies: Glover M. Allen's *Extinct and Vanishing Mammals of the Western Hemisphere* and Francis Harper's *Extinct and Vanishing Animals of the Old World.* The Survival Service Commission of the IUCN will issue its own definitive listing in the near future.

CODA FOR EXTINCT MAMMALS

Hunted for meat or fat	A
Hunted for hides or feathers	B
Hunted for sport or pleasure	C
Persecuted because of superstitious beliefs	D
Combatted as an alleged pest	E
Habitat altered through destruction of the forest	F
Habitat altered through civilization or monocultures	G
Denaturalized fauna through feral dogs	H
Denaturalized fauna through feral cats	I
Denaturalized fauna through rats	J
Denaturalized fauna through foxes	K
Denaturalized fauna through mongoose forms	L

EXTINCT MAMMALS

Marsupials		
Freckled marsupial mouse (Antechinus apicalis)	Australia	20 G
Eastern barred bandicoot (Perameles fasciata)	Australia	20 I K
Western barred bandicoot (Perameles myosura myosura)	Australia	20 K I
Gaimard's rat-kangaroo (Bettongia gaimardi)	Australia	20 K I

EXTINCT MAMMALS (cont.)

Gilbert's rat-kangaroo (Potorous gilberti)	Australia	19 A
Broad-faced rat-kangaroo (Potorous platyops)	Australia	20 K I
Toolach wallaby (Wallabia greyi)	Australia	20 K
Tasmanian wolf (Thylacinus cynocephalus)	Tasmania	20 E
Insectivores		
Antillean insectivores: 6 forms (Nesophontidae)	Antilles	17–19 J L
Christmas Island musk-shrew (Crocidura fuliginosa trichura)	Christmas Island	20 I
Bats		
7 forms	West Indies	19–20 F
Lemurs		
Hairy-eared mouse lemur (Cheirogaleus trichotis)	Madagascar	19 F
Rodents		
Spiny rats: 15 forms (Echimyidae)	Antilles	17–20 L I
Hamsterlike rodents: 8 forms (Cricetidae)	Antilles	17–20 L I
Old World rats: 3 forms (Muridae)	Malay Archipelago and Australia	20 K I
Giant rats: 2 forms (Dinomyidae)	Central America and Antilles	19 A
Sea Cows		
Steller's sea cow (Hydrodamalis gigas)	Bering Islands	1768 A
Carnivores		
Sea mink (Mustela macrodon)	Northeast coast of the U. S. A.	19 B
Grizzly bear: 17 races (Ursus horribilis)	North America	19–20 A·E
Atlas bear (Ursus crowtheri)	North Africa	19 A E F
Long-eared kit fox (Vulpes macrotis macrotis)	Southern U. S. A.	19 E
Japanese wolf (Canis hodophilax)	Japan	20 E
Antarctic wolf (Dusicyon australis)	Falkland Islands	19 E
Newfoundland wolf (Canis lupus beothucus)	Newfoundland	20 E
Florida wolf (Canis niger niger)	Florida	20 E

EXTINCT MAMMALS (cont.)

Eastern cougar (Felis concolor couguar)	Eastern U. S. A.	20 E
European lion (Panthera leo europaea)	Greece	1-2 H E
Cape lion (Panthera leo melanochaitus)	South Africa	1865 E
Barbary lion (Panthera leo barbarus)	North Africa	1922 E
Horses and relatives (Perissodactyla)		
Syrian wild ass (Equus hemionus hemippus)	Syria, Persia	1927 A
Algerian wild ass (Equus asinus atlanticus)	North Africa	?
Quagga (Equus quagga)	South Africa	1878 E
Burchell's zebra (Equus burchelli burchelli)	South Africa	20 E
Cattle and relatives (Artiodactyla)		
Arizona wapiti (Cervus canadensis merriami)	Arizona	1906 C F
Eastern wapiti (Cervus canadensis canadensis)	Eastern U. S. A.	19 F
Schomburgk's deer (Rucervus schomburgki)	Siam	20 D
Badlands bighorn sheep (Ovis canadensis auduboni)	American middle west	20 A C
Pyrenean ibex (Capra pyrenaica pyrenaica)	Pyrenees	1910 A
Portuguese ibex (Capra pyrenaica lusitanica)	Western Pyrenees	1892 A C
Rufous gazelle (Gazella rufina)	Algeria	20 A C
Blue buck (Hippotragus leucophaeus)	South Africa	19 E
Bubal Hartebeest (Alcelaphus alcelaphus)	North Africa	20 A
Auroch (Bos primigenius)	Europe	1627 A F
Eastern bison (Bison bison pensylvanicus)	North America	1825 A C
Oregon bison (Bison bison oregonus)	North America	19 A C
Caucasian wisent (Bison bonasus caucasicus)	Caucasus	1930 A F

Extinct Birds

The IUCN published a detailed listing of extinct birds in 1965 (*IUCN Bulletin,* Special Supplement, No. 16, July/September 1965). Compiled by Jack Vincent, Liaison Officer of the International Council for Bird Preservation at the IUCN, it classifies extinct species (since 1600) according to several designations which are summarized here according to popular and scientific name, location if not included with the latter, the date of extinction and the cause, if known.

CODA FOR EXTINCT BIRDS

Destroyed by cats	A
Hunted by man	B
Destroyed by goats	C
Destroyed by volcanic eruption	D
Destroyed through introduction of domestic animals	E
Destroyed by rats	F
Destroyed by rabbits	G
Habitat altered or destroyed by man	H
Destroyed by dogs	I
Destroyed by mongooses	J
Destroyed through the introduction of predators	K
Destroyed by pigs	L
Captured for wild animal trade	M
Destroyed by monkeys	N

LIST OF BIRDS EITHER KNOWN OR THOUGHT TO HAVE BECOME EXTINCT SINCE 1600[1]

Arabian ostrich (Struthio camelus syriacus)	Africa	1941
Great elephant bird (Aepyornis maximus)	Madagascar	c. 1649
Tasmania race of emu (Dromiceius novaehollandiae diemenensis)		1838
Kangaroo Island race of emu (Dromiceius novaehollandiae diemenianus)		1803
A lesser moa (Megalapteryx didinus)	South Island, New Zealand	1773
Jamaica race of diablotin (Pterodroma hasitata caribbea)		1880
Guadalupe storm petrel (Oceanodroma macrodactyla)		1912 A
Spectacled cormorant (Phalacrocorax perspicillatus)	Bering Island	1852 B
Flightless night heron (Nycticorax megacephalus)	Rodriguez Island	1730

LIST OF BIRDS EITHER KNOWN OR THOUGHT TO HAVE BECOME EXTINCT SINCE 1600 (cont.)

Bonin Islands race of nankeen night heron (Nycticorax caledonicus crassirostris)		1889
Príncipe Island race of olive ibis (Lampribis olivacea rothschildi)		1901 B
Chatham Island swan (Cygnus sumnerensis)	New Zealand	between 1590 and 1690
Bering Island race of Canada goose (Branta canadensis asiatica)		1900
Crested shelduck (Tadorna cristata)	Japan	1943
Washington Island race of gadwall (Anas strepera couesi)		1874
Pink-headed duck (Rhodonessa caryophyllacea)	India	1944 B
Labrador duck (Camptorhynchus labradorium)		1875
Auckland Island merganser (Mergus australis)		1905
Guadalupe caracara (Caracara lutosa)	Southwest United States and Mexico	1900 C
Kermadec Islands megapode (Megapodius sp. ?)		1876 D
Virginia race of heath hen (Tympanuchus cupido cupido)	New England and Middle Atlantic States	1932
New Zealand quail (Coturnix novae-zelandiae)		1875
Himalaya mountain quail (Ophrysia superciliosa)		1868
Auckland Island race of Australian rail (Rallus pectoralis muelleri)		1865 E
Macquarie Island race of banded rail (Rallus philippensis macquariensis)	Oceania	1880
Tahiti Red-billed rail (Rallus ecaudata)		1925 A,F
Wake Island rail (Rallus wakensis)		1945
Chatham Island banded rail (Nesolimnas dieffenbachii)		1840 A,F
Chatham Island rail (Cabalus modestus)		1900 A,C,G,H
New Caledonia wood rail (Tricholimnas lafresnayanus)		1904 A,F,I

[1] "The list, which in each instance shows the date of disappearance, is of birds known from specimens or sound descriptions. It excludes those known only from fanciful accounts or osseous remains. It also omits those subspecies whose extinction, although not entirely confirmed, has almost certainly come about in various islands of the Pacific, particularly in the western groups of the Izu, Ryukyu, Bonin, Volcano and Borodino Islands."

LIST OF BIRDS EITHER KNOWN OR THOUGHT TO HAVE BECOME EXTINCT SINCE 1600 (cont.)

Jamaica race of wood rail (Amaurolimnas concolor concolor)		1890 A,F,J
Fiji bar-winged rail (Nesoclopeus poecilopterus)		1890 K
Van den Broecke's red rail (Aphanapteryx bonasia)	Mauritius	1675
Flightless blue rail (Aphanapteryx leguati)	Rodriguez Island	1730
Ascension flightless crake (Crecopsis sp.)		1656 F
Laysan Island rail (Porzanula palmeri)		1944 F,H
Hawaii Island rail (Pennula sandwichensis)		1893
Kusaie Island crake (Aphanolimnas monasa)		1828 F
Iwo Jima race of white-browed rail (Poliolimnas cinereus brevipes)		1925 A,F,H
Tristan da Cunha Island race of island hen (Porphyriornis nesiotis nesiotis)		1872 F,L
Samoa wood rail (Pareudiastes pacificus)	Savaii Island	1873 E
Lord Howe Island race of Old World purple gallinule (Porphyrio porphyrio albus)		1834
Little Barrier Island race of New Zealand snipe (Coenocorypha aucklandica barrierensis)		1870
Tahiti sandpiper (Prosobonia leucoptera)		1777 F
Cooper's sandpiper (Pisobia cooperi)	New York	1833
Jerdon's courser (Cursorius bitorquatus)	Central India	1900
Great auk (Pinguinus impennis)	Iceland	1844 B
Cebu Island race of amethyst brown fruit dove (Phapitreron amethystina frontalis)		1892
Mauritius blue pigeon (Alectroenas nitidissima)		1830
Rodriguez pigeon (Alectroenas rodericana)		1867
Norfolk Island race of kereru (Hemiphaga novaeseelandiae spadicea)		1801
Lord Howe Island race of metallic wood pigeon (Columba vitiensis godmanae)		1790
Bonin wood pigeon (Columba versicolor)		1889 B
Bourbon pink pigeon (Columba dubosi)	Réunion	1669

LIST OF BIRDS EITHER KNOWN OR THOUGHT TO HAVE BECOME EXTINCT SINCE 1600 (cont.)

Passenger pigeon (Ectopistes migratorius)	United States	1914 B
Tanna ground dove (Gallicolumba ferruginea)	Tanna Island, New Hebrides	1774
St. Helena blue dove ('Columbinae generis incerti')		1775
Choiseul crested pigeon (Microgoura meeki)		1904
Dodo (Raphus cucullatus)	Mauritius	1681
Solitaire (Raphus solitarius)	Réunion	1746
Rodriguez solitaire (Pezophaps solitaria)		1791
Norfolk Island race of kaka (Nestor Meridionalis productus)		1851 B
New Caledonia lorikeet (Charmosyna diadema)		1860
Lord Howe Island race of kakariki (Cyanoramphus novaezelandiae subflavescens)		1869
Macquarie Island race of kakariki (Cyanoramphus novaezelandiae erythrotis)		1913
Tahiti parakeet (Cyanoramphus zealandicus)		1844
Raiatea parakeet (Cyanoramphus ulietanus)		1774
Mascarene parrot (Mascarinus mascarinus)		1834
Mauritius broad-billed parrot (Lophopsittacus mauritianus)		1638
Rodriguez parakeet (Necropsittacus rodericanus)		1760
Bourbon parakeet (Necropsittacus borbonicus)	Réunion	1669
Seychelles Islands race of Alexandrine parakeet (Psittacula eupatria wardi)		1870 B
Réunion race of ring-necked parakeet (Psittacula krameri eques)		1800
Rodriguez ring-necked parakeet (Psittacula exsul)		1875
Cebu Island race of Philippines hanging parakeet (Loriculus philippensis chrysonotus)		1906 H
Culebra Island race of Puerto Rico parrot (Amazona vittata gracilipes)		1899
Guadeloupe parrot (Amazona violacea)		early 18th century
Martinique parrot (Amazona martinica)		early 18th century B,H,M

LIST OF BIRDS EITHER KNOWN OR THOUGHT TO HAVE BECOME EXTINCT SINCE 1600 (cont.)

Puerto Rico race of Hispaniola conure (Aratinga chloroptera maugei)		1892
Guadeloupe conure (Aratinga labati)		early 18th century
Carolina parakeet (Conuropsis carolinensis)		1914 B
Cuba red macaw (Ara tricolor)		1885
Jamaica red macaw (Ara gossei)		1765
Jamaica green and yellow macaw (Ara erythrocephala)		early 19th century
Guadeloupe red macaw (Ara guadeloupensis)		early 18th century
Dominica green and yellow macaw (Ara atwoodi)		late 18th century
Mysterious macaw (Ara erythrura)	West Indies	1658
Martinique macaw (Ara martinica)		1640
Guadeloupe violet macaw (Ara purpurascens)		1640
Madagascar coucal (Coua delalandei)		1930 B
Mauritius scops owl (Otus commersoni)		1837
North Island race of New Zealand laughing owl (Sceloglaux albifacies rufifacies)		1889
Rodriguez little owl (Athene murivora)		1730
Forest spotted owlet (Athene blewitti)	Central India	1872
Antigua race of burrowing owl (Speotyto cunicularia amaura)		1890 } B,J
Guadeloupe race of burrowing owl (Speotyto cunicularia guadeloupensis)		1890 } B,J
New Caledonia owlet frogmouth (Aegotheles savesi)		1880
Jamaica race of least pauraque (Siphonorhis americanus americanus)		1859 K
Ryukyu Island kingfisher (Halcyon miyakoensis)		1887
Guadalupe Island race of redshafted flicker (Colaptes cafer rufipileus)		1906 A,H
Stephen Island wren (Xenicus lyalli)		1894 F
Cebu Island race of dark-throated oriole (Oriolus xanthonotus assimilis)		1906 H

LIST OF BIRDS EITHER KNOWN OR THOUGHT TO HAVE BECOME EXTINCT SINCE 1600 (cont.)

Lord Howe Island race of Norfolk Island starling (Aplonis fuscus hullianus)		1918 F
Kusaie Island starling (Aplonis corvina)		1828 F
Mysterious starling (Aplonis mavornata)	? Pacific	1774
Leguat's starling (Fregilupus rodericanus)	Rodriguez	1832
Bourbon crested starling (Fregilupus varius)	Réunion Island	1862
Huia (Heteralocha acutirostris)	New Zealand	1907 H
Cebu Island race of barred graybird (Coracina striata cebuensis)		1906 H
Cebu Island race of black graybird (Coracina coerulescens altera)		1906 H
San Benedicto Island race of rock wren (Salpinctes obsoletus exsul)		1952 A
Guadalupe Island race of Bewick's wren (Thryomanes bewickii brevicauda)		1897 C
Guadeloupe race of house wren (Troglodytes aëdon quadeloupensis)		1914 K
Martinique race of house wren (Troglodytes aëdon martinicensis)		1886 K
Cebu Island race of slaty-crowned bulbul (Hypsipetes siquijorensis monticola)		1906 H
Kittlitz's thrush (Zoothera terrestris)	Peel Island, Beechey Group Bonin Islands	1828 K
Lanai Island race of Hawaii thrush (Phaeornis obscurus lanaiensis)		1931 F,H
Molokai Island race of Hawaii thrush (Phaeornis obscurus rutha)		1936 F,H
Oahu Island race of Hawaii thrush (Phaeornis obscurus oahensis)		1825 F,H
Lord Howe Island race of grey-headed blackbird (Turdus poliocephalus vinitinctus)		1918 E,F
Lifu Island race of grey-headed blackbird (Turdus poliocephalus pritzbueri)		1939 E,F
Maré Island race of grey-headed blackbird (Turdus poliocephalus mareensis)		1939 E,F
Raiatea thrush (Turdus ulietensis)	Society Island	1774
Southern Burma race of Jerdon's babbler (Moupinia altirostris altirostris)		1941 H
Laysan Island race of millerbird (Acrocephalus familiaris familiaris)		1923 G
Chatham Islands race of fernbird		1900 F

LIST OF BIRDS EITHER KNOWN OR THOUGHT TO HAVE BECOME EXTINCT SINCE 1600 (cont.)

(Bowdleria punctata rufescens)			
Long-legged warbler (Trichocichla rufa)	Vitilevu, Fiji	c. 1890	J
Lord Howe Island race of grey warbler (Gerygone igata insularis)		1919	F
Lord Howe Island race of grey fantail (Rhipidura fuliginosa cervina)		1928	F
Tongatabu Island race of Tahiti flycatcher (Pomarea nigra tabuensis)		1773	
Four-coloured flowerpecker (Dicaeum quadricolor)	Cebu Island Philippines	1906	H (bracketed with next)
Cebu Island race of orange-breasted flowerpecker (Dicaeum trigonostigma pallidius)		1906	
Molokai Island o-o (Moho bishopi)		1915	F,H,M
Hawaii Island o-o (Moho nobilis)		1934	F,H,M (bracketed with next)
Oahu Island o-o (Moho apicalis)		1837	
Kioea (Chaetoptila angustipluma)	Hawaii Island	1859	
Chatham Island race of bellbird (Anthornis melanura melanocephala)		1906	
Seychelles Islands race of chestnut-flanked white-eye (Zosterops mayottensis semiflava)		1888	
Cebu Island race of Everett's white-eye (Zosterops everetti everetti)		1906	H
Lord Howe Island white-eye (Zosterops strenula)		1928	F

The most authoritative classification of the Hawaiian honeycreepers shows 39 names, made up of 15 monotypic species with another 7 divided into 24 subspecies. The 16 extinct ones listed below, therefore, mean that 41 percent of the birds have now disappeared. Knowledge of this interesting family began when Captain Cook discovered the Hawaiian Islands in 1778 and collected some specimens. Birds of often specialized feeding habits, the Drepaniidae show striking examples of evolution and adaptation, and have been the subject of many detailed studies; much has also been written about the extinction of so large a proportion of them. Some of the causative factors are known or surmised, others quite unknown but, generally speaking, the losses seem to have been occasioned by a combination of disease, domestic predators, competition with introduced birds and destruction of forest.

Great amakihi (Loxops sagittirostris)	Hawaii Island	1900	
Lanai Island race of alauwahio (Loxops maculata montana)		1937	
Molokai Island race of alauwahio (Loxops maculata flammea)		1949	
Oahu Island race of akepa (Loxops coccinea rufa)		1893	
Hawaii Island race of akialoa (Hemignathus obscurus obscurus)		1895	

LIST OF BIRDS EITHER KNOWN OR THOUGHT TO HAVE BECOME EXTINCT SINCE 1600 (cont.)

Oahu Island race of akialoa (Hemignathus obscurus ellisianus)		1837
Lanai Island race of akialoa (Hemignathus obscurus lanaiensis)		1894
Maui Island race of nukupuu (Hemignathus lucidus affinis)		1896
Oahu Island race of nukupuu (Hemignathus lucidus lucidus)		1860
Hopue (Psittirostra palmeri)	Hawaii Island	1896
Lesser Koa finch (Psittirostra flaviceps)	Hawaii	1891
Kona finch (Psittirostra kona)	Hawaii	1894
Laysan Island race of apapane (Himatione sanguinea freethii)		1923
Ula-ai-hawane (Ciridops anna)	Hawaii	1892
Mamo (Drepanis pacifica)	Hawaii	1898
Black mamo (Drepanis funerea)	Molokai Island	1907
São Thomé Island grosbeak weaver (Neospiza concolor)		1888 H
Réunion Island fody (Foudia bruante)		1776
Bonin Islands grosbeak (Chaunoproctus ferreorostris)		1890 A,C,F,I
St. Christopher Island race of Puerto Rico bullfinch (Loxigilla portoricensis grandis)		1880
Townsend's finch (Spiza townsendii)	Pennsylvania, United States	1833
Guadalupe Island race of rufous-sided towhee (Pipilo erythrophthalmus consobrinus)		1897

Extinct Amphibians

No amphibians are known to be extinct since 1600. Several species are endangered though, and they are listed in Part 3.

Extinct Fishes

Not much research has been expended on extinct fishes. A list of fishes extinct in America, however, does appear in *Rare and Endangered Fish and Wildlife of the United States.* That list follows.

EXTINCT FISHES

San Gorgonio trout (Salmo evermanni). Santa Ana River in California. Extinct about 1935.

Pahranagat spinedace (Lepidomeda altivelis). Outflow of Ash Spring and chain of lakes in the Pahranagat Valley in Nevada. Extinct between 1938 and 1959.

Big Spring spinedace (Lepidomeda mollispinis pratensis). Spring-fed marsh, Lincoln County, Nevada. Extinct between 1938 and 1959.

Harelip sucker (Lagochila lacera). Found in a few clear streams of the upper Mississippi Valley; Scioto River in Ohio, Tennessee River in Georgia and the White River in Arkansas; also in the Lake Erie drainage, Blanchard and Auglaize Rivers in northwestern Ohio. Not seen since 1900.

Leon Springs pupfish (Cyprinodon bovinus). Leon Springs, Pecos County, Texas. Not seen since 1938.

Ash Meadows killifish (Empetrichthys merriami). Isolated waters of Death Valley in southern Nevada. Not seen since 1942.

3. RARE AND ENDANGERED ANIMALS

Mammals

This list of rare and endangered animals encompasses all those species and subspecies included in the 1970 Index of Volume I (Mammalia) of the *Red Data Book* as well as those mammal forms similarly classified in the 1968 edition of *Rare and Endangered Fish and Wildlife of the United States.*

CODA FOR RARE AND ENDANGERED ANIMALS

Both the Red Data Book and Rare and Endangered Fish and Wildlife of the United States define the categories "Rare," "Endangered" and "Indeterminate" (RDB) or "Status Undetermined" (REFWUS), according to the same general criteria.

The Red Data Book's "Depleted" category has no counterpart in Rare and Endangered Fish and Wildlife in the United States.

Except in the cases of a few amphibians, Rare and Endangered Fish and Wildlife of the United States does not provide complete data sheets for its "Peripheral" category and no sheets are offered for any form in the "Status Undetermined" category. Therefore a simple listing of "Peripheral" and "Status Undetermined" U.S. forms will be found at the end of each of the four animal divisions.

Since the individual data sheets in both the Red Data Book and Rare and Endangered Fish and Wildlife of the United States contain more information than could possibly be used in this book (see facsimile pages), we have reduced the data here to six essentials: scientific and common names, location, legal protection, population and status.

CODA FOR RARE AND ENDANGERED FORMS

LEGAL PROTECTION Some forms are protected by national or state laws in the whole or part of their range. The existence of legal protection is marked by the letter P. The absence of legal protection is marked by a dash (–).

POPULATION It is often difficult to fix the exact population of rare and endangered forms. The letter U means that the population of a particular form is unknown.

* Form listed in both the Red Data Book and Rare and Endangered Fish and Wildlife of the United States.

‡ Form listed only in Rare and Endangered Fish and Wildlife of the United States.

CLASSIFICATION OF STATUS RARE AND ENDANGERED FORMS

Red Data Book	Rare and Endangered Fish and Wildlife of the United States
E ENDANGERED. In immediate danger of extinction: continued survival unlikely without the implementation of special protective measures. Three asterisks (***) indicate the form is "critically endangered."	E ENDANGERED. An endangered species or subspecies is one whose prospects of survival and reproduction are in immediate jeopardy. Its peril may result from one or many causes—loss of habitat or change in habitat, overexploitation, predation, competition, disease. An endangered species must have help, or extinction will probably follow.
R RARE. Not under immediate threat of extinction, but occurring in such small numbers and/or in such a restricted or specialized habitat that it could quickly disappear. Requires careful watching.	R RARE. A rare species or subspecies is one that, although not presently threatened with extinction, is in such small numbers throughout its range that it may be endangered if its environment worsens. Close watch of its status is necessary.
D DEPLETED. Although still occurring in numbers adequate for survival, the species has been heavily depleted and continues to decline at a rate which gives cause for serious concern.	P PERIPHERAL. A peripheral species or subspecies is one whose occurrence in the United States is at the edge of its natural range and which is rare or endangered within the United States although not in its range as a whole. Special attention is necessary to assure retention in our nation's fauna.
I INDETERMINATE. Apparently in danger, but insufficient data currently available on which to base a reliable assessment of status. Needs further study.	U STATUS UNDETERMINED. A status-undetermined species or subspecies is one that has been suggested as possibly rare or endangered, but about which there is not enough information to determine its status. More information is needed.

Scientific name	Common name
MARSUPIALIA (Order)	
DASYURIDAE (Family) Marsupial mice, dasyures, etc.	
(Planigale tenuirostris)	Southern planigale
(Planigale subtilissima)	Kimberley planigale
(Phascogale calura)	Red-tailed phascogale
(Sminthopsis longicuadata)	Long-tailed sminthopsis
(Antechinomys laniger)	Eastern jerboa marsupial
(Dasyurus viverrinus)	Eastern native cat
(Dasyurinus geoffroyi-geoffroyi)	Western native cat
(Thylacinus cynocephalus)	Thylacine
(Myrmecobius fasciatus rufus)	Rusty numbat
PERAMELIDAE (Family) Bandicots	
(Perameles fasciata)	Eastern barred-bandicoot
(Perameles bougainvillei)	Western barred-bandicoot
(Macrotis lagotis)	Rabbit bandicoot
(Chaeropus ecaudatus)	Pig-footed bandicoot
PHALANGERIDAE (Family) Phalangers, cuscuses, etc.	
(Phalanger orientalis peninsulae)	Grey cuscus
(Gymnobelideus leadbeateri)	Leadbeater's possum
(Wyulda squamicaudata)	Scaly-tailed possum
(Pseudocheirus occidentalis)	Western ring-tail
VOMBATIDAE (Family) Wombats	
(Vombatus ursinus ursinus)	Flinders Island wombat
(Lasiorhinus barnardi)	Barnard's hairy-nosed wombat
MACROPODIDAE (Family) Kangaroos and wallabies	
(Lagorchestes hirsutus)	Western hare-wallaby
(Lagostrophus fasciatus)	Banded hare-wallaby
(Petrogale xanthopus xanthopus)	Ring-tailed rock-wallaby
(Onychogalea fraenata)	Bridled nail-tail wallaby
(Onychogalea lunata)	Crescent nail-tail wallaby
(Macropus parma)	White-throated wallaby
(Bettongia penicillata)	Brush-tailed rat-kangaroo
(Bettongia lesueuri)	Lesueur's rat-kangaroo
(Caloprymus campestris)	Desert rat-kangaroo
(Potorous tridactylus tridactylus)	Long-nosed rat-kangaroo
(Hypsiprymnodon moschatus)	Musky rat-kangaroo
INSECTIVORA (Order)	
SOLENODONTIDAE (Family) Solenodons	
(Atopogale cubana)	Cuban solenodon
(Solenodon paradoxus)	Haitian solenodon

Location	Legal protection	Population	Status
New South Wales, Australia	P	U	I
Northwest Australia	P	U	I
Southwest Australia	P	U	I
West Australia	P	U	I
Australia	P	U	I
Australia, Tasmania	P	U	I
Central Australia	–	U	I
Australia	P	U	E***
South and West Australia	P	U	I
West Australia	–	U	I
Australia	P	U	I
West and North Australia	P	U	E
Central Australia	–	U	I
Cape York, Peninsula, Australia	–	U	I
Victoria, Australia	P	U	I
Western Australia	P	U	I
	P	U	I
Flinders Island, Australia	–	U	I
Queensland, Australia	P	U	R
Bernier and Dorre Islands, West Australia	P	U	I
Bernier and Dorre Islands, West Australia	P	U	I
Flinders Range, South Australia	P	U	I
Australia	P	U	I
Nullarbor Plain, Australia	–	U	I
Kauwa Island, New Zealand	P	U	R
Southwest Australia	–	U	I
Northwest and Central Australia	P	U	I
Lake Eyre Basin, South Australia	–	U	I
New South Wales, Australia	P	U	I
Queensland, Australia	P	U	I
Oriente, Province, Cuba	P	401	E***
Dominican Republic	P	U	E

Scientific name	Common name
ERINACEIDAE (Family) Hedgehogs	
(Podogymnura truei)	Mindanao gymnure
TALPIDAE (Family) Moles and desmans	
(Galemys pyrenaicus)	Pyrenean desman
CHIROPTERA (Order)	
VESPERTILIONIDAE (Family) Common bats	
*(Myotis sodalis)	Indiana bat
*(Euderma maculatum)	Spotted bat
PRIMATES (Order)	
LEMURIDAE (Family) Lemurs	
(Hapalemur griseus)	Grey gentle lemur
(Hapalemur simus)	Broad-nosed gentle lemur
(Lemur macaco macaco)	Black lemur
(Lemur macaco flavifrons)	Sclater's lemur
(Lemur macaco rufus)	Red-fronted lemur
(Lemur macaco sanfordi)	Sanford's lemur
(Lemur mongoz mongoz)	Mongoose lemur
(Lemur mongoz coronatus)	Crowned lemur
(Lepilemur mustelinus ruficaudatus)	Red-tailed weasel lemur
(Lepilemur mustelinus dorsalis)	Nossi-Be weasel lemur
(Lepilemur mustelinus leucopus)	White-footed weasel lemur
(Allocebus trichotis)	Hairy-eared dwarf lemur
(Cheirogaleus medius)	Fat-tailed lemur
(Microcebus coquereli)	Coquerel's mouse lemur
(Phaner furcifer)	Fork-marked mouse lemur
INDRIIDAE (Family) Avahis, sifakas, indri	
(Avahi laniger occidentalis)	Western woolly avahi
(Propithecus diadema perrieri)	Perrier's sifaka
(Propithecus verreauxi verreauxi)	Verreaux's sifaka
(Propithecus verreauxi coquereli)	Coquerel's sifaka
(Propithecus verreauxi deckenii)	Decken's sifaka
(Propithecus verreauxi coronatus)	Crowned sifaka
(Propithecus verreauxi majori)	Forsyth-Major's sifaka
(Indri indri)	Indris
DAUBENTONIIDAE (Family) Aye-aye	
(Daubentonia madagascariensis)	Aye-aye
CEBIDAE (Family) New world monkeys	
(Cacajao calvus)	Bald uakari

[1] Rated "Endangered" in Rare and Endangered Fish and Wildlife of the United States.

Location	Legal protection	Population	Status
Mindanao, Philippines		U	R
Southwest France, Spain, Portugal	–	U	R
Midwest, Eastern United States	–	500,000	I[1]
Southwest United States	–	U	R
East and West Madagascar	–	U	I
Lake Alaotra, Didy Marshes, Madagascar	–	U	R
Northwest Madagascar	--	U	I
West Coast, Madagascar	–	U	I
Northwest Madagascar	–	U	I
North Madagascar	–	U	I
Northwest Madagascar	–	U	I
Northeast Madagascar	–	U	I
West Madagascar	–	U	I
Northwest Madagascar	–	U	I
Southeast Madagascar	–	U	I
East Coast, Madagascar	–	U	R
West Madagascar	–	U	I
Southwest Madagascar	–	U	E
West Madagascar	–	U	I
Northwest Madagascar	–	U	R
Analamera Forest, Madagascar	–	U	I
Southwest Coast, Madagascar	–	U	I
Northwest Madagascar	–	U	I
Northwest Madagascar	–	U	I
West of Mahavavy River, Madagascar	–	U	I
Southwest Madagascar	–	U	I***
East Madagascar	–	U	E
East Coast, Madagascar	–	50–	E***
West Brazil	–	U	E***

Scientific name	Common name
(Cacajao rubicundus)	Red uakari
(Cacajao melanocephalus)	Black-headed uakari
(Chiropotes albinasus)	White-nosed saki
(Brachyteles arachnoides)	Woolly spider monkey
CALLITHRICIDAE (Family) Marmosets and tamarins	
(Callimico goeldii)	Goeldi's tamarin
(Leontideus rosalia)	Golden lion marmoset
(Leontideus chrysomelas)	Golden-headed tamarin
(Leontideus chrysopygus)	Golden-rumped tamarin
CERCOPITHECIDAE (Family) Old world monkeys	
(Cercocebus galeritus galeritus)	Tana River mangabey
(Pygathrix nemaeus)	Douc langur
(Rhinopithecus roxellanae)	Snub-nosed monkey
(Simias concolor)	Pig-tailed langur
(Colobus badius kirkii)	Zanzibar red colobus
(Colobus badius rufomitratus)	Tana River red colobus
(Colobus badius gordonorum)	Uhehe red colobus
(Colobus verus)	Green colobus
PONGIDAE (Family) Gibbons and great apes	
(Hylobates lar pileatus)	Indo-Chinese lar gibbon
(Hylobates klossi)	Dwarf gibbon
(Pongo pygmaeus)	Orang-utan
(Pan paniscus)	Pygmy chimpanzee
(Gorilla gorilla beringei)	Mountain gorilla
EDENTATA (Order)	
MYRMECOPHAGIDAE (Family) Anteaters	
(Myrmecophaga tridactyla)	Giant anteater
BRADYPODIAE (Family) Sloths	
(Bradypus torquatus)	Maned sloth
DASYPODIDAE (Family) Armadillos	
(Priodontes giganteus)	Giant armadillo
(Tolypeutes tricinctus)	Brazilian three-banded armadillo
(Chlamyphorus truncatus)	Lesser pichiciego
(Burmeisteria retusa)	Greater pichiciego

Location	Legal protection	Population	Status
West Brazil, East Peru	–	U	E***
Banks of Rio Negro and Rio Braneo,	–	U	E***
Northwest Brazil, Brazil	–	U	I
Coastal area, Southeast Brazil	–	U	I***
Western Brazil	–	U	I
Coast of states, Rio de Janeiro and Guanabara, Southeast Brazil	P	U	E***
South Bahia State, East Brazil	–	U	E***
State of Sao Paulo, Brazil	–	U	E***
Lower Tanyo, region of Kenya	P	U	I***
Laos, Vietnam, Hainan Island	–	U	I***
West China	P	U	I
Mentawai Islands off Sumatra	–	U	I
East Coast, Zanzibar	–	200 (1964)	I
Forests, Lower Tana River, Kenya	P	U	I
Tanganyika	P	U	I
West Coast of Africa from Sierre Leone to Togo	P	U	E
Thailand, Cambodia, Laos	–	U	I
Mentawai Islands off Sumatra	–	U	I
Sumatra, Sarawak, Borneo, Kalimantan	–	5000 (1966)	R
Congo (Kinshasa)	–	U	I
Congo (Kinshasa), Rwanda, Uganda	P	5-15,000	R
From Venezuela and the Guayana to Peru, North Argentina and South Brazil	–	U	D
East Brazil	–	U	I
Eastern South America	–	U	D
Northeastern Brazil	–	U	I
Central West Argentina	–	U	I
Province of Formosa, Argentina	–	U	I

Scientific name	Common name
LAGOMORPHA (Order)	
LEPORIDAE (Family) Hares and rabbits	
(Pentalagus furnessi)	Ryukyu rabbit
(Romerolagus diazi)	Volcano rabbit
(Caprolagus hispidus)	Hispid hare
(Nesolagus netscheri)	Short-eared rabbit
RODENTIA (Order)	
SCIURIDAE (Family) Squirrels	
*(Sciurus kaibabensis)	Kaibab squirrel
*(Sciurus niger cinereus)	Delmarva Peninsula fox squirrel
(Sciurus niger vulpinus)	Eastern fox squirrel
(Epixerus ebii)	Ebian palm squirrel
(Epixerus wilsoni)	Wilson's palm squirrel
(Lariscus hosei)	Four-striped ground squirrel
(Marmota marmota menzbieri)	Menzbier's marmot
(Cynomys mexicanus)	Mexican prairie dog
*(Cynomys parvidens)	Utah prairie dog
(Cynomys ludovicianus)	Black-tailed prairie dog
HETEROMYIDAE (Family) Pocket mice, kangaroo rats	
(Dipodomys elephantinus)	Big-eared kangaroo rat
(Dipodomys elator)	Texas kangaroo rat
CRICETIDAE (Family) Lemmings, hamsters, voles, etc.	
(Reithrodontomys raviventris)	Salt marsh harvest mouse
*(Microtus pennsylvanicus provectus)	Block Island meadow vole
*(Microtus breweri)	Beach meadow vole
MURIDAE (Family) Old world rats	
(Tokudaia osimensis muenninki)	Ryukyu spiny rat
ERETHIZONTIDAE (Family) New world porcupines	
(Chaetomys subspinosus)	Thin-spined porcupine

[2] Rated "Endangered" in Rare and Endangered Fish and Wildlife of the United States.
[3] Rated "Rare" in Rare and Endangered Fish and Wildlife of the United States.
[4] Rated "Rare" in Rare and Endangered Fish and Wildlife of the United States.

Location	Legal protection	Population	Status
Amami Oshima and Toku-no-Shima Islands, Japan	P	500–900 (1964)	R
Valley of Mexico	P	U	R
Assam	–	U	I***
Southwest Sumatra	–	U	I
Grand Canyon, Arizona	P	1,000 (1965)	R
East shore of Maryland	–	low thousands (1964)	E[2]
Maryland, West Virginia, South Pennsylvania, Northern Virginia	–	U	I
Sierre Leone, Liberia, Ghana Ivory Coast		U	R
Gabon, Cameroon, Congo (Brazzaville)	–	U	R
North and Northwest Borneo	–	U	I
U.S.S.R.	P	low thousands (1962)	D
Mexico	P	U	I
South Central Utah	–	6,000 (1968)	E
Plains and foothills from South Saskatchewan to South Central Texas	–	U	E
San Benito and Monterey counties, California	–	U	I
San Benito and Monterey counties, California	–	U	I
San Francisco Bay	–	U	R
Block Island, Rhode Island	–	U	I[3]
Muskeget, Island off Martha's Vineyard, Massachusetts	–	U	I[4]
Okinawa	–	U	I
Southeast Bahia State, Brazil	–	U	I

Scientific name	Common name
CHINCHILLIDAE (Family) Chinchillas	
(Chinchilla laniger)	Chinchilla
CAPROMYDIAE (Family) Coypu and hutias	
(Capromys melanurus)	Bushy-tailed hutia
(Capromys nana)	Dwarf hutia
(Plagiodontia aedium)	Cuvier's hutia
(Plagiodontia hylaeum)	Dominican hutia
(Geocapromys brownii brownii)	Jamaican hutia
(Geocapromys brownii thoracatus)	Little Swan Island hutia
(Geocapromys ingrahami)	Bahaman hutia
CETACEA (Order)	
BALAENOPTERIDAE (Family) Rorquals	
‡(Eschrichtius glaucus)	Gray Whale
(Balaenoptera physalus)	Fin whale
*(Balaenoptera musculus musculus)	Blue whale
(Balaenoptera musculus brevicauda)	Pygmy blue whale
*(Megaptera novaeangliae)	Humpback whale
BALAENIDAE (Family) Right whales	
*(Balaena mysticetus)	Greenland right whale
(Eubalaena glacialis)	North Atlantic right whale
(Eubalaena sieboldii)	North Pacific right whale
(Eubalaena australis)	Southern right whale
CARNIVORA (Order)	
CANIDAE (Family) Dogs, wolves and foxes	
‡(Canis lupus lycaon)	Eastern timber wolf
*(Canis rufus)	Red wolf
(Simenia simensis simensis)	Northern Simien fox
(Vulpes velox hebes)	Northern kit fox
*(Vulpes marcotis mutica)	San Joaquin kit fox
(Atelocynus microtis)	Small eared dog
(Chrysocyon brachyurus)	Maned wolf
(Speothos venaticus)	Bush dog
(Cuon alpinus alpinus)	Eastern Asiatic wild dog
(Cuon alpinus hesperius)	Western Asiatic wild dog

[5] Rated "Endangered" in Rare and Endangered Fish and Wildlife of the United States.
[6] Rated "Endangered" in Rare and Endangered Fish and Wildlife of the United States.
[7] Rated "Endangered" in Rare and Endangered Fish and Wildlife of the United States.

Location	Legal protection	Population	Status
Andes Mountains, Chile and Bolivia	P	U	I
Sierra Maestra Mountains, Cuba	P	U	E***
Crengaga de Zapata, Cuba	P	U	E***
Dominican Republic Haiti	—	U	I
Northeast Dominican Republic	P	U	I
Jamaica	P	U	I
Little Swan Island	—	U	D
Plana Keys, Bahama Archipelago	P	U	R
North Pacific	P	8,000 (1965)	D
Northern and Southern Hemispheres	P	32,000 (1964)	R
Antarctic Ocean, North to Tropical Seas	P	65-1950 (1963)	E***
South Indian Ocean	—	2-3000 (1965)	R
Arctic to Antarctic Oceans	P	U	R[5]
Arctic Ocean	P	U	D
Temperate North Atlantic	P	few hundred (1959)	D[6]
Japan to Northwest North America	P	U	D[7]
Southern Oceans	P	U	D
Michigan, Minnesota	P	300-400 (1964)	E
Gulf Coast, Texas	P	U	E***
Ethiopia	—	"low" (?)	E***
Cypress Hills, Southwest Saskatchewan	—	U	E***
San Joaquin Valley, California	P	113 dens (1966)	E***
Southwest Saskatchewan	—	U	R
Amazonian Basin in Brazil, Peru, Ecuador and Colombia	—	1580-2300 (1968)	D
Panama, Colombia, Guianas, Brazil, Paraguay, Peru, Bolivia	—	U	I
U.S.S.R., China	—	U	E
U.S.S.R.	—	U	E

Scientific name	Common name
URSIDAE (Family) Bears	
(Tremarctos ornatus)	Spectacled bear
(Selenarctus thibetanus gedrosianus)	Baluchistan bear
(Ursus arctos syriacus)	Syrian brown bear
*(Ursus americanus emmonsi)	Glacier bear
(Ursus horribilis nelsoni)	Mexican grizzly bear
‡(Ursus horribilis (Ord))	Grizzly bear
(Ursus richardsoni)	Barren ground grizzly bear
(Thalarctos maritimus)	Polar bear
PROCYONDIAE (Family) Pandas and racoons	
(Ailuropoda melanoleuca)	Giant panda
MUSTELIDAE (Families) Otters, martens and weasels	
*(Mustela nigripes)	Black-footed ferret
(Martes flavigula chrysospila)	Formosan yellow-throated marten
(Lutra felina)	Marine otter: chingungo
(Lutra platensis)	La Plata otter
(Lutra provocax)	Southern river otter: huillin
(Pteronura brasiliensis)	Giant otter
(Paraonyx microdon)	Cameroun clawless otter
*(Enhydra lutris nereis)	Southern sea otter
VIVERRIDAE (Family) Civets and mongooses	
(Viverra megaspila civettina)	Malabar civet
(Fossa fossa)	Malagasy civet
(Chrotogale owstoni)	Owston's banded civet
(Cynogale bennetti)	Otter civet
(Eupleres goudoti)	Falanouc
(Cryptoprocta ferox)	Fossa
HYANIDAE (Family) Hyaenas	
(Hyaena brunnea)	Brown hyaena
(Hyaena hyaena barbara)	Barbary hyaena
FELIDAE (Family) Cats	
(Felis caracal michaelis)	Turkmenian caracal lynx

[8] Rated "Rare" in Rare and Endangered Fish and Wildlife of the United States.
[9] Rated "Rare" in Rare and Endangered Fish and Wildlife of the United States.

Location	Legal protection	Population	Status
Mountains in Colombia, Ecuador, Peru, Venezuela, Bolivia	–	U	I
Pakistan	–	U	I
Syria, Lebanon, Iraq, Iran, U.S.S.R.	–	U	E
Alaska	P	about 500 (1966)	D[8]
Mexico	–	Nil (1969)	E***
Montana, Wyoming, Idaho, Colorado, Alaska	P	850 outside Alaska (1963)	R
Canada	–	500–1000 (1965)	I
Canada, Alaska, U.S.S.R.	P	5–15,000 (1962–64)	R
Western China	P	U	D
Interior Plains, North America	P	U	E***
Central Formosa	–	U	E
Pacific Coast, South America	–	U	I
South Brazil, Paraguay, North Argentina, Uruguay	–	U	I
Central and South Chile	–	U	I
South America	–	U	E***
Cameroun	–	U	E
Southern California coast	–	850–900 (1965)	R[9]
South India	–	U	I***
East Coast, Madagascar	–	U	I
Vietnam, Laos	–	U	I
Borneo, Cambodia, Laos, Vietnam, Sumatra, Malaya	–	U	I
Coasts, Madagascar	–	U	R
Madagascar	–	U	D
Southern Africa	P	U	R
Morocco	P	400–500 (1964)	E
U.S.S.R.	–	U	R

Scientific name	Common name
(Felis lynx pardina)	Spanish lynx
(Felis serval constantina)	Barbary serval
(Felis pardalis albescens)	Texas ocelot
(Felis wiedii cooperi)	Texas margay
(Felis concolor couguar)	Eastern panther
*(Felis concolor coryi)	Florida cougar (or panther)
(Neofelis nebulosa brashyurus)	Formosan clouded leopard
(Panthera leo persica)	Asiatic lion
(Panthera tigris virgata)	Caspian tiger
(Panthera tigris altaica)	Siberian tiger
(Panthera tigris sondaica)	Javan tiger
(Panthera tigris amoyensis)	Chinese tiger
(Panthera tigris balica)	Bali tiger
(Panthera tigris sumatrae)	Sumatran tiger
(Panthera pardus panthera)	Barbary leopard
(Panthera pardus nimr)	South Arabian leopard
(Panthera pardus tulliana)	Anatolian leopard
(Panthera pardus orientalis)	Amur leopard
(Panthera pardus jarvisi)	Sinai leopard
(Panthera uncia)	Snow leopard
(Acinonyx jubatus venaticus)	Asiatic cheetah
PINNIPEDIA (Order)	
OTARIIDAE (Family) Fur seals and sea lions	
(Arctocephalus a. galapagoensis)	Galapagos fur seal
(Arctocephalus philippii philippii)	Juan Fernandez fur seal
*(Arctocephalus philippii townsendi)	Guadalupe fur seal
(Zalophus californianus japonicus)	Japanese sea lion
ODOBENIDAE (Family) Walrus	
(Odobenus rusmarus rosmarus)	Atlantic walrus
PHOCIDAE (Family) Seals	
‡(Histriophoca fasciata)	Ribbon seal
(Phoca kurilensis)	Kurile harbour seal
(Phoca hispida saimensis)	Saimaa seal
(Ommatophoca rossi)	Ross seal
(Monachus monachus)	Mediterranean monk seal
*(Monachus tropicalis)	Caribbean monk seal
*(Monachus schauinslandi)	Hawaiian monk seal

[10] Rated "Endangered" in Rare and Endangered Fish and Wildlife of the United States.
[11] Rated "Endangered" in Rare and Endangered Fish and Wildlife of the United States.
[12] Rated "Rare" in Rare and Endangered Fish and Wildlife of the United States.

Location	Legal protection	Population	Status
Spain	–	several hundred (1958)	E***
Algeria	–	U	E***
South Texas, Mexico	–	U	I
Texas, Mexico	–	U	I
Eastern Canada	–	U	D
Everglades National Park, Florida	P	100– (1964)	E[10]
Taiwan	–	U	E***
India, Iran	P	162+ (1968)	E
U.S.S.R., Iran, Afghanistan	P	60-80 (1959)	E***
Far East, U.S.S.R., China, Korea	P	100-140 (1964)	E***
Java, Indonesia	–	12 (1968)	E***
China	–	U	E
Bali, Indonesia (?)	–	U	E***
Sumatra, Indonesia	–	U	I
Morocco, Algeria, Tunis	P	100+	E
Saudi Arabia	–	U	R
Turkey, U.S.S.R.	–	U	E***
Korea, China, U.S.S.R.	–	40-55 (1969)	E***
North Saudi Arabia	–	U	E***
U.S.S.R., China, India, Tibet, Afghanistan	P	400±	E
Afghanistan, Pakistan, U.S.S.R., Iran	P	U	E***
Galapagos Islands	–	U	D
Juan Fernandez Islands off Chile	–	30+ (1969)	R
Guadalupe Island	P	U	R[11]
Sea of Japan	–	Probably nil	E***
Arctic Ocean	P	25,000 (1966)	R
Arctic Ocean	–	U	D
Kurile Islands North Kokkaido	–	2,000-2,500 (1956)	I
Saimaa Lake system, Finland	P	200-250	I
Antarctic Ocean	–	20,000-50,000 (1958)	I
Shores of Mediterranean and Black Seas, Coasts of Northwest Africa	P	500 (1964)	E***
Caribbean Sea	–	U	E***
Hawaiian Islands	P	1,500 (1963)	R[12]

Scientific name	Common name
PROBOSCIDEA (Order)	
ELEPHANTIDAE (Family) Elephants	
(Elephas maximus maximus)	Ceylon elephant
SIRENIA (Order)	
DUGONGIDAE (Family) Dugongs	
(Dugong dugon)	Dugong
TRICHECHIDAE (Family) Manatees	
(Trichechus manatus manatus	West Indian manatee
(Trichechus manatus latirostris)	Florida manatee
(Trichechus inunguis)	Amazonian manatee
(Trichechus senegalensis)	West African manatee
PERISSODACTYLA (Order)	
EQUIDAE (Family) Horses, asses, zebras	
(Equus przewalskii)	Przewalski's horse
(Equus hemionus hemionus)	Mongolian wild ass
(Equus hemionus onager)	Persian onager
(Equus hemionus khur)	Indian wild ass
(Equus hemionus kiang)	Tibetan wild ass
(Equus hemionus hemippus)	Syrian wild ass
(Equus asinus africanus)	Nubian wild ass
(Equus asinus somalicus)	Somali wild ass
(Equus zebra zebra)	Cape mountain zebra
(Equus zebra hartmannae)	Hartmann's mountain zebra
TAPIRIDAE (Family) Tapirs	
(Tapirus pinchaque)	Mountain tapir
(Tapirus bairdii)	Central American tapir
RHINOCEROTIDAE (Family) Rhinoceroses	
(Rhinoceros unicornis)	Great Indian rhinoceros
(Rhinoceros sondaicus)	Javan rhinoceros
(Didermoceros sumatrensis)	Sumatran rhinoceros

Location	Legal protection	Population	Status
Ceylon	P	100–1,500 (1963)	D
North and South Pacific Ocean	P	U	D
Coasts and coastal rivers of West Indies	P	"some thousands" (1963)	D
South Coast, Florida	P	U	I
Lower reaches of Amazon tributaries	P	U	E***
Coastal lagoons and lower reaches of West African rivers from Senegal to Angola	P	U	I
China	–	"scores" (1968)	D
Mongolia, China, U.S.S.R.	P	"several thousand"	I
		(1965)	I
Iran, Afghanistan	P	400–100	
	P	(1959)	I
Gujarat States, India	–	870 (1962)	E
Tibet, Nepal, Sikkim, India	P	U	I
Syria, Turkey	P	U ("believed nil")	I
Chad, Sudan, Egypt, Lybia	P	U	I***
Somalia, Ethiopia, U.S.S.R.	–	"few hundred" (1968)	E***
South Africa	P	75 (1965)	R
Southwest Africa	P	7000 (1967)	D
Colombia, Ecuador, Peru, West Venezuela	–	200–300 (1968)	E
Central America, Ecuador, Colombia	P	U	I
India, Nepal	P	740 (1966)	R
Java	P	40's (1964)	E***
Burma, Thailand, Malaya, Sumatra and Sabah, India, East Pakistan, Laos, Vietnam	P	100–170 (1965)	E***

Scientific name	Common name
(Ceratotherium simum cottoni)	Northern square-lipped rhinoceros
(Diceros bicornis)	Black rhinoceros
ARTIODACTYLA (Order)	
SUIDAE (Family) Old world pigs	
(Sus salvanius)	Pygmy hog
HIPPOPOTAMIDAE (Family) Hippopotamuses	
(Choeropsis liberiensis)	Pygmy hippopotamus
CAMELIDAE (Family) Llamas, camels, etc.	
(Vicugna vicugna)	Vicuña
(Camelus bactrianus ferus)	Wild Bactrian camel
CERVIDAE (Family) Deer	
(Muntiacua crinifrons)	Black muntjac
(Muntiacus feae)	Fea's muntjac
(Dama dama mesopotamica)	Persian fallow deer
(Cervus duvauceli)	Swamp deer
(Cervus duvauceli branderi)	Brander's swamp deer
(Cervus eldi eldi)	Manipur brow-antlered deer
(Cervus eldi siamensis)	Thailand brow-antlered deer
(Cervus nippon taiouanus)	Formosan sika
(Cervus nippon mandarinus)	North China sika
(Cervus nippon kopschi)	South China sika
(Cervus nippon grassianus)	Shansi sika
(Cervus nippon keramae)	Ryukyu sika
(Cervus albirostris)	Thorold's deer
(Cervus elaphus corsicanus)	Corsican red deer
(Cervus elaphus wallichi)	Shou
(Cervus elaphus barbarus)	Barbary stag
(Cervus elaphus hanglu)	Kashmir stag
(Cervus elaphus yarkandensis)	Yarkand stag
(Cervus elaphus bactrianus)	Bactrian wapiti
(Cervus elaphus macneilli)	M'Neill's deer
(Cervus nannodes)	Tule elk
(Elaphurus davidianus)	Père David's deer
(Odocoileus virginianus clavium)	Key deer
(Odocoileus virginianus leucurus)	Columbia white-tailed deer
(Blastoceros dichotomus)	Marsh deer

Location	Legal protection	Population	Status
Southwest Sudan, Uganda, Congo (Kinshasa)	P	U	E***
Eighteen countries in South, West and East Africa	P	11,000-13,500 (1960)	R
India, Nepal, Bhutan	–	U	I
Nigeria, Ivory Coast, Liberia, Sierra Leone, Guinea, Portuguese Guinea	P	U	D
Andes Mountains in Peru, Northeast Argentina and Chile	P	400,000 (1957)	R
China, Mongolia	P	400-500 (1963)	D
State of Chekiang, Southeast China	–	U	I
Thailand	–	U	I
Iran	P	35+ (1968)	E***
India, Nepal	P	3,000-4,000 (1965)	D
Kanha National Park, Madhya Pradesh	P	73 (1969)	E***
Manipur State, India	P	"about 100" (1961)	D
Thailand, Vietnam, Cambodia	P	U	I
Southern Formosa	–	"few" (1966)	I***
China	–	U	I***
China	P	U	I***
China	–	U	E***
Ryukyu Islands	P	30 (1965)	E***
West Coast, Corsica, Sardinia	P	65 (1965-66)	D
Tibet, Bhutan	–	U	E***
Tunisia, Algeria	P	150 (1967)	I
Vale of Kashmir, India, Nepal	–	150 (1968)	E***
Basin of the Tarim, Lob-nor Lake, China	–	U	I
U.S.S.R., North Afghanistan	P	400-500 (1968)	E***
Tibet, China	P	U	E***
California	P	308+ (1964)	D
Unknown in wild state	–	542 in captivity (1968)	R
Monroe County, Florida	P	300 (1963)	D
Columbia River Lowlands, U.S.A.	–	U	E
Central South America	P	U	D

Scientific name	Common name
(Ozotoceros bezoarticus)	Pampas deer
(Pudu pudu)	Chilean pudu
(Rangifer tarandus pearsoni)	Novaya Zemlya reindeer
ANTILOCAPRIDAE (Family) Pronghorns	
(Antilocapra americana peninsularis)	Lower California pronghorn
(Antilocapra americana sonoriensis)	Sonora pronghorn
BOVIDAE (Family) Antelopes, cattle, sheep and goats	
(Taurotragus derbianus derbianus)	Western giant eland
(Bubalus bubalis)	Asiatic buffalo
(Anoa mindorensis)	Tamaraw
(Anoa depressicornis depressicornis)	Lowland anoa
(Anoa depressicornis fergusoni)	Mountain anoa
(Anoa depressicornis quarlesi)	Quarles' anoa
(Bos gaurus hubbacki)	Seladang
(Bos sauveli)	Kouprey
(Bos grunniens mutus)	Wild yak
(Bison bonasus)	European bison
(Bison bison athabascae)	Wood bison
(Cephalophus jentinki)	Jentink's duiker
(Kobus leche smithemani)	Black lechwe
(Hippotragus niger variani)	Giant sable antelope
(Oryx leucoryx)	Arabian oryx
(Oryx tao)	Scimitar-horned oryx
(Addax nasomaculatus)	Addax
(Damaliscus dorcas dorcas)	Bontebok
(Alcelaphus buselaphus tora)	Tora hartebeest
(Alcelaphus buselaphus swaynei)	Swayne's hartebeest
(Nesotragus moschatus moschatus)	Zanzibar suni
(Dorcatragus megalotis)	Beira antelope
(Aepyceros melampus petersi)	Black-faced impala
(Gazella subgutturosa marica)	Sand gazelle

Location	Legal protection	Population	Status
Central Eastern Brazil	–	U	D
Lower slopes of Andes in Argentina and Brazil	–	U	I
Eastern and northeastern parts of northern island, Novaya Zemlya, U.S.S.R.	P	"few dozen" (1950)	E***
Baja California, Mexico	P	U	E***
Southwest Arizona; Sonor State, Mexico	P	U	E***
West Africa	P	180 in Senegal (1965)	E***
North India, Nepal, Assam	P	"under 2000" (1966)	R
Mount Iglit, Mount Calavite, hinterland of The Sablayon Penal Settlement, Philippine Islands	P	100 (1969)	E***
Swampy forest of northern Celebes	–	U	E***
Central mountains of Celebes	–	U	I***
Toradja, Celebes	–	U	I***
Malaya	P	350 (1968)	E***
Cambodia, Vietnam	P	U	E***
Northern parts of Tibet above 4500 meters	P	U	E
Bialowieza Forest, Poland	P	790-800 (1965)	D
Upper Nyarling River, Canada	P	100– (1965)	E
Liberia, Sierra Leone, Ivory Coast	–	"few hundred" (1968)	E
Bangweulu area of Zambia	P	4500 (1966)	R
Southern part of the Luanda Reserve in the Malange district of Angola	P	500-700 (1964)	I
Oman, Saudi Arabia	P	200– (1969)	E***
From Mauritania to Red Sea fringing narrow strip of land south of Sahara Desert	–	4000 in Tchad (1964)	D
Mauritania, Mali, Algeria, Libya, Sudan, Chad	–	6450 (1967)	D
Swellendam district; Bontebok National Park, South Africa	–	750± (1965)	D
Ethiopia	–	200– (1967)	I
Ethiopia, Sudan	–	U	E***
Zanzibar Island	–	U	I
Lower hills in northern Somalia	–	U	I
Banks of Kunene River, Angola; Southwest Africa	P	1000– (1965)	E
Eastern deserts of Jordan, Kuwait, Saudi Arabia	–	U	D

Scientific name	Common name
(Gazella dorcas massaesyla)	Moroccan dorcas gazelle
(Gazella dorcas saudiya)	Saudi Arabian dorcas gazelle
(Gazella gazella arabica)	Arabian gazelle
(Gazella gazella cuvieri)	Cuvier's gazelle
(Gazella leptoceros)	Slender-horned gazelle
(Gazella pelzelni)	Pelzeln's gazelle
(Gazella dama mhorr)	Mhorr gazelle
(Gazella dama lozanoi)	Rio de Oro dama gazelle
(Capricornis S. sumatraensis)	Sumatran serow
(Capricornis crispus crispus)	Japanese serow
(Capricornis crispus swinhoei)	Formosan serow
(Budorcas taxicolor tibetana)	Szechwan takin
(Budorcas taxicolor bedfordi)	Golden takin
(Hemitragus jayakari)	Arabian tahr
(Hemitragus hylocrius)	Nilgiri tahr
(Capra walie)	Walia ibex
(Capra pyrenaica pyrenaica)	Pyrenean ibex
(Capra falconeri jerdoni)	Straight-horned markhor
(Ovis orientalis ophion)	Cyprian mouflon
(Ovis canadensis cremnobates)	Peninsular bighorn

PERIPHERAL MAMMALS

listed in Rare and Endangered Fish and Wildlife of the United States

Coatimundi or chula (Nasua narica molaris)
Southern Arizona, New Mexico and Texas; subject to epidemics and periodic fluctuations in population.

Jaguar (Felis onca veraecrucis)
Eastern and southeastern Mexico north to Central Texas.

Jaguarundi (Felis yagouaroundi cacomitli)
Tampico, Tamaulipas, Mexico, north to extreme southern Texas; reported seen at Platt National Park in Oklahoma.

Ocelot (Felis pardalis albescens)
Northeastern Mexico into northern Texas.

Margay (Felis wiedii cooperi)
Northeastern Mexico into southeastern Texas.

Location	Legal protection	Population	Status
Northeastern Morocco, Algeria	–	U	E***
Saudi Arabia, Kuwait, Israel, Jordan, Iraq	P	U	D
Saudi Arabia, Yemen, Oman, Sinai	–	U	D
Morocco, Tunisia, Algeria	P	600-700 (1961-64)	E***
Algeria, Libya, Egypt, Sudan	–	U	E***
Maritime plains of Berbera, northern Somaliland	–	U	R
Morocco, Spanish Sahara	–	U	E***
Adrar Sutuf in southwestern Rio de Oro, Spanish Sahara	–	"half a hundred" (1968)	E
Higher regions of Sumatra	P	U	I
Mountain areas all over Honshu, Shikoku and Kyushu Islands, Japan	P	2000-3000 (1968)	D
Formosa	–	U	D
Western China	–	U	I
Isolated area in the Tsing Ling Range, China	P	200-300 (1937)	I
Mountains of Oman	–	U	I
Southern India	–	820+ (1963)	R
North and Northwest escarpment of Semien, Ethiopia	P	150+ (1964)	E***
Northern extreme of Huesca Province, Spain	P	"perhaps 20" (1965)	E***
Afghanistan, Pakistan	P	U	I
Northwestern Cyprus	P	100+ (1964)	E
Northern Baja California Peninsula	P	900 (1966)	I

Woodland caribou (Rangifer tarandus caribou)
Northern Great Lakes states to Hudson Bay, Canada.

Mountain caribou (Rangifer tarandus montanus)
Pacific northwest United States to British Columbia, Canada; a transient group of 25 to 100 in extreme northern Idaho.

Musk ox (Ovibos moschatus moschatus)
Northern Canada and Greenland; on Nunivak Island, Alaska.

STATUS-UNDETERMINED MAMMALS

listed in Rare and Endangered Fish and Wildlife of the United States

Hawaiian bat (Lasiurus cinereus semotus) (Allen)
Islands of Kaui, Oahu and Hawaii.

Arizona prairie dog (Cynomys ludovisianus arizonensis) (Mearns)
Southeastern Arizona, southern and central New Mexico, southwestern Texas.

Chiricahua squirrel (Sciurus chiricahuae) (Goldman)
Chiricahua Mountains of southeast Arizona.

Apache fox squirrel (Sciurus apache)
Chiricahua Mountains of southeast Arizona and adjacent areas in Mexico.

Eastern fox squirrel (Sciurus niger vulpinus)
Southern Pennsylvania, eastern West Virginia, northern Virginia and Maryland exclusive of the Eastern Shore.

Texas kangaroo rat (Dipodomys elator)
North-central Texas and southwestern Oklahoma.

Big-eared kangaroo rat (Dipodomys elephantinus)
Central California.

Salt-marsh harvest mouse (Reithrodontomys raviventris)
Central California.

Guadalupe mountain vole (Microtus mexicanus guadalupensis)
El Paso County in Texas and Sacramento Mountains in New Mexico.

Louisiana vole (Microtus ludovicianus)
Southeastern Texas and southwestern Louisiana.

Florida water rat or round-tailed muskrat (Neofiber alleni)
Bogs and marshes of Florida and extreme southern Georgia.

Northern swift fox (Vulpes velox hebes)
Dakotas, eastern Montana and Wyoming and adjacent areas in Canada.

Polar bear (Thalarctos maritimus)
Circumpolar; in Western Hemisphere, northern Alaska, Canada and Greenland. International research program is underway to determine status.

Pine marten (Martes americana)
Alaska and Northern United States, south in mountains to central California and northern New Mexico. Reintroduced in Wisconsin, Michigan and New Hampshire. Protected by law in Michigan.

Fisher (Martes pennanti)
Northern United States. Reintroduced in Idaho, Oregon, Michigan and Wisconsin. Increasing in recent years in Massachusetts, New Hampshire and northern New York. Protected by law in Michigan.

Everglades mink (Mustela vison evergladensis)
Mangrove and cypress swamps of Florida Everglades and the Ten Thousand Islands.

Wolverine (Gulo luscus)
Alaska and northern United States, south in mountains to central California, Utah and Colorado. Rare in Idaho. Completely protected in California, Colorado and Washington.

Mississippi Valley red wolf (Canis rufus gregoryi)
Formerly in Mississippi Valley from Illinois and Indiana south to Louisiana and west to eastern Texas, and probably in adjacent Kentucky, Tennessee and Mississippi and in Ozark Mountains of Arkansas and Missouri, to southeastern Oklahoma. Present status over former range, particularly Gulf coast, needs investigation.

Canada lynx (Lynx canadensis)
Alaska, Canada and northern States. Rare in Idaho; making a comeback in northern Michigan; protected in Wisconsin and Michigan; still carries a $20 bounty in New Hampshire.

Elephant seal (Mirounga angutirostris)
Alaska southward to Baja California, Mexico; breeding from Año Nuevo Island, California, southward.

BOX 2-1. Sample Biography

RARE

GRIZZLY BEAR (Ursus horribilis) (Ord)

Order: CARNIVORA Family: URSIDAE

Distinguishing characteristics: Large bear, average about 600 pounds for males; grizzled brown, hump on shoulder, huge front claws, concave facial profile.

Present distribution: Montana, Wyoming, remnants in Idaho and San Juan range of southwest Colorado. Still widespread in Alaska.

Former distribution: Western North America from Arctic to Mexico and east to Great Plains.

NOTE: The taxonomic status of the grizzly is confused (see remarks, below). The grizzly and big brown bear of Alaska are closely allied, and 77 species of the two combined have been described. Some of these are now extinct, while others are doubtless synonyms. What we here refer to as the grizzly bear, Ursus horribilis (with 4 subspecies included), represents populations from Idaho, Colorado, Montana, and Wyoming.

Status: Rare in the conterminous United States.

Estimated numbers: About 850 in Colorado, Idaho, Montana and Wyoming.

Breeding rate in the wild: Usually 1-2 cubs in alternate years.

Reasons for decline: Persecution with guns, traps, dogs and poisons as predator and menace to man and his livestock. Human activity continues to intrude on the habitat of this wilderness species.

Protective measures already taken: Managed as a trophy animal or given complete protection in all states. Complete protection in national parks where they occur, and is given management emphasis on national forests.

Measures proposed: Wilderness areas most needed, with cessation of any unnecessary persecution as a predator.

Number in captivity: 33 males, 53 females in 31 American zoos (1963).

Breeding potential in captivity: Good.

Remarks: Last grizzly reported in California in 1922. Estimated population in 1940 about 1,100 in U. S. exclusive of Alaska. The taxonomy of the grizzly and brown bears is confused and clarification is greatly needed. It is currently being reviewed by E. R. Hall and has been studied previously by R. L. Rausch.

References:

Animal Census, 1963.
Allen, G. M., 1942: 139-165.
Beard, 1943: 40-47.
National Wildlife Federation, 1956: 3-4.
Matthiessen, 1959: 87-90.
Palmer, 1954: 83-88.
Rausch, Robert L., 1953. On the status of some arctic mammals. Arctic, 6 (2): 91-148.
———, 1962. Geographic variation in size in North American brown bears . . . Canadian Journal of Zoology, 41: 33-45.
U. S. Fish and Wildlife Service, 1964. Big Game Inventory for 1963. Wildlife Leaflet 461, 4 pp.

BOX 2-2. Sample Biography from the Red Data Book

Survival Service Commission Red Data Book © January 1966
International Union for Conservation of Nature and Natural Resources

ORANG UTAN

(Pongo pygmaeus) (Hoppius, 1763)

Order: PRIMATES Family: PONGIDAE

Distinguishing characteristics: "The adult Orang-utan is a large shaggy animal, of dark rufous color. The profile of the skull is much more sloping than in the African anthropoids, the skull showing very little of the brow ridges so prominent in the latter. The arms are very long, reaching to the ankles when the animal is erect; foot long and narrow, the great toe very short. Tail absent. Prominent cheek callosities sometimes present in adult males . . ." (2:164–165)

Present distribution: Sumatra: Carpenter stated that in 1937 orangs were found "throughout an estimated fifty percent of the primary forests in the former State of Atjeh," northern Sumatra. (1:19) Milton concludes that the present day population is mainly confined to the Löser Reserve. "In addition, however, there is an area to the north which I was unable to visit, another area on the coast on the west slopes of the Löser, and a third area directly west of Medan, all of which are known to contain orang-utan." (6:182)

Sarawak: distribution is limited to about 2,000 sq. miles. (3:82)

Sabah: the Orang occurs in "extensive sections of Borneo." (3:82)

Kalimantan: confined to limited areas in the north-east and west. (5:247)

Former distribution: At one time the Orang-utan occurred on the Asiatic mainland. "Remains have been found in Stone Age archaeological sites from Peking to the Celebes." (5:11) ". . . remains of anthropoids resembling the Orang are known from the Siwilak Hills of India, but there seems to be no evidence of their survival to the historic period." (2:164) "Even within these two islands [Sumatra and Borneo] they were much commoner and more widespread in the recent past." (5:11) "There are none left in the State of Brunei, between North Borneo and Sarawak." (5:199)

Status: "Although no population estimates are available prior to 1959, it is apparent from the earlier literature that orang-utans have declined drastically in the past hundred years." (3:75)

Estimated numbers:				
	Sabah	approx.	2000	
	Sarawak	"	700	
	Kalimantan	"	1000	
	Sumatra	"	1000	
	Total	"	5000	(8)

Breeding rate in wild: Gestation period 210–270 days. Has a single infant probably every fourth year. Female remains fertile for as long as 23–25 years. Thus, allowing for an infant mortality rate of 40%, the average lifetime reproductive rate may be 2–3 young per female. (8)

Reasons for decline: Sumatra: "As large clearings are made in the rather level lowlands, these apes are being destroyed or forced into the hills and mountains where it is questionable whether or not conditions, including food supply, are sufficiently suitable for the maintenance of the present population level . . . the most serious inroads being made by commercial developments in the areas suitable for orang-utan habitats." (1:19) "The situation in Sumatra . . . is accentuated by the presence there of soldiers with rifles, and by the proximity of the Asian mainland and the difficulty of controlling smugglers in sailing sampans." (5:199) "The biggest menace to orang conservation is the Indonesian Army . . . They hunt orangs in Sumatra with automatic weapons and sell the babies to smugglers." (9)

Sarawak: "Hunting has been the major cause of their decline in the past and habitat destruction threatens them at present in their major area of concentration." (3:82)

Sabah: The large illicit trade in young orangs and the high mortality rate during the process of capture which usually involves killing the mothers, have resulted in a substantial numerical decline. An important contributory factor is the extensive commercial exploitation of the natural habitat for forestry purposes. (4:241–242)

Kalimantan "Such meagre evidence as is now available from the large area of Indonesian Borneo territory indicates a continuing, almost uncontrolled exploitation of Orangs there—whatever intentions and regulations are in force on paper." (5:199)

Protective measures already taken: The International Union of Directors of Zoological Gardens has agreed to introduce stringent regulations prohibiting the purchase of orangs through illicit channels.

Measures proposed: Schaller makes the important point that "it is doubtful if the orang-utan will ever adapt to habitat other than primary forest and old secondary forest. . . . The only hope for the remaining orang-utans . . . lies in the preservation of the forest reserves which still harbor animals. These reserves are at present being logged in the accessible portions . . . logging has damaged some sectors so heavily that expansion of this activity can only be detrimental to the remaining animals. All hunting, too, must cease if the orang-utan is expected to survive." (3:77) Regulations governing the importation of orangs into Singapore and other eastern ports require strengthening and active enforcement. (8) "Close cooperation among the countries of South-East Asia is necessary to control the illegal trade. There is also an urgent need to establish fully protected sanctuaries in the Mount Löser Reserve (Acheen), in Sarawak, and in the Sampit Reserve (Borneo)." (10) The IUCN Conference on Conservation of Nature and Natural Resources in Tropical South-East Asia, Bangkok, (4/12/65) passed a resolution recommending the establishment of a 700 sq. mile sanctuary at Ulu Segama, eastern Sabah. The Conference also recommended that the Governments concerned should appoint research officers to undertake long-term studies of the breeding biology and behaviour of the species. (11)

Number in captivity: The total number of orangs in zoos throughout the world is estimated at 133♂♂ and 141♀♀ + 4 in 96 zoos. (7:377) A breeding colony has been established at the Yerkes Laboratory with the object of attempting to perpetuate the species and to carry out psychological studies. (9)

Breeding potential in captivity: Of the above, 10♂♂ and 16♀♀ + 11 were born in captivity. (7:377) The rearing of captive orangs is difficult. (4:259)

References:

1. Carpenter, 1938
2. Harper, 1945
3. Schaller, 1961
4. Harrisson, 1961
5. Harrisson, 1962
6. Milton, 1964
7. Jarvis, 1965
8. B. Harrisson in verbis 29/11/63
9. G. Bourne in litt. 26/2/64
10. H. Basjarudin in litt. 28/10/65
11. IUCN Bulletin No. 18, Jan/Mar 1966

Birds

The *Red Data Book* includes over 300 bird forms listed as endangered. Many of these species are arcane and familiar only to specialists. For this reason and in order to keep this chapter at a manageable

Scientific name	Common name
AVES	
PROCELLARIIFORMES (Order)	
PROCELLARIIDAE (Family) Petrels and shearwaters	
(Puffinus puffinus newelli)	Newell's manx shearwater
(Pterodroma phaeopygia sandwichensis)	Hawaiian dark-rumped petrel
CHARIDRIFORMES (Order)	
LARIDAE (Family) Gulls and terns	
(Sterna albifrons browni)	California beast tern
CICONIIFORMES (Order)	
ARDEIDAE (Family) Herons, egrets and bitterns	
(Ardea o. occidentalis)	Florida great white heron
ANSERIFORMES (Order)	
ANATIDAE (Family) Ducks, geese and swans	
(Branta sandvicensis)	Nene (Hawaiian goose)
(Branta canadensis leucoprareia)	Aleutian Canada goose
(Anser albifrons gambelli)	Tule white-fronted goose
(Anas laysanensis)	Laysan duck
(Anas wyvilliana)	Hawaiian duck
(Anas diazi)	Mexican duck
FALCONIFORMES (Order)	
CATHARTIDAE (Family) New world vultures	
(Gymnogyps californianus)	California condor
ACCIPITRIDAE (Family) Hawks, eagles, harriers, old world vultures	
(Rostrhamus sociabilis plumbeus)	Florida Everglades kite (Florida snail kite)
(Buteo solitarius)	Hawaiian hawk
(Buteo brachyurus)	Short-tailed hawk
(Haliaeetus l. leucocephalus)	Southern bald eagle

length, we have restricted our listing of endangered birds to only those forms named in the *Rare and Endangered Fish and Wildlife of the United States.*

Location	Legal protection	Population	Status
Kauai	P	"low thousands" (1967)	R
Hawaii and Maui	P	800 adults on Maui	E
Pacific Coast from central California to southern Baja California	P	U	E
Florida Keys, Florida Bay, southern peninsular Florida	P	2000 adults	R
Lava flows between 5,000 and 8,000 feet on the slopes of Mauna Loa and Hualalai	P	300-400	E
Aleutian Islands	–	250-300	E
Yukon, Oregon, California, Texas, Louisiana, Northwest Mexico	–	U	E
Laysan Island, Hawaii	P	133 (1968)	E
Kauai Island, Hawaii	P	3,000	E
Southeast Arizona, South New Mexico, central West Texas, south in Mexican Highlands to Puebla and Michoacan	–	500 U. S. A., "several thousand" Mexico	E
California	P	60-80 (1968)	E
Fresh-water marshes of southern Florida	–	47 + (1967)	E
Island of Hawaii	P	"low hundreds"	E
From northern Florida and eastern Mexico south to northern Argentina	P	200+ U. S.	R
Nests in estuarine areas of Atlantic and Gulf Coasts; lower Mississippi Valley	P	U	E

Scientific name	Common name
FALCONIDAE (Family) Falcons, caracaras	
(Falco mexicanus)	Prairie falcon
(Falco peregrinus anatum)	American peregrine falcon
GALLIFORMES (Order)	
TETRAONIDAE (Family) Grouse	
(Tympanuchus cupido pinnatus)	Northern greater prairie chicken
(Tympanuchus cupido attwateri)	Attwater's greater prairie chicken
(Tympanuchus pallidicinctus)	Lesser prairie chicken
PHASIANIDAE (Family) Pheasants, francolins, quails and peafowl	
(Colinus virginianus ridgwayi)	Masked bobwhite
GRUIFORMES (Order)	
GRUIDAE (Family) Cranes	
(Grus americana)	Whooping crane
(Grus canadensis tabida)	Greater sandhill crane
(Grus canadensis pratensis)	Florida sandhill crane
RALLIDAE (Family) Rails	
(Rallus longirostris yumanensis)	Yuma clapper rail
(Rallus longirostris obsoletus)	California clapper rail
(Rallus longirostris levipes)	Light-footed clapper rail
(Laterallus jamaicensis coturniculus)	California black rail
(Gallinula chloropus sandvicensis)	Hawaiian gallinule
(Fulica americana alai)	Hawaiian coot
CHARADRIIFORMES (Order)	
SCOLOPACIDAE (Family) Snipes, woodcocks and sandpipers	
(Numenius borealis)	Eskimo curlew

Location	Legal protection	Population	Status
Central British Columbia to southern Saskatchewan and south to Baja California and northern Texas	–	U	R
Non-Arctic regions of Alaska and Canada south to Baja California	P	U	E
Prairie habitation in central southern Canada and midwest U. S.	P	U	R
Gulf coastal prairie of Texas	P	1,000 (1967)	R
Brush grassland prairies of western U. S. A.	P	U	R
Sonora State, Mexico; central southern Arizona	–	400-1,000	E
Breeds in Wood Buffalo National Park, Mackenzie, Canada; winters on Gulf Coast, Texas	P	67 (1968)	E
Southwest and South Central Canada; California, Nevada, Utah, Wyoming, Minnesota, Wisconsin, Michigan	P	about 6,000	R
Wet prairies of Florida and extreme southern Georgia	P	2,000-3,000 (1964)	R
Marshes of the lower Colorado River	–	200–	E
Salt marshes along the coast of West Central California	P	U	R
Tidal salicornia marshes from Santa Barbara County, California to the Mexican border	P	U	E
Tidal marshes from Tomales Bay and San Francisco south to Baja California	–	U	R
All main Hawaiian Islands except Lanai and Niihau	P	U	E
Islands of Oahu, Maui, Kauai, Molokai and Hawaii	P	"probably 1,500"	E
Last seen on Texas coast in 1962	P	U	E

Scientific name	Common name
RECURVITOSTRIDAE (Family) Avocets, stilts	
(Himantopus humantopus knudseni)	Hawaiian stilt
COLUMBIFORMES (Order)	
COLUMBIDAE (Family) Pigeons, doves	
(Columba inornata wetmorei)	Puerto Rican plain pigeon
PSITTACIFORMES (Order)	
PSITTACIDAE (Family) Lories, parrots and macaws	
(Amazona vittata)	Puerto Rican parrot
CAPRIMULGIFORMES (Order)	
CAPRIMULGIDAE (Family) Nightjars	
(Caprimulgus noctitherus)	Puerto Rican whippoorwill
PICIFORMES (Order)	
PICIDAE (Family) Woodpeckers	
(Campephilus p. principalis)	American ivory-billed woodpecker
(Dendrocopus borealis borealis)	Northern red-cockaded woodpecker
(Dendrocopus borealis hylonomus)	Southern red-cockaded woodpecker
PASSERIFORMES (Order)	
CORVIDAE (Family) Crows	
(Corvus tropicus)	Hawaiian crow (alala)
TURDIDAE (Family) Thrushes	
(Phaeornis palmeri)	Small Kauai thrush
(Phaeornis obscurus myadestina)	Large Kauai thrush
SYLVIDAE (Family) Old world warblers	
(Acrocephalus kingi)	Nihoa millerbird
MELIPHAGIDAE (Family) Honey-eaters	
(Moho braccatus)	Kauai oo (oo aa)

Location	Legal protection	Population	Status
Islands of Kauai, Niihau, Maui, Hawaii, Molokai and Oahu	P	"about 1,500"	E
Woodland near Cidra, Puerto Rico	–	"possibly several thousand"	E
National Forest, Puerto Rico	–	"less than 200"	E
Guanica Forest, Puerto Rico	–	"probably 100–200"	R
Scattered in Southeast Texas, Louisiana, Florida, Georgia, South Carolina	P	U	E
Pine woodlands from South Mississippi, West Kentucky, and Southeast Virginia south to Gulf Coast and North Florida	P	U	E
Pine woodlands in Central and South Florida	–	U	E
Island of Hawaii	P	"perhaps 100"	E
Unknown	P	"probably low"	E
Island of Kauai, Hawaii	P	U	R
Nihoa Island, Hawaii	P	500–600 (1967)	E
Island of Kauai, Hawaii	P	"very few"	E

Scientific name	Common name
DREPANIDIDAE (Family) Hawaiian honeycreepers	
(Palmeria dolei)	Crested honeycreeper (Akohekohe)
(Loxops maculata flammea)	Molokai creeper (Kakawahie)
(Hemignathus wilsoni)	Akiapolaau
(Hemignathus procerus)	Kauai akialoa
(Hemignathus lucidus hanapepe)	Kauai nukupuu
(Hemignathus lucidus affinus)	Maui nukupuu
(Psittirostra c. cantans)	Laysan finch
(Psittirostra cantans ultima)	Nihoa finch
(Psittirostra psittacea)	Ou
(Psittirostra bailleui)	Palila
(Pseudonestor xanthophrys)	Maui parrotbill
PARULIDAE (Family) Wood warblers	
(Vermivora bachmanii)	Bachman's warbler
(Dendroica chrysoparia)	Golden-cheeked warbler
(Denroica kirtlandii)	Kirtland's warbler
FRINGILLIDAE (Family) Grosbeaks, finches	
(Passerculus princeps)	Ipswich sparrow
(Ammospiza nigrescens)	Dusky seaside sparrow
(Ammospiza mirabilis)	Cape sable sparrow

Location	Legal protection	Population	Status
Island of Maui, Hawaii	P	U	E
Island of Molokai, Hawaii	P	U	E
Mauna Kea and Mauna Loa, Island of Hawaii	P	U	E
Island of Kauai, Hawaii	P	U	E
Island of Kauai, Hawaii	P	U	E
Island of Maui, Hawaii	P	U	E
Island of Laysan Hawaii	P	8,000-10,000 (1967)	E
Island of Nihoa, Hawaii	P	4,800-5,000 (1967)	E
Islands of Kauai and Hawaii	P	U	E
Island of Hawaii	P	"low hundred"	E
Island of Maui	P	U	E
Swamp river forests of southeastern Mississippi, northeastern Arkansas, western Kentucky, northern Alabama, and South Carolina	P	U	E
Edwards Plateau in central Texas	P	15,000 (1962)	R
Breeds in lower peninsula of Michigan, winters in the Bahamas	P	"less than 1,000"	E
Breeds on Sable Island, Nova Scotia, winters on sand dunes along Atlantic Coast from Nova Scotia south to Georgia	–	U	R
Salt marshes on Merritt Island, Florida	–	900-1,200 (1968)	E
Fresh and brackish water marshes in southwestern Florida	P	"perhaps less than 500"	E

BOX 2-3. Sample Biography

ENDANGERED

CALIFORNIA CONDOR (Gymnogyps californianus) Shaw
Order: FALCONIFORMES Family: CATHARTIDAE

Distinguishing characteristics: North America's largest soaring land bird. Weighs 20-25 pounds and has a wing spread of 9-9½ feet. It has dark brown plumage with a large white patch under each wing and a bare orange head in the adult. The young birds have dark heads and go through three plumage stages. The juvenile and subadult are similar to the adult, but the immature bird is entirely dark underneath.

Present distribution: Southern coast ranges from Monterey County south to the Transverse Mountains and north in the Sierra Nevada foothills to Fresno County.

Former distribution: In historical times, from the Columbia River in Oregon, south to northern Baja California, east to southwest Utah and Arizona. Prehistoric remains found east to Texas, and known as a fossil form east to Florida.

Status: Endangered. Very small population slowly declining in numbers.

Estimated numbers: Minimum counts of 51 in 1966 and 52 in 1968 indicate a population of 60-80.

Breeding rate in the wild: One young every other year. If unsuccessful one year renesting usually occurs the next year. Approximately three young reach flying stage each year.

Reasons for decline: Disturbance by man, including habitat modification and shooting. Some may be killed by eating strychnine bait or strychnine poisoned animals.

Protective measures already taken: Shooting prohibited by California State law with penalties up to a year in jail or $1,000 fine or both. Use of poison prohibited on Federal lands within the range of the condor. Two sanctuaries established by the U. S. Forest Service to protect major nesting areas. Development of a condor management plan for the Los Padres National Forest by a full-time condor biologist. An annual condor survey conducted by the California Department of Fish and Game. Appointment of a condor naturalist by the National Audubon Society. Initiation of a 5-year research study by the U. S. Fish and Wildlife Service.

Measures proposed: Constant cooperation of State and Federal government and private conservation agencies in law enforcement, public education, land management, and research studies. Increased protection of nesting areas through modification of management plans, including withdrawal and closure of key areas, prohibition of firearms, meaningful restrictions on oil drilling, rerouting of trails, and purchase of private lands within the Sespe Condor Sanctuary. Determine the possible benefits of supplemental feeding either in restricting wandering or providing food during critical periods. Experiments with propagation of related South American condor are in progress at the Patuxent Wildlife Research Center near Laurel, Maryland.

Number in captivity: One in the Los Angeles Zoo. Brought to the zoo as a fledgling in February 1967 after being deserted by its parents.

Breeding potential in captivity: Unknown, but based on experience with South American condors, thought to be good. Two unmated female California condors at the National Zoo, Washington, D.C., during several decades laid about two dozen eggs.

References:

Koford, C. B., The California Condor. National Audubon Society Research Report No. 4, 1953 154 pp.

Miller, A. H., McMillan, I., McMillan, E., 1965. The Current Status and Welfare of the California Condor. National Audubon Society Research Report No. 6, 61 pp.

PERIPHERAL BIRDS

listed in Rare and Endangered Fish and Wildlife of the United States

Green-throated arctic loon (Gavia arctica viridigularis)
Breeds from Cape Prince of Wales, Alaska, west to Khatanga River, Kamchatka and Sakhalin Island, U.S.S.R. Winters south to Baltic Sea and Japan.

Northeastern least grebe (Podiceps dominicus brachypterus)
Resident from southern Texas south to Panama.

Red-faced cormorant (Phalacrocorax urile)
Breeds from Pribilof Islands and Aleutian Islands west to Komandorskie Islands and Siberia, U.S.S.R. Winters from Pribilof and Aleutian Islands south to Japan.

Eastern reddish egret (Dichromanassa r. rufescens)
Breeds along Texas coast and in Florida Keys south to Hispaniola. Winters from southern Texas south to Venezuela.

Wood ibis (Mycteria americana)
Breeds and winters from Florida and coast of Texas south along both coasts of Mexico and Central and South America, Cuba and the Dominican Republic.

Roseate spoonbill (Ajaia ajaja)
Breeds and winters from coastal Texas, Louisiana and South Florida south to Central Argentina.

Northern black-bellied tree duck (Denrocygna autumnalis fulgens)
Breeds from southeastern Arizona and Gulf Coast of Texas south to Panama. Winters from Mexico south to Panama.

Masked duck (Oxyura dominica)
Resident in Puerto Rico and Mexico south to Argentina, casual in South Texas.

Zone-tailed hawk (Buteo albonotatus)
Resident from northern Baja California, central Arizona, southwestern New Mexico, and central western Texas, southward to northern South America.

Sennett's white-tailed hawk (Buteo albicandatus hypospodius)
Resident in South Arizona and South Texas south to North Colombia and western Venezuela.

Northern gray hawk (Buteo nitidus maximus)
Breeds from South Arizona, South New Mexico and South Texas south to northern Mexico. Winters in Mexico.

Northern black hawk (Buteogallus a. anthracinus)
Resident from South Arizona, South New Mexico, and South Texas south to northern Colombia.

Northern chachalaca (Ortalis vetula macalli)
Resident from lower Rio Grande region of Texas south to northern Vera Cruz.

Richardson's blue grouse (Dendragapus obscurus richardsonii)
Resident from extreme northern Idaho and Northwest Montana to Yukon Territory.

Northern white-tailed ptarmigan (Lagopus l. leucurus)
Resident from North Yukon south to Northwest Montana.

Gould's turkey (Meleagris gallopavo mexicana)
Resident in mountains from Southwest New Mexico south to northern Jalisco, Mexico.

Northern jacana (Jacana s. spinosa)
Resident from southern Texas south to Panama.

Rufous-necked sandpiper (Erolia ruficollis)
Breeds in vicinity of Wales, western Alaska to Northeast Siberia, U.S.S.R. Winters from southern China to islands of Southwest Pacific, Australia and New Zealand.

Atlantic sooty tern (Sterna f. fuscata)
Breeds from Gulf Coast of Texas, Louisiana, Florida and Virgin Islands south to Ascension Island and South Trinidad. Nonbreeding season ranges at sea through breeding range.

Atlantic noddy tern (Anous s. stolidus)
Breeds on Dry Tortugas, Florida and West Indies south to islands of South Atlantic Ocean.

Northern Xantus' murrelet (Endomychura hypoleuca scrippsi)
Breeds from Southern California to central Baja California. Winters on coast of Southern California and Baja California.

Whiskered auklet (Aethia pygmaea)
Breeds on western Aleutian Islands west to Komandorskie Islands and southern Kurile Islands. Winters on waters surrounding breeding range.

Northern red-billed pigeon (Columba f. flavirostris)
Resident from lower Rio Grande Valley in Texas south to Nicaragua.

Northern white-fronted dove (Leptotila verreauxi angelica)
Resident in lower Rio Grande Valley of Texas south to northern Vera Cruz and Chiapas.

Florida mangrove cuckoo (Coccyzus minor maynardi)
Breeds from southeast coast of Florida to Bahama Islands and Cuba. Winters in breeding range south of Florida.

Northern Groove-billed ani (Crotophaga s. sulcirostris)
Resident from lower Rio Grande Valley in Texas to Colombia and British Guiana.

Ferruginous owl (Glaucidium brasilianum)
Resident from southern Arizona and lower Rio Grande Valley, Texas, southward in lowlands to southern South America.

West Indian nighthawk (Chordeiles minor vicinus)
Breeds in Florida Keys, Bahamas, Hispaniola and Puerto Rico. Winters presumably in south America.

Blue-throated hummingbird (Lampornis clemenciae)
Resident mountains of southern Arizona and central western Texas south to southern Mexico.

Eastern blue-throated hummingbird (Lampornis c. clemenciae)
Breeds in mountains of central western Texas south to southern Mexico. Winters in lowlands of Mexico.

Western blue-throated hummingbird (Lampornis clemenciae bessophilus)
Breeds in mountains of southeastern Arizona and southwestern New Mexico south to central western Mexico. Winters at lower elevations.

Northern buff-bellied hummingbird (Amazilia yucatanensis chalconota)
Breeds from lower Rio Grande Valley in Texas south to San Luis Potosi and Vera Cruz, Mexico. Winters in southern Tamaulipas and Vera Cruz, Mexico.

Northern violet-crowned hummingbird (Amazilia verticalis ellioti)
Breeds from southern Arizona south to Colima and Hidalgo, Mexico. Winters in Mexico.

Coppery-tailed Elegant Trogon (Trogon elegans canescens)
Breeds from central southern Arizona south to Sinaloa. Winters in Northwest Mexico.

Northeastern Elegant Trogon (Trogon elegans ambiguus)
Resident in lower Rio Grande Valley of Texas south to Isthmus of Tehuantepec, Mexico.

Northeastern green kingfisher (Chloroceryle americana septentrionalis)
Resident from southern Texas south to Guatemala and El Salvador.

Northwestern green kingfisher (Chloroceryle americana hachisukai)
Resident from central western Texas south to Nayarit, Mexico.

Northwestern rose-throated becard (Platypsaris aglaiae richmondi)
Breeds from southern Arizona south to southern Sonora, Mexico. Winters in Mexico.

Northeastern rose-throated becard (Platypsaris aglaiae gravis)
Resident from lower Rio Grande Valley, Texas, south to San Luis Potosi and North Vera Cruz, Mexico.

Northeastern tropical kingbird (Tyrannus melancholicus couchii)
Resident from extreme southern Texas south to Puebla and central Vera Cruz, Mexico.

Northwestern tropical kingbird (Tyrannus melancholicus occidentalis)
Breeds from southeastern Arizona south to Guerrero, Mexico. Winters in Guatemala.

Northern thick-billed kingbird (Tyrannus crassirostris pompalis)
Resident South Arizona and North Sonora.

Northern buff-breasted flycatcher (Empidonax fulvifrons pygmaeus)
Breeds from southeastern Arizona south to southwestern Chihuahua. Winters in Mexico.

Northeastern beardless flycatcher (Camptostoma i. imberbe)
Breeds from extreme southern Texas south to Costa Rica. Winters in Mexico and Costa Rica.

Northwestern cave swallow (Petrochelidon fulva pallida)
Breeds from Southeast New Mexico and South Central Texas, in the vicinity of certain caves, south to Coahuila and Tamaulipas, Mexico. Winter range unknown.

Couch's Mexican jay (Aphelocoma ultramarina couchii)
Resident in mountains of Big Bend of Texas south to central Nuevo Leon and Tamaulipas, Mexico.

Northern green jay (Cyanocorax yncas luxuosus)
Resident from lower Rio Grande Valley, Texas, south to Guanajuato and central Vera Cruz, Mexico.

Cascade boreal chickadee (Parus hudsonicus cascadensis)
Resident from central southern British Columbia south to central northern Washington.

Azure eastern bluebird (Sialia sialis fulva)
Resident from central southern Arizona south to southern Mexico.

Red-spotted bluethroat (Luscinia s. svecica)
Breeds from coast of northern Alaska west to northern Asia and Europe. Winters from northern Africa to Northwest India.

Cuban black-whiskered vireo (Vireo altiloquus barbatulus)
Breeds along coast of southern Florida to Bahamas, Cuba and Isle of Pines. Winters in Amazon Basin, South America.

Colima warbler (Vermivora crissalis)
Breeds from Southwest Texas to Southwest Tamaulipas, Mexico. Winters from southern Sinaloa south to Guerrero, Mexico.

Olive warbler (Peucedramus taeniatus arizonae)
Breeds from central and southeastern Arizona and southwestern New Mexico south to central Mexico.

Cuban yellow warbler (Dendroica petechia gundlachi)
Resident in lower Florida Keys, Cuba and Bahamas.

Northern olive-backed warbler (Parula pitiayumi nigrilora)
Resident from lower Rio Grande Valley, Texas, south to northern Hidalgo and northern Vera Cruz, Mexico.

Alta Mira Lichtenstein's oriole (Icterus gularis tamaulipensis)
Resident from extreme southern Texas south to Campeche, Mexico.

Audubon's black-headed oriole (Icterus graduacauda audubonii)
Breeds from southern Texas south to central Tamaulipas, Mexico. Winters in breeding range and southward to San Luis Potosi, Mexico.

Dickey's varied bunting (Passerina versicolor dickeyae)
Breeds from central southern Arizona to Colima. Winters in Northwest Mexico.

Northern white-collared seedeater (Sporophila torqueola sharpei)
Resident from extreme southern Texas south to San Luis Potosi and northern Vera Cruz.

Southeastern pine grosbeak (Pinicola enucleator eschatosus)
Breeds from northern New England north to central Quebec and Newfoundland. Winters in breeding range and occasionally south to Virginia.

Northern olive sparrow (Arremonops r. rufivirgata)
Resident from southern Texas south to eastern Coahuila and central Tamaulipas.

Arizona grasshopper sparrow (Ammodramus savannarum ammolegus)
Breeds in Southeast Arizona and North Sonora.

Northern rufous-winged sparrow (Aimophila c. carpalis)
Resident from southern Arizona south to central Sonora.

Northeastern Botteri's sparrow (Aimophila botterii texana)
Resident from lower Rio Grande Valley, Texas, south to Northeast Tamaulipas, Mexico.

Western Botteri's sparrow (Aimophila b. botterii)
Breeds from southeastern Arizona south to southern Mexico. Winters in southern part of breeding range.

STATUS-UNDETERMINED BIRDS

listed in Rare and Endangered Fish and Wildlife of the United States

California brown pelican (Pelecanus occidentalis californicus)
Breeds on Anacapa Island off the coast of California and possibly on some islands off the coast of Baja California, in the Gulf of California and south to Tres Marias Islands off Nayarit.

Red-bellied red-shouldered hawk (Buteo lineatus elegans)
Resident in Sacramento and San Joaquin Valleys and southern coastal lowlands of California south to northern Baja California.

Ferruginous hawk (Buteo regalis)
Breeds from East Washington and Southwest Manitoba south to Nevada and West Oklahoma. Winters chiefly from Southwest United States south to northern Mexico.

American osprey (Pandion haliaetus carolinensis)
Breeds from North Alaska south to Baja California and Sonora, east to South Labrador, Newfoundland and South Florida. Winters from southern United States south to South America.

Northern aplomado falcon (Falco femoralis septentrionalis)
Bred formerly from southern Arizona, southwestern New Mexico and southern Texas south to southern Mexico.

Townsend's rock ptarmigan (Lagopus mutus townsendi)
Resident on Kiska and Little Kiska and possibly Buldir Islands, Aleutian Islands.

Yunaska rock ptarmigan (Lagopus mutus yunaskensis)
Resident on Yunaska Island, possibly also Amukta Island and Islands of the Four Mountains, Aleutian Islands.

Sanford's rock ptarmigan (Lagopus mutus sanfordi)
Resident on Tanaga and Kanaga Islands, Aleutian Islands.

Dixon's rock ptarmigan (Lagopus mutus dixoni)
Resident in southern Alaska from Yakutat Bay south to Baranof and Admiralty Islands.

Columbian sharp-tailed grouse (Pedioecetes phasianellus columbianus)
Resident from north-central British Columbia south to Northwest Nevada east to West Colorado and North New Mexico.

Texas Gambel's quail (Lophortyx gambelii ignoscens)
Resident in Rio Grande Valley in western Texas.

Mountain plover (Eupoda montana)
Breeds in Great Plains from Montana and North Dakota to southeastern New Mexico and western Texas. Winters from central California, southern Arizona and central and coastal Texas south to southern Baja California.

Bristle-thighed curlew (Numenius tahitiensis)
Breeds locally in mountains of southwestern Alaska. Winters in islands of central and Southwest Pacific.

Alaskan short-billed dowitcher (Limnodromus griseus caurinus)
Breeds along south-central Alaskan coast from Nushagak Bay to Yakutat Bay. Winters south along the Pacific coast to Baja California.

Pacific bar-tailed godwit (Limosa lapponica baueri)
Breeds from Kuskokwim delta to Colville delta, western Alaska. Winters in Southwest Asia and Malaysia to Australia and New Zealand.

Red-legged kittiwake (Rissa brevirostris)
Breeds on Komandorskie and Pribilof Islands, Bering Sea. Winters on adjoining seas.

St. Thomas screech owl (Otus nudipes newtoni)
Resident on St. Thomas, St. John and St. Croix, Virgin Islands.

Florida Burrowing owl (Speotyto cunicularia floridana)
Resident prairie central and southern Florida.

Hawaiian short-eared owl (Asio flammeus sandwichensis)
Resident on all main islands of Hawaii.

Puerto Rican short-eared owl (Asio flammeus portoricensis)
Puerto Rico where apparently now localized in the area of the Anegardo Lagoon and some swamps in the west of the island.

Pribilof winter wren (Troglodytes t. alascensis)
Resident in Pribilof Islands, Alaska.

Semidi winter wren (Troglodytes t. semidiensis)
Resident on Semidi Islands, Southeast Alaska.

Unalaska winter wren (Troglodytes t. petrophilus)
Resident on Unalaska and other islands in Fox Islands, Alaska.

Kiska winter wren (Troglodytes t. kiskensis)
Resident on Kiska, Little Kiska, Amchitka, Ogliuga and Semisopochnoi Islands, Aleutian Islands.

Tanaga winter wren (Troglodytes t. tanagensis)
Resident in Andreanof Islands in the central Aleutian Islands.

Seguam winter wren (Troglodytes t. seguamensis)
Resident on Seguam, Amukta, Yunaska, Islands of the Four Mountains, Aleutian Islands.

Black-capped vireo (Vireo atricapilla)
Breeds locally from north-central Oklahoma through central Texas to central northern Mexico. Winters on the west coast of Mexico from southern Sonora to Guerrero.

Hawaii thrush (Phaeornis o. obscurus)
Resident Island of Hawaii, Hawaii.

Kauai creeper (Loxops maculatus bairdii)
Resident Island of Kauai, Hawaii.

Oahu creeper (Loxops m. maculata)
Resident Island of Oahu, Hawaii.

Maui creeper (Loxops maculata newtoni)
Resident Island of Maui, Hawaii.

Pribilof gray-crowned rosy finch (Leucosticte tephrocotis umbrina)
Resident on St. Paul, St. George, St. Matthew and Otter Islands, Bering Sea.

Wallowa gray-crowned rosy finch (Leucosticte tephrocotis wallowa)
Breeds in Wallowa Mountains, northeastern Oregon. Winters south to central western Nevada.

Puerto Rican bullfinch (Loxigilla p. portoricensis)
Puerto Rico.

Florida grasshopper sparrow (Ammodramus savannarum floridanus)
Resident central peninsula Florida.

Yakutat fox sparrow (Passerella iliaca annectens)
Breeds in coastal Alaska, in the vicinity of Yakutat Bay. Winters from Southwest British Columbia south to Southern California.

Samuel's song sparrow (Melospiza melodia samuelis)
Resident in salt marshes on northern side of San Francisco and San Pablo Bays central western California.

San Francisco song sparrow (Melospiza melodia pusillula)
Resident in salt marshes surrounding south area of San Francisco Bay, California.

Suisun song sparrow (Melospiza melodia maxillaris)
Resident in brackish marshes surrounding Suisun Bay, central California.

Amak song sparrow (Melospiza melodia amaka)
Resident on Amak Island, Aleutian Islands.

McKay's bunting (Plectrophenax hyperboreus)
Breeds on Hall and St. Matthew Islands, Bering Sea. Winters there and in western coastal Alaska.

Amphibians and Reptiles

The following list of rare and endangered amphibian and reptilian

Scientific name	Common name
AMPHIBIA	
CAUDATA (Order)	
CRYPTOBRANCHIDAE (Family) Giant Salamanders	
(Megalobatrachus japonicus japonicus)	Japanese giant salamander
(Megalobatrachus japonicus davidianus)	Chinese giant salamander
AMBYSTOMATIDAE (Family) Mole Salamanders	
(Ambystoma dumerilii dumerilii)	Lake Patzcuaro salamander
(Ambystoma lermaensis)	Lake Lerma salamander
(Ambystoma macrodactylum croceum)	Santa Cruz long-toed salamander
○(Ambystoma mexicanum)	Axototl
(Ambystoma tigrinum californiense)	
SALAMANDRIDAE (Family) Salamandrids, newts	
(Chioglossa lusitanica)	Goldstriped salamander
PLETHODONTIDAE (Family) Lungless salamanders	
(Plethodon larselli)	Larch Mountain salamander
○ (Plethodon nettingi)	Cheat Mountain salamander
○ (Typhlotriton spelaeus)	Grotto salamander
*(Typhlomolge rathbuni)	Texas blind salamander
○ (Haideotriton wallacei)	Georgia blind salamander
(Hydromantes shastae)	Shasta salamander
*(Hydromantes bruñus)	Limestone salamander
SALIENTIA (Order)	
LEIOPELMATIDAE (Family) New Zealand Frogs	
(Leiopelma archeyi)	Coromandel Leiopelma
(Leiopelma hamiltoni)	Stephen's Island Leiopelma
(Leiopelma hochstetteri)	North Island Leiopelma

○ Data sheet with biographical information unavailable.

[1] Listed as "Rare" in Rare and Endangered Fish and Wildlife of the United States.

forms is collated from the *Red Data Book* and *Rare and Endangered Fish and Wildlife of the United States.*

Location	Legal protection	Population	Status
Western part of Honshu and (limited) in Central Kyushu	–	U	R
Southwest China	–	U	I
Lake Patzcuaro, Michoacan, Mexico	–	U	R
Near Tenango, Santa Maria Jajalpa and San Pedro, Mexico	–	U	R
Valencia Lagoon, Rio del Mar near Aptos and four miles west of Watsonville, Santa Cruz County, California	–	U	E
Central West California	–	U	D
Northwest Spain and Portugal	–	U	I
Larch Mountains, Lower Columbia between Troutdale and Hood River, Oregon, United States	–	U	I
In caves of Hays County, Texas	–	U	E
Near McCloud River, U.S.F.S. Station, Southwest tip of McCloud limestone formation, Low Pass Creek, and Brock Mountain, United States	–	U	R
At the confluence of Bear Creek and Merced River and along the tributaries of Bear Creek, at altitudes of 1,200 to 2,500 feet, in the vicinity of Briceburg, Mariposa County, California	–	U	I[1]
Coromandel Peninsula New Zealand	P	U	R
Stephens and Maud Islands, New Zealand	P	U	R
Various parts of North Islands, New Zealand, including the Coromandel Peninsula	P	U	R

Scientific name	Common name
PIPIDAE (Family) Pipid Frogs	
(Xenopus gilli)	Cape platana
DISCOGLOSSIDAE (Family) Fire-bellies, midwife toads	
(Discoglossus nigriventer)	Israel discoglossus, Israel painted frog
LEPTODACTYLIDAE (Family) Leptodactylids	
○ (Batrachophrynus macrostomus)	Lake Junin frog
BUFONIDAE (Family) Toads	
(Bufo boreas nelsoni)	Amargosa toad
*(Bufo boreas exsul)	Black toad
*(Bufo houstonensis)	Houston toad
(Bufo retiformis)	Sonoran green toad
○ (Bufo superciliaris)	
○ (Nectophrynoides occidentalis)	Mount Nimba viviparous toad
HYLIDAE (Family) Tree frogs	
*(Hyla andersoni)	Pine Barrens tree frog
(Pseudacris streckeri illinoensis)	Illinois chorus frog
SOOGLOSSIDAE (Family) Seychelles frogs	
(Nesomantis thomasseti)	Seychelles frog
(Sooglossus seychellensis)	Seychelles frog
(Sooglossus gardineri)	Seychelles frog
RANIDAE (Family) True Frogs	
(Rana pipiens fisheri)	Vegas Valley leopard frog

[2] Listed as "Rare" in Rare and Endangered Fish and Wildlife of the United States.
[3] Listed as "Rare" in Rare and Endangered Fish and Wildlife of the United States.

Location	Legal protection	Population	Status
Forelands around Cape Town, South Africa	–	U	I
Lake Huleh (Hula), eastern shore, in North Israel and possibly in adjacent part of Syria	P	Possibly extinct (1955)	E
South and East Nye County and North Lincoln County, Nevada, to Owen's Valley, California	–	U	I
Deep Springs Valley, Inyo County, California	–	10,000 adults (1961)	R
Nine known isolated, relict population in Southcentral Texas	–	U	E***
Southwest Arizona to West-Central Sonora, Mexico	–	U	I
Pine barrens area of southern New Jersey, a few small colonies in North Carolina	–	U	E[2]
Sand prairie of West Central Illinois, sand prairie of extreme Southwest Missouri, adjacent Illinois and Northeast Arkansas	–	U	I
Mahe and Silhouette Islands, Seychelles, Indian Ocean	–	U	I
Mahe and Silhouette Islands, Seychelles, Indian Ocean	–	U	I
Mahe and Silhouette Islands, Seychelles, Indian Ocean	–	U	I
Vicinity of Las Vegas, Vegas Valley, Dark County, South Nevada	–	U	E[3]

Scientific name	Common name
RHACOPHORIDAE (Family) Tachophorids	
(Megalixalus seychellensis)	Seychelles tree frog
REPTILIA	
TESTUDINES (Order)	
Cryptodira	
EMYDIDAE (Family) Freshwater turtles	
(Batagur baska)	River terrapin, Tuntong
(Clemmys muhlenbergii)	Bog turtle
○(Pseudemys ornata callirostris)	South American red lined turtle
(Terrapene coahuila)	Aquatic box turtle
TESTUDINIDAE (Family) Land tortoises	
(Gopherus polyphemus agassizii)	Desert tortoise, western gopher tortoise
(Gopherus polyphemus berlandieri)	Berlandier's gopher tortoise, Texas tortoise
○ (Gopherus polyphemus flavomarginatus)	Mexican giant gopher tortoise
○ (Malacochersus tornieri)	Pancake tortoise
○ (Pyxis arachnoides)	Madagascar spider tortoise
(Testudo elephantopus elephantopus)	South Albemarle tortoise
(Testudo elephantopus abingdonii)	Abingdon saddlebacked tortoise
(Testudo elephantopus becki)	North Albemarle saddlebacked tortoise
(Testudo elephantopus chathamensis)	Chatham Island tortoise
(Testudo elephantopus darwini)	James Island tortoise
(Testudo elephantopus ephippium)	Duncan saddlebacked tortoise
(Testudo elephantopus guentheri)	Vilamil Mountain tortoise, Southwest Albemarle tortoise
(Testudo elephantopus hoodensis)	Hood saddlebacked tortoise
(Testudo elephantopus microphyes)	Tagus Cove tortoise
(Testudo elephantopus nigrita)	Indefatigable Island tortoise, Porter's black tortoise
(Testudo elephantopus phantastica)	Narborough saddlebacked tortoise
(Testudo elephantopus vandenburghi)	Cowley Mountain tortoise
(Testudo elephantopus wallacei)	Jervis Island tortoise
(Testudo geometrica)	Geometric tortoise

Location	Legal protection	Population	Status
Mahe and Praslin Islands, Seychelles, Indian Ocean	–	U	I
Southeast Asia from Bengal to Sumatra	–	U	E
Isolated freshwater marshes, meadows and bogs from Connecticut to West Pennsylvania and in Southwestern North Carolina	–	U	R
Northeast Mexico	P	U	R
Southwest U. S.	P	U	R
South Texas and Northeastern Mexico	P	U	D
Cerro Azul, eastern part of Isabela (Albemarle Island), Bermuda	P	U	E***
Minta, Abingdon Islands, Galapagos	P	U	E***
Volcano Wolf, Isabela (Albemarle Island)	P	U	E
San Cristobal (Chatham Island), Galapagos	P	69 (1969)	E***
San Salvador (James Island), Galapagos	P	"very rare or extinct" (1966)	E***
Pinzon (Duncan Island), Galapagos	P	92 (1967)	E***
Volcano Santo Tomas, Southern Isabela (Albemarle Island)	P	26 (1967)	E***
Espanola (Hood Island), Galapagos	P	U	E***
Southern slopes of Volcano Darwin, Taugus Cove, Isabela (Albemarle Island), Galapagos	P	69 (1967)	E***
Santa Cruz (Indefatigable Island), Galapagos	P	2,000 (1964)	E
Fernandina (Narborough Island), Galapagos	P	U	E
Alcedo Volcano, East Isabela (Albemarle Island), Galapagos	P	174 (1964)	E***
Rabida (Jervis Island), Galapagos	P	U	E***
South Africa (extreme southwest of Cape Province)	P	U	E

Scientific name	Common name
(Testudo graeca graeca)	Mediterranean spur-thighed tortoise
(Testudo radiata)	Radiated tortoise
○(Testudo planicauda)	Madagascar flat-shelled tortoise
(Testudo yniphora)	Madagascar tortoise
CHELONIIDAE (Family) Bea Turtles	
(Caretta caretta)	Loggerhead turtle
(Chelonia depressa)	Flatback green turtle
*(Chelonia mydas)	Green turtle
(Eretmochelys imbricata)	Hawksbill turtle
(Lepidochelys kempii)	Atlantic ridley turtle
(Lepidochelys olivacea)	Olive turtle or Pacific ridley
DERMOCHELYIDAE (Family) Leatherback Turtle	
(Dermochelys coriacea)	Leathery turtle, Luth
PLEURODIRA (Order)	
PELOMEDUSIDAE (Family) Side-necked Turtles	
○ (Podocnemis cayennensis)	Redheaded Amazon turtle
○ (Podocnemis dumeriliana)	Giant river turtle, Duméril's greaved turtle
(Podocnemis expansa)	South American river turtle, Arrau
○ (Podocnemis lewyana)	Magdalena River turtle
○ (Podocnemis madagascariensis)	Madagascar greaved turtle
(Podocnemis unifilis)	Terecay turtle
○ (Podocnemis sextuberculata)	Yellow-headed side-necked turtle
○ (Podocnemis vogli)	Orinoco greaved turtle
CHELIDAE (Family) Snake-rucked turtles	
(Pseudemydura umbrian)	Short-necked turtle, Swamp turtle

RHYNCHOCEPHALIA

SPHENODONTIDAE (Family) Tautara

[4] Listed as "Peripheral" in Rare and Endangered Fish and Wildlife of the United States.

Location	Legal protection	Population	Status
Southwestern Europe (South Spain and Pityusae Islands) and North Africa Morocco east to Cyrenaika)	–	(from "more than 5 million in Morocco" (1969)	D
South Madagascar	P	U	D
Region west of Majunga	P	U	I
Southeast coast of United States between North Carolina and Florida Keys; along coast of Natal (South Africa); coast of East Australia	P	U	D
North Australia waters	P	U	R
Tortuguero (Costa Rica); Isla Aves in Caribbean; Ascension Island in South Atlantic; Trinidad and Surinam	P	U	D[4]
Mediterranean, Atlantic, Pacific and Indian Oceans in very few places	P	U	E
Gulf of Mexico, Atlantic coast from central Florida to Massachusetts	–	world pop. of female 5,000-10,000 (1970)	E***
Indian (except for western shores), Pacific and parts of Atlantic Oceans	P	U	R
Atlantic, Pacific and Indian Oceans	P	U	E***
Throughout tropical South America	P	U	E
Colombia	P	U	D
Upper Swan and Bullbrook area, Southwest Australia	–	200-300 in Ellen Brook and Twin Swamps Reserves	E

Scientific name	Common name
(Sphenodon punctatus punctatus) (Sphenodon punctatus guntheri) (Sphenodon punctatus reischeki)	Tautars
SQUAMATA (Order)	
Sauria	
GEKKONIDAE (Family) Geckos	
(Oedura reticulata)	Reticulated velvet gecko
(Phelsuma guentheri)	Round Island day gecko
(Phelsuma newtoni)	Rodriguez day gecko
○ (Uroplatus alluaui) ○ (Uroplatus enebaui) ○ (Uroplatus fimbriatus) ○ (Uroplatus guentheri) ○ (Uroplatus lineatus) ○ (Uroplatus phantasticus)	Madagascar leaf-tailed gecko
AGAMIDAE (Family) Agamids	
○ (Amphibolurus maculatus griseus)	
○ (Gonocephalus spinipes)	Dragon lizard
(Hydrosaurus pustulatus)	Sail-fin lizard, soa-soa water lizard
IGUANIDAE (Family) Iguanids	
(Amblyrhynchus cristatus cristatus)	Narborough Island marine iguana
○ (Amblyrhynchus cristatus albemarlensis)	Albemarle marine iguana
○ (Amblyrhynchus cristatus hassi)	Santa Cruz marine iguana
○ (Amblyrhynchus cristatus mertensi)	San Cristobal marine iguana
○ (Amblyrhynchus cristatus nanus)	Genovese marine iguana
○ (Amblyrhynchus cristatus sielmanni)	Pinta marine iguana
○ (Amblyrhynchus cristatus venustissimus)	Hood Island marine iguana
(Brachylophus fasciatus)	Fiji iguana
(Conolophus pallidus)	Barrington land iguana
(Conolophus subcristatus)	Galapagos land iguana
(Crotaphytus wislizenii silus)	Blunt nosed leopard lizard, San Joaquin leopard lizard
(Cyclura baeolopha)	Andros Island ground iguana

Location	Legal protection	Population	Status
Twenty islets around the New Zealand coast	P	over 10,000	R
Southwest of West Australia	P	15 specimens known (1969)	R
Round Island, north, 25 kilometers northeast from Mauritius	–	150-200 (1970)	R
Rodrigues, east of Mauritius	–	U	E
Philippine Islands	–	U	I
Galapagos Islands, Pacific Ocean	P	U	R
Fiji and Tonga Islands, South Pacific	–	U	R
Santa Fe (Barrington, Island), south of Santa Cruz in the Galapagos	P	about 300	E***
Found on seven islands of the Galapagos Group: Fernandina (Narborough), Isabela (Albemarle), Santiago (James), Santa Cruz (Indefatigable), Seymour, and South Plaza	P	U	R
In and near San Joaquin Valley, California: Fresno, Kern, Madera, Merced, San Luis Obispo and Tulare Counties	–	U	E***
Andros Islands, Bahamas	P	in excess of 5,000 in 1961	D

Scientific name	Common name
(Cyclura carinata carinata)	Turks and Caicos ground iguana
(Cyclura carinata bartschi)	Mayaguana iguana
(Cyclura cornuta cornuta)	Rhinoceros iguana
(Cyclura cornuta stejnegeri)	Mona Island rhinoceros iguana
(Cyclura cristata)	White Cay ground iguana
(Cyclura figginsi)	Exuma Island ground iguana
(Cyclura inornata)	Allen Cays ground iguana
(Cyclura macleayi macleayi)	Cuban ground iguana
(Cyclura macleayi caymanensis)	Cayman Island iguana
(Cyclura macleayi lewisi)	Grand Cayman iguana
(Cyclura nuchalis)	Acklins Island ground iguana
(Cyclura pinguis)	Virgin Island iguana
(Cyclura ricordii)	Ricord's ground iguana
(Cyclura riley)	Watlings Island ground iguana
(Phrynosoma coronatum blainvillei)	San Diego horned lizard
LACERTIDAE (Family) Lacertids	
(Lacerta filfolensis filfolensis)	Filfola lizard
○ (Lacerta lilfordi lilfordi)	Ayre Island lizard
○ (Lacerta sicula coerulea)	Faraglione lizard
TEIIDAE (Family) Teiid lizards	
* (Ameiva polops)	St. Croix ground lizard
(Cnemidophorus hyperythrus)	Orange-throated race runner, orange-throated whiptail
SCINCIDAE (Family) Skinks	
(Leiolopisma telfairii)	Round Island skink

[5] Listed as "Peripheral" in Rare and Endangered Fish and Wildlife of the United States.

Location	Legal protection	Population	Status
Long Cay, Six Hill Cay, Pine Cay	P	thousands	D
Booby Cay and other small islands off Mayaguana, Bahamas	P	U	D
Hispaniola (Haiti and Dominican Republic), La Gouva, Petit Gonave and Beata Islands	–	more than 10,000 in the wild	D
Mona Island between Puerto Rico and Hispaniola	P	U	D
White Cay at extreme southern end of the Exuma Islands chain, Bahamas	P	fewer than 1,000	D
Bitter Guana Cay, Guana Cay off Norman Pond Cay, Prickly Pear Cay and Allen Cay, in the Exuma Islands chain, Bahamas	P	U	D
The Allen Cay group in the northern end of the Exuma Islands chain, Bahamas	P	U	D
Cuba and Isle of Pines	–	over 10,000	D
Cayman Brac and Little Cayman Islands (Jamaica)	P	over 10,000	D
Grand Cayman Island, south of Cuba	P	fewer than 30 specimens	D
Fortune Island and Guana Cay in the bight of Acklins, Bahamas	P	fewer than 1,000	D
Anegada, British Virgin Islands	P	U	D
Isla Cabritos and hills bordering Lago de Enriquillo, Dominican Republic	P	over 5,000	D
Watlings Island, and Green Cay, and White Cay off Watlings, Bahamas	P	several thousand	D
Scattered localities in southern California, U. S., and northern Maja California, Mexico	–	U	D
Filfola Island, 4 kilometers southwest of Malta	–	about 3,000 specimens all ages	R
The beach at Frederiksted, St. Croix; Protestant and Green Cays, U. S. Virgin Islands	–	about 200	D[5]
In California from Riverside south into Maja California	–	U	R
Round Island, North-northeast from Mauritius	–	U	R

Scientific name	Common name
◯ (Macroscincus coctaei)	Cape Verde giant skink
◯ (Scelotes braueri)	Seychelle Island skink
◯ (Scelotes veseyfitzgeraldi)	Seychelle Island skink
◯ (Tiliqua adelaidensis)	Miniature blue-tongued skink
ANGUIDAE (Family) Anguid lizards	
(Gerrhonotus panamintinus)	Panamint alligator lizard
ANNIELLIDAE (Family) Legless lizards	
(Aniella pulchra nigra)	Black legless lizard, California legless lizard
XENOSAURIDAE (Family) Xenosauarids, Shinisaurids	
◯ (Shinisaurus crocodilurus)	Chinese crocodile lizard
HELODERMATIDAE (Family) Gila monsters, beaded lizards	
(Heloderma horridum horridum)	Mexican beaded lizard }
(Heloderma horridum alvarezi)	Chiapan beaded lizard }
(Heloderma horridum exasperatum)	Rio Fuerto beaded lizard }
◯ (Heloderma suspectum suspectum)	Reticulated gila monster
◯ (Heloderma suspectum cinctum)	Banded gila monster
VARANIDAE (Family) Monitor lizards	
◯ (Varanus griseus caspius)	
(Varanus komodoensis)	Komodo dragon, Komodo Island monitor
SERPENTES (Order)	
BOIDAE (Family) Giant snakes	
◯ (Acrantophis dumerili)	Dumeril's Madagascar boa
◯ (Acrantophis madagascariensis)	Madagascar boa
(Bolyeria multocarinata)	Round Island boa
(Casarea dussumieri)	Round Island boa or keel-scaled boa
◯ (Epicrates angulifer)	Cuban boa
(Epicrates inornatus)	Puerto Rican boa
◯ (Epicrates subflavus)	Jamaica boa
◯ (Python molurus molurus)	Indian python
◯ (Python molurus bivittatus)	Burmese python
(Sanzinia madagascariensis)	Madagascar boa, Sanzinia

Location	Legal protection	Population	Status
Mountains east of Sierra Nevada, Surprise Canyon on Telescope Peak and an isolated location some 40 miles northwest	–	U	I
Antioch, near San Francisco Bay, California, south to northern Baja California	–	U	E
Pacific drainage, from central Sinaloa to Acapetagua in Chiapas, central depressions of Chiapas and the arid central Guatemala, and South Sonora and Sinaloa.	P	U	I
Komodo, Rintja, Padar Islands and west coast of Flores, Indonesia	P	2,000–5,000	R
Round Island 15 miles northwest of Mauritius	–	U	R
Round Island 15 miles northwest of Mauritius	–	50	R
Puerto Rico	–	200– (P.R.)	E

Scientific name	Common name
COLUBRIDAE (Family) Colubrid snakes	
○(Elaphe triaspis)	Mexican rat snake, neo-tropical rat snake
ALLIGATORIDAL (Family) Alligators, caimans	
(Alligator mississippiensis)	American alligator, Mississippi alligator
(Alligator sinensis)	China alligator
(Caiman crocodilus crocodilus)	Spectacled caiman
○ (Caiman crocodilus apaporiensis)	Rio Apaporis caiman
(Caiman crocodilus fuscus)	Magdalena caiman, Central American caiman
○ (Caiman crocodilus yacare)	Paraguay caiman
○(Caiman latirostris)	Broad-nosed caiman
(Melanosuchus niger)	Black caiman
○ (Paleosuchus palpebrosus)	Dwarf caiman
○ (Paleosuchus trigonatus)	Smooth-fronted caiman
CROCODYLIDAE (Family) Crocodiles, false gavial	
*(Crocodylus acutus)	American crocodile
(Crocodylus cataphractus)	African slender-snouted crocodile
(Crocodylus intermedius)	Orinoco crocodile
(Crocodylus johnsoni)	Australian freshwater crocodile
(Crocodylus moreletii)	Morelet's crocodile
(Crocodylus niloticus)	Nilotic crocodile, Nile crocodile
(Crocodylus novaeguineae novaeguineae)	New Guinean crocodile
○ (Crocodylus novaeguineae mindorensis)	Mindoro crocodile
○ (Crocodylus palustris palustris)	Mugger, marsh crocodile
○ (Crocodylus palustris kimbula)	Ceylon crocodile
(Crocodylus porosus)	Estuarine crocodile, saltwater crocodile
(Crocodylus rhombifer)	Cuban crocodile
○ (Crocodylus siamensis)	Siamese crocodile
○ (Osteolaemus tetraspis)	West African dwarf crocodile
○ (Tomistoma schlegelii)	False gavial

[6] Listed as "Peripheral" in Rare and Endangered Fish and Wildlife of the United States.

Location	Legal protection	Population	Status
Texas (Corpus Christi) on coast to North Carolina (Tyrrell County), north in Mississippi drainage to Arkansas and Southeast Oklahoma	P	U	E***
Wuhu in Anhwei Province, Changhsing in Chekiang, and along small section of lower reaches of the Yangtze River	–	U	I
Venezuela, Guianas and Lower Amazon River	–	U	E
Colombia	–	U	E
Peru, Ecuador, Brazil, Colombia	–	U	E
Florida, Colombia, Mexico, British Honduras and Venezuela	P	U	E[6]
Colombia	–	U	D
Northeast Australia from the Kimberley Division of the state of Western Australia east to the Northern Territory and the north of the state of Queensland	P	U	R
Central America (east coast of Mexico, British Honduras and Guatemala)	–	U	E***
Africa	–	U	E
Swamps of Territory of Papua and New Guinea	–	U	R
South India, Ceylon, Sunda Archipelago, Philippines, Moluccas, Timar-Laut, Arucanc Kei Islands, Papua-New Guinea, Bismarck Archipelago, Solomon Islands, New Hebrides, Northern Australia	P	U	R
Swamps of Zapata Peninsula, Cuba	P	500 estimate (1965)	E***

Scientific name	Common name
GAVIALIDAE (Family) Gavial	
○ (Gavialis gangeticus)	Gavial
○ (Langaha nasuta)	Madagascar rear-fanged snake
○ (Masticophis flagellum ruddocki)	San Joaquin whipsnake
(Masticophis lateralis euryxanthus)	Alameda striped racer
○ (Natrix sipedon insularum)	Lake Erie water snake
(Thamnophis elegans gigas)	Giant garter snake
(Thamnophis elegans hammondi)	Two-striped garter snake
(Thamnophis sirtalis tetrataenia)	San Francisco garter snake

STATUS-UNDETERMINED AMPHIBIANS AND REPTILES

listed in Rare and Endangered Fish and Wildlife of the United States

Georgia blind salamander (Haideotriton wallacei)
Shasta salamander (Hydromantes shastae)
Larch mountain salamander (Plethodon larselli)
Cheat mountain salamander (Plethodon nettingi)
Jemez mountain salamander (Plethodon neomexicanus)
Grotto salamander (Typhlotriton spelaeus)
Amargosa toad (Bufo boreas nelsoni)
Illinois chorus frog (Pseudacris streckeri illinoensis)

Location	Legal protection	Population	Status
Coast range of California, near San Francisco Bay	–	U	I
Great Valley of California, United States south of Sacramento	–	U	D
Coastal mountains and slope from Monterey Bay, California, through the Sierra San Pedro Martir in northern Baja California, Mexico	–	U	D
San Francisco area	–	U	E***

Desert tortoise (Gopherus agassizi)
Key blacksnake (Coluber constrictor haasti)
Lake Erie water snake (Natrix sipedon insularum)
Giant garter snake (Thamnophis elegans gigas)
Two-striped garter snake (Thamnophis elegans hammondi)
Arizona ridge-nosed rattlesnake (Crotalus willardi willardi)
Black Legless Lizard (Anniella pulchra nigra)
Gila Monster (Heloderma suspectum)

BOX 2-3A.

ENDANGERED

AMERICAN ALLIGATOR (Alligator mississippiensis) (Daudin)

Order: CROCODILLA Family: CROCODILIDAE

Distinguishing characteristics: Huge, roughbacked reptile, with a broad rounded snout; fourth tooth on lower jaw fits into notch in upper jaw.

Present distribution: Tyrrell County, North Carolina, on coast to Corpus Christi, Texas, North in Mississippi drainage to Arkansas and Southeast Oklahoma.

Former distribution: To Rio Grande in Texas.

Status: Endangered by heavy poaching. "Seems to be increasing in numbers in Everglades" (Duellman and Schwartz); probably declining slightly in other parts of range.

Estimated numbers: Unknown.

Breeding rate in the wild: Once a year; 15-85 eggs per nesting female.

Reasons for decline: Heavy poaching by collectors of commercial skins; destruction of habitat; young heavily subject to predator and human pressure.

Protective measures already taken: Protected by law in every state where found except Texas; in Texas six counties have established protective legislation. Florida spends about $300,000 a year on alligator law enforcement; Louisiana now spends $100,000 a year for enforcement, research, and sanctuary care. (Alligator Symposium, 1968)

Measures proposed: The Alligator Symposium, made up of individuals interested in the protection and survival of the alligator, indicated the following measures as desirable: (1) Elimination of markets for alligator hides, (2) provision of additional funds for law enforcement, (3) establishment of added reserves, sanctuaries, and management areas, (4) increase in education of public concerning problem, (5) establishment of central clearing house for information on alligators, (6) increase in basic research on biology of species, and (7) strengthened legislation on local and national levels.

Number in captivity: Probably thousands. The alligator farm in Buena Park, California, alone, probably has several thousand. There are 35 registered alligator farmers in Louisiana; Florida has many so-called "farms." These farms are usually only holding pens for animals captured in the wild, and the alligator is not yet truly farmed in the sense of breeding, hatching, and raising individuals to a size suitable for sale or skinning. The latter may soon be achieved in refuge areas, where successful cropping of wild populations will soon be appropriate, both for restocking depleted areas and for skins.

Breeding potentialities in captivity: Good—extensively cultivated in some places.

References:

Duellman and Schwartz, Amphibians and Reptiles of Southern Florida, Bull. Fla. St. Mus., 3, 1958.
J. Oliver, Natural History of North American Amphibians and Reptiles, 1955.
Francis Harper (FH).
Alligator Symposium, Winter Park, Florida, September 6, 1968.

Fishes

Fish are neither as approachable nor as easily identified as mammals and birds. Consequently, we know less concerning their survival status and their endangered list is comparatively shorter.

The following list of endangered fishes is collated from the *Red Data Book* and *Rare and Endangered Fish and Wildlife of the United States.*

Scientific name	Common name
PISCES	
ASCIPENSERIFORMES (Order)	
ACIPENSERIDAE (Family) Sturgeons	
*(Acipenser brevirostrum)	Shortnose sturgeon
*(Acipenser fulvescens)	Lake sturgeon
*(Acipenser oxyrhynchus)	Atlantic sturgeon
(Acipenser schrencki)	Amur sturgeon
(Huso dauricus)	Kaluga
OSTEOGLOSSIFORMES (Order)	
OSTEOGLOSSIDAE (Family) Bonytongues	
(Scleropages formosus)	Asian bonytongue
SALMONIFORMES (Order)	
SALMONIDAE (Family) Trouts, whitefishes, graylings	
*(Coregonus alpenae)	Longjaw cisco
‡(Coregonus johannae)	Deepwater cisco
‡(Coregonus n. nigripinnis)	Blackfin cisco
(Salmo chrysogaster)	Mexican golden trout
*(Salmo clarki henshawi)	Lahontan cutthroat trout
*(Salmo clarki seleniris)	Piute cutthroat trout
*(Salmo clarki stomias)	Greenback cutthroat trout
(Salmo clarki utah)	Bonneville cutthroat trout
(Salmo clarki virginalis)	Rio Grande cutthroat trout
*(Salmo clarki subsp.)	Humboldt cutthroat trout
(Salmo gairdneri gilberti)	Kern rainbow trout
*(Salmo gilae)	Gila trout
(Salmo platycephalus)	Ala balik
(Salmo sp.)	Apache trout
‡(Salmo salar)	Atlantic salmon
*(Salvelinus alpinus aureolus)	Sunapee trout
*Salvelinus alpinus oquassa)	Blueback trout

[1] Rated "Endangered"
[2] Rated "Endangered"
[3] Rated "Endangered"
[4] Rated "Rare"
} in Rare and Endangered Fish and Wildlife of the United States.

Location	Legal protection	Population	Status
St. John River, New Brunswick, Canada, Hudson River, New York	–	U	Eq R[1]
Great Lakes	P	U	R
Atlantic Coast	–	U	R
Amur River and Gulf, U.S.S.R.	P	2000+	R
Basin of Amur River and Gulf	P	2000+	R
Streams and lakes of Borneo, Banka and Sumatra		2000–	D
Lakes Michigan, Huron, Erie	–	U	E
Unknown if extant	–	U	R
Unknown if extant in Lakes Michigan and Huron	–	U	R
Rio Fuerte, Sinaloa, Culiacan	–	U	R
Independence Lake, California and four other Western streams	P	5-6000	R[2]
Two tributaries to Silver King Creek, California	–	1-200	E
Unknown	–	10	E***
Reservoir Canyon, Utah	–	2-300	E
Trinehera Ranch to Rio Grande, Colorado	–	U	R
20-30 small tributaries in Humboldt River, Nevada	–	few thousand	R[3]
Little Kern River, California	–	few thousand	R
Gila Creek, Gila River, New Mexico	–	U	E
Zamanti River, Turkey	–	U	E***
Salt River drainage of White Mountains, Fort Apache Indian Reservation, Arizona	–	U	E
Eight coastal streams, Maine Ord, Deep and Firebox Creek, Arizona	–	U	E
Flood's Pond, Maine, Tewksbury Pond, New Hampshire	–	U	E[4]
Lakes of headwaters, St. John and Penobscot Rivers, Maine	–	U	R

Scientific name	Common name
(Stenodus leucichthys leucichthys)	Beloribitsa
‡(Thymallus arctictus)	Arctic grayling
UMBRIDAE (Family) Mudminnows	
*(Novumbra hubbsi)	Olympic mudminnow
CYPRINIFORMES (Order)	
CYPRINIDAE (Family) Minnows, carps	
(Acanthorutilus handlirschi)	Cicek
*(Eremichthys acros)	Desert dace
*(Gila cypha)	Humpback chub
*(Gila (Siphateles) mohavensis)	Mohave chub
*(Lepidomeda albivallis)	White River spinedace
‡(Lepidomeda vittata)	Little Colorado spinedace
(Meda fulgida)	Spikedace
*(Moapa coriacea)	Moapa dace
(Plagopterus argentissimus)	Woundfin
(Probarbus jullieni)	Ikan temoleh-pla eesok (Thai) Ikan temelian (Malay)
(Tanakia tanago)	Miyako tanago or Tokyo bitterling
(Tylognathus klatti)	
CATOSTOMIDAE (Family) Suckers	
*(Catostomus microps)	Modoc sucker
*(Chasmistes brevirostris)	Shortnose sucker
(Chasmistes cujus)	Cui-ui
COBITIDAE (Family) Loaches	
(Hymenophysa curta)	Ayumodoki
SILURIFORMES (Order)	
ICTALURIDAE (Family) North American catfishes	
(Prietella phreatophila)	Mexican blindcat
*(Satan eurystomus)	Widemouth blindcat
*(Trogloglanis pattersoni)	Toothless blindcat

[5] Rated "Endangered" in Rare and Endangered Fish and Wildlife of the United States.
[6] Rated "Undetermined" in Rare and Endangered Fish and Wildlife of the United States.
[7] Rated "Undetermined" in Rare and Endangered Fish and Wildlife of the United States.
[8] Rated "Endangered" in Rare and Endangered Fish and Wildlife of the United States.

Location	Legal protection	Population	Status
Caspian Sea	–	2000–	R
Lakes in Montanta, Utah, Wyoming, Washington, Colorado	–	U	R
Puget Sound, Olympic Peninsula, Washington	–	U	R
Lake Egridir, Turkey	–	U	E***
Soldier Meadows, Nevada	–	100,000	R[5]
Green and Colorado Rivers, Utah and Colorado	–	U	E
Zzyzx Mineral Springs Resort, California	–	U	R[6]
White River, Nevada	–	U	R[7]
East Clear Creek, tributary Clear Creek, tributary Little Colorado River	–	fewer than 1,000 (1963)	E
Salt River, Upper Gila River, New Mexico	P	U	E
Moapa River, Nevada	–	500–1000	R[8]
Virgin River, Utah	–	U	E***
Menam River (Thailand), Mecong River (Cambodia, Laos, Vietnam), Pahang Rivers (Malaya)	–	2500	D
Kanto district, Japan	–	U	E
Lakes Egridir, Golcuk, Turkey	–	U	E
Rush Creek, California	–	U	E[9]
Copco Reservoir, California	–	U	E[10]
Pyramid Lake, Nevada	P	U	R
Lake Biwa, Yodo River, few rivers in Okayama, Japan	–	U	E
Well at base of Sierra de Santa Rosa, Mexico	–	U	E
Artesian wells of Edwards Limestone, Texas	–	U	R[11]
Artesian wells in or near San Antonio, Texas	–	U	R[12]

[9] Rated "Undetermined" in Rare and Endangered Fish and Wildlife of the United States.
[10] Rated "Undetermined" in Rare and Endangered Fish and Wildlife of the United States.
[11] Rated "Undetermined" in Rare and Endangered Fish and Wildlife of the United States.
[12] Rated "Undetermined" in Rare and Endangered Fish and Wildlife of the United States.

Scientific name	Common name
BAGRIDAE (Family) Asiatic catfishes	
(Coreobagrus ichikawai)	Nekogigi
SCHILBEIDAE (Family) Oriental Catfishes	
(Pangasianodon gigas)	Giant catfish
(Pangasius sanitwongsei)	Catfish
PERCOPSIFORMES (Order)	
AMBLYOPSIDAE (Family) Cavefishes	
(Amblyspsis rosae)	Ozark cavefish
ATHERINIFORMES (Order)	
CYPRINODONTIDAE (Family) Killifishes	
(Cynolebias constanciae)	
(Cynolebias marmoratus)	
(Cynolebias minimus	
(Cynolebias opalescens)	
(Cynolebias splendens)	
(Cyprinodon diabolis)	Devils Hole pupfish
(Cyprinodon elegans)	Comanche Springs pupfish
(Cyprinodon nevadensis calidae)	Tecopa pupfish
*(Cyprinodon nevadensis miononectes)	Nevada pupfish
(Cyprinodon nevadensis pectoralis)	Warm Spring pupfish
(Cyprinodon radiosus)	Owens Valley pupfish
(Empetrichthys latos)	Pahrump killifish
(Kosswigichthys asquamatus)	Scaleless killifish
(Micropanchax schoelleri)	
(Orestias cuvieri)	
POECILIDAE (Family) Livebearers	
(Gambusia gaigei)	Big Bend gambusia
(Gambusia heterochir)	Clear Creek gambusia
*(Gambusia nobilis)	Pecos gambusia

[13] Rated "Undetermined" in Rare and Endangered Fish and Wildlife of the United States.
[14] Rated "Undetermined" in Rare and Endangered Fish and Wildlife of the United States.

Location	Legal protection	Population	Status
Miya River, Japan	–	U	E
Mecong River Basin	–	very few	E
Largest rivers in basin of the Menam Chao Phoya, Thailand	–	2000 –	E
Few caves and wells in Southwest Missouri and Northwest Arkansas	–	U	R
Single pond east of Rio de Janeiro, Brazil	–	U	I
Ditches along old Petropolis Road at foot of Organ Mountains, near Rio de Janeiro, Brazil	–	U	I
Ditches near Rio de Janeiro, Brazil	–	U	I
	–	U	I
	–	U	I
Single pool in Ash Meadows, Nevada	–	300-800	R
Outflow of Phantom Lake Springs, Texas	–	U	R
Reservoir, small creek flowing from well at Jed's Motel, Tecopa Hot Springs, California	–	U	E
Warm springs of Ash Meadows, Nevada	–	500-20,000	R[13]
Schoolhouse and Scruggs Springs, Nevada	–	U	E
Marshy pool 10 miles north of Bishop, California	P	U	R
Spring-fed pool on Manse (Bowman) Ranch Pahrump Valley, Nevada	–	1300 (1967)	E***
Lake Hazer, Turkey	–	many thousands	D
Lake Chad basin	–	U	I
Lake Titicaca	–	U	I
Big Bend National Park, Texas	–	1000±	R
Headwaters of Clear Creek, Texas	–	1,000 –	R
Ditches about Toyahvale and spring near Fort Stockton, Texas	–	U	E[14]

Scientific name	Common name
(Gambusia sp. nov.)	San Marcos gambusia
(Poeciliopsis occidentalis occidentalis)	Gila topminnow
(Xiphophorus couchianus)	Monterrey platyfish
ATHERINIDAE (Family) Silversides	
*(Menidia extensa)	Waccamaw silverside
NEOSTETHIDAE (Family)	
(Gulaphallus mirabilis)	
(Neostethus siamensis)	
PHALLOSTETHIDAE (Family)	
(Phallostethus dunckeri)	
(Phenacostethus smithi)	
GASTEROSTEIFORMES (Order)	
GASTEROSTEIDAE (Family) Sticklebacks	
(Gasterosteus aculeatus williamsoni)	Unarmored threespine stickleback
SCORPAENIFORMES (Order)	
COTTIDAE (Family) Sculpins	
*(Cottus asperrimus)	Rough sculpin
PERCIFORMES (Order)	
CENTRARCHIDAE (Family)	
*(Ambloplites cavifrons)	Roanoke bass
(Micropterus notius)	Suwannee Bass

Location	Legal protection	Population	Status
San Marcos River, U. S. Mexico	–	1000	R
2 locations in Arizona	–	U	E***
3 locations in Nuevo Leon, Mexico	–	1000 –	R
Lake Waccamaw, North Carolina	–	U	I
Philippines	–	U	I
Unknown	–	U	I
Muar River, Malay Peninsula	–	U	I
Canals in Bangkok, Thailand	–	U	I
Headwaters of the Santa Clara River, California	–	U	E
Pit River port of Sacramento River, California	–	U	I
Tar and Neuse River watersheds, North Carolina	–	U	I
Ichtucknee Springs and adjacent springs, Florida	–	U	I

BOX 2-4. Sample Biography

RARE

ATLANTIC STURGEON (Acipenser oxyrhynchus) Mitchill, 1814

Order: ACIPENSERIFORMES Family: ACIPENSERIDAE

Distinguishing characteristics: A large sturgeon (adults average over 100 pounds), olive gray in color, snout nearly as long as head, short barbels midway between snout tip and mouth, with bony shields of the mid-dorsal line touching or overlapping.

Present distribution: Atlantic Coast from the St. Lawrence River to northern Florida and along the northern Gulf Coast.

Former distribution: Same as present.

Status: Rare. Commercial catch declined from 726,000 pounds recorded from ten states in 1908 to 170,000 pounds from fourteen states in 1962. Maine catch declined from an annual catch of eight to ten thousand pounds fifty to sixty years ago to one or two fish presently.

Estimated numbers: Unknown. About 1,700 adults were taken in 1962.

Fecundity: Adult females produce from a million to 2½ million eggs per year.

Reasons for decline: Pollution of rivers and estuaries and obstructions in spawning streams.

Protective measures already taken: Some states have imposed commercial fishing restrictions. Measures which are being taken to improve conditions for Atlantic salmon, striped bass and shad will aid in sturgeon restoration.

Measures proposed: Pollution abatement, improved fish passage facilities and stream flow fluctuation control.

Number in captivity: Unknown.

Culture potential in captivity: In both the United States and Europe sturgeon culture has been almost a complete failure.

Remarks: Growth is slow in rivers and estuaries. Seven- to eight-year-old fish are from 24 to 34 inches long. Growth rate increases rapidly after they go to sea where eleven- to twelve-year-old fish reach 75 to 100 inches in length. Data submitted by the Maine Department of Inland Fisheries and Game, Division of Fishery Research and Management.

References:

Bigelow, Henry B., and Schroeder, William G. Fishes of the Gulf of Maine. U. S. Fish and Wildlife Service, Fishery Bulletin 74, Vol. 53, 1953, pp. 80–84.

Breder, Charles M. Field Book of Marine Fishes of the Atlantic Coast. G. P. Putnam's Sons, N.Y., 1929, pp. 41–42.

Dees, Lola T. Sturgeons. U. S. Fish and Wildlife Service Fishery Leaflet 526, 1961, 8 pp.

PERIPHERAL FISHES

listed in Rare and Endangered Fish and Wildlife of the United States

Mexican stoneroller (Campostoma orantum)
Big Bend region of Rio Grande in Texas and in limited range in Arizona; common in Mexico.

Sonora chub (Gila ditaenia)
Rio de la Concepcion in Mexico; Sycamore Canyon, Coronado National Forest, southern Arizona.

Chihuahua shiner (Notropis chihuahua)
Rio Grande drainage in Texas and Mexico.

Rio Grande darter (Etheostoma grahami)
Tributaries of the Rio Grande in Mexico and Texas.

STATUS-UNDETERMINED FISHES

listed in Rare and Endangered Fish and Wildlife of the United States

White sturgeon (Acipenser transmontanus)
West Coast.

Pallid sturgeon (Scaphirhynchus albus)
Mississippi Valley.

Shortnose cisco (Coregonus reighardi)
Lake Superior, Lake Michigan and Lake Ontario.

Colorado cutthroat trout (Salmo clarki pleuriticus)
Headwaters of the Colorado River.

Utah cutthroat trout (Salmo clarki utah)
Utah, west of Wasatch Mountains, and White Pine County in Nevada.

Yellowfin cutthroat trout (Salmo clarki macdonaldi)
Twin Lakes, Colorado.

Eagle Lake rainbow trout (Salmo gairdnerii aquilarum)
Eagle Lake and other waters in Lassen and Modoc Counties, California.

Thicktail chub (Gila crassicauda)
Formerly in lower Sacramento and San Joaquin Rivers in California.

Yaqui chub (Gila purpurea)
San Bernardino Creek of Yaqui River in Arizona.

White River spinedace (Lepidomeda albivallis)
Springs in White Pine and Nye Counties, Nevada.

Kanawha minnow (Phenacobius teretulus)
Kanawha River in West Virginia, Virginia, and North Carolina.

Mohave chub (Siphateles mohavensis)
Mohave River and pool near Baker, California.

Lost River sucker (Catostomus luxatus)
Klamath Lakes in Oregon and California.

June sucker (Chasmistes liorus)
Utah Lake, Utah.

Modoc sucker (Catostomus microps)
Rush Creek in Modoc County, California.

Shortnose sucker (Chasmistes brevirostris)
Klamath and Tule Lake System in California and Oregon.

Rustyside sucker (Moxostoma hamiltoni)
Roanoke River in Virginia.

Humpback sucker (Xyrauchen texanus)
Colorado System in Arizona and California.

Widemouth blindcat (Satan eurystomus)
Artesian wells at San Antonio, Texas.

Toothless blindcat (Trogloglanis pattersoni)
Artesian wells at San Antonio, Texas.

Nevada pupfish (Cyprinodon nevadensis)
Desert springs in Nye County, Nevada, and San Bernardino County, California.

Salt Creek pupfish (Cyprinodon salinus)
Salt Creek in Death Valley, California.

Waccamaw killifish (Fundulus waccamensis)
Lake Waccamaw in North Carolina.

Pecos gambusia (Gambusia nobilis)
Pecos River System in Texas and New Mexico.

Unarmored threespine stickleback (Gasterosterus aculeatus williamsoni)
Headwaters of Santa Clara River in California.

Roanoke bass (Ambloplites cavifrons)
Roanoke River in Virginia.

Sacramento perch (Archoplites interruptus)
Lakes in California, Nebraska, Arizona, Nevada and Utah.

Guadalupe bass (Micropterus treculi)
Colorado River, San Marcos River and Guadalupe River, and western tributaries of the Brazos River in Texas.

Blenny darter (Etheostoma blennius)
Tennessee River System in Tennessee and Alabama.

Fountain darter (Etheostoma fonticola)
San Marcos and Comal Springs in Texas.

Tuckasegee darter (Etheostoma gutselli)
Tennessee River System in Tennessee and North Carolina.

Waccamaw darter (Etheostoma perlongum)
Lake Waccamaw in North Carolina.

Backwater darter (Etheostoma zoniferum)
Catoma and Big Swamp Creeks near Montgomery, Alabama.

Yellow darter (Percina aurantiaca)
Tennessee River System in Tennessee, North Carolina and Virginia.

Bluestripe darter (Percina cymatotaenia)
Southern Missouri and northern Arkansas.

Freckled darter (Percina lenticula)
Alabama River System in Alabama and Georgia.

Longnose darter (Percina nasuta)
Southern Missouri, northern Arkansas, and eastern Oklahoma.

Sharpnose darter (Percina oxyrhyncha)
Mountain streams of Kanawha River drainage in Virginia and West Virginia.

Leopard darter (Percina pantherina)
Little River System in Oklahoma and Arkansas.

Slenderhead darter (Percina phoxocephala)
In a few streams in the Mississippi River system.

Olive darter (Percina squamata)
Tennessee River System in Tennessee and North Carolina.

Tidewater goby (Eucyclogobius newberryi)
Corte Madera Creek in California.

Rough sculpin (Cottus asperrimus)
Few tributaries of Pit River in Shasta and Modoc Counties, California.

Tidewater silverside (Menidia beryllina)
Atlantic Coast.

Waccamaw silverside (Menidia extensa)
Lake Waccamaw in North Carolina.

SELECTED BIBLIOGRAPHY

Although articles abound on individual forms, not many books have been written on the general problem of endangered species. The *Red Data Book* contains an exhaustive bibliography of expert studies on just about every endangered species and subspecies listed in its pages.

References

Rare and Endangered Fish and Wildlife of the United States, Committee on Rare and Endangered Wildlife Species, Bureau of Sport Fisheries and Wildlife, U. S. Department of the Interior, Revised Edition, Washington, D.C., 1968.

The definitive listing of endangered forms native and peripheral to the fauna of the United States. The bureau of Sport Fisheries and Wildlife is presently considering a new five-volume format which may be retitled *Wildlife Data Book.* For further information concerning this publication and endangered U. S. species, write to the Office of Endangered Species, Bureau of Sports Fisheries and Wildlife, U. S. Department of the Interior, Washington, D.C. 20402.

Red Data Book, Vol. 1 (Mammalia), Vol. 2 (Aves), Vol. 3 (Amphibia & Reptilia), Vol. 4 (Pisces), Survival Service Commission, International Union for the Conservation of Nature and Natural Resources, Morges, Switzerland, 1966.

The *sine qua non* of animal conservation. A complete international listing of every form identified as endangered. For further information write the Survival Service Commission, IUCN, 1110 Morges, Switzerland.

Standard Texts

Allen, G. M., *Extinct and Vanishing Mammals of the Western Hemisphere with the Marine Species of All the Oceans,* American Committee for International Wildlife Protection, New York, 1942. Individual biographies of extinct and vanishing mammal forms.

Greenway, J. C., *Extinct and Vanishing Birds of the World,* American Committee for International Wildlife Protection, New York, 1958.

Individual accounts of extinct and vanishing bird forms with good bibliography and list of museums where extinct birds can be found.

Harper, F., *Extinct and Vanishing Mammals of the Old World,* American Committee for International Wildlife Protection, New York, 1945.

Individual biographies of extinct and vanishing mammal forms.

Popular Books

Fisher, J., Simon, N., and Vincent, J., *Wildlife in Danger,* Viking, New York, 1969.

An excellent popular treatment of the critically endangered forms listed in the *Red Data Book* by three expert members of the IUCN's Survival Service Commission. The best of its kind.

Prince Philip, Duke of Edinburgh, and Fisher, J., *Wildlife Crisis,* Cowles, New York, 1970.

A less rigorous book than the above but sufficient.

Ziswiler, Vincenz, *Extinct and Vanishing Animals,* Springer-Verlag, New York, 1967.

A brief, direct survey of the causes of animal extinction with lists of mammals and birds which have become extinct since 1600.

Organizations

Friends of Animals, Inc.
11 West Sixtieth Street
New York, N.Y. 10023

Activist pressure group which lobbies in support of animal conservation and against needless slaughter of certain species.

International Union for the Conservation of Nature and Natural Resources
1110 Morges
Switzerland

The clearing house for animal conservation on the international scale.

The World Wildlife Fund
1110 Morges
Switzerland

American Office:
Suite 728
910 Seventeenth Street, N.W.
Washington, D.C. 20006

Works with the advice of the IUCN on certain critical conservation problems; specifically—conservation of endangered habitats, preservation of critically endangered species, encouragement of conservation programs in critical regions or countries.

III Pollution

1. AIR

There are between 5 and 6 quadrillion tons of air in the earth's atmosphere and no more. Air cannot be increased but it is constantly recycled. Wind, rain and temperature changes combine to purify the air and keep it moving. Globally, air pollution has not yet had a lethal effect. The air crisis is mainly restricted to the industrial West whose ambient effluence rises into the skies in ever-increasing tonnage. The United States, for example, by far the number one ravager of the atmosphere, launched approximately 200 million tons of pollutants in 1968 (Table 3-1, 2). As ominous as this statistic appears, it is dwarfed by those residual 5 or 6 quadrillion tons of air, a figure 25 or 30 million times larger. And since some major pollutants tend to disappear in a matter of days while others portend no evil in their accumulations, the weight factor is misleading (Figure 3-1).

Toxicity and climatic effects are the more telling measures of air pollution, putting aside the most immediate oppression—aesthetics. There is considerable evidence building which identifies air pollution as a killer—directly in specific incidents and indirectly as an abettor of certain respiratory conditions; and even when air pollution doesn't kill, it can inflict various levels of discomfort.

Climatically, there is some fear among scientists that a prolonged increase in the amount of carbon dioxide (resulting from the conversion of carbon monoxide) could affect the earth's heat balance (there has already been a slight worldwide rise in temperature in recent decades), the ultimate consequence of which would be the melting of the icecaps and the flooding of the land.

Principle Types of Air Pollutants[1]

Carbon Monoxide (CO)—a colorless, odorless, tasteless and poisonous gas, slightly lighter than air, that is produced by the incomplete combustion of the carbon in fuels. Carbon monoxide is emitted into the atmosphere in larger quantities than any other urban air pollutant.

[1]Descriptions of air pollutants are taken from the *First Annual Report of the Council on Environmental Quality,* 1970, with slight emendations.

TABLE 3-1. Estimated Emissions of Air Pollutants by Weight, Nationwide, 1969
(In millions of tons per year)

Source	CO	Particulates	SO_x	HC	NO_x	Total	Percent change 1968-69[1]
Transportation	111.5	0.8	1.1	19.8	11.2	144.4	−1.0
Fuel combustion in stationary sources	1.8	7.2	24.4	.9	10.0	44.3	+2.5
Industrial processes	12.0	14.4	7.5	5.5	.2	39.6	+7.3
Solid waste disposal	7.9	1.4	.2	2.0	.4	11.9	−1.0
Miscellaneous	18.2	11.4	.2	9.2	2.0	41.0	+18.5
Total	**151.4**	**35.2**	**33.4**	**37.4**	**23.8**	**281.2**	**+3.2**
Percent change	**+1.3**	**+10.7**	**+5.7**	**+1.1**	**+4.8**		

[1]Computed by the 1969 method from the difference between 1969 estimates and 1968 estimates. The new method results in higher values for 1968 than those computed by EPA for 1968.
Source: The Mitre Corp. MTR-6013. Based on Environmental Protection Agency data.

TABLE 3-2. Industry Pollution (Partial List)
(In millions of tons per year)

Source	Tonnage	Pollutants
Cement manufacture	.85	Particulates
Coal cleaning and refuse	2.35	Particulates, sulphur oxides, carbon monoxide
Coke (in steel manufacture)	2.2	Particulates, sulphur oxides, carbon monoxide
Grain mills and handling	1.1	Particulates
Iron foundries	3.7	Particulates and carbon monoxide
Iron and steel mills	1.8	Particulates and carbon monoxide
Kraft pulp and paper mills	3.3	Particulates, carbon monoxide, sulphur oxides
Pertroleum refining	4.2	Particulates, sulphur oxides, hydrocarbons, carbon monoxide
Phosphate fertilizer plants	.3	Particulates and fluorides
Smelters (aluminum, copper, lead, zinc)	4.15	Particulates and sulphur oxides

Source: After Esposito, Vanishing Air, Grossman, 1970.

Background concentrations from CO (from natural and technological sources) are presently estimated in the range from .029 to 1.15 milligrams per cubic meter (mg/m^3), that is, .025 to 1 part per million (ppm).

The mean residence time of atmospheric CO has been estimated to be between one month and five years.

Almost two-thirds of the carbon monoxide which ascends annually

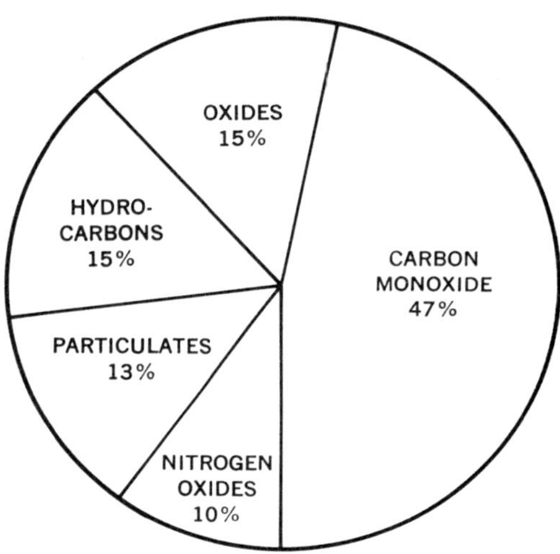

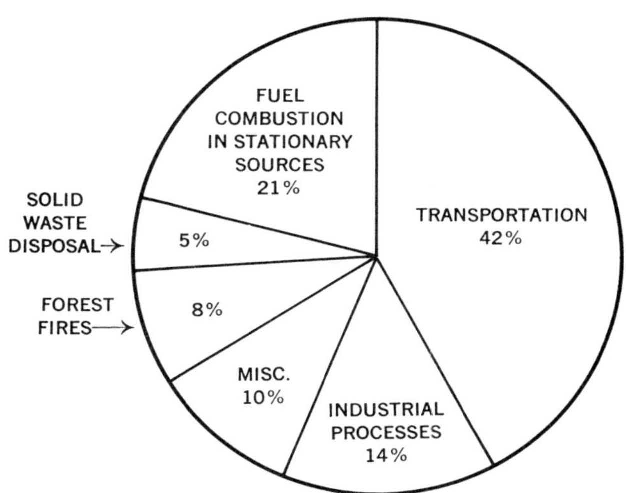

FIGURE 3-1. Air Pollution Emissions in the United States, 1968. Percentage by Weight

Source: National Air Pollution Control Administration, HEW

into American air space comes from internal combustion engines, mainly from gasoline-powered motor vehicles. Carbon monoxide emissions can be prevented by supplying enough air to insure complete combustion.

Globally, CO does not threaten the atmosphere in the long range view. However, CO's rate of conversion to carbon dioxide (CO_2) is unknown and so the accumulation of CO bears watching.

Particulate Matter includes particles of solid or liquid substances in a very wide range of sizes, from those visible as soot and smoke to microscopic particles. Particulates may be so small that they stay in the air for long periods and can be transported great distances by the winds. Dust from volcanic eruptions of Krakatoa and Agung, for example, once circled the globe.

Some common particulates—fluorides, beryllium, lead, asbestos—are directly toxic, although not at levels routinely found in the atmosphere today.

Particulates are produced primarily by stationary fuel combustion, industrial processes, forest fires and miscellaneous sources.

Established techniques for controlling particulates include filtering, washing, centrifugal separation and electrostatic precipitation. Complete removal of the very finest particles is technically difficult as well as expensive.

Globally, particulates present no danger as long as they are evenly dispersed. Very large or very intense concentrations, however, can affect the weather by altering the earth's albedo and the altitude at which heat is released in the atmosphere.

Sulphur Oxides (SO_x)—acrid, corrosive, poisonous gases produced when fuel containing sulphur is burned. Electric utilities and industrial plants are the principal producers since their most abundant fuels are coal and oil, which contain sulphur as an impurity.

About two-thirds of the nation's sulphur oxides are emitted in urban areas. Factories and apartment buildings are big offenders. Densely populated cities with cold winters are especially prone to have large emission rates (Table 3-3).

Sulphur dioxide (SO_2) is the most prevalent oxide. It is a nonflammable, nonexplosive colorless gas that most people can taste at concentrations from .3 ppm to 1 ppm (about .9 mg/m^3 to 3 mg/m^3) in air. In the atmosphere, sulphur dioxide is partly converted to sulphur trioxide or to sulphuric acid and its salts by photochemical or catalytic processes.

The degree of oxidations of sulphur dioxide in the atmosphere is dependent on a number of factors, including residence time, amount of moisture present and the intensity and duration of sunlight and its

TABLE 3-3. Annual Arithmetic Average of Sulfur Dioxide Concentrations (ppm) for 30 Cities (1964–1969)*

	1964	1965	1966	1967	1968	1969	Increase or decrease from previous year
New York City	0.171	0.143	0.134	0.139	0.15	0.11	−.04
Philadelphia	0.080#	0.084	0.091	0.098	0.077	0.075	−.002
Dayton	0.047#	0.053	0.055	0.064	0.069	0.070	+.001
Boston	0.023#	0.026	0.061	0.045	0.046	0.069	+.023
Providence	0.043	0.042	N.A.	0.015	0.021	0.046	+.025
Washington, D.C.	0.047	0.046	0.044	0.045	0.037	0.035	−.002
St. Louis	0.059#	0.047	0.043	0.029	0.028	0.034	+.006
New Haven	0.017	N.A.	0.038	0.052	0.042	0.032	−.01
Pittsburgh	0.034	0.034	0.035	0.025	0.029	0.029	NONE
Newark	0.078	0.055	0.066	0.049	0.043	0.029	−.014
Chicago	0.060#	0.050	0.053	0.043	0.028	0.026	−.002
Cleveland	0.033	0.034	0.029	0.023	0.032	0.025	−.007
Baltimore	0.038	0.032	0.040	N.A.	N.A.	0.022	NONE
Hartford	0.031	0.028	0.024	0.032	0.021	0.021	NONE
Detroit	0.009	0.003	0.006	0.016	0.025	0.021	−.004
Youngstown	0.024	0.022	0.025	0.022	0.016	0.020	+.004
Los Angeles County	0.011	0.015	0.016	0.020	0.023	0.019	−.004
Indianapolis	0.025	0.018	0.020	0.020	0.015	0.016	+.001
Seattle	0.013	0.013	0.013	0.008	0.010	0.013	+.003
Charleston	0.009	0.006	0.010	0.012	0.011	0.013	+.002
Denver	N.A.	0.018	0.011	0.005	0.013	0.010	−.003
Minneapolis	0.010	0.013	0.018	0.018	0.011	0.010	−.001
Salt Lake City	0.006	0.004	0.007	0.006	0.006	0.010	+.004
Nashville	0.008	0.009	N.A.	0.009	0.011	0.008	−.003
Des Moines	0.005	0.004	N.A.	0.006	0.005	0.006	+.001
Milwaukee	0.008	0.006	0.011	0.016	0.015	0.006	−.009
Kansas City	0.003	0.002	0.005	0.005	0.004	0.005	+.001
Chattanooga	0.017	0.012	0.013	0.011	0.011	0.005	−.006
Houston	N.A.	N.A.	N.A.	0.007	0.005	0.005	NONE
Buffalo	0.014	0.015	0.010	N.A.	0.010	0.004	−.006

*Data from National Air Sampling Network, Division of Air Quality and Emission Data, NAPCA, unless noted (#). In these cases, data is from county or city air pollution control agency.

spectral distribution. The amounts of catalytic material, hydrocarbons and nitrogen oxides, and the amounts of sorptive and alkaline materials present also affect the oxidation process.

Sulphur dioxide has been involved in major pollution emergencies (Donora, Pennsylvania, 1948; London, 1942; New York, 1966) which resulted in alarming increases in death rates.

Sulphur oxide emissions can be reduced in three ways: (1) switching to low-sulphur fuels (less than 1 percent sulphur); (2) removing sulphur from fuels entirely and (3) removing sulphur oxides from the combustion gases.

Globally, sulphur dioxide does not pose grave danger. Much of it is oxidized or neutralized by airborne alkalies. Rain washes away the sulphur salts. All told, sulphur dioxide lasts probably less than fifty days in the atmosphere. But locally, it is the most toxic and dangerous pollutant of the air.

Hydrocarbons (HC)—like carbon monoxide—represent unburned and wasted fuel. Unlike carbon monoxide, gaseous hydrocarbons at concentrations normally found in the atmosphere are not toxic, but they are a major pollutant because they assist in forming photochemical smog. More than half the tonnage of hydrocarbons produced each year comes from transportation sources, mainly gasoline-fueled vehicles.

The control of hydrocarbon emissions rests upon the basic principles of: (1) combustion process optimization, (2) recovery by mass transfer principles, (3) restriction of evaporative loss and (4) process material and fuel substitution. The first three principles are all applied with varying degrees of success in the control of automobile emissions.

Nitrogen Oxides (NO_x) are produced when fuel is burned at very high temperatures.

Internal combustion engines operate at very high temperatures, and so do efficient, large electric power and industrial boilers. Nitrogen that is ordinarily inert combines with oxygen in high temperature flames and tends to stay combined if the exhaust gases are cooled too quickly. The control of NO_x from stationary sources requires careful adjustment of flame and stack gas temperatures. Control of nitrogen oxides from automobiles is more difficult because reducing other pollutants can increase the output of NO_x.

Globally, nitrogen oxides are not expected to do serious damage in the atmosphere in the near future.

Under the influence of sunlight, nitrogen oxides combine with gaseous hydrocarbons to form a complex variety of secondary pollutants called *photochemical oxidants.* These oxidants, together with solid and liquid particles in the air, make up what is commonly known as smog.

Photochemical Oxidants result from a complex series of atmospheric reactions initiated by sunlight. When reactive organic substances and nitrogen oxides accumulate in the atmosphere and are exposed to the ultraviolet component of sunlight, the formation of new compounds, including ozone and peroxyacyl nitrates, takes place.

Since photochemical oxidants are the products of atmospheric chemical reactions, the relationship between precursor emissions and atmospheric oxidant concentrations is much less direct than is the case for primary pollutants. A further complicating situation is the dependence of these photochemical reactions on intensity and duration of sunlight, and on temperature.

Globally, the accumulation of photochemical air pollution is not likely to be hazardous for several years.

Air Pollution and Human Health

Air pollution kills. This statement is no longer a slogan to be accepted or rejected according to one's disposition. It is a medical fact. Numerous studies indicate a definite correspondence between the increase in pollution ratings and the rise in respiratory disease deaths. Cardiovascular disease, infant mortality rates and the death rates of those over sixty-five have also been linked with air pollution.[2] Emphysema is the fastest growing cause of death in the United States. Lung

TABLE 3-4. Health Effects Attributed to Specific Pollutants

Air pollutant	Effects
Particulates	speed chemical reactions; obscure vision; corrode metals; cause grime on belongings and buildings; aggravate lung illness
Sulfur Oxides	cause acute and chronic leaf injury; attack wide variety of trees; irritate upper respiratory tract; destroy paint pigments; erode statuary; corrode metals; ruin hosiery; harm textiles; disintegrate book pages and leather
Hydrocarbons (in solid and gaseous states)	may be cancer-producing (carcinogenic); retard plant growth; cause abnormal leaf and bud development
Carbon Monoxide	causes headaches, dizziness, nausea; absorbed into blood, reduces oxygen content; impairs mental processes
Nitrogen Oxides	cause visible leaf damage; irritate eyes and nose; stunt plant growth even when not causing visible damage; create brown haze; corrode metals
Oxidants: Ozone	discolors upper surface of leaves of many crops, trees, shrubs; damages and fades textiles; reduces athletic performance; hastens cracking of rubber; disturbs lung function; irritates eyes, nose, throat; induces coughing
PAN (peroxyacetyl nitrate)	discolors lower leaf surface; irritates eyes; disturbs lung function

Source: HEW, National Air Pollution Control Administration, The Effects of Air Pollution, No. 1556, revised 1967. [2]NAPCA, Air Pollution Injury to Vegetation, No. AP-71, 1970. [3]American Association for the Advancement of Science, Air Conservation, Pub. No. 80, 1965. [4]National Tuberculosis and Respiratory Disease Association, Air Pollution Primer, 1969.

[2]Lester B. Lave and Eugene Seskin, *Air Pollution and Human Health,* (*Science,* Vol. 169, No. 3947, pp. 723–33).

TABLE 3-4a. Effects of Air Pollutants

	Receptors					
Air pollutants	**Health**	**Materials**	**Soiling**	**Esthetics**	**Vegetation**	**Animal**
Particulates	X	X	X	X	X	X
Sulfur oxides	X	X		X	X	X
Oxidants	X	X		X	X	
Carbon monoxide	X					
Hydrocarbons	X			X	X	
Nitrogen oxides	X	X		X	X	
Fluorides	X				X	X
Lead	X				X	X
Polycyclic, organic matter	X					X
Odors (including hydrogen sulfide)		X		X		
Asbestos	X					
Beryllium	X				X	X
Hydrogen chloride	X	X			X	
Chlorine	X	X			X	X
Arsenic	X				X	X
Cadmium	X					X
Vanadium	X					
Nickel	X					
Manganese	X					
Zinc	X					X
Copper	X					
Barium	X					
Boron	X					
Mercury	X	X			X	X
Selenium	X					X
Chromium	X	X				
Pesticides	X				X	X
Radioactive substances	X					X
Aeroallergens	X					

Source: Environmental Protection Agency.

cancer has increased a hundredfold in Great Britain in the last sixty years.

Epidemiologically then, the problem of air pollution is real. Fortunately, disasters involving high casualties are rare. However, we are not certain at this stage in the research what the long-term consequences of urban air pollution will be. We are the first air-polluted generation. What comes after us we do not know. The findings recorded in Tables 3-4, 5, 6 as to the present effects of air pollution, do not allow for much cheer.

TABLE 3-5. Air Pollutants with Recognized or Potential Long-term Effects on Health at Usual Air-pollution Levels

Substances with known effects on health (acute or chronic)	Substances thought to have long-term effects per se[a]	Potential long-term effects of combinations
Arsenic	Arsenic (arsenical dermatitis)	
Asbestos	Asbestos (asbestosis, mesothelioma)	
Beryllium	Beryllium (berylliosis)	Be + F (fluorides potentiate pulmonary changes in berylliosis)
Carbon monoxide		Synergistic in pO_2 depression
Carcinogens		Carcinogens produce tumours in presence of promotors
Fluoride	Fluoride (fluorosis)	Fluoride (promotes or accelerates lung disease)
Hydrocarbons		HC + $O_3 \rightarrow$ tumorigen + influenza $\rightarrow$ cancer
Hydrogen sulfide (possibly with mercaptans)		Antagonizes pollutants (strictly speaking not detrimental to health)
Inorganic particulates	Inorganic particulates (pulmonary sclerosis)	
Lead		
Nitric oxide		
Nitrogen dioxide	Nitrogen dioxide (mild accelerator of lung tumours)	NO_2 + micro-organisms (pneumonia) + HNO_3 (bronchiolitis, fibrosa obliterans) + tars (smoker's lung cancer)
Organic oxidants (peroxyacylnitrates)		
Organic particulates (asthmagenic agents)	Asthmagenic agents (asthma)	
Ozone	Ozone (chronic lung changes, accelerated aging)	O_3 + micro-organisms (lung-tumour accelerator)
Sulfur dioxide, sulfur trioxide		SO_2, SO_3 + particulates aggravate lung disease

[a] Effects are given in parentheses.
Source: Research into Environmental Pollution, World Health Organization, 1968.

TABLE 3-6. Adverse Health Affects of Major Air Pollutants (October 1970)

Pollutant	Conc. level producing adverse health effects	Adverse health effects
Carbon Monoxide (CO)	(1) 58 mg/m^3 (50 ppm) for 90 minutes (similar effects upon exposures to 10 to 17 mg/m^3 (10 to 15 ppm) for 8 or more hours).	(1) Impaired time interval discrimination.
	(2) Effects upon equivalent exposure to 35 mg/m^3 (30 ppm) for 8 or more hours.	(2) Impaired performance in psychomotor tests.
	(3) Effects upon equivalent exposure to 35 mg/m^3 (30 ppm) for 8 or more hours.	(3) Increase in visual threshold.
Particulates and Sulfur Oxides	(1) 80–100 μg/m^3 particulates (annual geometric mean) with sulfation levels of about 0.3 mg/cm^2-mo.	(1) Increased death rates for persons over 50 years of age.
	(2) 130 μg/m^3 (0.046 ppm) of SO_2 (annual mean) accompanied by particulate concentrations of 130 μg/m^3.	(2) Increased frequency and severity of respiratory diseases in school children.
	(3) 190 μg/m^3 (0.068 ppm) of SO_2 (annual mean) accompanied by particulate concentrations of about 177 μg/m^3.	(3) Increased frequency and severity of respiratory diseases in school children.
	(4) 105–265 μg/m^3 (0.037 to 0.092 ppm) of SO_2 (annual mean) accompanied by particulate concentrations of 185 μg/m^3.	(4) Increased frequency of respiratory symptoms and lung disease.
	(5) 140–260 μg/m^3 (0.05–0.09 ppm) of SO_2 (24-hour average).	(5) Increased illness rate of older persons with severe chronic.
	(6) 300–500 μg/m^3 (0.11–0.19 ppm) of SO_2 (24-hour mean) with low particulate levels.	(6) Increased hospital admissions for respiratory disease and absenteeism from work of older persons.
	(7) 300 μg/m^3 particulates for 24 hours accompanied by SO_2 concentrations of 630 μg/m^3 (0.22 ppm).	(7) Chronic bronchitis patients suffer acute worsening of symptoms.
Photochemical Oxidants	(1) In excess of 130 μg/m^3 (0.07 ppm).	(1) Impairment of performance by student athletes.
	(2) 490 μg/m^3 (0.25 ppm) maximum daily value. (This value would be expected to be associated with a maximum hourly average concentration as low as 300 μg/m^3 (0.15 ppm).	(2) Aggravation of asthma attacks.
	(3) 200 μg/m^3 (0.1 ppm) maximum daily value.	(3) Eye irritation.

Source: Air Quality Criteria Documents' Sum Public Health Service, 1970.

Research reporting adverse health effect data

(1) Beard, R. R., and Wertheim, G. A.—"Behavioral Impairment Associated with Small Doses of Carbon Monoxide", Amer. J. Public Health, 57:2012-2022, November 1967.

(2) Schulte, J. H.—"Effects of Mild Carbon Monoxide Intoxication", Arch. Environ. Health 7(5):524-530, November 1963.

(3) McFarland, R. A., et al.—"The Effects of Carbon Monoxide and Altitude on Visual Thresholds", Aviation Med. 15(6):381-394, December 1944.

(1) Winkelstein, W.—"The Relationship of Air Pollution and Economic Status to Total Mortality and Selected Respiratory System Mortality in Man", Arch. Environ. Health 14:162-169, 1967.

(2) Douglas, J. W. B., & Waller, R. E.—"Air Pollution and Respiratory Infection in Children", Brit. J. Prevent. Soc. Med. 20:1-8, 1966.

(3) Lunn, J. E., Knowelden, J., and Handyside, A. J.—"Patterns of Respiratory Illness in Sheffield Infant School Children", Brit. J. Prevent. Soc. Med. 21:7-16, 1967.

(4) Petrilli, R. L., Agnese, G., and Kanitz, S.—"Epidemiology Studies of Air Pollution Effects in Genoa, Italy", Arch. Environ. Health 12:733-740, 1966.

(5) Carnow, B. W., Lepper, M. H., Shekelle, R. B., and Stamler, J.—"The Chicago Air Pollution Study: SO_2 Levels and Acute Illness in Patients with Chronic Bronchopulmonary Disease", Arch. Environ. Health 18:768-776, 1969.

(6) Brasser, L. J., Joosting, P. E., and Von Zuilen, D.—"Sulfur Dioxide—To What Level Is It Acceptable?", Research Institute for Public Health Engineering, Delft, Netherlands, Report G-300, July 1967.

(7) Lawther, P. J.—"Climate: Air Pollution and Chronic Bronchitis", Proc. Roy Soc. Med. 51:262-264, 1958.

(1) Wayne, W. S., Wehrle, P. F., and Carroll, R. E.—"Oxidant Air Pollution and Athletic Performance", J. Amer. Med. Assoc. 199(12):901-904, March 20, 1967.

(2) Schoettlin, C. E., and Landau, E.—"Air Pollution and Asthmatic Attacks in the Los Angeles Area", Public Health Reports 76:545-548, 1961.

(3) Renzetti, N. A., and Gobram, V.—"Studies of Eye Irritation Due to Los Angeles Smog 1954-1956", Air Pollution Foundation, San Marino, Calif., July 1957.

Air Pollution Ratings

It is presently impossible to obtain true air pollution ratings for U.S. cities. The reason is twofold: (1) methodologically, no system has yet been devised which can accurately measure the total air pollution mix swirling together in the skies in ever-changing ratios; (2) physically, not enough testing equipment has been spread around in any case, a situation that also serves to impede the measurement of specific pollutants. Thus, those lists that attempt to rank cities according to their over-all air quality are scientifically suspect. Until someone discovers an air pollution index which can account for the variables of place, time, toxicity, the interaction between different pollutants, temperature, relative humidity, sunlight, the concentration of pollutants and topographical and meteorological characteristics, not to mention health effects, economics and aesthetics, city rankings must remain very rough estimates.

The last attempt at a nationwide ranking was in 1967. Despite the risks entailed in air pollution comparisons, the Public Health Service of the Department of Health, Education and Welfare issued a document entitled "Relative Severity of Air Pollution in the 65 Standard Metropolitan Statistical Areas with Industrial Populations of 40,000 or More" (Table 3-7).

Several significant qualifications were listed: (1) air pollution is not the same from place to place or even necessarily from time to time in the same place; (2) optimum areas for measuring air pollution do not coincide with political boundaries and therefore a Standard Metropolitan Statistical Area—"a socially and economically integrated area with a central city (or twin central cities) containing 10,000 or more"—is introduced; (3) adequate data on photochemical smog is lacking; (4) the list is not static and (5) the available data in every case is not the most desirable.

What this document did was total up eight air pollution factors (dealing only with particulates, sulphur oxides, hydrocarbons and carbon monoxides)—to which were assigned equal weight on a descending scale of severity from 65 down—for each of the 65 Standard Metropolitan Statistical Areas. The addition was expressed in a Rank Sum. While this sort of rating game was scientifically imprecise for reasons cited above, it was at least suggestive. Without stressing the inaccuracy of the Rank Sums, it would not be rash to suppose New York's air pollution worse than Worcester's or Worcester's worse than Wichita's.

Mindful of the difficulties in establishing a multiple-pollutant air quality index which would allow for a comparative measurement of cities, four National Air Pollution Control Administration scientists recently made a tentative stab in that uncharted direction. In a paper entitled "The Development and Utilization of an Air Quality Index," the group supplied known emissions data for sulphur oxides, carbon monoxides and total particulates with a diffusion model to arrive at

TABLE 3-7. Relative Severity of Air Pollution in the 65 Standard Metropolitan Statistical Areas with Industrial Population of 40,000 or more

SMSA	Rank sum	SMSA	Rank sum
New York	457½	Nashville	253
Chicago	422	San Francisco-Oakland	253
Philadelphia	404½	Seattle	252½
Los Angeles-Long Beach	393½	†Lawrence-Haverhill	
Cleveland	390½	New Haven	246
Pittsburgh	390	York	246
Boston	389	Springfield-Chicopee-Holyoke	241
Newark	376½	Allentown-Bethlehem-Easton	239
Detroit	370	Worcester	234½
St. Louis	369	Houston	233½
Gary-Hammond-East Chicago	368½	Chattanooga	232½
Akron	367½	Memphis	232
Baltimore	355	Columbus, Ohio	231½
Indianapolis	351	Richmond	230½
Wilmington	342	San Jose	217½
Louisville	338	Portland, Oregon	210½
Jersey City	333½	Syracuse	209
Washington	327½	Atlanta	208
Cincinnati	325½	Grand Rapids	204
Milwaukee	301½	Rochester	200½
*Paterson-Clifton-Passaic	304	Reading	196½
*Canton	302	Albany-Schenectady-Troy	187½
Youngstown-Warren	294½	Lancaster	181
Toledo	287	Dallas	178
Kansas City	285½	Flint	171½
Dayton	280	New Orleans	160½
Denver	280	Fort Worth	156½
Bridgeport	261	San Diego	151½
Providence-Pawtucket	261	Utica-Rome	130
Buffalo	260	Miami	117
Birmingham	259½	Wichita	102
Minneapolis-St. Paul	257	High Point-Greensboro	87
Hartford	254½		

*Paterson-Clifton-Passaic and Canton are tentatively listed below Milwaukee despite the fact that the Rank Sum for these SMSA's is greater than Milwaukee's. The sulfur dioxide data available for these areas has been used in making the table despite the fact that too little of it is available. Giving these data equal weight with the rest of the sulfur dioxide data is unreasonable, and the National Center believes that adequate sulfur dioxide data would put the two SMSA's in question into the positions they occupy.

†Gasoline data is lacking for Lawrence-Haverhill. Its position in the list is tentative and a matter of judgment based on the six available factors and an estimate of the gasoline factors.

Source: Public Health Service, 1967.

"gross ambient concentrations for a particular pollutant in a community." These concentrations were then standardized into individual pollutant indexes which were added together to produce a single Air Quality Index. "This paper," wrote the authors, "presents a method that would relate any predicted concentration under consideration, regardless of pollutant, to a standard reference group. Such a method is the first step toward achievement of a multi-pollutant Air Quality Index." Table 3-8 lists twenty-nine major metropolitan areas according to the new quality index worked out in the joint study.

SELECTED BIBLIOGRAPHY

American Association for the Advancement of Science, *Air Conservation,* 1965. Study of air pollution with emphasis on public policy, present scientific knowledge.

Carr, D., *The Breath of Life,* W. W. Norton & Co., Inc., New York, 1965. A general discussion of air pollution.

TABLE 3-8. Air Quality Index for Various Metropolitan Areas Pollutant–index

Metropolitan area	SO_x	CO	Particulate	Air quality index
Chicago	54.93	42.03	53.73	150.69
New York	48.83	56.93	32.23	137.99
Detroit	44.43	43.83	41.93	130.19
Steubenville	56.43	23.43	46.23	126.09
Philadelphia	44.73	43.03	34.73	122.49
Los Angeles	25.53	65.33	27.43	118.29
Birmingham	24.13	27.83	65.23	117.19
Cleveland	40.63	33.73	42.03	116.39
St. Louis	38.83	38.43	34.73	111.99
Boston	40.33	38.43	30.93	109.69
Pittsburgh	39.03	27.23	42.53	108.79
Louisville	38.13	27.13	41.93	107.19
Buffalo	39.23	28.63	39.03	106.89
Cincinnati	38.53	28.13	31.73	98.39
San Francisco	24.93	43.63	26.83	95.39
Baltimore	30.03	31.63	31.33	92.99
Washington	29.63	27.13	24.63	91.39
Dayton	26.63	25.33	34.83	86.79
Milwaukee	28.73	27.63	29.83	86.19
Hartford	30.63	29.63	25.73	85.99
Providence	28.43	30.53	25.23	84.19
Minneapolis-St. Paul	27.63	31.23	25.03	83.89
Indianapolis	26.33	29.03	27.83	83.19
Kansas City	24.93	28.03	25.83	78.79
Houston	23.73	26.33	27.73	77.79
Denver	22.93	29.83	24.73	77.49
San Antonio	21.83	23.03	26.93	71.79
Dallas	22.03	26.03	23.23	71.29
Seattle-Tacoma	24.33	23.73	22.23	70.29

Source: Fensterstock, Goodman, Duggan and Baker, "The Development and Utilization of an Air Quality Index," unpublished, 1969.

Department of Health, Education and Welfare, *Air Quality Criteria for Carbon Monoxide,* Washington, D.C., 1970.
Air Quality Criteria for Particulate Matter, Washington, D.C., 1969.
Air Quality Criteria from Chemical Oxidants, Washington, D.C., 1970.
Air Quality Criteria for Sulphur Oxides, Washington, D.C., 1969.
Department of Health, Education and Welfare, "Relative Severity of Air Pollution in 65 Standard Metropolitan Statistical Areas With Industrial Populations of 40,000 or More," Washington, D.C., 1967. The most recent comparative national ranking of cities on air pollution. Precision of comparison highly questionable.
Environmental Protection Agency, "National Primary and Secondary Ambient Air Quality Standards and Air Pollution Controls," *Federal Register,* Vol. 36, No. 21, Part II, pp. 1502–15, Washington, D.C., January 30, 1971.
Esposito, J. C., *Vanishing Air,* Grossman, New York, 1970. Ralph Nader's study group reports on air pollution. Excellent history of the failure of air pollution control.
Fensterstock, J. C.; Goodman, K.; Duggan, G. M.; and Baker, W. S., "The Development and Utilization of an Air Quality Index," Unpublished, 1969.
Lave, L. B., and Seskin, E., "Air Pollution and Human Health," *Science Magazine,* Vol. 169, No. 3947, pp. 723–33. A detailed academic overview with broad documentation.
National Tuberculosis and Respiratory Disease Association, *Air Pollution Primer,* New York, 1969. Pamphlet guide to health dangers of air pollution.
Population Reference Bureau. "The Thin Slice of Life." *Population Bulletin,* Vol. XXIV, No. 5 (December 1968). 24pp.
U. S. Department of Health, Education and Welfare. *National Conference on Air Pollution: Proceedings.* Government Printing Office, Washington, D.C., 1963.
The proceedings of a conference on air pollution at which many approaches to the problems were presented.
World Health Organization, *Research into Environment Pollution,* Geneva, 1968. Excellent booklet outlining basic pollution concerns by group of international scientists.

2. RIVERS, LAKES AND STREAMS

Water pollution is just as insidious a national problem as air pollution. American rivers, lakes and beaches are incontestably fouled, even more so than our skies (Table 3-9, 9a, 10; Map 3-1). Hardly any major water body is exempt. "The only conspicuously unsullied streams in the country," writes Gladwin Hill in *The New York Times* (March 17, 1970), "are the few that have been insulated in the Federal 'Wild Rivers' wilderness preservation program."

People may not be dying from polluted waters (despite the impure quality of drinking water that obtains in many areas) but the potential health hazards are there nonetheless. For no one knows exactly the long term effect of the mounting chemical ingredients in our water supplies.

Unless something is done about water pollution, and rather swiftly, there is the distinct possibility that we will run out of usable water in the United States. Fresh water is a limited quantity and the demand for it rises every year (Figures 3-3, 4; Table 3-11). Scientist Georg

TABLE 3-9. Polluted Lakes and Rivers in the United States

Percent of stream miles polluted in regions of the United States

	Percent		Percent
Northern Plains	42	Southern Plains	29
Northeast	40	Pacific States	25
Lake States	35	Southeast	8

Official ratings on some major waterways

[Percentage of miles polluted]

Kansas River	90	North Platte River (Nebraska)	30
Lower Missouri River	90	San Joaquin River (California)	25
Calument River (Illinois, Indiana)	90	Upper Colorado River	25
James River (North Dakota, South Dakota)	80	Lake Huron, western shore	25
Illinois River	80	Lake Ontario	25
Grand River (Michigan)	80	Yellowstone River	20
Kennebec River (Maine)	70	Susquehanna River (Pennsylvania, Maryland)	20
Red River of the North (Minnesota, North Dakota)	70	Middle Hudson River	20
Lower Platte River (Nebraska)	70	Lake Huron, northern shore	20
Lake Michigan, western shore	70	Lower Columbia River	20
Washita River (Oklahoma)	70	Kentucky River	20
Upper Snake River (Idaho)	65	Upper Missouri River	15
Narragansett Bay	65	Potomac River	15
Monongahela River (Pennsylvania, West Virginia)	65	Cumberland River (Tennessee, Kentucky)	15
Lake Erie, western shore	60	Sacramento River	15
Housatonic River (Connecticut, Massachusetts)	55	Upper Mississippi, Rock Island to Cairo, Illinois	10
Fox River (Wisconsin)	50	Arkansas River	10
San Francisco Bay	50	Lower Tombigbee River (Alabama, Mississippi)	10
North Canadian River (Oklahoma)	50	Pee Dee River (North Carolina, South Carolina)	10
Des Moines/Skunk Rivers	50	Upper Chesapeake Bay	10
Lower Hudson River	50	Lake Michigan, northern shore	10
Savannah River	50	Mobile Bay	10
Lower Colorado River	50	Lake Superior	8
Red River from Denison, Texas, to Mississippi River	40	St. Croix River (Minnesota, Wisconsin)	5
Mohawk River (New York)	40	Little Colorado River (Arizona)	2
Rock River (Illinois, Wisconsin)	40	White River (Arkansas)	2
Allegheny River (Pennsylvania)	40	Middle Mississippi River, Cairo, Illinois, to Helena, Arkansas	2
Ohio River	40	Lower Mississippi, Helena, Arkansas, to Natchez	1
Central Snake River	35	Quachita River (Louisiana, Arkansas)	0
Connecticut River	35	St. Johns River (Florida)	0
Lake Ontario	30	Tampa Bay	0
Genesee River (New York)	30		
Wabash River (Indiana, Illinois)	30		
Rio Grande	30		

Source: Water Quality Administration.

TABLE 3-9a. Estimated Prevalence of Water Pollution, by Region, 1970

Region	Percent of stream miles polluted	Percent of watersheds polluted			
		Predominantly polluted[1]	Extensively polluted[2]	Locally polluted[3]	Slightly polluted[4]
Pacific Coast	33.9	14.8	59.3	22.2	3.7
Northern Plains	40.0	37.5	33.3	25.0	4.2
Southern Plains	38.8	27.3	51.5	18.2	6.1
Southeast	23.3	14.3	41.1	16.1	28.6
Central	36.6	23.2	51.8	21.4	3.6
Northeast	43.9	36.1	55.6	5.6	2.8
East of Mississippi River	31.6	23.0	48.7	15.5	12.8
West of Mississippi River	35.5	24.1	47.1	20.7	4.6
United States	32.6	23.7	48.5	17.7	9.9

[1]Predominantly polluted: $\geq 50\%$ of stream miles polluted.
[2]Extensively polluted: 20–49.9% of stream miles polluted.
[3]Locally polluted: 10–19.9% of stream miles polluted.
[4]Slightly polluted: $\leq 10\%$ of stream miles polluted.
Source: Environmental Protection Agency, Water Quality Office.

MAP 3-1. Polluted Waters

Extent of Pollution

Virtually every U. S. stream, river, lake and estuary is polluted to some degree. Our Great Lakes are all polluted; Lake Erie is worst, followed by Ontario, Michigan, Huron and Superior

Source: National Wildlife Federation

TABLE 3-10. Beach Closings: 1970

Location	Beach/(Water body)
	GREAT LAKES REGION
ILLINOIS	
Lake Forest	"Swim-at-own-risk" signs posted.
North Chicago	Foss Park Beach has been closed all summer.
Lake Bluff	Lifeguards present, swimmers are warned to enter water at their own risk.
Highland Park	No-swimming signs are posted at Rosewood, Cory Avenue, and Park Avenue beaches.
Waukegan	Central Beach has been closed all summer. The other public beach closed July 28, 1970.
Winthrop Harbor	The one public beach has signs mentioning swim at own risk.
Zion	Hosah Beach has signs "swim at your own risk."
Evanston-North Shore	The Evanston-North Shore Health Department reported that beaches in Evanston, Wilmette, Kenilworth, Winnetka and Glencoe are open for swimming.
Chicago Beaches	None of the Chicago beaches have been closed according to Park District information.
INDIANA	
Hammond	Closed for a number of years.
Whiting	Closed in the summer of 1970 by local health department.
IOWA None	
MINNESOTA No beach closings	
MICHIGAN None	
OHIO	
Toledo	Reno Beach et al.
Cleveland	Peruins
(in or near Cleveland, there are no natural beaches which are not exclusively polluted.)	Edgewater
	White City
	Wildwood
	Euclid
	Lloyd Road
	Lakewood
	Rocky River
NEW YORK	
Rochester	Ontario Beach—Lake Ontario
Rochester	Durand-Eastman—Lake Ontario
Webster	Webster Beach—Lake Ontario
Ithaca	Stewart Beach Park—Cayuga Lake
Buffalo	Woodlawn Beach, Times Beach—Lake Erie
Geneva	Geneva City Beach—Seneca Lake
Baldwinsville	Mercer Park Beach—Seneca River

TABLE 3-10. Beach Closings (cont.)

Location	Beach/(Water body)
WISCONSIN	
Milwaukee	Beaches are closed after heavy rain.
The Department of Natural Resources has recommended all recreation be restricted on 300 miles of the Wisconsin River because of the mercury situation. However, no beaches have been closed.	
NORTHWEST REGION	
IDAHO	
Shoshone County	South Fork of the Coeur d'Alene (about 25 miles of stream).
MONTANA	
No closeouts in 1970 in part of state included in Northwest Region.	
OREGON	
Oregon reported no beaches posted as unsafe for recreational purposes but mentioned the Tualatin River and parts of the Willamette Harbor as not recommended for water contact sports. No information available on usage, closing dates, etc.	
WASHINGTON	
Clark County	Burnt Bridge Creek
	Columbia River (Washington shore 25-30 miles)
	Salmon Creek
Kitsap County	Southern portion of Dies Inlet west of Bremerton
Lewis County	Lake at Fort Borst Park closed July 17, 1970 (temporary closure expected)
SOUTHEAST REGION	
There have been no ocean, lake or river beaches in this region closed by health authorities because of pollution.	
SOUTH CENTRAL REGION	
ARKANSAS	
The Arkansas State Board of Health does not recommend body contact sports in Lake Hamilton and Lake Catherine, near Hot Springs. The beaches are in effect open. The State Board of Health also recommends that the Arkansas River not be used for body contact sports.	
LOUISIANA	
At New Orleans there is one beach and several supervised access areas on Lake Pontchartrain. Warnings of possible beach pollution, especially after rains, are posted at these sites, which are permitted to remain open.	
MISSISSIPPI	
The Mississippi State Health Department, the Park System and the Air & Pollution Control Commission reported no beach closings this summer.	

TABLE 3-10. Beach Closings (cont.)

Location	Beach/(Water body)
TENNESSEE	
McKellar Lake, a slack-water area of the Mississippi River near Memphis, is highly polluted with municipal and industrial waste waters. The Memphis Health Department does not recommend recreational use of McKellar Lake. However, there is a marina and the lake is used for water skiing and swimming.	
	MISSOURI BASIN
COLORADO, WYOMING, NORTH DAKOTA, KANSAS, IOWA, MONTANA — no closings reported	
MISSOURI	
Near Troy	Crooked Creek
	Cuivre River
Tarkio	Nishnabotna
NEBRASKA	
Near Omaha	Carter Lake
SOUTH DAKOTA	
Letcher	Letcher Lake
	PACIFIC SOUTHWEST
CALIFORNIA	
Coastal bay beach about 20 miles northwest of San Francisco.	Bolinas Lagoon
Almost entire river between cities of Napa and Vallejo, Napa County.	Napa River
Peninsula west of city of Vallejo, on San Francisco Bay.	Mare Island Straits
City of San Francisco, on San Francisco Bay.	Aquatic Park Beach
On Stanislaus River, about 12 miles north of city of Modesto.	Caswell Memorial State Park
Pebble Beach.	Stillwater Cove Beach
Point Pinos in Pacific Grove.	(Unnamed)
Various locations along Laguna de Santa Rose, 5-7 miles north of Sebastopol.	(Unnamed)
On Santa Ana River about 5 miles northeast of Anaheim.	Sycamore Flats Regional Park
Pacific Coast at Oceanside.	Oceanside Small Craft Harbor
On Pacific Coast, near Del Mar.	Torrey Pines State Park Slough (also known as Penasquito Slough)
UTAH	
Utah County	Utah Lake

TABLE 3-10. Beach Closings (cont.)

Location	Beach/(Water body)
HAWAII AND PACIFIC POSSESSIONS	
State of Hawaii	(fresh-water streams and lakes)
Territory of Guam	Agana Bay
Territory of Guam	Talafofo Bay
American Samoa	Pago Pago Bay
Trust Territory of the Pacific	Benjo bays, Six Districts
Trust Territory of the Pacific	Koror Lagoon
Trust Territory of the Pacific	Ebeye Beach
OHIO BASIN REGION	
There were no reported closings of any beaches in the summer of 1970 in the portion of the eleven states within the Ohio Basin Region.	
NORTHEAST REGION	
MAINE	
Norway	Lake Pennesseewassee
Winthrop	Winthrop Beach
NEW HAMPSHIRE	
Laconia	Bartlett Beach
Laconia	Weirs, Lake Winnipesaukee
VERMONT	
Wallingford	Elfin Lake
Fairfield	Fairfield Pond
Burlington	North Beach, Lake Champlain
MASSACHUSETTS	
Stowe	Brierly Pond
Webster	Webster Lake
Wendell	Tributary to Lake Wyola
Agawam	Silver Lake
Needham	Rosemary Pond
Lowell	Merrimack River
Boston	Boston Harbor, Tenean Beach
RHODE ISLAND	
Jamestown	East Ferry
Jamestown	West Ferry
Bristol	Bristol Harbor
Warwick	North of Conimicut Point
Warwick	Gaspee Point
Barrington	Providence River
CONNECTICUT	
Stamford	Southfield Beach

TABLE 3-10. Beach Closings (cont.)

Location	Beach/(Water body)
NEW YORK	
New York City—Brooklyn	Coney Island
New York City—Staten Island	South Beach
	Ocean Edge Colony
	Clearwater Beach
	Graham Beach
	Midland Beach
	Chelsea Beach
	Tottenville
Schuylerville	Hudson River
Westport Village	Lake Champlain
Westport Village	Westport Inn Co., Lake Champlain
Plattsburgh, AFB	Lake Champlain
NEW JERSEY	
No closures in state, according to state.	
DELAWARE	
Dover	Silver Lake
State Park	Killen's Pond
Port Penn	Augustine Beach
MIDDLE ATLANTIC REGION	
MARYLAND	
Baltimore County located on Bear Creek	Merritt Park Beach
	Iverness Beach
	Turners Beach
	Watersedge Beach
Baltimore County located on Back River	Dembows Beach
	Wilson Point Beach
	Lynch Point Beach
	Middleview Beach and Boat Marina
Baltimore County located on Middle River	Holly Beach
	Chesapeake Village Beach
	Bowley's Resort
Baltimore County Bird River	Harewood Park Beach
Baltimore County Gunpowder River	Oliver Beach
VIRGINIA	
Chesterfield County	Unnamed beach (this beach was closed because of amoebic pollution in the summer of 1969 after two deaths occurred.)
WASHINGTON, D.C.	
District of Columbia	No recognized beaches (D.C. Department of Public Health has for many years forbidden swimming in the Potomac River and its tributaries.)

TABLE 3-10. Beach Closings (cont.)

Location	Beach/(Water body)
PENNSYLVANIA	
Honeybrook Township, Chester County	Two Logs Camp
Limerick Township, Montgomery County	Lake View Amusement Park
Jackson Township, Huntingdon County	Greenwood Furnace
NORTH CAROLINA None reported	
SOUTH CAROLINA	
Unnamed beach	Sullivans Island, Charleston

Source: Environmental Protection Administration.

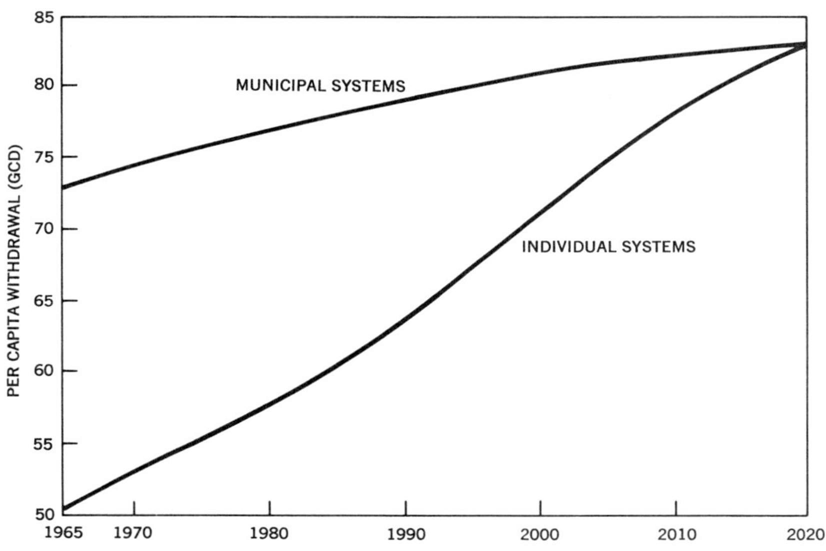

FIGURE 3-3

Source: The Nation's Water Resources, Water Resources Council, 1968

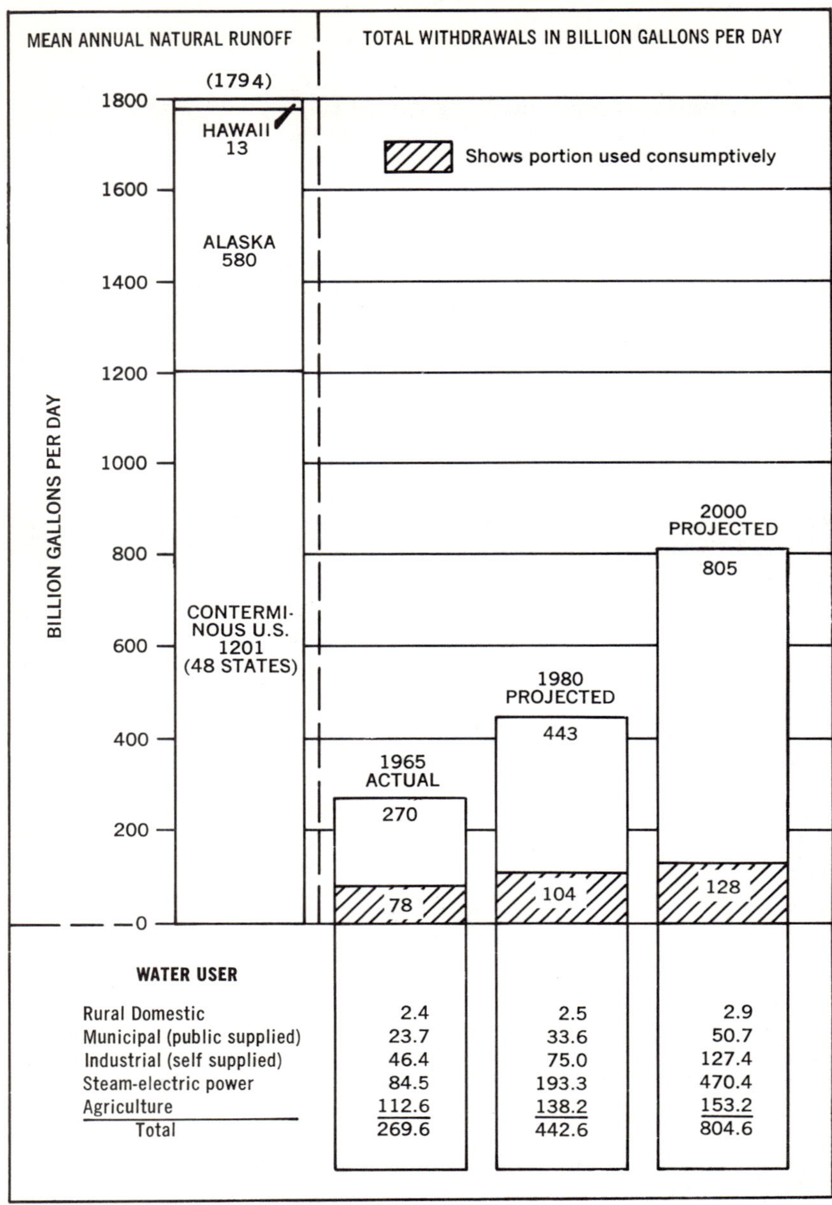

FIGURE 3-4. U. S. Water Supply and Projected Water Use
Source: Water Resources Council, 1968 National Water Assessment

TABLE 3-11. Estimated Water Use and Projected Requirements, by Purpose, United States
(Million gallons daily)

Type of use	Used	Projected requirements			Used	Projected requirements		
	1965	1980	2000	2020	1965	1980	2000	2020
	Withdrawals				Consumptive use			
Rural domestic	2,351	2,474	2,852	3,334	1,636	1,792	2,102	2,481
Municipal (public-supplied)	23,745	33,596	50,724	74,256	5,244	10,581	16,478	24,643
Industrial (self-supplied)	46,405	75,026	127,365	210,767	3,764	6,126	10,011	15,619
Steam-electric power:								
Fresh	62,738	133,963	259,208	410,553	659	1,685	4,552	8,002
Saline	21,800	59,340	211,240	503,540	157	498	2,022	5,183
Agriculture:								
Irrigation	110,852	135,852	149,824	160,978	64,696	81,559	89,964	96,919
Livestock	1,726	2,375	3,397	4,660	1,626	2,177	3,077	4,238
Total	269,617	442,626	804,610	1,368,088	77,782	104,418	128,206	157,085

Source: The Nation's Water Resources, Water Resources Council, 1968.

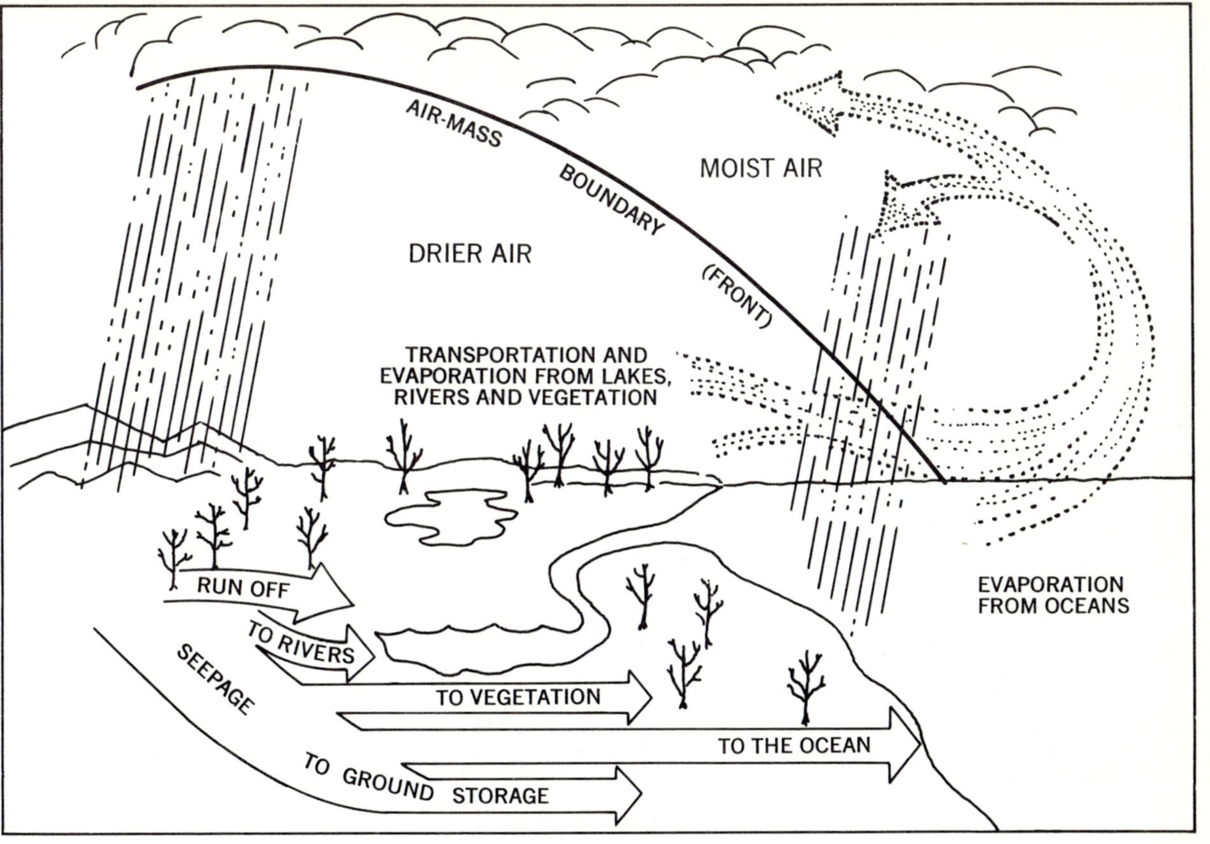

FIGURE 3-2. Hydrologic Cycle Source: The Nation's Water Resources, Water Resources Council, 1968

BOX 3-1. Polluted Beaches in Western Europe

Paris' Center for Research in Biology and Oceanography released a study in 1970 of French, Italian, Dutch and Belgian beaches. Beaches were classified on a 1 to 5 scale in ascending order of pollution:

3 "Better not swim here."
4 "You are playing with your health."
5 "You are playing with your life."

The diseases connected with categories 3 and 4 are conjunctivitis, sinusitis and laryngitis. Swimming in number 5 waters exposes one to hepatitis, typhoid and cholera.

On the Dutch coast: Scheveningen and Vlissingen (4).

On the Belgian coast: Westende, Ostende, Knokke, Koksijde (3).

On the Italian coast (summarized): Ostia (4), Naples (3), Sorrento (3), Bari (4), Ravenna (4), Trieste (4) and various coastlines in the area of Genoa and Venice (3-5).

On France's northern coast: Calais (4), Boulogne (5), Equihen (5), Yport (5), Cap de la Hève (5) . . . and from Le Havre to Mont Saint Michel Bay, all beaches are classified (5).

On France's Atlantic coast: Plougastel (4), Morgat (3), Tréboul (4), Saint-Pierre (5), Les Sables-d'Olonne (3), Pyla-sur-Mer (3), Vieux Boucau (4).

On France's Mediterranean coast: Etang de Berre (3-5), Marseille (5), Sanary-sur-Mer (5), Fréjus (3), Cannes (1-5, depending on location), Nice (5), Monaco (4), Monte Carlo (4).

Borgstrom of Michigan State University estimates that twice as much water is being removed from ground water reserves than is being returned by the natural hydrologic cycle (Figure 3-2). We would not have to risk exhaustion of these precious reserves, however, if other available sources were not so polluted. Three times as much water as New York City needs each day, for example, passes right by it untapped in the filthy Hudson River.

Sources of Water Pollution

Industrial Wastes: Industry contributes 60 percent of all U.S. water pollution. Water-using factories which number over 300,000 discharge three to four times the amount of oxygen-demanding wastes as all the sewered population in the country. The principle industrial offenders are by category—paper, organic chemicals, petroleum and steel (Figure 3-5). The growing need for electrical power threatens our waters with another scare. Thermal pollution, a by-product of the water-cooling process necessary for the production of electrical power, raises the water temperature of the streams with all sorts of bad aquatic consequences.

The regions victimized the most by industrial waste are the Northeast, the Ohio River Basin, the Great Lakes States and the Gulf Coast States, and to a lesser extent the Southeast and Pacific Coast States.

TABLE 3-12. Typical Water Pollutants

Pesticides	Copper
DDE	Cyanides
DDT	Dissolved gases
Dieldrin	Detergents and dyes
Endrin	Fluorides
Heptachlor	Hydrogen sulfide
2, 4-D	Iron
Radioactive Materials	Lead
Radium-226	Manganese
Strontium-90	Nitrates and nitrites
Chemicals	Nickel
Acids	Phenols
Alkalies and hydroxides	Phosphorous
Ammonia	Potassium
Arsenic	Selenium
Barium	Silver
Boron	Sulfides and Sulfates
Cadmium	Tars
Chlorides	Urea
Chromium	Zinc

Municipal Wastes: Wastes from cities account for 25 percent of the water pollution.[3] Sixty-eight percent of the population lives in just under 13,000 sewered communities, 1,000 of which outgrow their treatment systems every year. And the Federal Water Quality Administration has judged only 40 percent of the sewage treatment systems in the nation as *adequate* (Figure 3-6).

The most seriously affected regions are the Northeast (New York, Boston, Rochester), Midwest (Chicago, Detroit, Cleveland) and to a lesser degree the Far West.

Agricultural Wastes: Agricultural wastes are two in kind: (1) feed lot and (2) runoff.

Modern animal husbandry techniques have inadvertently created an enormous problem concerning animal wastes. By confining animals—expecially beef cattle, dairy cows, poultry and hogs—to a minimum of space and feeding them a concentrated ration, farmers wind up with an unwieldy bulk of waste impervious to natural decomposition or assimilation in pastures.

Once this waste works itself into the water supply, it can: "add excessive nutrients that unbalance natural ecological systems, causing

[3]Fifty-five percent of city waste, that is, waste processed by municipal treatment plants, originates in homes and commercial establishments. The other 45 percent comes from industry.

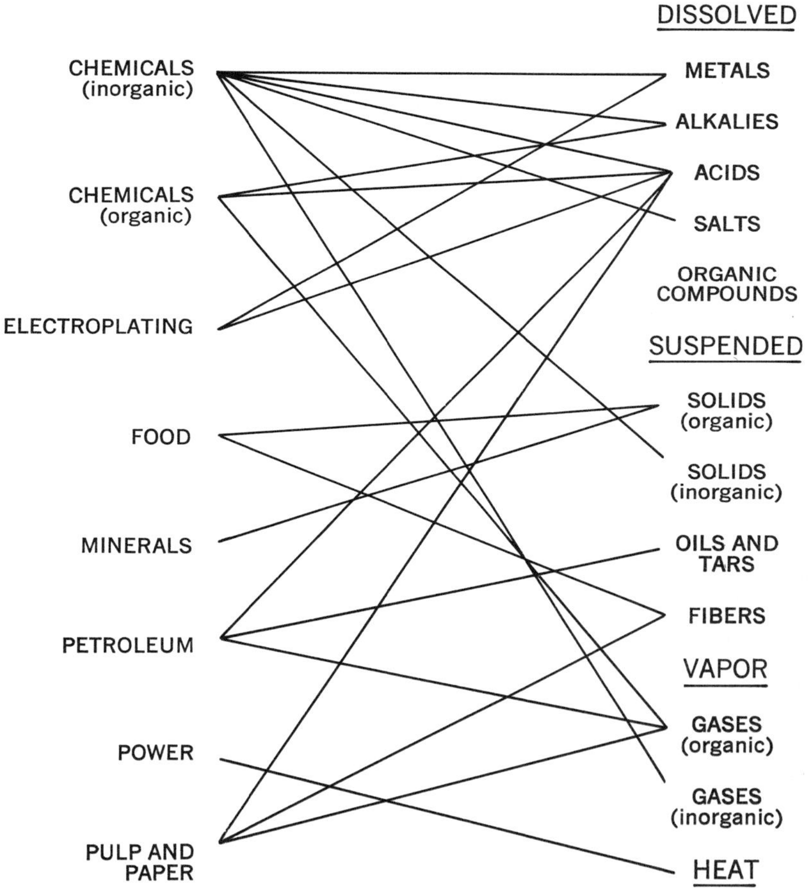

FIGURE 3-5. Major Industries and Their Water Pollutants

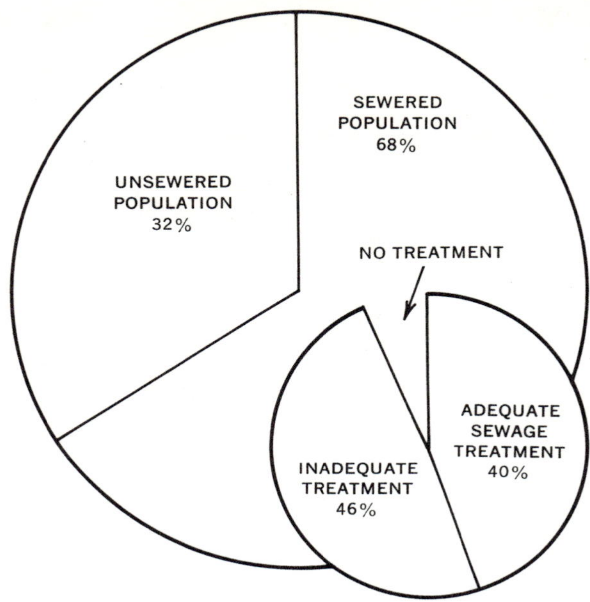

FIGURE 3-6. Sewered and Unsewered Population

excessive aquatic plant growth and fish kills; load water filtration systems with solids, complicating water treatment; cause undesirable tastes and odors in waters; add chemicals that are detrimental to both man and animals; increase consumption of dissolved oxygen, producing stress on aquatic populations and occasionally resulting in septic conditions; and add micro-organisms that are pathogenic to animals and to man" (*Clean Water for the 70's,* Federal Water Quality Administration, 1970).

As U.S. population increases, so will the demand for meat and milk consumption and so too the increase in animal wastes.

Agricultural waste sources are scattered around the country with cattle in the Midwest, West and Southeast; poultry in the South and some of the Middle Atlantic States; hogs in the Midwest and South and cows in New York, Pennsylvania, Wisconsin, Minnesota, Iowa and California.

Sediment and Erosion: Sediments produced by erosions are by far the most extensive pollutants in U.S. surface waters (700 times the discharge from sewers). These sediments flow into rivers and streams

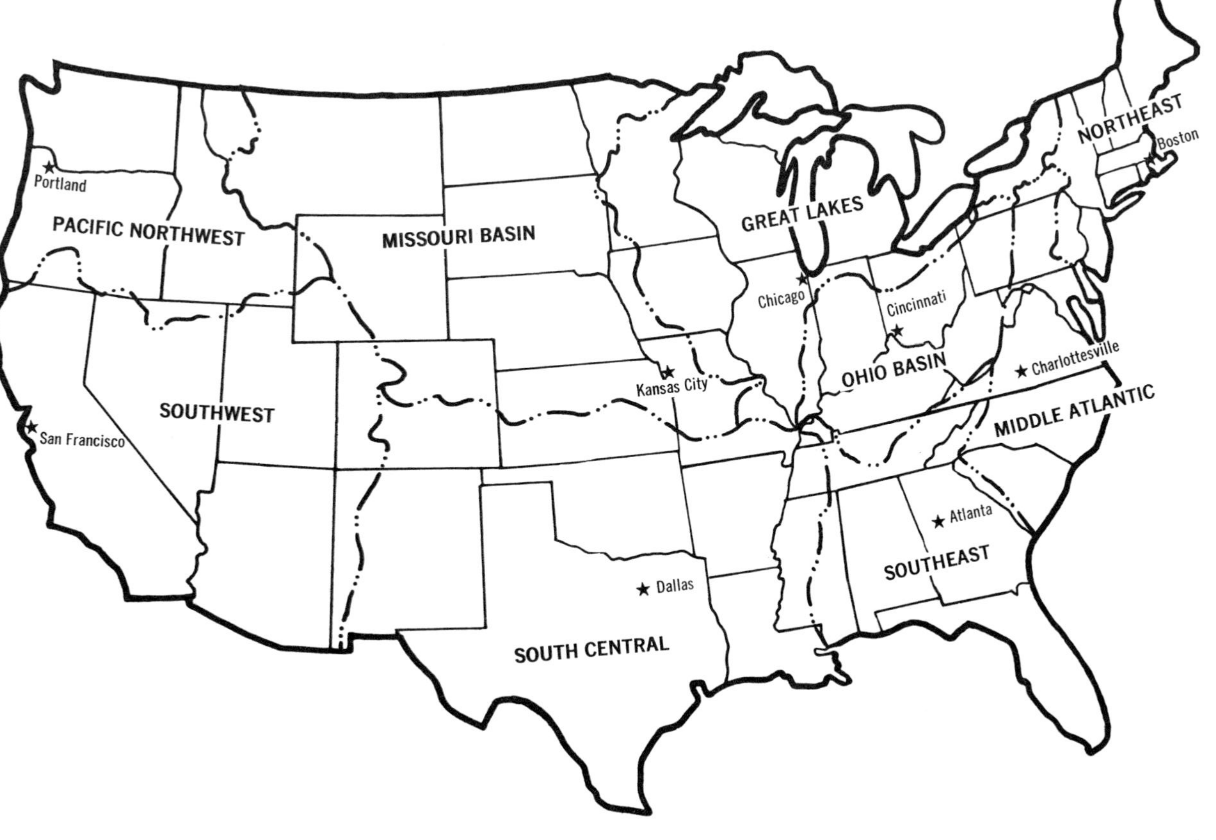

MAP 3-2. Federal Water Quality Administration Regions

Source: Clean Water for the 1970's, Federal Water Quality Administration, 1970

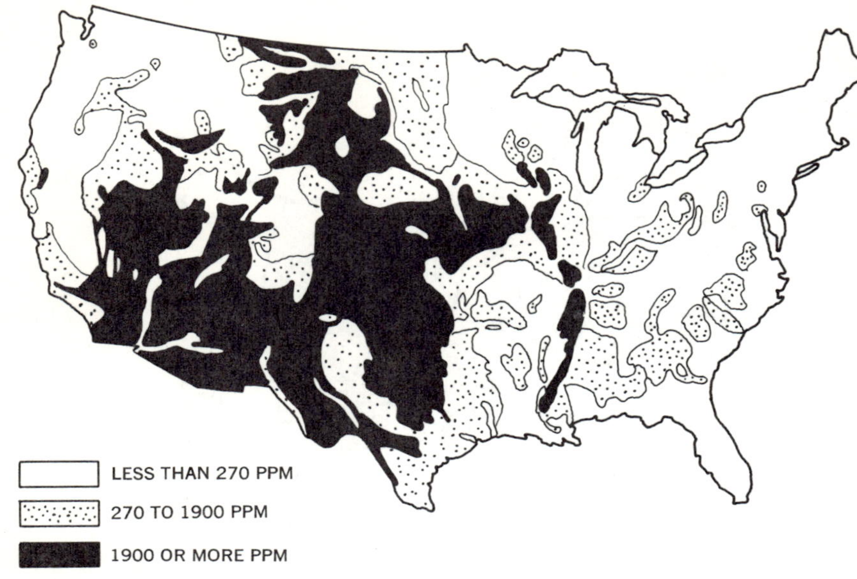

MAP 3-3. Concentration of Sediment in Streams

Source: Clean Water for the 1970's, Federal Water Quality Administration, 1970

from croplands, unprotected forest soils, overgrazed pastures, strip mines, roads and bulldozed urban areas. Agricultural development increases erosion at a rate four to nine times that of natural cover. Construction can increase erosion a hundredfold.

Erosion is a serious water pollution factor on at least 300,000 miles of the nation's stream banks. Only New England, New York, Florida, the Great Lakes States and the Pacific Northwest seem to be relatively free of the problem (Map 3-3).

Oil and Hazardous Substances: Oil spillage, whether by deliberate dumping, accident, pipeline, drilling rig and storage facility leaks or the breakup of transportation equipment has recently joined the growing cost of major water pollutants. Ten thousand spills of oils and other hazardous substances are estimated every year in the United States.

The damage from such spillage affects marine life and recreation, ruins wildlife habitats, kills birds and contaminates water supplies.

Mine Drainage: Mine drainage disturbs water quality in Appalachia and the Ohio Basin States. This drainage (principally sulphuric acid and iron compounds created by the reaction of water and air with sulphur-bearing minerals in mines and refuse piles) leaks into ponds and streams with particularly adverse effects. In Appalachia, for example, 10,500 miles of streams (6,700 miles of which are continuously degraded) are reduced below desirable standards by acid mine drainage.

The more than 2 million acres of strip mining land contribute to the acid pollution of our waters as well as adding substantially to sediment pollution (up to 94 million tons of sediment a year). An additional 153,000 acres are disturbed every year by surface mining.

Watercraft Wastes: Ordinary watercraft cannot be overlooked in connection with water pollution, especially since the total vessel population in the United States is estimated at over 8 million. Although this pollution source is quite minor over-all, it can be a considerable local annoyance in some harbors and recreational areas.

SELECTED BIBLIOGRAPHY

Briggs, P., *Water, The Vital Essence,* Harper & Row, New York, 1967.
Discussion of present water supply and quantity throughout the world, with special emphasis on the United States.

Federal Water Quality Administration, *Clean Water for the 1970's: A Status Report,* Government Printing Office, Washington, D.C., 1970. Rather thorough governmental report on water pollution in United States.

Federal Water Pollution Control Administration, *Water Quality Criteria: Report of the National Technical Advisory Committee,* Government Printing Office, Washington, D.C., 1968. Encyclopedic study of water and its contaminants.

Graham, F. Jr., *Disaster by Default. Politics and Water Pollution,* M. Evans & Co., Inc., New York, 1966.

Goldman, M. I., ed, *Controlling Pollution,* Prentice-Hall, Englewood Cliffs, N.J., 1967.
Collection of readings on the problems of water pollution and the ways in which government and industry might work together to control it.

Lindsay, S. "How Safe Is the Nation's Drinking Water?" *Saturday Review,* May 2, 1970, pp. 54–55.

National Council on Marine Resources and Engineering Development. *Marine Science Affairs.* Government Printing Office, Washington, D.C., 1967.
Recommendations for more effective use of U.S. water supplies and a description of federal programs concerned with water problems.

Moss, Sen. F. E., *The Water Crisis,* Frederick A. Praeger, New York, 1967.
Analysis of the water crisis in the United States and the demographic and economic pressures which brought it about.

Water Resources Council, *The Nation's Water Resources: A Summary Report.* Government Printing Office, Washington, D.C., 1968. Useful information and graphs.

3. OCEANS

The oceans have always been treated as eternal receptacles of waste. It was once thought they could absorb infinite matter in their deep. We are now learning, however, that the oceans are indeed frail. Although the facts and figures are not sufficient to confirm scientific suspicions absolutely, it is rather self-evident that we can no longer regard the seas as immune to our effluence.

We know, for example, that toxic wastes like pesticides and oil affect fish reproduction; that oxygen demanding wastes alters the diversity of marine organisms by depleting the oxygen supply; that the nutrients in sewage sludge can cause biostimulation—the accelerated fertilization of plant life—which creates blooms of algae and thereby changes the nature of bottom sediments and consequently whole communities of bottom organisms; that dumping sewage sludge and polluted dredge spoils drastically upsets marine habitats.

The human impact of ocean pollution is all too apparent. The poisons we blithely put to sea are now coming back to haunt us in our seafood. Fish species are infected with human pathogens by exposure to our wastes. Several beaches have been closed owing to the high coliform bacteria count and visual and odoriferous pollution make others less amenable. Fish catches of almost every variety are down and the culprit is pollution again.

The oceans, then, are in clear and present danger. If they are to be salvaged from death-dealing pollution, the dumping has to stop.

TABLE 3-13. Estimated Vessels in the United States

Federally registered commercial vessels	46,000
Unregistered commercial fishing vessels	65,000
Federally owned vessels	1,600
Recreational vessels	8,000,000

Ocean Dumping

In 1968, 48.2 million tons of waste were dumped into our off shore waters from 246 sites on the Atlantic, Pacific and Gulf Coasts. Dredging spoils from harbor-deepening operations accounted for 80 percent of the waste (34 percent of which material was polluted to begin with), followed mainly by industrial wastes, often highly toxic (10 percent) and sewage sludge (9 percent).

TABLE 3-14. Ocean Dumping: Site Location Summary (22, 66)

Coastal area	Number of sites	Active Corps disposal permits
Atlantic Coast	122	136
Gulf Coast	56	50
Pacific Coast	68	71
Total	246	257

TABLE 3-15. Composition of Solid Waste (28)

Type of waste	Average (percent)
Paper products	43.8
Food wastes	18.2
Metals	9.1
Glass and ceramics	9.0
Garden wastes	7.9
Rock, dirt and ash	3.7
Plastics, rubber and leather	3.1
Textiles	2.7
Wood	2.5
Total	100.0

Ocean dumping is definitely a trend. There was a fourfold increase in total tonnage from 1949 to 1960, and the future looks equally unpromising. The populations in coastal regions are going up and consequently so will waste of every sort—along with a declining capacity to meet it in terms of land disposal sites.

Let's look at the coastal wastes projections of the future as given in *Ocean Dumping: A National Policy,* a document prepared by the Council on Environmental Quality to advise the President on this crucial problem. This booklet is a comprehensive source on ocean pollution and the principal source of information for this section.

Solid Waste—by the year 2000, the 65 million tons of solid waste now generated in the coastal regions will have escalated to close to 200 million tons. Several cities are already contemplating the ocean as a future panacea for their garbage.

Sewage Sludge—the 1970 figure of 1.4 million tons of sludge disposed of at sea will rise 50 percent to 2.1 million tons by 2000.

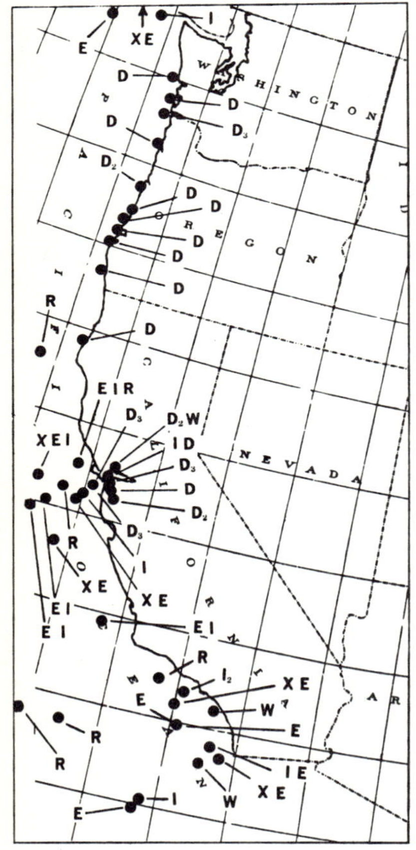

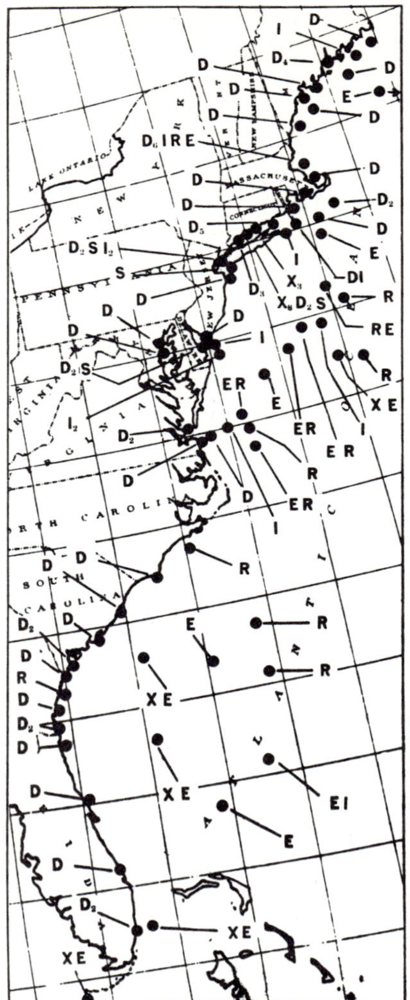

MAP 3-4. Known Dumping Sites Off U. S. Coasts

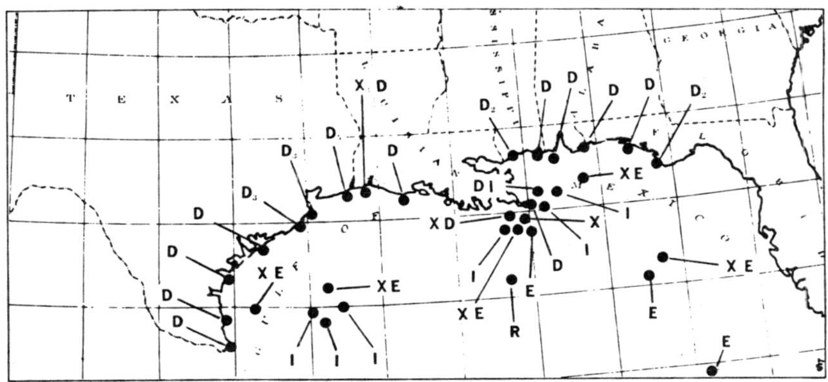

MAP 3-5. Known Dumping Sites Off U. S. Coasts

Industrial Wastes—industrial production grows 4.5 percent a year and its waste grows accordingly; thus, the potential for increased industrial waste dumping at sea is quite large.

Dredge Spoils—as a long-range problem, dredge spoils should be neutralized as soon as water quality standards force the reduction of polluted discharge from municipal and industrial sources: for the next five or ten years, however, while the demand for deeper harbors lasts, dredge spoils will remain an ocean pollution factor.

Tables and maps on ocean dumping are from *Ocean Dumping: A National Policy.*

SELECTED BIBLIOGRAPHY

Council On Environmental Quality, *Ocean Dumping: A National Policy,* Government Printing Office, Washington, D.C., 1970. A report to the President prepared by the Council on Environmental Quality. The best summary available on ocean dumping, detailed statistics.

Cornwell, J., "Is the Mediterranean Dying?" *The New York Times Magazine,* February 21, 1971. Frightening account of the demise of the Mediterranean—a microcosm of the world's oceans.

Marx, W., *The Frail Ocean,* Ballantine Books, New York, 1967. An ecological classic.

Olson, T. A., and Burgess, F. J. (eds.), *Pollution and Marine Ecology.* Interscience Publishers, New York, 1967.

TABLE 3-16. Industrial Wastes by Method of Disposal (66)
(In tons)

Coastal area	Number of sites	Bulk wastes	Container-ized wastes	Total
Atlantic Coast	10	3,011,000	2,200	3,013,200
Gulf Coast	6	690,000	6,000	696,000
Pacific Coast	7	981,000	300	981,300
Total	23	4,682,000	8,500	4,690,500

TABLE 3-17. Ocean Dumping: Types and Amounts, 1968 (66)
(In tons)

Waste type	Atlantic	Gulf	Pacific	Total	Percent of total
Dredge spoils	15,808,000	15,300,000	7,320,000	38,428,000	80
Industrial wastes	3,013,200	696,000	981,300	4,690,500	10
Sewage sludge	4,477,000	0	0	4,477,000	9
Construction and demolition debris	574,000	0	0	574,000	<1
Solid waste	0	0	26,000	26,000	<1
Explosives	15,200	0	0	15,200	<1
Total	23,887,400	15,966,000	8,327,300	48,210,700	100

TABLE 3-18. Industrial Wastes by Manufacturing Process (66)

Type of waste	Estimated tonnage	Percent
Waste acids	2,720,500	58
Refinery wastes	562,900	12
Pesticide wastes	328,300	7
Paper mill wastes	140,700	3
Other wastes	938,100	20

TABLE 3-19. Ocean Dumping: Historical Trends, 1949–1968[1] (66)

	1949-1953		1954-1958		1959-1963		1964-1968	
Coastal area	**Total**	**Avg./Yr.**	**Total**	**Avg./Yr.**	**Total**	**Avg./Yr.**	**Total**	**Avg./Yr.**
Atlantic Coast	8,000,000	1,600,000	16,000,000[2]	3,200,000	27,270,000	5,454,000	31,100,000	6,200,000
Gulf Coast	40,000[3]	8,000	283,000	56,000	860,000	172,000	2,600,000	520,000
Pacific Coast	487,000	97,000	850,000	170,000	940,000	188,000	3,410,000	682,000
Total	8,527,000	1,705,000	17,133,000	3,426,000	29,070,000	5,814,000	37,110,000	7,422,000

[1] Figures do not include dredge spoils, radioactive wastes, and military explosives.
[2] Estimated by fitting a linear trend line between data for preceding period and data for succeeding period.
[3] Disposal operations in the Gulf of Mexico began in 1952.

TABLE 3-20. Estimated Polluted Dredge Spoils

Coastal area	**Total spoils (in tons)**	**Estimated percent of total polluted spoils[1]**	**Total polluted spoils (in tons)**
Atlantic Coast	15,808,000	45	7,120,000
Gulf Coast	15,300,000	31	4,740,000
Pacific Coast	7,320,000	19	1,390,000
Total	38,428,000	34	13,250,000

[1] Estimates of polluted dredge spoils consider chlorine demand; BOD; COD; volatile solids; oil and grease; concentrations of phosphorous, nitrogen, and iron; silica content; and color and odor of the spoils.

TABLE 3-21. Reported Oil Spills in U. S. Waters (Over 100 barrels)

	1968	**1969**
Vessels	347	532
Shore facilities	295	331
Unidentified	72	144
Total	714	1007

4. THERMAL POLLUTION

One of nature's delicate balances is its thermal property. Weather, climate, atmosphere depend enormously on the thermal interrelation of winds and waters, persons and things. The problem is that this balance is being disturbed by the input into waters and the atmosphere of man-made energies of startling amounts. The Council on Environmental Quality explains:[4]

In a primitive society, energy utilization consists mostly of the food consumed by the individual. This corresponds to a power output of about 100 thermal watts per person. The world average—including primitive and technologically advanced regions—is somewhat more than 1000 thermal watts per person. In the highly industrialized United States, energy consumption is equivalent to 10,000 watts for each individual. If world population grows to 5 billion and if the worldwide average of energy use increases to 10,000 watts per person, manmade energy input into the atmosphere would reach almost one-hundredth that of the natural net radiation balance over land areas. If energy consumption continues to increase at the present rate of 4 percent per year, then in 200 years artificial energy input into the atmosphere would equal one-third of the natural radiation balance. This level would be reached in only 100 years with a 10 percent yearly increase.

These figures, as the Council notes, are significant, as an increase of just a few tenths of 1 percent in the radiation balance of the planet would, if long sustained, cause polar ice to disappear completely, unless other natural or man-made changes compensated for the energy gain.

What would happen if the ice cap melted? Great flooding, the inundation of islands, coastal areas and cities and the submergence of resources in the line of the rising waters. The melting of the ice cap in toto would lift sea levels about seven meters, roughly 23 feet. Some conceive of the possibility of the world freezing as a result of the unloosing of the ice cap, but this possibility is not taken seriously. Nevertheless, the melting of just the thinner polar ice would tend to let the warm waters of the Gulf Stream continue northward. This would mean that the Gulf Stream would no longer be deflected eastward to warm the coasts of Europe.[5]

It would be alarmist to speak of the melting of the ice cap in terms of its imminence. On the other hand, sea levels have been rising, ever so gradually, over the last 20,000 years, under conditions infinitely more natural than those which exist today. The process could be accelerated,

[4]First Annual Report, August 1970, p. 100.

[5]Professor Carroll S. Wilson of the Massachusetts Institute of Technology in discussing the findings of a panel of 30 ecological specialists from 14 countries at the United Nations, September 22, 1971.

to the point of great speed, by the artificial energy forces being released by man. It is one reason why some scientists advise against overcrowding and overconcentration of urban development in low coastal areas.[6]

Some of the thermal forces generated by man and unleashed on the environment are discussed in the pages following.

THE "HOT" CITY

Whatever the calendar season, urban areas seem to be climatically warmer than suburban and rural areas. This is no delusion; they are. Direct energy input from home heating units, industrial plants, air conditioning, automobiles, etc., causes the annual mean temperature of the city to rise in both summer and winter; spring and fall, too, for that matter. Other factors are the tall and tightly spaced buildings, which cut down wind speeds and lock in energy from moving weather systems, thus slowing heat dispersement. The net result is that cities are 0.9 to 1.4 degrees warmer, on the average, than suburban and rural areas. In winter the differential is the more pronounced, the city being as much as 2 to 3 degrees warmer than surrounding areas. (This is by Fahrenheit measurement.)

The differences have a marked effect on weather. Heats rising from cities modify atmospheric properties in several ways. They will push the natural air up vertically to colder levels over the city; they will seed the immediate skies with particulate matter.[7] One result is a higher precipitation for cities of rain or ice crystals, depending upon the season. The Council on Environmental Quality has drawn up a parameter table (3-22) detailing climatic changes produced by cities.[8]

The Council on Environmental Quality describes the elevation of heat over cities as a "thermal mountain."[9] It is an apt coupling of words. The point is, however, that with large parts of the world growing

[6]*Resources and Man,* Committee on Resources and Man, National Academy of Sciences-National Research Council; Freeman and Co., San Francisco, 1969, p. 152.

[7]General Electric proposed what may be one solution to the thermal polluting of the air by power-plant and other industrial installations at a meeting of the American Society for Public Administration in Albany, New York, on April 7, 1971. G.E.'s proposal is for new cooling towers which would be hollow, about 60 feet tall and 600 feet in diameter. The towers would propel thermal exhaust thousands of feet into the air, where the waste heat would be dispersed in the upper atmosphere. Present cooling towers, smaller and weaker, propel thermal wastes only to low altitudes, where they become diluted with outside air, and have warming as well as sedimentary effects. G.E.'s tower, according to company officials, would "literally drill holes through inversion layers that periodically cover many cities." On-site testing in a major U.S. city had yet to be done.

[8]First Annual Report, August 1970.

[9]Ibid. 101–2.

TABLE 3-22.

Parameter	City as compared with rural surroundings
Temperature:	
Annual mean	0.9° to 1.4° F. higher.
Winter minimum	2° to 3° F. higher.
Cloudiness:	
Clouds	5 to 10 percent more.
Fog, winter	100 percent more.
Fog, summer	30 percent more.
Dust particles	10 times more.
Wind speed:	
Annual mean	20 to 30 percent lower.
Extreme gusts	10 to 20 percent lower.
Precipitation	5 to 10 percent more.

into back-to-back cities (e.g., the Boston-Washington corridor), heat input escaping from these cities is going to effect climatic changes—on a regional and perhaps eventually on a global scale. Inadvertent changes have already occurred; other more radical changes may not be far off. Is the phenomenon being watched and studied carefully? Unfortunately, no. Only about 1 percent of federal research monies for weather modification was going in 1970 to programs investigating the effects of man's thermal mountain.

Heating the Waters

Nuclear power plants are a major cause of thermal pollution, producing as much as 50 and 60 percent more pollution in the form of waste heat per kilowatt hour of capacity as the ordinary fossil fuel plant (coal, petroleum, natural gas). A nuclear power plant's cooling operation (cooling waters are run through condenser tubing, then returned to the water source) can raise the temperature of river, lake or sound, whatever the cooling source, from 10 to 20 degrees at distances several miles from the point of outflow. The effects of the process on the character of the waters and adjacent environments are staggering. The warmer waters hold less dissolved oxygen, nourish heavier growths of algae in the water and can alter plant, insect, fungi and other growths of the shore areas. There is also danger of a radiation build-up in the cooling source.

The waters lose attractiveness as swimming and recreational resources; the reproductive cycles of fish are threatened or destroyed; the well-being of wildlife of immediate and contiguous areas is placed in jeopardy.

Horror stories are multiple of the toll exacted by thermal pollution from nuclear power plants. Thus far they concern fish primarily. But they are not to be minimized on that account—particularly when by

1980 it is estimated that nuclear power plants will require some 200 billion gallons of water per day, mostly for cooling purposes. Such usage—the inevitable consequence of demands for more electrical power and a concomitant proliferation of nuclear power plants—will mean the tapping of virtually every large fresh-water system in the country for cooling purposes.[10] The basic marine and shoreline ecology of the nation could be devastated in the process.

Indeed, Charles F. Luce, chairman of the New York's Consolidated Edison Company, declared on April 20, 1971,[11] that power demands were expected to be such by the 1980s that Con Edison would need to use the Atlantic Ocean as sites for its new stations. He envisioned stations as many as ten miles at sea, because shoreline and inland plants by then would have used up all the cooling waters. It is prospects such as that which contribute to forecasts like that of Swiss marine scientist Jacques Piccard that at the current rate of pollution there will be no life in the world's oceans in a quarter-century.[12]

Oiling the Oceans

Another major devastator of the ecology of the water, and of oceans especially, is oil. The world has been plagued in recent years with huge oil spills, frequently from tankers colliding or running aground. The tendency has been to view these mishaps in terms of what the oil does to beaches and wildlife and fish. Forgotten largely is the fact that these spills also have thermal effects.

Oceans are a major determinant of weather, helping to equalize the temperature of the globe. A complicated interaction is involved here between air, wind and sea. The very thinnest of oil films can throw that interaction off by upsetting the surface roughness of the water, its evaporation and natural radiation emissions.

An international convention seeks to prevent pollution of the sea by oil,[13] but it has limited effectiveness. In 1970, ships, including those of the U. S. Navy, were still dumping oil wastes in so-called international waters. It was only when some spills reached beaches that a public alarm was raised. Few individuals thought to wonder whether the oils were also disturbing weather, water patterns and temperatures. Enough of these oils could do so.

[10]*Perils of the Peaceful Atom,* by Richard Curtis and Elizabeth Hogan; The Museum of Natural History, 1969; Ballantine Books, 1970; p. 183 in Ballantine edition.

[11]Annual briefing for news media; *The New York Times,* April 21, 1971, p. 1.

[12]*The New York Times,* October 26, 1971, p. 5.

[13]The International Convention for the Prevention of Pollution of the Sea by Oil, 1954, amended in 1962. The United States Senate ratified the Convention in 1961, and President Kennedy formalized U.S. participation on December 8, 1961.

SELECTED BIBLIOGRAPHY

(*thermal pollution*)

Bryerton, G., *Nuclear Dilemma*, Ballantine Books, 1970.

Callendar, G. S., "Temperature Fluctuations and Trends over the Earth," Q. J. Royal Meteorological Society, 87:1–12, 1961.

Curtis, R., and Hogan, E., *Perils of the Peaceful Atom*, The American Museum of Natural History, 1969; Ballantine Books, 1970.

Darling, F. F., and Milton, J. P., eds., *Future Environments of North America; Transformation of a Continent*, The Natural History Press, 1966.

Foreman, H. (ed.), *Nuclear Power and the Public*, University of Minnesota Press, 1971.

Goldberg, E. D., "The Oceans as a Chemical System," *The Sea*, M. N. Hill, ed., Vol. 2, p. 3–25, Wiley, New York, 1963.

Mitchell, J. M., "On the Worldwide Pattern of Secular Temperature Change," in *Changes of Climate, Proceedings*, Rome Symposium, UNESCO and World Meteorological Organization: 161–81, 1963.

Resources and Man, Committee on Resources and Man, National Academy of Sciences-National Research Council; Freeman, San Francisco, 1969.

5. NUCLEAR POWER

Perhaps the greatest twentieth-century threat to man and nature is posed by nuclear power—not in the form of nuclear military weapons only, but through the peaceful adaptations of the power of the atom as well. In a way, the second is the more perverse of the two threats, as by introducing nuclear power into everyday life, man unwittingly makes himself the victim of one of the terrible effects of nuclear war itself—radiation. By the same token, he lays himself open to the frightening possibility of a nuclear "accident," which could be no less catastrophic than a nuclear military encounter. He is already in the grips of the radiation eventuality.[14]

Radiation is nothing new to man. Some cosmic radiation enters the earth's atmosphere naturally from the spaces outside earth. There is radiation in radioactive isotopes found in water and mineral deposits. There is low-level radiation in medical and occupational usages of certain kinds. Fallout from nuclear testing and experimentation adds to dosages. The first annual report of the Council on Environmental Quality included a chart (Table 3-23) itemizing the sources of radiation dosage of the average individual.

But now the new element enters the equation, the one which threatens (1) to increase substantially man's radiation intake, with subsequent increased danger of cancer, leukemia, genetic disturbance, etc.; and

[14]See chapter on thermal pollution for a description of the heat effects of nuclear power plants on the environment.

TABLE 3-23. Average Annual Genetically Significant Dose to General Population From Various Environmental Sources[1]

Source	Dose (mrem)[2]	Percent— Of total from all sources	Percent— Of manmade sources
Natural background	125	68.3	
Medical sources	55.2	30.1	93.8
Diagnostic X-ray	(50.0)	(27.3)	(85.0)
Therapeutic X-ray	(5.0)	(2.7)	(8.5)
Radioisotopes	(0.2)	(0.1)	(0.3)
Other sources	1.7	0.9	2.9
Occupational	(0.2)	(0.1)	(0.3)
Fallout	(1.5)	(0.8)	(2.6)
Miscellaneous (includes TV sets, luminous markings on watches, etc.)	2.0	1.1	3.4
Total		100.4	100.1

[1] Based on data reported by John B. Little, "Environmental Hazards—Ionizing Radiation," New England Journal of Medicine, 275, 929–38 (1966) and the United Nations Scientific Committee on the Effects of Atomic Radiation.

[2] mrem = millirem (1/1000 rem). ("Rem" stands for "roentgen equivalent man" and reflects the amount of radiation absorbed in human tissues and also the quality of the type of radiation.)

The Federal Radiation Council advises that the public not be exposed to more than 500 whole-body millirems of radiation a year. One chest X-ray is gauged at 100 millirems; a complete dental X-raying at 5,000 millirems. The natural background of Denver, Colorado, is placed at 500 millirems. The figures are from the Westinghouse Electric Corporation booklet, Infinite Energy. As for diagnostic X-rays, the Food and Drug Administration was concerned to the point of proposing new performance standards in October, 1971, for medical X-ray machines, in order to cut down exposure of individuals to man-made radiation. Food and Drugs Commissioner Charles E. Edwards said at the time that "more than 90 percent of all human exposure to man-made radiation comes from diagnostic use of X-rays . . ."

(2) to place over man's head the risk of a holocaust resulting from some accidental peacetime catastrophe. This element again: nuclear power plants.

According to Atomic Energy Commission statistics of December 31, 1970, no less than 109 nuclear power plants are operational or in the building or planning stages in the United States. The plants are spread through twenty-nine states and Puerto Rico; in 1971, those plants which were operational were supplying 7,497,800, or 2 percent, roughly, of the kilowatt power used in the country. This was small by electric utility standards. But the picture is changing drastically. The Atomic Energy Commission estimates that nuclear power plants will be providing 25 percent of all electrical power by 1980, and between 60 and 70 percent by the year 2000. (Table 3-24; Map 3-6)

The implications of this are staggering.

Effluents from nuclear power reactors contain two significant isotopes: krypton-85, which is fed into the atmosphere and possesses a half-life of 10.76 years; and tritium, a liquid discharge which passes into receiving waters and which possesses a half-life of 12.26 years. ("Half-life" is the rate at which radioactivity decays or disappears. This means that half the radioactivity in krypton-85 will still be there after 10.75 years; half of that half in 21.50 years, etc.)

To date, public authorities have taken an exceedingly benign view toward both elements. The Council on Environmental Quality, for instance, said in its 1970 report that "there is no evidence that it (krypton-85) can concentrate through food chains," and that "there is no known mechanism by which tritium can concentrate in fish and shellfish or other food chains."[15] It did concede, on the other hand, that by the year 2000 the average genetic dose to the population from krypton-85 will be about 0.02 mrem, assuming that the element continues to be fed into the atmosphere, and that the population dosage of tritium will be 0.002 mrem per year by the same time. Since by the A.E.C.'s own literature "any amount of radiation will produce some measure of harm,"[16] since radionuclides have very long half-lives and thus can build up radioactive totals year by year, and since individual exposure to radiation is steadily increasing through X rays and common electronic devices of work and home (e.g., color television sets, luminous wrist watches, etc.), to minimize radiation health hazards from nuclear power plants is foolhardy, indeed. The additional millirems could prove disastrous.

Then there is that terrifying hazard: the possibility of nuclear accident. The Council of Environmental Quality plays down the possibility of a major nuclear accident,[17] but there is still the Brookhaven Report to sober the populace.[18] According to its findings, a reactor accident in a small nuclear plant in a nonurban location would kill some 3,400 persons, injure 43,000 more and inflict property damage of $7 billion. Deaths would be caused at distances of up to fifteen miles and injuries as far away as forty-five miles. Land contaminations might cover as much as 150,000 square miles, thus necessitating agricultural restrictions for an indefinite period. Proponents of nuclear power plants argue

[15]*Environmental Quality,* first annual report, August 1970.

[16]"Fallout from Nuclear Tests," June 1963, rev. June 1966.

[17]First Annual Report, 1970, p. 144.

[18]The Brookhaven Report is a study published by the Atomic Energy Commission in March 1957 under the title, "Theoretical Possibilities and Consequences of Major Accidents in Large Nuclear Plants." It takes the name Brookhaven from the fact that many of the forty scientists and engineers participating in the study were from Brookhaven National Laboratory.

that the Brookhaven is outdated, and that safety controls have become enormously sophisticated since 1957, the date of the report's issuance. Critics of nuclear power agree that the report is outdated, but because the situation has changed for the worse, not the better. The location of nuclear plants on the edges of large population concentrations (and sometimes in the very heart of metropolitan communities) and the phenomena of nuclear chain reactions provide more uneasiness over the wisdom of nuclear plant development. Not even a billion-to-one chance per year per reaction is a good gamble when the stakes are as high as they are.

Finally, there is the perplexing problem of the storage and disposal of the radioactive wastes from nuclear power plants, a problem which can only get progressively worse as nuclear power volume increases. The common practice at the moment is to store these wastes in huge steel tanks, encased in concrete and buried in the earth; the waste is so hot that it boils itself. Nuclear waste is a mighty problem now, when nuclear energy is supplying over 2 percent of the nation's kilowatt power; what of thirty years from now, when this percentage is between 60 and 70? Nuclear cemeteries will be as common and as vast as cemeteries for deceased humans. And what guarantee is there that these nuclear cemeteries will themselves not be accident prone? Will the steel caskets hold indefinitely? Will an earthquake disturb a nuclear cemetery and set off a devastating nuclear shower? These are questions which should be faced now, but which are being blissfully put off. Instead of sticking with fossil fuels until viable power alternatives are developed, the country presses ahead with the nuclear power scheme, and thus plays a kind of roulette game with millions of lives and millions of square miles of land, sea and air.

A U.S. Court of Appeals ruling of July 23, 1971, may have turned things around, however—though it is still too early to say definitely. On that date, Judge J. Skelly Wright of the District of Columbia handed down a decision delaying the nuclear power plant slated for construction by the Baltimore Gas and Electric Company at Calvert Cliffs on Chesapeake Bay in Maryland. Judge Wright ruled that the Atomic Energy Commission's regulations regarding the environment have made "a mockery" of the National Environmental Protection Act, and he ordered the agency to revise its rules completely. An outshoot of the ruling was the announcement on October 20, 1971, by Dr. James R. Schlesinger of the A.E.C. that the agency's role had shifted from promoting atomic energy to protecting the public interest in nuclear affairs.[19] Environmentalists breathed a small sigh of relief and expressed the hope that deeds would match words.

[19]"A.E.C. Shifts Role to Protect Public," Richard D. Lyons, *The New York Times,* October 21, 1971.

TABLE 3-24. Nuclear Power Plants

Site	Plant name	Capacity (Net kilowatts)	Utility	Initial design power
ALABAMA				
Decatur	Browns Ferry Nuclear Power Plant: Unit 1	1,064,500	Tennessee Valley Authority	1972
Decatur	Browns Ferry Nuclear Power Plant: Unit 2	1,064,500	Tennessee Valley Authority	1972
Decatur	Browns Ferry Nuclear Power Plant: Unit 3	1,064,500	Tennessee Valley Authority	1973
Dothan	Joseph M. Farley Nuclear Plant: Unit 1	829,000	Alabama Power Co.	1975
Dothan	Joseph M. Farley Nuclear Plant: Unit 2	829,000	Alabama Power Co.	1977
ARKANSAS				
London	Arkansas Nuclear One: Unit 1	820,000	Arkansas Power & Light Co.	1973
London	Arkansas Nuclear One: Unit 2	950,000	Arkansas Power & Light Co.	1975
CALIFORNIA				
Humboldt Bay	Humboldt Bay Power Plant: Unit 3	68,500	Pacific Gas & Electric Co.	1963
San Clemente[1]	San Onofre Nuclear Generating Station: Unit 1	430,000	So. Calif. Ed. & San Diego Gas & El. Co.	1967
San Clemente	San Onofre Nuclear Generating Station: Unit 2	1,140,000	So. Calif. Ed. & San Diego Gas & El. Co.	1975
San Clemente	San Onofre Nuclear Generating Station: Unit 3	1,140,000	So. Calif. Ed. & San Diego Gas & El. Co.	1977
Diablo Canyon	Diablo Canyon Nuclear Power Plant: Unit 1	1,060,000	Pacific Gas & Electric Co.	1973
Diablo Canyon	Diablo Canyon Nuclear Power Plant: Unit 2	1,060,000	Pacific Gas & Electric Co.	1974
Clay Station	Rancho Seco Nuclear Generating Station	804,000	Sacramento Municipal Utility District	1972
COLORADO				
Platteville	Ft. St. Vrain Nuclear Generating Station	330,000	Public Service Co. of Colorado	1972
CONNECTICUT				
Haddam Neck	Haddam Neck Plant	575,000	Conn. Yankee Atomic Power Co.	1967
Waterford	Millstone Nuclear Power Station: Unit 1	652,100	Northeast Utilities	1970
Waterford	Millstone Nuclear Power Station: Unit 2	828,000	Northeast Utilities	1974
FLORIDA				
Turkey Point	Turkey Point Station: Unit 3	651,500	Florida Power & Light Co.	1971
Turkey Point	Turkey Point Station: Unit 4	651,500	Florida Power & Light Co.	1972

Red Level	Crystal River Plant: Unit 3	858,000	Florida Power Corp.	1972
Ft. Pierce	Hutchinson Island: Unit 1	813,000	Florida Power and Light Co.	1973
GEORGIA				
Baxley	Edwin I. Hatch Nuclear Plant: Unit 1	786,000	Georgia Power Co.	1973
Baxley	Edwin I. Hatch Nuclear Plant: Unit 2	786,000	Georgia Power Co.	1976
ILLINOIS				
Morris	Dresden Nuclear Power Station: Unit 1	200,000	Commonwealth Edison Co.	1960
Morris	Dresden Nuclear Power Station: Unit 2	809,000	Commonwealth Edison Co.	1970
Morris	Dresden Nuclear Power Station: Unit 3	809,000	Commonwealth Edison Co.	1971
Zion	Zion Nuclear Plant: Unit 1	1,050,000	Commonwealth Edison Co.	1972
Zion	Zion Nuclear Plant: Unit 2	1,050,000	Commonwealth Edison Co.	1973
Cordova	Quad-Cities Station: Unit 1	809,000	Comm. Ed. Co.–Ia.–Ill. Gas & Elec. Co.	1971
Cordova	Quad-Cities Station: Unit 2	809,000	Comm. Ed. Co.–Ia.–Ill. Gas & Elec. Co.	1972
Seneca	LaSalle Co. Nuclear Station: Unit 1	1,078,000	Comm. Ed. Co.–Ia.	1975
Seneca	LaSalle Co. Nuclear Station: Unit 2	1,078,000	Comm. Ed. Co.–Ia.	1976
INDIANA				
Dune Acres	Bailly Generating Station	660,000	Northern Indiana Public Service Co.	1976
IOWA				
Cedar Rapids	Duane Arnold Energy Center: Unit 1	545,000	Iowa Electric Light and Power Co.	1973
LOUISIANA				
Taft	Waterford Generating Station: Unit 3	1,165,000	Louisiana Power & Light Co.	1976
MAINE				
Wiscasset	Maine Yankee Atomic Power Plant	790,000	Maine Yankee Atomic Power Co.	1972
MARYLAND				
Lusby	Calvert Cliffs Nuclear Power Plant: Unit 1	800,000	Baltimore Gas and Electric Co.	1973
Lusby	Calvert Cliffs Nuclear Power Plant: Unit 2	800,000	Baltimore Gas and Electric Co.	1974

[1] The San Onofre nuclear power plant is only one mile distant from the Christianitos fault, which cuts inland from the Pacific Ocean and northward, just west of Richard Nixon's California "White House" at San Clemente. According to geologists, the fault has been dormant for at least 100,000 years. However, the Los Angeles earthquake of February 1971 activated conservationists to the possibility that the plant—Unit 1 and proposed Units 2 and 3—could accidentally trigger a disturbance of the fault. Neither the existing Unit 1 nor the proposed new units contain any special design features to cope with earthquakes. Atomic Energy Commission standards require reinforced, anti-rupture reactor vessels only when a nuclear power plant is within a quarter-mile of a fault.

TABLE 3-24. Nuclear Power Plants (cont.)

Site	Plant name	Capacity (Net kilowatts)	Utility	Initial design power
MASSACHUSETTS				
Rowe	Yankee Nuclear Power Station	175,000	Yankee Atomic Electric Co.	1961
Plymouth	Pilgrim Station	654,000	Boston Edison Co.	1971
MICHIGAN				
Big Rock Point[2]	Big Rock Point Nuclear Plant	70,300	Consumers Power Co.	1963
South Haven	Palisades Nuclear Power Station	700,000	Consumers Power Co.	1970
Lagoona Beach	Enrico Fermi Atomic Power Plant: Unit 1	60,900	Detroit Edison Co.	1970
Lagoona Beach	Enrico Fermi Atomic Power Plant: Unit 2	1,123,000	Detroit Edison Co.	1973
Bridgman	Donald C. Cook Plant: Unit 1	1,054,000	Indiana & Michigan Electric Co.	1973
Bridgman	Donald C. Cook Plant: Unit 2	1,060,000	Indiana & Michigan Electric Co.	1974
Midland	Midland Nuclear Power Plant: Unit 1	492,000	Consumers Power Co.	1974
Midland	Midland Nuclear Power Plant: Unit 2	818,000	Consumers Power Co.	1975
MINNESOTA				
Monticello	Monticello Nuclear Generating Plant	545,000	Northern States Power Co.	1970
Red Wing	Prairie Island Nuclear Generating Plant: Unit 1	530,000	Northern States Power Co.	1972
Red Wing	Prairie Island Nuclear Generating Plant: Unit 2	530,000	Northern States Power Co.	1974
*	—	1,201,000	Tennessee Valley Authority	1977
*	—	1,201,000	Tennessee Valley Authority	1978
NEBRASKA				
Fort Calhoun	Ft. Calhoun Station: Unit 1	457,400	Omaha Public Power District	1972
Brownville	Cooper Nuclear Station	778,000	Nebraska Public Power District and Iowa Power and Light Co.	1972
NEW JERSEY				
Toms River	Oyster Creek Nuclear Power Plant: Unit 1	560,000	Jersey Central Power & Light Co.	1969
Lacey Township	Forked River Generating Station: Unit 1	1,140,000	Jersey Central Power & Light Co.	1975
Salem	Salem Nuclear Generating Station: Unit 1	1,050,000	Public Service Electric and Gas, N.J.	1972
Salem	Salem Nuclear Generating Station: Unit 2	1,050,000	Public Service Electric and Gas, N.J.	1973
Newbold Island	Newbold Nuclear Generating Station: Unit 1	1,088,000	Public Service Electric and Gas, N.J.	1975
Newbold Island	Newbold Nuclear Generating Station: Unit 2	1,088,000	Public Service Electric and Gas, N.J.	1977

NEW YORK				
Indian Point	Indian Point Station: Unit 1	265,000	Consolidated Edison Co.	1963
Indian Point	Indian Point Station: Unit 2	873,000	Consolidated Edison Co.	1971
Indian Point	Indian Point Station: Unit 3	965,000	Consolidated Edison Co.	1973
Scriba	Nine Mile Point Nuclear Station	500,000	Niagara Mohawk Power Co.	1970
Rochester	R.E. Ginna Nuclear Power Plant: Unit 1	420,000	Rochester Gas & Electric Co.	1970
Brookhaven	Shoreham Nuclear Power Station	819,000	Long Island Lighting Co.	1975
Lansing	Bell Station	838,000	New York State Electric & Gas Co.	1978
Verplanck	Verplanck: Unit 1	1,115,000	Consolidated Edison Co.	1977
Scriba	James A. Fitzpatrick Nuclear Power Plant	821,000	Power Authority of State of N.Y.	1973
NORTH CAROLINA				
Southport	Brunswick Steam Electric Plant: Unit 1	821,000	Carolina Power and Light Co.	1976
Southport	Brunswick Steam Electric Plant: Unit 2	821,000	Carolina Power and Light Co.	1974
*	–	821,000	Carolina Power and Light Co.	–
Cowans Ford Dam	Wm. B. McGuire Nuclear Station: Unit 1	1,150,000	Duke Power Co.	1975
Cowans Ford Dam	Wm. B. McGuire Nuclear Station: Unit 2	1,150,000	Duke Power Co.	1976
OHIO				
Oak Harbor	Davis-Besse Nuclear Power Station	872,000	Toledo Edison-Cleveland Electric Illuminating Co.	1974
Moscow	Wm. H. Zimmer Nuclear Power Station: Unit 1	810,000	Cincinnati Gas & Electric Co.	1974
OREGON				
Rainier	Trojan Station	1,130,000	Portland General Electric Co.	1974
PENNSYLVANIA				
Peach Bottom	Peach Bottom Atomic Power Station: Unit 1	40,000	Philadelphia Electric Co.	1967
Peach Bottom	Peach Bottom Atomic Power Station: Unit 2	1,065,000	Philadelphia Electric Co.	1972
Peach Bottom	Peach Bottom Atomic Power Station: Unit 3	1,065,000	Philadelphia Electric Co.	1973
Pottstown	Limerick Generating Station: Unit 1	1,065,000	Philadelphia Electric Co.	1975
Pottstown	Limerick Generating Station: Unit 2	1,065,000	Philadelphia Electric Co.	1977
Shippingport	Shippingport Atomic Power Station: Unit 1	90,000	Duquesne Light Co.	1957
Shippingport	Beaver Valley Power Station: Unit 1	847,000	Duquesne Light Co.–Ohio Edison Co.	1973

[2] In March 1971, Glenn T. Seaborg, chairman of the Atomic Energy Commission, conceded under pressure from consumer advocate Ralph Nader that the Big Rock Point plant had actually been used for a time as an Air Force practice target in simulated low-level bombing runs. Nader had protested that a "nuclear catastrophe" could result if a plane accidentally plunged into a nuclear plant and caused a release of radioactive material. Seaborg said that Big Rock Point had been removed from the Air Force's practice target list some time before. The fact that the Air Force has once engaged in practice "dry runs" against the nuclear plant sent chills down the backs of safety officials and environmentalists.

*Site not selected.

TABLE 3-24. Nuclear Power Plants (cont.)

Site	Plant name	Capacity (Net kilowatts)	Utility	Initial design power
Middletown	Three Mile Island Nuclear Station: Unit 1	810,000	Metropolitan Edison Co.	1972
Middletown	Three Mile Island Nuclear Station: Unit 2	810,000	Jersey Central Power & Light Co.	1974
Berwick	Susquehanna Steam Electric Station: Unit 1	1,052,000	Pennsylvania Power and Light	1977
Berwick	Susquehanna Steam Electric Station: Unit 2	1,052,000	Pennsylvania Power and Light	1979
SOUTH CAROLINA				
Hartsville	H.B. Robinson S.E. Plant: Unit 2	700,000	Carolina Power & Light Co.	1971
Seneca	Oconee Nuclear Station: Unit 1	841,000	Duke Power Co.	1971
Seneca	Oconee Nuclear Station: Unit 2	886,000	Duke Power Co.	1972
Seneca	Oconee Nuclear Station: Unit 3	886,000	Duke Power Co.	1973
TENNESSEE				
Daisy	Sequoyah Nuclear Power Plant: Unit 1	1,124,000	Tennessee Valley Authority	1974
Daisy	Sequoyah Nuclear Power Plant: Unit 2	1,124,000	Tennessee Valley Authority	1974
Rhea County	Watts Bar Nuclear Plant: Unit 1	1,170,000	Tennessee Valley Authority	1976
Rhea County	Watts Bar Nuclear Plant: Unit 2	1,170,000	Tennessee Valley Authority	1977
VERMONT				
Vernon	Vermont Yankee Generating Station	513,900	Vermont Yankee Nuclear Power Corp.-Green Mt. Power Corp.	1971
VIRGINIA				
Gravel Neck	Surry Power Station: Unit 1	780,000	Virginia Electric & Power Co.	1971
Gravel Neck	Surry Power Station: Unit 2	780,000	Virginia Electric & Power Co.	1972
Mineral	North Anna Power Station: Unit 1	845,000	Virginia Electric & Power Co.	1974
Mineral	North Anna Power Station: Unit 2	845,000	Virginia Electric & Power Co.	1975
WASHINGTON				
Richland	N-Reactor/WPPSS Steam	790,000	Washington Public Power Supply System	1966
WISCONSIN				
Genoa	LaCrosse Boiling Water Reactor	50,000	Dairyland Power Cooperative	1969
Two Creeks	Point Beach Nuclear Plant: Unit 1	497,000	Wisconsin Michigan Power Co.	1970
Two Creeks	Point Beach Nuclear Plant: Unit 2	497,000	Wisconsin Michigan Power Co.	1971
Carlton	Kewaunee Nuclear Power Plant: Unit 1	527,000	Wisconsin Public Service Co.	1972
PUERTO RICO				
Central Aguirre	Aguirre Nuclear Power Plant	583,000	Puerto Rico Water Resources Authority	1975

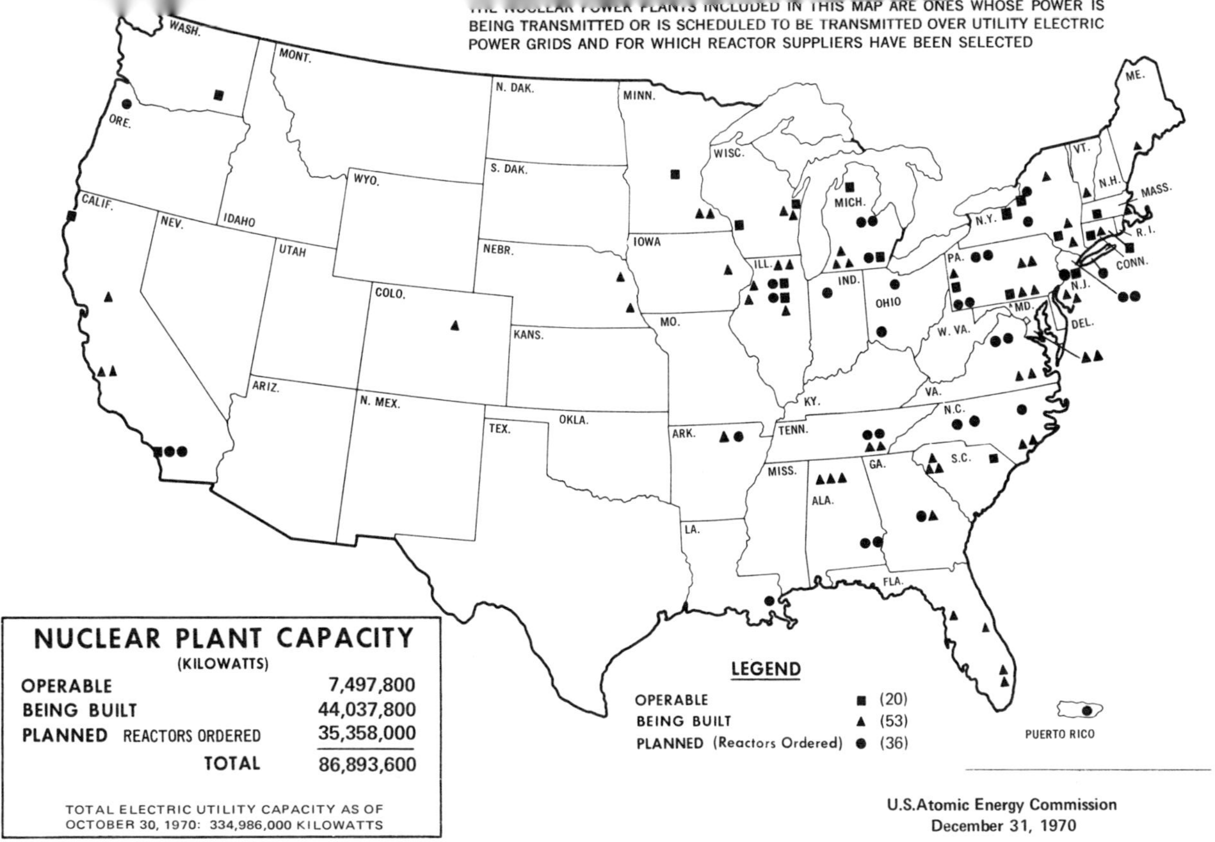
INCLUDED IN THIS MAP ARE ONES WHOSE POWER IS
BEING TRANSMITTED OR IS SCHEDULED TO BE TRANSMITTED OVER UTILITY ELECTRIC
POWER GRIDS AND FOR WHICH REACTOR SUPPLIERS HAVE BEEN SELECTED
WASH.
MONT.
N. DAK.
MINN.
ORE.
S. DAK.
WISC.
WYO.
MICH.
ME.
VT.
N.H.
MASS.
CALIF.
NEV.
IDAHO
N.Y.
R. I.
UTAH
NEBR.
IOWA
PA.
CONN.
ILL.
IND.
N.J.
COLO.
OHIO
MD.
MO.
DEL.
KANS.
W. VA.
ARIZ.
VA.
KY.
N. MEX.
N.C.
TEX.
OKLA.
ARK.
TENN.
S.C.
GA.
MISS.
ALA.
LA.
FLA.
PUERTO RICO
LEGEND
OPERABLE (20)
BEING BUILT (53)
PLANNED (Reactors Ordered) (36)
NUCLEAR PLANT CAPACITY
(KILOWATTS)
OPERABLE 7,497,800
BEING BUILT 44,037,800
PLANNED REACTORS ORDERED 35,358,000
TOTAL 86,893,600
TOTAL ELECTRIC UTILITY CAPACITY AS OF
OCTOBER 30, 1970: 334,986,000 KILOWATTS
U.S.Atomic Energy Commission
December 31, 1970

Map 3-6.

SELECTED BIBLIOGRAPHY

Advisory Task Force on Power Reactor Emergency Cooling, "Emergency Core Cooling," U. S. Atomic Energy Commission, Division of Technical Information Extension, Oak Ridge, Tennessee, 1967.

Beckerley, J. G., and Hilberry, N., review of *Perils of the Peaceful Atom,* in *INFO,* publication of the Atomic Industrial Forum, New York, July 1969, special issue.

Boffey, P. M., "Radioactive Pollution: Minnesota Finds AEC Standards Too Lax," *Science Magazine,* American Association for the Advancement of Science, Washington, D.C., March 7, 1969.

Bryerton, G., *Nuclear Dilemma,* A Friends of the Earth/Ballantine Book, New York, 1970.

Brezina, E. R., "The Effects of Heated Water Discharge and Acid Mine Drainage on the Water Quality, Biota and Community Metabolism in a 1500-Acre Missouri Reservoir"; thesis, University of Missouri Graduate School, Columbia, Missouri, June 1968.

Cairns, J., Jr., "Pollution's Eternal Triangle," *The Association of Southeastern Biologists Bulletin,* Philadelphia, Pennsylvania, April 1965.

Curtis, R., and Hogan, E., *Perils of the Peaceful Atom,* Doubleday, New York, 1969; Ballantine, 1970.

Federal Water Pollution Control Agency, "Industrial Waste Guide on Thermal Pollution," Northwest Region, Pacific Northwest Water Laboratory, Corvallis, Oregon, September 1968 (rev.).

Foreman, H., ed., *Nuclear Power and the Public,* University of Minnesota Press, 1971.

Hedgpeth, J. W., "The Era of Environmental Concern," *Science Magazine,* May 1969.

Iowa State University, "Genetic Effects of Irradiating Swine," ninth annual report of work in progress under contract with the U. S. Atomic Energy Commission, Clearinghouse for Federal Scientific and Technical Information, Springfield, Virginia, June 1969.

Jacobs, D. G., "Sources of Tritium and Its Behavior Upon Release to the Environment," Oak Ridge National Laboratory, Oak Ridge, Tennessee, distributed by the Clearinghouse for Federal Scientific and Technical Information, Springfield, Virginia, 1968.

Lederberg, Joshua, Affidavit, Public Service Board of Vermont, Docket #3445, on the Vermont Yankee Nuclear Power Plant, September 8, 1970.

Minnesota Committee for Environmental Information, "The Costs and Benefits of Nuclear Electric Power Plants," Minneapolis, Minnesota, February 8, 1969.

Novick, S., *The Careless Atom,* Houghton Mifflin, Boston, 1969.

"Nuclear Plant Used as Target in Simulated Bombing," John D. Morris in *The New York Times,* April 1, 1971, p. 27.

Pauling, Linus, Affidavit, Public Service Board of Vermont, Docket #3445, on the Vermont Yankee Nuclear Power Plant, September 9, 1970.

Ramparts, Editors of, *Eco-Catastrophe,* Harper & Row, New York, 1970.

Ritchie-Calder, Lord, "Polluting the Environment," *The Center Magazine,* Santa Barbara, California, May 1969.

Russell, R. S., et al., *Radioactivity and Human Diet,* Pergamon Press, London, 1966.

Snow, J. A., "Radioactive Waste from Reactors: The Problem That Won't Go Away," *Scientist and Citizen Magazine,* Committee for Environmental Information, St. Louis, Missouri, May 1967.

Thompson, T. J., and Beckerley, J. G., *The Technology of Nuclear Reactor Safety,* M.I.T. Press, Cambridge, 1964.

Tremmel, E. B., "The Growth of Nuclear Power in the United States," address at the Hill Foundation Seminar for Newsmen, University of Oregon, Eugene, Oregon, June 19, 1969.

U. S. Atomic Energy Commission, "Major Activities in the Atomic Energy Programs," U. S. Government Printing Office, January 1969.

U. S. Atomic Energy Commission. *The New Force of Atomic Energy—Its Development and Use.* USAEC Division of Technical Information Extension. Oak Ridge, Tennessee, n.d.

U. S. Atomic Energy Commission, "Rules and Regulations, Title 10—Atomic Energy; Part 20, Standards for Protection Against Radiation." Washington, D.C.

U. S. Atomic Energy Commission. "Theoretical Possibilities and Consequences of Major Accidents in Large Nuclear Power Plants." WASH-740, USAEC. March 1957. (Brookhaven Report)

United States Atomic Energy Commission, *Understanding the Atom* series, including:

Asimov, Isaac, and Dobzhansky, Theodosius. "The Genetic Effects of Radiation," September 1968.

Comar, C. L. "Fallout from Nuclear Tests," June 1963, rev. June 1966.

Fox, Charles H. "Radioactive Wastes," 1966, rev. 1969.

Frigerio, Norman A. "Your Body and Radiation," March 1969.

Glasstone, Samuel. "Controlled Nuclear Fusion," October 1968.

Hogerton, John F. "Atomic Power Safety," December 1967.

———, "Nuclear Radiation Environment, 1968.

Kastner, Jacob. "The Natural Radiation Environment," 1968.

Lyerly, Ray L., and Mitchell III, Walter. "Nuclear Power Plants," October 1968.

Lyman, James D., and USAEC staff members. "Nuclear Terms: A Brief Glossary," 2d ed. December 1967.

Martens, Frederick H., and Jacobson, Norman H. "Research Reactors," September 1968.

Ricciuti, Edward R. "Animals in Atomic Research," August 1967.

Singleton Jr., Arthur L. "Sources of Nuclear Fuel," June 1968.

Urrows, Grace M. "Nuclear Energy for Desalting," September 1967.

U. S. Department of the Interior. "An Appraisal of the Petroleum Industry of the United States," Office of Oil and Gas, Washington, D.C., January 1965.

U. S. Department of the Interior, Federal Water Pollution Control Administration, "Compendium of Department of the Interior Statements of Non-degradation of Interstate Waters." Washington, D.C., August 1968.

U. S. Department of the Interior. "United States Petroleum Through 1980," Department of the Interior, Office of Oil and Gas, Washington, D.C., July 1968.

U. S. Joint Committee on Atomic Energy. "Selected Materials on Environmental Effects of Producing Electric Power," U. S. Government Printing Office, Washington, D.C., August 1969.

U. S. Congress, Senate Committee on Public Works. "Amending the Federal Water Pollution Control Act, As Amended, and for Other Purposes," U. S. Government Printing Office, August 1969.

6. NOISE

No pollutant comes so close to embracing everyone, yet none is appreciated so little, as noise. Noise has so much become a part of the living and working condition of modern man as to take on an aspect of the inevitable. It should not be the case, but nevertheless it is. The housewife takes pretty much for granted the whirling and grinding of her appliances, the buzz of automobiles and clanging of machinery in the street outside her window, the drone of the television set or the hi-fi which follows her from room to room. The worker copes with noise on the job, noise going to and from work, noise at home and noise during his leisure. Noise comes from the sky, via airplanes; from underground, via trains and subways; from the neighbor's yard, via power mowers; from youngsters strolling along the sidewalk, via transistor radios. Noise is everywhere. Oscar Wilde remarked in 1882 that "America is the noisiest country that ever existed." He should be here in 1970. It is the difference between two in the morning and high noon. In the last fifteen years alone, the noise level of the country has doubled.[20]

Perhaps noise is so little appreciated as a pollutant because individuals have accepted it as inevitable and adjusted to it, even to the point of building up psychological tolerances. But anyone who thinks he is not adversely affected by noise is likely to be deluding himself. The Federal Council of Science and Technology estimates that as many as 16 million men and women workers in America are threatened with irreversible hearing loss by the noise of their work environment. Even entertainment carries its threat. Rock music and electronic musical instruments, for instance, are so demonstrably dangerous to hearing that at least one manufacturer has placed warning labels on his products. Noise damages hearing; it can also cause ulcers, hypertension, involuntary muscular responses, allergies and a variety of other biological and psychological disturbances. Noise can bring harm to unborn fetuses, and so upset animals as to threaten their survival. Rats exposed to high-level noise have turned homosexual and cannibalistic, then died of heart failure.

The quality of noise, that which gives it its pitch, is frequency. Frequency is measured by units of cycle per second. These units are described as Hertz (Hz), after Heinrich Hertz (1857–1894), the German physicist who first established the presence of electromagnetic waves in the air. The range of the human ear is from 15 Hertz to 20,000 Hertz. Noises such as shrieks or whistles which exceed 20,000 Hz will be heard by pigeons, dogs, bats and other animals, but are ultrasonic so far as the human ear is concerned, and will not be heard by humans.

The intensity of noise is measured in units called decibels, after Alexander Graham Bell (1847–1922), inventor of the telephone and an important researcher into the nature of sound. The decibel (dB) measurement is logarithmic, which means that every increase of ten is a ten-time increase in the level of noise. Thus, a noise pressure of 130 decibels is ten times greater than that of 120 decibels, and 100 times greater than that of 110 decibels. Thirty decibels is considered very quiet; 50, moderately quiet; 80, annoying, and 95, very annoying. At 100 decibels, noise begins to become intolerable. At 140 decibels,

[20]*In Quest of Quiet,* by Henry Still, Stackpole Books, 1970.

the individual has reached the threshold of pain. At 180 decibels, the noise is lethal. (See Table 3-25 for a decibel measurement of the sounds of America.)

The most direct health threat from noise is, obviously, to one's hearing. Studies show that the most dangerous noises are those which are audibly the loudest, highest pitched, purest in tone and longest lasting.[21] Police-car and fire-engine sirens are precisely such noises. To be damaging, however, noise need not be steady. Occasional blasts of noise will also be damaging.

The initial warning of noise damage to hearing is ear discomfort. At 85 decibels, there may be a ringing in the ear or some temporary inability to hear. These are signals to the individual to take care. The ear will recover from occasional jarring noises, but if noise is experi-

TABLE 3-25. Comparative Noise Levels (by decibel measure)

(Increases in decibels are not arithmetical but logarithmic. Therefore, every increase of ten decibels is a ten-time increase in noise. Eighty decibels is considered loud, and 100 decibels the level at which a high percentage of people will find the noise intolerable and begin to react strongly.)

	Perceived decibel level
Room in a quiet city dwelling at midnight	32
Average city residence	40
House party with 4-piece rock band	115
Power lawn mower, operator's position	96
Traffic at a residential intersection	82
Small 2-engine private plane (sideline noise @ 1,500 feet)	80-85
Heavy truck, 25 feet away	90
Train whistle, 500 feet away	90
Subway train, 20 feet away	95
DC-3 (sideline noise @ 1,500 feet)	95-100*
Loud outboard motor	102
Loud motorcycle	110
Boeing 707, DC-8 (sideline noise @ 1,500 feet)	110-115
Large pneumatic 3-inch riveter	125
Sports car moving in street	86
SST—Supersonic Transport Plane (sideline noise @ 1,500 feet)	122-129**
Threshold of pain	140

Source: Noise—The Third Pollution, by Theodore Berland, New York, New York; et al.

*The judgment of 100 decibels as intolerable noise is shared by the Federal Aviation Agency. Yet new FAA noise standards allow 108 decibels.

**The SST also will produce a noise of over 100 decibels for 13 miles in either direction from its flight path.

[21] *Noise—The Third Pollution,* by Theodore Berland. Public Affairs Pamphlet No. 449, of Public Affairs Committee, Inc., 381 Park Avenue South, New York, New York, 10016, 1970.

enced too often and too steadily permanent damage that will make the ear deaf to certain frequencies of sound will begin to occur. Long-term exposure to noise over 80 decibels is for most people the courting of degrees of deafness.

The first sounds lost to the ear from excess noise, it is found, are the fricative consonants: *f, s, th, ch* and *sh* sounds. Then the explosive consonants are likely to go: *b, t, p, k* and *d.* Curiously, hearing losses from noise do not coincide with the offending frequencies, but are a half an octave higher. Accordingly, an individual suffering from noise deafness will still be able to hear the offending frequencies, but not the frequencies just a bit higher.[22]

Noise is not an unrecognized problem in the United States. A number of states and cities have adopted statutes and codes in attempts to bring noise under control. The Department of Labor drew up federal standards for occupational exposure to noise in May 1969, and in November 1969 the Department of Transportation issued the first of a series of noise standards under Public Law 90-411. The Department of Housing and Urban Development (HUD) has entered noise into equations for determining the quality of proposed housing sites. However, the adoption of statutes and codes is not the solving of the problem of noise; as the first report of the Council on Environmental Quality commented, "these regulations are almost impossible to enforce."[23] Primarily it comes down to the fact that noise is still an intangible.

But codes or no codes, enforcement or no enforcement, health authorities are unanimous in recommending that people protect themselves against noise, and that they create as little noise themselves as possible. Health officials would like to see individuals use earplugs and ear protectors as commonly and instinctively as they do sunglasses. They advise noiseproof walls in construction, and noise-deadening appointments in the home, like window drapes, carpets, upholstered furniture and acoustical ceilings. These will both absorb sound and reduce its reverberation. They advise, too, that in making purchases for blenders, appliances or any power-driven machine or apparatus, the buyer take into consideration the noise levels of the various brands and favor the quieter item. Most especially, health authorities ask that people themselves be quiet in a conscientious way. Even small details, like restraint in blowing one's automobile horn (105 dB at three feet) can improve appreciably the livability of a neighborhood.

The Supersonic Airplane

The development which finally aroused the public to the problem of noise was that which threatened to devastate whatever hope there

[22]Ibid. p. 7.

[23]*Environmental Quality.* August 1969, p. 129.

was left to establish a quiet in the country—the commercial supersonic transport plane (SST). The SST is designed to travel routinely at speeds vastly exceeding those of sound. At sea level and 60 degrees Fahrenheit, the sound barrier is exceeded at 760 miles per hour; at 65,000 feet, where the temperature is lower (minus 80 degrees) and the speed of sound correspondingly lower, the figure drops to 650 mph. The Boeing SST, the U.S. experiment in a supersonic airplane aborted by Congress in 1971, would have traveled at speeds of up to 1800 mph at heights of from 60,000 to 80,000 feet. This would be 2.7 times the speed of sound.

The most immediate effect of an aircraft exceeding the speed of sound is the creation of a sonic boom, or pressure disturbance, sending shock waves toward earth capable of breaking windows, cracking walls, stampeding cattle and seriously unsettling human, animal and fish life. People have learned to live with all sorts of rackets, but a sonic boom is something else. A series of forty-nine test flights flown over Chicago in 1965 resulted in 6,000 complaints, 3,000 damage claims and a total of $114,763 being paid out in damages; in Switzerland, a herd of prize cattle raced off a cliff when frightened by a sonic boom; simulated booms have altered birth patterns among test rats at the University of Oklahoma.

The sonic boom is not a phenomenon of the SST alone. A number of military planes fly at speeds greater than sound, but because of their lighter weight (only 10–20 percent the SST's gross weight of 375 tons), their booms are less intense and of lesser duration than those of an SST. Also, the military plane is not flying the usual commercial routes, and thus not exposing as many people to its boom as would an SST.

The SST would produce no boom during the first 100 and last 100 miles of its trip, when it is accelerating and decelerating. But over the remainder of its flight, it would carve out a boom, or bang-zone, fifty miles wide. If the SST ever entered domestic service, a single New York to Los Angeles trip, a distance of 2,000 miles, would mean the banging of a 100,000-square-mile area and the disturbance of anywhere from 10 to 40 million people.

But the boom is only one problem connected with the SST. On take-off and landing, the SST would make 2.5 times more sideline noise than the largest subsonic jets. Because it would require larger quantities of fuel for its propulsion (one ton per minute on take-off), the SST would add appreciable amounts of toxic pollutants to the environment. A regular jet airplane dirties the environment in one landing with as much soot as 2,500 automobiles produce in an entire day; an SST would top that. The SST would not help the upper atmosphere either. Because of the windless altitudes at which the plane would fly, the water vapor, sulphur and soot which the plane would emit could lie virtually dead over the earth, building itself eventually into a permanent cloud cover. This could radically alter radiation and temperature balances over the whole planet.

There is the possibility, too, that the SST would be a serious health menace to passengers. The SST is designed to cruise at heights where ionization from cosmic radiation is at its highest. No passenger could be comforted by the fact that between him and this ionization was the metal shield of the plane. The metal body of the aircraft would be no protection at all; in fact, the reverse. The metal would actually multiply the charged particles (protons, alpha particles, etc.) of the radiation belt, by a process known as shower production. At cruising altitudes, this would increase radiation levels inside the SST as much as 100 times those of sea level.

In addition to all this, there are engineering and operating liabilities, among them:

Metal fatigue (quickened by the high temperatures caused by impacting supersonic airflow);

Landing speeds (a dangerous 180 mph);

Poor maneuverability (the SST is comparable in size to a football field);

Limited visibility and, therefore, limited reaction time (at 1800 mph, the SST would be traveling one mile in two seconds, five miles in ten seconds, ten miles in 20 seconds);

Inability to "hold" for long periods (at a half-ton of fuel per cruise minute, options in times of distress would be drastically restricted);

Limited emergency landing opportunities (the SST would need extra-long runways—10,300 feet, or almost two miles—and surfaces of extra strength).

The United States began development of an SST during the Kennedy Administration, when Congress approved $11 million for research. That was in August 1961. Several administrations and $700 million later, the project was moving steadily ahead. Then in December 1970 the Senate surprisingly denied a Nixon Administration request for $290 million more to continue work on two prototypes of the Boeing SST. After long and intense congressional debate, emergency funding was provided to carry the project until the following March, when a new Congress, rather than a "lame-duck" Congress, could decide its fate. The decision again was negative. On March 18, 1971, the House voted 215–204 to cut off federal funding of the SST as of March 30, 1971. The Senate concurred by a 51–46 vote five days later. The reasons for the SST's defeat were environmental and economic; with respect to the latter, technological refinements necessary to overcome such difficulties as noise had skyrocketed costs and made it unlikely that the plane could ever be operated on a profit basis.

The Nixon Administration was bitter about the congressional deci-

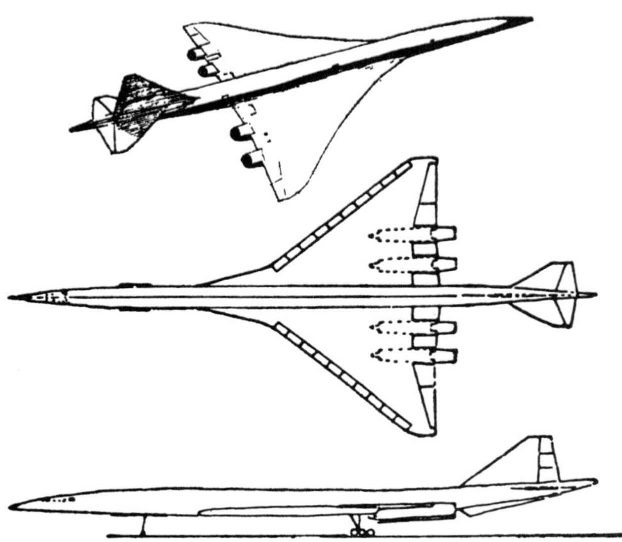

FIGURE 3-7. Design of the Boeing SST (B-2707-300)

sion, but there was nothing it could do except to pledge to the aircraft industry and to the 14,000 SST workers that one day the project would again be alive. "We may have lost this one," Mr. Nixon told workers in Seattle and Wichita by telephone on March 25, 1971, "but we're going to win the next one."[24] The comment may have been rhetoric, but only in so far as Mr. Nixon did not have a Plan B to put into operation once Plan A had been scuttled by Congress. It can be said almost without question that the future will bring pressures anew for an SST.

It is not going to be easy to resist this pressure. The British and French were flying prototypes of their Concorde supersonic in 1970, and the Russians announced that their supersonic TU-144 would be operational about the end of 1973. The British and French are aiming for commerical service in 1974. Thus the matter becomes more than one of environmental concern. It becomes one of national prestige—and the foreign trade market. The United States, which sells four out of every five planes bought in the noncommunist world, has never been one to turn its back on new business, and the SST market will be worth an estimated $125 billion to someone by 1990. There will undoubtedly be those who will want the United States to get back into the SST business to capture a corner of that market.

[24]*The New York Times,* March 26, 1971, p. 23.

One way to lessen that pressure, and at the same time to defuse foreign industry and reckless enthusiasm over the SST, would be to pass laws banning the SST from one's national air space. Scandinavian countries have taken the initiative here; the United States should also act. If enough nations act, the horizons of the SST can be so limited as to make construction and operation impractical.

Herewith is a depiction of the bang zone which fifty SSTs serving eleven Western Hemisphere cities and twenty one European and African cities would create over the Atlantic. The map was prepared by Citizens League Against the Sonic Boom, and is calculated according to individual bang-zone widths of 100 miles each. The cities proposed as future SST airport communities were: Atlanta, Baltimore, Boston, Miami, Montreal, New York, Ottawa, Philadelphia, Washington, San Juan, Bermuda, and Amsterdam, Bergen, Bordeaux, Brussels, Dublin, Frankfort, Helsinki, Keflavik, Lisbon, London, Madrid, Manchester, Milan, Oslo, Paris, Prestwick, Stockholm, Zurich, Azores, Casablanca, Las Palmas.

The routes shown are great-circle routes, with occasional deviations required for avoidance of peninsulas and islands. Final specifications of routes have not yet been decided by the airlines and the FAA (Federal Aviation Agency).

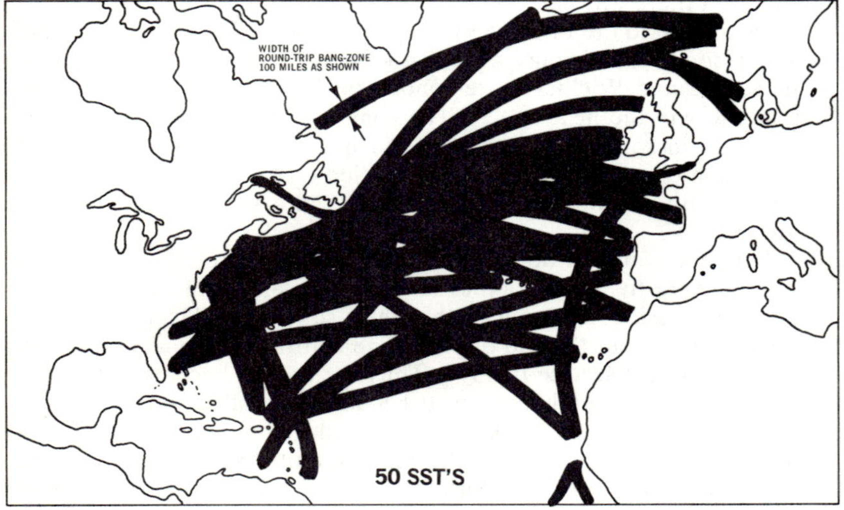

MAP 3-7.
This is what 50 SSTs' paths of destruction would look like. Everything in the blackened area would be damaged or destroyed

SELECTED BIBLIOGRAPHY

Acoustical Society of America, Proceedings of the Sonic Boom Symposium, *Journal of the Acoustical Society of America,* No. 39, May 1966.

American Speech and Hearing Association, *Proceedings,* National Conference on "Noise as a Public Health Hazard," June 13–14, 1968.

Baker, L., *The Guaranteed Society,* Macmillan, New York, 1968.

Baron, Robert Alex, *The Tyranny of Noise,* St. Martin's Press, New York, 1970.

Baxter, W. F., "The SST: From Watts to Harlem in Two Hours," *Stanford Law Review,* November 1968.

Beranek, Leo L. (ed.), *Noise Reduction,* McGraw-Hill, New York, 1960.

Berland, Theodore, *Noise—The Third Pollution,* Public Affairs Pamphlets, No. 449, New York, 1970.

———, *The Fight for Quiet,* Prentice-Hall, Englewood Cliffs, N.J., 1970.

Bolt, Beranek and Newman, Inc., *Laboratory Tests of Subjective Reactions to Sonic Booms,* by K. S. Pearsons and K. D. Kryter, Report NASA-CR-187, March 1965.

Burns, William, *Noise and Man,* John Murray, Lodon, 1968.

Chacona, C. J., "The High and the Mighty: the SST Charivari," a thesis, Harvard University, 1968.

Dwiggins, D., *The SST: Here It Comes, Ready or Not,* Doubleday, New York, 1969.

Gleason, G. K., "The Supersonic Transport and the Boom Problem," thesis for Harvard Law School Seminar on Legal Protection of Environmental Quality, May 31, 1968.

Harris, H. L., "Assault on Emotional Health," *American Journal of Psychiatry, 125,* September 3, 1968.

Huard, L. A., "The Roar, the Whine, the Boom and the Law: Some Legal Concerns about the SST," *Santa Clara Lawyer,* Spring 1969.

Institute for Defense Analyses, Inc., *Economic Effects of the Sonic Boom,* N. J. Asher, *et al.,* AD-655608, December 1964.

Institute for Defense Analyses, Inc., *Demand Analysis for Air Travel by Supersonic Transport,* Report R-118, two volumes, AD-652309 and AD-652310, December 1966.

International Commission on Radiological Protection, Task Group on the Biological Effects of High-Energy Radiation, *Radiobiological Aspects of the Supersonic Transport, Health Physics 12,* 209–226, 1966.

Kryter, K. D., "Sonic Booms from Supersonic Transport," *Science,* January 24, 1969.

———, "Sonic Boom—Results of Laboratory and Field Studies," Stanford Research Institute, June 1968.

Landis, C., and Hunt, W. A., *The Startle Reaction,* Farrar and Rinehart, New York, 1939.

Library of Congress, *Policy Planning for Aeronautical Research and Development,* Document 90, 89th Congress, 2nd Session, May 19, 1966.

Lundberg, B., "Supersonic Aviation, a Testcase for Democracy," NATO's Fifteen Nations, April–June 1965 issues.

———, "The Menace of the Sonic Boom to Society and Civil Aviation," Aeronautical Research Institute of Sweden, Report FFA-PE-19, May 1966.

———, "Acceptable Nominal Sonic Boom Overpressure in SST Operation Over Land and Sea," paper presented at June 14, 1968, National Conference on Noise as a Public Health Hazard, American Speech & Hearing Association.

———, "Implications and Justification of the SST," from "The Sonic Boom," October 2, 1968 symposium, Nederlands Akoestisch Genootschap, Delft, Netherlands. Postbus 162, Publication No. 15, April 1969, pp. 33–69.

———, "Summary Statement on the Unacceptability of the SST Sonic Boom Over Land and Sea and the Economic Losses of SST Operation Confined to Oversea Routes," BL Report 118, October 24, 1969, 16 pages.

Murphy, C. J. V., "Boeing's Ordeal with the SST," *Fortune,* October 1968.
National Academy of Sciences, Committee on SST-Sonic Boom, *Generation and Propaganda of Sonic Boom,* October 1967.
National Academy of Sciences, Committee on SST-Sonic Boom, *Physical Effects of the Sonic Boom,* February 1968.
National Academy of Sciences, Committee on SST-Sonic Boom, *Human Responses to the Sonic Boom,* June 1968.
National Academy of Sciences, Clarifying material called "Statement of the Committee on SST-Sonic Boom," August 19, 1968. (Prepared to correct a false conclusion in an earlier report.)
"Noise Around Us, Findings and Recommendations," report of the Panel on Noise Abatement, U. S. Government Printing Office, 1971.
Pao, Y. H., and Goldburg, A., *Clear Air Turbulence,* Consultants Bureau, New York, 1969.
Parkhurst, F. S., Jr., *Noise, Jets and the Sonic Boom,* Guilford College, Greensboro, North Carolina, August 11, 1967.
President's SST Ad Hoc Review Committee, Report of March 1969, *Congressional Record,* October 31, 1969, pp. H-10432–H-10446.
Shurcliff, W. A., *S/S/T and Sonic Boom Handbook,* Ballantine Books, 1970.
Standford Research Institute Report, "Preliminary Study of the Awakening and Startle Effects of Simulated Sonic Booms," J. S. Lukas and K. D. Kryter, contract NAS-1-6193, April 1968.
Still, Henry, *In Quest of Quiet, Meeting the Menace of Noise Pollution,* Stackpole Books, Harrisburg, Pennsylvania, 1970.
———, *The Dirty Animal,* Hawthorn, New York, 1967.
———, *Will the Human Race Survive?,* Hawthorn, New York, 1966.
U. S. Army Human Engineering Laboratories, *Criteria for Assessing Hearing Damage Risk from Impulse-Noise Exposure,* Technical Memorandum 13-67 AD-666206. August 1967.
U. S. Department of the Interior, Sonic Boom Study Group: "Noise and Sonic Boom in Relation to Man," November 4, 1968.
U. S. Department of Transportation, FAA Report "Final Program Summary: Oklahoma City Sonic Boom Study," Report SST-65-3, AD459601, March 21, 1965.
U. S. Department of Transportation, Federal Aviation Administration, "U.S. Supersonic Transport: Economic Feasibility Report," April 1967.
U. S. Federal Aviation Agency "United States Supersonic Transport Program," Report SST-65-10, July 1965.
U. S. National Aeronautics and Space Administration Report "Result of USAF-NASA-FAA Flight Program to Study Community Response to Sonic Booms in the Greater St. Louis Area," C. W. Nixon and H. H. Hubbard, NASA TN-D-2705, May 1965.
U. S. National Aeronautics and Space Administration Report "Sonic Boom Measurements During Bomber Training Operations in the Chicago Area," D. A. Hilton, V. Huckel and D. J. Maglieri, NASA TN-D-3655, October 1966.
Welch, B. L., and Welch, A. S. (eds.), *Psychological Effects of Noise,* Plenum Press, New York, 1970.

GENERAL BIBLIOGRAPHY FOR POLLUTION

Council on Environmental Quality, *Environmental Quality: First Annual Report of the Council on Environmental Quality,* Government Printing Office, Washington, D.C., 1970. The best general overview of U. S. pollution and environmental issues.
Study of Critical Environmental Problems (SCEP), *Man's Impact on the Global Environ-*

ment: Assessment and Recommendations for Action, M.I.T. Press, Cambridge, 1970. Clear, pragmatic look at various environmental problems by interdisciplinary team of experts. One of the most valuable contributions to the field.

American Chemical Society (ACS), *Cleaning Our Environment: The Chemical Basis For Action,* Washington, D.C., 1969. Chemical view of pollution crisis, excellent documentation.

McHale, John, *The Future of the Future,* George Braziller, New York, 1969. *The Ecological Context,* George Braziller, New York, 1970. Two eclectic studies of wide-ranging interest offering multi-faceted approach to environment.

Reinow, R., and Reinow, L. T., *Moment in the Sun,* Ballantine Books, New York, 1967. Popular, well-written introduction to the American environmental situation.

Erlich, P., and Erlich, Ann H., *Population, Resources, Environments,* W. H. Freeman and Company, San Francisco, 1970. The best ecology textbook on the market.

IV Detergents

When radio and television personality Arthur Godfrey bit the hand that fed him in February 1970 by publicly criticizing the Colgate-Palmolive Company because of its Axion product, he dramatized the problem of pollution of waters by phosphates in a manner which congressional hearings and warnings by scientists and environmentalists had to that time barely approximated. For long months consumers had been softened by the Godfrey pitch for Axion, an "enzyme active" for pre-soaking laundry. Godfrey had been selling Axion under assurances from Colgate-Palmolive that it ate the dirt out of clothes and polluted nothing. A newspaper article recapitulating hearings of a congressional subcommittee alerted Godfrey that it was all a fiction. Axion was not only a pollutant, but one of the heaviest of its type, having a sodium tripolyphosphate percentage level of 63.2. Godfrey's protestations, his threat to refuse to do further commercials for Axion were widely publicized and had the effect of making millions of persons suddenly detergent-conscious.

What concerned Godfrey, and what concerns ecologists generally, is the phosphate content in laundry products like Axion. Phosphates, basically, are a nutrient, essential to plant life. In excessive equations, however, phosphates take on negative characteristics, producing most immediately an overenrichment of the waters with which they blend. Science defines this as eutrophication. The consequences include an accelerated growth of waterweeds and algae, the microscopic organisms that populate lakes and rivers, with a correlative depletion of the dissolved oxygen needed to sustain fish life and, ultimately, aquatic plant life itself. This leads to clogged filters and drainage systems as plants die and wash away, useless recreational areas as channels and shorelines become constricted with weeds, foul odors and dead waters.

Waters polluted by phosphates frequently take on a striking coloration. The stretch of the Allegheny River along Route 8 north of Pittsburgh, for instance, is a rich green during some months of the year. But the brightness is a deception. It is a telltale sign of algae disordinately nourished by phosphates, choking life out of the water just as surely as a garrote does out of a human body.

Phosphates enter the waters through a combination of sources: domestic sewage, industrial effluents, agricultural drainage, ground water, rainfall, bird and animal wastes, decomposition of plant and animal life—and detergents. Wesley O. Pipes, professor of civil engineering and biological sciences at Northwestern University, claims that approximately 75 percent of the phosphate in sewage is derived from material added to commercial detergents.[1] An American Chemical Society study estimates that 280 million pounds of phosphorus flow into the surface waters of the United States each year from detergents. Its removal, however, would still leave 680 million pounds mixing with the waters through other means. Equally distributed in the total stream flow of the United States, these 680 million pounds would average to a concentration more than ten times the amount believed to induce excessive algae growth.[2]

Whatever these other factors, detergents remain a prime cause of phosphate pollution, so much so that the Conservation and Natural Resources Subcommittee of the House Committee on Government Operations urged a complete elimination of phosphates from detergents by 1972. The International Joint Commission combating the pollution of Lake Erie, Lake Ontario and the international section of the St. Lawrence River has established a similar deadline for the replacement of phosphorus compounds in detergents emptying into those waters.[3]

Concern reached to the highest level of government. The White House appealed in April 1970 to the detergent industry to find a substitute for phosphates. Two months later, on June 8, 1970, the Department of the Interior awarded a $344,000 grant to the Gillette Company's Research Institute in Rockville, Maryland, for the development of a phosphate-free detergent. In its first annual report, trans-

[1] Letter to Donald Perkins, president, Jewel Tea Company, Melrose Park, Illinois, April 24, 1970.

[2] *Cleaning Our Environment: The Chemical Basis for Action;* a report by the Subcommittee on Environmental Improvement, Committee on Chemistry and Public Affairs. American Chemical Society, Washington, D.C., 1969.

[3] A ban on the manufacture of detergents containing more than 20 percent phosphates went into effect in Canada on August 1, 1970. Similar action is being pursued legislatively in the United States on a number of levels of government. Suffolk County, Long Island, banned the sale of most laundry detergents, effective March 1, 1971. And Governor Nelson Rockefeller of New York, in January 1971, said he would seek legislation curbing phosphate detergents in the state by 1972.

The City of Chicago has an ordinance banning sale of detergents with more than 25 units phosphate and requiring those with less to list phosphate content on the package, after February 1, 1971, and banning sale of detergents containing any phosphate after June 30, 1972.

On March 22, 1971, Governor Nelson Rockefeller sent a similar bill to the New York State Legislature. It would ban the sale of detergents containing phosphates by June 1, 1973.

mitted to the Congress in August 1970, the Council on Environmental Quality recommended the phasing of phosphates out of detergents "as soon as feasible."

For a time it appeared that phosphates would eventually be phased out completely from household use. But on September 15, 1971, Federal officials reversed directions and told housewives to return to the use of phosphate detergents. Health and environmental spokesmen acknowledged that phosphates cause ecological damage, but they said phosphates were a lesser evil than cleaners that contain either caustic soda or the chemical NTA (nitrilotriacetic acid). Environmentalists were upset, but the detergent industry, which now has two-thirds of the laundry market, was overjoyed. (The industry has increased its profits from 31 percent of sales in 1947 to 54 percent in 1967 by emphasizing the sale of detergents over soaps, according to environmental expert Barry Commoner.[4])

Industry's professed reasons for pushing detergents over soaps, which are relatively harmless, are that the phosphates in detergents provide the "muscle" to get clothes clean, and that they "materially contribute to the reduction of germs in clothes, thereby reducing the danger of cross infection."[5] Indeed, phosphates do the cleaning job so well that for some time industry resisted formula changes, preferring that the phosphate problem, such as it might be, be handled through the development of new municipal waste-treatment processes. However, a combination of pressures—public opinion, restrictive legislation and, in fairness to some portions of the industry, a quickened sense of ecological responsibility—partially altered hard positions. Procter & Gamble is experimenting with reduced phosphate strengths out of concern for "the natural environment of the country." Spokesmen for Lever Brothers and Sears announced that their firms would be marketing phosphate-free products before 1972.[6]

On the other hand, Lever Brothers joined Colgate-Palmolive on October 27, 1971, in urging Congress to set what was termed "reasonable" levels for phosphorus content in detergents. The urging itself

[4] *The Closing Circle,* by Barry Commoner, Knopf, New York, 1971.

[5] Procter & Gamble ad in *The New York Times,* March 31, 1970.

[6] Sears beat its deadline handily. It was advertising "a phosphate-free laundry detergent" by fall 1970. Early tests on the product showed it to be more effective at soil removal than phosphate detergents in hard water and only slightly less effective in soft water. It is considered comparable to phosphates on dyed fabrics and is less corrosive than phosphate detergents on laundry equipment.

Lever Brothers, somewhat less altruistically, went into U.S. District Court in Portland, Maine, April 6, 1971, seeking an injunction against the Federal Trade Commission and a proposed rule which would require detergent makers to list ingredients on packages and to display pollution warnings in advertisements. The case was dismissed April 19, 1971. Lever Brothers immediately announced an appeal.

seemed reasonable, but the 8.7 percent phosphate which the companies requested actually represents 34 percent phosphate content in a compound form. The industry maintains that 34 percent is the minimum phosphate level necessary for an effective laundering; environmental groups have established a tolerance point of 25 phosphate units per washload. The Congressional request was undertaken by the companies in an effort to avert impending state and local bans on phosphate detergents. Curiously enough, Procter & Gamble, a giant in the detergents field, did not join in the request. Instead, in what seemed a reversal of its earlier stance, a company spokesman declared that elimination of phosphates from detergents "will have little or no effect" on the problems of eutrophication; the solution, he remarked, is in the development of adequate sewage treatment.

Actions such as these caused not a few persons to wonder precisely how serious the detergents industry is about solving the phosphate dilemma.

The quickening of concern over pollution from detergents brought to consumer markets a number of new products, on behalf of which extravagant claims were made but which were eventually seized by health authorities as harmful. Two such detergents were "Bohack's No-Phosphates" and "Ecolo-G," products of the North American Chemical Corporation of Paterson, New Jersey. Supplies of the two items were seized on March 8, 1971, in raids in New York and Maryland, because both products showed signs of being "extremely dangerous." Said Fred S. Halverson, an official in the bureau of product safety of the Food and Drug Administration, "They're toxic, corrosive to intact skin, and produce, on contact, a severe eye irritation . . . They create an open wound on the skin, an actual burn."[7] The manufacturer angrily said that it would fight the government on the issue, but its words were not such as to rally the public to its side. "This product is only for clothes and washing machines," commented Joseph Yankler of North American Chemical. "It doesn't matter whether it's toxic or not. What are you going to do? Eat it?"[8]

The manufacturer apparently won his point, for supermarkets and stores continued to carry the suspect detergents. Nevertheless the case stands as a perfect example of the care which must be exercised by the public and the skepticism which must be attached to manufacturers' claims until tests are carried out and contents and performance verified by reputable agencies of government or responsible private groups.

Actually, there is not much doubt but that with time and research the detergents industry can come up with an effective phosphate-free

[7] Lacey Fosburgh in *The New York Times,* March 9, 1971.

[8] Ibid.

product, if it really wants to. Ten years ago the industry was equally challenged, by a foam resulting from alkyl benzene sulfonate, a surface-active agent in common use in synthetic detergents. Alkyl benzene sulfonate was building up mountains of soap bubbles in waste-treatment plants, in lakes and streams. The bubbles were even appearing in tap water. Industry solved the difficulty in 1965 by switching to a much more biodegradable substance, linear alkylate sulfate. If it could meet that challenge, industry should also be able to meet the challenge of phosphates.

At one point, some believed that the sodium salt of nitrilotriacetic acid would prove an adequate substitute for phosphates, but hopes invested in it were routed in December 1970, when, under federal prodding, the nation's major soap manufacturers agreed to remove items containing nitrilotriacetic acid (NTA) from their products on the grounds that NTA can be hazardous to humans, particularly pregnant women, and particularly in areas where wells and septic tanks are in use.

Meanwhile, as the research proceeds, private and public agencies are circulating consumer guides, urging consumers to purchase products of low-phosphate content and asking stores to feature such brands. The response has been encouraging, with some food chains even posting information in their stores identifying detergents by phosphorus content. Canada Safeway and Jewel Food Stores in this country are two of these chains.

A number of guides are in circulation, the data of some varying slightly according to analytical methods used in testing the individual products. Perhaps the most authoritative is one released May 1, 1970, by the Federal Water Quality Administration, based on Method D-820 of the American Society for Testing Materials. (Table 4-1) It covers the more popular name-brand products, as follows:

TABLE 4-1.

Type of material	Product	Percentage phosphates as STPP (sodium tripolyphosphate)
Pre-soaks	Biz	73.9
	Axion	63.2
Laundry Detergents	Salvo	56.6
	Tide	49.8

TABLE 4-1. (cont.)

	Drive	47.4
	Oxydol	46.6
	Bold	45.4
	Cold Water All	45.4
	Ajax Laundry	44.6
	Cold Power	44.6
	Punch	44.2
	Dreft	41.9
	Gain	39.5
	Duz	38.3
	Bonus	37.5
	Breeze	37.2
	Cheer	36.3
	Fab	34.8
	Diaper Pure	19.8
	Wisk (liquid)	14.2
	Trend	7.1
Automatic Dishwasher Detergents	Cascade	54.5
	All	54.0
	Calgonite	49.4
	Electrosol	34.8

A research, education and action group involving the Northwestern University community—Northwestern Students for a Better Environment (NSBE)—has taken phosphate studies a step further and compiled a use-guide per wash load. NSBE recommends that consumers buy low-phosphate detergents, that they stay below 25 units (grams) of phosphates per wash load, and that they use measuring cups so that detergents will not be applied in quantities above those specified on the box. The NSBE guide (Table 4-2) follows:

TABLE 4-2. (In Circulation as of Fall 1971)

Units are grams of phosphate as phosphate. Values between zero and one half unit are reported as zero units. Error is plus or minus ten percent of value reported. Data represent products found in U. S. markets. For best data on products in Canadian markets, consult compilation by Pollution Probe at University of Toronto.

	Amount per washload	Phosphate units per washload
DETERGENTS		
Add-It	½ c.	0
Cold Water All (liq.)	½ c.	0
Modway	½ c.	0
Neo-Kleen Plus	¼ c.	0
Nu-Wash	2 tbsp.	0
Purewater	½ c.	0

TABLE 4-2. (cont.)

	Amount per washload	Phosphate units per washload
Sears	½ c.	0
Trend	1½ c.	6
Special-T	½ c.	7
Instant Fels	1½ c.	8
Tetra D	¼ c.	9
Twin Oaks	¼ c.	12
Basic L	¼ c.	14
Nutriclean CLC	2 oz.	14
Wisk	½ c.	15
Amway SA-8 Plus	¼ c.	17
Cold Power	1¼ c.	17
Blue Magic	1¼ c.	19
Bestline B-7	¼ c.	20
Nutrilite Conc.	¼ c.	20
Montgomery Wards	⅔ c.	21
Launder Maid Blue	1 c.	25
- - - - - - - -	- - - - - - - -	- - - - Tolerance Point
Cheer	1¼ c.	27
Dreft	1½ c.	27
Silver Dust	2 c.	28
Surf	1¼ c.	28
Bold	1¼ c.	29
Gain	1¼ c.	29
Rinso	1¼ c.	29
Bonus	2 c.	30
Easy Life Heavy Duty	1½ c.	32
Drive	1¼ c.	33
Fab	1½ c.	34
Oxydol Plus	1¼ c.	34
Cold Water All	1¼ c.	35
Punch	1¼ c.	35
Ajax	1¼ c.	36
Breeze	2 c.	36
Field 222	¾ c.	37
Concentrated All	1 c.	38
Ad	1 c.	38
Easy Life Enzyme	1½ c.	38
Duz	1½ c.	39
Easy Life Blue	1½ c.	39
Tide XK	1¼ c.	40
American Family	1¼ c.	40
Fluffy All	1½ c.	42
Burst	1 c.	42
HLD	½ c.	44
Vim	4 tblts.	44
Salvo	2 tblts.	51
Dash	1 c.	60

TABLE 4-2. (cont.)

	Amount per washload	Phosphate units per washload	
SOAPS			
Culligan	any	0	
Diaper Sweet	any	0	
Ivory Flakes	any	0	
ServiSoft Soap	1 c.	1	
Diaper Pure	1¼ tbsp.	1	
Gray-Gone	1 c.	3	
ENZYME PRESOAKS			
Trizyme	¼ c.	15	
Axion	½ c.	27	
Brion	½ c.	30	
Biz	½ c.	35	
Sears	½ c.	55	
FABRIC SOFTENERS			
generally have no phosphates			
ADDITIVES			
Fels Naphtha Bar	any	0	
Borateem	any	0	
Borax	any	0	
Washing Soda	any	0	
- - - - - - - -	- - - - - - - -	- - - - - - - -	Tolerance Point
Calgon	½ c.	57	
Rain Crystals	1 pkt.	66	
Starches	generally no phosphates		
BLEACHES & BLUING			
Liquid Chlorine type	1 c.	generally 0	
LaFrance Bluing	½ c.	0	
Miracle White Bleach	½ c.	0	
LaFrance Enzyme	½ c.	2	
Action	1 pkt.	5	
Amway Dry Bleach	2 tbsp.	6	
Snowy	¾ c.	10	
Beads O' Bleach	2 oz.	16	
- - - - - - - -	- - - - - - - -	- - - - - - - -	Tolerance Point
Stardust	1 c.	41	
BOOSTERS			
Miracle White	½ c.	11	
Smashing White	¼ c.	12	
Laundry White	¼ c.	13	
Climalene	¼ c.	14	
Easy White	½ c.	24	
- - - - - - - -	- - - - - - - -	- - - - - - - -	Tolerance Point
Anything Goes	½ c.	27	
ALL PURPOSE CLEANERS			
Bestline	¼ c.	0	

TABLE 4-2. (cont.)

	Amount per washload	Phosphate units per washload	
Amway L.O.C.	¼ c.	0	
Pinesol	¼ c.	0	
20 Mule Team	¼ c.	0	
Whistle	¼ c.	0	
E-Z Par	¼ c.	0	
Basic H	¼ c.	0	
Nu-All	any	0	
Bo-Peep Ammonia	any	0	
Fantastik	¼ c.	1	
Formula 409	¼ c.	1	
Impac Clean All	¼ c.	2	
Janitor in a Drum	¼ c.	2	
Willex	¼ c.	2	
Ajax All Purpose	¼ c.	4	
Lysol Cleaner	¼ c.	4	
Basic I	¼ c.	5	
Handy Andy	¼ c.	6	
Ajax Floor & Wall	¼ c.	8	
Top Job	¼ c.	8	
Mr. Clean	¼ c.	9	
Spic & Span	¼ c.	12	
Spoilax	¼ c.	16	
CLEANSERS			
Babbitt's	can (14 oz)	3	
Bon Ami	can	5	
Hep	can	6	
Ajax	can	10	
Air Maid	can	12	
Kitchen Klenzer	can	17	
- - - - - - - -	- - - - - - - -	- - - - - - - -	Tolerance Point
Comet	can	30	
DISHWASHING LIQUIDS			
generally have no phosphates			
AUTOMATIC DISHWASHING CPDS			
Basic D	1 tsp.	1	
Special-T	1 tbsp.	1	
Amway	1 tbsp.	5	
Calgonite	2 tbsp.	6	
Advance	2 tbsp.	6	
Finish	1½ tbsp.	6	
Electra Sol	2 tbsp.	6	
Dishwasher All	2 tbsp.	9	
Cascade	2½ tbsp.	11	
Jet Dry Liquid	bottle	21	
Jet Dry Solid	cake	21	

TABLE 4-2. (cont.)

BATH AIDS		
Shampoos	generally no phosphates	
Bar Soaps	generally no phosphates	
Calgon Oil Beads	3 tbsp.	13
Calgon Bouquet	3 tbsp.	15
MISC. PRODUCTS		
Decor-lite		0
Hosiery Care		0
Sparkle Glass Cleaner		0
Woolite (liq.)	½ c.	2
- - - - - - - - - - Tolerance Point		
Woolite	½ c.	28

Many manufacturers are reformulating their products and bringing out new low-phosphate detergents as a result of consumer pressures and publicity. Most manufacturers keep their formulations secret to protect themselves from competitors.

Following are changes tested as of December 1, 1970, by Northwestern Students for a Better Environment. (Table 4-3) Values are plus or minus 10 percent of listed number of units.

TABLE 4-3.

	Amount per washload	Phosphate units per washload
DETERGENTS		
Great Lakes	–	0
Dairi Brite	¼ c.	0
Concern	4 oz.	0
Basic L	⅛ c.	0
Somethin' Else	–	0
HLD (PO_4 free)	–	0
Swipe	–	0
Topco	½ c.	0
Sears	½ c.	0
K-50	¼ c.	11
Malco	¼ c.	13
Miracle White Creamed Detergent	½ c.	17
Liquid Cold Power	½ c.	17
Bonus	1½ c.	30
Supersuds	1½ c.	31
Squire Enzyme	1½ c.	32
Justrite	1½ c.	34
Co-op Controlled Suds	½ c.	37
A & P Controlled Suds	1¼ c.	50
Spring Controlled Suds	1 c.	51

TABLE 4-3. (cont.)

ALL PURPOSE		
Hazel	–	0
Tomorrow's Lestoil	½ c.	2
Original Lestoil	½ c.	2
Sky Blue	1 c.	16
BLEACHES		
Daybrite	½ c.	13
Clorox II	½ c.	20
BOOSTERS		
Miracle White	¼ c.	11
DISHWASHING COMPOUNDS		
Spring Dishwashing	2 tbsp.	14

SUFFOLK'S LAWS

Perhaps the most stringent laws relating to detergents are those of Suffolk County, Long Island, New York. As of March 1, 1971, all detergents—liquid and powder—were banned. Suffolk County has very few sewers, and its water supply is entirely underground. Officials found that the water was being polluted and made unpotable (often coming out of taps with a head of foam on it) by detergents that did not break down chemically as they filtered into the ground through septic tanks and cesspools. Thus the decision for laws which will undoubtedly be forerunners for legislation in numbers of communities.

Following is the status table (4-4) of general-purpose cleaners in Suffolk County:

TABLE 4-4.

Acceptable	Not acceptable
Soaps	Pre-soaks
Bleaches	Cold water detergents
Washing sodas	Hot water detergents
Borax	Liquid detergents for hand-dishwashing
Baking soda	Heavy duty detergents if label indicates use for laundry
Starch	
Bluing	Detergents manufactured especially for wool
Ammonia	
Water softeners	
Whiteners	
Fabric softeners	

SELECTED BIBLIOGRAPHY
(detergents)

"A Sudden Boom for Detergents That Don't Pollute," Richard D. Lyons, *The New York Times* (Week in Review), January 31, 1971.

"An Acid Removed from Detergents," Paul Delaney, *The New York Times,* December 19, 1970, p. 1.

"Canada to Ban All Phosphates in Detergents over 2-Year Span," Jay Walz, *The New York Times,* February 20, 1970, p. 2.

Carson, Rachel, *Silent Spring,* Boston, 1962 (Houghton Mifflin); New York, 1970 (Fawcett Crest).

Cleaning Our Environment, the Chemical Basis for Action, a report by the Subcommittee on Environmental Improvement, Committee on Chemistry and Public Affairs of the American Chemical Society; Washington, D.C., 1969.

"Deadly Detergents," editorial, *The New York Times,* August 4, 1970.

"Detergent Curb Begins in Canada," Jay Walz, *The New York Times,* August 2, 1970, p. 26.

"Detergents Held Pollution Factor," Paul Delaney, *The New York Times,* December 15, 1969, p. 1.

"Detergents Safe Now—But What of Future?" Gannett News Service, *The Daily Times,* Mamaroneck, New York, July 29, 1970.

Federal Water Pollution Control Administration, "Tests Determine Levels of Phosphates in Detergents," Washington, D.C., May 1, 1970.

"Governor Seeking a Curb on Phosphate Detergents," Thomas P. Ronan, *The New York Times,* January 8, 1971, p. 1.

Heuper, W. C., "Cancer Hazards from Natural and Artifical Water Pollutants," *Proceedings,* Conference on Physiological Aspects of Water Quality, Washington, D.C., September 8–9, 1960, p. 181–93, U. S. Public Health Service.

"Less-Is-Better List Ranks Laundry Items by Phosphate Content," *Wall Street Journal,* May 4, 1970.

"Return to Detergents With Phosphates Urged by Government in Shift of Policy," Richard D. Lyons, *The New York Times,* September 16, 1971, p. 1.

"Suffolk Accepts Detergents Ban," Carter B. Horsley, *The New York Times,* November 12, 1970.

"Suffolk Forbids Detergents' Sale," Carter B. Horsley, *The New York Times,* November 11, 1970, p. 1.

V Food: A Crisis in Supply

The insufficiency of food supply is not new in human history. Starvation, undernourishment and malnourishment have always been with us. Periodic famines have wiped out tens of millions in the past and still continue to cut a wide swath of death in this century—e.g., 5 to 10 million victims in Russia (1918–22 and 1932–34); 4 million in China (1920–21) and 2 to 4 million in West Bengal, India (1943).

Despite the horror and suffering attached to such occurrences, large-scale famines have been at least spasmodic and somewhat containable in earlier times. Now, however, no such consolation is assured. According to many food and population scientists, the world is presently heading into a dangerous period in which the dreaded specter of global starvation seems more and more real.

It is estimated that already between 10 and 20 million die every year from starvation or the effects of malnutrition. (This statistic is truly staggering when one considers it represents from one-sixth to one-third of the annual human mortality of 60 million dead.) It is further estimated that another 1½ to 2½ billion, mainly in underdeveloped regions, have inadequate diets of varying degrees of deficiency. Caught in this predicament, the world can ill afford slumps or even a standstill in food production. Steady yearly gains are necessary merely to keep up with current population growth.

In the decade prior to 1968 the 3 percent average annual increase in food production stayed a little ahead of population growth rate. But in 1969 this upward trend leveled off to zero—a very ominous sign (Box 5-1).

The Geography of Hunger

Hunger can be referred to in two ways—undernourishment (insufficient intake of calories) and malnourishment (deficiency in essential nutrients, principally protein). According to the United Nations FAO Second World Food Survey, all of Asia, Africa and Latin America (except Argentina, Chile and Uruguay) are lacking in caloric intake. This means that two-thirds of the human population is undernourished. The FAO report, however, can be criticized for both underestimating caloric intake and overestimating caloric requirements in underdeveloped countries.

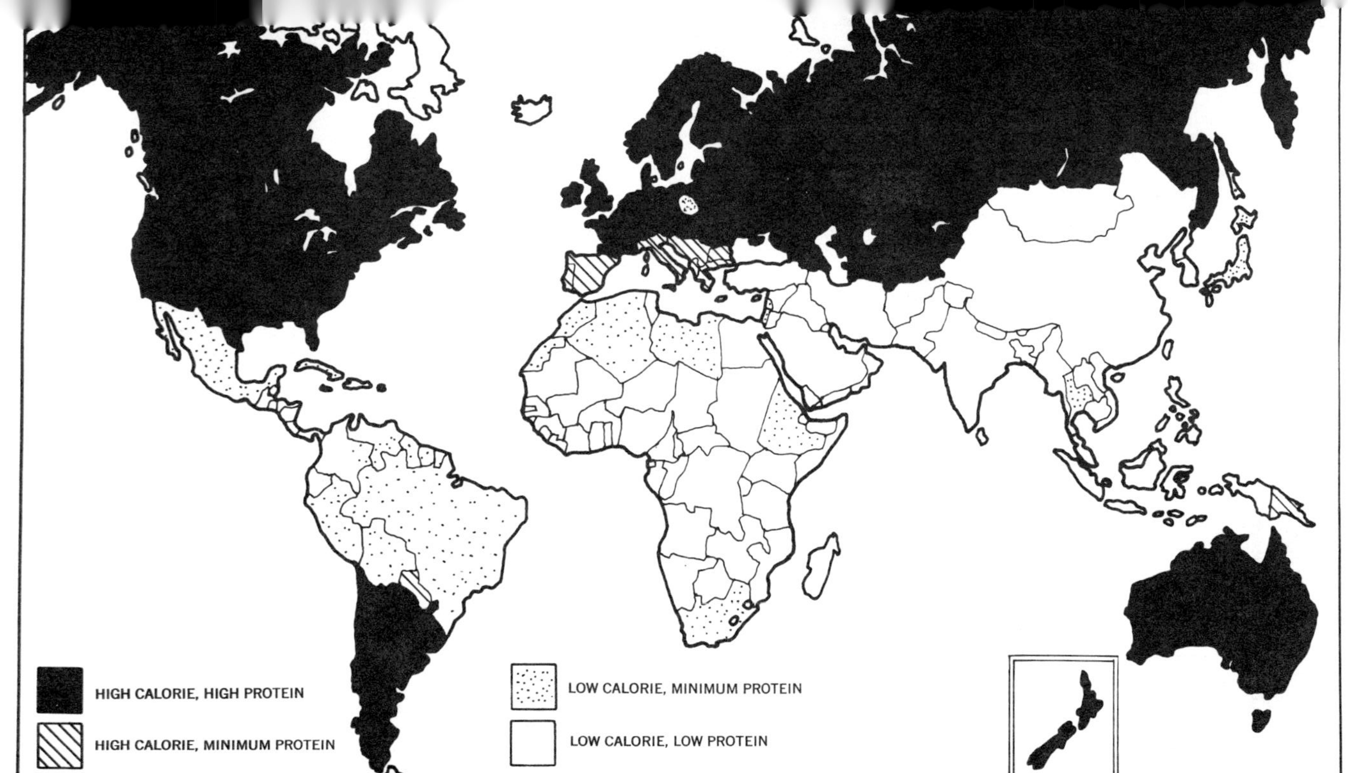

MAP 5-1. The Geography of Hunger

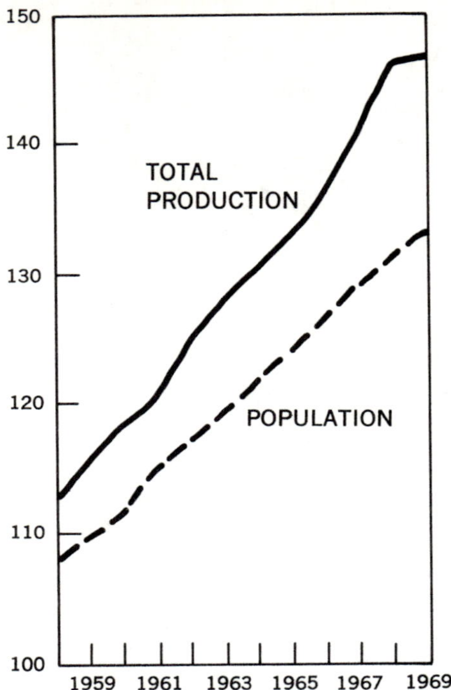

BOX 5-1. World Food Crop Said to Stagnate

The New York Times. October 4, 1970

Solid line shows how the combined output of farms, fisheries and forests has grown. It does not include data from Communist China or other Asian lands that engage in central planning

Source: The New York Times, October 4, 1970

In 1967, the President's Science Advisory Committee Panel on the World Food Supply proposed a more conservative, but nonetheless frightening, picture of nutrition in underdeveloped areas by speculating that 20 percent of the population therein was undernourished while 60 percent was malnourished. In this case, we are talking about a billion and a half or so under- or malnourished people rather than the FAO's 2 billion.

Malnourishment is the greater obstacle in the battle against hunger not simply because it affects six times the number as undernourish-

BOX 5-2. What Happens to Food Surpluses

The harvest of 1969 was the greatest mass of wheat the world has ever known. This was due primarily to the chance occurrence of favorable weather in all the wheat countries, but in part to the influence of better practices and new strains in Mexico, India and Pakistan. The result is a massive surplus and a crash of world market prices. In Canada, where storage bins were full with a record 850 million bushels, a new crop of 650 million bushels was harvested. Her communist customers canceled their annual standing order because their own wheat crops fulfilled their needs. So one might think that this year the hungry people of the world will be well fed and able to produce a larger crop of children. But the world's wheat surplus will not go to feed hungry people. With a wheat glut and falling prices the exporter nations cannot afford to give their grain to starving people even if they wanted to. Only the US has been able to give away grain.

The Canadian farmer is in serious trouble because of wheat prices. With $65 million in last year's loans still unpaid the Canadian government has increased its cash advances against unsold wheat to $6000 per farm. Obviously the Canadians must sell their wheat to the highest bidder and take their losses; the wheat will go to produce meat for Americans and Europeans.

Here we can see one of the simple lessons of agricultural economics which should help the reader to understand why the farmers never get a fair deal and why we are always hopelessly bogged down in federal controls, price supports and crop surpluses. The farmer's customers are every person on earth. But with most of the world's people in grinding poverty which deepens every year, the average customer cannot be expected to provide daily margin of profit which could be considered a generous contribution to the standard of living of a Canadian farmer. On the other hand, he who markets automobiles, jewelry or furs has only selected customers who are known to be well off and his margin of profit is substantial. As long as our system demands that every person alive be fed but not that he be supplied with automobiles, jewelry, furs, etc., the farmer will be poor while the merchants become wealthy.

So we will feed the wheat to farm animals. Wheat is not a feed grain; feeding it exclusively leads to digestive problems in livestock. Nevertheless, farm experts have developed programs to use up the wheat which the starving people cannot afford. Thus the Farm Journal for October says to feed wheat to cattle and in November to feed wheat to pigs. It also says that Canada plans to export grain surplus as beef. She brings in feeder cattle from the United States, fattens them on wheat, and sells them back to us.

Source: Wayne H. Davis, "More or Less People?" The New Republic, June 20, 1970.

ment, but rather because it is harder to combat. Only protein—an item of limited source and severe maldistribution—can fight malnourishment successfully.

Protein doesn't grow on trees. It comes chiefly from animal products (meat, poultry, fish, milk, eggs, etc.), certain cereal grains (rice, wheat, corn, etc.) and legumes (like soybeans and peanuts). Animals furnish the highest quality protein. The quality of plant protein varies greatly and even at its best cannot match that of animal protein. Thus the population in underdeveloped countries are shortchanged twice. For not only do they share disproportionately in the world supply of livestock and therefore in protein-bearing animals, but their principal protein source—grains—offers them protein of inferior quality. Figures 5-2 and 3 show precisely the difference between developed and underdeveloped countries in the crucial protein count.

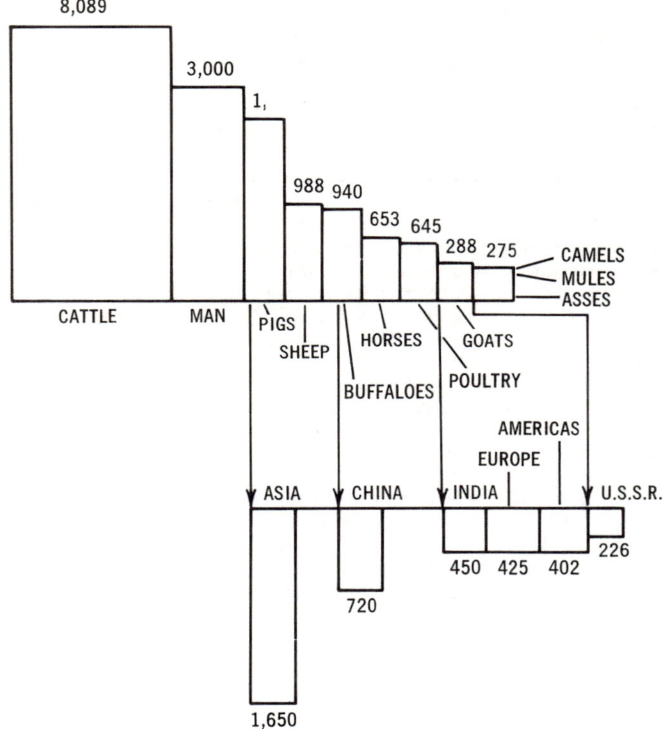

FIGURE 5-1. World Biomass (Human Sphere) 1958–59 Mil. Pop. Equiv.

The living mass which directly is part of the human biosphere. Besides man are the various livestock categories required for traction and other work but largely for the raising of animal products (milk, meat, eggs, etc.). Indirectly, man is enjoying the support of a far greater biomass, represented by the lengthy biochains of oceans and fresh waters, terrestrial wildlife, as well as soil organisms and a wealth of micro-organisms

Source: Borgstrom, The Hungry Planet, Macmillan, 1967

Compounding this regrettable imbalance is what Georg Borgstrom calls "the protein swindle." In his book *Too Many,* Borgstrom notes that protein-starved underdeveloped nations are actually exporting this essential nutrient to protein-rich developed nations. Ninety percent of

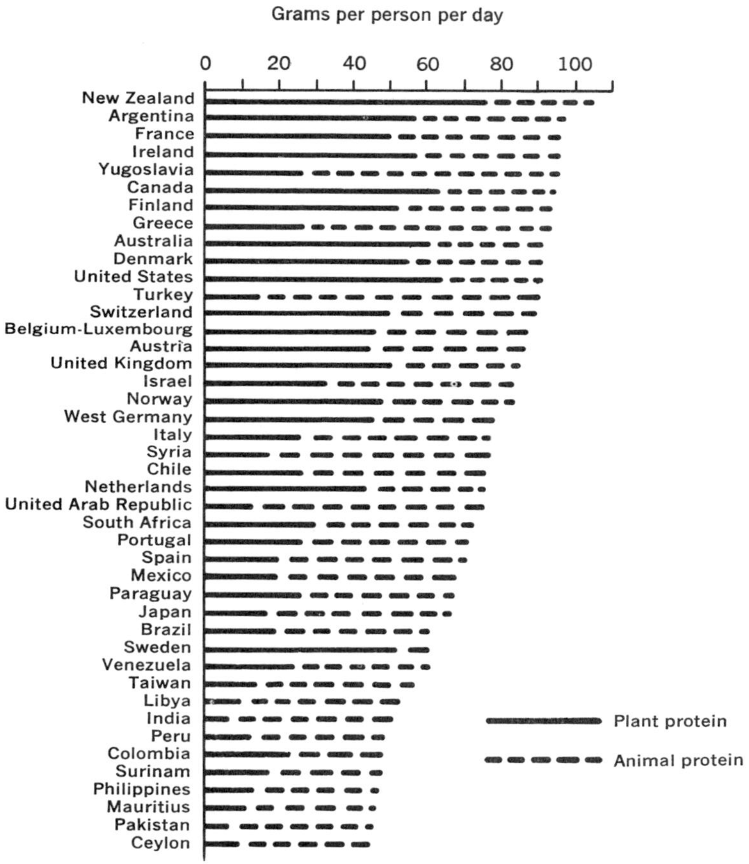

FIGURE 5-2. Daily per Capita Total Protein Supplies in Forty-three Countries

After Introduction to Livestock Production, by H. H. Cole. W. H. Freeman & Company. Copyright © 1966

the world's fish meal catch (used in feeding dairy cattle and poultry), for example, is exported to the developed lands. "Sometimes one wonders," complains Borgstrom, how many Americans and western Europeans have grasped the fact that quite a few of their beef steaks, quarts of milk, dozens of eggs, and hundreds of broilers are the result, *not of their agriculture, but rather of the approximately two million metric tons of protein, mostly of high quality,* which astute Western businessmen channel away from the needy and hungry."

LAND MASSES
In million hectares

	Total Land Area	Deserts, Wasteland and Built-On Land		Inaccessible Forest		Potentially Tillable Acreage		Potentially Tillable Acreage							
								Not Utilized Acreage		Presently Tilled Acreage		Pastures		Accessible Forest	
			%		%		%		%		%		%		%
Europe	493	117	23.7	5	1.0	371	75.3	7	1.4	153	31.0	78	15.8	133	27.0
U.S.S.R.	2,240	679	30.3	545	24.3	1,016	45.4	—	—	221	9.9	370	16.5	425	19.0
North and Central America	2,426	867	35.7	468	19.3	1,091	44.9	115	4.7	256	10.5	364	15.0	356	14.7
South America	1,776	451	25.4	622	35.0	703	39.6	52	2.9	73	4.1	292	16.4	286	16.1
Asia*	1,739	638	36.7	127	7.3	974	56.0	90	5.2	329	18.9	243	14.0	312	17.5
China	976	612	62.7	49	5.0	315	32.3	—	—	109	11.2	178	18.2	28	2.9
Africa	3,027	1,349	44.5	445	14.5	1,233	40.5	114	3.7	239	7.8	596	19.5	284	9.3
Oceania	854	325	38.1	33	3.8	496	55.8	1	0.1	28	3.8	447	49.5	20	2.4
Total	13,531	5,038	37.8	2,294	16.2	6,199	46.0	379	2.9	1,408	10.5	2,568	19.1	1,844	13.5

It should be noted that neither the U.S.S.R. nor China has any remaining agricultural reserve listed in the table above other than what can be obtained through the plowing of forest or pasture land.

***Exclusive of China.**

TABLE 5-1. Land Masses (in Million Hectares)

Source: FAO statistics, 1965, as compiled by Borgstrom, Too Many, Macmillan, 1969

Food and Land

The limitation of land is the single most inhibiting factor in the quest for increased food production. We don't grow more food largely because there isn't much more good land to grow more food on (Table 5-1). The best land is already being tilled and the remainder tends to be marginal, that is, unconducive to agricultural development. Owing to mismanagement, even the quality of presently cultivated land has deteriorated over the years (Table 5-3). Instead of making the most of what we have, population and other allied pressures of industrial civilization actually work to reduce the amount of available arable land. In the seventy-years between 1880 and 1950, according to Georg Borgstrom's calculations, roads, cities, airports and industries have absorbed 1 billion hectares (2.5 billion acres). In the United States, we now turn over 2 million acres of rural land every year to non-agricultural uses (Figure 5-4).

Solutions to the World Food Crisis: Irrigation, Improvement of Crop Yields, Harvesting the Seas. Some food scientists maintain that the earth's abundance, if exploited rationally and with maximum efficiency, could feed a population of 20 billion or more, that is, six times the present population. Widespread irrigation, drastic improvement of crop yields and harvesting the seas are often mentioned as component parts in the solution of the world food crisis.

Irrigation

Irrigation, it is said, could turn the vast deserts of the earth into blooming gardens. True enough. But where will the water come from? The price of irrigation is quite high and the availability of water reserves quite low. After citing the treadmill character of the most ambitious of irrigation schemes—The North American Water and Power Alliance[1]—Paul Ehrlich writes in *Population, Resources, Environment* ". . . [I]t should be clear that even the most massive water projects can make but a token contribution to the long-term solution of the world food problem. And in the crucial short-term, the years preceding 1980, *no* additional people will be fed by projects that exist only on the drawing board today."

Desalinization? Again, prohibitive economics as well as primitive technology.

[1]The North American Water and Power Alliance, a twenty-year, $100 billion project, will route the waters of large Canadian rivers to locations all over the United States. But despite the grandeur of the Alliance's design, it would only serve to increase U.S. water consumption 21 percent upon completion, while U.S. population is expected to have a concomitant rise of between 25 and 43 percent.

WORLD CLIMATE AND FOOD POTENTIAL

		APPROPRIATE SYSTEMS & FOOD PRODUCTS	AREAS OF UNEXPLOITED POTENTIAL	MEASURES REQUIRED
POLAR	EF Ice Cap	*NIL*	NIL	
	ET Tundra	*Reindeer (Nomadic)*		
COOLER HUMID	Dc Dd Subarctic	*Barley, Oats, Rye, Cattle, Forage Crops*	°Canada, Siberia: Northern river valleys	*D, F, C* Stone removal *Quick growing strains*
	Db Continental Cool Summer	*Dairy Cattle, Forage Crops, Barley, Oats, Rye, Spring Wheat, Potatoes*	°°N. Canadian prairie °°Central European Russia	
	Da Continental Warm Summer	*Wheat, Millet, Maize, Soybeans, Forage Crops, Cattle, Sheep*	°Manchuria	*P, F, Flood control Improved husbandry*
WARMER HUMID	Cb Cc Marine West Coast	*Dairy Cattle, Sheep, Fodder Crops, Horticulture, Wheat, Barley, Oats*	°°°New Zealand °°°S.E. Australia	*D, F, P More intensive farming*
	Ca Humid Subtropical	*Cattle Ranching, Wheat, Maize, Rice, Truck Farming*	°°°Uruguay °°°Australia: E. coast plains	*A, E, F, P Selective breeding*
	Cs Mediterranean	*Horticulture, Viticulture, Citrus, Wheat, Sheep, Goats*	°°°S. Australia °°°S. Africa °°Mediterranean littoral	*I, E, F, M, A Restoration and preservation of pasture*
DRY	BS Steppe	*Cattle, Sheep, Fodder Crops, Wheat, Maize, Millet*	°°°USSR: Steppe °°°China: Northern loess °°°Queensland (NSW) °°N. American prairies	*I, F, P Selective breeding*
	BW Desert	*Sheep, Goats, Millet, Wheat, Date Palms*	°°°Great American desert °°°Soviet Central Asia °°°Upper Egypt °°S.W. Asia: River basins °Sahara NW & SE (aquifers)	*Provision of water Prevention of salinity I, F, M*
TROPICAL HUMID	Aw As Savanna	*Cattle, Pigs, Poultry, Millet, Maize, Padi Rice, Vegetable Oils, Sugar Cane*	°°Ethiopia, W. Madagascar °African savanna °Llanos and campos °Northern Australia	*Water conservation Fire control Disease control Selective breeding E, F, C*
		Padi Rice, Fish Farming	°°S.E. Asia: Great river basins	*Soil and water conservation A, F*
	Af Am Rain forest	*Rice, Vegetable Oils, Citrus, Bananas, Coffee, Tea, Cocoa, Fish Farming, Pigs, Poultry*	°°Malaysia °°Guinea Coast °Amazon basin °Indonesia °Congo °Central America	*Penetration, C Maintenance of fertility, F Mixed cropping, Bush fallowing Water and erosion control Disease and weed control*
		NOTES Ease of exploitation: °°°Most practical °°Possible °Difficult	A Agrarian reform C Communications D Drainage E Erosion control F Fertilizers I Irrigation	M Mechanization P Pasture improvement: Controlled grazing, Selected species, Rotation with fodder crops

TABLE 5-2. World Climate and Food Potential

The main factors of environment which determine plant development and distribution are those provided by climate and the soil. Climate thus imposes limits to agricultural systems according to the varying conditions of temperature, moisture and light

Source: Times Atlas of the World, John Bartholomew & Son, Ltd., and Times Newspapers, Limited

TABLE 5-3. Quality Classification of Tilled Land

	1882 Percent	1952 Percent
Good	85.0	41.2
Half of original humus lost	9.9	38.5
Marginal soils	5.1	20.3

Source: Doane, World Balance Sheet, Harper and Row, 1957.

TABLE 5-4. World Catch of Marine Fish and Other Products[a]

Year	Catch in millions of metric tons[b]
1850	1.50–2.25
1900	4.00
1930	10.00
1938	17.50
1948	17.02
1955	21.21
1956	22.61
1957	26.44
1958	27.64
1959	30.56
1960	33.39
1961	36.44
1962	40.22
1963	41.26
1964	45.46
1965	45.75
1966	49.17
1967	52.28
1968	57.40

[a] Source: Food and Agriculture Organization Yearbooks of Fishery Statistics.
[b] One metric ton = 2204 pounds.

TABLE 5-5. World Catch by Groups of Species, 1967[a]

Species	Catch in metric tons[b]
Herring, sardines, anchovies, etc.	19,680,000
Cod, hake, haddock, etc.	8,150,000
Redfish, bass, etc.	3,140,000
Mackerel, billfish, etc.	2,680,000
Jack, mullet, etc.	2,030,000
Tuna, bonita, etc.	1,330,000
Flounders, halibut, sole, etc.	1,200,000
Salmon, trout	1,070,000
Sharks, rays, etc.	440,000
Crustaceans	1,350,000
Mollusks	3,080,000
Unsorted and unidentified	8,290,000

[a] Source: Food and Agriculture Organization Yearbook of Fishery Statistics, Vol. 24.
[b] One metric ton = 2204 pounds.

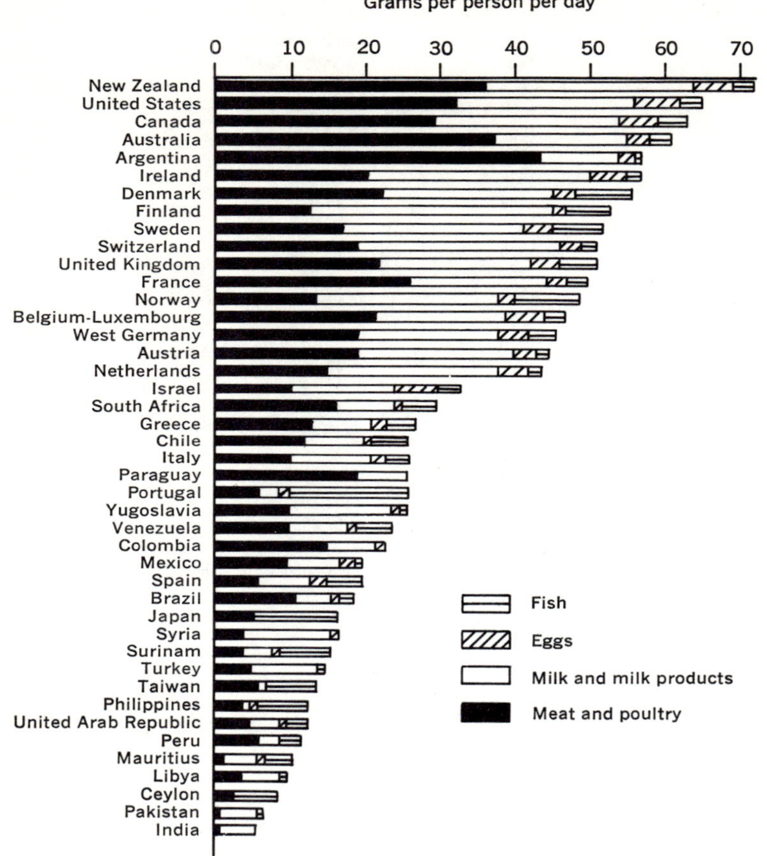

FIGURE 5-3. Daily per Capita Animal Protein Supplies in Forty-three Countries

After Introduction to Livestock Production, by H. H. Cole. W. H. Freeman & Company. Copyright © 1966

Improvement of Crop Yields

The improvement of crop yields is a very tempting idea. Theoretically, the chances would seem rather good for some underdeveloped countries to double, treble and even quadruple their yields. After all, developed countries get 2 to 5 times or more their harvest per acre for certain crops. What works in developed countries should work elsewhere.

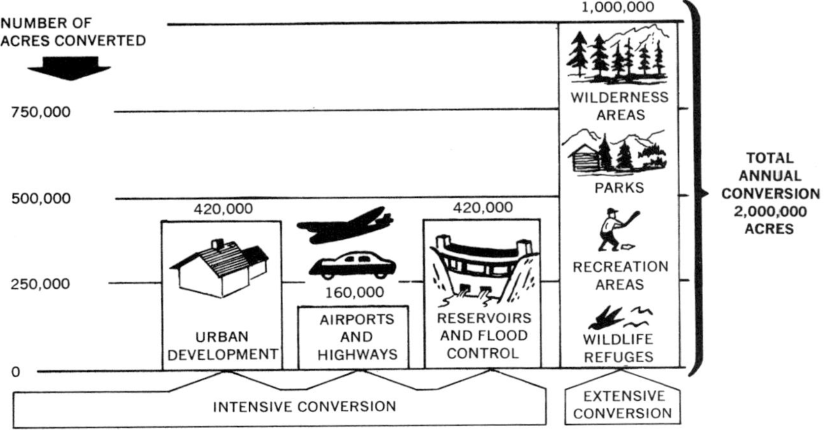

FIGURE 5-4. Annual Conversion of Rural Land in the United States to Nonagricultural Uses

Source: Department of Agriculture

The problem is that Western technology and know-how are very expensive to import. And even if the West's equipment and expertise were cheap, sometimes there's just not enough to go around. For example, in its fantastically fruitful agriculture Holland employs a hundred times as much fertilizer per capita as India. And if India were to equal Holland's fertilizer use proportionately, it would consume one-half of the present world output.

Uncontrolled spreading of fertilizer too has its disadvantages, as illustrated by Figure 5-5.

The introduction of high-yield strains of food crops has dramatically increased some harvests in some underdeveloped areas. However, these increases are not expected to keep apace of population growth, let alone make a dent in the generally poor and pervasive nutritional state that exists in so many lands.

High-yield strains bring with them greater demands for water, fertilizer pesticides and machinery. In the market place, they can create more trouble that they are worth. When a high-yield harvest turns into a glut, the rickety economic systems in underdeveloped countries may not be up to the task of handling the surplus. Finally a high yield is no guarantee of a good yield. Some of these new crops have been of lesser quality, taste and strength.

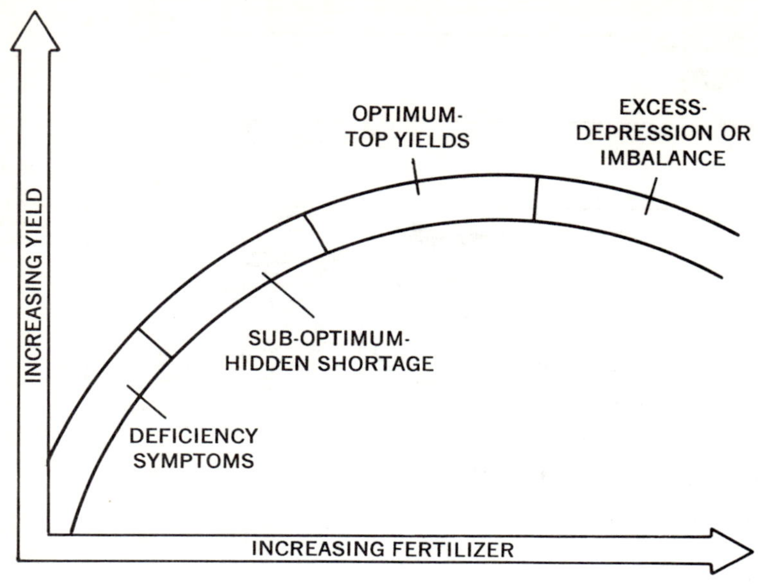

FIGURE 5-5. The Limits of Fertilizer Use

The law of diminishing returns. The effect upon productivity of various amounts of input such as water, fertilizers, etc., gradually levels off and may even reverse itself. The higher the yield, the smaller the net return of each additional identical amount of input

Source: Borgstrom, Too Many, Macmillan, 1969

Harvesting the Seas

Contrary to popular mythology, the seas are not bottomless reservoirs of food merely waiting to be dragged by man. The seas are rather restricted preserves. In 1967, approximately 60 million metric tons of fish products were extracted from the oceans, providing one-fifth of the world's animal protein. The most optimistic projections foresee a possible 2 to 2½ times increase in catch, but not before the year 2000, not without overfishing certain species (an unfortunate state of affairs which has already happened) and not without a tremendous enlargement of the fish industry—five to six times the present equipment would be necessary to reach 150 million tons. A jump to a catch of 70 million metric tons by 1980 is a more likely prospect.

Why the ceiling on fish catches? The answer is simple: the fish population is finite and does not reproduce to suit human designs. If a species is overfished, that is, if its population is so reduced that

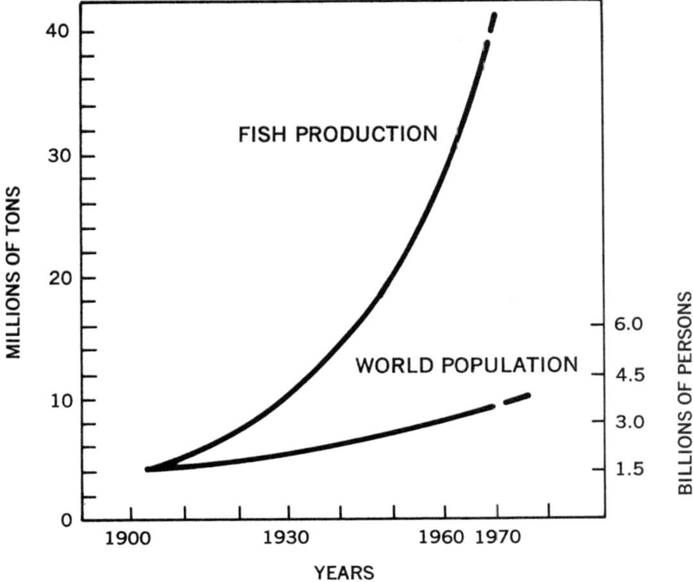

FIGURE 5-6. Growth in Fish Production and World Population Compared

Source: Fisheries of North America

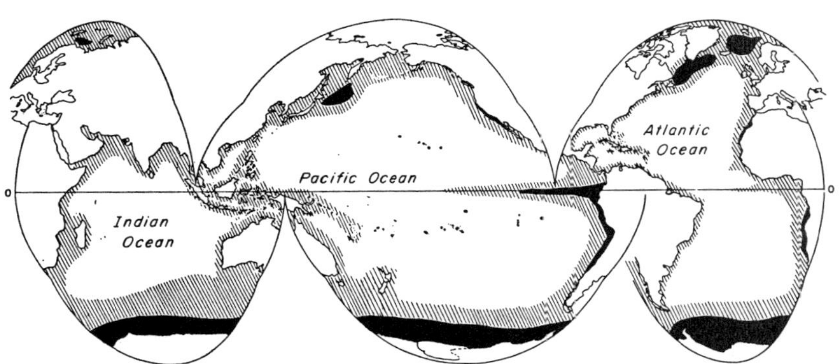

MAP 5-3. Fishing Grounds

Distribution of mineral nutrients over the world ocean. The black areas are the richest, the white the poorest

Source: Gullion, Uses of the Seas, Prentice-Hall, 1968

normal reproduction rates can't restore the species to its optimum number, then sustainable yields will fall accordingly. Overfishing has already pushed several important fish stocks up to and past the limit of sustainable yield (Table 5-6). And there are not many new stocks left to exploit.

TABLE 5-6. Overfishing: The Take of the Following Species Has Declined Appreciably and Has Not Recovered to Date.

Species	Approximate date of decline
Antarctic blue whales	1935
Eastern Asian sardines	1945
California sardine	1946
Northwest Pacific salmon	1950
Atlanto-Scandian herring	1961
Barents Sea cod	1962
Antarctic fin whales	1962

Several more species are presently showing signs of strain. They include Newfoundland cod, North Sea herring, menhaden, British Columbia herring, Bering Sea flatfishes, yellowfin tuna in the Eastern Pacific.

Source: Ricker, "Food from the Sea" in Resources and Man.

Where Do We Go from Here?

Now that the outline of the world food crisis has been sketched, it is well to ask what happens next. Is mass starvation inevitable or is there a chance new ways will be devised to stave off the beast of hunger? Edward A. Ackerman examines the dimensions of the food source crisis in an article entitled "Population, Natural Resources and Technology." He proposes to answer the following two questions:

(1) Can technology alleviate problems of population "pressure" existing in several regions of the world in the near future, and, if so, under what conditions?

(2) What hope can technology provide for the support of the world's population over the long run, that is, indefinitely into the future?

First, Ackerman settles the matter of technology—which nations have it and which have not and to what degree—before determining the role of technology in attempting to solve the food crisis. Instead of the crude developed-underdeveloped dichotomy, he comes up with the more sophisticated classification of *technology-source* and *technology-deficient* areas which are further broken down according to high-population resource ratios and low-population resource ratios (a population resource ratio being the ration between the technological resources, including food-producing resources, and and the number of people that share in them). Within this framework, Ackerman plots out five basic types of countries and regions:

(1) technology-source areas of high population-potential resource ratios (European type);
(2) technology-source areas of low population-potential resource ratio (United States type);
(3) technology-deficient areas of low population-resource ratios (Brazil type);
(4) technology-deficient areas of high population-resource ratio (India-China type); and
(5) the arctic-desert type, technology-deficient and with few potential food-producing resources (Map 5-4, Table 5-7).

Ackerman's cartography puts one-half of the human race in technology-deficient areas with a high ratio of population to its potential resources. The main countries in this category are China, India, Java, Korea, Egypt, Pakistan and Iran, most of whose food-producing resources are especially subject to the misfortunes of weather—droughts, floods, monsoons, etc.

The other half lives in roughly equal shares in the other categories: one-sixth in technology-deficient countries of low population-potential resource ratios (much of Africa and Latin America); one-sixth in technology-source areas of high population-resource ratios such as Western Europe and Japan, where industrial organization and world trade cancel out the inadequacy of domestic resources; and one-sixth in technologically advanced countries with territories large enough to allow for relatively low ratios of population to potential resources (United States, Canada, Australia, etc.).

According to this scheme, the greater part of the world's population not only lacks proper food amounts but also the technology resources sufficient to tackle the situation head on. These two factors—inadequate food and technology—seem to go together around the globe. "Every country with daily caloric intakes of less than 2700 calories per person," writes Ackerman, "may be assumed to have a resource adequacy problem in supporting all or part of its population. Technological deficiency and adequacy of *employed* resources as distinguished from potential resources thus appear to be con-variant."

Given the gap between technology-source and technology-deficient countries (of either high or low population-resource ratios), Ackerman wonders what hope the former can afford the latter regarding the food crisis. In other words, how can source countries help deficiency countries feed themselves?

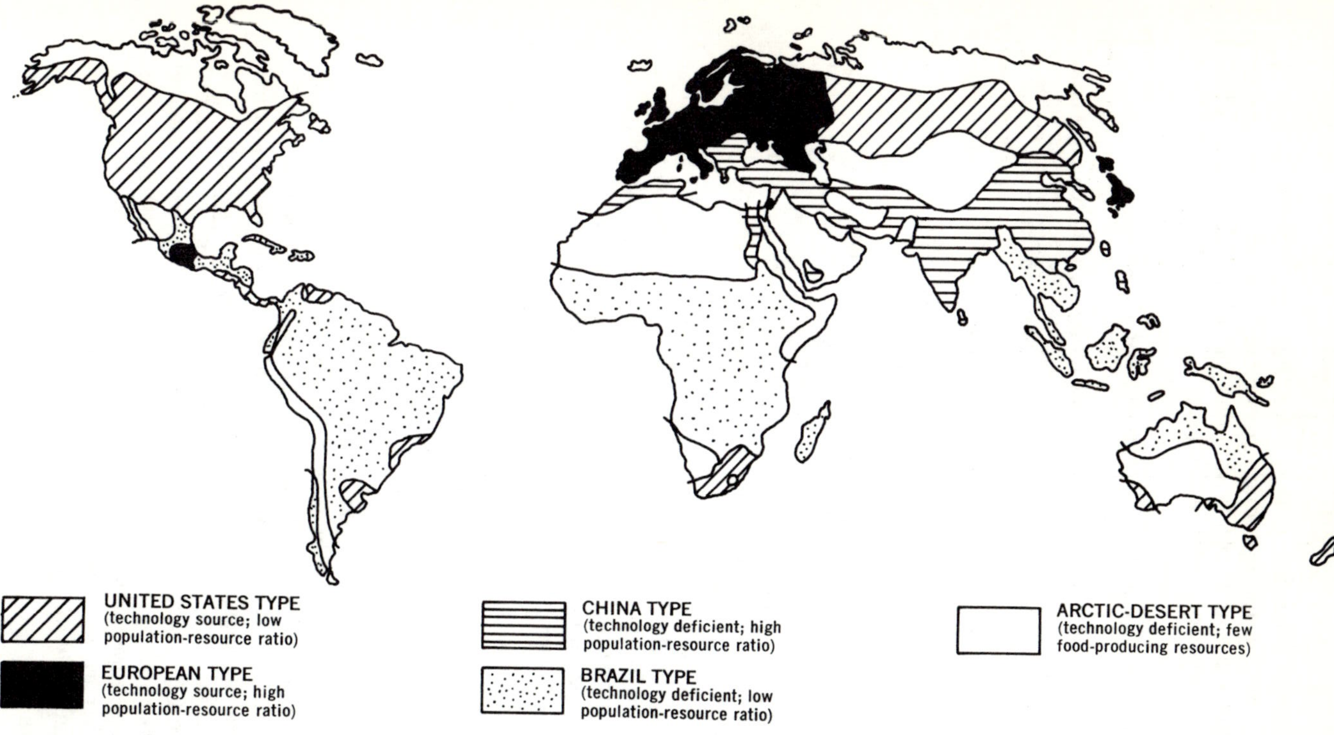

MAP 5-4. Type Areas of Resource-Population Correlation in the World

Source: Ackerman, "Population and Natural Resources," in Hauser and Duncan, The Study of Population, University of Chicago Press, 1959

Type	Application of Technology	Land Productivity	Mineral Productivity	Standard of Living	Numbers of People	Pressure for Use of Foreign Resources	Summary Characteristics
1. United States	U+	U+	U	U+	U	U	Little resource limitation on numbers, some on standard of living; economically strong competition for product of foreign resources
2. European	U+	U—	D	U—	U—	U+	Strong pressure for attachment to foreign resources; where frustrated, crisis possible
3. Brazil	U	U+	U+	U	U+	N	Little resource limitation on numbers; domestic orientation
4. China	U	U	U	U—	U	U	Continued consciousness of impending crisis; increasing pressure for attachment to foreign resources
5. Arctic-desert	U	N	U+	U	N	N	Development by type 1, 2, 4 countries inevitable; strong competition for resources; however, few people

U+ strong upward trend
U, U— upward trend
D downward trend
N very little or very few

TABLE 5-7. Trends Affecting Resource Adequacy in Five Type Areas of the World

Source: Ackerman, "Population and Natural Resources," in Hauser and Duncan, The Study of Population, University of Chicago Press, 1959

TABLE 5-8. Gross Food Needs and Requirements (1975–2000)

Year	Increase in total food supply needed to maintain present diet levels	Increase in food supply necessary to improve present diet levels: Total supply	Increase in food supply necessary to improve present diet levels: Animal foods
1975	35%	50%	60%
1985	50%	85%	130%
2000	75%	124%	210%

Required Production Increases (1975–2000)

Product	Increases 1975	Necessary 2000
Cereals	35%	110%
Pulses & nuts	85%	225%
Animal products	60%	210%

Source: Ozbekau, "Role of Goals and Planning," in Jungk and Galtung, Mankind 2000, Allen & Unwin, 1969.

Ackerman sees the improvement of agricultural yield as the most encouraging possibility in increasing the food production in deficiency areas. In this connection, however, he calls the technology transfer from source to deficiency countries disappointing. For yields are rising considerably faster in the latter. For example, in 1967 Japan's per acre rice yield was three times that of India. Furthermore, Ackerman points out the incredible fact that India's rice output in 1960–63 was only about 5 percent greater than in the years 1936–39.

The task of turning a populous nation's agriculture around, Ackerman is quick to admit, it no small undertaking. The obstacles are almost insuperable—the sheer number of farmers (hundreds of millions in technology-deficient areas), rampant illiteracy (82 percent illiteracy in Africa, 54 percent in Asia and 34 percent in South America), the want of capital for land improvement, equipment and fertilizer and the native economic and cultural resistance.

Ackerman summarizes:

(1) The technology exists for vast improvements in the agricultural production of the technology-deficient countries;

(2) there are few obstacles, if any, to the export of needed technology from the technology-source areas; and

(3) the main obstacles to flow of technical improvements to the farmers of the technology-deficient areas lie with those countries. A higher level of literacy, economic systems that give farmers incentives to produce, and adequate capital formation appear to be keys to the situation.

Another means of increasing agricultural production is assayed—the expansion of the food-producing resources of the world—principally an extension of the land area under cultivation. Ackerman summarizes his brief exposition:

(1) Middle-latitude technology-source low-population areas—some tens of millions of acres are available in the near future if either migration or world trade can be so organized as to stimulate their use. Under present world trade and migration outlooks, however, few of these lands appear scheduled for use within this century.

(2) Desert and semiarid areas of the middle latitudes and tropics—modest land extensions will be possible in the near future, depending on the availability of capital. The technology for development exists and is easily exportable, and new techniques for discovery and assessment of water supplies have materially expanded the prospect of development, but in world terms the potential additions to cultivated areas are very modest.

(3) The lands of the podsolized areas of the North, and the rain forest and savanna lands of the tropics—except for some alluvial oases, these must be generally regarded as longer-range possibilities for expansion and cultivation in any great amount, probably beyond the turn of the century. A vast task of local exploration and of agronomic experimentation appears to be prerequisite if expensive failures and dislocations are to be avoided, particu-

larly in tropical areas. Among the interesting aspects of developing the tropics is application of technology to extracting leaf protein.

Returning to the first question posed by Ackerman at the outset of his article. Can technology alleviate [the food] problems of population pressure in the near future? The response is negative.

> *Until formidable problems of raising the level of literacy have been surmounted* [Ackerman observes], *until capital formation is much increased in comparison with the present, until many institutional changes have been made, or until rates of population natural increases have declined, the flow of technology to increase yields is not as much favored as population growth.*

What about the long range? Can technology provide for the support of the world's growing population in the indefinite future?—the second question. No, again. Not if population continues to multiply at 2 percent a year, which would give us 16 billion people in just more than 2½ centuries. Not if living levels continue to rise in both source and deficient countries, placing intolerable demands on exhaustible natural resources.

SELECTED BIBLIOGRAPHY

Ackerman, E. A., "Population, Natural Resources, and Technology," *The Annals of the American Academy of Political and Social Science,* 369, 1967, pp. 84–97.

Borgstrom, G., *Hungry Planet,* Collier-Macmillan, Toronto, 1967.

———, *Too Many,* Macmillan, New York, 1969. Borgstrom exposes the biological limitations of the earth; a lucid advocate of agricultural reform.

Brown, R., *Man, Land and Food: Looking Ahead at World Food Needs,* Government Printing Office, Washington, D.C., 1963.

Clawson, M., Landsberg, H. H., Alexander, L. T., "Desalted seawater for agriculture: is it economic?" *Science,* Vol. 164, pp. 1141–48. Detailed critique of desalting procedure.

Cochrane, W. W. *The World Food Problem: A Guardedly Optimistic View,* Thomas Y. Crowell, New York, 1969.

Cole, H. H. (ed.), *Introduction to Livestock Production, Including Dairy and Poultry,* 2nd ed., W. H. Freeman and Company, San Francisco, 1966.

Dumont, R., and Rosier, Bernard, *The Hungry Future,* Praeger, New York, 1969.

Food and Agriculture Organization of the United Nations, 1968, *Production Yearbook 1967.* FAO-UN, Rome. A basic source for statistical data.

Hendricks, S. B., "Food from the Land," in P. E. Cloud, Jr. (ed.), *Resources and Man,* W. H. Freeman and Company, San Francisco, 1969.

Idyll, C. P., *The Sea Against Hunger,* Thomas Y. Crowell, 1970. Nonutopian view of sea's role in food crisis.

Johnson, D., *The Struggle Against World Hunger.* Foreign Policy Association, New York, 1967.

Kristensen, T., *The Food Problem in Developing Countries,* Organization for Economic Cooperation and Development Publications Center, Washington, D.C., 1968.

Paddock, W., and Paddock, P., *Hungry Nations.* Little, Brown & Company, Boston, 1964.

______ *Famine 1975!,* Little, Brown & Company, Boston, 1967.

President's Science Advisory Committee Panel on the World Food Supply, 1967. *The World Food Problem* (3 vols.). Washington, D.C. A very detailed, basic source.

Ricker, W. E., "Food from the Sea," *In* P. E. Cloud, Jr. (ed.), *Resources and Man.* W. H. Freeman and Company, San Francisco, 1969.

Robinson, H. F., Dimensions of the world food crisis. *BioScience,* Vol. 19, no. 1, January 1969, pp. 24–29.

Ryther, J. H., Photosynthesis and fish production in the sea. *Science,* Vol. 166, 1969 pp. 72–76.

Wharton, C. R., Jr., "The green revolution: cornucopia or Pandora's box?" *Foreign Affairs,* Vol. 47, April 1969, pp. 464–476. An excellent summary of economic and social consequences of the Green Revolution.

VI Pesticides

No one item demonstrates more dramatically the double effects of human "progress" and the subtle toll which "miracle" developments can exact than do pesticides. These wonder chemical formulations controlling insects and pests improve crops, make lawns beautifully green and impart such blessings as added comfort during the mosquito season. But the damages they cause, silently and multidirectionally, border on the catastrophic. Pesticides have killed fresh- and salt-water fish, contaminated marine invertebrates and threatened whole species of animals, including the American bald eagle. That is only the beginning. Under laboratory conditions, some pesticides have been shown to produce cancers, birth defects and genetic mutations among rats, mice, hamsters, dogs and monkeys. There is no reason to believe they are not similarly harmful to humans. Indeed, the deaths of some humans have been laid to accumulations of pesticides in the body's system.

Rachel Carson rang her sobering alarm on pesticides back in 1962, a whole decade ago. But pesticides remain a large fact of American life. Further, the extent of their negative side effects is as yet only infinitesimally researched—the effects of pesticides on animals, for instance, have been studied on less than 1 percent of the species in the United States. Pesticides remain as American as apple pie.

As of December 1969, approximately 900 active pesticidal chemicals were formulated into more than 60,000 preparations in the United States.[1] Production and sales of synthetic organic pesticides for 1968 alone amounted to 1.2 billion pounds, 80 percent of which was for domestic usage. These pesticides were marketed as dusts, sprays, aerosols, granules, pellets and baits; they were sprayed on trees to control disease, fed to animals to control parasites, sold to housewives to improve room odors, promoted among growers to increase the quality and yield of their crops; and added to clothing as moth-proofing. Pesticides, in a word, were and are everywhere. And their popularity grows. They have a usage-growth rate in the United States

[1]"Pesticides and Their Relationship to Environmental Health"; a report of the Department of Health, Education and Welfare, 1970.

of 15 percent a year. Farming accounts for just more than half of the pesticides manufactured; government agencies use about 5 percent; residential and industrial users, the remainder.

Synthetic organic pesticides are classified into three broad groups—chlorinated hydrocarbons, organophosphates and carbamates—and categorized on four persistence levels.

Nonpersistent pesticides (e.g., parathion, schradan and EPN) are those which last from several days to about twelve weeks.

Moderately persistent pesticides (e.g., 2,4-D and atrazine) have a lifetime of from one to eighteen months, and are measurably more dangerous.

Persistent pesticides (most of the chlorinated hydrocarbons—DDT, aldrin, dieldrin, endrin, heptachlor, toxaphene) are more dangerous still and may persist in the environment for years. (Present research indicates that DDT may have a toxic life of twenty years or more.)

Permanent pesticides (based on toxic, inorganic elements such as mercury, lead and arsenic) are among the most dangerous of all; they may linger in the environment indefinitely.

The complicating factor in evaluating pesticides is that even those which are nonpersistent, and which may degrade rapidly, are not without ecological liabilities. For instance, the application of a light insecticide may eliminate a family of insects; but it also may strip the area of the predators, or natural enemies, of the intended targets. Thus, rather than the area being cleared of pests, it becomes more vulnerable to new attacks by the same family of pests from nearby areas. Since pests multiply more rapidly than their predators, the area treated with the insecticide may end up worse off than before.

There are other complications. For one thing, pests build up a resistance to pesticides, thus tempting the introduction of stronger new pesticides, or heavier dosages of the old pesticide at more frequent intervals. In fact, a study carried out by the World Health Organization (WHO) of the United Nations and made public in July 1971 revealed that more than 200 species of insects had developed resistance to one or more of the insecticides used against them; 105 of the total carry disease to man and animals.

By the same token, every pesticide compound seems to have one or more boomerang effects. A pesticide like carbaryl, for instance, has a relatively low toxicity for mammals, but it is deadly to the honeybee and related insects. Zectran, on the other hand, is not so disturbing to the latter, but it is deadly to mammals.

Unfortunately, no pesticide is so marvelously effective as to be all benefit.

Pesticides enter the ecosystem in a number of ways. Pesticide sprays can be carried long distances by winds and dust particles (spraying in the United States is known to have affected remote nesting places of the bald eagle in Canada). They can build up in the soil, from there to wash into water supplies, or be drawn into vegetable crops through leaching, thus reaching humans themselves (.20 parts per million of DDT have been found in mother's milk by University of California scientists). Pesticides can cling to vegetation, be ingested by animals and pass to humans through meat (one of the biggest problems with DDT is that its danger increases as its residues accumulate along the food chain). Also, pesticides can circulate via the waste discharge of pesticide producers. From clothing they can be taken into the body through the pores of the skin.

Public authority is alert at last to the fact that pesticides are bane as well as blessing to man. Controls have tightened on the federal and state levels. The first of the big targets was DDT, initially banned in many states and then brought under tightening restriction by Washington itself.[2] Other bans followed. The Department of Agriculture in 1970 cancelled all uses of aldrin and dieldrin in aquatic environments, and the Department of the Interior ordered a stop of the use of DDT, aldrin, 2,4,5-T, dieldrin, endrin, DDD, mercury and nine other pesticides on the 356 million acres of land controlled by the department. States like New York ban many pesticides outright and impose a commerical or purchase permit on the use of many more.

Even with steps such as these, the problem is being scratched only on the surface. Only a relative handful of the total number of pesticides has been dealt with. Pesticides abound in such number (there are over 100 commonly used insecticides and some 1,000 different formulations), are used in so many ways (even in paints and floor waxes) and have so many unknown side effects that the challenges they pose have hardly been categorized. (Tables 6-7, 6-8)

What is to be done?

The Council on Environmental Quality in its first report[3] recommended that high priority be given four steps:

1. Legislative and administration proposals for more effective pesticide regulation, including measures to assure adoption of less persistent

[2]William D. Ruckelshaus, administrator of the Environmental Protection Agency, declined, however, to place DDT (and the herbicide 2,4,5-T) under a total suspension, March 18, 1971. Ruckelshaus said that he did not consider DDT or 2,4,5-T "imminent" hazards to humans. He did, though, order an administrative review of their safety, and said he hoped the review would be completed in a year. The Ruckelshaus decision disappointed environmentalists, who had believed Ruckelshaus to be inclined toward suspension.

[3]*Environmental Quality;* first annual report, August 1970, p. 140.

or toxic materials, limit the availability of certain types of pesticides and regulate disposal of unused pesticides.

2. Ensurance that information on the dangers of pesticides and on innovations in pest control is spread worldwide, with consideration given to international control over use and shipment of pesticides. ("Although the need for pesticides may be great in developing countries, the risks to human and environmental health are very great also, and knowledge, techniques, and standards developed in the United States do not necessarily apply elsewhere. For example, recent studies have shown that application of the non-selective, persistent pesticides under tropical conditions in some cases aggravate the pest condition rather than the reverse.")

3. Exploration of incentives to industry to stimulate research and development by the private sector on substitutes for persistent pesticides and on nonchemical control.

4. Study of the effects of pesticides on man and the environment to be vigorously pursued, particularly through controlled exposure experiments.

What of the individual, in the meantime? The individual can help in several ways. He should:

—Use pesticides sparingly and dispose of empty containers or excess preparation with great care,

—Question community-wide spraying programs, particularly for mere nuisance targets, such as the mosquito,

—Protect wet lands and waters as much as possible from pesticide contaminants,

—Avoid pesticide compounds that will destroy insect predators,

—Be wary of general purpose pesticides,

—Try pesticide substitutes before going to pesticides themselves (sometimes easy sprays of water will clear a plant of pests),

—Avoid herbicides completely,

—Avoid poisonous products (usually marked with skull and crossbones),

—Be familiar with the tolerance ratings of the Food and Drug Administration (see pages following).

Food and Drug Administration (FDA) Pesticide Tolerances

FDA tolerances for pesticide chemicals in or on raw agricultural commodities established in the code of federal regulations, Sections 120.101 through 120.275 under the Pesticide Amendment.

Unless otherwise stated, tolerances apply only to residues from pre-harvest or pre-slaughter applications of pesticide chemicals.

The list on the pages following is from the National Agricultural Chemicals Association's sixteenth annual revision of FDA tolerances. It is used with permission from the NACA, 1155 Fifteenth Street, N.W., Washington, D.C. 20005 (202-296-1585).

The list in these pages is selective. It itemizes the more common agricultural commodities of professional and amateur fruit and vegetable growers. It does not list smaller, more special or more exotic crop items, such as hay, forage, nuts, tropical fruits, etc. (Table 6-1)

The complete listing may be had by writing to the National Agricultural Chemicals Association and requesting a copy of its official FDA tolerances. Copies are available at 50 cents per copy, with a minimum order of four copies. Remittance should be included with order.

The term, "negligible residue," as used in these pages is defined by Federal Pesticide Regulations. It means any amount of pesticide chemical remaining in or on a raw agricultural commodity or group of raw agricultural commodities that would result in a daily intake regarded as toxicologically insignificant on the basis of scientific judgment of adequate safety data. Ordinarily this will add to the diet an amount which will be less than 1/2,000 of the amount that has been demonstrated to have no effect from feeding studies of the most sensitive animal species tested. Such toxicity studies shall usually include at least ninety-day feeding studies in two species of mammals.

A pesticide residue is the amount of the active chemical in or on a food product. This is expressed in the tables as p.p.m., *parts per million,* which is a measure of the amount of chemical in relation to the total weight of the product sample. The residue tendency of a pesticide is not the same as its toxicity. Rather it is the persistence factor, or tendency of the chemical to break down slowly, or not at all, under field conditions. Long-lived chemicals present more of a residue problem than short-lived chemicals. The Food, Drug and Cosmetic Act of 1938 and the Miller Amendment of 1954 require that safe residues must be determined before a chemical can be marketed commercially. These safe residues' levels are termed "tolerances."

TABLE 6-1.

I FRUITS

APPLES, PEARS AND QUINCES	
Aldrin and its expoxidation product dieldrin	Zero (total residues resulting from application of aldrin).
Benzene hexachloride	5 p.p.m.
1,1-bis (p-Chlorophenyl)-2,2,2-trichloroethanol	5 p.p.m.
Captan (pre-harvest and/or post-harvest uses)	25 p.p.m.
Carbophenothion	0.8 p.p.m.
Chlorbenside	3 p.p.m.
Chlordane	0.3 p.p.m.
DDT	7 p.p.m.
2,4-D	5 p.p.m.
Dicyclohexylamine salt of dinitro-o-cyclohexylphenol	1 p.p.m.
Dieldrin	0.1 p.p.m.
O,O-dimethyl S-[4-oxo-1,2,3-benzotriazin-3(4H)-ylmethyl] phosphorodithioate	2 p.p.m.
Dioxathion	4 p.p.m.
EPN	3 p.p.m.
Ferbam	7 p.p.m.
Fluorine compounds	7 p.p.m. of combined fluorine.
Lead arsenate	7 p.p.m. of combined lead.
Lindane	10 p.p.m.
Malathion	8 p.p.m.
Methyl bromide (post-harvest fumigation)	5 p.p.m. of inorganic bromides calculated as Br.
Methoxychlor	14 p.p.m.
Methyl parathion (and/or parathion)	1 p.p.m.
α-naphthaleneacetic acid	1 p.p.m.
Nicotine-containing compounds	2 p.p.m. of nicotine.
Parathion (and/or methyl parathion)	1 p.p.m.
Phenothiazine	7 p.p.m.
TDE	7 p.p.m.
Tetradifon	5 p.p.m.
Toxaphene	7 p.p.m.
Zinc ion and Maneb (coordination product)	10 p.p.m. calculated as zineb on the whole product.
Zineb	7 p.p.m.
Ziram	7 p.p.m.
APPLES AND PEARS	
Allethrin (post-harvest use)	4 p.p.m.
Ammonium sulfamate	5 p.p.m.
2-(p-tert-butylphenoxy)cyclohexyl 2-propynyl sulfite	3 p.p.m.
2-(p-tert-butylphenoxy)-isopropyl-2-chloroethyl sulfite	Zero.
Carbaryl	10 p.p.m.
p-chlorophenyl phenyl sulfone	8 p.p.m.
Dalapon sodium salt	3 p.p.m. as 2,2-dichloropropionic acid
Demeton	0.75 p.p.m.
Dichlobenil and its metabolite	0.15 p.p.m. (negligible residue).
1,1-dichloro-2,2-bis (p-ethylphenyl) ethane	15 p.p.m.
O,O-diethyl O-(2-isopropyl-4-methyl-6-pyrimidinyl) phosphorothioate	0.75 p.p.m.

TABLE 6-1. (cont.)

Dimethoate and its oxygen analog	2 p.p.m.
Diuron	1 p.p.m.
Dodine	5 p.p.m.
Endosulfan and its metabolite	2 p.p.m.
Ethoxyquin (pre-harvest or post-harvest use)	3 p.p.m.
Ethyl 4,4′-dichlorobenzilate	5 p.p.m.
Glyodin	5 p.p.m.
Isopropyl 4,4′-dichlorobenzilate	5 p.p.m.
N-(mercaptomethyl)phthalimide S-(O,O-dimethyl phosphorodithioate) and its oxygen analog	10 p.p.m.
1-methoxycarbonyl-1-propen-2-yl dimethylphosphate and its beta isomer	0.5 p.p.m.
Ovex	3 p.p.m.
Paraquat	0.05 p.p.m. (negligible residue) derived from application of either the bis(methyl sulfate) or dichloride salt, both calculated as the cation.
o-phenylphenol and sodium o-phenylphenate (post-harvest application)	25 p.p.m. expressed as o-phenylphenol on each.
Phosalone	10 p.p.m.
Piperonyl butoxide (post-harvest use)	8 p.p.m.
Pyrethrins (post-harvest use)	1 p.p.m.
Simazine	0.25 p.p.m.
Terbacil	0.1 p.p.m.
APPLES	
Ammoniates of [ethylenebis (dithiocarbamato)] zinc (5.2 parts by weight) with ethylenebis [dithiocarbamic acid] bimolecular and trimolecular cyclic anhydrosulfides and disulfides (1 part by weight)	7 p.p.m. calculated as zineb.
2-chloro-1-(2,4,5-trichlorophenyl) vinyl dimethyl phosphate, and its related conversion products	10 p.p.m.
p-chlorophenyl-2,4,5-trichlorophenyl sulfide	0.1 p.p.m. (negligible residue).
Dichlone	3 p.p.m.
Diphenylamine (pre-harvest or post-harvest use)	10 p.p.m.
Ethion and its oxygen analog	2 p.p.m.
Folpet	25 p.p.m.
Heptachlor (and its epoxide)	Zero.
Maneb	7 p.p.m.
Manganous dimethyldithiocarbamate	7 p.p.m. as zinc ethylene-bisdithiocarbamate.
Mercaptobenzothiazole	0.1 p.p.m. as 2,2′-dithiobisbenzothiazole.
Phosphamidon and all of its related cholinesterase-inhibiting compounds	1 p.p.m. expressed as phosphamidon.
Succinic acid 2,2-dimethylhydrazide	30 p.p.m.
Thiram	7 p.p.m.
2,3,5-triiodobenzoic acid and its dimethylamine salt	0.05 p.p.m. calculated as 2,3,5-triiodobenzoic acid (negligible residue).
PEARS	
Basic copper carbonate (post-harvest application)	3 p.p.m. of combined copper.
Ethion and its oxygen analog	1 p.p.m.

TABLE 6-1. (cont.)

CRABAPPLES	
Allethrin (post-harvest use)	4 p.p.m.
1,1-bis (p-chlorophenyl)-2,2,2-trichloroethanol	5 p.p.m.
Captan (pre-harvest and/or post-harvest uses)	25 p.p.m.
Carbophenothion	0.8 p.p.m.
Chlorbenside	3 p.p.m.
O,O-dimethyl S-[4-oxo-1,2,3-benzotriazin-3(4H)-ylmethyl] phosphorodithioate	2 p.p.m.
Folpet	25 p.p.m.
Piperonyl butoxide (post-harvest use)	8 p.p.m.
Pyrethrins (post-harvest use)	1 p.p.m.
Tetradifon	5 p.p.m.
Zinc ion and Maneb (coordination product)	10 p.p.m. calculated as zineb on the whole product.
APRICOTS	
Aldrin and its epoxidation product dieldrin	Zero (total residues resulting from application of aldrin).
Benzene hexachloride	5 p.p.m.
1,1-bis (p-chlorophenyl)-2,2,2-trichloroethanol	10 p.p.m.
Captan (pre-harvest and/or post-harvest uses)	50 p.p.m.
Carbophenothion	0.8 p.p.m.
Chlordane	0.3 p.p.m.
cis-N-[(1,1,2,2-tetrachloroethyl)thio]-4-cyclohexene-1,2-dicarboximide	30 p.p.m.
Dalapon sodium salt	1 p.p.m. as 2,2-dichloropropionic acid.
DDT	7 p.p.m.
Demeton	0.75 p.p.m.
1,2-dibromo-3-chloropropane	5 p.p.m. of inorganic bromides calculated as Br.
2,6-dichloro-4-nitroaniline	20 p.p.m.
Dicyclohexylamine salt of dinitro-o-cyclohexyl-phenol	1 p.p.m.
Dieldrin	0.1 p.p.m.
O,O-diethyl O-(2-isopropyl-4-methyl-6-pyrimidinyl) phosphorothioate	0.75 p.p.m.
O,O-dimethyl S-[4-oxo-1,2,3-benzotriazin-3-(4H)-ylmethyl] phosphorodithioate	2 p.p.m.
Endosulfan and its metabolite	2 p.p.m.
EPN	3 p.p.m.
Ferbam	7 p.p.m.
Fluorine compounds	7 p.p.m. of combined fluorine.
Lead arsenate	7 p.p.m. of combined lead.
Lindane	10 p.p.m.
Malathion	8 p.p.m.
Maneb	10 p.p.m.
Methoxychlor	14 p.p.m.
Methyl bromide (post-harvest fumigation)	20 p.p.m. of inorganic bromides calculated as Br.
Methyl parathion (and/or parathion)	1 p.p.m.
Nicotine-containing compounds	2 p.p.m. of nicotine.
Paraquat	0.05 p.p.m. (negligible residue) derived from application of either the bis(methyl sulfate) or dichloride salt, both calculated as the cation.

TABLE 6-1. (cont.)

Parathion (and/or methyl parathion)	1 p.p.m.
TDE	7 p.p.m.
Tetradifon	5 p.p.m.
Toxaphene	7 p.p.m.
Zineb	7 p.p.m.
Ziram	7 p.p.m.
GRAPEFRUIT, LEMONS, LIMES, ORANGES, TANGERINES	
Aldrin and its epoxidation product dieldrin	0.05 p.p.m.[1] (total residues resulting from application of aldrin).
Benzene hexachloride	5 p.p.m.
1,1-bis (p-chlorophenyl)-2,2,2-trichloroethanol	10 p.p.m.
Captan (pre-harvest and/or post-harvest uses)	25 p.p.m.[1]
Carbophenothion	2 p.p.m.
Chlordane	0.3 p.p.m.
Dicyclohexylamine salt of dinitro-o-cyclohexylphenol	1 p.p.m.
Dieldrin	0.05 p.p.m.[1]
Dinitro-o-cyclohexylphenol	1 p.p.m.
Dioxathion	2.8 p.p.m.
Ethylene dibromide (USDA Quarantine Program)	10 p.p.m. of inorganic bromides calculated as Br.
EPN	3 p.p.m.
Fluorine compounds	7 p.p.m. of combined fluorine.
Lead arsenate	1 p.p.m. of combined lead.
Lindane	10 p.p.m.
Malathion	8 p.p.m.
Methyl bromide (post-harvest fumigation)	30 p.p.m. of inorganic bromides calculated as Br.
Monuron	1 p.p.m.
Nicotine-containing compounds	2 p.p.m. of nicotine.
Tetradifon	2 p.p.m.
Tartar emetic	3.5 p.p.m. of combined antimony trioxide.
Toxaphene	7 p.p.m.
Zineb	7 p.p.m.
GRAPEFRUIT, LEMONS, ORANGES, TANGERINES	
Naled and its conversion product 2,2-dichlorovinyl dimethyl phosphate	3 p.p.m. expressed as naled.
Ovex	5 p.p.m.
Phosphamidon and all of its related cholinesterase-inhibiting compounds	0.75 p.p.m. expressed as phosphamidon.
GRAPEFRUIT, LEMONS, ORANGES	
2-(p-tert-butylphenoxy)-isopropyl-2-chloroethyl sulfite	Zero.
Demeton	0.75 p.p.m.
1-methoxycarbonyl-1-propen-2-yl-dimethylphosphate and its beta isomer	0.25 p.p.m.
Simazine	0.25 p.p.m.
GRAPEFRUIT, LIMES, ORANGES, TANGERINES	
Dalapon sodium salt	5 p.p.m. as 2,2-dichloropropionic acid.

TABLE 6-1. (cont.)

LEMONS	
Dimethoate and its oxygen analog	2 p.p.m.
ORANGES	
Allethrin (post-harvest use)	4 p.p.m.
Dimethoate and its oxygen analog	2 p.p.m.
Piperonyl butoxide (post-harvest use)	8 p.p.m.
Pyrethrins (post-harvest use)	1 p.p.m.
CITRUS CITRON	
Methyl bromide (post-harvest fumigation)	30 p.p.m. of inorganic bromides calculated as Br.
Monuron	1 p.p.m.
Tetradifon	2 p.p.m.
KUMQUATS	
1,1-bis (p-chlorophenyl)-2,2,2-trichloroethanol	10 p.p.m.
Malathion	8 p.p.m.
Methyl bromide (post-harvest fumigation)	30 p.p.m. of inorganic bromides calculated as Br.
Monuron	1 p.p.m.
TANGELOS	
1,1-bis (p-cholorophenyl)-2,2,2-trichloroethanol	10 p.p.m.
Captan (pre-harvest and/or post-harvest uses)	25 p.p.m.[1]
Carbophenothion	2 p.p.m.
Dioxathion	2.8 p.p.m.
Malathion	8 p.p.m.
Methyl bromide (post-harvest fumigation)	30 p.p.m. of inorganic bromides calculated as Br.
Monuron	1 p.p.m.
Tetradifon	2 p.p.m.
GRAPES	
Aldrin and its epoxidation product dieldrin	0.1 p.p.m. (total residues resulting from application of aldrin).
Allethrin (post-harvest use)	4 p.p.m.
Benzene hexachloride	5 p.p.m.
1,1-bis (p-chlorophenyl)-2,2,2-trichloroethanol	5 p.p.m.
2-(p-tert-butylphenoxy)-isopropyl-2-chloroethyl sulfite	Zero.
Captan (pre-harvest and/or post-harvest uses)	50 p.p.m.
Carbaryl	10 p.p.m.
Carbophenothion	0.8 p.p.m.
Chlordane	0.3 p.p.m.
Dalapon sodium salt	3 p.p.m. as 2,2-dichloropropionic acid.
DDT	7 p.p.m.
Demeton	1.25 p.p.m.
1,2-dibromo-3-chloropropane	25 p.p.m. of inorganic bromides calculated as Br.
Dichlobenil and its metabolite	0.15 p.p.m. (negligible residue).
2,6-dichloro-4-nitroaniline	10 p.p.m.
Dicyclohexylamine salt of dinitro-o-cyclohexylphenol	1 p.p.m.
Dieldrin	0.1 p.p.m.

TABLE 6-1. (cont.)

0,0-diethyl 0-(2-isopropyl-4-methyl-6-pyrimidinyl) phosphorothioate	0.75 p.p.m.
0,0-dimethyl S-[4-oxo-1,2,3-benzotriazin-3(4H)-ylmethyl] phosphorodithioate	5 p.p.m.
Dioxathion	2.1 p.p.m.
Diuron	1 p.p.m.
Ethion and its oxygen analog	2 p.p.m.
Endosulfan and its metabolite	2 p.p.m.
EPN	3 p.p.m.
Ferbam	7 p.p.m.
Fluorine compounds	7 p.p.m. of combined fluorine.
Folpet	25 p.p.m.
Gibberellic acid	0.15 p.p.m. (negligible residue).
Heptachlor (and its epoxide)	Zero.
Lead arsenate	7 p.p.m. of combined lead.
Lindane	10 p.p.m.
Malathion	8 p.p.m.
Maneb	7 p.p.m.
1-methoxycarbonyl-1-propen-2-yl dimethylphosphate and its beta isomer	0.5 p.p.m.
Methoxychlor	14 p.p.m.
Methyl bromide (post-harvest fumigation)	20 p.p.m. of inorganic bromides calculated as Br.
Methyl parathion (and/or parathion)	1 p.p.m.
Monuron	1 p.p.m.
Nicotine-containing compounds	2 p.p.m. of nicotine.
Paraquat	0.05 p.p.m. (negligible residue) derived from application of either the bis(methyl sulfate) or dichloride salt, both calculated as the cation.
Parathion (and/or methyl parathion)	1 p.p.m.
Phosalone	10 p.p.m.
Piperonyl butoxide (post-harvest use)	8 p.p.m.
Pyrethrins (post-harvest use)	1 p.p.m.
Simazine	0.25 p.p.m.
Sodium arsenate	3.5 p.p.m. of combined As_2O_3.
Succinic acid 2,2-dimethylhydrazide	10 p.p.m.
Tartar emetic	3.5 p.p.m. of combined antimony trioxide.
TDE	7 p.p.m.
Tetradifon	5 p.p.m.
Trifluralin	0.05 p.p.m. (negligible residue).
Zinc ion and Maneb (coordination product)	7 p.p.m. calculated as zineb on the whole product.
Zineb	7 p.p.m.
Ziram	7 p.p.m.
PEACHES	
Allethrin (post-harvest use)	4 p.p.m.
2-(p-tert-butylphenoxy)cyclohexyl 2-propynyl sulfite	7 p.p.m.
2-(p-tert-butylphenoxy)-isopropyl-2-chloroethyl sulfite	Zero.
p-chlorophenyl phenyl sulfone	8 p.p.m.

TABLE 6-1. (cont.)

cis-N-[(1,1,2,2-tetrachloroethyl)thio]-4-cyclohexene-1,2-dicarboximide	30 p.p.m.
Dalapon sodium salt	15 p.p.m. as 2,2-dichloropropionic acid.
Dichlone	3 p.p.m.
2,6-dichloro-4-nitroaniline (pre- and post-harvest application)	20 p.p.m.
Dodine	5 p.p.m.
Glyodin	5 p.p.m.
Heptachlor (and its epoxide)	Zero.
Maneb	7 p.p.m.
N-(mercaptomethyl)phthalimide S-(O,O-dimethyl phosphorodithioate) and its oxygen analog	10 p.p.m.
1-methoxycarbonyl-1-propen-2-yl dimethylphosphate and its beta isomer	1 p.p.m.
Ovex	3 p.p.m.
o-phenylphenol and sodium o-phenylphenate (post-harvest application)	20 p.p.m. expresses as o-phenylphenol on each.
Piperonyl butoxide (post-harvest use)	8 p.p.m.
Pyrethrins (post-harvest use)	1 p.p.m.
Simazine	0.25 p.p.m.
Succinic acid 2,2-dimethylhydrazide	30 p.p.m.
Terbacil	0.1 p.p.m.
Thiram	7 p.p.m.
Zinc sulfate (basic)	30 p.p.m. calculated as elemental zinc.
PEARS (for tolerances established for pesticide residues on pears, see "Apples, pears and quinces.")	
RASPBERRIES, BLACKBERRIES, LOGANBERRIES AND RELATED BERRIES	
Allethrin (post-harvest use)	4 p.p.m.
1,1-bis (p-chlorophenyl)-2,2,2-trichloroethanol	5 p.p.m.
Calcium arsenate	3.5 p.p.m. of combined As_2O_3.
Carbaryl	12 p.p.m.
Chlordane	0.3 p.p.m.
DDT	1 p.p.m.
2,4-dichloro-6-o-chloroanilino-s-triazine	10 p.p.m.
Dicyclohexylamine salt of dinitro-o-cyclohexylphenol	1 p.p.m.
O,O-dimethyl S-[4-oxo-1,2,3-benzotriazin-3(4H)-ylmethyl] phosphorodithioate	2 p.p.m.
Diuron	1 p.p.m.
EPN	3 p.p.m.
Ferbam	7 p.p.m.
Fluorine compounds	7 p.p.m. of combined fluorine.
Folpet	25 p.p.m.
Lead arsenate	7 p.p.m. of combined lead.
Malathion	8 p.p.m.
Methoxychlor	14 p.p.m.
Methyl parathion (and/or parathion)	1 p.p.m.
Nicotine-containing compounds	2 p.p.m. of nicotine.
Parathion (and/or methyl parathion)	1 p.p.m.
Piperonyl butoxide (post-harvest use)	8 p.p.m.
Pyrethrins (post-harvest use)	1 p.p.m.
TDE	3.5 p.p.m.

TABLE 6-1. (cont.)

Toxaphene	7 p.p.m.
Zineb	7 p.p.m.
Ziram	7 p.p.m.
RHUBARB	
Captan (pre-harvest and/or post-harvest uses)	25 p.p.m.
2,6-dichloro-4-nitroaniline	10 p.p.m.
Maneb	10 p.p.m.
STRAWBERRIES	
Aldrin and its epoxidation product dieldrin	0.1 p.p.m. (total residues resulting from application of aldrin).
Benzene hexachloride	5 p.p.m.
1,1-bis (p-chlorophenyl)-2,2,2-trichloroethanol	5 p.p.m.
2-(p-tert-butylphenoxy)-isopropyl-2-chloroethyl sulfite	Zero.
Calcium arsenate	3.5 p.p.m. of combined As_2O_3.
Captan (pre-harvest and/or post-harvest uses)	25 p.p.m.
Carbaryl	10 p.p.m.
Carbophenothion	0.8 p.p.m.
Chlordane	0.3 p.p.m.
3-[p-(p-chlorophenoxy)phenyl]-1,1-dimethylurea	0.1 p.p.m. (negligible residue).
Combinations of chloropicrin, methyl bromide, and propargyl bromide (soil treatment)	25 p.p.m. of inorganic bromides calculated as Br.
DDT	1 p.p.m.
Demeton	0.75 p.p.m.
1,2-dibromo-3-chloropropane	10 p.p.m. of inorganic bromides calculated as Br.
Dichlone	15 p.p.m.
2,4-dichloro-6-o-chloroanilino-s-triazine	10 p.p.m.
2,6-dichloro-4-nitroaniline	15 p.p.m.
Dicyclohexylamine salt of dinitro-o-cyclohexylphenol	1 p.p.m.
Dieldrin	0.1 p.p.m.
O,O-diethyl O-(2-isopropyl-4-methyl-6-pyrimidinyl) phosphorothioate	0.75 p.p.m.
O,O-diethyl O-2-pyrazinyl phosphorothioate and its oxygen analog	0.1 p.p.m. (negligible residue).
O,O-dimethyl S-[4-oxo-1,2,3-benzotriazin-3(4H)-ylmethyl] phosphorodithioate	2 p.p.m.
Dimethyl 2,3,5,6-tetrachloroterephthalate and its metabolites	2 p.p.m. calculated as dimethyl 2,3,5,6-tetrachloroterephthalate.
Diphenamid and its desmethyl metabolite	1 p.p.m.
Dodine	5 p.p.m.
Endosulfan and its metabolite	2 p.p.m.
EPN	3 p.p.m.
Ethion and its oxygen analog	2 p.p.m.
S-ethyl dipropylthiocarbamate	0.1 p.p.m. (negligible residue).
Ethylene dibromide (soil treatment)	5 p.p.m. of inorganic bromides calculated as Br.
Ferbam	7 p.p.m.
Fluorine compounds	7 p.p.m. of combined fluorine.
Folpet	25 p.p.m.
Lead arsenate	7 p.p.m. of combined lead.

TABLE 6-1. (cont.)

Lindane	10 p.p.m.
Malathion	8 p.p.m.
1-methoxycarbonyl-1-propen-2-yl dimethylphosphate and its beta isomer	1 p.p.m.
Methoxychlor	14 p.p.m.
Methyl bromide	30 p.p.m. of inorganic bromides calculated as Br.
Methyl parathion (and/or parathion)	1 p.p.m.
Naled and its conversion product 2,2-dichlorovinyl dimethyl phosphate	1 p.p.m. expressed as naled.
Nicotine-containing compounds	2 p.p.m. of nicotine.
Parathion (and/or methyl parathion)	1 p.p.m.
Sesone	2 p.p.m.
Simazine	0.25 p.p.m.
Sodium dehydroacetate (post-harvest application)	65 p.p.m. calculated as dehydroacetic acid.
TDE	3.5 p.p.m.
Tetradifon	5 p.p.m.
Thiram	7 p.p.m.
Toxaphene	7 p.p.m.
Zineb	7 p.p.m.
Ziram	7 p.p.m.

II VEGETABLES

ARTICHOKES

DDT	1 p.p.m.
O,O-dimethyl S-[4-oxo-1,2,3-benzotriazin-3(4H)-ylmethyl] phosphorodithioate	2 p.p.m.
O,O-dimethyl 2,2,2-trichloro-1-hydroxyethyl phosphonate	0.1 p.p.m. (negligible residue).
Diuron	1 p.p.m.
Endosulfan and its metabolite	2 p.p.m.
Gibberellic acid	0.15 p.p.m. (negligible residue).
1-methoxycarbonyl-1-propen-2-yl dimethylphosphate and its beta isomer	1 p.p.m.
Methyl bromide (post-harvest fumigation)	30 p.p.m. of inorganic bromides calculated as Br.
Methyl parathion (and/or parathion)	1 p.p.m.
Nicotine-containing compounds	2 p.p.m. of nicotine.
Parathion (and/or methyl parathion)	1 p.p.m.
Simazine	0.5 p.p.m.

ASPARAGUS

Aldrin and its epoxidation product dieldrin	0.1 p.p.m. (total residues resulting from application of aldrin).
Benzene hexachloride	5 p.p.m.
Calcium arsenate	3.5 p.p.m. of combined As_2O_3.
Carbaryl	10 p.p.m.
Chlorosulfamic acid (post-harvest application)	8 p.p.m. of sulfamate ion expressed as sulfamic acid.
Dalapon sodium salt	30 p.p.m. as 2,2-dichloropropionic acid.
DDT	1 p.p.m.

TABLE 6-1. (cont.)

Dieldrin	0.1 p.p.m.
Diuron	7 p.p.m.
S-ethyl dipropylthiocarbamate	0.1 p.p.m. (negligible residue).
Ethylene dibromide (soil treatment)	10 p.p.m. of inorganic bromides calculated as Br.
O-ethyl S-phenyl ethylphosphonodithioate and its oxygen analog	0.1 p.p.m. (negligible residue).
Ferbam	7 p.p.m.
Lead arsenate	7 p.p.m. of combined lead.
Lindane	10 p.p.m.
Malathion	8 p.p.m.
Methoxychlor	14 p.p.m.
Methyl bromide (USDA Quarantine Program)	100 p.p.m. of inorganic bromides calculated as Br.
Monuron	7 p.p.m.
Nicotine-containing compounds	2 p.p.m. of nicotine.
Sesone	2 p.p.m.
Simazine	10 p.p.m.
Sodium 2,4-dichlorophenoxyacetate	5 p.p.m. as 2,4-D.
Zinc ion and Maneb (coordination product)	0.1 p.p.m. calculated as zineb on the whole product (negligible residue).
BEANS	
Aldrin and its epoxidation product dieldrin	Zero (total residues resulting from application of aldrin).
Benzene hexachloride	5 p.p.m.
Calcium arsenate	3.5 p.p.m. of combined As_2O_3.
Carbaryl	10 p.p.m.
Chlordane	0.3 p.p.m.
Chloroneb and its metabolite	0.1 p.p.m. calculated as chloroneb (negligible residue).
DDT	7 p.p.m.
Demeton	0.3 p.p.m.
Dichlone	3 p.p.m.
Dicyclohexylamine salt of dinitro-o-cyclohexylphenol	1 p.p.m.
Dieldrin	Zero.
Endosulfan and its metabolite	2 p.p.m.
EPN	3 p.p.m.
Ethion and its oxygen analog	2 p.p.m.
Ferbam	7 p.p.m.
Fluorine compounds	7 p.p.m. of combined fluorine.
Lindane	10 p.p.m.
Magnesium arsenate	3.5 p.p.m. of combined As_2O_3.
Malathion	8 p.p.m.
1-methoxycarbonyl-1-propen-2-yl dimethylphosphate and its beta isomer	0.25 p.p.m.
Methoxychlor	14 p.p.m.
Methyl parathion (and/or parathion)	1 p.p.m.
Nicotine-containing compounds	2 p.p.m. of nicotine.
Parathion (and/or methyl parathion)	1 p.p.m.
Piperonyl butoxide (post-harvest use)	8 p.p.m.
Pyrethrins (post-harvest use)	1 p.p.m.

TABLE 6-1. (cont.)

TDE	7 p.p.m.
Toxaphene	7 p.p.m.
Zineb	7 p.p.m.
Ziram	7 p.p.m.
BEANS (green beans, lima beans, snap beans, and blackeyed peas)	
Methyl bromide (post-harvest fumigation)	50 p.p.m. of inorganic bromides calculated as Br.
BEANS (dried)	
Amiben	0.1 p.p.m. (negligible residue).
1,1-bis (p-chlorophenyl)-2,2,2-trichloroethanol	5 p.p.m.
Captan (pre-harvest and/or post-harvest uses)	25 p.p.m.[1]
0,0-diethyl S-[2-(ethylthio)ethyl] phosphorodithioate and its cholinesterase-inhibiting metabolites	0.75 p.p.m. calculated as demeton.
Dimethoate and its oxygen analog	2 p.p.m.
0,0-dimethyl 2,2,2-trichloro-1-hydroxyethyl phosphonate	0.1 p.p.m. (negligible residue).
Hydrogen cyanide (post-harvest fumigation)	25 p.p.m.
Maneb	7 p.p.m.
BEANS (except lima beans)	
4-(methylsulfonyl)-2,6-dinitro-N,N-dipropylaniline	0.1 p.p.m. (negligible residue).
BEANS (succulent)	
Captan (pre-harvest and post-harvest uses)	25 p.p.m.[1]
Maneb	10 p.p.m.
FIELD BEANS (dry), MUNG BEANS (dry), AND SNAP BEANS (succulent)	
Dimethyl 2,3,5,6-tetrachloroterephthalate and its metabolites	2 p.p.m. calculated as dimethyl 2,3,5,6-tetrachloroterephthalate.
GREEN BEANS	
2-(p-tert-butylphenoxy)-isopropyl-2-chloroethyl sulfite	Zero.
Ethylene dibromide (USDA Quarantine Program)	10 p.p.m. of inorganic bromides calculated as Br.
LENTILS	
Barban	0.1 p.p.m. (negligible residue).
Malathion	8 p.p.m.
LIMA BEANS AND SNAP BEANS	
1,1-bis (p-chlorophenyl)-2,2,2-trichloroethanol	5 p.p.m.
Carbophenothion	0.8 p.p.m.
2-chloroallyl diethyldithiocarbamate	0.2 p.p.m. (negligible residue).
0,0-diethyl S-[2-(ethylthio)ethyl] phosphorodithioate and its cholinesterase-inhibiting metabolites	0.75 p.p.m. calculated as demeton.
0,0-diethyl 0-(2-isopropyl-4-methyl-6-primidinyl phosphorothiate	0.75 p.p.m.
Dimethoate and its oxygen analog	2 p.p.m.
0,0-dimethyl 2,2,2-trichloro-1-hydroxyethyl phosphonate	0.1 p.p.m. (negligible residue).

TABLE 6-1. (cont.)

LIMA BEANS	
Amiben	0.1 p.p.m. (negligible residue).
Ethylene dibromide (soil treatment)	5 p.p.m. of inorganic bromides calculated as Br.
Heptachlor (and its epoxide)	Zero.
MUNG BEAN SPROUTS	
p-chlorophenoxyacetic acid (from use as a plant regulator on the beans to inhibit embryonic root development)	2 p.p.m.
Trifluralin	2 p.p.m.
SNAP BEANS	
1,2-dibromo-3-chloropropane	75 p.p.m. of inorganic bromides calculated as Br.
2,6-dichloro-4-nitroaniline	20 p.p.m.
O,O-dimethyl S-[4-oxo-1,2,3-benzotriazin-3(4H)-ylmethyl] phosphorodithioate	2 p.p.m.
Heptachlor (and its epoxide)	0.1 p.p.m.
BLACKEYED PEAS	
Aldrin and its epoxidation product dieldrin	Zero (total residues resulting from application of aldrin).
Dieldrin	Zero.
Dimethyl 2,3,5,6-tetrachloroterephthalate and its metabolites	2 p.p.m. calculated as dimethyl 2,3,5,6-tetrachloroterephthalate.
Heptachlor (and its epoxide)	Zero.
BEETS (garden) (with or without tops) OR BEET GREENS ALONE	
Aldrin and its epoxidation product dieldrin	Zero (total residues resulting from application of aldrin).
Carbophenothion	0.8 p.p.m.
Chlordane	0.3 p.p.m.
Dieldrin	Zero.
O,O-diethyl O-(2-isopropyl-4-methyl-6-pyrimidinyl) phosphorothioate	0.75 p.p.m.
EPN	3 p.p.m.
S-ethyl cyclohexylethylthiocarbamate	0.05 p.p.m. (negligible residue).
Ferbam	7 p.p.m.
Fluorine compounds	7 p.p.m. of combined fluorine.
Malathion	8 p.p.m.
1-methoxycarbonyl-1-propen-2-yl dimethylphosphate and its beta isomer	1 p.p.m.
Methyl parathion (and/or parathion)	1 p.p.m.
Methoxychlor	14 p.p.m.
Nicotine-containing compounds	2 p.p.m. of nicotine.
Parathion (and/or methyl parathion)	1 p.p.m.
Ziram	7 p.p.m.
BEETS (garden) ROOTS ONLY	
Captan (pre-harvest and/or post-harvest uses)	2 p.p.m.
Carbaryl	5 p.p.m.

TABLE 6-1. (cont.)

DDT	1 p.p.m.
0,0-dimethyl 2,2,2-trichloro-1-hydroxyethyl phosphonate	0.1 p.p.m. (negligible residue).
Heptachlor (and its epoxide)	Zero.
Methyl bromide (post-harvest fumigation)	30 p.p.m. of inorganic bromides calculated as Br.
Zinele	7 p.p.m.
BEETS (garden) TOPS ONLY	
Captan (pre-harvest and/or post-harvest uses)	100 p.p.m.
Carbaryl	12 p.p.m.
DDT	7 p.p.m.
Zineb	25 p.p.m.
SUGAR BEETS AND SUGAR BEET TOPS	
Aldrin and its epoxidation product dieldrin	Zero (total residues resulting from application of aldrin).
Barban	0.1 p.p.m. (negligible residue).
Benzadox	0.1 p.p.m. (negligible residue).
Carbophenothion	5 p.p.m.
Chloroneb and its metabolite	0.1 p.p.m. calculated as chloroneb (negligible residue).
2,4-dichlorophenyl p-nitrophenyl ether	0.05 p.p.m. (negligible residue).
Dalapon sodium salt	5 p.p.m. as 2,2-dichloropropionic acid.
Endrin	Zero.
S-ethyl cyclohexylethylthiocarbamate	0.05 p.p.m. (negligible residue).
Paraquat	0.5 p.p.m. derived from application of either the bis(methyl sulfate) or the dichloride salt, both calculated as the cation.
S-propyl butylethylithiocarbamate	0.1 p.p.m. (negligible residue).
SUGAR BEETS (but not tops)	
2-chloro-N-isopropylacetanilide and its metabolites	0.2 p.p.m. calculated as 2-chloro-N-isopropylacetanilide.
Demeton	0.5 p.p.m.
0,0-diethyl S-[2-ethylthio)ethyl] phosphorodithioate and its cholinesterase-inhibiting metabolites	0.5 p.p.m. calculated as demeton.
0,0-diethyl 0-(2-isopropyl-4-methyl-6-pyrimidinyl) phosphorothioate	0.75 p.p.m.
0,0-dimethyl 2,2,2-trichloro-1-hydroxyethyl phosphonate	0.1 p.p.m. (negligible residue).
EPN	3 p.p.m.
Heptachlor (and its epoxide)	Zero.
Malathion	1 p.p.m.
Methyl bromide (post-harvest fumigation)	30 p.p.m. of inorganic bromides calculated as Br.
Phorate and its cholinesterase-inhibiting metabolites	0.3 p.p.m.
Zinc ion and Maneb (coordination product)	2 p.p.m. calculated as zineb on the whole product.

TABLE 6-1. (cont.)

SUGAR BEET TOPS	
Carbaryl	100 p.p.m.
2-chloro-N-isopropylacetanilide and its metabolites	1 p.p.m. calculated as 2-chloro-N-isopropylacetanilide.
Demeton	5 p.p.m.
0,0-diethyl S-[2-(ethylthio)ethyl] phosphorodithioate and its cholinesterase-inhibiting metabolites	2 p.p.m. calculated as demeton.
0,0-diethyl 0-(2-isopropyl-4-methyl-6-pyrimidinyl) phosphorothioate	10 p.p.m.
0,0-dimethyl 2,2,2-trichloro-1-hydroxyethyl phosphonate	12 p.p.m.
0-ethyl S-phenyl ethylphosphonodithioate and its oxygen analog	0.1 p.p.m. (negligible residue).
Malathion	8 p.p.m.
Maneb	45 p.p.m.
Phorate and its cholinesterase-inhibiting metabolites	3 p.p.m.
Zinc ion and Maneb (coordination product)	65 p.p.m. calculated as zineb on the whole product.
BROCCOLI	
Aldrin and its epoxidation product dieldrin	0.1 p.p.m. (total residues resulting from application of aldrin).
Benzene hexachloride	5 p.p.m.
Calcium arsenate	3.5 p.p.m. of combined As_2O_3.
Captan (pre-harvest and/or post-harvest uses)	2 p.p.m.
Carbaryl	10 p.p.m.
Chlordane	0.3 p.p.m.
2-chloroallyl diethyldithiocarbamate	0.2 p.p.m. (negligible residue).
Combinations of chloropicrin, methyl bromide, and propargyl bromide (soil treatment)	25 p.p.m. of inorganic bromides calculated as Br.
DDT	1 p.p.m.
Demeton	0.75 p.p.m.
1,2-dibromo-3-chloropropane	50 p.p.m. of inorganic bromides calculated as Br.
1,1-dichloro-2,2-bis (p-ethylphenyl) ethane	15 p.p.m.
2,4-dichlorophenyl p-nitrophenyl ether	0.75 p.p.m.
Dieldrin	0.1 p.p.m.
0,0-diethyl S-[2-(ethylthio)ethyl] phosphorodithioate and its cholinesterase-inhibiting metabolites	0.75 p.p.m. calculated as demeton.
0,0-diethyl 0-(2-isopropyl-4-methyl-6-pyrimidinyl) phosphorothioate	0.75 p.p.m.
0,0-diethyl 0-2-pyrazinyl phosphorothioate and its oxygen analog	0.1 p.p.m. (negligible residue).
Dimethoacte and its oxygen analog	2 p.p.m.
0,0-dimethyl S-[4-oxo-1,2,3-benzotriazin-3(4H)-ylmethyl] phosphorodithioate	2 p.p.m.
Dimethyl 2,3,5,6-tetrachloroterephthalate and its metabolites	1 p.p.m. calculated as dimethyl 2,3,5,6-tetrachloroterephthalate.
Endosulfan and its metabolite	2 p.p.m.
Endrin	Zero.

TABLE 6-1. (cont.)

Ethylene dibromide (soil treatment)	75 p.p.m. of inorganic bromides calculated as Br.
Ferbam	7 p.p.m.
Fluorine compounds	7 p.p.m. of combined fluorine.
Lindane	10 p.p.m.
Malathion	8 p.p.m.
Maneb	10 p.p.m.
1-methoxycarbonyl-1-propen-2-yl dimethylphosphate and its beta isomer	1 p.p.m.
Methoxychlor	14 p.p.m.
Methyl parathion (and/or parathion)	1 p.p.m.
4-(methylsulfonyl)-2,6-dinitro-N,N-dipropylaniline	0.1 p.p.m. (negligible residue).
Naled and its conversion product 2,2-dichlorovinyl dimethyl phosphate	1 p.p.m. expressed as naled.
Nicotine-containing compounds	2 p.p.m. of nicotine.
Parathion (and/or methyl parathion)	1 p.p.m.
Phosphamidon and all of its related cholinesterase-inhibiting compounds	0.5 p.p.m. expressed as phosphamidon.
TDE	1 p.p.m.
Toxaphene	7 p.p.m.
Zineb	7 p.p.m.
Ziram	7 p.p.m.
BRUSSELS SPROUTS, KOHLRABI, CAULIFLOWER	
DDT	1 p.p.m.
Heptachlor (and its epoxide)	Zero.
Maneb	10 p.p.m.
CABBAGE	
DDT	7 p.p.m.
Dimethoate and its oxygen analog	2 p.p.m.
Heptachlor (and its epoxide)	0.1 p.p.m.
Maneb	10 p.p.m.
Methyl bromide (USDA Quarantine Program)	50 p.p.m. of inorganic bromides calculated as Br.
CABBAGE, BRUSSELS SPROUTS, KOHLRABI, CAULIFLOWER	
Benzene hexachloride	5 p.p.m.
Calcium arsenate	3.5 p.p.m. of combined As_2O_3.
Carbaryl	10 p.p.m.
Chlordane	0.3 p.p.m.
Copper arsenate	3.5 p.p.m. of combined As_2O_3.
1,1-dichloro-2,2-bis (p-ethylphenyl) ethane	15 p.p.m.
2,4-dichlorophenyl p-nitrophenyl ether	0.75 p.p.m.
Ferbam	7 p.p.m.
Fluorine compounds	7 p.p.m. of combined fluorine.
Lindane	10 p.p.m.
Malathion	8 p.p.m.
Methoxychlor	14 p.p.m.
Methyl parathion (and/or parathion)	1 p.p.m.
Nicotine-containing compounds	2 p.p.m. of nicotine.
Parathion (and/or methyl parathion)	1 p.p.m.

TABLE 6-1. (cont.)

TDE	1 p.p.m.
Toxaphene	7 p.p.m.
Zineb	7 p.p.m.
Ziram	7 p.p.m.
CABBAGE, BRUSSELS SPROUTS, CAULIFLOWER	
Aldrin and its epoxidation product dieldrin	0.1 p.p.m. (total residues resulting from application of aldrin).
Captan (pre-harvest and/or post-harvest uses)	2 p.p.m.
2-chloroallyl diethyldithiocarbamate	0.2 p.p.m. (negligible residue).
Demeton	0.75 p.p.m.
1,2-dibromo-3-chloropropane	50 p.p.m. of inorganic bromides calculated as Br.
Dieldrin	0.1 p.p.m.
0,0-diethyl S-[2-(ethylthio)ethyl] phosphorodithioate and its cholinesterase-inhibiting metabolites	0.75 p.p.m. calculated as demeton.
0,0-diethyl 0-(2-isopropyl-4-methyl-6-pyrimidinyl) phosphorothioate	0.75 p.p.m.
0,0-dimethyl 2,2,2-trichloro-1- and its oxygen analog	0.1 p.p.m. (negligible residue).
0,0-dimethyl S-[4-oxo-1,2,3-benzotriazin-3(4H)-ylmethyl] phosphorodithioate	2 p.p.m.
Dimethyl 2,3,5,6-tetrachloroterephthalate and its metabolites	1 p.p.m. calculated as dimethyl 2,3,5,6-tetrachloroterephthalate.
0,0-dimethyl 2,2,2-trichloro-1-hydroxyethyl phosphonate	0.1 p.p.m. (negligible residue).
Endosulfan and its metabolite	2 p.p.m.
Endrin	Zero.
1-methoxycarbonyl-1-propen-2-yl dimethylphosphate and its beta isomer	1 p.p.m.
4-(methylsulfonyl)-2,6-dinitro-N,N-dipropylaniline	0.1 p.p.m. (negligible residue).
Naled and its conversion product 2,2-dichlorovinyl dimethyl phosphate	1 p.p.m. expressed as naled.
CARROTS	
Aldrin and its epoxidation product dieldrin	Zero (total residues resulting from application of aldrin).
Calcium arsenate	3.5 p.p.m. of combined As_2O_3.
Captan (pre-harvest and/or post-harvest uses)	2 p.p.m.
Carbaryl	10 p.p.m.
Chlordane	0.3 p.p.m.
3-[p-(p-chlorophenoxy)phenyl]-1,1-dimethylurea	0.1 p.p.m. (negligible residue).
Chlorosulfamic acid (post-harvest application)	8 p.p.m. of sulfamate ion expressed as sulfamic acid.
Copper arsenate	3.5 p.p.m. of combined As_2O_3.
DDT	3.5 p.p.m.
1,2-dibromo-3-chloropropane	75 p.p.m. of inorganic bromides calculated as Br.
2,6-dichloro-4-nitroaniline (post-harvest application)	10 p.p.m.
2,4-dichlorophenyl p-nitrophenyl ether	0.75 p.p.m.
Dieldrin	0.1 p.p.m.
0,0-diethyl 0-(2-isopropyl-4-methyl-6-pyrimidinyl) phosphorothioate	0.75 p.p.m.

TABLE 6-1. (cont.)

O,O-dimethyl 2,2,2-trichloro-1-hydroxyethyl phosphonate	0.1 p.p.m. (negligible residue).
Endosulfan and its metabolite	0.2 p.p.m.
Ethylene dibromide (soil treatment)	75 p.p.m. of inorganic bromides calculated as Br.
Ferbam	7 p.p.m.
Fluorine compounds	7 p.p.m. of combined fluorine.
Heptachlor (and its epoxide)	Zero.
Linuron	1 p.p.m.
Malathion	8 p.p.m.
Maneb	7 p.p.m.
1-methoxycarbonyl-1-propen-2-yl dimethylphosphate and its beta isomer	0.25 p.p.m.
Methoxychlor	14 p.p.m.
Methyl bromide (post-harvest fumigation)	30 p.p.m. of inorganic bromides calculated as Br.
Methyl parathion (and/or parathion)	1 p.p.m.
Parathion (and/or methyl parathion)	1 p.p.m.
o-phenylphenol and sodium o-phenylphenate (post-harvest application)	20 p.p.m. expressed as o-phenylphenol on each.
TDE	1 p.p.m.
Toxaphene	7 p.p.m.
Trifluralin	1 p.p.m.
Zinc ion and Maneb (coordination product)	2 p.p.m. calculated as zineb on the whole product.
Zineb	7 p.p.m.
Ziram	7 p.p.m.
CORN (fresh vegetable)	
Benzene hexachloride	5 p.p.m.
Calcium arsenate	3.5 p.p.m. of combined As_2O_3.
Chlordane	0.3 p.p.m.
DDT	3.5 p.p.m. (determined on kernels plus cob after removing any husk present when marketed.)
EPN	3 p.p.m.
Ethylene dibromide (soil treatment)	50 p.p.m. of inorganic bromides calculated as Br.
Ferbam	7 p.p.m.
Flourine compounds	7 p.p.m. of combined fluorine.
Heptachlor	Zero.
Lindane	10 p.p.m.
1-methoxycarbonyl-1-propen-2-yl dimethyl-phosphate and its beta isomer	0.25 p.p.m.
Methoxychlor	14 p.p.m.
Methyl parathion (and/or parathion)	1 p.p.m.
Nicotine-containing compounds	2 p.p.m. of nicotine.
Paraquat	0.05 p.p.m. (negligible residue) derived from application of either the bis(methyl sulfate) or dischloride salt, both calculated as the cation.

TABLE 6-1. (cont.)

Parathion (and/or methyl parathion)	1 p.p.m.
Toxaphene	7 p.p.m.
Zineb	7 p.p.m.
FRESH CORN INCLUDING SWEET CORN (kernels plus cobs with husk removed)	
Atrazine	0.25 p.p.m.
2,4-bis(isopropylamino)-6-methylthio-s-triazine	0.25 p.p.m.
Dalapon sodium salt	5 p.p.m. as 2,2-dichloropropionic acid.
S-ethyl diisobutylthiocarbamate	0.1 p.p.m. (negligible residue).
O-ethyl S-phenyl ethylphosphonodithioate and its oxygen analog	0.1 p.p.m. (negligible residue).
Methomyl	0.1 p.p.m. (negligible residue).
Simazine	0.25 p.p.m.
Zinc ion and Maneb (coordination product)	0.5 p.p.m. calculated as zineb on the whole product.
SWEET CORN (kernels plus cob with husk removed)	
Captan (pre-harvest and/or post-harvest uses)	2 p.p.m.
2-chloro-N-isopropylacetanilide and its metabolites	0.1 p.p.m. calculated as 2-chloro-N-isopropylacetanilide (negligible residue).
Dimethyl 2,3,5,6-tetrachloroterephthalate and its metabolites	0.05 p.p.m. calculated as dimethyl 2,3,5,6-tetrachloroterephthalate (negligible residue).
Endosulfan and its metabolite	0.2 p.p.m.
Phorate and its cholinesterase-inhibiting metabolites	0.1 p.p.m.
TDE	3.5 p.p.m.
SWEET CORN (kernels and forage thereof)	
2-(p-tert-butylphenoxy)-isopropyl-2-chloroethyl sulfite	Zero.
CORN (kernels plus cob with husk removed)	
Carbaryl	5 p.p.m.
Carbophenothion	0.2 p.p.m.
2-chloroallyl diethyldithiocarbamate	0.2 p.p.m. (negligible residue).
O,O-diethyl O-(2-isopropyl-4-methyl-6-pyrimidinyl) phosphorothioate	0.75 p.p.m.
O,O-dimethyl 2,2,2-trichloro-1-hydroxyethyl phosphonate	0.1 p.p.m. (negligible residue).
Malathion	2 p.p.m.
Maneb	7 p.p.m.
Methyl bromide (post-harvest fumigation)	50 p.p.m. of inorganic bromides calculated as Br.
CUCUMBERS	
Aldrin and its epoxidation product dieldrin	0.1 p.p.m. (total residues resulting from application of aldrin).
Ammoniates of [ethylenebis (dithiocarbamato)] zinc (5.2 parts by weight) with ethylenebis [dithiocarbamic acid] bimolecular and trimolecular cyclic anhydrosulfides and disulfides (1 part by weight)	5 p.p.m. calculated as zineb.
Benzene hexachloride	5 p.p.m.
1,1-bis (p-chlorophenyl)-2,2,2-trichloroethanol	5 p.p.m.
2-(p-tert-butylphenoxy)-isopropyl-2-chloroethyl sulfite	Zero.

TABLE 6-1. (cont.)

Calcium arsenate	3.5 p.p.m. of combined As_2O_3.
Captan (pre-harvest and/or post-harvest uses)	25 p.p.m.
Carbaryl	10 p.p.m.
Carbophenothion	0.8 p.p.m.
Chlordane	0.3 p.p.m.
2-chloroallyl diethyldithiocarbamate	0.2 p.p.m. (negligible residue).
cis-N-[1,1,2,2-tetrachloroethyl)thio]-4-cyclohexene-1,2-dicarboximide	2 p.p.m.
DDT	7 p.p.m.
1,2-dibromo-3-chloropropane	25 p.p.m. of inorganic bromides calculated as Br.
2,4-dichloro-6-o-chloroanilino-s-triazine	10 p.p.m.
2,6-dichloro-4-nitroaniline	5 p.p.m.
Dieldrin	0.1 p.p.m.
O,O-diethyl O-(2-isopropyl-4-methyl-6-pyrimidinyl) phosphorothioate	0.75 p.p.m.
S-(O,O-diisopropyl phosphorodithioate) of N-(2-mercaptoethyl) benzenesulfonamide and its oxygen analog	0.1 p.p.m. (negligible residue).
O,O-dimethyl S-[4-oxo-1,2,3-benzotriazin-3(4H)-ylmethyl] phosphorodithioate	2 p.p.m.
Dimethyl 2,3,5,6-tetrachloroterephthalate and its metabolites	1 p.p.m. calculated as dimethyl 2,3,5,6-tetrachloroterephthalate.
Endosulfan and its metabolite	2 p.p.m.
Endrin	Zero.
Ethion and its oxygen analog	0.5 p.p.m.
Ethylene dibromide (soil treatment)	30 p.p.m. of inorganic bromides calculated as Br.
Ethylene dibromide (USDA Quarantine Program)	10 p.p.m. of inorganic bromides calculated as Br.
Ferbam	7 p.p.m.
Fluorine compounds	7 p.p.m. of combined fluorine.
Folpet	15 p.p.m.
Lindane	10 p.p.m.
Malathion	8 p.p.m.
Maneb	7 p.p.m.
1-methoxycarbonyl-1-propen-2-yl dimethylphosphate and its beta isomer	0.25 p.p.m.
Methoxychlor	14 p.p.m.
Methyl bromide (post-harvest fumigation)	30 p.p.m. of inorganic bromides calculated as Br.
Methyl parathion (and/or parathion)	1 p.p.m.
4-(methylsulfonyl)-2,6-dinitro-N,N-dipropylaniline	0.1 p.p.m. (negligible residue).
Naled and its conversion product 2,2-dichlorovinyl dimethyl phosphate	0.5 p.p.m. expresses as naled.
Nicotine-containing compounds	2 p.p.m. of nicotine.
Parathion (and/or methyl parathion)	1 p.p.m.
o-phenylphenol and sodium o-phenylphenate (post-harvest application)	10 p.p.m. expressed as o-phenylphenol on each.
	0.5 p.p.m. expressed as phosphamidon.
TDE	7 p.p.m.
Tetradifon	1 p.p.m.

TABLE 6-1. (cont.)

Toxaphene	7 p.p.m.
Zinc ion and Maneb (coordination product)	7 p.p.m. calculated as zineb on the whole product.
Zineb	7 p.p.m.
Ziram	7 p.p.m.
EGGPLANT	
Aldrin and its epoxidation product dieldrin	0.1 p.p.m. (total residues resulting from application of aldrin).
Benzene hexachloride	5 p.p.m.
1,1-bis (p-chlorophenyl)-2,2,2-trichloroethanol	5 p.p.m.
Calcium arsenate	3.5 p.p.m. of combined As_2O_3.
Captan (pre-harvest and/or post-harvest uses)	25 p.p.m.
Carbaryl	10 p.p.m.
Carbophenothion	0.8 p.p.m.
Chlorbenside	3 p.p.m.
Chlordane	0.3 p.p.m.
Combinations of chloropicrin, methyl bromide, and propargyl bromide (soil treatment)	60 p.p.m. of inorganic bromides calculated as Br.
DDT	7 p.p.m.
Demeton	0.3 p.p.m.
1,2-dibromo-3-chloropropane	50 p.p.m. of inorganic bromides calculated as Br.
Dieldrin	0.1 p.p.m.
0,0-dimethyl S-[4-oxo-1,2,3-benzotriazin-3(4H)-ylmethyl] phosphorodithioate	0.3 p.p.m.
Dimethyl 2,3,5,6-tetrachloroterephthalate and its metabolites	1 p.p.m. calculated as dimethyl 2,3,5,6-tetrachloroterephthalate.
Endosulfan and its metabolite	2 p.p.m.
Endrin	Zero.
Ethion and its oxygen analog	1 p.p.m.
Ethylene dibromide (soil treatment)	50 p.p.m. of inorganic bromides calculated as Br.
Ferbam	7 p.p.m.
Fluorine compounds	7 p.p.m. of combined fluorine.
Lead arsenate	7 p.p.pm. of combined lead.
Lindane	10 p.p.m.
Malathion	8 p.p.m.
Maneb	7 p.p.m.
1-methoxycarbonyl-1-propen-2-yl dimethylphosphate and its beta isomer	0.25 p.p.m.
Methoxychlor	14 p.p.m.
Methyl bromide (post-harvest fumigation)	20 p.p.m. of inorganic bromides calculated as Br.
Methyl parathion (and/or parathion)	1 p.p.m.
Naled and its conversion product 2,2-dichlorovinyl dimethyl phosphate	0.5 p.p.m. expressed as naled.
Nicotine-containing compounds	2 p.p.m. of nicotine.
Parathion (and/or methyl parathion)	1 p.p.m.
TDE	7 p.p.m.

TABLE 6-1. (cont.)

Toxaphene	7 p.p.m.
Zineb	7 p.p.m.
Ziram	7 p.p.m.
ENDIVE AND ESCAROLE	
Aldrin and its epoxidation product dieldrin	Zero (total residues resulting from application of aldrin).
Carbaryl	10 p.p.m.
2-chloroallyl diethyldithiocarbamate	0.2 p.p.m. (negligible residue).
DDT	1 p.p.m.
1,2-dibromo-3-chloropropane	130 p.p.m. of inorganic bromides calculated as Br.
Dieldrin	Zero.
O,O-diethyl O-(2-isopropyl-4-methyl-6-primidinyl) phosphorothioate	0.75 p.p.m.
Dimethoate and its oxygen analog	2 p.p.m.
Malathion	8 p.p.m.
Maneb	10 p.p.m.
Methyl parathion (and/or parathion)	1 p.p.m.
Parathion (and/or methyl parathion)	1 p.p.m.
Zineb	25 p.p.m.
HANOVER SALAD	
2-chloroallyl diethyldithiocarbamate	0.2 p.p.m. (negligible residue).
KALE AND COLLARDS	
Aldrin and its epoxidation product dieldrin	Zero (total residues resulting from application of aldrin).
Benzene hexachloride	5 p.p.m.
Calcium arsenate	3.5 p.p.m. of combined As_2O_3.
Captan (pre-harvest and/or post-harvest uses)	2 p.p.m.
Carbaryl	12 p.p.m.
Chlordane	0.3 p.p.m.
2-chloroallyl diethyldithiocarbamate	0.2 p.p.m. (negligible residue).
DDT	7 p.p.m.
Dieldrin	Zero.
O,O-diethyl O-(2-isopropyl-4-methyl-6-pyrimidinyl) phosphorothioate	0.75 p.p.m.
Dimethoate and its oxygen analog	2 p.p.m.
Dimethyl 2,3,5,6-tetrachloroterephthalate and its metabolites	2 p.p.m. calculated as dimethyl 2,3,5,6-tetrachloroterephthalate.
Endosulfan and its metabolite	2 p.p.m.
Ferbam	7 p.p.m.
Fluorine compounds	7 p.p.m. of combined fluorine.
Lindane	10 p.p.m.
Malathion	8 p.p.m.
Maneb	10 p.p.m.
1-methoxycarbonyl-1-propen-2-yl dimethylphosphate and its beta isomer	1 p.p.m.
Methoxychlor	14 p.p.m.
Methyl parathion (and/or parathion)	1 p.p.m.
Nicotine-containing compounds	2 p.p.m. of nicotine.

TABLE 6-1. (cont.)

Parathion (and/or methyl parathion)	1 p.p.m.
Toxaphene	7 p.p.m.
Zineb	25 p.p.m.
Ziram	7 p.p.m.
COLLARDS	
O,O-dimethyl 2,2,2-trichloro-1-hydroxyethyl phosphonate	0.1 p.p.m. (negligible residue).
LETTUCE	
Aldrin and its epoxidation product dieldrin	0.1 p.p.m. (total residues resulting from application of aldrin).
Benzene hexachloride	5 p.p.m.
N-butyl-N-ethyl-α,α,α-trifluoro-2,6-dinitro-p-toluidine	0.05 p.p.m. (negligible residue).
Captan (pre-harvest and/or post-harvest uses)	100 p.p.m.
Carbaryl	10 p.p.m.
Chlordane	0.3 p.p.m.
2-chloroallyl diethyldithiocarbamate	0.2 p.p.m. (negligible residue).
DDT	7 p.p.m.
Demeton	0.75 p.p.m.
1,2-dibromo-3-chloropropane	130 p.p.m. of inorganic bromides calculated as Br.
1,1-dichloro-2,2-bis (p-ethylphenyl) ethane	15 p.p.m.
2,6-dichloro-4-nitroaniline	10 p.p.m.
Dieldrin	0.1 p.p.m.
O,O-diethyl S-[2-(ethylthio)ethyl] phosphorodithioate and its cholinesterase-inhibiting metabolites	0.75 p.p.m. calculated as demeton.
O,O-diethyl O-(2-isopropyl-4-methyl-6-pyrimidinyl) phosphorothioate	0.75 p.p.m.
S-(O,O-diisopropyl phosphorodithioate) of N-(2-mercaptoethyl) benzenesulfonamide and its oxygen analog	0.1 p.p.m. (negligible residue).
Dimethoate and its oxygen analog	2 p.p.m.
Dimethyl 2,3,5,6-tetrachloroterephthalate and its metabolites	2 p.p.m. calculated as dimethyl 2,3,5,6-tetrachloroterephthalate.
O,O-dimethyl 2,2,2-trichloro-1-hydroxyethyl phosphonate	0.1 p.p.m. (negligible residue).
Endosulfan and its metabolite	2 p.p.m.
EPN	3 p.p.m.
Ethylene dibromide (soil treatment)	30 p.p.m. of inorganic bromides calculated as Br.
Ferbam	7 p.p.m.
Fluorine compounds	7 p.p.m. of combined fluorine.
Folpet	50 p.p.m.
Heptachlor (and its epoxide)	0.1 p.p.m.
Lindane	10 p.p.m.
Malathion	8 p.p.m.
Maneb	10 p.p.m.
1-methoxycarbonyl-1-propen-2-yl dimethylphosphate and its beta isomer	0.5 p.p.m.
Methoxychlor	14 p.p.m.
Methyl parathion (and/or parathion)	1 p.p.m.

TABLE 6-1. (cont.)

Naled and its conversion product 2,2-dichlorovinyl dimethyl phosphate	1 p.p.m. expressed as naled.
Nicotine-containing compounds	2 p.p.m. of nicotine.
Paraquat	0.05 p.p.m. (negligible residue) derived from application of either the bis(methyl sulfate) or dichloride salt, both calculated as the cation.
Parathion (and/or methyl parathion)	1 p.p.m.
Phorate and its cholinesterase-inhibiting metabolites	0.1 p.p.m.
TDE	1 p.p.m.
Toxaphene	7 p.p.m.
Zineb	25 p.p.m.
Ziram	7 p.p.m.
MUSHROOMS	
DDT	1 p.p.m.
Lindane	10 p.p.m.
Malathion	8 p.p.m.
Methoxychlor	14 p.p.m.
Nicotine-containing compounds	2 p.p.m. of nicotine.
Zineb	7 p.p.m.
ONIONS (including green onions and garlic)	
Aldrin and its epoxidation product dieldrin	0.1 p.p.m. (total residues resulting from application of aldrin).
Benezene hexachloride	5 p.p.m.
Chlordane	0.3 p.p.m.
DDT	7 p.p.m.
2,6-dichloro-4-nitroaniline	5 p.p.m.
Dieldrin	0.1 p.p.m.
O,O-diethyl O-(2-isopropyl-4-methyl-6-pyrimidinyl) phosphorothioate	0.75 p.p.m.
O,O-dimethyl S-[4-oxo-1,2,3-benzotriazin-3(4H)-ylmethyl] phosphorodithioate	2 p.p.m.
Dimethyl 2,3,5,6-tetrachloroterephthalate and its metabolites	1 p.p.m. calculated as dimethyl 2,3,5,6-tetrachloroterephthalate.
Ethion and its oxygen analog	1 p.p.m.
Ferbam	7 p.p.m.
Heptachlor (and its epoxide)	Zero.
Lindane	10 p.p.m.
Malathion	8 p.p.m.
Maneb	7 p.p.m.
1-methoxycarbonyl-1-propen-2-yl dimethylphosphate and its beta isomer	0.25 p.p.m.
Methyl bromide (post-harvest fumigation)	20 p.p.m. of inorganic bromides calculated as Br.
Methyl parathion (and/or parathion)	1 p.p.m.
Nicotine-containing compounds	2 p.p.m. of nicotine.
Parathion (and/or methyl parathion)	1 p.p.m.
Tartar emetic	3.5 p.p.m. of combined antimony trioxide.

TABLE 6-1. (cont.)

Toxaphene	7 p.p.m.
Zineb	7 p.p.m.
Ziram	7 p.p.m.
GREEN ONIONS	
Captan (pre-harvest and/or post-harvest uses)	50 p.p.m.
Carbophenothion	0.8 p.p.m.
2,4-dichloro-6-o-chloroanilino-s-triazine	10 p.p.m.
Folpet	50 p.p.m.
PEAS	
Aldrin and its epoxidation product dieldrin	Zero (total residues resulting from application of aldrin).
Barban	0.1 p.p.m. (negligible residue).
Benzene hexachloride	5 p.p.m.
Carbophenothion	0.8 p.p.m.
Chlordane	0.3 p.p.m.
DDT	7 p.p.m.
Demeton	0.75 p.p.m.
Dieldrin	Zero.
0,0-diethyl S-[2-(ethylthio)ethyl] phosphorodithioate and its cholinesterase-inhibiting metabolites	0.75 p.p.m. calculated as demeton.
Dimethoate and its oxygen analog	2 p.p.m.
Diuron	1 p.p.m.
Ferbam	7 p.p.m.
Fluorine compounds	7 p.p.m. of combined fluorine.
Heptachlor (and its epoxide)	Zero.
Lindane	10 p.p.m.
Malathion	8 p.p.m.
1-methoxycarbonyl-1-propen-2-yl dimethylphosphate and its beta isomer	0.25 p.p.m.
Methoxychlor	14 p.p.m.
Methyl bromide (post-harvest fumigation)	50 p.p.m. of inorganic bromides calculated as Br.
Methyl parathion (and/or parathion)	1 p.p.m.
Nicotine-containing compounds	2 p.p.m. of nicotine.
Parathion (and/or methyl parathion)	1 p.p.m.
Piperonyl butoxide (post-harvest use)	8 p.p.m.
Pyrethrins (post-harvest use)	1 p.p.m.
TDE	1 p.p.m.
Toxaphene	7 p.p.m.
Zineb	7 p.p.m.
Ziram	7 p.p.m.
PEPPERS	
Aldrin and its epoxidation product dieldrin	0.1 p.p.m. (total residues resulting from application of aldrin).
Amiben	0.1 p.p.m. (negligible residue).
Benzene hexachloride	5 p.p.m.
1,1-bis (p-chlorophenyl)-2,2,2-trichloroethanol	5 p.p.m.
Calcium arsenate	3.5 p.p.m. of combined As_2O_3.

TABLE 6-1. (cont.)

Captan (pre-harvest and/or post-harvest uses)	25 p.p.m.
Carbaryl	10 p.p.m.
Carbophenothion	0.8 p.p.m.
Chlordane	0.3 p.p.m.
Combinations of chloropicrin, methyl bromide, and propargyl bromide (soil treatment)	25 p.p.m. of inorganic bromides calculated as Br.
DDT	7 p.p.m.
Demeton	0.75 p.p.m.
1,2-dibromo-3-chloropropane	50 p.p.m. of inorganic bromides calculated as Br.
Dieldrin	0.1 p.p.m.
0,0-diethyl 0-(2-isopropyl-4-methyl-6-pyrimidinyl) phosphorothioate	0.75 p.p.m.
Dimethoate and its oxygen analog	2 p.p.m.
0,0-dimethyl S-[oxo-1,2,3-benzotriazin-3(4H)-ylmethyl] phosphorodithioate	0.3 p.p.m.
0,0-dimethyl 2,2,2-trichloro-1-hydroxyethyl phosphonate	0.1 p.p.m. (negligible residue).
Dimethyl 2,3,5,6-tetrachloroterephthalate and its metabolites	2 p.p.m. calculated as dimethyl 2,3,5,6-tetrachloroterephthalate.
Endosulfan and its metabolite	2 p.p.m.
Endrin	Zero.
Ethion and its oxygen analog	1 p.p.m.
Ethylene dibromide (soil treatment)	30 p.p.m. of inorganic bromides calculated as Br.
Ethylene dibromide (USDA Quarantine Program)	10 p.p.m. of inorganic bromides calculated as Br.
Ferbam	7 p.p.m.
Fluorine compounds	7 p.p.m. of combine fluorine.
Lead arsenate	7 p.p.m. of combined lead.
Lindane	10 p.p.m.
Malathion	8 p.p.m.
Maneb	7 p.p.m.
1-methoxycarbonyl-1-propen-2-yl dimethylphosphate and its beta isomer	0.25 p.p.m.
Methoxychlor	14 p.p.m.
Methyl bromide (post-harvest fumigation)	30 p.p.m. of inorganic bromides calculated as Br.
Methyl parathion (and/or parathion)	1 p.p.m.
Naled and its conversion product 2,2-dichlorovinyl dimethyl phosphate	0.5 p.p.m. expressed as naled.
Nicotine-containing compounds	2 p.p.m. of nicotine.
Paraquat	0.05 p.p.m. (negligible residue) derived from application of either the bis(methyl sulfate) or dichloride salt, both calculated as the cation.
Parathion (and/or methyl parathion)	1 p.p.m.
o-phenylphenol and sodium o-phenylphenate (post-harvest application)	10 p.p.m. expressed as o-phenylphenol on each.
Phosphamidon and all of its related cholinesterase-inhibiting compounds	0.5 p.p.m. expressed as phosphamidon.

TABLE 6-1. (cont.)

TDE	7 p.p.m.
Toxaphene	7 p.p.m.
Zineb	7 p.p.m.
Ziram	7 p.p.m.
POTATOES	
Aldrin and its epoxidation product dieldrin	0.1 p.p.m. (total residues resulting from application of aldrin).
3-(p-bromophenyl)-1-methoxy-1-methylurea	0.2 p.p.m.
Captan (pre-harvest and/or post-harvest uses)	25 p.p.m.[1]
Chlordane	0.3 p.p.m.
2-chloroallyl diethyldithiocarbamate	0.2 p.p.m. (negligible residue).
Chlorosulfamic acid (post-harvest application)	8 p.p.m. of sulfamate ion expressed as sulfamic acid.
CIPC (post-harvest application)	50 p.p.m.
Dalapon sodium salt	10 p.p.m. as 2,2-dichloropropionic acid.
Demeton	0.75 p.p.m.
2,4-dichloro-6-O-Chloroanilino-s-triazine	1 p.p.m.
2,6-dichloro-4-nitroaniline	0.25 p.p.m.
DDT	1 p.p.m. after washing off soil present when marketed.
Dieldrin	0.1 p.p.m.
O,O-diethyl S-[2-(ethylthio)ethyl] phosphorodithioate and its cholinesterase-inhibiting metabolites	0.75 p.p.m. calculated as demeton.
O,O-diethyl O-(2-isopropyl-4-methyl-6-pyrimidinyl) phosphorothioate	0.1 p.p.m.
Dimethoate and its oxygen analog	0.2 p.p.m.
Dimethyl 2,3,5,6-tetrachloroterephthalate and its metabolites	2 p.p.m. calculated as dimethyl 2,3,5,6-tetrachloroterephthalate
Diphenamid and its desmethyl metabolite	1 p.p.m.
Diuron	1 p.p.m.
Endrin	Zero.
2-ethylamino-4-isopropylamino-6-methylthio-s-triazine	0.25 p.p.m. (negligible residue).
Ethylene dibromide (soil treatment)	75 p.p.m. of inorganic bromides calculated as Br.
O-ethyl S-phenyl ethylphosphonodithioate and its oxygen analog	0.1 p.p.m. (negligible residue).
Heptachlor (and its epoxide)	Zero.
Linuron	1 p.p.m.
Malathion	8 p.p.m.
Maleic hydrazide	50 p.p.m.
Maneb	0.1 p.p.m.
1-methoxycarbonyl-1-propen-2-yl dimethylphosphate and its beta isomer	0.25 p.p.m.
Methoxychlor	1 p.p.m.
Methyl bromide (post-harvest fumigation)	75 p.p.m. of inorganic bromides calculated as Br.
Paraquat	0.5 p.p.m. derived from application of either the bis(methyl sulfate) or dichloride salt, both calculated as the cation.
Phorate and its cholinesterase-inhibiting metabolites	0.5 p.p.m.

TABLE 6-1. (cont.)

Sesone	6 p.p.m.
2,4,5,6-tetrachloroisophthalonitrile and its metabolite	0.1 p.p.m. (negligible residue).
2,3,5,6-tetrachloronitrobenzene (post-harvest application	25 p.p.m.
Triphenyltin hydroxide	0.05 p.p.m. (negligible residue).
PUMPKINS	
Aldrin and its epoxidation product dieldrin	0.1 p.p.m. (total residues resulting from application of aldrin).
Amiben	0.1 p.p.m. (negligible residue).
Benzene hexachloride	5 p.p.m.
1,1-bis (p-chlorophenyl)-2,2,2-trichloroethanol)	5 p.p.m.
Calcium arsenate	3.5 p.p.m. of combined As_2O_3.
Captan (pre-harvest and/or post-harvest uses)	25 p.p.m.
Carbaryl	10 p.p.m.
2,4-dichloro-6-o-chloroanilino-s-triazine	10 p.p.m.
DDT	7 p.p.m.
S-(O,O-diisopropyl phosphorodithioate) of N-(2-mercaptoethyl) benzenesulfonamide and its oxygen analog	0.1 p.p.m. (negligible residue).
O,O-dimethyl 2,2,2-trichloro-1 hydroxyethyl phosphonate	0.1 p.p.m. (negligible residue).
Endosulfan and its metabolite	2 p.p.m.
Ferbam	7 p.p.m.
Fluorine compounds	7 p.p.m. of combined fluorine.
Folpet	15 p.p.m.
Lindane	10 p.p.m.
Malathion	8 p.p.m.
Maneb	7 p.p.m.
Methoxychlor	14 p.p.m.
Methyl bromide (post-harvest fumigation)	20 p.p.m. of inorganic bromides calculated as Br.
Methyl parathion (and/or parathion)	1 p.p.m.
Naled and its conversion product 2,2-dichlorovinyl dimethyl phosphate	0.5 p.p.m. expressed as naled.
Nicotine-containing compounds	2 p.p.m. of nicotine.
Parathion (and/or methyl parathion)	1 p.p.m.
TDE	7 p.p.m.
Tetradifon	1 p.p.m.
Zineb	7 p.p.m.
Ziram	7 p.p.m.
RADISHES (with or without tops) OR RADISH TOPS	
Chlordane	0.3 p.p.m.
Dieldrin	0.1 p.p.m.
O,O-diethyl O-(2-isopropyl-4-methyl-6-pyrimidinyl) phosphorothioate	0.75 p.p.m.
Ferbam	7 p.p.m.
Fluorine compounds	7 p.p.m. of combined fluorine.
Methoxychlor	14 p.p.m.
Methyl parathion (and/or parathion)	1 p.p.m.

TABLE 6-1. (cont.)

Nicotine-containing compounds	2 p.p.m. of nicotine.
Parathion (and/or methyl parathion)	1 p.p.m.
Toxaphene	7 p.p.m.
Zineb	7 p.p.m.
Ziram	7 p.p.m.
RADISH TOPS	
DDT	7 p.p.m.
RADISHES	
Aldrin and its epoxidation product dieldrin	Zero (total residues resulting from application of aldrin).
Carbaryl	5 p.p.m.
Chlorosulfamic acid (post-harvest application)	8 p.p.m. of sulfamate ion expressed as sulfamic acid.
DDT	1 p.p.m.
1,2-dibromo-3-chloropropane	75 p.p.m. of inorganic bromides calculated as Br.
Heptachlor (and its epoxide)	Zero.
Malathion	8 p.p.m.
Methyl bromide (post-harvest fumigation)	30 p.p.m. of inorganic bromides calculated as Br.
SPINACH	
Aldrin and its epoxidation product dieldrin	Zero (total residues resulting from application of aldrin).
Benzene hexachloride	5 p.p.m.
Calcium arsenate	3.5 p.p.m. of combined As_2O_3.
Captan (pre-harvest and/or post-harvest uses)	100 p.p.m.
Carbaryl	12 p.p.m.
Carbophenothion	0.8 p.p.m.
2-chloroallyl diethyldithiocarbamate	0.2 p.p.m. (negligible residue).
DDT	7 p.p.m.
1,1-dichloro-2,2-bis (p-ethylphenyl) ethane	15 p.p.m.
Dieldrin	Zero.
O,O-diethyl S-[2-(ethylthio)ethyl] phosphorodithioate and its cholinesterase-inhibiting metabolites	0.75 p.p.m. calculated as demeton.
O,O-diethyl O-(2-isopropyl-4-methyl-6-pyrimidinyl) phosphorothioate	0.75 p.p.m.
Dimethoate and its oxygen analog	2 p.p.m.
O,O-dimethyl S-[4-oxo-1,2,3-benzotriazin-3(4H)-ylmethyl] phosphorodithioate	2 p.p.m.
Endosulfan and its metabolite	2 p.p.m.
EPN	3 p.p.m.
S-ethyl cyclohexylethylthiocarbamate	0.05 p.p.m. (negligible residue).
Ferbam	7 p.p.m.
Lindane	10 p.p.m.
Malathion	8 p.p.m.
Maneb	10 p.p.m.
1-methoxycarbonyl-1-propen-2-yl dimethylphosphate and its beta isomer	1 p.p.m.
Methoxychlor	14 p.p.m.

TABLE 6-1. (cont.)

Methyl parathion (and/or parathion)	1 p.p.m.
Monuron	1 p.p.m.
Naled and its conversion product 2,2-dichlorovinyl dimethyl phosphate	3 p.p.m. expressed as naled.
Nicotine-containing compounds	2 p.p.m. of nicotine.
Norea	0.2 p.p.m. (negligible residue).
Parathion (and/or methyl parathion)	1 p.p.m.
TDE	1 p.p.m.
Toxaphene	7 p.p.m.
Zineb	25 p.p.m.
Ziram	7 p.p.m.
SQUASH	
DDT	7 p.p.m.
Methyl parathion (and/or parathion)	1 p.p.m.
Parathion (and/or methyl parathion)	1 p.p.m.
TDE	7 p.p.m.
SQUASH (summer and winter squash)	
Aldrin and its epoxidation product dieldrin	0.1 p.p.m. (total residues resulting from application of aldrin).
Amiben	0.1 p.p.m. (negligible residue).
Benzene hexachloride	5 p.p.m.
1,1-bis (p-chlorophenyl)-2,2,2-trichloroethanol	5 p.p.m.
Calcium arsenate	3.5 p.p.m. of combined As_2O_3.
Captan (pre-harvest and/or post-harvest uses)	25 p.p.m.
Carbaryl	10 p.p.m.
Chlordane	0.3 p.p.m.
2,4-dichloro-6-o-chloroanilino-s-triazine	10 p.p.m.
0,0-diethyl 0-(2-isopropyl-4-methyl-6-pyrimidinyl) phosphorothioate	0.75 p.p.m.
Dimethyl 2,3,5,6-tetrachloroterephthalate and its metabolites	1 p.p.m. calculated as dimethyl 2,3,5,6-tetrachloroterephthalate.
Endosulfan and its metabolite	2 p.p.m.
Ferbam	7 p.p.m.
Fluorine compounds	7 p.p.m. of combined fluorine.
Folpet	15 p.p.m.
Lindane	10 p.p.m.
Malathion	8 p.p.m.
Maneb	7 p.p.m.
Methoxychlor	14 p.p.m.
Naled and its conversion product 2,2-dichlorovinyl dimethyl phosphate	0.5 p.p.m. expressed as naled.
Nicotine-containing compounds	2 p.p.m. of nicotine.
Zineb	7 p.p.m.
Ziram	7 p.p.m.
SUMMER SQUASH	
Carbophenothion	0.8 p.p.m.
DDT	7 p.p.m.
1,2-dibromo-3-chloropropane	25 p.p.m. of inorganic bromides calculated as Br.

TABLE 6-1. (cont.)

Dieldrin	0.1 p.p.m.
S-(O,O-diispopropyl phosphorodithioate) of N-(2-mercaptoethyl) benzenesulfonamide and its oxygen analog	0.1 p.p.m. (negligible residue).
Endrin	Zero.
Ethion and its oxygen analog	0.5 p.p.m.
Ethylene dibromide (soil treatment)	50 p.p.m. of inorganic bromides calculated as Br.
1-methoxycarbonyl-1-propen-2-yl dimethylphosphate and its beta isomer	0.25 p.p.m.
Methyl bromide (post-harvest fumigation)	30 p.p.m. of inorganic bromides calculated as Br.
Methyl parathion (and/or parathion)	1 p.p.m.
Parathion (and/or methyl parathion)	1 p.p.m.
TDE	7 p.p.m.
Zinc ion and Maneb (coordination product)	7 p.p.m. calculated as zineb on the whole product.
WINTER SQUASH	
Methyl bromide (post-harvest fumigation)	20 p.p.m. of inorganic bromides calculated as Br.
Tetradifon	1 p.p.m.
TOMATOES	
Aldrin and its epoxidation product dieldrin	0.1 p.p.m. (total residues resulting from application of aldrin).
Allethrin (post-harvest use)	4 p.p.m.
Amiben	0.1 p.p.m. (negligible residue).
Ammoniates of [ethylenebis (dithiocarbamato)] zinc (5.2 parts by weight) with ethylenebis [dithiocarbamic acid] bimolecular and trimolecular cyclic anhydrosulfides and disulfides (1 part by weight)	5 p.p.m. calculated as zineb.
Benzene hexachloride	5 p.p.m.
1,1-bis (p-chlorophenyl)-2,2,2-trichloroethanol	5 p.p.m.
2-(p-tert-butylphenoxy)-isopropyl-2-chloroethyl sulfite	Zero.
Calcium arsenate	3.5 p.p.m. of combined As_2O_3.
Captan (pre-harvest and/or post-harvest uses)	25 p.p.m.
Carbaryl	10 p.p.m.
Carbophenothion	0.8 p.p.m.
Chlordane	0.3 p.p.m.
2-chloroallyl diethyldithiocarbamate	0.2 p.p.m. (negligible residue).
cis-N-[(1,1,2,2-tetrachloroethyl)thio]-4-cyclohexene-1,2-dicarboximide	15 p.p.m.
Combinations of chloropicrin, methyl bromide, and propargyl bromide (soil treatment)	40 p.p.m. of inorganic bromides calculated as Br.
Copper arsenate	3.5 p.p.m. of combined As_2O_3.
Demeton	0.75 p.p.m.
1,2-dibromo-3-chloropropane	50 p.p.m. of inorganic bromides calculated as Br.
Dichlone	3 p.p.m.
2,4-dichloro-6-o-chloroanilino-s-triazine	10 p.p.m.

TABLE 6-1. (cont.)

2,6-dichloro-4-nitroaniline	5 p.p.m.
2,2-dichlorovinyl dimethyl phosphate (post-harvest application)	0.5 p.p.m. expressed as naled.
DDT	7 p.p.m.
Dieldrin	0.1 p.p.m.
O,O-diethyl S-[2-(ethylthio)ethyl] phosphorodithioate and its cholinesterase-inhibiting metabolites	0.75 p.p.m. calculated as demeton.
O,O-diethyl O-(2-isopropyl-4-methyl-6-pyrimidinyl) phosphorothioate	0.75 p.p.m.
Dimethoate and its oxygen analog	2 p.p.m.
O,O-dimethyl S-[4-oxo-1,2,3-benzotriazin-3(4H)-ylmethyl] phosphorodithioate (pre-harvest and/or post-harvest uses)	2 p.p.m.
Dimethyl 2,3,5,6-tetrachloroterephthalate and its metabolites	1 p.p.m. calculated as dimethyl 2,3,5,6-tetrachloroterephthalate.
O,O-dimethyl 2,2,2-trichloro-1-hydroxyethyl phosphonate	0.1 p.p.m. (negligible residue).
Endosulfan and its metabolite	2 p.p.m.
Endrin	Zero.
EPN	3 p.p.m.
Ethion and its oxygen analog	2 p.p.m.
Ethylene dibromide (soil treatment)	50 p.p.m. of inorganic bromides calculated as Br.
Ferbam	7 p.p.m.
Fluorine compounds	7 p.p.m. of combined fluorine.
Folpet	25 p.p.m.
Heptachlor (and its epoxide)	Zero.
Lead arsenate	7 p.p.m. of combined lead.
Lindane	10 p.p.m.
Malathion	8 p.p.m.
Maneb	7 p.p.m.
1-methoxycarbonyl-1-propen-2-yl dimethylphosphate and its beta isomer	0.25 p.p.m.
Methoxychlor	14 p.p.m.
Methyl bromide (post-harvest fumigation)	20 p.p.m. of inorganic bromides calculated as Br.
Methyl parathion (and/or parathion)	1 p.p.m.
Naled and its conversion product 2,2-dichlorovinyl dimethyl phosphate	0.5 p.p.m. expressed as naled.
Nicotine-containing compounds	2 p.p.m. of nicotine.
Paraquat	0.05 p.p.m. (negligible residue) derived from application of either the bis(methyl sulfate) or dichloride salt, both calculated as the cation.
Parathion (and/or methyl parathion)	1 p.p.m.
o-phenylphenol and sodium o-phenylphenate (post-harvest application)	10 p.p.m. expressed as o-phenylphenol on each.
Piperonyl butoxide (post-harvest use)	8 p.p.m.
S-propyl butylethylthiocarbamate	0.1 p.p.m. (negligible residue).
Pyrethrins (post-harvest use)	1 p.p.m.
TDE	7 p.p.m.

TABLE 6-1. (cont.)

Tetradifon	1 p.p.m.
Thiram	7 p.p.m.
Toxaphene	7 p.p.m.
Zinc ion and Maneb (coordination product)	7 p.p.m. calculated as zineb on the whole product.
Zineb	7 p.p.m.
Ziram	7 p.p.m.
III GRAIN CROPS	
GRAIN CROPS	
S-ethyl dipropylthiocarbamate	0.1 p.p.m. (negligible residue).
BARLEY	
Allethrin (post-harvest use)	2 p.p.m.
Barban	0.1 p.p.m. (negligible residue).
Carbaryl	Zero.
Ethylene dibromide (post-harvest fumigation)	50 p.p.m. of inorganic bromides calculated as Br.
Heptachlor (and its epoxide)	Zero.
Hydrogen cyanide (post-harvest fumigation)	100 p.p.m.
Methoxychlor (storage bin treatment)	2 p.p.m.
Methyl bromide (post-harvest fumigation)	50 p.p.m. of inorganic bromides calculated as Br.
Methyl parathion (and/or parathion)	1 p.p.m.
Parathion (and/or methyl parathion)	1 p.p.m.
Phosphine, from fumigation with aluminum phosphide	0.1 p.p.m.
Piperonyl butoxide (post-harvest application)	20 p.p.m.
Pyrethrins (post-harvest application)	3 p.p.m.
Toxaphene	5 p.p.m.
BARLEY GRAIN, OAT GRAIN	
O,O-diethyl S-[2-(ethylthio)ethyl] phosphorodithioate and its cholinesterase-inhibiting metabolites	0.75 p.p.m. calculated as demeton.
BARLEY GRAIN, OAT GRAIN, WHEAT GRAIN	
Demeton	0.75 p.p.m.
Dicamba and its metabolite	0.5 p.p.m.
O,O-dimethyl 2,2,2-trichloro-1-hydroxyethyl phosphonate	0.1 p.p.m. (negligible residue).
BARLEY GRAIN, OAT GRAIN, RYE GRAIN, WHEAT GRAIN	
Aldrin and its epoxidation product dieldrin	0.02 p.p.m.[1] (total residues resulting from application of aldrin).
Calcium cyanide (post-harvest use)	25 p.p.m. calculated as hydrogen cyanide.
2,4-D	0.5 p.p.m. from application of 2,4-D in acid form, or in the form of one or more of its inorganic salts, amine salts, or esters.
Dieldrin	0.02 p.p.m.[1]
O,O-dimethyl S-[4-oxo-1,2,3-benzotriazin-3(4H)-ylmethyl] phosphorodithioate	0.2 p.p.m.
Diuron	1 p.p.m.

TABLE 6-1. (cont.)

Linuron	0.25 p.p.m.
Malathion (accumulative pre- and post-harvest applications)	8 p.p.m.
Zinc ion and Maneb (coordination product)	5 p.p.m. calculated as zineb on the whole product.
BUCKWHEAT	
Calcium cyanide (post-harvest use)	25 p.p.m. calculated as hydrogen cyanide.
Hydrogen cyanide (post-harvest fumigation)	100 p.p.m.
Piperonyl butoxide (post-harvest application)	20 p.p.m.
Pyrethrins (post-harvest application)	3 p.p.m.
CORN	
Phosphine, from fumigation with aluminum phosphide	0.1 p.p.m.
CORN IN GRAIN OR EAR FORM (including field corn, sweet corn and popcorn)	
O-ethyl S,S-dipropylphosphorodithioate	0.02 p.p.m. (negligible residue).
Linuron	0.25 p.p.m.
CORN GRAIN (includes popcorn)	
Aldrin and its epoxidation product dieldrin	Zero (total residues resulting from application of aldrin).
Atrazine	0.25 p.p.m.
2,4-bis(isopropylamino)-6-methylthio-s-triazine	0.25 p.p.m.
Dieldrin	Zero.
Dimethyl 2,3,5,6-tetrachloroterephthalate and its metabolites	0.05 p.p.m. calculated as dimethyl 2,3,5,6-tetrachloroterephthalate (negligible residue).
Diuron	1 p.p.m.
Ethylene dibromide (post-harvest fumigation)	50 p.p.m. of inorganic bromides calculated as Br.
S-ethyl diisobutylthiocarbamate	0.1 p.p.m. (negligible residue).
O-ethyl S-phenyl ethylphosphonodithioate and its oxygen analog	0.1 p.p.m. (negligible residue).
Hydrogen cyanide (post-harvest fumigation)	100 p.p.m.
Methomyl	0.1 p.p.m. (negligible residue).
1-methoxycarbonyl-1-propen-2-yl dimethylphosphate and its beta isomer	0.25 p.p.m.
Mineral oil (post-harvest application)	200 p.p.m.
Piperonyl butoxide (post-harvest use)	20 p.p.m.
Pyrethrins (post-harvest application)	3 p.p.m.
Simazine	0.25 p.p.m.
Zinc ion and Maneb (coordination product)	0.5 p.p.m. calculated as zineb on the whole product.
CORN GRAIN	
Allethrin (post-harvest use)	2 p.p.m.
Calcium cyanide (post-harvest use)	25 p.p.m. calculated as hydrogen cyanide.
Carbofuran and its metabolite	0.1 p.p.m.
2-chloroallyl diethyldithiocarbamate	0.2 p.p.m. (negligible residue).
2-chloro-2′,6′-diethyl-N-(methoxymethyl) acetanilide and its metabolites	0.2 p.p.m. calculated as 2-chloro-2′,6′-diethyl-N-(methoxymethyl) acetanilide (negligible residue).

TABLE 6-1. (cont.)

2-chloro-N-isopropylacetanilide and its metabolites	0.1 p.p.m. calculated as 2-chloro-N-isopropylacetanilide (negligible residue).
Dalapon sodium salt	10 p.p.m. as 2,2-dichloropropionic acid.
Dicamba and its metabolite	0.5 p.p.m.
Heptachlor (and its epoxide)	Zero.
Malathion (post-harvest application)	8 p.p.m.
Methoxychlor (storage bin treatment)	2 p.p.m.
Methyl bromide (post-harvest fumigation)	50 p.p.m. of inorganic bromides calculated as Br.
Mixture of 75% m-(1-methylbutyl)phenyl methylcarbamate and 25% m-(1-ethylpropyl)phenyl methylcarbamate	0.05 p.p.m. (negligible residues of both components).
Paraquat	0.05 p.p.m. (negligible residue) derived from application of either the bis(methyl sulfate) or dichloride salt, both calculated as the cation.
Phorate and its cholinesterase-inhibiting metabolites	0.1 p.p.m.
CORN GRAIN, INCLUDING FIELD CORN AND SWEET CORN (kernels plus cob with husk removed)	
O,O-diethyl S-[2-(ethylthio)ethyl] phosphorodithioate and its cholinesterase-inhibiting metabolites	0.3 p.p.m. calculated as demeton.
Trichlorobenzyl chloride and its metabolite	0.02 p.p.m. (negligible residue).
POPCORN GRAIN	
O,O-diethyl S-[2-(ethylthio)ethyl] phosphorodithioate and its cholinesterase-inhibiting metabolites	0.3 p.p.m. calculated as demeton.
Methyl bromide (post-harvest fumigation)	240 p.p.m. of inorganic bromides calculated as Br.
Trichlorobenzyl chloride and its metabolite	0.02 p.p.m. (negligible residue).
FIELD CORN GRAIN	
Amiben	0.1 p.p.m. (negligible residue).
O,O-diethyl O-[p-(methylsulfinyl)phenyl] phosphorothioate and its cholinesterase-inhibiting metabolites	0.1 p.p.m.
Dimethyl 2,3,5,6-tetrachloroterephthalate and its metabolites	0.05 p.p.m. calculated as dimethyl 2,3,5,6-tetrachloroterephtalate (negligible residue).
1-methoxycarbonyl-1-propen-2-yl dimethylphosphate and its beta isomer	0.25 p.p.m.
MILLET	
Phosphine, from fumigation with aluminum phosphide	0.1 p.p.m.
OATS	
Allethrin (post-harvest use)	2 p.p.m.
Carbaryl	Zero.
Ethylene dibromide (post-harvest fumigation)	50 p.p.m. of inorganic bromides calculated as Br.
Heptachlor (and its epoxide)	Zero.
Hydrogen cyanide (post-harvest fumigation)	100 p.p.m.
Methoxychlor (storage bin treatment)	2 p.p.m.
Methyl bromide (post-harvest fumigation)	50 p.p.m. of inorganic bromides calculated as Br.

TABLE 6-1. (cont.)

Methyl parathion (and/or parathion)	1 p.p.m.
Parathion (and/or methyl parathion)	1 p.p.m.
Phosphine, from fumigation with aluminum phosphide	0.1 p.p.m.
Piperonyl butoxide (post-harvest use)	8 p.p.m.
Pyrethrins (post-harvest use)	1 p.p.m.
Toxaphene	5 p.p.m.
RICE	
Carbaryl	5 p.p.m.
Carbofuran and its metabolite	0.2 p.p.m.
O,O-diethyl S-[2-(ethylthio)ethyl] phosphorodithioate and its cholinesterase-inhibiting metabolites	0.75 p.p.m. calculated as demeton.
Ethylene dibromide (post-harvest fumigation)	50 p.p.m. of inorganic bromides calculated as Br.
S-ethyl hexahydro-1H-azepine-1-carbothioate	0.1 p.p.m. (negligible residue).
Hydrogen cyanide (post-harvest fumigation)	100 p.p.m.
Methoxychlor (storage bin treatment)	2 p.p.m.
Methyl bromide (post-harvest fumigation)	50 p.p.m. of inorganic bromides calculated as Br.
Methyl parathion (and/or parathion)	1 p.p.m.
Naled and its conversion product 2,2-dichlorovinyl dimethyl phosphate	0.5 p.p.m. expressed as naled.
Parathion (and/or methyl parathion)	1 p.p.m.
Phorate and its cholinesterase-inhibiting metabolites	0.1 p.p.m.
Phosphine, from fumigation with aluminum phosphide	0.1 p.p.m.
Piperonyl butoxide (post-harvest application)	20 p.p.m.
Pyrethrins (post-harvest application)	3 p.p.m.
Toxaphene	5 p.p.m.
RICE GRAIN	
Aldrin and its epoxidation product dieldrin	0.05 p.p.m.[1] (total residues resulting from application of aldrin).
Calcium cyanide (post-harvest use)	25 p.p.m. calculated as hydrogen cyanide.
Malathion (accumulative pre- and post-harvest applications)	8 p.p.m.
RYE	
Allethrin (post-harvest use)	2 p.p.m.
Carbaryl	Zero.
Ethylene dibromide (post-harvest fumigation)	50 p.p.m. of inorganic bromides calculated as Br.
Heptachlor (and its epoxide)	Zero.
Hydrogen cyanide (post-harvest fumigation)	100 p.p.m.
Methoxychlor (storage bin treatment)	2 p.p.m.
Methyl bromide (post-harvest fumigation)	50 p.p.m. of inorganic bromides calculated as Br.
Phosphine, from fumigation with aluminum phosphide	0.1 p.p.m.
Piperonyl butoxide (post-harvest application)	20 p.p.m.
Pyrethrins (post-harvest application)	3 p.p.m.
Toxaphene	5 p.p.m.

TABLE 6-1. (cont.)

WHEAT	
Allethrin (post-harvest use)	2 p.p.m.
Barban	0.1 p.p.m. (negligible residue).
Calcium cyanide (post-harvest use)	25 p.p.m.
Carbaryl	Zero.
Ethylene dibromide (post-harvest fumigation)	50 p.p.m. of inorganic bromides calculated as Br.
Heptachlor (and its epoxide)	Zero.
Hydrogen cyanide (post-harvest fumigation)	100 p.p.m.
Methoxychlor (storage bin treatment)	2 p.p.m.
Methyl bromide (post-harvest fumigation)	50 p.p.m. of inorganic bromides calculated as Br.
Methyl parathion (and/or parathion)	1 p.p.m.
Parathion (and/or methyl parathion)	1 p.p.m.
Phosphine, from fumigation with aluminum phosphide	0.1 p.p.m.
Piperonyl butoxide (post-harvest application)	20 p.p.m.
Pyrethrins (post-harvest application)	3 p.p.m.
Toxaphene	5 p.p.m.
Zineb	1 p.p.m.
WHEAT GRAIN	
Atrazine	0.25 p.p.m.
2-tert-butylamino-4-ethylamino-6-methylthio-s-triazine	0.1 p.p.m. (negligible residue).
0,0-diethyl S-[2-(ethylthio)ethyl] phosphorodithioate and its cholinesterase-inhibiting metabolites	0.3 p.p.m. calculated as demeton.
SORGHUM	
Phosphine, from fumigation with aluminum phosphide	0.1 p.p.m.
SORGHUM GRAIN	
Atrazine	0.25 p.p.m.
Calcium cyanide (post-harvest use)	25 p.p.m. calculated as hydrogen cyanide.
Carbaryl	10 p.p.m.
Carbophenothion	2 p.p.m.
2-chloro-N-isopropylacetanilide and its metabolites	0.25 p.p.m. calculated as 2-chloro-N-isopropylacetanilide.
2-chloro-4,6-bis(isopropylamino)-s-triazine	0.25 p.p.m. (negligible residue).
Demeton	0.2 p.p.m.
Dicamba and its metabolite	0.3 p.p.m.
0,0-diethyl S-[2-(ethylthio)ethyl] phosphorodithioate and its cholinesterase-inhibiting metabolites	0.75 p.p.m. calculated as demeton.
0,0-diethyl 0-(2-isopropyl-4-methyl-6-pyrimidinyl) phosphorodithioate	0.75 p.p.m.
Diuron	1 p.p.m.
Ethion and its oxygen analog	2 p.p.m.
Malathion (accumulative pre- and post-harvest applications)	8 p.p.m.
1-methoxycarbonyl-1-propen-2-yl dimethylphosphate and its beta isomer	1 p.p.m.
Methoxychlor (storage bin treatment)	2 p.p.m.
Norea	0.2 p.p.m. (negligible residue).

TABLE 6-1. (cont.)

Paraquat	0.05 p.p.m. (negligible residue) derived from application of either the bis(methyl sulfate) or dichloride salt, both calculated as the cation.
Toxaphene	5 p.p.m.
SORGHUM GRAIN (Milo)	
Linuron	0.25 p.p.m.
GRAIN SORGHUM (Milo)	
Allethrin (post-harvest use)	2 p.p.m.
Ethylene dibromide (post-harvest fumigation)	50 p.p.m. of inorganic bromides calculated as Br.
Heptachlor (and its epoxide)	Zero.
Hydrogen cyanide (post-harvest fumigation)	100 p.p.m.
Methyl bromide (post-harvest fumigation)	50 p.p.m. of inorganic bromides calculated as Br.
IV EGGS, MEAT, MILK AND POULTRY	
EGGS	
Atrazine	0.02 p.p.m. (negligible residue).
Carbaryl	Zero.
2-chloro-2′,6′-diethyl-N-(methoxymethyl) acetanilide and its metabolites	0.02 p.p.m. calculated as 2-chloro-2′,6′-diethyl-N-(methoxymethyl) acetanilide (negligible residue).
2-chloro-N-isopropylacetanilide and its metabolites	0.02 p.p.m. calculated as 2-chloro-N-isopropylacetanilide (negligible residue).
Coumaphos and its oxygen analog	0.1 p.p.m.
Dodecachlorooctahydro-1,3,4-metheno-2H-cyclobuta[cd]pentalene	0.1 p.p.m. (negligible residue).
Malathion (application to poultry)	0.1 p.p.m.
Simazine	0.02 p.p.m. (negligible residue).
FAT OF MEAT FROM CATTLE, GOATS, HOGS, HORSES, POULTRY AND SHEEP	
Dodecachlorooctahydro-1,3,4-metheno-2H-cyclobuta[cd]pentalene	0.1 p.p.m. (negligible residue).
FAT OF MEAT FROM CATTLE, GOATS, HOGS, HORSES AND SHEEP	
DDT	7 p.p.m.
Dioxathion	1 p.p.m.
Methoxychlor	3 p.p.m.
Toxaphene	7 p.p.m.
FAT OF MEAT FROM CATTLE, GOATS, HORSES, AND SHEEP	
Lindane	7 p.p.m.
FAT OF MEAT OF CATTLE, GOATS, HOGS AND SHEEP	
Carbophenothion	0.1 p.p.m.
FAT OF MEAT FROM HOGS	
Lindane	4 p.p.m.

TABLE 6-1. (cont.)

FAT OF CATTLE	
Ethion and its oxygen analog	2.5 p.p.m.
KIDNEY AND LIVER	
Zinc ion and Maneb (coordination product)	0.5 p.p.m. calculated as zineb on the whole product.
MEAT AND FAT OF MEAT OF CATTLE, GOATS, HOGS AND SHEEP	
N-(mercaptomethyl)phthalimide S-(O,O-dimethyl phosphorodithioate) and its oxygen analog	0.2 p.p.m.
MEAT, FAT, AND MEAT BYPRODUCTS OF CATTLE, GOATS, HOGS, HORSES, POULTRY, AND SHEEP	
Atrazine	0.02 p.p.m. (negligible residue).
2-chloro-2′,6′-diethyl-N-(methoxymethyl) acetanilide and its metabolites	0.02 p.p.m. calculated as 2-chloro-2′,6′-diethyl-N-(methoxymethyl) acetanilide (negligible residue).
2-chloro-N-isopropylacetanilide and its metabolites	0.02 p.p.m. calculated as 2-chloro-N-isopropylacetanilide (negligible residue).
Coumaphos and its oxygen analog	1 p.p.m.
Malathion	4 p.p.m. (which level shall not be exceeded in any cut of such meats or any meat byproduct).
Simazine	0.02 p.p.m. (negligible residue).
MEAT, FAT, AND MEAT BYPRODUCTS OF CATTLE, GOATS, HOGS, HORSES AND SHEEP	
Chloroneb and its metabolite	0.2 p.p.m. calculated as chloroneb.
Diuron	1 p.p.m.
Endosulfan and its metabolite	0.2 p.p.m.
Linuron	1 p.p.m.
Phorate and its cholinesterase-inhibiting metabolites	0.05 p.p.m. (negligible residue).
Pyrethrins	0.1 p.p.m. (negligible residue).
MEAT, FAT, AND MEAT BYPRODUCTS OF CATTLE, GOATS AND SHEEP	
O,O-dimethyl S-[4-oxo-1,2,3-benzotriazin-3(4H)-ylmethyl] phosphorodithioate	0.1 p.p.m.
S,S,S,-tributyl phosphorotrithioate	0.02 p.p.m. (negligible residue).
MEAT, FAT AND MEAT BYPRODUCTS OF CATTLE AND POULTRY	
Fenthion and its cholinesterase-inhibiting metabolites	0.1 p.p.m.
MEAT, FAT AND MEAT BYPRODUCTS OF CATTLE AND SHEEP	
O,O-diethyl O-(2-isopropyl-4-methyl-6-pyrimidinyl) phosphorothioate	0.75 p.p.m.
Ethyl 4,4′-dichlorobenzilate	0.5 p.p.m.
MEAT, FAT AND MEAT BYPRODUCTS OF CATTLE	
Dimethoate and its oxygen analog	0.02 p.p.m. (negligible residue).
O,O-dimethyl O-p-(dimethylsulfamoyl)phenyl phosphorothioate and its oxygen analog	0.1 p.p.m.
O,O-dimethyl 2,2,2-trichloro-1-hydroxyethyl phosphonate (from topical application to cattle)	0.1 p.p.m. (negligible residue).

TABLE 6-1. (cont.)

MEAT AND MEAT BYPRODUCTS OF CATTLE	
Ethion and its oxygen analog	0.75 p.p.m.
MEAT (uncooked) OR MEAT BYPRODUCTS FROM CATTLE	
Ronnel	Zero.
MEAT AND FAT OF POULTRY	
Carbaryl	5 p.p.m.
MEAT	
Tetradifon	Zero.
MEAT AND MILK	
Dalapon sodium salt	Zero as 2,2-dichloropropionic acid.
1,1-dichloro-2,2-bis (p-ethylphenyl) ethane	Zero.
Diphenylamine	Zero.
Dodine	Zero.
Heptachlor (and its epoxide)	Zero.
MILK	
Atrazine	0.02 p.p.m. (negligible residue).
Carbophenothion	Zero.
2-chloro-2′,6′-diethyl-N-(methoxymethyl) acetanilide and its metabolites	0.02 p.p.m. calculated as 2-chloro-2′,6′-diethyl-N-(methoxymethyl) acetanilide (negligible residue).
2-chloro-N-isopropylacetanilide and its metabolites	0.02 p.p.m. calculated as 2-chloro-N-isopropylacetanilide (negligible residue).
Chloroneb and its metabolite	0.05 p.p.m. calculated as chloroneb (negligible residue).
DDT, DDD and DDE (for each or any combination of the same)	0.05 p.p.m. (These tolerances are not established to provide for residues from the purposeful use of DDT, DDD, or DDE on dairy cattle, in dairy barns, or on the crops intended to be used for feeding dairy cattle.)
Dicamba and its metabolite	0.05 p.p.m. (negligible residue).
Dimethoate and its oxygen analog	0.002 p.p.m. (negligible residue).
O,O-dimethyl S-[4-oxo-1,2,3-benzotriazin-3(4H)-ylmethyl] phosphorodithioate	Zero.
O,O-dimethyl 2,2,2-trichloro-1-hydroxyethyl phosphonate (from topical application to cattle)	0.01 p.p.m. (negligible residue).
Dioxathion	Zero.
Ethion and its oxygen analog	Zero.
Fenthion and its cholinesterase-inhibiting metabolites	0.1 p.p.m. (negligible residue).
Methoxychlor	Zero.
Phorate and its cholinesterase-inhibiting metabolites	0.02 p.p.m. (negligible residue).
Simazine	0.02 p.p.m. (negligible residue).
Tetradifon	Zero.
S,S,S,-tributyl phosphorotrithioate	0.002 p.p.m. (negligible residue).
MILK-FAT	
Coumaphos and its oxygen analog	0.5 p.p.m. (reflecting negligible residues in milk).

TABLE 6-1. (cont.)

Dodecachlorooctahydro-1,3,4-metheno-2H-cyclobuta[cd]pentalene	0.1 p.p.m. (reflecting negligible residues in milk).
Endosulfan and its metabolite	0.5 p.p.m. (reflecting negligible residues in milk).
Malathion (application to dairy cows)	0.5 p.p.m. (reflecting negligible residues in milk).
Pyrethrins	0.5 p.p.m. (reflecting negligible residues in milk).

[1]These tolerances are established on an interim basis pending reevaluation of new toxicity and related data by FDA.

Pesticide Chemicals for Which Tolerances on Raw Agricultural Commodities Are Not Required Under the Pesticide Amendment:

A. Pesticide Chemicals Found by FDA to be Generally Recognized as Safe

The following pesticide chemicals have been declared generally recognized as safe and require no formal tolerances or exemptions for pesticidal use: benzaldehyde (as a bee repellant), ferrous sulfate, lime, limesulfur, potassium polysulfide, sodium carbonate, sodium chloride, sodium polysulfide, and sulfur, and as postharvest fungicides, citric acid, fumaric acid, oil of lemon, oil of orange, sodium benzoate, and sodium propionate.

B. Pesticide Chemicals Exempted by FDA from the Tolerance Requirement

1. *Active Ingredients Applied to Growing Crops*
   a) The following copper compounds:
      Bordeaux mixture
      copper abietate
      copper acetate
      basic copper carbonate (malachite)
      copper hydroxide
      copper-lime mixtures
      copper linoleate
      copper oleate
      copper oxychloride
      copper silicate
      copper sulfate basic
      copper sulfate monohydrate
      copper sulfate pentahydrate
      copper-zinc chromate
      cupric oxide
      cuprous oxide
      tetra copper calcium oxychloride

b) Allethrin (allyl homolog of cinerin I) on apples, beans, broccoli, brussels sprouts, cabbage, cauliflower, citrus, collards, horseradish, kale, kohlrabi, lettuce, mushrooms, mustard greens, peaches, pears, peppers, radishes, rutabagas, tomatoes, turnips.
c) *N*-Octylbicyclo-(2,2,1)-5-heptene-2,3-dicarboximide
d) Petroleum oils
e) Piperonyl butoxide
f) Piperonyl cyclonene
g) *N*-Proply isome
h) Pyrethrum and pyrethrins
i) Rotenone or derris or cubé roots
j) Ryania
k) Sabadilla
l) *Bacillus thuringiensis* Berliner (as specified in paragraph (a) of the official tolerance order), in or on alfalfa, apples, artichokes, bananas, beans, broccoli, cabbage, cauliflower, celery, collards, cottonseed, cucumbers, eggplants, grapes, kale, lettuce, melons, mustard greens, oranges, potatoes, spinach, strawberries, sweet corn, tomatoes, turnip greens.
m) Sodium propionate (exempt when used as a fungicide in the production of garlic.)
n) Ethylene (exempt when used before harvest as a plant regulator on fruit and vegetable crops.)
o) Ammonium nitrate formulated with ammonium chloride or ammonium thiosulfate as a desiccant or defoliant in the production of cottonseed, grain sorghum, peppers, potatoes, sweetpotatoes.

2. *Active Ingredients Applied After Harvest.*
a) Carbon disulfide (exempt when used as post-harvest fumigant on barley, corn, oats, popcorn, rice, rye, sorghum (milo), wheat.)
b) Ammonia (exempt for post-harvest use on grapefruit, lemons, oranges.)
c) Carbon tetrachloride (exempt when used as post-harvest fumigant on barley, corn, oats, popcorn, rice, rye, sorghum (milo), wheat.)
d) Ethylene dichloride (exempt when used as post-harvest fumigant on barley, corn, oats, popcorn, rice, rye, sorghum (milo), wheat.)
e) Ethylene dibromide (organic bromide residues exempt when used as a fumigant on barley, corn, oats, popcorn, rice, rye, sorghum (milo), wheat.)

A tolerance of 50 p.p.m. of inorganic bromide residues (calculated as Br.) from ethylene dibromide when used as a grain fumigant has been set on the same crops.
f) Chloropicrin (exempt when used as a fumigant for the following grains: barley, buckwheat, corn, oats, rice, rye, grain sorghum, wheat.)
g) Chloroform (exempt when used as post-harvest fumigant on barley, corn, oats, popcorn, rice, rye, sorghum (milo), wheat.)
h) Methylene chloride (exempt when used as a fumigant for the following grains: barley, corn, oats, popcorn, rice, rye, sorghum

(milo), wheat, and when used in the postharvest fumigation of citrus fruits.)

i) 1,1,1 - Trichloroethane (exempt when used in the post-harvest fumigation of citrus fruits.)

j) Sulfur dioxide in liquid grain-fumigant formulations for marker or fire-retardant purposes at levels not exceeding 5 percent by weight of such formulations (exempt when used in the fumigation of barley, buckwheat, corn, oats, popcorn, rice, rye, grain sorghum (milo), wheat.)

k) Pentane (exempt when used as an adjuvant in liquid grain formulations for the fumigation of the following grains: barley, corn, oats, popcorn, rice, rye, sorghum [milo], wheat.)

l) Ethylene (exempt when used after harvest as a plant regulator on fruit and vegetable crops.)

m) Diatomaceous earth (exempt when used against insect pests on the following stored grains: barley, buckwheat, corn, oats, rice, rye, sorghum [milo], wheat; also, beans, peas, and soybeans.)

n) Sodium propionate (exempt when used as preservative on salad greens and vegetables intended for consumption as salads.

Safe and Unsafe Pesticides for Home and Garden

The following thumbnail guide to the use of pesticides around home and garden was prepared by Shirley A. Briggs, and appeared as part of a longer article in the *Atlantic Naturalist,* publication of the Audubon Naturalist Society of the Central Atlantic States, Inc.; Vol. 22, No. 2, April–June 1967. It appears here with permission of the author.

Some Acceptable Pesticides

While these include some potent poisons, they do not persist in food chains or in the environment generally, and they have not been shown dangerous to wildlife except as noted. They are fairly selective in their targets, and will not spread indiscriminately through the environment. Most have been used for a long time, and their effects are generally well-known. Some of these, as with any pesticide, can be irritating to people with allergies. Avoid any large-scale spraying, never spray or dust on windy days. Keep applications as local as possible. (See Table 6-2).

TABLE 6-2.

Bordeaux mixture (copper sulphate-calcium hydroxide) if not fortified with lead or calcium arsenate	Fungicide and insecticide.
Copper-lime mixtures	
Pyrethrum (Allethrin is a synthetic analogue)	Be careful of applications that could lead to human allergic reactions
Rotenone (derris, cube)	Toxic to fish; avoid applications that could drain into ponds or streams.
Ryania	
Sabadilla	Toxic to bees, but not in the usual low dosage.
Sulphur, lime-sulphur	
Nicotine sulphate (use with caution)[1]	Highly toxic, but non-persistent. Has not been shown dangerous to wildlife, but must be handled with great care to avoid human poisoning.
BACTERIAL INSECTICIDES	
"Bacillus thuringiensis" Berliner	Specific for a variety of species of moths and certain other Lepidoptera.
Milky spore disease	Specific for Japanese beetle grubs.
DESICCANTS	
Silica aerogel—in brand names Dri-Die, or with pyrethrum, as Drione.	A desiccant powder, especially for use in the house, as it is non-toxic to humans or pets, though it can be drying if inhaled much. Effective on insects because it penetrates their waxy exoskeleton. This particular kind of silica aerogel absorbs lipids and is thus most effective.
Diatomaceous earth	Also kills insects by contact and desiccation.
RODENTICIDES	
Anti-coagulants, such as Warfarin	Selective for rats and mice if only they have a chance to get repeated doses. Use a locked bait-box which children and pets cannot get into.
Red squill	

[1]Shirley A. Briggs, in letter to authors, March 4, 1971, said she is "still leery" of suggesting nicotine sulphate for home use, even though it does not damage the environment too much.

Some Pesticides to Avoid:

Persistent, Broad-Spectrum Pesticides (Avoid)

These remain in the ecosystem with little change for many years, accumulating in soil and organisms, and tending to concentrate in animals at the end of food chains. They are toxic to a wide range of organisms, and cannot be confined to the target species once they are released in an environment. (Tables 6-3, 6-4)

TABLE 6-3. Chlorinated Hydrocarbons

Aldrin BHC (benzene hexachloride, lindane) Chlordane DDD (TDE) DDT Dieldrin Endrin Heptachlor Toxaphene	Act as nerve poisons, and are stored in the fat of animals; can be released suddenly into other tissues when stress or reduction of food intake depletes fat reserves, thus reaching critical areas like the brain long after initial exposure. They are synthetic compounds, not ever found in nature before their wide use since 1946. Have little-understood metabolic and other physiological effects. Can disrupt soil ecology, and are very persistent. Some give evidence of carcinogenic effects.

Methoxychlor is less toxic than the others to warm-blooded animals, but it has known hormonal effects, with estrogenic capabilities. Carcinogenic effects are considered very low in normal use. Toxic to fish.

TABLE 6-4. General Protoplasmic Poisons

Arsenic, in many forms (used as insecticides, herbicide, rodenticide)	A cumulative poison in animals and soil; can make soil sterile to plants and soil organisms. Carcinogenic.
Mercury, organic and inorganic	Increasingly used as a fungicide, often on golf courses and cemeteries. Has caused a variety of problems with wildlife and food supplies in Sweden, where it has been much used in pesticides.
DINITRO COMPOUNDS	
Dinitrophenol (DNBP, DNOSBP) Dinitrocresol	Cumulative poisons, used as fungicides, insecticides, miticides, or herbicides. Very toxic, can be absorbed through skin.
PENTACHLOROPHENOL	Action similar to the dinitrophenols. Also used as a bactericide. Symptoms of poisoning similar to those of organic phosphate poisoning, but treatment must be different.
RODENTICIDES	
Alpha naphthythiourea (ANTU)	Evidence of carcinogenic effects.
Phosphorus, white or yellow Sodium fluoracetate (1080) Thallium	Extremely toxic; poisons with these active ingredients are not registered for home use, except for phosphorus, which may not be in or on anything resembling human food.

Non-Persistent, Broad-Spectrum Pesticides (Undesirable)

These are new synthetic chemicals, as are chlorinated hydrocarbons. They include highly poisonous compounds, but may have less total effect on the environment than the preceding kinds because they break down into non-toxic materials fairly quickly. Their indiscriminate effects make them undesirable for home or garden use. (Tables 6-5, 6-6)

TABLE 6-5. Organic Phosphates

Chlorthion *Demetron *Diazinin Dimethoate EPN Parathion Phosdrin Schradan TEPP	A group of chemicals originally developed as chemical warfare agents. Toxic chiefly through cholinesterase inhibition, and resultant breakdown in nerve and muscle response. Some may show potentiation: combinations with other chemicals may be many times more toxic than the original components would indicate. Sublethal effects and full impact on the environment not well known, as is also true of the chlorinated hydrocarbons.

Malathion is usually listed as much less toxic to warm-blooded animals than are the other organic phosphates. In home use, acute poisoning is possible from malathion, however, and severe kills of birds and other wildlife have resulted from indiscriminate spraying with it.

TABLE 6-6. Carbamates

Carbaryl Methyl carbamate herbicides	Carbamates are still under study, and while evidence so far does not indicate serious danger in their use, some doubts have not yet been dispelled. They are not cumulative, act through cholinesterase inhibition, and are now considered of medium toxicity to humans. They may be very toxic to bees.
FUNGICIDES	
Captan Folpet	Recent experiments with animals show high incidence of birth deformities following exposure to these, whose chemical structure is similar to that of thalidomide.

Herbicides (Avoid)

Growing suspicions about health hazards from the herbicides formerly thought safest have led to the recent restrictions on 2,4,5-T, and there are doubts about the similar 2,4-D. Any chemicals so physiologically active with one form of protoplasm should have had more study than these received before being released widely into our environment. Other herbicides on the market are suspect as carcinogens, mutagens, or they may interfere with embryological development. Older types, such as arsenic, have the added hazards of persistence. In the home environment, where no pressing reasons exist for chemical controls of this sort except as a convenience, cultural methods to destroy unwanted plants are thus much to be preferred. Competent botanists have used 2,4-D, 2,4,5-T, and Dalapon sodium salts effectively, and relatively safely, in the very selective control of vegetation, applying the chemicals precisely to the vulnerable parts of individual plants. Over-all spraying or distributing of herbicide-containing materials is not recommended by these experts. It is often not much harder to remove such plants by other means.

As usually applied, herbicides can create serious problems with drift, killing plants not intended. Even on calm days, sprays of these materials can be detected surprising distances away, and damage may occur a mile or more from point of application. Danger can also arise from the use of lawn conditioners which contain herbicides such as 2,4-D, and 2,4,5-T in granular form. In hot weather these can volatolize and affect susceptible plants nearby. Your neighbor's lawn treatment may deform your roses, grapes, or tomatoes, especially if he has overdone the dosage.

Federal regulations for farmers have prohibited concentration of 2,4-D at more than two pounds per acre, and the state of Iowa limits this to one pound because of the volatility problem. Homeowners should practice converting the directions for their garden chemicals from the usual "per 1000 square feet" formula to the "pounds per acre" rule applied to farm use. There are no federal regulations governing amounts permissible in home and garden use, so alarmingly high rates are sometimes recommended. Some weed-killers marketed for home use have contained arsenic compounds at a proportion 60 times that permitted on the farm.

Even more problems can arise from use of "weed bars" which are usually 2,4-D and wax. Placing or dragging these bars near such plants as roses, grapes, or petunias can be damaging. Herbicides have been considered less dangerous than more persistent chemicals, since they break down fairly soon in the environment, but once plants have been exposed to them no remedies are known, and you can only hope the harm will not be fatal.

TABLE 6-7. Common and Chemical Names for Pesticide Chemicals

(The Federal Regulations Relating to Each; Proprietary trade marks or trade names for certain of them)

Common name	Chemical name	21 CFR part 120 section No.	Trade name
aldicarb	2-methyl-2-(methylthio)propionaldehyde O-(methylcarbamoyl)oxime	120.269	Temik
aldrin	1,2,3,4,10,10-hexachloro-1,4,4a,5,8,8a-hexahydro-1, 4-endo,exo-5,8-dimethano-naphthalene	120.135	
allethrin	allyl homolog of cinerin I	120.113; 120.1002	
	aluminum phosphide	120.225	Phostoxin
amiben	3-amino-2,5-dichlorobenzoic acid	120.266	Vegiben
	ammonia	120.1003	
	ammoniates of [ethylenebis(dithiocarbamato)] zinc and ethylenebis [dithiocarbamic acid] bimolecular and trimolecular cyclic anhydrosulfides and disulfides	120.217	Polyram
	ammonium nitrate formulated with ammonium chloride or ammonium thiosulfate	120.1018	
	ammonium sulfamate	120.188	Ammate
atrazine	2-chloro-4-ethylamino-6-isopropylamino-s-triazine	120.220	
	Bacillus thuringiensis Berliner	120.1011	Thuricide, Bakthane L-69
barban	4-chloro-2-butynyl m-chlorocarbanilate	120.268	Carbyne
benzadox	benzamidooxyacetic acid	120.270	Topcide
benzene hexachloride (BHC)	1,2,3,4,5,6-hexachlorocyclohexane	120.140	
biphenyl, diphenyl	biphenyl	120.141	
	2,4-bis(isopropylamino)-6-methylthio-s-triazine	120.222	Prometryne
borax	sodium tetraborate decahydrate	120.271	
	boric acid	120.271	
bromacil	5-bromo-3-sec-butyl-6-methyluracil	120.210	Hyvar
	3-(p-bromophenyl)-1-methoxy-1-methylurea	120.250	Metobromuron
	N-butyl-N-ethyl-α,α,α-trifluro-2,6-dinitro-p-toluidine	120.208	Balan
	1,1-bis(p-chlorophenyl)-2,2,2-trichloroethanol	120.163	Kelthane
	2-tert-butylamino-4-ethylamino-6-methylthio-s-triazine	120.265	Igran
	2-(p-tert-butylphenoxy)cyclohexyl 2-propynyl sulfite	120.259	Omite

	2-(p-tert-butylphenoxy)-isopropyl-2-chloroethyl sulfite	120.107	Aramite
	calcium arsenate	120.192	
	calcium cyanide	120.125	
captan	N-trichloromethyl mercapto-4-cyclohexene-1,2-dicarboximide	120.103	
carbaryl	1-naphthyl N-methylcarbamate	120.169	Sevin
carbofuran	2,3-dihydro-2,2-dimethyl-7-benzofuranyl N-methylcarbamate	120.254	Furadan
carbofuran metabolite	2,3-dihydro-2,2-dimethyl-3-hydroxy-7-benzofuranyl N-methylcarbamate	120.254	
carbon disulfide	carbon disulfide	120.1004	
carbon tetrachloride	carbon tetrachloride	120.1005	
	3-[p-(p-chlorophenoxy)phenyl]-1,1-dimethylurea	120.216	Tenoran
carbophenothion	S-(p-chlorophenylthiomethyl)O,O-diethyl phosphorodithioate	120.156	Trithion
chlorbenside	p-chlorobenzyl p-chlorophenyl sulfide	120.168	Mitox
chlordane	1,2,4,5,6,7,8,8-octachloro-2,3,3a,4,7,7a-hexahydro-4,7-methanoindene, containing not more than 1 percent of the intermediate compound hexachloro-cyclopentadiene	120.122	
	2-chloroallyl diethyldithiocarbamate	120.247	Vegadex
	2-chloro-4,6-bis(isopropylamino)-s-triazine	120.243	Propazine
	2-chloro-2′,6′-diethyl-N-(methoxymethyl) acetanilide	120.249	Lasso
chloroform	trichloromethane	120.1009	
	2-chloro-N-isopropylacetanilide	120.211	Ramrod
	p-chlorophenoxyacetic acid	120.202	
	p-chlorophenyl phenyl sulfone	120.112	Sulphenone
chloroneb	1,4-dichloro-2,5-dimethoxybenzene	120.257	
chloroneb metabolite	2,5-dichloro-4-methoxyphenol	120.257	
	p-chlorophenyl-2,4,5-trichlorophenyl sulfide	120.256	Animet
chloropicrin	trichloronitromethane	120.199; 120.1008	
	chlorosulfamic acid	120.201	
	2-chloro-1-(2,4,5-trichlorophenyl)vinyl dimethyl phosphate, and its related conversion products 2-chloro-1-(2,4,5-trichlorophenyl) vinyl methylphosphoric acid, 2,2′,4′,5′-tetrachloroacetophenone, and conjugates of the latter two	120.252	Gardona, Rabon
CIPC	isopropyl N(3-chlorophenyl) carbamate	120.181	
	cis-N-[(1,1,2,2-tetrachloroethyl)thio]-4-cyclohexene-1,2-dicarboximide	120.267	Difolatan
	combination of chloropicrin, methyl bromide, and propargyl bromide	120.199; 120.1008	Trizone
	copper arsenate	120.193	

TABLE 6-7. Common and Chemical Names for Pesticide Chemicals (cont.)

Common name	Chemical name	21 CFR part 120 section No.	Trade name
copper carbonate (basic)	basic copper carbamate	120.136; 120.1001	
copper compounds (other)	Bordeaux mixture, copper abietate, copper acetate, copper carbonate, copper hydroxide, copper-lime mixtures, copper linoleate, copper oleate, copper oxychloride, copper silicate, copper sulfate (basic), copper sulfate monohydrate, copper sulfate pentahydrate, copper-zinc chromate, cupric oxide, cuprous oxide, tetra copper calcium oxychloride	120.1001	
coumaphos	0,0-diethyl 0-3-chloro-4-methyl-2-oxo-2H-1-benzopyran-7-yl phosphorothioate	120.189	Co-Ral
coumaphos oxygen analog	0,0-diethyl 0-3-chloro-4-methyl-2-oxo-2H-1-benzopyran-7-yl phosphate	120.189	
dalapon sodium salt	sodium 2,2-dichloropropionate	120.150	Dowpon
DDD (or TDE)	1,1-dichloro-2,2-bis(p-chlorophenyl) ethane	120.147(c); 120.187	
DDE	1,1-dichloro-2,2-bis(p-chlorophenyl) ethylene	120.147(c)	
DDT	a mixture of 1,1,1-trichloro-2,2-bis(p-chlorophenyl) ethane and 1,1,1-trichloro-2-(o-chlorophenyl)-2-(p-chlorophenyl) ethane	120.147	
demeton	a mixture of 0,0-diethyl 0-(and S-)[2-(ethylthio)ethyl] phosphorothioates	120.105	Systox
diatomaceous earth	diatomaceous earth	120.1017	Permaguard
	1,2-dibromo-3-chloropropane	120.197	Nemagon, Fumazone
dicamba	3,6-dichloro-o-anisic acid	120.227	Banvel, Banvel D
dichlobenil	2,6-dichlorobenzonitrile	120.231	Casoron
dichlobenil metabolite	2,6-dichlorobenzoic acid	120.231	
dichlone	2,3-dichloro-1,4-naphthoquinone	120.118	Phygon
	1,1-dichloro-2,2-bis(p-ethylphenyl) ethane	120.139	Perthane
	2,4-dichloro-6,o-chloroanilino-s-triazine	120.158	Dyrene
	3,6-dichloro-5-hydroxy-o-anisic acid	120.227	
	2,6-dichloro-4-nitroaniline	120.200	Botran
	2,4-dichlorophenyl p-nitrophenyl ether	120.223	Tok

2,4-D	2,4-dichlorophenoxyacetic acid	120.142	
	2,2-dichlorovinyl dimethyl phosphate	120.235	Vapona
	dicyclohexylamine salt of dinitro-o-cyclohexylphenol	120.143	
dieldrin	1,2,3,4,10,10-hexachloro-6,7-epoxy-1,4,4a,5,6,7,8,8a-octahydro-1,4-endo,exo-5,8-dimethanonaphthalene	120.137	
	0,0-diethyl S-[2-(ethylthio)ethyl] phosphorodithioate and its cholinesterase-inhibiting metabolites	120.183	Di-System
	0,0-diethyl 0-(2-isopropyl-4-methyl-6-pyrimidinyl) phosphorothioate	120.153	Diazinon
	0,0-diethyl 0-[p-(methylsulfinyl)phenyl] phosphorothioate	120.234	Dasanit
	diethyl 2-pyrazinyl phosphate	120.264	
	0,0-diethyl 0-2-pyrazinyl phosphorothioate	120.264	Zinophos
	S-(0,0-diisopropyl phosphorodithioate) of N-(2-mercaptoethyl)benzenesulfonamide	120.241	Prefar
	S-(0,0-diisopropyl phosphorothioate) of N-(2-mercaptoethyl)benzenesulfonamide	120.241	
	0,0-dimethyl 0-p-(dimethylsulfamoyl)phenyl phosphate	120.233	Warbex
	0,0-dimethyl 0-p-(dimethylsulfamoyl)phenyl phosphorothioate	120.233	
dimethoate	0,0-dimethyl S-(N-methylcarbamoylmethyl) phosphorodithioate	120.204	Cygon
dimethoate oxygen analog	0,0-dimethyl 0-(N-methylcarbamoylmethyl) phosphorodithioate	120.204	
	0,0-dimethyl S-[4-oxo-1,2,3-benzotriazin-3(4H)-ylmethyl] phosphorodithioate	120.154	Guthion
	dimethyl 2,3,5,6-tetrachloroterephthalate	120.185	Dacthal
	0,0-dimethyl 2,2,2-trichloro-1-hydroxyethyl phosphonate	120.198	Dipterex, Dylox, Neguvon
	dinitro-o-cyclohexylphenol	120.144	
dioxathion	2,3-p-dioxanedithiol S,S-bis(0,0-diethyl phosphorodithioate)	120.171	Delnav
diphenamid	N,N-dimethyl-2,2-diphenylacetamide	120.230	Dymid
diphenamid desmethyl metabolite	N-methyl-2,2-diphenylacetamide	120.230	
diphenylamine	diphenylamine	120.190	
diquat	6,7-dihydrodipyrido (1,2-a:2′,1′-c) pyrazidiinium	120.226	
diuron	3-(3,4-dichlorophenyl)-1,1-dimethylurea	120.106	Karmex
	dodecachlorooctahydro-1,3,4-metheno-2H-cyclobuta[cd]pentalene	120.251	Mirex
dodine	n-dodecylguanidine acetate	120.172	Cyprex
endosulfan	6,7,8,9,10,10-hexachloro-1,5,5a,6,9,9a-hexahydro-6,9-methano-2,4,3-benzodioxathiepin-3-oxide	120.182	Thiodan
endosulfan sulfate	6,7,8,9,10,10-hexachloro-1,5,5a,6,9,9a-hexahydro-6,9-methano-2,4,3-benzodioxathiepin-3,3-dioxide	120.182	

TABLE 6-7. Common and Chemical Names for Pesticide Chemicals (cont.)

Common name	Chemical name	21 CFR part 120 section No.	Trade name
endrin	1,2,3,4,10,10-hexachloro-6,7-epoxy-1,4,4a,5,6,7,8,8a-octahydro-1,4-endo-endo-5,8-dimethanonaphthalene	120.131	
	2-ethylamino-4-isopropylamino-6-methylthio-s-triazine	120.258	Ametryne
	S-ethyl cyclohexylethylthiocarbamate	120.212	Ro-Neet
	ethyl 4,4′-dichlorobenzilate	120.109	Chlorobenzilate
	S-ethyl diisobutylthiocarbamate	120.232	Sutan
	O-ethyl S,S-dipropylphosphorodithioate	120.262	Mocap
	S-ethyl dipropylthiocarbamate	120.117	Eptam
EPN	O-ethyl O-p nitrophenyl benzene thiophosphonate	120.119	
	O-ethyl S-phenyl ethylphosphonodithioate	120.221	Dyfonate
	O-ethyl S-phenyl ethylphosphonothiolate	120.221	
ethion	O,O,O,′O′-tetraethyl S,S′-methylene bisphosphorodithioate	120.173	
ethion oxygen analog	S-[[(diethoxyphosphinothioyl)thio] methyl] O,O-diethyl phosphorothioate	120.173	
ethoxyquin	1,2-dihydro-6-ethoxy-2,2,4-trimethylquinoline	120.178	
	ethylene	120.1016	
	ethylene dibromide	120.126; 120.146; 120.1006	
	ethylene dichloride	120.1007	
	ethylene oxide	120.151	
	S-ethyl hexahydro-1H-azepine-1-carbothioate	120.228	Ordram
fenthion	O,O-dimethyl O-[4-(methylthio)-m-tolyl] phosphorothioate	120.214	Baytex, Tiguvon
ferbam	ferric dimethyldithiocarbamate	120.114	Fermate
	ferrous sulfate	120.2	
fluometuron	1,1-dimethyl-3-(α,α,α-trifluoro-m-tolyl)urea	120.229	Cotoran
fluorine compounds	cryolite, synthetic cryolite (sodium aluminum fluoride)	120.145	
folpet	N-(trichloromethylthio)phthalimide	120.191	Phaltan
	gibberellic acid	120.224	
glyodin	2-heptadecyl glyoxalidine acetate or 2-heptadecyl glyoxalidine (base)	120.124	
heptachlor and heptachlor epoxide	heptachlor (1,4,5,6,7,8,8-heptachloro-3a,4,7,7a-tetrahydro-4,7-methanoindene) and its oxidation product heptachlor epoxide (1,4,5,6,7,8,8-heptachloro-2,3-epoxy-2,3,3a,4,7,7a-hexahydro-4,7-methanoindene)	120.104	

HCN	hydrogen cyanide	120.130	
	4-hydroxy-2,5,6-trichloroisophthalonitrile	120.275	
	isopropyl 4,4′-dichlorobenzilate	120.218	Chloropropylate, Acaralate
	lead arsenate	120.194	
lime	calcium oxide	120.2	
lime sulfur	mixture of calcium polysulfide, water, free sulfur, and calcium thiosulphate	120.2	
lindane	gamma isomer of benzene hexachloride	120.133	
	magnesium arsenate	120.195	
linuron	3-(3,4-dichlorophenyl)-1-methoxy-1-methylurea	120.184	Lorox
malathion	0,0-dimethyl dithiophosphate of diethyl mercaptosuccinate	120.111	
maleic hydrazide	1,2-dihydro-3,6-pyridazinedione	120.175	MH-30
maneb	manganous ethylenebisdithiocarbamate	120.110	
	manganous dimethyldithiocarbamate	120.161	
	mercaptobenzothiazole	120.160	
	N-(mercaptomethyl)phthalimide S-(0,0-dimethyl phosphorodithioate)	120.261	Imidan, Prolate
	1-methoxycarbonyl-1-propen-2-yl dimethylphosphate and its beta isomer	120.157	Phosdrin
methomyl	S-methyl N-[(methylcarbamoyl)oxy]thioacetimidate	120.253	
methoxychlor	2,2-bis-(p-methoxyphenyl)-1,1,1-trichloroethane	120.120	
	methyl bromide	120.123; 120.199	
methyl parathion (methyl homolog of parathion)	0,0-dimethyl 0-p-nitrophenyl thiophosphate	120.121	Metacide
	methylene chloride	120.1010	
	2-methyl-2-(methylsulfinyl)propionaldehyde 0-(methylcarbamoyl)oxime	120.269	
	2-methyl-2-(methylsulfonyl)propionaldehyde 0-(methylcarbamoyl)oxime	120.269	
	4-(methylsulfonyl)-2,6-dinitro-N,N-dipropylaniline	120.237	Planavin
mineral oil	refined petroleum oil	120.149	
	mixture of 75% m-(1-methylbutyl)phenyl methylcarbamate and 25% m-(1-ethylpropyl)phenyl methylcarbamate	120.255	BUX
	monomethyl 2,3,5,6-tetrachloroterephthalate	120.185	
monuron	3-(p-chlorophenyl)-1,1-dimethylurea	120.108	Telvar
	α-naphthaleneacetic acid	120.155	
	β-naphthoxyacetic acid	120.148	

TABLE 6-7. Common and Chemical Names for Pesticide Chemicals (cont.)

Common name	Chemical name	21 CFR part 120 section No.	Trade name
naled	1,2-dibromo-2,2-dichloroethyl dimethyl phosphate	120.215	Dibrom
	neodecanoic acid (a mixture of 10-carbon trialkyl acetic acids (calculated as $C_9H_{19}COOH$))	120.248	Wiltz 65
nicotine containing compounds	nicotine and nicotine sulfate	120.167	
norea	3-(hexahydro-4,7-methanoindan-5-yl)-1,1-dimethyl urea	120.260	Herban
	N-octylbicyclo-(2,2,1)-5-heptene-2,3-dicarboximide	120.1001	MGK 264
	Orthoarsenic acid	120.180	
ovex	p-chlorophenyl-p-chlorobenzenesulfonate	120.134	Ovotran
paraquat	1,1′-dimethyl-4,4′-bipyridinium	120.205	
parathion	0,0-diethyl 0-p-nitrophenyl thiophosphate	120.121	
	pentane	120.1014	
petroleum oils		120.1001	
phenothiazine	thiodiphenylamine	120.170	
	o-phenylphenol	120.129	
phorate	0,0-diethyl S-(ethylthio)methyl phosphorodithioate	120.206	Thimet
phosalone	S-(6-chloro-3-(mercaptomethyl)-2-benzoxazolinone) 0,0-diethyl phosphorodithioate	120.263	Zolone
phosphamidon	2-chloro-2-diethylcarbamoyl-1-methylvinyl dimethyl phosphate including all of its related cholinesterase-inhibiting compounds	120.239	
	phosphine	120.225	
piperonyl butoxide	(butyl carbityl) (6-propyl piperonyl) ether	120.127; 120.1001	
piperonyl cyclonene	mixture of 3-alkyl-6-carbethoxy-5-(3,4-methylenedioxyphenyl)-2-cyclohexene-1-one and 3-alkyl-5-(3,4-methylenedioxyphenyl)-2-cyclohexene-1-one	120.1001	
	potassium polysulfide	120.2	
	S-propyl butylethylthiocarbamate	120.238	Tillam
	S-propyl dipropylthiocarbamate	120.240	Vernam
n-propyl isome	dipropyl 5,6,7,8-tetrahydro-7-methylnaphtho(2,3)-1,3-dioxole-5,6-dicarboxylate	120.1001	
pyrethrins	insecticidally active principles of Chrysanthemum cinerariaefolium	120.128; 120.1001	

ronnel	O,O-dimethyl O-(2,4,5-trichlorophenyl) phosphorothioate	120.177	
rotenone	principal insecticidal constituent of derris root, cubé	120.1001	
ryania	ryania	120.1001	
sabadilla	sabadilla	120.1001	
schradan	octamethylpyrophosphoramide (OMPA)	120.166	
sesone	sodium 2,4-dichlorophenoxyethyl sulfate	120.102	SES
simazine	2-chloro-4,6-bis(ethylamino)-s-triazine	120.213	
	sodium arsenate	120.196	
	sodium carbonate	120.2	
	sodium chloride	120.2	
	sodium dehydroacetate	120.159	
2,4-D sodium salt	sodium 2,4-dichlorophenoxyacetate	120.165	
	sodium dimethyldithiocarbamate	120.152	
	sodium o-phenylphenate	120.129	
	sodium polysulfide	120.2	
	sodium propionate	120.1015	
	streptomycin	120.245	
	succinic acid 2,2-dimethylhydrazide	120.246	Alar
	sulfur	120.2	
	sulfur dioxide	120.1013	
tartar emetic	potassium antimonyl tartrate	120.179	
TDE (or DDD)	1,1-dichloro-2,2-bis(p-chlorophenyl) ethane	120.147(c);	
		120.187	Rhothane
terbacil	3-tert-butyl-5-chloro-6-methyluracil	120.209	Sinbar
terpene polychlorinates	terpene polychlorinates containing 65-66% chlorine	120.164	Strobane
tetradifon	2,4,5,4′-tetrachlorodiphenyl sulfone	120.174	Tedion
	2,4,5,6-tetrachloroisophthalonitrile	120.275	Daconil
	2,3,5,6-tetrachloronitrobenzene	120.203	Fusarex
	2,3,5,6-tetrachloroterephthalic acid	120.185	
	tetraiodoethylene	120.162	
thiabendazole	2-(4-thiazolyl)-benzimidazole	120.242	
thiram	tetramethyl thiuram disulfide	120.132	

TABLE 6-7. Common and Chemical Names for Pesticide Chemicals (cont.)

Common name	Chemical name	21 CFR part 120 section No.	Trade name
toxaphene	chlorinated camphene containing 67-69% chlorine	120.138	
	S,S,S,-tributyl phosphorotrithioate	120.272	DEF
	tributylphosphorotrithioite	120.186	Merphos
	trichlorobenzoic acid	120.273	
	trichlorobenzyl chloride	120.273	Randox
	1,1,1-trichloroethane	120.1012	
	2,3,5-triiodobenzoic acid	120.219	Floraltone
trifluralin	α,α,α-trifluoro-2,6-dinitro-N,N-dipropyl-p-toluidine	120.207	Treflan
	triphenyltin hydroxide	120.236	DU-TER
zinc ion and maneb (coordination product)		120.176	Dithane M-45
zineb	zinc ethylenebisdithiocarbamate	120.115	
ziram	zinc dimethyldithiocarbamate	120.116	
	zinc sulphate (basic)	120.244	

TABLE 6-8. Recommended Chemical Control of Some Problem Pests

Pest	Control
Ants	in woodwork—desiccant powders (Drione, Dri-Die, etc.); in lawns—chlordane (minimal)
Aphids	wash off with slightly soapy (not detergent) warm water; introduce lady-bugs; apply rotenone, pyrethrum; nicotine sulfate (last resort)
Fleas, silverfish, bedbugs, roaches	desiccants, malathion, diazinon
Caterpillars	rotenone, Biotrol, diazinon, methoxychlor, Sevin
Cutworms	diazinon, Sevin
Flies	in the house—flypaper or a fly swatter
Grasshoppers	diazinon
Gypsy moth	an overrated pest—Biotrol or Sevin by spot treatment
Japanese beetle	grubs—milky spore disease; adults—malathion
Lawn moths	diazinon, Sevin
Leafhoppers, leafminers, leafrollers	diazinon
Mice, rats	mouse (or rat) trap, Warfarin
Mites (red spider)	oil spray, wash with warm, soapy (no detergent) water
Mosquitoes	larvae—eliminate stagnant, standing water, in which larvae are born; adults—apply repellents to your exposed skin; spray pyrethrin or methoxychlor in outdoor areas (patios, under picnic tables, etc.)
Scale insects	diazinon, malathion
Spittlebugs	malathion
Termites	chlordane (minimal—as for severe ant problem); better left to professional exterminator
Thrips	rotenone, nicotine sulfate, diazinon, malathion
Wasps, hornets	dangerous when aroused! Apply rotenone at dusk when nest is quiet (weather cold or rainy) and cover tightly with plastic bag for several hours
Wireworms	diazinon
Wood borers	diazinon

(Compiled from National Audubon Society and FOE lists)

SELECTED BIBLIOGRAPHY

Borror, D.J., and LeLong, D.M., *An Introduction to the Study of Insects,* Holt, Rinehart and Winston, New York, 1964 (revised edition).

Carson, R. L., *Silent Spring,* Houghton Mifflin, Boston, 1962; extensive source listing included.

Clark, L. R., Geier, P. W., Hughes, R. D., and Morris, R. F., *The Ecology of Insect Populations in Theory and Practice,* Methuen and Company, Ltd., London, 1967.

Conway, G. R., "Pests Follow the Chemicals in the Cocoa of Malaysia," *Natural History,* 78 (2) :46-51; 1969.

DeBach, P. (ed.), *Biological Control of Insect Pests and Weeds,* Reinhold Corporation, New York, 1964. 844 pp.

Environmental Quality, first annual report of the Council on Environmental Quality, U. S. Government Printing Office, Washington, D.C., 1970.

Egler, F. E., "Pesticides in Our Ecosystem," *American Scientist,* 52:110-136, 1964.

———, "Pesticides in Our Ecosystem: Communication II," *Bioscience,* 14 (11):29-36, 1964.

Frost, J., "Earth, Air, Water," *Environment,* 11(6):14–33, 1969.

Geier, P. W., "Management of Insect Pests," *Annual Review of Entomology,* 11:471–90, 1966.

Graham, Jr., F., *Since Silent Spring,* Houghton Mifflin, Boston, 1970; 333pp. Fawcett Crest Book, 1970; extensive source references.

Jukes, T. M., "People and Pesticides," *American Scientist,* 51:335–61, 1963.

Kilgore, W. W., and Doutt, R. L. (eds.), *Pest Control: Biological, Physical, and Selected Chemical Methods,* Academic Press, New York, 1967.

McLean, L. A., "Pesticides and the Environment," *Bioscience,* 17(9):613–17, 1967.

Miller, M. W., and Borg, G. G. (eds.), *Chemical Fallout: Current Research on Persistent Pesticides,* Charles C. Thomas, Springfield, Illinois, 1969.

Peterle, T. J., "Pyramiding Damage," *Environment,* 11(6):34–40, 1969.

Rudd, R. L., *Pesticides and the Living Landscape,* University of Wisconsin Press, Madison, 1964.

Scientists Institute for Public Information, *Pesticides,* a workbook by Donald L. Dahlsten, Richard Garcia, John E. Laing and Robert van den Bosch, New York, 1970.

Sladen, W. J. L., Menzie, C. M., and Reichel, W. L., "DDT Residues in Adelie Penguins and a Crabeater Seal from Antarctica: Ecological Implications," *Nature,* 210, 670–73, 1966.

Whitten, J. L., *That We May Live,* Van Nostrand Company, Princeton, New Jersey, 1966.

Woodwell, G. M., "Toxic Substances and Ecological Cycles," *Scientific American,* 216(3):24–31 (Offprint No. 1066), 1967.

Wurster, C. F., "DDT Goes to Trial in Wisconsin," *Bioscience,* 19(9):809–13, 1969.

Wurster, D. H., Wurster, C. F., and Strickland, W. N., "Bird Mortality Following DDT Spray for Dutch Elm Disease," *Ecology,* 46, 488–99, 1965.

Young, L. A., and Nicholson, H. P., "Stream Pollution Resulting from the Use of Organic Insecticides," *Progressive Fish Culturist,* Vol. 13, No. 4, 193–98, 1951.

GOVERNMENT PUBLICATIONS

(U. S. Government Printing Office, Public Documents Department, Washington, D.C., 20402.)

On Insecticides:

Contact, Residue, and Vapor Toxicity of New Insecticides to Stored-Product Insects, II, U. S. Government Printing Office, 1970. A 1.82:885; 35¢.

On Pesticides:

Farmers' Pesticide Expenditures in 1966, U. S. Government Printing Office, 1970; 50¢.

Fish, Wildlife, and Pesticides, Fish and Wildlife Service, 1966; 10¢.

Hayes, W. J., Jr., *Clinical Handbook on Economic Poisons;* Department of Health, Education and Welfare; Public Health Service Publication No. 476; 1963; 55¢.

"Pesticides—What Are Pecticides?" U. S. Government Printing Office, revised, 1971, 10¢.

Safe Use of Agricultural and Household Pesticides; Department of Agriculture Handbook No. 321; 1967; 50¢.

Use of Pesticides; President's Science Advisory Committee; 1963; 15¢.

On Rodenticides:

(On request from Superintendent of Documents, Government Printing Office)

Controlling Rats and Mice: Use of Anticoagulant Poisons; No. 318.

Controlling Rats and Mice: Use of Bait Stations; No. 319.

Characteristics of Common Rodenticides; Wildlife Leaflet 337.

Anticoagulant Rodenticides for Control of Rats and Mice; Wildlife Leaflet 402.

VII Nonrenewable Mineral Resources

Perhaps the thinnest thread in the whole ecosystem web is the mineral situation. What has taken eons to join together in the crust of the earth, industrial man promises to break asunder in one or two centuries. For the world is fast running out of its fossil fuels and key metals.

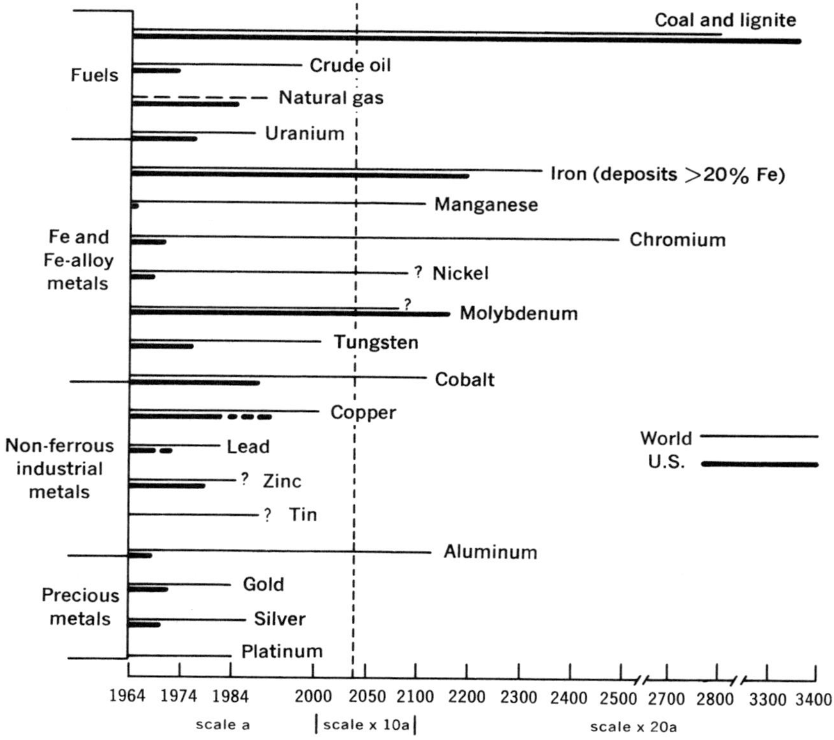

FIGURE 7-1.

Lifetimes of estimated recoverable reserves of mineral resources at current mineable grades and rates of consumption (no allowance made for increasing populations and rates of consumption, or for submerged or otherwise concealed deposits, use of now submarginal grades or imports

Source: Cloud, "Realities of Mineral Distribution," The Texas Quarterly, 1969

Figure 7-1 indicates the sinking mineral reserve. Although it does not take into account the possible discovery of new deposits or the exploitation of submarginal ores, there is no allowance either for the mounting demands on mineral consumption. The thin line is based on a world population of roughly 3.3 billion and the thick line on a U.S. population of about 200 million—both keyed to 1965 rates of use. It would seem that the chances of finding new mineral sources in the ground or in technology are balanced off by the certain consumptive requirements of an expanding technology in both the developed and underdeveloped countries.

Geologist Preston E. Cloud drew a line through this figure in 1968 to represent the year 2038—a point then seventy years hence when only eight of the nineteen commodities considered would exist in world supply and only three in U.S. supply.

There is nothing apocalyptic about these projections. The statistics are on the wall and probably underestimated. Optimists may point to new or lower grade reserves, synthesized substitutes or recycling. To these people Cloud suggests the following questions: "(1) how do we deduce these generalities to specifics; (2) can we do so fast enough to sustain current rates of consumption; (3) can we increase and sustain production of industrial materials at a rate sufficient to meet the rising expectations of a world population of 3½ billion, now growing with a doubling time of about thirty to thirty-five years, and for how long; and (4) if the answer to the last question is no, what then?"

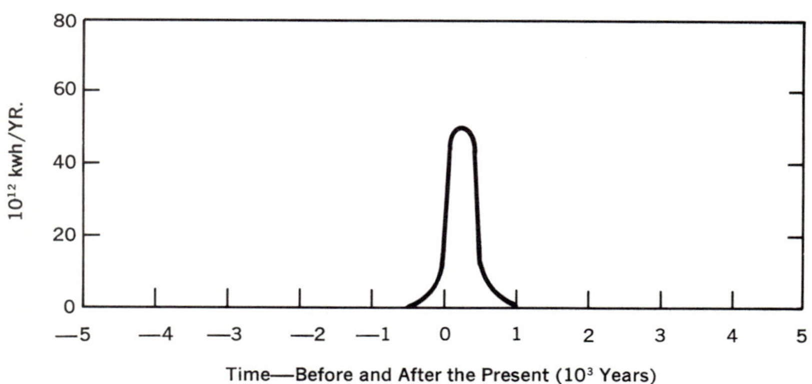

FIGURE 7-2.

Epoch of exploitation of fossil fuels in historical perspective from minus to plus 5,000 years from present

Source: Hubbert, Energy Resources, National Academy of Sciences, 1962

FIGURE 7-3.

	Geological time required to produce 1 ton (Millions of years)	Man's removal rate (Millions of tons per year)
Petroleum	250	600
Coal	1000	2000
Iron	2000	200
Lead	4000	4

Source: McHale, The Ecological Context, Braziller, 1970.

SELECTED BIBLIOGRAPHY

Barnett, H. J., and Morse, Chandler, *Scarcity and Growth,* Johns Hopkins Press, Baltimore, 1963.

Discussion of population growth and the scarcity of resources, using recent statistical data.

Cloud, P. E., Jr., "Realities of mineral distribution," *Texas Quarterly,* 1969, Vol. 11, pp. 103–26. A brief summary of the nonrenewable resource situation.

Cloud, P. E., Jr. (ed.), *Resources and Man.* W. H. Freeman and Company, San Francisco, 1969. See especially Chapter 8 on energy resources, Chapter 6 on mineral resources from the land and Chapter 7 on the mineral resources of the sea.

Fisher, J. L., and Potter, N., *World Prospects for Natural Resources: Some Projections of Demand and Indicators of Supply to the Year 2000,* Resources for the Future, Washington, D.C., 1964.

Landsberg, H. H., *et al., Resources in America's Future: Pattern of Requirements and Availabilities, 1960–2000.* Johns Hopkins Press, Baltimore, 1963.

A projection of America's resource use to the year 2000; includes discussion of products, services, and land, water and mineral resources.

Mudd, Stuart (ed.), *The Population Crisis and the Use of World Resources.* Bloomington, Indiana University Press, 1964.

Park, Charles F., Jr., *Affluence in Jeopardy,* San Francisco, Freeman, Cooper & Company, 1968.

VIII Solid Wastes

British naturalist Peter Scott, at a London gathering in November 1970,[1] labeled the United States the world's biggest polluter. Each American, he said, accounts for more toxic wastes poured into rivers and oceans than 1,000 Asians; the nation as a whole, he added, generates more industrial and municipal waste than any other country.

There is no argument.

In 1920, the average American created 2.75 pounds of solid waste per day; in 1970, the figure was 5 pounds per day; by 1980, it will be 8 pounds per day. The over-all tonnage is staggering. For 1969, the total was 4,340,000,000 tons, according to the Council on Environmental Quality.[2] The breakdown was as follows:

TABLE 8-1.

	Million tons
Residential, commercial and institutional wastes	250
collected	(190)
uncollected	(60)
Industrial wastes	110
Mineral wastes	1,700
Agricultural wastes	2,280
Total	4,340

To collect the residential, commercial and institutional wastes alone cost about $3.5 billion in 1969, an average of $18 per ton. This is a cost in excess of the annual budget of the United Nations and many countries of the world. The solid waste collected annually includes 30 million tons of paper and paper products; 4 million tons of plastics; 100 million rubber or rubber-composition tires; 30 billion bottles; 60 billion cans; millions of tons of demolition debris, grass and tree trimmings, food wastes and sewage sludge; and millions of discarded appliances and automobiles. (Tables 8-3, 8-4)

[1] The Second International Congress of the World Wildlife Fund.

[2] First Annual Report, August 1970.

A waste-composition profile, drawn from a Public Health Service study of municipal refuse for the years 1966–68, shows a waste picture by percentage, as follows:

TABLE 8-2.

Item	Percentage by weight
Paper products (The largest categories of this division are: corrogated paper boxes, 23.8%; newspapers, 9.4%; magazines, 6.8%; brown paper, 5.6%; paper food cartons, 2%; tissue paper, 1.98%; mail, 2.8%.)	55.0%
Glass/ash	7.7
Metals (e.g., tin cans)	6.8
Vegetable wastes	2.9
Meat scraps	2.9
Other foods	2.9
Leaves, grass, etc.	10.0
Other	2.8
Adjusted moistures	9.0
	100.0%

Approximately 77 percent of these collected solid wastes end up in one of the 14,000 open dumps of the country; 13 percent is deposited in what is known as sanitary landfill areas (areas where wastes are covered each day with a layer of earth to enter into biodegradation); 10 percent is burned in municipal incinerators. (Figure 8-1)

However the wastes are disposed of, they present an enormous problem. Incineration results in air pollution; dumping results in exhaustion of land and space. There is hardly a city in the United States whose dumps are not clogged, and which is not looking for new places where it can haul its refuse. The complication is that communities with open space have little disposition to let others in for dumping purposes. Who wants to be his neighbor's garbage can? So it is back to the old dumping grounds for most. Westchester County's (N.Y.) experience is typical. Its one dump at Croton-on-Hudson, sated and reeking, was scheduled to be closed on January 1, 1969; authorities ruled that it could not take any more refuse without becoming a serious health menace. But extensions to its closing have had to be granted. There is just nowhere else to be found to take the waste. The same situation exists in San Francisco, Milwaukee, Philadelphia, New York City—almost any city one can name.

A number of proposals are on the books to meet the problem, at least partially—ideas such as incentive and subsidy programs promoting waste-reclaiming processes; a use tax and/or deterrent tax on packaging; the education of the consumer on efficient disposal proce-

TABLE 8-3. Generation of Solid Wastes from Five Major Sources in 1967*

Source	Solid wastes generated	
	lbs/cap./day	million tons/yr.
Urban		
domestic	3.5	128
municipal	1.2	44
commercial	2.3	84
sub-total	7.0	256
Industrial	3.0	110
Agricultural		
vegetation	15.0	552
animal	43.0	1563
sub-total	58.0	2115
Mineral	30.8	1126
Federal	1.2	43
Totals	100.0	3650

*Source: Public Health Service, Department of Health, Education and Welfare.

TABLE 8-4. Range in Composition of Residential Solid Wastes in 21 U. S. Cities*

Component	Percent composition by net weight		
	Low	High	Average
Food waste	0.8	36.0	18.2
Garden waste	0.3	33.3	7.9
Paper products	13.0	62.0	43.8
Metals	6.6	14.5	9.1
Glass and ceramics	3.7	23.2	9.0
Plastics, rubber and leather	1.6	5.8	3.0
Textiles	1.4	7.8	2.7
Wood	0.4	7.5	2.5
Rock, dirt, ash, etc.	0.2	12.5	3.7

*Source: Public Health Service, Department of Health, Education and Welfare.

dures; the recycling and reuse of items such as glass, cans, paper, etc. But none of these proposals is being pushed strongly. Nor is technology being put to work on the problem in any marked manner. The key is in developing techniques for separating and recovering waste materials. But these remain as primitive as they are costly. Unless something is done quickly, Americans will be knee-deep in plastic detergent containers, beer cans and the other diarrhea of affluence.[3]

MILLION TONS, ESTIMATED

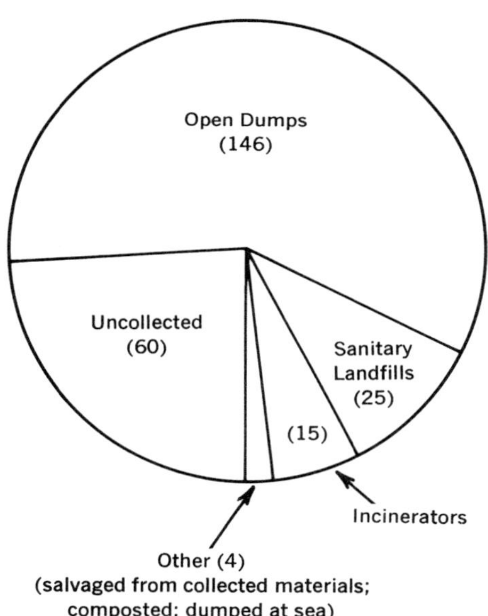

Total—250 million tons

FIGURE 8-1. Disposal of Residential, Commercial, and Institutional Solid Wastes, 1969

Source: Bureau of Solid Waste Management, HEW

[3]The Federal Bureau of Solid Waste Management, pursuant to Section 204(b) of the Solid Waste Disposal Act (P.L. 89–272), has prepared a listing of 115 publications reporting on research, development and demonstrations-in-progress relating to solid wastes. The listing is collected into a booklet, *Solid Waste Management: A List of Available Literature,* single copies of which are available from the Bureau of Solid Waste Management, Office of Information, 5555 Ridge Avenue, Cincinnati, Ohio 45213.

1. AGRICULTURAL, MINERAL, INDUSTRIAL WASTES

Agricultural and mineral wastes comprise the two largest sources of solid wastes in the United States—a fact sometimes unappreciated because their volumes are not concentrated, as a rule, in urban centers, and because the collection and disposal of these wastes do not involve municipal energies and facilities. These circumstances do not, however, mean that agricultural and mineral wastes are any less of a problem. Quite the contrary. They take an enormous toll on the quality of air and water, to say nothing of aesthetics.

Of all solid waste categories, the largest by far is *agricultural waste.* It was 2.2 billion tons in 1969. The accumulation builds from animal and slaughterhouse wastes, residues from crop harvests, vineyard and orchard prunings, vegetable parings and greenhouse refuse.

The new methods of raising meat cattle point up the complexities of the manure problem alone. At one time, meat cattle grazed over wide open spaces, where nature could readily handle animal wastes. Today these animals are often matured and fattened in enclosed feedlots of limited size. The result is fatter cattle and perhaps more tender meat—and mountains of manure, not easily disposed of and not readily assimilated by the earth of the feedlots. As a consequence, the manure works its way into water resources, poisoning wells, killing fish, despoiling aquifers, contaminating reservoirs and causing eutrophication in lakes and rivers. At the same time, the feedlot fouls the air with smells, dusts and pests of multiple kinds. There was a period when fertilizer demands relieved a large part of the manure load, but this is no longer the case because of the increasing preferences for chemical fertilizers.

How great is the total amount of animal wastes in the United States?

According to the Council on Environmental Quality,[4] it is the equivalent of the wastes of 2 billion people. Beef cattle, poultry, hogs, sheep and horses are the major sources of animal wastes. The number of these animals, their waste equivalents to humans and the total waste equivalent are totaled in Table 8-5.[5]

Mineral Waste: 39 percent of the solid waste total, is generated primarily from mineral and fossil fuel mining, milling and processing industries. According to the Council on Environmental Quality,[6] eighty mineral industries generate solid waste, with eight of these industries

[4]First Annual Report, August 1970.

[5]The figures are not to be interpreted as an estimate of the potential pollution from feedlots. They are a measure of the total amount of animal wastes, part of which causes water pollution and solid waste problems.

[6]First Annual Report, August 1970.

TABLE 8-5.

	Animal population (in millions) (1)	Ratio of waste output of single animal to output of a human (2)	Total animal wastes expressed as equivalent number of humans (in millions of humans) (3)
Cattle	107	16.40	1,754.8
Horses	3	11.30	33.9
Hogs	53	1.90	100.7
Sheep	26	2.45	63.7
Chickens	375	0.14	52.5
Total[1]	564		2,005.6

[1] Col. 1 times col. 2 equals total in col. 3.
Source: Data derived from Federal Water Pollution Control Administration, "Cost of Clean Water," Vol. 2, 1968.

responsible for 80 percent of the total. The eight, in the order of their waste contribution, are:

— Copper
— Iron and steel
— Bituminous coal
— Phosphate rock
— Lead
— Zinc
— Alumina
— Anthracite

Mineral waste for 1970 was estimated at 1.7 billion tons. The Council on Environmental Quality predicts that by 1980 the nation's mineral industries will be generating at least 2 billion tons of waste every year.[7] These wastes generally accumulate as slag heaps, culm piles and mill tailings. Besides being a frightful eyesore, these wastes are drained off by rains and winds to pollute air and water elsewhere.

Industrial Waste: Weighs in behind agriculture and mineral wastes, as well as behind residential, commercial and industrial wastes. But it still amounts to 110 million tons a year. This waste includes paper and paper products, plastics, rags, bales and drums of useless by-products, slags, metals and assorted other items. Scrap metals alone amount to 15 million tons. Heavy as this tonnage might seem, it is only half the amount of waste fly ash produced by the electric utility industry. The latter total is placed at 30 million tons.[8] With the growing

[7] Ibid.

[8] Figure for 1969; First Annual Report, Council on Environmental Quality, August 1970.

and almost insatiable public demands for more power, this total is expected to rise one-third in the next ten years—to 40 million tons.

2. THE PACKAGE AS PROBLEM

No one, not even the most conscientious of conservationists, escapes completely from becoming a polluter of the environment. Merely as a consumer of goods he figures as a statistic in the solid waste problem. For goods come in packages, and packaging accounts for 13 percent of the total volume of solid waste in the United States. This packaging comprises everything from tin cans and beer bottles to paper bags, cereal boxes and large wooden containers.

Some 51.7 million tons of packaging materials were manufactured and marketed in the United States in 1966, an average of 525 pounds per American. By 1976, these amounts will rise to 73.5 million tons and 661 pounds, respectively. Approximately 90 percent of all this will end as solid waste, to be disposed of one way or another by refuse and sanitation departments.

The basic packaging materials are paper and paperboard, metals, glass, wood, plastics and textiles. Their percentage of packaging's solid waste tonnage for 1966 and their percentage projection for 1976 are as follows:

TABLE 8-6.

	1966	1976
Paper and paperboard	54.75%	56.86%
Metals	15.56%	12.96%
Glass	17.91%	18.32%
Wood	8.83%	6.81%
Plastics	2.39%	4.82%
Textiles	.55%	.23%

Each material is discussed in the following section.

Glass

When the nation observed its first Earth Day on April 22, 1970, a Coca-Cola newspaper advertisement featured the message, "If you love me, don't leave me." It was Coke's plaintive plea on behalf of the "ecologically sound" returnable bottle, lately rendered near obsolete by the no-deposit container. "The returnable bottle," Coke's ad exclaimed, "can make as many as 50 round trips in its useful life"; the nonreturnable bottle presents "a real litter [and disposal] problem," since it goes to market one time only.

Only on point one did the Coca-Cola ad exaggerate. According to the Federal Bureau of Solid Waste Management, the returnable container will average about nineteen trips to market; the Glass Container Manufacturers Institute estimates fourteen trips for the returnable soft-drink bottle, twenty for the returnable beer bottle. The figures are a distance from fifty, but they still make point two a fact beyond dispute: the disposable glass container—or, the "throwaway bottle," as the beer business called it in less sensitive days—is a major contributor to solid-waste pollution.

Over the past fifteen years, glass container shipments in the United States have more than doubled. In 1969 they reached 36 billion units, 178 glass containers per American. Much of this ends as solid waste in already dense dumping areas, much as castoff litter along highways, in beaches, parks and recreational areas. Studies indicate that glass accounts for up to 17.91 percent of the total tonnage of packaging's solid waste.[9]

Barring a dramatic turnaround, it is a percentage that is almost sure to rise. Consumer preference for containers that need not be returned, the reluctance of merchants to handle deposit bottles, industry determination to exploit its lighter weight, tougher durability product—factors such as these give glass containers a fat future. The growth projection for 1976 is 45.7 billion units, with the big gains being in the soft-drink and beer markets. As is the case now with baby foods, powdered coffee and spices, virtually all the containers will be of the nonreturnable type. By 1976, the deposit bottle will be ready to take its place on the curio shelves of antique stores alongside the old snap-top preserve jar. (Table 8-7; Figure 8-2)

As an item for packaging, glass possesses attractive properties. It is transparent, chemically inert and resistant to all external influences except temperature and light. Also, its manufacture is no great drain on natural resources. Glass is made of plentiful raw materials—silica sand, limestone and soda ash. About 73 percent of container glass, for instance, is silica. Finally, glass is salvageable. It can be reused or recycled. If properly ground up, it can even be made an ingredient of compost, its component parts thus returning to the land in an almost original state.

The trouble is that glass is relatively so simple and inexpensive to make that the impulse to bother about salvage has not been strong—at least it had not been before June 30, 1970, when the glass industry announced a bottle redemption program aimed at salvaging 11 billion

[9]Midwest Research Institute, as cited in Public Health Service Publication No. 1855. The glass industry places the percentage between 6 and 8.5—*The Litter Fact Book* and *The Solid Waste Fact Book,* both published by the Glass Container Manufacturers Institute, Inc.; undated.

TABLE 8-7. Shipments of Glass Containers by End Use: 1955 to 1976

(In millions of units)

End use	1955	1956	1957	1958	1959	1960	1961	1962	1963	1964	1965	1966	1970	1973	1976
Food, total	8,051	8,167	8,395	8,669	8,998	9,189	9,584	10,068	10,072	10,508	11,024	10,754	11,500	12,100	12,730
Narrow neck	2,065	2,165	2,198	2,221	2,338	2,538	2,578	2,734	2,768	2,999	3,103	3,111	3,025	3,000	2,950
Wide mouth	5,584	5,627	5,870	6,171	6,373	6,389	6,760	7,102	7,085	7,304	7,739	7,479	8,350	9,000	9,700
Dairy	402	376	327	277	287	261	246	232	219	205	182	164	125	100	80
Beverage, total	4,905	5,178	4,989	5,073	5,703	6,180	7,135	8,077	8,902	9,745	10,611	12,045	17,090	21,090	26,820
Wine	661	678	664	653	708	727	731	713	754	784	784	769	2,730 (Wine and Liquor)	2,890	3,060
Liquor	1,335	1,457	1,365	1,361	1,504	1,420	1,500	1,539	1,577	1,629	1,703	1,766			
Beer, total	1,506	1,542	1,561	1,627	1,865	2,377	3,164	3,775	4,239	4,788	5,203	5,608	6,760	7,800	9,060
Beer returnable	352	357	337	388	435	431	375	353	388	415	503	577	530	490	460
Beer nonreturnable	1,154	1,185	1,223	1,239	1,430	1,946	2,790	3,421	3,851	4,373	4,700	5,031	6,230	7,310	8,600
Soft drink, total	1,403	1,501	1,401	1,432	1,627	1,656	1,740	2,051	2,332	2,544	2,921	3,902	7,600	10,400	14,700
Soft drink returnable	1,233	1,330	1,217	1,240	1,415	1,407	1,338	1,574	1,772	1,912	1,914	1,922	1,600	1,400	1,200
Soft drink nonre-	[illegible]	[illegible]	[illegible]	[illegible]	[illegible]	[illegible]	[illegible]	[illegible]	[illegible]	[illegible]	[illegible]	1,980	6,000	9,000	13,500

			[illegible]	[illegible]	[illegible]	[illegible]	[illegible]	[illegible]	[illegible]	5,294	5,387	5,760	5,760	5,760	5,760
Medicinal and health	2,955	3,054	3,262	2.985	3,100	3,011	3,119	3,253	3,109	3,188	3,393	3,429	3,560	3,610	3,660
Toiletry and cosmetic	1,767	1,751	1,811	1,843	1,939	2,002	2,039	2,045	2,026	2,106	2,194	2,331	2,200	2,150	2,100
Chemical, household and industrial, total	1,686	1,710	1,767	1,658	1,925	1,893	1,740	1,358	1,278	1,061	991	837	630	500	400
Narrow neck	1,386	1,399	1,449	1,391	1,644	1,620	1,494	1,143	1,067	846	784	658			
Wide mouth	301	311	318	267	281	273	246	216	210	214	207	179			
Glass domestic shipments, total[a]	19,364	19,861	20,225	20,228	21,667	22,275	23,617	24,803	25,387	26,608	28,213	29,396	34,980	39,450	45,710

[a] Categories may not add to total due to rounding.

Sources: U. S. Department of Commerce, Bureau of the Census. Glass containers. Current Industrial Reports, Series M32G(56-13)—M32G(66-13). Washington, D.C., 1957-1967. Glass Container Manufacturers Institute, Glass Containers—1966. New York, July 1967. p. 40-49. Forecasts by Midwest Research Institute.

Chart from The Role of Packaging in Solid Waste Management 1966 to 1976, written for the Bureau of Solid Waste Management by Arsen Darnay and William E. Franklin. Public Health Service Publication No. 1855.

bottles a year. The industry acted out of an alleged public consciousness, but it is fact that it was under pressure. Just a few months before, the President's Special Assistant for Consumer Affairs, Mrs. Virginia H. Knauer, had scored the Glass Container Manufacturers Institute for "public relations flackery" for its $7.5 million campaign to promote no-return soft-drink bottles.

The bottle redemption program is one answer to the waste glass problem. Industry will pay a half-cent each—or about a penny a pound—for used bottles, then crush these for reuse as cullet in the bottlemaking process. The difficulties are (1) the redemption centers are too few—between 75 and 100 at or near glass container plants in 21 states; (2) there is no regulatory authority. Each company is individually responsible for establishing a collection center and purchasing the bottles. Obviously, manufacturers with faint interest in glass salvage could neutralize the effort for sizable areas of the country.[10]

What other possibilities are there?

To Develop Waste Glass into a Resource: With 15 million tons annually to capitalize upon, the Bureau of Mines is financing research for the utilization of waste glass in the manufacture of lightweight, pre-cast building elements, structural blocks, rods and sheeting and in lightweight aggregates for use in construction of low-cost housing and roads. Significant breakthroughs have been made, but widespread introduction of the new developments seems a distance in time.

A Legislative Ban on the Nonreturnable Bottle: Bills providing for such bans crop up regularly in assemblies, but do not get far, encountering first the opposition of lobbyists and second the citation of Vermont's experience. Vermont voted a four-year ban on nonreturnable glass beverage containers in 1953 but repealed the ban after one year of enforcement when it was realized that the ban only boosted sales of the exempted no-return containers—e.g., cans—and did not appreciably diminish the litter problem over-all.

In 1971, conservation officials, including William D. Ruckelshaus of the Environmental Protection Agency, were telling of a federally aided program in California to test the public on returnable bottles. Preliminary reports showed the program not going well. Even with a high deposit of 11 cents a bottle, bottles were not being returned; the heavier experimental bottle was allegedly adding more to the solid waste burden, as the bottle was more durable; finally, the 11-cent deposit had reportedly activated counterfeiters who were manufacturing bottles merely to collect deposit returns. The program study was

[10] In February 1971, the Coca-Cola Bottling Company of New York announced that it would open collection points at seventeen locations in the metropolitan area, and pay one-half cent a bottle or can, regardless of brand, for glass bottles and aluminum cans, and five cents on returnable Coke bottles.

to be completed in February 1972. Then it would not be ready until April. At last, the Environmental Protection Agency's deputy assistant administrator, Samuel Hale, Jr., wrote to *The New York Times:* the experiment never existed. "From all indications," Mr. Hale said, "it appears that erroneous information was received on this matter from somewhere within the agency." Mr. Ruckelshaus, he said, had mistaken a conversation about the possibility of bottle counterfeiting and "had apparently seized on some information and taken it way further than was true." *The New York Times* publicized the Hale letter in its February 5, 1972, issue, page 14. The Hale explanation was received cynically by environmentalists, who have believed right along that the government's enthusiasm has been deficient on the returnable-bottle issue, Mrs. Knauer's previously cited concern notwithstanding.

So how then do you keep glass containers out of open dumping areas, where the glass becomes almost as permanent as stone, and out of municipal incinerators, where it can cause real damage by liquefying and depositing on incinerator wall and floor, forming a bond with the firebrick greater than the adhesion of the brick itself? The key is with the consumer. If the consumer forgot about convenience and dealt in two-way bottles, the waste glass problem would be fractioned immediately.[11] The consumer would be making a concrete contribution ecologically; he would also be realizing an economy. For products in returnable bottles are cheaper. Coca-Cola costs 0.85 cents/fluid ounce in 16-ounce deposit bottles, 1.02 cents/ounce in 16-ounce one-way bottles and 1.36 cents/ounce in 12-ounce aluminum cans.[12]

A major consumer education effort is necessary, however, in order to bring the public back to returnable bottles. The nonreturnable container had so completely converted the public by 1971 that studies showed people throwing away returnable bottles just as much as they were disposable bottles.

Metal Cans

Ecologists who warn that America stands in danger of burying itself in tin cans may be speaking in hyperbole, but only relatively so. Americans purchase and consume the contents of 131 million cans a day. The average American family uses 850 cans a year; the average American, 252 cans a year.

[11] *Ecotactics: The Sierra Club Handbook for Environmental Activists* recommends that consumers save six-packs of empty one-way containers and ship them back to the board of directors of the company that manufactured the product, telling them they are tired of "no-deposit, no-return" bottles. (Edited by John G. Mitchell with Constance L. Stallings; Pocket Books, 1970).

[12] "What Can I Do?" Rodale Press, Inc., Emmaus, Pennsylvania 18049

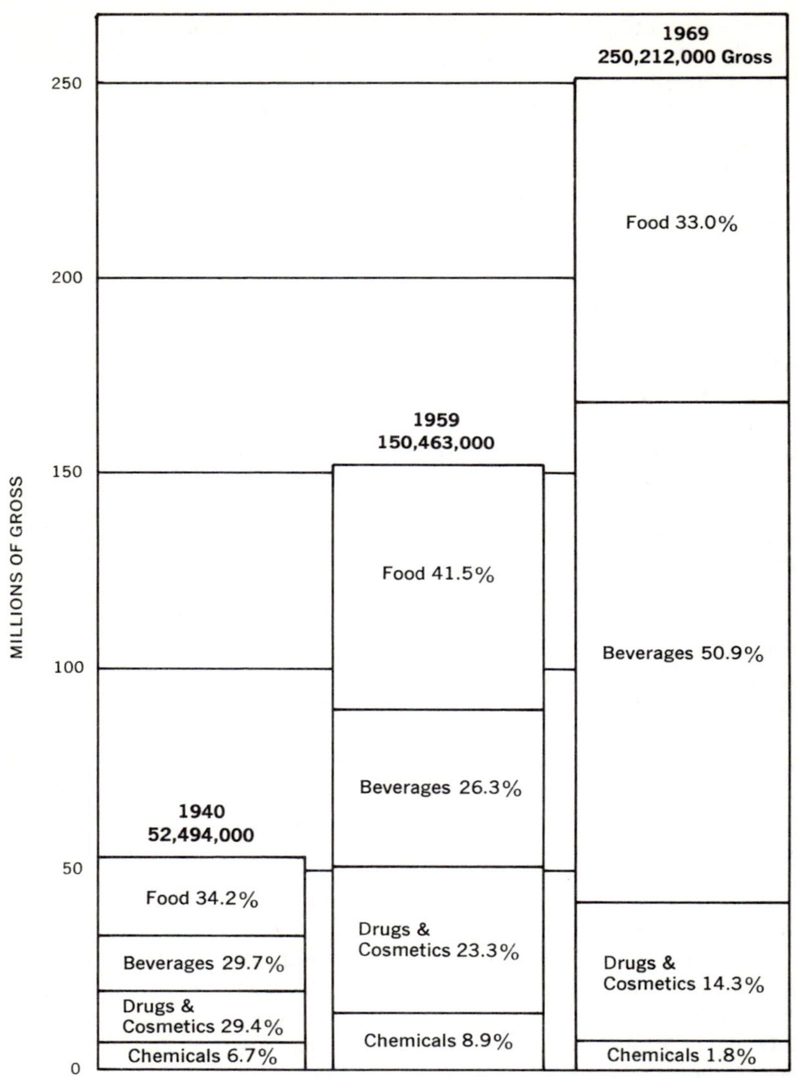

FIGURE 8-2. End-Use Categories in the Manufacture of Glass Containers for the Years 1940, 1959 and 1969

Source: U. S. Department of Commerce

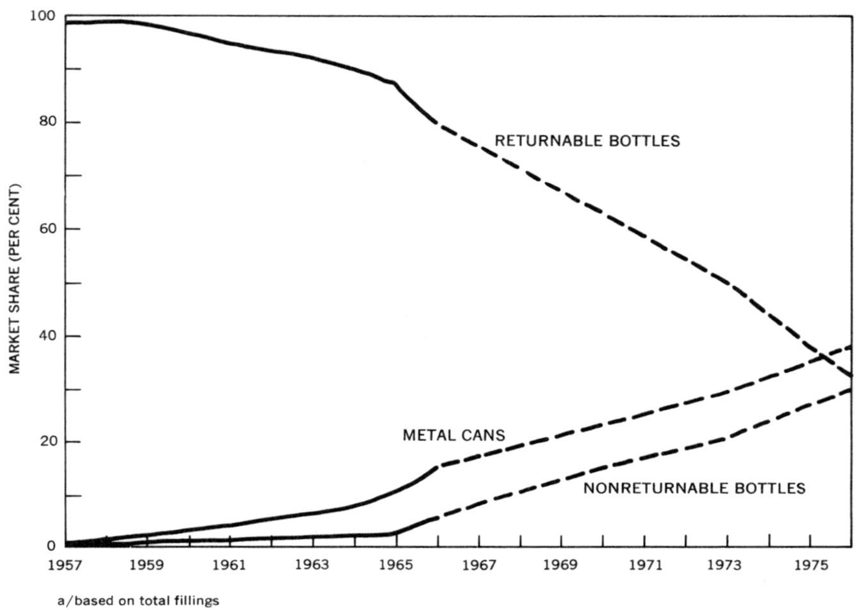

FIGURE 8-3. Trend in Distribution of Soft Drinks, 1957–76

Source: Midwest Research Institute

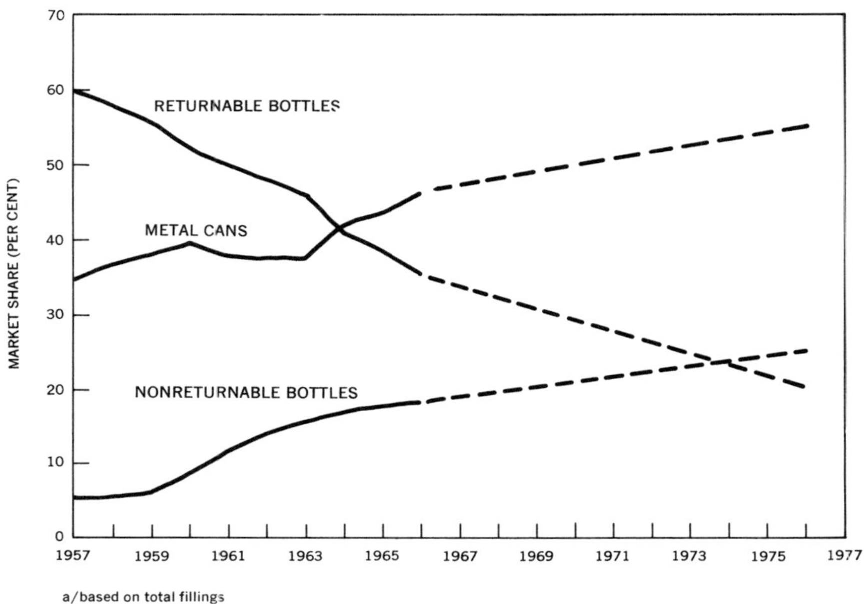

FIGURE 8-4. Trend in Distribution of Beer, 1957–76

Source: Midwest Research Institute

Metal cans are utilized by 135 industries for the marketing of 2,500 products. Food and beverages account for the bulk of the cans—84 percent. Beer accounts for the largest percentage, claiming 21 percent of the total metal cans manufactured in 1968. Vegetables and vegetable juices added to 16.8 percent. Soft drinks, which ten years ago took only 1 percent of the metal can total, had risen by 1968 to 13.7 percent of the total. The remainder of the can output is used for packaging meat, fish, coffee, oil, antifreeze, etc.

Metal cans come in all shapes and sizes, and eat up enormous quantities of valuable raw materials. In 1966, 10.35 billion pounds of steel went into the making of metal cans, and 0.33 billion pounds of aluminum. By 1976, these totals will grow to 11.42 billion pounds of steel and 1.40 billion pounds of aluminum. In units, this translates to an increase from 54.4 billion cans in 1966 to 78.3 billion cans in 1976. (Table 8-8; Figures 8-3, 8-4)

As things stand now, virtually all of this metal will end as solid waste refuse. The steel can (commonly called the "tin can") is one of the lowest forms of metallurgical life and of minimal salvage value; it attracts only the manufacturer of cheap metallic goods, such as window-sash weights and ballast. Aluminum can be readily recycled, but the aluminum scrap markets are limited and the prices which aluminum scrap bring are not yet such as to make the metal economically alluring as an item of scrap. Through 1976, analysts project a recovery rate of only 5 percent of aluminum packaging waste, and that projection is predicated on the most optimistic of estimates.

Thus the metal can will continue to be a vexing solid waste problem. It now comprises about 15 percent of the solid waste tonnage of packaging materials, a percentage likely to remain constant for the years immediately ahead. These cans will rust, corrode and eventually decompose, but the process is a slow one and amounts to little when the waste-can deposit is being endlessly renewed.

Can the consumer do anything to help alleviate the problem? Yes, he can:

Pressure for the Marketing of a Tin-Free Steel Can: Without tin, a steel can would become acceptable for scrap iron bundles. The tin content of the ordinary metal can is only about 0.5 percent of the weight of the can, but this amount suffices to void the can as a scrap commodity. (Tin, the intolerable impurity in salvaging metals, is employed in the first place to form a solder bond for the metal can; it serves no other purpose.) In recent years, industry has experimented with a tin-free can, primarily as a result of price fluctuations and political instabilities in Bolivia and Malaysia, the principal source locations of tin.[13] A tin-free can has actually been developed, but it accounts for less than 10 percent of all steel cans in production. By 1976, the tin-tainted can will still claim more than 50 percent of a 78.3 billion can market.[14]

Salvage Aluminum Cans: Aluminum is a vital national resource, too precious really to be exploited as a tin-can substitute. On the other hand, the aluminum can is salvageable. Scrap aluminum brings $200 a ton, and depots for collecting this scrap are being established in many parts of the country.[15] If there is no scrap depot as yet in one's area, the aluminum cans can be flattened and stored until such time as there is one. Clean and dry before storing. The aluminum can is easily identified. Many will say "all-aluminum" somewhere on the can; if not, the aluminum can is recognized by its smooth, seamless sides and rounded bottom. It will not hold a magnet. (Do not be fooled by some "flip-top" cans that say "aluminum" on top. This may refer only to the lid of the can; it may not mean that the can is all aluminum.)

Flatten All Tin Cans before Throwing Them Away: This will substantially reduce the volume of trash in dumps. Nearly 98 percent of the space taken up by uncompacted empty cans is space within and between the cans.

Resist Purchasing by Cans: When there is a choice, for instance, between soft drinks in cans and in returnable bottles, select the returnable bottle. When there is a choice between canned food and fresh food, select the fresh food. It will be tastier and likely be better value for the money, even out of season.

Bypass Aerosol Cans: The aerosol container is convenient, but its

[13]Bureau of Mines statistics for 1968 place domestic consumption of tin for that year for the manufacturing of tinplate at 32,280 short tons. This was a reduction of about 5 percent from 1967's figure of 33,000 short tons.

[14]Arsen Darnay and William E. Franklin of the Midwest Research Institute, Kansas City, Missouri, have suggested that government spur commercialization of a tin-free steel can by stipulating that that after a certain date canned goods purchased by the government must be in tin-free cans, or that tin-free cans will be given preference in competitive bidding for contracts. Federal spending on packaging materials for 1966 alone was in excess of $1 billion.

[15]The principal promoter of aluminum scrap is Reynolds Aluminum. After experimenting in salvaging used aluminum cans in Miami and Los Angeles, and being pleased with the results, Reynolds has expanded its salvage effort to 16 states. It has formed a working arrangement with Adolph Coors Co. of Colorado to help reclaim that firm's used aluminum beer cans in Arizona, Colorado, New Mexico, Wyoming, Utah, Nevada, Kansas, Oklahoma, Texas and California. In April 1971, Reynolds announced an arrangement with Mobil Oil Company for the collection of aluminum scrap in the New York-New Jersey area. Reynolds is urging Boy Scouts, hospital charity groups and other organizations to raise funds by collecting and returning aluminum scrap. For details: Reynolds Metals Company, P.O. Box 2346-LK, Richmond, Virginia 23218.

TABLE 8-8. Number of Cans Consumed by End Use: 1958 to 1976

(Millions of cans)

End use	1958	1959	1960	1961	1962	1963	1964	1965	1966	1970	1973	1976	1966 to 1976 rate of change (percent)
Food—beverage:													
Fruit and fruit juices, vegetable and vegetable juices	14,582	14,340	14,262	14,248	15,560	13,817	14,267	14,345	14,434	14,960	15,370	15,790	0.9
Evaporated milk and other dairy products	3,002	2,937	2,569	2,585	2,439	2,229	2,248	2,199	2,257	2,000	1,820	1,670	−3.0
Meat and poultry, fish and seafood	2,854	2,851	2,957	3,089	3,206	3,153	3,203	3,143	3,268	3,470	3,630	3,790	1.5
Lard and shortening	306	299	331	396	413	339	339	347	335	280	250	220	−4.1
Baby food and formulae, all other foods	4,818	4,937	6,394	6,477	6,525	6,558	6,939	5,664	5,870	6,480	6,980	7,520	2.5
Total foods	25,562	25,364	26,513	26,795	28,143	26,096	26,996	25,698	26,164	27,190	28,050	28,990	1.0
Coffee	939	993	993	1,053	1,054	1,130	1,042	1,044	998	940	900	860	−1.5
Beer	8,337	9,156	8,888	8,761	9,075	9,324	10,896	11,382	12,947	15,100	16,930	19,000	3.9
Soft drinks	409	548	812	1,225	1,651	2,058	2,795	3,841	5,612	9,000	12,300	17,000	11.7
Total beverages	9,685	10,697	10,693	11,039	11,780	12,512	14,733	16,267	19,557	25,040	30,130	36,860	6.5
Pet food	1,968	2,051	2,136	2,131	2,216	2,202	2,301	2,551	2,740	3,160	3,510	3,900	3.6
Pressure packing			743	786	1,042	1,000	1,220	1,577	1,580	1,810	2,300	2,700	5.5
Nonfood:													
Oil	1,575	1,693	1,429	1,507	1,576	1,080	866	856	873	1,070	1,240	1,510	5.6
All other nonfood	4,500	4,869	2,859	3,334	3,404	3,013	3,008	3,515	3,522	3,940	4,070	4,310	2.0
Total metal cans	43,290	44,674	44,373	45,592	48,161	45,903	49,124	50,464	54,436	62,210	69,300	78,270	3.7

Source: Can Manufacturers Institute. Annual Report, Metal Can Shipments—1966. Washington, D.C., 1967. Forecasts by Midwest Research Institute. Public Health Service Publication 1855.

added parts—valve, dispenser spout, actuator device, etc.—complicate salvage possibilities immeasurably. Besides, the price of a product in an aerosol can is considerably higher than the same product in another container.

Use Aluminum Foil Sparingly. This "semi-rigid" container is popular and effective for numerous kitchen duties; in thickness above 0.001 inch it is almost totally impermeable. But because it is an alloy it has no salvage value. It also resists decomposition.

Plastics

No American industry came more completely into its own in the 1960s than plastics. As one official pointed out: "The completion of the Houston astrodome in plastics from top (sheathed in acrylic) to bottom (the playing field is carpeted with grass-like fiber of nylon) convinced the skeptics that there is more to plastics than a cheap toy."[16] With increasing usages in home and school, in automobiles and sea and air travel and in medical procedures, industry is predicting a production output by the mid-1980s of $75 billion—larger than steel, petroleum or textiles.

A major part of the plastics business—and the part which more directly affects the environment since it ends as solid waste—is packaging. Plastics have moved from a relatively insignificant 736 million pounds for packaging applications in 1958 to 2.5 billion pounds in 1967. By 1980, an 8 billion pound total is foreseen. Tonnage, however, is not the full measure of plastics' strength. Plastics represented but 2.4 percent of the poundage of the 1966 packaging market, but in dollars this translated to 10 percent of the business. (Figure 8-5)

Most of the major varieties of plastics are made from ethylene, a prolific petroleum raw material. Ethylene is the base for polyethylene, polyvinyl chloride and polystyrene, the three so-called "workhorse" plastics. These reach the household as flexible or rigid bottles, molded containers, garment bags, etc. By 1980, 1.5 billion pounds of plastics will go into the production of bottles alone. They will be one-way containers. (Table 8-9)

The trouble with plastics in the waste context is that they do not decompose. Neither do they incinerate satisfactorily. Darnay and Franklin note the problem of plastics at low-temperature points in an incinerator: the plastics melt, flow down to the grates and there, coming in contact with cool air entering the burner, solidify again, clogging

[16]E. Eugene Winne, vice-president of plastics and fibers, Enjay Chemical Company, in *Enjay Magazine.* Reprinted by The Society of the Plastics Industry, Inc., New York. Undated.

the grates.[17] And several sources warn of harmful effects to the individual from the burning of plastics. Polystyrene gives off carbon monoxide and carbon black; polyvinyl chloride emits hydrogen chloride.[18]

Under pressure from the public, the plastics industry underwrote in February 1970 an $82,800 research project at New York University designed to pinpoint the effect of burning plastics on incinerator systems and the general environment. But the industry's basic impulse is still to lean strongly on a 1967 industry-sponsored study, which claimed there was "no quantitative evidence of [solid waste] problems uniquely assignable to the presence of plastics."[19] Three months after voting the NYU study it began putting together a $300,000 fund, one purpose of which is "to combat increasing irresponsible or uninformed criticism of the industry as a polluter."[20]

One of industry's big worries seems to be legislation regulating plastic products. It has opposed state bills, such as that in California which would require the affixing of a warning label on polyvinyl chloride containers, reading: "Do not burn this container. Fumes are extremely hazardous to human beings." And it lobbied in Illinois against a bill placing restrictions on plastic containers. The plastics industry usually finds such bills arbitrary, discriminatory and of limited effectiveness with regard to over-all purpose.

Plastic waste, meanwhile, piles on the landscape. By 1976 it will comprise an estimated 4.82 percent of the total tonnage of solid waste attributable to packaging, although here, too, tonnage is not an absolute measure, for the light weight of plastics means greater bulk in the waste heap.

Several cautions are in order:

Plastics Should Not Be Burned Indiscriminately: Whatever industry's claims about the burn-offs from plastics being of no appreciable danger, burning plastics can still emit gases injurious to respiratory systems and thus to health generally.

Plastics Should Not Be Consigned Indiscriminately to Municipal Incinerators: Many incinerators are ill-equipped to burn properly some new forms of refuse, including plastics. Consumers should inform

[17] Public Health Service Publication No. 1855.

[18] Industry itself concedes that noxious gases result from the burning of plastics, but maintains that they are minor compared to the burning of coal, auto exhausts and metal treating.

[19] Prepared for The Society of the Plastics Industry, Inc., by Battelle Memorial Institute.

[20] *Plastics and the Environment,* newsletter of The Society of the Plastics Industry; May 18, 1970.

TABLE 8-9. Consumption of Plastics by End Use: 1958 to 1976

(In millions of pounds)

End use	1958	1959	1960	1961	1962	1963	1964	1965	1966	1970	1973	1976
Rigid and semi-rigid:												
Bottles	23	32	65	125	175	195	227	270	304	730	1,150	1,700
Tubes					([a])	3	3	10	15	30	35	40
Formed and molded	61	73	120	140	175	213	288	375	478	800	1,000	1,400
Closures	22	22	22	53	58	65	66	72	85	120	160	210
Total	106	127	207	318	408	456	584	727	882	1,680	2,345	3,350
Film: [aa]												
Polyethylene film	175	247	280	340	380	440	500	615	730	1,280	1,610	2,030
Other plastic film	52	54	57	65	84	104	116	133	192	300	400	560
Total	227	301	337	405	464	544	616	748	922	1,580	2,010	2,590
Plastics total	333	428	544	723	872	1,000	1,200	1,475	1,804	3,260	4,355	5,940

[a] Not available.

[aa] Cellophane poundage not included, as cellophane is not a plastic in the conventional use of the term.

Source: Modern Packaging Encyclopedia. William C. Simms, ed. Vol. 40, No. 13A. New York, McGraw-Hill, Inc., September 1967. 879 p. Modern Plastics, 45(5): 93–94, January 1968. Midwest Research Institute. Public Health Service Publication No. 1855 (op. cit.).

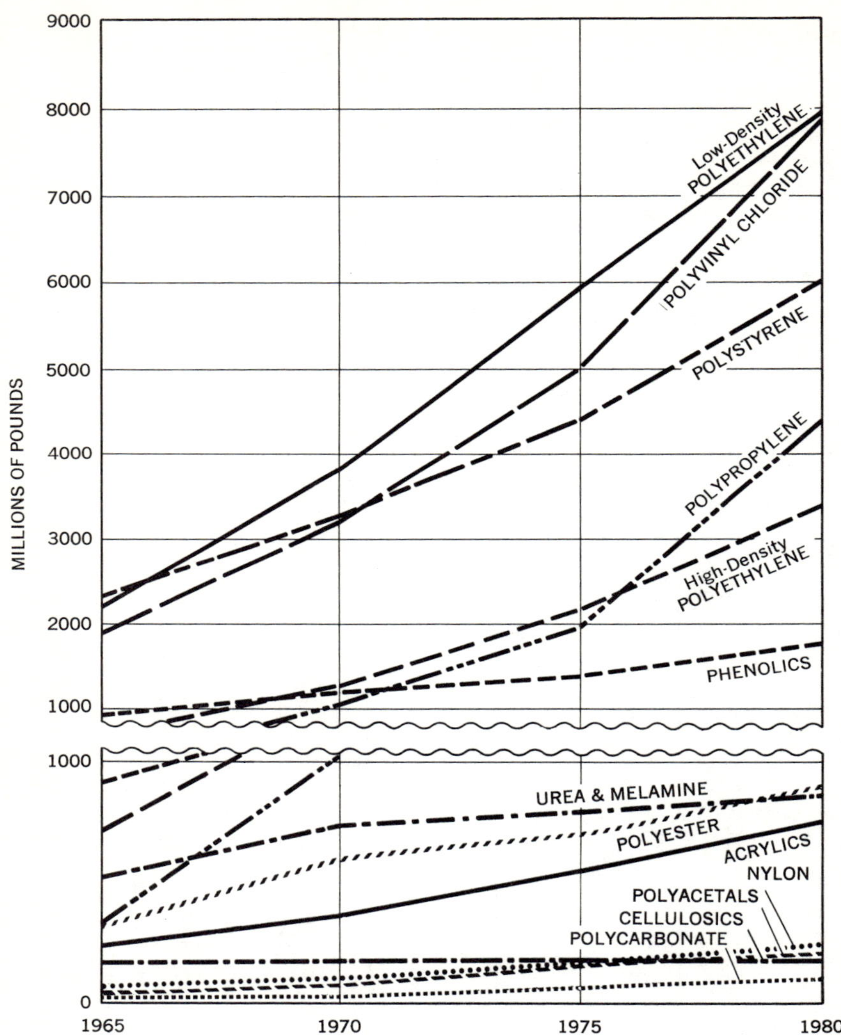

FIGURE 8-5. Plastics—Where They Are Headed

Source: Plastics: A 15 Year Outlook. A Modern Plastics Presentation, Spring 1968, McGraw-Hill

themselves about the capabilities of their local waste disposal system before consigning large quantities of waste plastic to it.

Products in Plastic Containers Should Be Bought Warily: An Evansville, Indiana, housewife was instrumental in persuading two supermarkets to return to the sale of eggs in cardboard boxes instead of in styrofoam containers. She acted after hearing of the "ill effects of burning polystyrene." Styrofoam is a polystyrene by-product.

Textiles

Modern packaging's two main trends—toward the "unit-of-use" size item and the disposable container—have cut into no material so markedly as the burlap bag and the cotton sack, once very common containers. As late as 1959, some 945 million yards of textiles were going into sacks and bags, carrying to the consumer such goods as flour, feed, potatoes, seeds, rice, beans, etc.; today sack and bulk packaging are as outmoded as the neighborhood grocer who reached into a fifty-pound burlap bag to weigh out a peck of potatoes for the housewife. By 1976, only 480 million yards of textiles will be used for packaging. Indeed, production would be closer than it is now to that figure were it not for Vietnam. The manufacture of sandbags for the war in that unhappy land slowed, at least momentarily, production declines in the textile-packaging industry.[21]

Nothing is going to save the textile container, however. Its fate is sealed by the cardboard box, by plastic bags and by heavy-duty paper, all of which combine economy and strength with handling convenience. Nevertheless, one sees the textile container disappear with a certain regret, for all the substitutes are one-way, one-time-use packages and thus contribute measurably to the waste load. The burlap bag, in its day, had a commercial reusability of a dozen times, and the cotton sack had valuable secondary usage as yard goods for the making of dish towels and other cloths. But, again, that was yesterday.

Paper

One ton of recycled waste paper is the sparing of seventeen trees; the recycling of 11.5 million tons—industry's figure for the paper recycled in 1969[22]—is the sparing of almost 200 million trees, a veritable forest.

[21] Darnay and Franklin note that sandbags rose from 0.5 percent of the textile packaging market in 1964 to 5.7 percent in 1965, to 9.9 percent in 1966. (Public Health Service Publication No. 1855.)

[22] Edwin A. Locke, Jr., president of the American Paper Institute before the Subcommittee on Air and Water Pollution, Senate Committee on Public Works, February 26, 1970.

Impressive as the figures are, however, they are fractional in terms of paper's demands on woodlands and paper's subsequent load on the environment. For 80 percent of the millions of tons of paper produced annually in the United States ends up being buried, burned or dumped on a waste heap, lost along with the millions of trees from which the paper is made. Less than 20 percent is utilized as secondary fiber in the production of new paper and paperboard. Japan, by comparison, reclaims and reprocesses nearly half its paper.[23]

The impulse is to think of paper primarily in the context of newspapers, perhaps because newsprint is in everyone's hands daily and seems forever to be accumulating around the house. Large as it is, newsprint is still only a small percentage of the paper industry itself; it comprised 3.3 million of 1970's 52.3 million-ton production. Half of the paper manufactured in the United States goes into packaging, and this half accounts in turn for some 55 percent of all the nation's packaging. (Figures 8-6, 8-7)

Everything from hat boxes to the sandwich bag is part of the paper industry and, ultimately, part of the waste problem. The average American uses 576 pounds of paper a year. Whether he litters it or disposes of it carefully, it causes difficulties.[24]

Paper has certain ecological advantages. It is biodegradable, combustible and, as noted, can be recycled. On the other hand, paper consumes a precious natural resource, wood—and the forests of the world are not endless, or forever renewable. Likewise, paper pollutes at multiple stages. Its manufacture pours sulphur oxides into the air and chemicals into the waters.[25] It constitutes nearly 60 percent of roadside litter, and it is 40 to 50 percent of mixed municipal refuse. Consigned as waste to incinerators, paper pollutes the air all over again. Waste-paper disposal costs are an estimated $900 million annually.

Industry is not oblivious to the environmental problems caused by

[23] *Environmental Quality,* first annual report of the Council on Environmental Quality, August 1970, p. 117.

[24] On April 1, 1971, a foundation dedicated to preserving trees urged Congress to pass lesislation banning the sale of "nonreturnable newspapers and magazines," and to provide incentives for recycling paper. Mrs. A. S. Hawthorn, president of the Sylvan Foundation, explained: "We urge such legislation to save millions of trees annually, substantially ease the growing problem of solid waste disposal, and force the print media to do something more about pollution than just write about it." The Foundation pointed out that a single issue of the Sunday *New York Times* weighs some five pounds, and that one Sunday's printing run of the paper consumes an estimated 68,000 trees—the equivalent of 425 acres of timberland.

[25] The Government's first victory against mercury pollution was in August 1970, and involved the Oxford Paper Company division of the Ethyl Corporation. Its plant was polluting the Androscoggin River at Rumford, Maine.

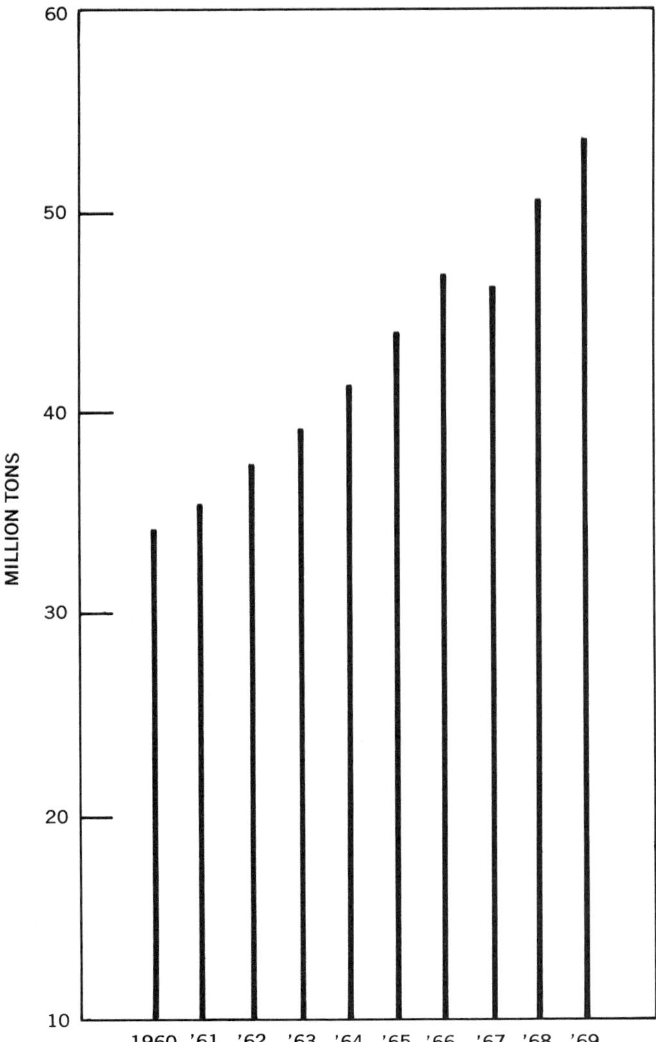

FIGURE 8-6. Total Paper and Paperboard Production, 1960–69

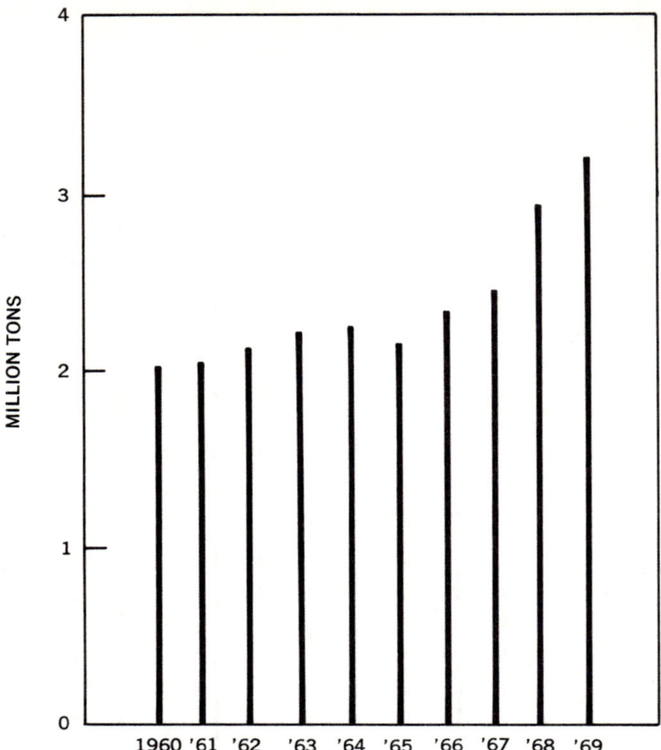

FIGURE 8-7. Newsprint Production, 1960–69

Source: How the American Paper Industry Performed in 1969, prepared by the American Paper Institute, New York, New York

paper, and in 1969 invested over $100 million in water-quality control facilities and another $30 million for air-quality equipment. By 1975, it will be $450 million (Figure 8-8). The industry is also encouraging salvage programs, and proud of the fact that the tonnage of recycled paper rises year by year. What is not always volunteered, however, is the detail that this tonnage is not apace with increases in production of whole new paper. In 1946, waste paper accounted for 35 percent of the paper market. By 1980, there will be a decrease to 17 percent.

The downward spiral in paper salvage is attributable to a number of factors. The coating of vast amounts of paper stock with wax-plastic combinations and other adhesives, for milk cartons, display boards, etc., contaminates that paper beyond possibility of reuse. At the same

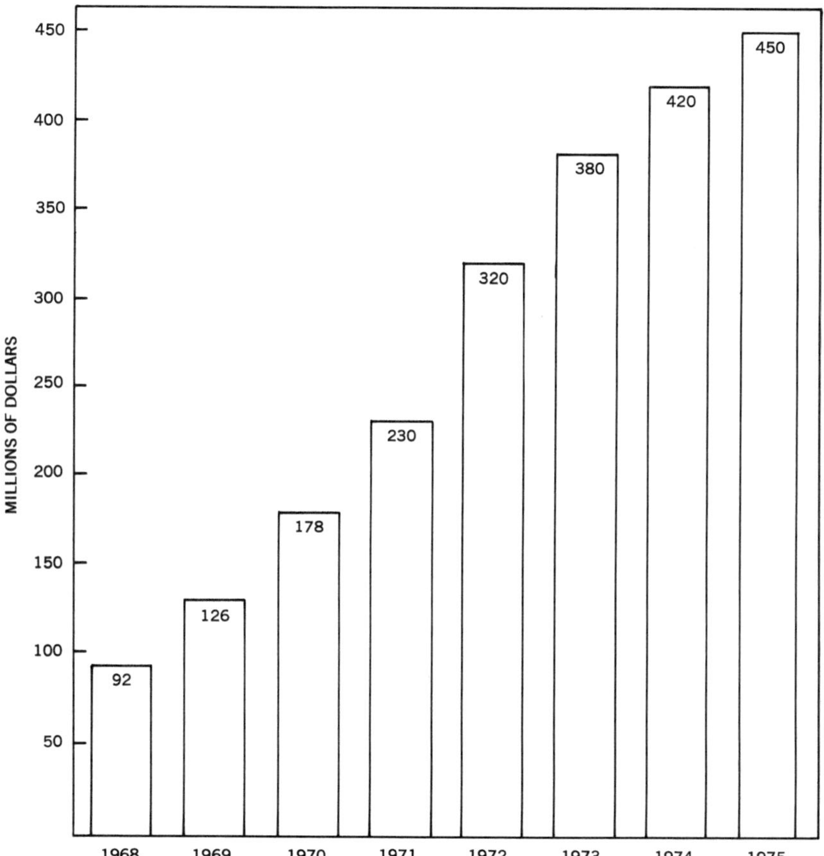

FIGURE 8-8. The Paper Industry's Capital Expenditures for Air and Water Pollution Control (expressed in millions of dollars)

Source: American Paper Institute

time, a large part of the profit has gone out of the salvage market. Old newspapers and corrugated boxes are easily recycled, but suburban sprawl and cartage costs have added to collection difficulties and cut margins for gain. Rounding up old paper was once a favorite and profitable activity for Boy Scouts and charity volunteers, but that was when Western Union still had messenger service.

The waste market is off, but some believe it is not entirely lost. If waste paper were sorted and graded at the generation source—in the household, notably—much more paper could be salvaged conveniently and economically. Madison, Wisconsin, believes so, and is promoting a citizen-participation project in connection with old newspapers. Individuals are asked to separate newspapers from trash, tie the papers into bundles and place them on the street curb. The bundles are then picked up, placed in bins built onto the sides of sanitation trucks and moved for recycling.

The success of the Madison project has not been fully determined. Even so, the practice of separating newspapers from trash and garbage is advisable. Many sanitation departments deal in waste newsprint, but newspapers that enter a compactor truck or are mixed with garbage are worthless because of contamination. Old newspapers should be separated at the source, if the only purpose served is to brighten the prospect of salvage.

Wood

Another of the major elements of the packaging market is wood, a material with extensive usages in agriculture and industry. Wood containers move the heaviest and lightest of items, from machinery, automobile parts and furniture on the one hand to berries, poultry and vegetables on the other. They account for only about 5 percent of the trade, but in weight this translates to more than 8 billion pounds of wood packaging a year.

It is not a growing business, however. Plastics and paperboard have made heavy inroads, leaving the wood container with a very modest 1970–76 growth projection—from 8.39 billion pounds to 8.84 billion.

The wood container has low-cost and high-strength qualities, and one more definite advantage: it is reusable and, in the case of many containers, repairable. Wooden boxes invariably have several cycles before being discarded. Nevertheless, they enter the waste stream in almost the same weight volume as their production, a detail which points up the fact that the most adaptable of possibilities in salvage and recycling can be counterbalanced by standing consumer demands.

3. THE MOST SOLID WASTE OF ALL: AUTOMOBILES

The automobile has brought many blessings to modern man, but the blessings are mixed at best. For the automobile is (1) an insatiable consumer of natural resources, (2) a prime polluter of the air and (3) one of the nation's most conspicuous solid waste problems.

(1) *Resources*
The automobile gobbles up:

—60 percent of all rubber used in the United States
—10 percent of all aluminum
—20 percent of all steel
— 7 percent of all copper
—13 percent of all nickel
—35 percent of all zinc
—50 percent of all lead

Many of these resources are in short supply; some are available only from Third World countries, where supplies are neither limitless nor renewable nor, given political antipathies toward the United States, forever exploitable.

In addition, the average uncontrolled car takes in 4,500 pounds of fuel a year and 60,000 pounds of air—much of which it gives back to the atmosphere in the form of pollution.

(2) *Air Pollution*
The automobile accounts for:

—60 percent of all air pollution in the United States (in some urban areas, air pollution from automobiles rises as high as 85 percent)
—91 percent of all carbon monoxide in the air
—63 percent of unburned hydrocarbons
—48 percent of nitrogen oxides
— 8 percent of particulate matter
— 4 percent of sulphur oxides

In tonnage, this residue weighs at 90 million tons a year.

(3) *Solid Waste*
There are in the United States more than 100 million registered vehicles.[26] No less than 9 million are retired from use each year. Most enter one or another of the nation's 33,000 auto-wrecking yards, but nowhere near all. Many are abandoned—2,500, on the average, per day; almost 1 million a year.

Abandoned or processed, the old automobile is a mighty waste problem. Those that are abandoned disfigure the landscape, clutter streets, make eyesores of empty lots; if arranged side by side, abandoned cars would cover six acres of land each new day. The Depart-

[26]The Department of Transportation estimated the number of registered vehicles in the United States by the end of 1970 as 108,977,000.

ment of Health, Education and Welfare estimates that from 12 to 20 million abandoned cars have accumulated during the last ten years.[27] Those cars which enter auto-wrecking yards are salvaged for parts, but only a small percentage is cycled for scrap. The explanation is a simple one: profit is marginal. It takes $51 worth of processing to retrieve $56 worth of scrap, a $5 profit which disappears if the car has already been relieved of its more valuable parts, such as its radiator, engine or transmission.

In addition, to accommodate its automobiles, the United States has paved over 3.71-million miles of good land as streets and roads, and the end is nowhere in sight. New roads are laid out daily. The Interstate Highway System, for instance, is adding upwards of 42,000 miles to the total. Before it is all over the quip which a Harvard savant made about the proclivities of a Secretary of Transportation may have come to pass: the United States will be black-topped from the Atlantic to the Pacific.

The automobile being a multiple pollutant, elimination of the negative by-effects requires a multiple approach. Numerous schemes have been proposed, and a few programs—such as the development of a nearly pollution-free car engine by 1977—are actually in motion. The programs are, however, invariably less than what environmentalists deem necessary.

What precisely do the environmentalists want with respect to the automobile?

Environmental Action, a Washington-based agency, outlined standards applying to pollution of the air in a letter to congressional legislators dated July 9, 1970[28]:

"—Drastically reduce pollution from automobiles to the much lower emission levels that can be achieved through alternatives to the internal combustion engine;[29]

[27] *The New York Times,* October 12, 1970.

[28] Co-signed by Denis Hayes, national coordinator, Environmental Action; Gary A. Soucie, executive director, Friends of the Earth; International Union of United Auto Workers; Cynthia Wilson, Washington representative, The National Audubon Society; Michael McCloskey, conservation director, Sierra Club; Stewart M. Brandborg, executive director, The Wilderness Society; Dr. Eugene Cohen, political director, Zero Population Growth.

[29] On December 16, 1970, the Senate and House completed a bill to eliminate nearly all pollution from car engines by 1977. The deadlines are 1975 for hydrocarbons and carbon monoxide; 1976 for nitrogen oxides, with a one-year extension, if necessary. Appropriations of $1.1 billion over three years were voted to finance administration of the bill's provisions and research projects. President Nixon signed the measure December 31, 1970.

"—Begin Federal testing of automobiles on the production line and on the road to ensure that the buyer gets a car which complies with anti-pollution regulations. Testing procedures must be more realistic than they are now; auto makers must warrant that devices will operate, as they are supposed to, for a minimum of 50,000 miles; and manufacturers should be required, if devices prove defective, to recall and repair them at no cost to the owner;

"—Empower the Department of Health, Education and Welfare to regulate oxides of nitrogen—a key element of smog—by 1973 instead of 1975 as now planned[30], and to ban dangerous fuel additives;

"—Require manufacturers to install, at no cost to customers, pollution-control devices on used cars;

"—Empower HEW to permit states with special air pollution problems to set automotive standards that are more stringent than the Federal regulations;

"—Require government agencies and owners of large fleets to purchase autos . . . which operate on lead-free gasoline;[31]

"—Require HEW to investigate immediately the availability of low-polluting fuels;[32]

"—Permit citizens to bring suit—either as individuals or as a class—to redress rights under the new air pollution laws;

"—Increase the budget of the National Air Pollution Control Administration to enable it to enforce the new laws effectively;

"—Simplify and shorten the process of judicial review of administrative decisions under the new law, in line with standard practices in administrative law."

The matter of automobile disposal and salvage, seemingly elementary on paper, becomes exceedingly complex when the problem of developing a master plan arises. President Nixon in his February 10, 1970, message on the environment asked the Council on Environmental Quality to take the lead in recommending a bounty payment or some other system to promote the prompt scrapping of all junk

[30] The date decided on in Congress was 1976, with a final deadline of January 1, 1977.

[31] President Nixon on October 26, 1970, ordered that all Federal vehicles must be operated on low-lead or unleaded gasoline, wherever practical, and he asked the governors of all states to adopt similar policy for state-owned vehicles. The Federal government operates some 600,000 cars throughout the country and buys .05 percent of all the gasoline purchased in the United States, or 905 million gallons a year. Then, on February 22, 1972, the Environmental Protection Agency proposed to require the sale of unleaded low-octane gasoline at most of the nation's gas stations by 1974.

[32] On December 30, 1970, the Federal Trade Commission issued a regulation requiring the posting of octane ratings on gasoline pumps in most of the country's gas stations. Gasolines which are either too high or too low in octane rating for a particular car create excessive emissions.

automobiles. The Council was not much help. In its first report, transmitted to Congress in August 1970, the Council argued that bounty payment, including one funded by a tax on the sale of automobiles, would work an "unfair burden" on the owners of the 85 percent of automobiles that are properly turned over to wreckers. Furthermore, the Council said it was "not persuaded that the demand for auto scrap would be improved by such a system, nor that it would in fact influence the economies affecting abandonment. The resulting fund of payments would divert billions of dollars from other investments in the private economy. Administration and enforcement of the system would require excessive increases in government personnel and expenditures."[33] The best the Council could recommend were firm penalties against abandonment of cars, and improvement of state title and transfer laws, particularly for cars of low value.

More helpful, though vaguer than some would like, is a model act proposed by Calvin Lieberman, second vice-president of the Institute of Scrap Iron and Steel, at a national conference on the abandoned automobile held March 31, 1970.[34] Lieberman holds that the problem of the abandoned auto must be attacked at three levels—Federal, state and local. These would be the respective responsibilities:

Federal: to encourage the states to adopt uniform and workable legislation; to provide for a continual and increasing usage of scrap iron resulting from the abandoned auto; to see that there are adequate railroad facilities for movement of scrap iron at reasonable freight rates; to insure financial aid to the states for the movement of vehicles to the processors.

States: eliminate roadblocks to prompt recycling of automobiles through (a) the removal of all title requirements, and (b) the removal of any form of storage requirement; to assume or cause local entities to assume the cost of moving the automobile to the processor, when necessary.

Local: to legislate against the abandonment of automobiles on private property, even when abandonment occurs with the property owner's permission (leaving to state and Federal authorities the problem of autos abandoned on public property); to recognize the need and promote scrap-processing operations in the community.

Mr. Lieberman's "Model Act" would read as follows:

> It is the intention of this Act to provide for the orderly, economic and prompt recycling of old vehicles without any impediments that would arise from storage or rehandling requirements of any kind.

[33] *Environmental Quality,* the first annual report of the Council on Environmental Quality; August 1970, page 116.

[34] proceedings available from the Institute of Scrap Iron and Steel, Inc., 1729 H Street, N.W., Washington, D.C., 20006.

To mitigate the impact on society of solid waste and to implement the Beautification Act of 1965 (Federal), this Act recognizes that there is no substantial security interest of any prior owner which is served by requiring the present holder of such a vehicle to produce a title certificate or to notify lien holders and the last owner when a vehicle of this character is only to be sold to a demolisher.

It is also the intention of this Act to allow the utilization of Federal or State funds, if available, by a public authority so designated, to cover the expense that might arise from the public movement of such vehicles described herein.

Notwithstanding any other provisions of the code referring to motor vehicles, any vehicle, described in this Act may be moved from its place where located directly to an establishment having facilities for processing iron or steel scrap and whose principle product is scrap iron and steel for sale for remelting purposes, without the necessity of obtaining or transferring a title of any kind:

A motor vehicle which is discarded, abandoned or in a wrecked, dismantled or worn-out condition and unfit for operation as a motor vehicle, located on public or private property and not displaying a current registration plate or license.

Nothing herein shall be construed to apply to any vehicle in an enclosed building or vehicle or premsies of a business enterprise being operated in a lawful place and manner and the vehicle is necessary to the operation of such business enterprise.

The State may require reasonable records to be kept by the public authority initiating the movement of the vehicle; the owner of a storage facility for such vehicles; or the former owners of such vehicles; as to the description or identification numbers of the vehicles, provided that this information is readily obtained and the vehicle is in such condition that identification numbers are available, and that this requirement does not impede the physical movement of the vehicle to the processor.

The State may determine which public authority, in whose jurisdiction such vehicles are located prior to removal, shall have the duty and responsibility of examining any vehicle to determine whether it properly fits the description of such a vehicle described herein.

There remains, finally, the exploding automobile population—the problem basic to all issues deriving from the automobile. There is at present one vehicle for every 2.1 persons in the United States, and the figure narrows as more people drive and as the automobile industry more and more pushes the concept of the two- and three-car family. This translates to a further drain of precious natural resources; more noise (85 percent of urban noise is traced to internal combustion engines); more air pollution (at least until 1977 when car engines should be largely emission-free); more solid waste on the landscape (barring some miracle of salvage and recycling); more land disappearing (1 million acres of land are paved over for roads, on the average, each year).

What can the individual do to correct the situation? Several things. He can:

—Rely more heavily on public transportation;

—Cut down on unnecessary driving;

—Walk when walking is possible (in the San Francisco area, 83 percent of automobile trips are of less than fifteen minutes' duration); walking is also one of the most healthful of exercises;

—Form car pools (the average car load in the United States is only 1.2 persons);

—When using one's automobile, do not leave motor idling or running unnecessarily;

—Always use lead-free or pollution-reducing gasolines;

—Make your car last longer; stretch its life by trading it in at a longer interval than has been your custom hitherto;

—Make your second vehicle of transportation a bicycle.

The Abandoned-car Capital

The most graphic illustration of the problem of the abandoned automobile is provided by the city of New York. The number abandoned during 1970 was 72,961, an increase of 15,000 over the year before and thirty times the number abandoned just a decade ago. This is the way the problem has escalated:

TABLE 8-10. Abandoned Cars Towed Away

1960	2,500
1961	5,117
1962	6,299
1963	13,579
1964	23,386
1965	21,943
1966	23,795
1967	25,842
1968	31,578
1969	57,742
1970	72,961

Some abandoned cars are stolen vehicles, stripped of tires, chrome and valuable parts, and left to rust and rot in some street or alley. Many others, however, are cars which the owners wish to be rid of, and which have no junk value and might even cost money to have towed to a junkyard. The owner of such a car just removes the license plates and departs.

SELECTED BIBLIOGRAPHY

Alarie, A., "Can Garbage Become a 'National Asset'?" *Compost Science,* 8(1):3–7, Spring-Summer 1967.

Alexander, T., "Where Will We Put All That Garbage?" *Fortune,* October 1967.
Alexander Hamilton Institute, Inc., "Spring and Billions of Waiting Cans," *Business Conditions Weekly,* 1963.
Aluminum Association, The, *Aluminum Statistical Review,* 1966.
"Aluminum Cans Recoverable," *Science News,* 91(18):428, May 1967.
American Paper and Pulp Association, *Statistics of Paper,* 8th ed., 1964.
American Paper Institute, Inc., *The Statistics of Paper,* 1967 supplement.
American Public Works Association Research Foundation. *Rail Transport of Solid Wastes: A Feasibility Study,* interim report, phase one. U. S. Department of Health, Education and Welfare, 1969.
"Applying Technology to Unmet Needs: A Report on the Solid Waste Problem." Appendix Vol. 5. *In* National Commission on Technology, Automation, and Economic Progress. *Technology and the American Economy; Report of the Commission.* Washington, D.C. U. S. Government Printing Office, 1966, pp. V161–V174.
Armstrong, W. L., *tr.,* and Wiley, J. S., *ed.,* International Research Group on Refuse Disposal (IRGR). Information Bulletins Nos. 13 and 14, Washington, D.C., U. S. Government Printing Office.
Arthur, D. Little, Inc., *The Role of Packaging in the U. S. Economy; A Report to the American Foundation for Management Research, Inc.,* 1966.
Associated Cooperage Industries of America, The, Inc., *The Wooden Barrel Manual,* 22(1), September 1951.
"Back to Bags," *Modern Packaging,* 39(9):113–18, May 1966.
"Battle over Cans Stiffens," *Chemical Week,* 95(16):85–86, October 1964.
Bishop, W. D., Carter, R. C., and Ludwig, H. F., "Gas Movement in Land-Filled Rubbish," *Public Works,* 64–68, November 1965.
Bjornson, B. F., and Bogue, M. D., "Keeping a Sanitary Landfill Sanitary," *Public Works,* 92(9):112–14, September 1961.
Boettcher, R. A., "Air Classification for Reclamation Processing of Solid Wastes," ASME Paper No. 69-WA/PID-9. Presented at Winter Annual Meeting, American Society of Mechanical Engineers, Los Angeles, 1969.
Bogue, M. D., *Municipal Incineration,* Cincinnati, U. S. Department of Health, Education and Welfare, 1968.
Braun, R., "Reutilization of Solid Waste by Composting," *Secondary Raw Materials,* 41–42, November 1967.
Broyles, H. C., "'Papercans' Versus Metal Cans," *Current Municipal Problems,* 5(4):75–81, May 1964.
Burkinshaw, L. D., "Polycarbons for Packaging," *Modern Packaging,* 37(9):147–50, June 1964.
Busch, T. W., "Paper Coating Additives," *Tappi,* 49(6):34–38, June 1966.
"CSMA notes trend to large can sizes." *Printer's Ink,* 290:31, March 1965.
Capp, J. P., "Fly Ash Utilization," *Combustion,* 37(8):36–40, February 1966.
"The Car Is Anti-City," brochure of the Environmental Protection Administration, *et al.,* City of New York, February 1971.
"Car Junkyards Try Sophistication," *Business Week,* 108–12, February 26, 1966.
"Coatings for Paper," *Chemical and Engineering News,* 86–93, September 1963.
Committee on Solid Wastes, American Public Works Association, *Municipal Refuse Disposal,* 2nd ed., Chicago, Public Administration Service, 1966.
———, 3rd ed., Chicago, Public Administration Service, 1966.
"Copolymer Plastic Refuse-Can Liners . . . Trim 20 Percent Off Refuse Collection Time," *American City,* 81(6):100–1, June 1966.
Cummins, R. L., *Effects of Land Disposal of Solid Wastes on Water Quality,* Cincinnati, U. S. Department of Health, Education and Welfare, 1968.
Darnay, A., and Franklin, W. E., *The Role of Packaging in Solid Waste Management,*

1966–1976, Public Health Service Publication No. 1855. Washington, D.C. U. S. Government Printing Office, 1969.

Davis, P. L., and Black, R. J., "Effects of Garbage Grinding on Sewage Systems and Environmental Sanitation," *APWA Reporter,* 29(12):16–18, December 1962.

Decker, W. M., and Steele, J. H., "Health Aspects and Vector Control Associated with Animal Wastes. *In* Management of Farm Animal Wastes; Proceedings; National Symposium on Animal Waste Management, East Lansing, Michigan, American Society of Agricultural Engineers, pp. 18–20.

Dooley, D. D., "Hot Melt Adhesives: Why They Are So Popular," *Material Handling Engineering,* 66–69, February 1966.

Engdahl, R. B., *Solid Waste Processing; A State-of-the-Art Report on Unit Operations and Processes.* Public Health Service Publication No. 1856. Washington, D.C., U. S. Government Printing Office, 1969.

"Establishment of a National Industrial Wastes Inventory, The," hearing held before Subcommittee of the House Committee on Government Operations, September 1970; U. S. Government Printing Office, Y 4.G 74/7:W 28; 1971.

Fehn, C. F., Hall, J. O., Rosenthal, M., Cain, J. R., Rigsby, J. H., and Farmer, H., "Bulk Storage and Mechanized Collection of Combined Refuse," *Public Works,* 95(9):130–31, September 1964.

Ferguson, Brooks and Kelly, *trs.,* and Wiley, J. S., *ed.,* International Research Group on Refuse Disposal (IRGR). Information Bulletins Nos. 15 and 16. Washington, D.C., U. S. Government Printing Office, 1964.

———, Information Bulletins Nos. 19 and 20. Washington, D.C., U. S. Government Printing Office, 1965.

"Forecast for PVC Bottles: Clearing," *Modern Plastics,* 44(1), 105–9, December 1966.

"Friends, Foes and Forecasts for the Old Tin Can" *Marketing Magazine,* 61–63, January 1967.

Fulmer, M. E., and Testin, R. F., *The Role of Plastics in Solid Waste,* a study done for the Society of the Plastics Industry, Inc., 1967.

Furlow, H. G., and Zollinger, H. A. "Reclamation of Refuse," *Current Municipal Problems,* January 1966.

"Future Boom Seen for Gas Incinerators," *American Gas Journal,* 49–52, October 1965.

"Garbage In, Merchandise Out, " *Scientific American,* 58, January 1967.

Gilbertson, W. E., and Black, R. J., "A National Solid Waste Program Is Created," *Compost Science,* 6(3):4–7, Autumn–Winter 1966.

Gilbertson, W. E., *et al., Solid Waste Handling in Metropolitan Areas,* Public Health Service Publication No. 1554. Washington, D. C., U. S. Government Printing Office, 1966.

"Glass: Fighting Back with New Strength," *Modern Packaging,* 112–16, January 1967.

Gordon, M., "Cities' Rubbish Woes Grow as Volume Rises, Dumping Sites Fill Up," *The Wall Street Journal,* October 18, 1961.

Gruenwald, A., and Reynolds, J. A., "Less Than $3,000 per Ton," *American City,* 80(10):100–1, October 1965.

Hanks, J. J., and Kube, H. D., "Industry Action to Combat Pollution," *Harvard Business Review,* 44:49–62, September–October 1966.

Hart, S. A., *Solid Waste Management/Composting; European Activity and American Activity,* Public Health Service Publication No. 1826, Washington, D.C., U. S. Government Printing Office, 1968.

———, "*Solid Wastes Management in Germany; Report of the U. S. Solid Wastes Study Team Visit, June 25–July 8, 1967,* Public Health Service Publication No. 1812, Washington, D.C., U. S. Government Printing Office, 1968.

"Heat Recovery Makes Garbage Less a Burden," *Chemical Engineering,* 74(16):72–73, August 1967.

Hickman, H. L., Jr., "Characteristics of Municipal solid Wastes, *Scrap Age,* 26(2):305–7, February 1969.
Hirsch, W. Z., "Cost Functions of an Urban Government Service: Refuse Collection," *Review of Economics and Statistics,* 87–92, February 1965.
"How Big Is Plastics in Packaging?" *Modern Plastics,* 44(9):98, May 1967.
"How to Dispose of Disposables?" *Chemical Week,* 101(11):32–33, September 1967.
"Industry Arms for War on Waste," *Chemical Week,* 78–80, January 1960.
Institute of Scrap Iron and Steel, *Landscape 1970,* a National Conference on the Abandoned Automobile, Proceedings, 1970.
Jensen, M. E., *Observations of Continental European Solid Waste Management Practices,* Public Health Service Publication No. 1880, Washington, D.C., U. S. Government Printing Office, 1969.
Kaiser, E. R., *Evaluation of the Melt-Zit High-Temperature Incinerator,* operation test report, August 1968, Cincinnati, U. S. Department of Health, Education and Welfare, 1969.
Kochtitzky, O. W., and Wiley, J. S., *"Composting Developments in the United States," Compost Science,* 6(2):5–9, Summer 1965.
Loehwing, D. A., "Flipping Their Lids," *Barron's,* 47:3–8, May 29, 1967.
McElwee, W., "From Landfills to Streets," *American City,* April 24, 1966.
Management Technology, Inc., *Automobile Scrapping Processes and Needs for Maryland; A Final Report on a Solid Waste Demonstration,* Public Health Service Publication No. 2027, Washington, D.C., U. S. Government Printing Office, 1970.
May, R. B., "Scrap-Steel Shedding Units Law Changes Could Solve Cities' Derelict Cars Problem," *The Wall Street Journal,* May 8, 1967.
Meller, F. H., *Conversion of Organic Solid Wastes Into Yeast; An Economic Evaluation,* Public Health Service Publication No. 1909, Washington, D. C., U. S. Government Printing Office, 1969.
Mix, S. A., "Solid Wastes: Every Day, Another 800 Million Pounds," *Today's Health,* 44(3):13–17, March 1966.
"More Refuse Collected with Less Work," *American City,* 80(7): July 26, 1965.
Neal, H. R., "Scrap Has a Bundle of Problems," *The Iron Age.,* 197(25):73–78, June 1966.
"New Heavy Duty Crusher-Disintegrator Solves Many Municipal Waste Disposal Problems," *Secondary Raw Materials,* 39–40, November 1967.
"New Incinerator Fights Pollution," *The Oil and Gas Journal,* 58–59, September 1967.
"The Old Trash Dump Is Obsolete," *Engineering News-Record,* 176:20, April 1966.
"Packaging—a 4.5 Billion-Lb. Plastics Market by 1970," *Modern Plastics,* 45(5):92–97, 191, January 1968.
"Packaging and Pollution," *Printer's Ink,* 294:61, April 1967.
"Packaging: Bottles Up to Scratch," *Economist,* 210:632, February 1964.
"Paper Bags for Household Refuse Handling—A Study in Depth," *Paper Trade Journal,* 39, October 1963.
Peterson, M. L., and Stutzenberger, F. J., "Microbiological Evaluation of Incinerator Operations," *Applied Microbiology,* 18(1):8–13, July 1969.
"Plastic Bootle Use Grows," *Chemical & Engineering News,* 44(44):20, October 1966.
"Plastics Industry Forecast for 1980: Nearly Eight Times Present Size," *Oil, Paint and Drug Reporter,* 7, February 1967.
Policies for Solid Waste Management, U. S. Department of Health Education and Welfare, 1970.
Prescott, J. H., "Composting Plant Converts Refuse into Organic Soil Conditioner," *Chemical Engineering,* 232–34, November 1967.
President's Science Advisory Committee, Environmental Pollution Panel, *Restoring the Quality of Our Environment,* Washington, D.C., The White House, 1965.

Proceedings of MECAR Symposium, "Incineration of Solid Wastes," New York, March 1967.
"Reclamation and Reuse of Industrial Waste," *Secondary Raw Materials,* 27, November 1967.
Rennicke, N. G., "Coorugated Box Manufacture—Its Growth and Prospects," *Paper Trade Journal,* 148(33):32–35, August 1964.
Rogus, C. A., "Collection and Disposal of Oversize Burnable Wastes," *Public Works,* 97(4):106–10, April 1966.
———, "European Developments in Refuse Incineration," *Public Works,* 97(5):113–17, May 1966.
Rosenthal, A. G., "Aluminum Broadens Beachhead in Can Market," *Modern Metals,* 21(8):24–25, September 1965.
"Scrap Shredding Offers Contamination solution," *Steel,* 25, May 1966.
Sebastian, F., "The Worldwide Rush to Incineration," *American City,* 40, December 1967.
Shell, G. L., and Boyd, J. L., *Composting Dewatered Sewage Sludge,* Public Health Service Publication No. 1936, Washington, D.C., U. S. Government Printing Office, 1970.
"Shredders Are Reshaping the Scrap Industry," *Steel,* 62–68, December 1966.
"Sintered Fly Ash goes to Market," *Electrical World,* 94–95, June 1965.
"Solid Wastes in Perspective," *Proceedings, Symposium on Research Needs,* American Public Works Association, Research Foundation, Philadelphia, 1966.
"Solid Wastes—The Job Ahead," *APWA Reporter,* 33(8):5–11, 25, August 1966.
Sponagle, C. E., *Summaries; Solid Waste Demonstration Grant Projects—1969,* Public Health Service Publication No. 1821, Washington, D.C., U. S. Government Printing Office, 1969.
Stanford Research Institute, *Refuse Disposal, Long Range Planning Service—Report No. 298,* September 1966.
Steiner, R. L., and Kantz, R., *Sanitary Landfill; A Bibliography,* Public Health Service Publication No. 1819, Washington, D.C., U. S. Government Printing Office, 1968.
"That's Not Junk; It's Billions of Dollars," *Forbes,* 51, April 1967.
"Tissue: 1967," *American Paper Industry,* 33–35, December 1966.
Townley, D. A., *Solid Waste Problems and Programs: A Challenge to the Professional Sanitarian,* Cincinnati, U. S. Department of Health, Education and Welfare, 1968.
"Turning Fly Ash from Onus to Bonus," *Chemical Engineering,* 98–302, May 1967.
U. S. Department of Commerce, Bureau of the Census, Current Industrial reports: glass Containers, 1966.
———, Metal Cans, Summary for 1959, 1960 and 1961.
———, Steel Shipping Barrels, Drums and Pails, Summary for 1959, 1960, 1961, 1965.
U. S. Department of Commerce, Business and Defense Services Administration, *Containers and Packaging,* Quarterly Industrial Reports, 17(4), January 1965; 18(1), April 1965; 18(3), October 1965; 18(4), January 1966; 19(1), April 1966; 19(4), January 1967; 20(1), April 1967; 20(2), July 1967; 20(3), October 1967, etc.
———, *Pulp, Paper, and Board,* Quarterly Industrial Reports, 21(2), June 1965; 21(3), September 1965; 21(4), January 1966; 22(1), April 1966; 22(2), July 1966; 22(3), October 1966; 22(4), January 1967; 23(1), April 1967; 23(2), July 1967; 23(3), October 1967, etc.
U. S. Department of the Interior, Bureau of Mines, *Automobile Disposal, A National Problem,* Case Studies of Factors That Influence the Accumulation of Automobile Scrap, Washington, D.C., U. S. Department of the Interior, 1967.
Vaughan, R. D., "The Federal Solid Wastes Program," *Civil Engineering,* 39(2):69–71, February 1969.
———, *Packaging and solid Waste Management,* Cincinnati, U. S. Department of Health, Education and Welfare, 1968.

Weaver, L., "The Sanitary Landfill," *American City,* March-May 1956.

———, ed., *Proceedings;* The Surgeon General's Conference on Solid Waste Management for Metropolitan Washington, July 19–20, 1967, Public Health Service Publication No. 1729, Washington, D.C., U. S. Government Printing Office, 1967.

Wiley, J. S., ed., International Research group on Refuse Disposal (IRGRD); Information Bulletin Nos. 1–12, November 1956 to September 1961, Washington, D.C., U. S. Department of Health, Education and Welfare, 1969.

———, Information Bulletin Nos. 13–20, December 1961 to May 1964, Washington, D.C., U. S. Government Printing Office, 1969.

Williams, E. R., and Black, R. J., *Refuse Collection and Disposal; An Annotated Bibliography, 1958–1959,* Public Health Service Publication No. 91, Washington, D.C., U. S. Government Printing Office 1961. Suppl. D.

Zausner, E. R., *An Accounting System for Incinerator Operations,* Public Health Service Publication No. 2032, Washington, D.C., U. S. Government Printing Office, 1970.

Appendixes

APPENDIX A

SOME NOTABLE COURT DECISIONS ON ENVIRONMENTAL CONTROL

I. Noise Pollution

United States v. Causby (328 U. S. 256; 1946).

Mr. Causby, a chicken farmer whose property was near the runway of a World War II air base, maintained that military planes had trespassed under the theory of *ad coelum* (to the sky). The Causby claim, thus, was that Mr. Causby's real property extended vertically as well as horizontally. The court agreed. This was a Supreme Court decision.

Griggs v. County of Allegheny (363 U. S. 84; 1962).

Here the Supreme Court ruled that the operator of the Pittsburgh, Pennsylvania, airport must buy and use its own land for the air approaches of low-flying jet planes, and not invade the airspace above private property.

Aaron v. City of Los Angeles (387 799 Superior Court, County of Los Angeles, February 5, 1970).

Landowners in the vicinity of Los Angeles Airport were upheld in allegation that by permitting noisy jet planes to take off and land directly over their residences, the city had taken free use of the airspace above said residences without compensation.

Board of Education, Elizabeth, New Jersey, v. State Department of Transportation (New Jersey Superior Court, September 27, 1971).

An award of $164,119 was made to the Board of Education for damages caused the William F. Halloran School No. 22 after Interstate Highway 278 was built next to it. Judge Milton Feller ruled that construction of the highway made it impossible to conduct classes normally in the school without extensive soundproofing.

Other noise pollution cases:

A. Nuisance

Landry v. Daley, 280 F. Supp. 968 (N. D. Ill. 1968), appeal dismissed 393 U. S. 220 (1968).

Greater Westchester Homeowners' Association v. City of Los Angeles, decided by California Supreme Court on April 17, 1970, 38 LW 2591.

Hooks v. International Speedways, Inc., 140 S.E. 2d 387 (N.C. 1965).

Connecticut Bank & Trust Company v. Mularik, 174 A.2d 128 (Conn. 1961).

Protokowicz v. Lesofski, 174 A. 2d 385 (N.J. 1961).

B. Occupational Deafness

Ciavarro v. Despatch Shops, Inc., 255 N.Y. Supp. 2d 48 (App. Div. 1964).
Comoletti v. Ideal Cement Company, 147 So. 2d 711 (La. 1962).

C. Inverse Condemnation

A. J. Industries, Inc., v. United States, 355 F. 2d 592 (Ct. of Cl. 1966).
Dennison v. State of New York, 22 N.Y. 2d 409 (Ct. of Ap. 1968).
Ferguson v. Keene, 108 N.H. 409 (1968).
City of Jacksonville v. Schumann, 167 So. 2d 95 (Fla. 1964).
Martin v. Port of Seattle, 391 P. 2d 540 (Wash. 1964).
Richmond County v. Williams, 137 S.E. 2d 343 (Ga. 1964).
Thornburg v. Port of Portland, 376 P. 2d 100 (Ore. 1962).

II. Scenic Beauty

Parker v. Citizens Committee for Hudson Valley (No. 614, U. S. Supreme Court, December 7, 1970).

The Supreme Court declined to disturb a lower court ruling barring Theodore W. Parker, commissioner of the New York Department of Transportation, from proceeding with construction of a proposed Hudson River Expressway between Tarrytown and Crotonville, New York. To have built the road, the state would have had to extend the roadbed into the river along a five-mile stretch of the bank. The court's ruling was based on the Refuse Act of 1899 that required the Army Corps of Engineers to get the consent of Congress before it approved construction of a "dike" on a navigable river.

Citizens to Preserve Overton Park, et al. v. Volpe et al. (No. 1066, U. S. Supreme Court, March 2, 1971).

The Supreme Court reversed decisions by the Federal District Court in Memphis and the U. S. Court of Appeals for the Sixth Circuit, which would have allowed the six-lane state highway No. 1-40 to cut through Overton Park in Memphis, a 342-acre city park containing zoo, golf course, outdoor theater, bridle path, etc., and 170 acres of forest. Twenty-six acres of the park would have been destroyed. The high court, in making its decision, ordered the lower court to determine whether two Secretaries of Transportation—Alan S. Boyd in the Johnson Administration and John A. Volpe in the Nixon Administration—had acted within the scope of their authority under the law in initially approving funds for the project, or whether their decision had been "arbitrary, capricious, an abuse of discretion, or otherwise not in accordance with law."

Road Review League, Town of Bedford v. Boyd. 270 F. Supp. 650 (S.D. N.Y. 1967).

Scenic Hudson Preservation Conference v. Federal Power Commission, 354 F. 2d 608 (2d Cir. 1965), cert. den. 384 U. S. 941 (1966). This is the so-called *Scenic Hudson* or *Storm King Case.*

Wes Outdoor Advertising Co. v. Goldburg, decided by the New Jersey Supreme Court on March 2, 1970, 38 LW 2488.

III. Animal Protection

Nettleton v. State of New York (N.Y. State Court of Appeals, October 16, 1970).

The state's highest tribunal upheld a new state law prohibiting importation or sale of skins of animals deemed to be near extinction. The challenge was brought against the Mason Act by A. E. Nettleton Company, a Syracuse shoe firm, some of whose products are made from alligator and crocodile skins. A lower court had held that the Mason Act represented an unreasonable exercise of police power. In a 5 to 2 decision the Court of Appeals ruled that "the protection of the animals listed in the Mason Act is necessary not only for their natural beauty and for the purpose of biological study, but for the key role that they play in the maintenance of the life cycle."

Reptile Products Association v. Diamond (No. 1225, U. S. Supreme Court, March 22, 1971).

High court let stand lower court ruling upholding the constitutionality of New York's 1970 law banning all sales in the state of items made of crocodile skins.

IV. Air Pollution

Boomer v. The Atlantic Cement Company, Inc. (N.Y. State Court of Appeals, March 4, 1970. 38 LW 2487).

This was a case charging a cement company with operating its plant without effective air pollution control equipment. A lower court denied an injunction restraining the company from operating its plant, but the Court of Appeals reversed the ruling, holding the defendants responsible for a public nuisance and awarding temporary damages. The injunction was granted, but its imposition suspended pending payment for damages resulting from the operations of the plant. Damages were found small in comparison to hurt which defendant and plant employees would suffer if the plant were closed by injunction.

Whalen v. Union Bag and Paper Company (208 N.Y. 1; 1913).

Case and problem similar to *Boomer v. The Atlantic Cement Company, Inc.*

United States v. Bishop Processing Company (287 F. Supp. 624; D. Md. 1968; cert. den., U. S. Supreme Court, May 18, 1970).

At issue was a chicken-rendering plant in the Selbyville and Bishop areas of Maryland, which residents claimed endangered health and welfare. On November 10, 1969, U. S. Court for the District of Maryland held the Bishop Processing Company responsible for thirty-one counts of air pollution (malodorous) and ordered rendering operations stopped as of February 16, 1970. The order was stayed pending appeal. On March 3, 1970, Judge Sobeloff of the Fourth Circuit Court affirmed the lower court ruling. The case was taken to the Supreme Court, which denied the petition, without comment, on May 18, 1970. Action was originated under the Federal Clean Air Act.

Oriental Boulevard Company v. Heller (No. 1275, U. S. Supreme Court, March 29, 1971).

High court let stand a lower court ruling upholding the constitutionality of a New York ordinance requiring apartment building owners to equip their incinerators and oil-burning furnaces with anti-smoke devices.

Other air pollution court cases:

County of Harris v. Ideal Cement Company, 290 F. Supp. 956 (S.D. Tex. 1968).
Reynolds Metals Company v. Lampert, 324 F. 2d 465 (9th Cir. 1963), cert. den. 376 U. S. 910 (1964).
Renken v. Harvey Aluminum (Incorporated), 226 F. Supp. 169 (D. Ore. 1963).
Fairview Farms, Inc. v. Reynolds Metals Company, 176 F. Supp. 178 (D. Ore. 1959).
Greyhound Corporation v. Blakley, 262 F. 2d 401 (9th Cir. 1958).

V. Water Pollution

Ohio v. Wyandotte Chemical Corporation (No. 41 [original] U. S. Supreme Court, March 23, 1971).

In an 8 to 1 ruling, the high court declined to hear a suit brought by the state of Ohio against companies accused of dumping mercury into Lake Erie, and served notice that it wanted such suits to pass in the future through the lower courts. The court declared that it lacked both time and expertise to play a major role in anti-pollution litigation, and that it could be inundated with actions if it agreed to be the first and last court of appeal. The net effect of the ruling was to serve notice that the Supreme Court would not exercise the original jurisdiction conferred upon it constitutionally to give states a forum to attack water and air pollution crossing national and state boundaries.

United States v. Oxford Paper Company (August 1970; Federal District Court for Maine).

Ethyl Corporation, parent company of the Oxford Paper Company, shut down a plant on the Androscoggin River at Rumford, Maine, following Justice Department action instituted against eight companies in seven states for discharging poisonous mercury into public waters. The action was brought under the Refuse Act of 1899, which prohibits the dumping of refuse, except in liquid form from streets and sewers, into navigable waters without a permit from the Army Corps of Engineers.

United States v. Chevron Oil Company (August 1970; U. S. District Court for Louisiana).

Chevron pleaded no contest to 500 of 900 counts in a case involving massive oil pollution of the Gulf of Mexico the previous winter. Chevron was charged with failing to install and maintain storm chokes or similar safety shutoff devices on ninety offshore oil wells in the Gulf southeast of New Orleans. The case was the first of its kind filed under the Outer Continental Shelf Lands Act of 1953. Chevron was fined $1 million. (On December 2, 1970, $500,000 in fines were levied against Humble Oil Company, Union Oil Company and Continental Oil Company also for failure to place safety valves on some offshore oil wells in the Gulf of Mexico. The indictments were brought by the federal government, and the cases were decided in federal court in New Orleans.)

Environmental Defense Fund v. Resor (Federal Reporter, 2nd Series; Civil No. 2394–70 D.D.C., filed August 12, 1970).

A temporary restraining order was sought seeking to restrain the military from dumping high-toxicity nerve gases in the waters off the Florida coast, until there was compliance with relevant policies, laws and treaties relating to the disposal of such agents. The motion was denied in the U. S. District Court (D.D.C.), and denied again by the U. S. Court of Appeals (District of Columbia Circuit). On August 18, 1970, the gases were loaded aboard an obsolete ship, moved to sea and sunk 283 miles off Florida's east coast.

Other water pollution cases:

State of New Hampshire v. Atomic Energy Commission, 406 F. 2d 170 (1st Cir. 1969), cert. den. 395 U. S. 962 (1969).

United States v. Interlake Steel Corporation, 297 F. Supp. 912 (N.D. Ill. 1969).

United States v. Esso Standard Oil Company of Puerto Rico, 375 F. 2d 621 (3rd Cir. 1967).

United States v. Standard Oil Company, 384 U. S. 224 (1966).

United States v. LeBeouf Bros. Barge Company, 368 F. 2d 221 (5th Cir. 1966).

United States v. Barge Boulder, 238 F. Supp. 748 (W.D. La. 1964), aff'd 343 F. 2d 175 (5th Cir. 1965).

Kernan v. Gulf Oil Corporation, 231 F. Supp. 339 (E.D. Pa. 1964), aff'd 341 F. 2d 920 (3rd Cir. 1965).

United States v. Steel Tank Barge Rainer, 235 F. Supp. 361 (W.D. La. 1964).

United States v. S.S. Mormacsaga, 204 F. Supp. 701 (E.D. Pa. 1962).

United States v. Republic Steel Corporation, 362 U. S. 482 (1960).

VI. Weather Modification

Southwest Weather Research, Inc., v. Jones, 327 S.W. 2d 417 (Tex. 1959).

Slutsky v. City of New York, 97 N.Y. Supp. 2d 238 (Sup. Ct. 1950).

VII. Nuclear Energy

Calvert Cliffs' Coordinating Committee, Inc., v. Atomic Energy Commission (U. S. Court of Appeals for the District of Columbia, July 23, 1971).

The Court of Appeals ruled that the Atomic Energy Commission's regulations regarding the environment have made a mockery of the National Environmental Protection Act, and ordered the agency to revise its rules completely. The decision involved construction of a nuclear power plant at Calvert Cliffs, Maryland. The court said that issues posed by nonradiological hazards must be settled before the Commission could grant construction and operating permits.

State of Minnesota v. Northern States Power Company (No. 71-650, U. S. Supreme Court, April 3, 1972).

The Supreme Court ruled 7 to 2 that states may not establish more rigid radiation-control standards for nuclear power plants than those set by the federal Atomic Energy Commission.

VIII. Miscellaneous

County of Santa Barbara v. Malley (No. 695, U. S. Supreme Court, January 11, 1971).

The Supreme Court let stand a lower court's decision that the Department of the Interior was not required to hold a public hearing before it granted permission for oil drilling to take place in the Santa Barbara (Calif.) channel.

APPENDIX B

GUIDELINES FOR TAX-EXEMPT ORGANIZATIONS

On November 12, 1970, the Internal Revenue Service announced the guidelines under which tax exemption will be granted to organizations engaged in litigation in the public interest. The guidelines were drawn up after the I.R.S. had drawn the fire of conservationists, environmentalists and consumer advocates for suspending new grants of exempt status to "public-interest law firms." The guidelines follow:

1. The engagement of the organization in litigation can reasonably be said to be in representation of a broad public interest rather than a private interest. The litigation is designed to present a position on behalf of the public at large on matters of public interest. Typical of such litigation may be class actions in the public interest, suits for injunction against action by government or private interests broadly affecting the public, similar representation before administrative boards and agencies, test suits where the private interest is small and the like. The activity would not normally extend to direct representation of litigants in actions between private persons where their financial interests at stake would warrant representation from private legal sources. In such cases, however, the organization may serve in the nature of a friend of the court.

2. The organization does not accept fees for its services except in accordance with procedures approved by the Internal Revenue Service.

3. The organization does not attempt to achieve its objectives through a program of disruption of the judicial system, illegal activity or violation of applicable canons of ethics.

4. The organization files with its annual information return a description of cases litigated and the rationale for the determinant that they would benefit the public generally.

5. The policies and programs of the organization are the responsibility of a board or committee representative of the public interest, which is not controlled by employees or persons who litigate on behalf of the organization or by any organization that is not itself an organization described in Section 501 (C) (3) of the Internal Revenue Code.

6. The organization is not operated, through sharing of office space or otherwise, in a manner so as to create identification or confusion with a particular private law firm.

7. There is no arrangement to provide, directly or indirectly, a deduction for the cost of litigation which is for the private benefit of the donor.

8. The organization must otherwise comply with the provisions of Section 501 (C) (3), that is, it may not participate in, or intervene in, any political campaign on behalf of any candidate for public office, no part of its net earnings may inure to the benefit of any private shareholder or individual and no substantial part of its activities may consist of "carrying on propaganda, or otherwise attempting, to influence legislation."

APPENDIX C

WHO'S CONCERNED ABOUT WHAT?

The number of conservation organizations and agencies is so large, one marvels that there are any conservation problems at all. *Conservation Directory 1970*[1] lists 640 American and 50 Canadian organizations and agencies concerned with natural-resource use and management. Some of these would seem to qualify only marginally as conservation bodies—the U. S. Department of Defense, for instance; and the National Rifle Association. Most, however, are bona fide, and there seems to be something for everyone's special interest.

Many conservation groups are single-unit associations. On the other hand, many have local and state chapters, which makes involvement in their cause easier and more direct. The National Wildlife Federation, for one, has more than 8,500 affiliates in 49 states, and a supporting constituency of some 2,250,000 persons.

New focuses on ecology and conservation have resulted in many groups which have not yet found their way into the *Conservation Directory*. In the pages following is a sampling of representative conservation organizations.

NATIONAL AND INTERNATIONAL ORGANIZATIONS

American Committee for International Wildlife Protection, Inc.; c/o The Wildlife Society, Suite S-176, 3900 Wisconsin Avenue, N.W., Washington, D.C. 20016 (202-363-2435). Seeks to coordinate interest of U. S. groups in international conservation activities. Has special interest in international conservation treaties, endangered species, fauna and flora habitats, national parks and reserves and ecological research.

American Conservation Association, Inc.; 30 Rockefeller Plaza, New York, New York 10020 (212-247-8141). Seeks to advance knowledge and understanding of conservation and to preserve and develop natural resources for public use.

American Fisheries Society; 1040 Washington Building, Fifteenth and New York Avenue, N.W., Washington, D.C. 20005 (202-347-9717). Promotes the conservation, development and wise utilization of fisheries, recreational and commerical.

American Forestry Association; 1319 Eighteenth Street, N.W., Washington, D.C. 20036 (202-638-1820). Advances the intelligent management and use of forests, soil, water, wildlife and other natural resources, and seeks to promote public appreciation of these resources.

American Water Resources Association; P.O. Box 434, Urbana, Illinois 61801. Collects and disseminates information in the field of water resources, science and technology. Seeks to establish a common meeting ground for engineers and physical, biological and social scientists concerned about water resources.

[1] Published as a conservation education service of the National Wildlife Federation, 1412 Sixteenth Street, N.W., Washington, D.C. 20036; 139 pp.

Boone and Crockett Club; c/o Carnegie Museum, 4400 Forbes Avenue, Pittsburgh, Pennsylvania 15213. Works for preservation of the wildlife of the United States, especially big game. Is especially concerned with furthering legislation toward that end.

Center for Study of Responsive Law; P.O. Box 19367, Washington, D.C. 20036 (202-833-3400). Founded in 1968 and headed by consumer advocate Ralph Nader, the center began as a watchdog of consumer interests and soon found itself engaged in pollution study and investigation.

Conservation Foundation; 1717 Massachusetts Avenue, N.W., Washington, D.C. 20036 (202-265-8882). Conducts research, education and information programs to develop knowledge, improve techniques and stimulate public and private decision-making and action to improve the quality of the environment.

Citizens League Against the Sonic Boom; 19 Appleton Street, Cambridge, Massachusetts 02138. Founded March 9, 1967, to combat the booms and other negative effects and noises of aircraft.

Conservation Law Society of America; 1500 Mills Tower, San Francisco, California 94104 (415-981-7800; Robert W. Jasperson, executive secretary and general counsel). Provides services of a legal staff on a fee basis to research and accumulate laws, decisions and other precedents relating to conservation problems; to advise conservation groups and represent these groups in court.

Council on Economic Priorities; 1127 Connecticut Avenue, N.W., Washington, D.C. 20036 (202-628-3016); 456 Greenwich Street, New York, New York 10013 (212-431-4770); P.O. Box 2210, San Francisco, California 94126 (415-383-3017). Research group which publishes "unbiased" data on corporate policies, practices and products "as they affect society." Available for contract work for organizations, usually for a fee. Publishes monthly newsletter and in-depth reports. Annual membership fee: $25 for individuals, $100 for institutions, $5 for students.

Defenders of Wildlife; 2000 N Street, N.W., Washington, D.C. 20036 (202-223-1993). Promotes protection and humane treatment of all mammals, birds, fish and other wildlife, and the elimination of painful methods of trapping, capturing and killing wildlife.

Ducks Unlimited; P.O. Box 66300, Chicago, Illinois 60666 (312-299-3334). Organized to perpetuate wild ducks and other wild waterfowl on the North American continent, principally by preservation and rehabilitation of wetland areas on the Canadian prairie breeding grounds.

Ecology Forum, Inc.; Suite 303 East, 200 Park Avenue, New York, New York 10017 (212-972-0523). Seeks to fill information and communication gaps by assembling and categorizing data on environmental conservation and pollution.

Environmental Action; Room 731, 1346 Connecticut Avenue, N.W., Washington, D.C. 20036. (202-833-1845). An outgrowth organization of Earth Day 1970, it investigates environmental abuse, presses for legislation, institutes lawsuits and keeps citizens informed on actions that can be taken individually and collectively to protect the environment.

Environmental Defense Fund; 162 Old Town Road, East Setauket, New York 11733. A nationwide coalition of scientists, lawyers and citizens dedicated to protection of environmental quality through legal action and through education of the public.

Environmental Law Institute; Dupont Circle Building, Suite 614, 1346 Connecticut Avenue, N.W., Washington, D.C. 20036 (202-659-8037). A nonprofit educational organization incorporated in 1969 as a clearinghouse for information regarding the law of the environment, including statute and regulatory law; cases and decisions of courts and other judicial or quasi-judicial bodies; briefs, memoranda, treatises, etc., by members of the legal profession and others.

Friends of the Earth; 30 East Forty-second Street, New York, New York 10017. A political action group—not tax-free, so can lobby for new environmental laws.

International Institute for Environmental Affairs; 600 Fifth Avenue, New York, New York 10020. An independent, nongovernment, nonprofit service organization, designed to assist a network of institutions throughout the world that are concerned with environmental policies and action. Also has Washington office at Jefferson Office Building, 1225 Nineteenth Street, N.W., Washington, D.C. 20036.

Izaak Walton League of America; 1800 North Kent Street, Suite 806, Arlington, Virginia 22209 (703-528-1818). Educates the public to conserve, maintain, protect and restore the soil, forest, water and other natural resources of the United States and promotes enjoyment and proper utilization of these resources.

Keep America Beautiful, Inc.; 99 Park Avenue, New York, New York 10016 (212-682-4564). Campaigns against littering and seeks the preservation and improvement of America's scenic and man-made beauty, urban and rural. Conducts a year-round program of public education to stimulate pride in clean surroundings.

League of Conservation Voters; 620 C Street, S.E., Washington, D.C. 20003 (202-543-4312). Nonpartisan political arm of Friends of the Earth (FOE). Raises money and recruits volunteers for candidates working to protect the environment.

National Audubon Society; 950 Third Avenue, New York, New York 10022 (212-369-2100). Aims to advance understanding of the value and need of conservation of wildlife, plants, soil and water, and the relationships of their wise use to human progress.

National Parks and Conservation Association; 1701 Eighteenth Street, N.W., Washington, D.C. 20009 (202-265-2717). Concerns itself not only with the protection of the great national parks and monuments of the United States, but also with the restoration of natural environment in general.

National Recreation and Park Association; 1700 Pennsylvania Avenue, N.W., Washington, D.C. 20006 (202-223-3030). Concerned with the development of professional and lay leadership to preserve and beautify the total American environment. Also educates in wholesome and meaningful leisure-time activities.

National Wildlife Federation; 1412 Sixteenth Street, N.W., Washington, D.C. 20036 (202-483-1550). Encourages an awareness among people of the United States of the need for wise use and proper management of those resources upon which the lives and welfare of man depend: soil, water, forest, minerals, plantlife and wildlife.

Natural Resources Council of America; Chairman: Richard H. Stroud, 719 Thirteenth Street, N.W., Washington, D.C. 20005 (202-737-0668). A society of major national and regional conservation organizations seeking to advance sound management of public resources in the public interest by providing member organizations with information on actions by Congress and the Executive Branch, by making available scientific data on conservation problems and by providing a medium of cooperation.

Natural Resources Defense Council; 36 West Forty-fourth Street, New York, New York 10036 (212-986-8310). Public-interest law center founded in 1969 to undertake legal and educational work in defense of the environment.

Nature Conservancy; Suite 800, 1800 North Kent Street, Arlington, Virginia 22209 (703-524-3151). Cooperates with colleges, universities, public and private organizations to acquire lands for scientific and educational purposes relating to conservation.

North American Wildlife Foundation; 709 Wire Building, Washington, D.C. 20005 (202-347-1775). Helps sponsor wildlife research through cooperating organizations and investigations into other phases of natural resource conservation, restoration and management.

Planned Parenthood—World Population; 515 Madison Avenue, New York, New York 10022 (212-752-2100). Federated agency uniting 166 affiliates in major cities of the United States. Sponsors medically supervised clinics providing family-planning information and services.)

Population Council; 245 Park Avenue, New York, New York 10017 (212-687-8330). Performs and supports research on contraceptive methods. Sponsors educational programs and films.

Population Crisis Committee; 1835 K Street, N.W., Washington, D.C. 20006 (202-659-1833). Rallies support for government programs aimed at meeting the challenge of world population growth.

Population Reference Bureau; 1755 Massachusetts Avenue, N.W., Washington, D.C. 20036 (202-232-2288). Disseminates facts on size, composition and dynamics of the world's population. Analyzes the impact of these factors on the quality of human life.

Rachel Carson Trust for the Living Environment; 8940 Jones Mill Road, Washington, D.C. 20015 (301-652-1877). Aims to further the causes and philosophy for which Rachel Carson lived and worked by promoting public interest in and knowledge of our environment; encouraging enlightened conservation measures; serving as a clearinghouse of information for scientists and laymen alike.

Sierra Club; 1050 Mills Tower, San Francisco, California 94104 (415-981-8634). Explores, enjoys and protects national scenic resources. Has thirty-five chapters across the country. Sponsors wilderness outings, white-water trips, skiing, mountaineering, knapsacking, films, exhibits and conferences.

Society for the Preservation of Birds of Prey; Box 293, Pacific Palisades, California 90272. Devoted solely to increasing interest and understanding of birds of prey, and promoting their protection on all continents.

Society of American Foresters; 1010 Sixteenth Street, N.W., Washington, D.C. 20036 (202-296-7820). Serves to represent, advance and protect the interests and standards of the forestry profession.

Soil Conservation Society of America; 7515 Northeast Ankeny Road, Ankeny, Iowa 50021 (515-289-2331). Promotes the science and art of good land use. Has 120 chapters.

Trout Unlimited; 4260 East Evans Avenue, Denver, Colorado 80222 (303-757-7144). Formed to preserve clear waters and to perpetuate and improve high-quality fishing.

Trustees for Conservation; 251 Kearny Street, San Francisco, California 94108 (415-392-2838); 235 Massachusetts Avenue, N.E., Washington, D.C. 20002 (202-547-1144). Secures support of people and government for the preservation of national parks and monuments, wildlife and wilderness areas.

Water Information Center, Inc.; 44 Sintsick Drive East, Port Washington, New York 11050 (516-883-6780). Publishers and consultants, particularly on questions relating to ground water. Its titles include *Water Atlas of the United States* and the *Water Encyclopedia.*

Water Pollution Control Federation; 3900 Wisconsin Avenue, N.W., Washington, D.C. 20016 (202-362-4100). Devoted to advancement of knowledge concerning the nature, collection, treatment and disposal of domestic and industrial waste waters, and the design, construction, operation and management of facilities for these purposes.

Whooping Crane Conservation Association, Inc.; R.R. 1, Box 485A, Kula, Maui, Hawaii 96790. Seeks to save the whooping crane from extinction.

Wilderness Society; 729 Fifteenth Street, N.W., Washington, D.C. 20005 (202-347-4132). Seeks the preservation of wilderness. Makes and encourages scientific studies of wilderness areas, and mobilizes cooperation in resisting their invasion.

Wildlife Management Institute; 709 Wire Building, Washington, D.C. 20005 (202-347-1774). Membership organization promoting better use of natural resources for the welfare of the nation.

Wildlife Restoration, Inc.; 17 West Sixtieth Street, New York, New York 10023 (212-245-4952). Membership organization established to restore and perpetuate game birds, animals and fish on the North American continent; to maintain wildlife sanctuaries; to encourage and assist educational research.

Wildlife Society; Suite S-176, 3900 Wisconsin Avenue, N.W., Washington, D.C. 20016 (202-363-2435). Professional association for those employed in the biological or related fields of wildlife conservation.

World Wildlife Fund; Suite 619, 910 Seventeenth Street, N.W., Washington, D.C. 20006 (202-296-0422). Makes grants to existing agencies, such as game and park departments, for surveys, habitat or protection of rare and vanishing species of the world. Coordinates projects through an international office in Switzerland.

Zero Population Growth; 343 Second Street, Los Angeles, California 94022 (415-942-3666); Suite 606, 917 Fifteenth Street, N.W., Washington, D.C. 20005 (202-737-8275). Political action and education organization concerned about overpopulation.

REGIONAL ORGANIZATIONS

Appalachian Trail Conference; 1718 N Street, N.W., Washington, D.C. 20036. Coordinates maintenance, preservation and general welfare of the Appalachian Trail, a 2,000-mile wilderness footpath extending from Maine to Georgia.

Audubon Naturalist Society of the Central Atlantic States; 8940 Jones Mill Road, Washington, D.C. 20015 (301-652-9188). Dedicated to conservation activities, environmental education and to the increase of public understanding of natural history and the importance of preserving and renewing natural resources.

Campaign Against Pollution; 600 West Fullerton, Chicago, Illinois 60614 (312-929-2922). A citizens' action organization with local neighborhood chapters in the Chicago area.

Caribbean Conservation Association; c/o Caribbean Research Institute, College of the Virgin Islands, St. Thomas, U. S. Virgin Islands 00801. Helps to foster a greater awareness of the value of the natural and cultural resources of the Caribbean area.

Citizens for Clean Air; 502 Park Avenue, New York, New York 10022 (212-935-1454). Citizens' research and action group working against pollution through attacking the automobile, incinerator and oil burner and power plant. Supplies information on these different aspects of air pollution and sends out speakers. Offers daily air pollution report for New York City (755-3300) and maintains a number for the reporting of polluters (227-1400).

Citizens for Environmental Improvement; 333 North Fourteenth Street, Lincoln, Nebraska 68508.

Clean Air Coordinating Committee; 1440 West Washington Boulevard, Chicago, Illinois 60607 (312-243-2000). Research and action group focusing on air pollution. Has coalition of over sixty community organizations, and volunteer legal staff to help the committee and other groups to file legal actions.

Conservation Law Foundation, Inc.; 506 Statler Office Building, Boston, Massachusetts 02116 (617-523-4828). Serves as clearinghouse for the New England area of conservation information with legal dimensions. Promotes the use of law, including law suits and legal research, for the wise use and conservation of natural resources.

Desert Protective Council, Inc.; P.O. Box 33, Banning, California, 92220. Seeks to safeguard desert areas with unique scenic features.

Federation of Western Outdoor Clubs; Betty Hughes, president, Box 2067, Carmel, California 93921. Group of forty-two clubs promoting proper use and enjoyment of America's scenic wilderness and outdoor recreational resources.

Goo, Inc. (Get Oil Out); 111 East De La Guerra Street, Santa Barbara, California 93101.

Inland Bird Banding Association; Roy Lukes, past-president, Box 152, Baileys Harbor, Wisconsin 54202. Engages in bird-banding and other activities for the protection and welfare of various bird species.

Lake Erie Cleanup Committee, Inc.; 3003 Eleventh Street, Monroe, Michigan 48161. Seeks to halt pollution of Lake Erie, and of other fresh-water lakes and streams. Promotes opinion for strong pollution controls.

Mid-Atlantic Council of Watershed Associations; P.O. Box 171, Pennington, New Jersey, 08534. Promotes exchange of ideas on citizen watershed association activities. Advises groups wishing to start new watershed associations.

New England Advisory Board for Fish and Game Problems; Dennis McCarthy, chairman, R.F.D. 2, North Kingstown, Rhode Island 02852. Promotes better hunting and fishing for sportsmen.

Northwestern Students for a Better Environment (NSBE); Room 157, Cresap Laboratory, Northwestern University, Evanston, Illinois 60201 (312-491-9627). Offers advice for environmental activists. Supplies speakers to clubs, churches, schools, neighborhood clubs, etc. Counsels consumers on household product usages so as to minimize pollution.

Resources Advisory Board, Southeast River Basins; Room 402, Walton Building, Atlanta, Georgia 30303 (404-522-9963). Engages in coordination and development of water and related land resources in the area from Savannah Basin to Pearl Basin.

Rocky Mountain Center on Environment; 4260 East Evans Avenue, Denver, Colorado 80222 (303-757-5439). Service center for environmental planning, communications, education, research, etc., which seeks to minimize the destructive forces of man's technology on the scenic, scientific, historical wilderness, wildlife, open-space and outdoor recreational resources of the eight-state Rocky Mountain region.

Save the Dunes Council; Sylvia Troy, executive vice-president, 1512 Park Drive, Munster, Indiana 46321 (219-838-5843). Concerned with protecting the ecological values of the Indiana dunes area and of Lake Michigan.

Southern Forest Institute; Suite 280, 1 Corporate Square, N.E., Atlanta, Georgia 30329 (404-633-5137). Encourages development of forest lands for multiple uses. Programs include forestry camps for youths.

Upper Mississippi River Conservation Committee; 322 Federal Building, Davenport, Iowa 52801; (319-324-1961). Advises conservation directorates of Illinois, Iowa, Minnesota, Missouri and Wisconsin, and the Bureau of Sport Fisheries and Wildlife, on the preservation and wise utilization of the natural and recreational resources of the upper Mississippi River.

Water Resources Association of the Delaware River Basin; 21 South Twelveth Street, Philadelphia, Pennsylvania 19107 (215-563-8572). Citizen federation devoted to the orderly development and equitable use and reuse of the water resources of the Delaware River Basin.

Western Forestry and Conservation Association; 1326 American Bank Building, Portland, Oregon 97205 (503-226-4562). Promotes the practice of forestry and forest conservation in western United States and western Canada. Fosters cooperations between federal, state, provincial and private forest agencies.

GOVERNMENT CONSERVATION AGENCIES AND COMMISSIONS[1]

Environmental Quality Council and Citizens' Advisory Committee on Environmental Quality; 722 Jackson Place, N.W., Washington, D.C. 20006 (202-382-5948). Established by Executive Order 11472 on May 29, 1969, to advise and assist the President on environmental-quality matters, improve interagency coordination, develop outdoor recreation and natural beauty policies and programs and to provide leadership in a nationwide effort to protect against pollution of the nation's air, water, land and living resources.

Environmental Protection Agency; Waterside Mall, 401 M Street, S.W., Washington, D.C. 20460 (202-755-2673). Coordinating agency charged with administering all federal anti-pollution programs and with enforcing anti-pollution laws. The agency became effective October 2, 1970. Agencies and functions transferred under its aegis follow:[2]

Federal Water Quality Administration (from the Department of the Interior). Charged with the control of pollutants which impair water quality, FWQA is broadly concerned with the impact of degraded water quality. It performs a wide variety of functions, including research, standard-setting and enforcement, and provides construction grants and technical assistance.

Pesticide Studies from the Department of the Interior. Authority for research on the effects of pesticides on fish and wildlife, provided under the pesticides act of 1958.

National Air Pollution Control Administration. As the principal federal agency concerned with air pollution, it conducts research on the effects of air pollution, operates a monitoring network and promulgates criteria which serve as the basis for setting air quality standards. Its regulatory functions are similar to those of the Federal Water Quality Administration. NAPCA is responsible for administering the Clean Air Act, which involves designating air quality regions, approving state standards, and providing financial and technical assistance to state control agencies to enable them to comply with the act's provisions. It also sets federal automotive emission standards.

Elements of the Environmental Control Administration. ECA is the focal

[1] Most listings here reflect the status of agencies and commissions as of April 1971. The function and even existence of some of these bodies may have been altered since as the result of reorganization programs proposed by the Nixon Administration, such as the transformation of the Department of the Interior into a Department of Natural Resources. However, the Nixon proposals had not been hammered into hard legislative recommendations as of the April 1971 date; their fate, therefore, is impossible to predict. It is possible that there may be no drastic changes at all. The proposal concerning a Department of Natural Resources, for instance, is actually as old as 1937, and the Brownlow Committee of the Franklin D. Roosevelt Administration. It went nowhere; the same could happen again.

[2] Divisions merged into the Environmental Protection Agency were left at their existing locations for the time being. Eventually it is expected that all of EPA will be housed under one roof. All departments, however, can be reached through the Waterside Mall address, allowing normal delay involved in any forwarding procedure.

point within the Department of Health, Education and Welfare for evaluation and control of a broad range of environmental health problems, including water quality, solid wastes, and radiation. Programs in the ECA involve research, development of criteria and standards and the administration of planning and demonstration grants. From the ECA, the activities of the Bureaus of Water Hygiene and Solid Waste Management and portions of the activities of the Bureau of Radiological Health are being transferred. (Other functions of the ECA including those related to the regulation of radiation from consumer products and occupational safety and health are to remain in HEW.)

Pesticides Research and Standard-setting Programs of the Food and Drug Administration. FDA's pesticides program consists of setting and enforcing standards which limit pesticide residues in food. EPA would have the authority to set pesticide standards and to monitor compliance with them, as well as to conduct related research. However, as an integral part of its food protection activities, FDA retains its authority to remove from the market food with excess pesticide residues.

General Ecological Research from the Council on Environmental Quality. This authority to perform studies and research relating to ecological systems is in addition to EPA's other specific research authorities, and it helps EPA to measure the impact of pollutants. (The Council on Environmental Quality retains its authority to conduct studies and research relating to environmental quality.)

Environmental Radiation Standards Programs. The Atomic Energy Commission was responsible for establishing environmental radiation standards and emission limits for radioactivity. Those standards have been based largely on broad guidelines recommended by the Federal Radiation Council. The Atomic Energy Commission's authority to set standards for the protection of the general environment from radioactive material is now transferred to the Environmental Protection Agency. The functions of the Federal Radiation Council are also transferred. (AEC retains responsibility for the implementation and enforcement of radiation standards through its licensing authority.)

Pesticides Registration Program of the Agricultural Research Service. The Department of Agriculture was traditionally responsible for several distinct functions related to pesticides use. It conducted research on the efficacy of various pesticides as related to other pest control methods and on the effects of pesticides on non-target plants, livestock and poultry. It registered pesticides, monitored their persistence and carried out an educational program on pesticide use through the extension service. It conducted extensive pest control programs which utilize pesticides. By transferring the Department of Agriculture's pesticides registration and monitoring function to the EPA and merging it with the pesticides programs being transferred from HEW and Interior, the new Environmental Protection Agency is given a broad capability for control over the introduction of pesticides into the environment. The Department of Agriculture continues to conduct research on the effectiveness of pesticides. The department furnishes this information to the EPA, which has the responsibility for actually licensing pesticides for use after considering environmental and health effects.

CONGRESSIONAL COMMITTEES

Committees of the United States Congress dealing with natural resources legislation and their areas of general concern:

Senate Committee on Agriculture and Forestry; Room 324 Old Senate Office Building, Washington, D.C. 20510 (202-225-2035);

House Committee on Agriculture; Room 1301, Longworth House Office Building, Washington, D.C. 20515 (202-225-2171): Agriculture generally; livestock and meat products; seeds, insect pests; protection of birds and animals in forest reserves; soils; rural electrification; forestry; dairy industry; etc.

Senate Committee on Interior and Insular Affairs; Room 3106, New Senate Office Building, Washington, D.C. 20510 (202-225-4971);

House Committee on Interior and Insular Affairs; Room 1324, Longworth House Office Building, Washington, D.C. 20515 (202-225-2761): Public lands generally; mineral resources, forest reserves and national parks; preservation of prehistoric ruins and objects of interest in the public domain; mining interests generally; petroleum conservation; care of Indian lands; etc.

Senate Committee on Public Works; Room 4204, New Senate Office Building, Washington, D.C. 20510 (202-225-6176);

House Committee on Public Works; Room 2167, Rayburn House Office Building, Washington, D.C. 20515 (202-225-4472): Flood control and improvement of rivers and harbors; oil and other pollution of navigable waters; water power; care of public reservations and parks within the District of Columbia, including Rock Creek Park and the Zoological Park; etc.

Senate Committee on Commerce; Room 5202, New Senate Office Building, Washington, D.C. 20510 (202-225-5115): Merchant Marine generally; registering and licensing of vessels and small boats; navigation and laws relating thereto; inland waterways; fisheries and wildlife, including research, restoration, refuges and conservation.

House Committee on Interstate and Foreign Commerce; Room 2125, Rayburn House Office Building, Washington, D.C. 20515 (202-225-2927): Regulation of interstate transmission of power, except the installation of connections between government water projects; inland waterways; interstate oil compacts, and petroleum and natural gas, except on public lands; interstate and foreign commerce generally.

House Committee on Merchant Marine and Fisheries; Room 1334, Longworth House Office Building, Washington, D.C. 20515 (202-225-4047): Merchant marine generally; coast and geodetic surveys; fisheries and wildlife; etc.

EXECUTIVE DEPARTMENTS

United States Department of Agriculture; Fourteenth Street and Jefferson Drive, S.W., Washington, D.C. 20250.

Agricultural Research Service, Washington, D.C. 20250. (Some functions transferred to the Environmental Protection Agency.)

Soil and Water Conservation Research Division; Plant Industry Station,

Beltsville, Maryland 20705. Conducts research in watershed engineering, soil management and water management.

Agricultural Quarantine Inspection Division; Federal Center Building, Hyattsville, Maryland 20782. Enforces quarantines affecting importations of plants and plant products from foreign countries, and the movement of plants between U. S. possessions and the mainland.

Plant Protection Division; Federal Center Building, Hyattsville, Maryland 20782. Administers programs for the control and eradication of insects, diseases and nematodes of economic importance. (Some functions transferred to EPA.)

Agricultural Stabilization and Conservation Service, Washington, D.C. 20250. Administers the following nationwide or regional programs: agricultural conservation, soil bank, cropland conversion and adjustment, Appalachian land stabilization and conservation, price stabilization, etc.

Cooperative State Research Service, Washington, D.C. 20250. Administers federal-grant funds for research in agriculture, forestry, resource conservation and rural life, made available to State Agricultural Experiment Stations in the fifty states and Puerto Rico.

Federal Extension Service; Washington, D.C. 20250. Has responsibility for and leadership in all general educational programs of the Department of Agriculture.

Forest Service; Washington, D.C. 20250. Administers national forests and grasslands. Cooperates in the enforcement of game laws on the national forests, and in the development and maintenance of wildlife resources. Promotes the application of sound forest-management practices.

Soil Conservation Service; Washington, D.C. 20250. Provides technical assistance in all land-use and rural areas development programs of the Department of Agriculture on farms and ranches and certain watersheds. Promotes development of wildlife habitat compatible with the primary use of the land.

United States Department of Commerce; Commerce Building, Fourteenth Street between Constitution Avenue and E Street, N.W., Washington, D.C. 20230.

Economic Development Administration; address above (202-967-5113). Conducts programs to help create permanent jobs in economically lagging areas. Provides public works grants and loans, planning and technical assistance.

National Oceanic and Atmospheric Administration; Washington, D.C. 20230. New agency established in 1970 to employ a unified approach to the problems of the ocean and atmosphere. The NOAA gathers into one department the following:

—The Environmental Science Services Administration (from within the Department of Commerce).
—Elements of the Bureau of Commercial Fisheries (from the Department of the Interior).
—The marine sport fish program of the Bureau of Sport Fisheries and Wildlife (from the Department of the Interior).
—The Marine Minerals Technology Center of the Bureau of Mines (from the Department of the Interior).

—The Office of Sea Grant Programs (from the National Science Foundation).
—Elements of the United States Lake Survey (from the Department of the Army).
—The National Oceanographic Data Center (from the Department of the Navy).
—The National Oceanographic Instrumentation Center (from the Department of the Navy).
—The National Data Buoy Project (from the Department of Transportation).

United States Department of Health, Education and Welfare; 330 Independence Avenue, S.W., Washington, D.C. 20201.

Consumer Protection and Environmental Health Service, 200 C Street, S.W., Washington, D.C. 20204. Established in 1968 to assess and help control environmental stresses affecting man's health and welfare. Operating agencies are the Food and Drug Administration, Environmental Control Administration and the National Air Pollution Control Administration.

Environmental Control Administration, 12720 Twinbrook Parkway, Rockville, Maryland 20852. Directs attention to such hazards as improper housing, noise, rodent and insect vectors, radiation, waste accumulation, improper sanitation and occupational disease and injury. (Some elements transferred to Environmental Protection Agency.)

United States Department of Housing and Urban Development; 451 Seventh Street, S.W., Washington, D.C. 20410.

Neighborhood Programs Division; same address. Concerned with open space land and urban beautification in the central city.

Division of Land Development; same address. Concerned with open space land and urban beautification outside the central city. Advances acquisition of land for public facilities.

United States Department of the Interior; Interior Building, C Street between Eighteenth and Nineteenth, N.W., Washington, D.C. 20240.[3]

Bureau of Land Management, Washington, D.C. 20240. Administers public domain lands, which are located primarily in the western states and which constitute about 60 percent of all federally owned lands.

Bureau of Mines, Washington, D.C. 20240. Conducts programs to promote conservation and development of mineral resources, discourage wasteful practices in mining and mineral processing and encourage safety and healthful working conditions. (Elements transferred to NOAA.)

Bureau of Outdoor Recreation, Washington, D.C. 20240. Administers Land and Water Conservation Fund Act of 1965. Through its Division of Water

[3]Since 1937, there has been talk of transforming the Department of the Interior into a coherent Department of Natural Resources. In 1971 the President's Advisory Council came up with concrete proposals, but they immediately ran into opposition. The opposition arises over the transfer of agencies. No department, it seems, is willing to hand over gracefully some part of itself to another department, no matter how logical the transfer might be.

Resources, it assesses needs in the area of water-oriented recreation, helps formulate action plans to help establish such recreational opportunities and strives to devise solutions to special problems, such as water pollution and conflicting land use.

Bureau of Reclamation, Washington, D.C. 20240. Administers the federal program in seventeen western states, Alaska and Hawaii, for water resource development and use so as to provide multiple-purpose projects furnishing fish and wildlife protection and recreational opportunities. Also concerned with farm irrigation, municipal and industrial use of water, hydroelectric power, etc.

Bureau of Commercial Fisheries, Washington, D.C. 20240. Aims to develop the nation's fishing industry. Seeks means of bringing the world's aquatic resources into economic and commercial production, and of contributing to man's understanding and control of aquatic living resources and their environment. (Elements transferred to NOAA.)

Bureau of Sport Fisheries and Wildlife, Washington, D.C. 20240. Aids in the conservation of the nation's migratory birds, certain mammals and sport and commercial fishes. (Elements transferred to NOAA.)

Fish and Wildlife Service, Washington, D.C. 20240. Established by the Fish and Wildlife Act of 1956, and consists of two separate bureaus: the Bureau of Commercial Fisheries and the Bureau of Sport Fisheries and Wildlife (above).

Geological Survey, GSA Building, Washington, D.C. 20242. Publishes and distributes maps and reports covering the nation's physical features and its mineral and water resources. Does typographic mapping and researches in geology, water resources and conservation.

National Park Service, Interior Building, Washington, D.C. 20240. Administers parks, monuments, etc., for their recreational, historic and natural values.

Advisory groups to the Department of the Interior are: the Advisory Board on National Parks, Historic Sites, Buildings and Monuments; the American Fisheries Advisory Committee; the National Advisory Board Council; the Water Pollution Control Board and the Bureau of Indian Affairs.

United States Department of Transportation; 400 Seventh Street, S.W., Washington, D.C. 20590 (202-426-4000): Composed of these main elements: the Coast Guard, the Federal Aviation Administration, the Federal Highway Administration, the Federal Railroad Administration, St. Lawrence Seaway Development Corporation, the National Transportation Safety Board and the Urban Mass Transportation Administration. The major objectives are to develop and improve a coordinated national transportation system and stimulate technological advances in the industry. Recent focuses on air and noise pollution, particularly in connection with automobiles and airplanes, have resulted in the introduction of another major objective: pollution control.

FEDERAL COMMITTEES

Commission on Population Growth and the American Future, 726 Jackson Place, N.W., Washington, D.C., 20506 (202-395-3417). Established March 16, 1970, to chart the probable course of population growth, internal migration and related demographic developments between now and the year 2000.

Federal Power Commission, 441 G Street, N.W., Washington, D.C. 20426. Licenses water-power projects; reviews plans for water development programs of the major federal construction agencies for conformance with the public interest.

General Services Administration, Eighteenth and F Streets, N.W., Washington, D.C. 20405 (202-343-1100). Concerned with the conveyance of surplus real property for wildlife conservation purposes to the Secretary of the Interior or to a state, pursuant to Public Law 537, Eightieth Congress.

National Council on Marine Resources and Engineering Development. Executive level group composed of the Vice President, Secretary of State, Secretary of the Navy, Secretary of the Interior, Secretary of Commerce, Secretary of the Treasury, Secretary of Health, Education and Welfare, the Chairman of the Atomic Energy Commission and the Director of the National Science Foundation.

Smithsonian Institution, 1000 Jefferson Drive, S.W., Washington, D.C. 20560 (202-628-4422). Sponsors programs of national and international cooperative research, conservation, education and training, with special emphasis on natural history and anthropology.

Tennessee Valley Authority, New Sprankle Building, Knoxville, Tennessee, 37902 (615-522-7181). Concerned with the development of the natural resources within the Tennessee Valley basin. Related activities include fish and wildlife development, water and air pollution control and reservoir ecology.

Water Resources Council, Suite 800, 2120 L Street, N.W., Washington, D.C. 20037 (202-254-6303). Executive level group headed by the Secretary of the Interior.

Working Group on Pesticides, Room 16B-30, 5600 Fishers Lane, Rockville, Maryland, 20852 (301-443-3230). Provides daily coordination of federal agency pesticide activities and policy programs. Responsible to the Council on Environmental Quality.

INTERNATIONAL, INTERSTATE AND NATIONAL COMMISSIONS

Atlantic Sea Run Salmon Commission, University of Maine, 5 Illinois Avenue, Bangor, Maine 04401 (207-947-8627). Charged by Maine legislature with the restoration and management of the Atlantic salmon in Maine waters. Represents the United States at international meetings concerning Atlantic salmon.

Great Lakes Commission, 5104 I.S.T. Building, 2200 North Campus Boulevard, Ann Arbor, Michigan 48105 (313-665-9135). Recommendatory and advisory agency for the eight Great Lakes states in regional water-resources matters.

Great Lakes Fishery Commission, 1451 Green Road, P.O. Box 640, Ann Arbor, Michigan 48107 (313-665-6847). Joint American-Canadian group on Great Lakes fishery. Established in 1954.

Inter-American Tropical Tuna Commission, Scripps Institution of Oceanography, La Jolla, California 92037 (714-453-2820). Established by convention between the United States and Costa Rica. Member nations include United States, Costa Rica, Canada, Mexico, Japan and Panama.

International Commission for the Northwest Atlantic Fisheries, P.O. Box 638, Dartmouth, Nova Scotia, Canada (902-466-7587). Fifteen-member nation compact to investigate, protect and conserve the fisheries of the northwest Atlantic Ocean.

International Commission on National Parks, P.O. Box 19347, Washington, D.C. 20036 (703-280-4086). Carries out activities concerning national parks and equivalent reserves and related subjects for parent organization: International Union for Conservation of Nature and Natural Resources (IUCN), IUCN Headquarters, 1110 Morges, Switzerland.

International North Pacific Fisheries Commission, 6640 Northwest Marine Drive, Vancouver 8, British Columbia, Canada (604-224-0722). Established by convention between Canada, Japan and the United States for the conservation of the fisheries resources of the northern Pacific Ocean.

International Pacific Halibut Commission, Marine Sciences No. 2, University of Washington, Seattle, Washington 98105 (206-634-1838). U. S.-Canadian agency charged with the investigation and scientific management of the halibut resource of the northern Pacific Ocean and Bering Sea.

International Pacific Salmon Fisheries Commission, Box 30, New Westminster, British Columbia, Canada (604-521-3771). U. S.-Canadian group concerned about the protection, preservation and extension of the sockeye and pink salmon fisheries of the Fraser River system.

International Whaling Commission, Great Westminster House, Horseferry Road, London S.W. 1, England. Member nations: United States, Argentina, Australia, Canada, Denmark, France, Iceland, Japan, Mexico, The Netherlands, New Zealand, Norway, Panama, South Africa, U.S.S.R. and United Kingdom.

Migratory Bird Conservation Commission, Interior Building, Washington, D.C. 20240 (202-343-4676). Considers, passes upon and fixes the prices for lands recommended by the Secretary of the Interior for purchase or lease by him under the Migratory Bird Conservation Act of 1929, as amended. Also concerned with migratory bird refuges in the national wildlife refuge system.

APPENDIX D

CONSERVATION PUBLICATIONS

Following is a listing of some of the major regional, national and international publications dealing primarily with ecology and conservation.

American Fishes and U. S. Trout News Magazine, publication of the U. S. Trout Farmers Association, 67 West 9000 South, Sandy, Utah 84070.

American Forests, publication of the American Forestry Association, 1319 Eighteenth Street, N.W., Washington, D.C. 20036.

Appalachia, publication of the Appalachian Mountain Club, 5 Joy Street, Boston, Massachusetts 02108.

Appalachian Trailway News, publication of the Appalachian Trail Conference, 1718 N Street, N.W., Washington, D.C. 20036.

Arctic Journal, publication of the Arctic Institute of North America, 3458 Redpath Street, Montreal 109, Quebec, Canada.

Atlantic Naturalist, publication of the Audubon Naturalist Society of the Central Atlantic States, 8940 Jones Mill Road, Washington, D.C. 20015.

Audubon, publication of the National Audubon Society, 950 Third Avenue, New York, N.Y. 10022.

BioScience, publication of the American Institute of Biological Sciences, Inc., 3900 Wisconsin Avenue, N.W., Washington, D.C. 20016.

California Condor, The, publication of the Society for the Preservation of Birds of Prey, Box 293, Pacific Palisades, California 90272.

Campfire Chatter, publication of the North American Family Campers Association, 76 State Street, Box 552, Newburyport, Massachusetts 01950.

Canadian Audubon, publication of the Canadian Audubon Society, 46 St. Clair Avenue, East, Toronto 7, Ontario, Canada.

Conservation News, semi-monthly publication of the National Wildlife Federation, 1412 Sixteenth Street, N.W., Washington, D.C. 20036.

Conservation Report, weekly publication while Congress is in session of the National Wildlife Federation, 1412 Sixteenth Street, N.W., Washington, D.C. 20036.

Ducks Unlimited Magazine, publication of Ducks Unlimited, P.O. Box 66300, Chicago, Illinois 60666.

Ecology Today, magazine-newsletter launched March 1, 1971, to report on problems, developments and action programs in the areas of population, food production, transportation, conservation of resources, environmental quality, etc.; P.O. Box 180, West Mystic, Connecticut 06388. $6 per year.

Environment, publication of the Scientists' Institute for Public Information, 30 East Sixty-eighth Street, New York, New York 10021. Editorial office: 438 North Skinker, St. Louis, Missouri 63130. Ten issues per year. Edited for nontechnical audience.

Environmental Action, bi-weekly publication of Environmental Action, Inc.; Room 731, 1346 Connecticut Avenue, N.W., Washington, D.C. 20036: $10 per year; student rate, $5.

Environmental Action Bulletin, weekly publication dramatizing action being done throughout the world of an ecological nature; stresses what the individual can do about pollution; Emmaus, Pennsylvania, 18049.

Environment Information ACCESS, bi-weekly intelligence, reference and research service of Ecology Forum, Inc., Suite 303 East, 200 Park Avenue, New York, New York, 10017.

Environmental Law Reporter, Dupont Circle Building, Suite 614, 1346 Connecticut Avenue, N.W., Washington, D.C. 20036. Loose-leaf monthly of the Environmental Law Institute. Aims to provide legal research tools and basic information useful to those confronting environmental issues as advocates, counselors, government officials and teachers.

Environmental Science & Technology, monthly journal published by the American Chemical Society and drawing on the society's world-wide news contacts in government, education and industry; 1155 Sixteenth Street, N.W., Washington, D.C. 20036; $7 per year.

Forest Farmer; Forest Farmer Manual, publications of the Forest Farmers Association Cooperative, Suite 307, 4 Executive Park East, N.E., Atlanta, Georgia 30329.

Forestry Chronicle, publication of the Canadian Institute of Forestry, P.O. Box 5000, MacDonald College, Quebec, Canada.

Great Lakes News Letter; Great Lakes Research Checklist, publications of the Great Lakes Commission, 5104 I.S.T. Building, 2200 North Campus Boulevard, Ann Arbor, Michigan 48105.

Hydata, publication of the American Water Resources Association, P.O. Box 434, Urbana, Illinois, 61801.

Journal of Forestry, publication of the Society of American Foresters, 1010 Sixteenth Street, N.W., Washington, D.C. 20006.

Journal of Geography, publication of the National Council for Geographic Education, Room 1226, 111 West Washington Street, Chicago, Illinois 60602.

Journal of Range Management, publication of the American Society of Range Management, 2120 South Birch Street, Denver, Colorado 80222.

Journal of Soil and Water Conservation, publication of the Soil Conservation Society of America, 7515 Northeast Ankeny Road, Ankeny, Iowa 50021.

Journal of Water Resources, publication of the American Water Resources Association, P.O. Box 434, Urbana, Illinois 61801. The association also publishes *Water Resources Newsletter* and *Water Resources Bulletin.*

Journal of Wildlife Management, publication of The Wildlife Society, Suite S-176, 3900 Wisconsin Avenue, N.W., Washington, D.C. 20016.

Journal Water Pollution Control Federation, publication of the Water Pollution Control Federation, 3900 Wisconsin Avenue, N.W., Washington, D.C. 20016.

Living Wilderness, The, publication of The Wilderness Society, 729 Fifteenth Street, N.W., Washington, D.C. 20005.

National Gardener, The, publication of the National Council of State Garden Clubs, Inc., 4401 Magnolia Avenue, St. Louis, Missouri 63110.

National Geographic; National Geographic School Bulletin, publications of the National Geographic Society, 1145 Seventeenth Street, N.W., Washington, D.C. 20036.

National Parks and Conservation Magazine, publication of the National Parks and Conservation Association, 1701 Eighteenth Street, N.W., Washington, D.C. 20009.

National Wildlife Magazine, bi-monthly publication of the National Wildlife Federation. Editorial office: 534 North Broadway, Milwaukee, Wisconsin 53202.

Nation's Agriculture, publication of the American Farm Bureau Federation, 1000 Merchandise Mart, Chicago, Illinois, 60654.

Oryx, publication of the Fauna Preservation Society, c/o Zoological Society of London, Regents Park, London N.W. 1, England.

Parks & Recreation Magazine, publication of the National Recreation and Park Association, 1700 Pennsylvania Avenue, N.W., Washington, D.C. 20006.

Ranger Rick's Nature Magazine, publication of the National Wildlife Federation. Editorial office: 1518 Walnut Street, Philadelphia, Pennsylvania 19102. Monthly except for July and September.

Reclamation News, publication of the National Reclamation Association, 897 National Press Building, Washington, D.C. 20004.

Rodale's Environment Action Bulletin, weekly coverage of health and human ecology news; published by Rodale Press, Inc., Emmaus, Pennsylvania 18049; subscription $10 per year; six months, $5.

Science, weekly publication of the American Association for the Advancement of Science, 1515 Massachusetts Avenue, N.W., Washington, D.C. 20005.

Shore and Beach, publication of the American Shore and Beach Preservation Association, Box 1246, Rockville, Maryland 20850.

Sierra Club Bulletin, publication of the Sierra Club, 1050 Mills Tower, San Francisco, California 94104.

Studies in Family Planning, publication of the Population Council, 245 Park Avenue, New York, New York 10017.

Transactions of the American Fishery Society, publication of the American Fisheries Society, 1040 Washington Building, Fifteenth and New York Avenue, N.W., Washington, D.C. 20005.

Trout Magazine, publication of Trout Unlimited, 4260 East Evans Avenue, Denver, Colorado 80222.

Tuesday Letter, publication of the National Association of Soil and Water Conservation Districts, 1025 Vermont Avenue, N.W., Washington, D.C. 20005.

Underwater Naturalist, publication of the American Littoral Society, Sandy Hook, Highlands, New Jersey 07732.

Water Newsletter; Research & Development News, Semi-monthly and monthly publications, respectively, of the Water Information Center, Inc., 44 Sintsink Drive East, Port Washington, New York 11050.

Water Sport, publication of the Boat Owners Council of America, 333 North Michigan Avenue, Chicago, Illinois 60601.

Whalewatcher, The, publication of the American Cetacean Society, 4725 Lincoln Boulevard, Marina del Rey, California 90291.

Wildlife Society News, publication of The Wildlife Society, Suite S-176, 3900 Wisconsin Avenue, N.W., Washington, D.C. 20016.

World Record Marine Fishes, publication of the International Game Fish Association, 3000 East Las Olas Boulevard, Fort Lauderdale, Florida 33316.

U. S. GOVERNMENT PUBLICATIONS

A valuable source of information is the Government Printing Office, which has approximately 25,000 publications available on a whole range of topics, including ecology and conservation. A listing of available publications in specific subject areas may be had by writing:

The Superintendent of Documents
Government Printing Office
Washington, D.C. 20402

The list is available free of charge. Prices range from a few cents to several dollars for individual items. The master list is revised yearly, although twice a month shorter lists of selected U. S. Government publications are issued. These are also available free of charge.

The most complete listing of current government publications is the *Monthly Catalogue of U. S. Government Publications,* available on subscription at $6 a year ($7.50 if foreign postage is required). This catalogue is primarily a library tool. It itemizes the publications of all departments issued during the month, whether for sale or otherwise.

Catalogues, price lists and indexes, as well as many government publications, may be consulted in most large libraries.

A word of caution is in order: not all government publications contain sound ecological advice. Many were prepared before conservation sensitivities were what they are now; some reflect institutional rather than human interests. But even these can be useful, once allowances are made and new environmental awareness applied.

Below is a subject list, which categorizes available government publications. Subjects checked will bring, free, titles and prices of specific documents. Orders for documents must include payment, else shipment will not be made.

10. *Laws, Rules, and Regulations.*
11. *Home Economics.* Foods and cooking.
15. *Geology.*
19. *Army.* Field manuals and technical manuals.
21. *Fish and Wildlife.*
25. *Transportation, Highways, Roads, and Postal Service.*
28. *Finance.* National economy, accounting, insurance, securities.
31. *Education.*
33. *Labor.*
33A. *Occupations.* Professions and job descriptions.
35. *National Parks.* Historic Sites, National Monuments.
36. *Government Periodicals and Subscription Services.*
37. *Tariff and Taxation.*

38. *Animal Industry.* Farm animals, poultry, and dairying.
41. *Insects.* Worms and insects harmful to man, animals, and plants.
42. *Irrigation, Drainage, and Water Power.*
43. *Forestry.* Managing and using forest and range land, including timber and lumber, ranges and grazing, American woods.
44. *Plants.* Culture, grading, marketing, and storage of fruits, vegetables, grass, and grain.
46. *Soils and Fertilizers.* Soil surveys, erosion, conservation.
48. *Weather, Astronomy, and Meteorology.*
50. *American History.*
51. *Health and Hygiene.* Drugs and sanitation.
51A. *Diseases.* Contagious and infectious diseases, sickness, and vital statistics.
53. *Maps.* Engineering, surveying.
54. *Political Science.* Government, crime, District of Columbia.
55. *Smithsonian Institution.* National Museum, and Indians.
58. *Mines.* Explosives, fuel, gasoline, gas, petroleum, minerals.
59. *Interstate Commerce.*
62. *Commerce.* Business, patents, trademarks, and foreign trade.
63. *Navy.* Marine Corps and Coast Guard.
64. *Scientific Tests, Standards.* Mathematics, physics.
65. *Foreign Relations of the United States.* Publications relating to foreign countries.
67. *Immigration, Naturalization, and Citizenship.*
68. *Farm Management.* Foreign agriculture, rural electrification, agricultural marketing.
70. *Census.* Statistics of agriculture, business, governments, housing, manufactures, minerals, population, and maps.
71. *Children's Bureau,* and other publications relating to children and youth.
72. *Homes.* Construction, maintenance, community development.
78. *Social Security.* Industrial hazards, health and hygiene, safety for workers, pensions, workmen's compensation and insurance.
79. *Air Force.* Aviation, civil aviation, naval aviation and Federal Aviation Administration.
79A. *Space, Missiles, the Moon, NASA, and Satellites.* Space education, exploration, research, and technology.
81. *Posters and Charts.*
82. *Radio and Electricity.* Electronics, radar, and communications.
83. *Library of Congress.*
84. *Atomic Energy and Civil Defense.*
85. *Defense.* Veterans' affairs.
86. *Consumer Information.* Family finances, appliances, recreation, gardening, health and safety, food, house and home, child care, and clothing and fabrics.
87. *States and Territories of the United States and Their Resources.* Including beautification, public buildings and lands, and recreational resources.

APPENDIX E

THE FOUNDATIONS

One of the positive indicators of expanding concern for the environment is the growing investment of foundation moneys in problem ecological areas. Files of The Foundation Center, a coordinating educational agency with offices in New York and Washington,[1] recorded $14,169,147 in new or current grants to environmental organizations for a host of studies, as of January 27, 1971. The center keeps a record of all grants of $10,000 or more. Following is a list of foundation grants for environmental study programs alone, and a brief description of these programs, when stated, from the files:

ALLEGHENY FOUNDATION (Pa.) $20,000 to Atlantic Council of the United States (D.C.) for an environmental conference.

BARTH (THEODORE H.) FOUNDATION (N.Y.) $10,000 to the Wildlife Management Institute (D.C.).

BIDDLE (MARY DUKE) FOUNDATION (N.Y.) $10,000 to the National Pollution Control Foundation (N.Y.).

CLEVELAND ASSOCIATED FOUNDATION, GREATER, (Ohio) $30,000 to Case Western Reserve University (Ohio) for research in separation problems of water pollutants.

——— $16,659 to Shaker Lakes Regional Nature Center (Ohio) for nature study program for school children.

CLEVELAND FOUNDATION (Ohio) $14,286 to Lake Erie Junior Nature and Science Center for building program.

DODGE (CLEVELAND H.) FOUNDATION (N.Y.) $15,000 to Wave Hill Center (N.Y.) for nature study groups and other cultural programs.

DONNER (WILLIAM H.) FOUNDATION (N.Y.) $25,000 to Thorne Ecological Foundation (Colo.) for seminars and studies on environmental arts and sciences, population growth, urbanization, pollution and other related subjects.

DREYFUS (CAMILLE AND HENRY) FOUNDATION (N.Y.) $10,000 to Environmental Research Institute (D.C.).

[1]The Foundation Center is an independent, tax-exempt organization, incorporated in 1956 as an educational institution under authority of the Board of Regents of the University of the State of New York. Formerly known as the Foundation Library Center, it is supported by twelve sponsoring foundations: Carnegie Coporation of New York, The Danforth Foundation, The William H. Donner Foundation, The Ford Foundation, W. K. Kellogg Foundation, Charles F. Kettering Foundation, Lilly Endowment, Richard King Mellon Foundation, Rockefeller Brothers Fund, The Rockefeller Foundation, Russell Sage Foundation, and Alfred P. Sloan Foundation.

The Foundation Center has five principal functions: information, research, publications, training, and consultation. Inquiries about any of these activities may be made by letter, telephone, or personal visit to the New York or Washington offices. New York offices are at 444 Madison Avenue, New York, New York 10022; Washington offices are at 1001 Connecticut Avenue, N.W., Washington, D.C. 20036.

EIGHTY MAIDEN LANE FOUNDATION (N.Y.) $100,000 to Continental Research Institute (N.Y.).

FELS (SAMUEL S.) FUND (Pa.) $10,000 to Academy of Natural Sciences (Pa.) for scientific research equipment.

——— $20,000 to Group for Environmental Education for preparation of textbook for eighth grade use.

FORD FOUNDATION (N.Y.) $20,500 to Association of American Law Schools (Ohio) for meeting with the American Association for the Advancement of Science dealing with the relation of law to environmental problems.

——— $18,500 to California Institute of Technology for student research on air pollution control.

——— $300,000 to Citizens for a Quieter City (N.Y.) for noise abatement project in New York City.

——— $23,500 to Citizens Union Research Foundation (N.Y.) for educational pamphlet on water pollution control.

——— $75,500 to Colorado Open Space Foundation for operation of Rocky Mountain Center on Environment.

——— $23,200 to Columbia University Center for Policy Research (N.Y.) for study of air pollution control in New York.

——— $500,000 to Conservation Foundation (D.C.) to stimulate informed action by citizens on behalf of environmental improvement.

——— $516,000 to Cornell University (N.Y.) to establish an interdepartmental program in ecology of pest management.

——— $152,000 to Environmental Law Institute for support of the monthly periodical, *Environmental Law Reporter.*

——— $36,850 to Harvard University to explore the use of advanced technology and community collaboration in more efficient and economical waste disposal.

——— $140,000 to International Center for Educational Development to develop environmental education in Los Angeles schools.

——— $858,000 to Johns Hopkins University (Md.) for graduate program in geography and environmental management.

——— $25,000 to Massachusetts Institute of Technology for studies preparatory to global environmental monitoring.

——— $450,000 to Michigan State University for construction of "tertiary" sewage treatment plant.

——— $25,000 to National Academy of Sciences (D.C.) for study on environmental problems.

——— $55,000 to New England Community Development Corporation (Mass.) for urban solid waste disposal demonstration project.

——— $180,150 to New England Community Development Corporation (Mass.) to explore use of advanced technology and community collaboration in more efficient and economical waste disposal.

——— $81,000 to North Jersey Conservation Foundation (N.J.) for in-service training in conservation and pollution problems at Rutgers University.

——— $23,500 to Northeast Illinois Natural Resources Service Center for natural resources information system.

——— $15,000 to Pennsylvania State University for symposium on statistical ecology concerning environmental problems.

——— $135,000 to Portland Public Schools (Ore.) for project on environmental education at Boise Elementary School.

——— $14,760 to Rutgers University (N.J.) for comparative study of municipal conservation commissions in New Jersey, New York and New England.

——— $182,000 to San Diego State College Foundation (Calif.) for undergraduate environmental biology program and student research in environmental problems.

——— $49,000 to San Francisco Planning and Urban Renewal Association to plan and set up rail-haul solid waste system.

——— $95,000 to Smithsonian Institution (D.C.) for comparative study of new state agencies dealing with environmental problems.

——— $368,000 to State University of New York (Stony Brook) for a program in applied environmental analysis and design.

——— $240,000 to Teachers College at Columbia University to study the influences of television on attitudes toward the environment.

——— $65,000 to Tilton School (N.H.) for a program on water pollution research for secondary school students.

——— $55,000 to the University of Alaska for survey of environmental and land use policy issues in Alaska.

——— $311,850 to the University of Arizona for a graduate program in water resource planning and decision making.

——— $10,000 to the University of California to defray publication costs of *Ecology Law Quarterly* dealing with problems of environmental law.

——— $176,000 to the University of Colorado to develop environmental education in elementary schools.

——— $100,000 to the University of Colorado School of Law for environmental quality control seminar.

——— $124,000 to the University of Illinois for a natural resources information system.

——— $79,000 to the University of Maine for an environmental research project on cleanup of the Penobscot River Basin.

——— $37,775 to the University of Michigan to study the role of courts in reviewing decisions affecting the environment.

——— $45,250 to the University of Southern California to document and evaluate work of the California Environmental Quality Study Council.

——— $75,000 to the University of Washington for an interdisciplinary workshop on the use of resource management computer simulation games.

——— $587,695 to the University of Washington for a graduate program in qualitative ecology and natural resource management.

——— $150,000 to Wave Hill Center for Environmental Studies (N.Y.) for an urban environmental education program.

——— $909,655 to Yale University for a graduate program in management of terrestrial environment.

GIFFORD (ROSAMOND) CHARITABLE FOUNDATION $49,200 to Onondaga

Nature Center (N.Y.) for environmental education program at Beaver Lake Nature Center.

GREENAWAY FOUNDATION (N.Y.) $11,700 to National Pollution Control Foundation (N.Y.).

HARTFORD FOUNDATION PUBLIC GIVING (Conn.) $15,000 to Capital Region Planning Agency for air pollution study.

HILL (LOUIS W. AND MAUD) FAMILY FOUNDATION (Minn.) $21,740 to Oregon State University Foundation for studies of tidal hydraulics and water quality at School of Engineering.

HOMELAND FOUNDATION (N.Y.) $30,000 to Johns Hopkins University for research in geography and environmental engineering.

JOHNSON (A. D.) FOUNDATION (N.Y.) $100,000 to the Foundation for Human Ecology (Ill.).

KALAMAZOO FOUNDATION (Mich.) $300,000 to Kalamazoo Nature Center (Mich.) for operation of a school program of environmental education.

KAUFMANN (EDGAR J.) CHARITABLE FOUNDATION (Pa.) $17,000 to the Center for Environmental Structure (Calif.) for research.

KELLOGG (W. K.) FOUNDATION (Mich.) $55,615 to Colorado State University Institute of Rural Environmental Health, for prevention of health problems with farmers' environment.

——— $700,000 to the National Academy of Sciences, Environmental Studies Board (D.C.), for studies to improve environmental quality.

——— $442,380 to National Sanitation Foundation (Mich.) for environmental quality study and action program.

——— $31,110 to University of Iowa Institute of Agricultural Medicine for prevention of health problems within farmers' environment.

——— $383,240 to Washington University Center for the Biology of Natural Systems (Mo.) to utilize basic sciences in solving environmental health problems.

LEAVITT FOUNDATION (N.Y.) $17,500 to the Environmental Health Research Institute.

MELLON (ANDREW W.) FOUNDATION (N.Y.) $15,000 to International Union for Conservation of Nature and Natural Resources (D.C.) for a general assembly on environmental problems and for equipment.

——— $15,000 to Park Association of New York City for programs of the Environmental Resource Council.

——— $200,000 to Polytechnic Institute of Brooklyn (N.Y.) for the Center for Urban Environmental Studies.

——— $150,000 to Smithsonian Institution for land acquisition for Chesapeake Bay Center for Environmental Studies.

MERRILL (CHARLES E.) TRUST (N.Y.) $25,000 to Continental Research Institute (N.Y.).

PICKER (JAMES) FOUNDATION (N.Y.) $10,000 to the National Council on Radiation Protection and Measurements (D.C.).

RESOURCES FOR THE FUTURE (D.C.) $10,000 to Carnegie-Mellon University (Pa.) to estimate level and cost of air pollution.

——— $14,818 to George Washington University (D.C.) to estimate cross-elasticities of outdoor recreation demands.

——— $21,925 to Harvard University for analysis of environmental perception and attitudes.

——— $59,510 to Indiana University Foundation to study effects of power structure and decision making on environmental quality programs.

——— $71,227 to Temple University for economic evaluation of alternative air resource management policies.

——— $35,205 to University of California for recognition, definition and use of landscape resources.

——— $10,000 to University of Illinois for formulation of comprehensive air pollution model.

——— $43,500 to University of Massachusetts for study of urban growth in rural countryside.

——— $19,734 to University of Michigan to study institutional aspects of managing lakes and bays.

——— $40,000 to University of Pennsylvania to explore statistical relationship between air pollutants and certain chronic disease mortality rates.

ROCKEFELLER FOUNDATION (N.Y.) $250,000 to Academy of Natural Sciences of Philadelphia for studies in water pollution problems.

——— $25,000 to Columbia University School of Engineering and Applied Science (N.Y.) for survey of environmental pollution.

——— $25,000 to Conservation Foundation (D.C.) for a conference on ecological aspects of international development.

——— $199,530 to Cornell University, University of California at Berkeley and Riverside and University of Illinois for research in nonpollutant insecticides.

——— $250,000 to Harvard University Laboratory of Insect Physiology for research in insect control to replace pesticides that pollute the environment.

——— $25,000 to Massachusetts Institute of Technology for study of global climatic and ecological effects of pollution of the atmosphere-ocean system.

——— $250,000 to Michigan State University to develop a series of lakes and ponds stocked with plants and fish to serve as a living filters for sewage effluent.

——— $45,000 to Monroe County Community College (Ohio) for training program for environmental control technicians.

——— $25,000 to National Academy of Sciences (D.C.) for summer study on environmental problems by the Environmental Studies Board.

——— $40,000 to National Academy of Sciences (D.C.) for exploratory studies in environmental science.

——— $50,000 to Princeton University Center of International Studies for study on ecological problems.

———$95,000 to University of Arizona for research to remove contaminants from industrial residues by soil filtration process.

——— $284,000 to University of California Division of Environmental Studies for interdisciplinary research and teaching.

——— $750,000 to University of Michigan for interdisciplinary program in environmental quality.

——— $200,000 to Williams College Center for Environmental Studies to enlarge faculty.

SCHMIDLAPP (JACOB G.) TRUST (Ohio) $700,000 to University of Cincinnati to establish a chair of environmental health.

SEARS FAMILY FOUNDATION (Ohio) $15,000 to Committee for Environmental Information (Ohio).

SLOAN (ALFRED P.) FOUNDATION (N.Y.) $10,000 to National Academy of Arts and Sciences (Mass.) for conference in Nairobi to determine feasibility of a center on insect physiology and endocrinology with implications for improved means for pest control.

——— $10,000 to Massachusetts Institute of Technology for summer study on critical environmental problems.

SPAULDING-POTTER CHARITABLE TRUSTS (N.H.) $100,000 to Controlled Environment Corporation (N.H.) for purchase of land.

——— $100,000 to New Hampshire-Tomorrow for environmental studies and demonstration projects.

STERN FUND (N.Y.) $20,000 to Center for the Study of Responsive Law (D.C.) for Savannah River Project, to study pollution.

——— $20,000 to Environmental Resources (D.C.) for project on occupational health and safety.

STRONG (HATTIE M.) FOUNDATION (D.C.) $30,000 to Chesapeake Bay Foundation (Md.) for conservation and environmental research and education.

——— $10,000 to Potomac Basin Center (D.C.) for conservation and environmental research and education.

WATERMAN (PHOEBE) FOUNDATION (Pa.) $95,583 to Academy of Natural Sciences (Pa.) for ecological research.

WOOD (SAMUEL J. AND EVELYN L.) FOUNDATION (N.Y.) $20,000 to Environmental Health and Light Research Institute (Ill.).

APPENDIX F

A CREED TO PRESERVE OUR NATURAL HERITAGE

Extract from President Johnson's message to Congress, February 1966

To sustain an environment suitable for man, we must fight on a thousand battlegrounds. Despite all of our wealth and knowledge, we cannot create a Redwood Forest, a wild river, or a gleaming seashore.

But we can keep those we have.

The science that has increased our abundance can find ways to restore and renew an environment equal to our needs.

The time is ripe to set forth a creed to preserve our natural heritage—principles which men and women of goodwill will support in order to assure the beauty and bounty of their land. Conservation is ethically sound. It is rooted in our love of the land, our respect for the rights of others, our devotion to the rule of law.

Let us proclaim a creed to preserve our natural heritage with rights and the duties to respect those rights:

The right to clean water—and the duty not to pollute it.

The right to clean air—and the duty not to befoul it.

The right to surroundings resonably free from man-made ugliness—and the duty not to blight.

The right of easy access to places of beauty and tranquillity where every family can find recreation and refreshment—and the duty to preserve such places clean and unspoiled.

The right to enjoy plants and animals in their natural habitats—and the duty not to eliminate them from the face of this earth.

These rights assert that no person, or company or government has a right in this day and age to pollute, to abuse resources, or to waste our common heritage.

The work to achieve these rights will not be easy. It cannot be completed in a year or five years. But there will never be a better time to begin.

Let us from this moment begin our work in earnest—so that future generations of Americans will look back and say:

1966 was the year of the new conservation, when farsighted men took farsighted steps to preserve the beauty that is the heritage of our Republic.

I urge the Congress to give favorable consideration to the proposals I have recommended in this message.

(signed) LYNDON B. JOHNSON

The White House
23 February 1966

APPENDIX G

Excerpts from President Nixon's State of the Union Address, January 22, 1970

I now turn to a subject which, next to our desire for peace, may well become the major concern of the American people in the decade of the seventies.

In the next ten years we shall increase our wealth by fifty percent. The profound question is—does this mean that we will be fifty percent richer in a real sense, fifty percent better off, fifty percent happier?

Or, does it mean that in the year 1980 the President standing in this place will look back on a decade in which seventy percent of our people lived in metropolitan areas choked by traffic, suffocated by smog, poisoned by water, deafened by noise and terrorized by crime?

These are not the great questions that concern world leaders at summit conferences. But people do not live at the summit. They live in the foothills of everyday experience. It is time for us all to concern ourselves with the way real people live in real life.

The great question of the seventies is, shall we surrender to our surroundings, or shall we make our peace with nature and begin to make reparations for the damage we have done to our air, our land and our water?

Restoring nature to its natural state is a cause beyond party and beyond factions. It has become a common cause of all the people of America. It is a cause of particular concern to young Americans—because they more than we will reap the grim consequences of our failure to act on programs which are needed now if we are to prevent disaster later.

Clean air, clean water, open spaces—these should once again be the birthright of every American. If we act now—they can be.

We still think of air as free. But clean air is not, and neither is clean water. The price tag on pollution control is high. Through our years of past carelessness we incurred a debt to nature, and now that debt is being called.

The program I shall propose to Congress will be the most comprehensive and costly program in this field ever in the nation's history.

It is not just a program for the next year. A year's plan in this field is no plan at all. This is a time to look ahead not a year, but five or ten years—whatever time is required to do the job.

I shall propose to this Congress a ten billion dollar nation-wide clean waters program to put modern municipal waste treatment plants in every place in America where they are needed to make our waters clean again, and to do it now.

We have the industrial capacity, if we begin now, to build them all within five years. This program will get them built within five years.

As our cities and suburbs relentlessly expand, those priceless open spaces needed for recreation areas accessible to their people are swallowed up—often forever. Unless we preserve these spaces while they are still available, we will have none to preserve. Therefore, I shall propose innovative financing methods for purchasing open space and park lands, now, before they are lost to us.

The automobile is our worst polluter of the air. Adequate control requires further advances in engine design and fuel composition. We shall intensify our research, set increasingly strict standards and strengthen enforcement procedures—and we shall do it now.

We no longer can afford to consider air and water common property, free to be abused by anyone without regard to the consequences. Instead, we should begin now to treat them as scarce resources, which we are no more free to contaminate than we are free to throw garbage in our neighbor's yard. This requires comprehensive new regulations. It also requires that, to the extent possible, the price of goods should be made to include the costs of producing and disposing of them without damage to the environment.

The argument is increasingly heard that a fundamental contradiction has arisen between economic growth and the quality of life, so that to have one we must forsake the other.

The answer is not to abandon growth, but to redirect it. For example, we should turn toward ending congestion and eliminating smog the same reservoir of inventive genius that created them in the first place.

Continued vigorous economic growth provides us with the means to enrich life itself and to enhance our planet as a place hospitable to man.

Each individual must enlist if this fight is to be won.

It has been said that no matter how many national parks and historical monuments we buy and develop, the truly significant environment for each of us is that in which we spend eighty percent of our time—that is, our homes, our places of work and the streets over which we pass.

Street litter, rundown parking strips and yards, dilapidated fences, broken windows, smoking automobiles, dingy working places, all should be the object of our fresh view.

We have been much too tolerant of our surroundings and too willing to leave it to others to clean up our environment. It is time for those who make massive demands on society to make some minimal demands on themselves. Each of us must resolve that each day he will leave his home, his property and the public places of his city or town a little cleaner, a little better, a little more pleasant for himself and those around him.

With the help of people we can do anything. Without their help we can do nothing. In this spirit, together, we can reclaim our land for ours and generations to come.

Between now and the year 2000, over one-hundred-million children will be born in the United States. Where they grow up—and how—will, more than any one thing, measure the quality of American life in these years ahead.

This should be a warning to us.

For the past thirty years our population has also been growing and shifting. The result is exemplified in the vast areas of rural America emptying out of people and of promise—a third of our counties lost population in the 1960s.

The violent and decayed central cities of our great metropolitan complexes are the most conspicuous area of failure in American life.

I propose that before these problems become insoluble, the nation develop a national growth policy. Our purpose will be to find those means by which Federal, state and local government can influence the course of urban settlement and growth so as positively to affect the quality of American life.

In the future, decisions as to where to build highways, locate airports, acquire land or sell land should be made with a clear objective of aiding a balanced growth.

In particular, the Federal government must be in a position to assist in the building of new cities and the rebuilding of old ones.

At the same time, we will carry our concern with the quality of life in America to the farm as well as the suburb, to the village as well as the city. What rural America most needs is a new kind of assistance. It needs to be dealt with, not as a separate nation, but as part of an over-all growth policy for all America. We must create a new rural environment that will not only stem the migration to urban centers but reverse it.

If we seize our growth as a challenge, we can make the 1970s an historic period when by conscious choice we transformed our land into what we want it to become.

America, which has pioneered in the new abundance, and in the new technology, is called upon today to pioneer in meeting the concerns which have followed in their wake—in turning the wonders of science to the service of man. . . .

APPENDIX H

President Nixon's Message on the Environment, February 10, 1970

To the Congress of the United States:

Like those in the last century who tilled a plot of land to exhaustion and then moved on to another, we in this century have too casually and too long abused our natural environment. The time has come when we can wait no longer to repair the damage already done, and to establish new criteria to guide us in the future.

The fight against pollution, however, is not a search for villains. For the most part, the damage done to our environment has not been the work of evil men, nor has it been the inevitable by-product either of advancing technology or of growing population. It results not so much from choices made, as from choices neglected: not from malign intention, but from failure to take into account the full consequences of our actions.

Quite inadvertently, by ignoring environmental costs we have given an economic advantage to the careless polluter over his more conscientious rival. While adopting laws prohibiting injury to person or property, we have freely allowed injury to our shared surroundings. Conditioned by an expanding frontier, we came only late to a recognition of how precious and how vulnerable our resources of land, water and air really are.

The tasks that need doing require money, resolve and ingenuity—and they are too big to be done by government alone. They call for fundamentally new philosophies of land, air and water use, for stricter regulation, for expanded government action, for greater citizen involvement, and for new programs to ensure that government, industry and individuals all are called on to do their share of the job and to pay their share of the cost.

Because the many aspects of environmental quality are closely interwoven, to consider each in isolation would be unwise. Therefore, I am today outlining a comprehensive, 37-point program, embracing 23 major legislative proposals and 14 new measures being taken by administrative action or Executive Order in five major categories:

—Water pollution control.
—Air pollution control.
—Solid waste management.
—Parklands and public recreation.
—Organizing for action.

As we deepen our understanding of complex ecological processes, as we improve our technologies and institutions and learn from experience, much more will be possible. But these 37 measures represent actions we can take *now,* and that can move us dramatically forward toward what has become an urgent common goal of all Americans: the rescue of our natural habitat as a place both habitable and hospitable to man.

Water Pollution

Water pollution has three principal sources: municipal, industrial and agricultural wastes. All three must eventually be controlled if we are to restore the purity of our lakes and rivers.

Of these three, the most troublesome to control are those from agricultural sources: animal wastes, eroded soil, fertilizers and pesticides. Some of these are nature's own pollutions. The Missouri River was known as "Big Muddy" long before towns and industries were built on its banks. But many of the same techniques of pest control, livestock feeding, irrigation and soil fertilization that have made American agriculture so abundantly productive have also caused serious water pollution.

Effective control will take time, and will require action on many fronts: modified agricultural practices, greater care in the disposal of animal wastes, better soil conservation methods, new kinds of fertilizers, new chemical pesticides and more widespread use of natural pest control techniques. A number of such actions are already underway. We have taken action to phase out the use of DDT and other hard pesticides. We have begun to place controls on wastes from concentrated animal feed-lots. We need programs of intensified research, both public and private, to develop new methods of reducing agricultural pollution while maintaining productivity. I have asked the Council on Environmental Quality to press forward in this area. Meanwhile, however, we have the technology and the resources to proceed *now* on a program of swift clean-up of pollution from the most acutely damaging sources: municipal and industrial waste.

MUNICIPAL WASTES

As long as we have the means to do something about it, there is no good reason why municipal pollution of our waters should be allowed to persist unchecked.

In the four years since the Clean Waters Restoration Act of 1966 was passed, we have failed to keep our promises to ourselves: Federal appropriations for constructing municipal treatment plants have totaled only about one-third of authorizations. Municipalities themselves have faced increasing difficulty in selling bonds to finance their share of the construction costs. Given the saturated condition of today's municipal bond markets, if a clean-up program is to work it has to provide the means by which municipalities can finance their share of the cost even as we increase Federal expenditures.

The best current estimate is that it will take a total capital investment of about $10 billion over a five-year period to provide the municipal waste treatment plants and interceptor lines needed to meet our national water quality standards. This figure is based on a recently-completed nationwide survey of the deficiencies of present facilities, plus projections of additional needs that will have developed by then—to accommodate the normal annual increase in the volume of wastes, and to replace equipment that can be expected to wear out or become obsolete in the interim.

This will provide every community that needs it with secondary waste treatment, and also special, additional treatment in areas of special need, including communities on the Great Lakes. We have the industrial capacity to do the job in five years if we begin now.

To meet this construction schedule, I propose a two-part program of Federal assistance:

—*I propose a Clean Waters Act with $4 billion to be authorized immediately, for Fiscal 1971, to cover the full Federal share of the total $10 billion cost on a matching fund basis. This would be allocated at a rate of $1 billion a year for the next four years, with a reassessment in 1973 of needs for 1975 and subsequent years.*

By thus assuring communities of full Federal support, we can enable planning to begin *now* for all needed facilities and construction to proceed at an accelerated rate.

—*I propose creation of a new Environmental Financing Authority, to ensure that every municipality in the country has an opportunity to sell its waste treatment plant construction bonds.*

The condition of the municipal bond market is such that, in 1969, 509 issues totaling $2.9 billion proved unsalable. If a municipality cannot sell waste treatment plant construction bonds, EFA will buy them and will sell its own bonds on the taxable market. Thus, construction of pollution control facilities will depend not on a community's credit rating, but on its waste disposal needs.

Providing money is important, but equally important is where and how the money is spent. A river cannot be polluted on its left bank and clean on its right. In a given waterway, abating *some* of the pollution is often little better than doing nothing at all, and money spent on such partial efforts is often largely wasted. Present grant allocation formulas—those in the 1966 Act—have prevented the spending of funds where they could produce the greatest results in terms of clean water. Too little attention has been given to seeing that investments in specific waste treatment plants have been matched by other municipalities and industries on the same waterway. Many plants have been poorly designed and inefficiently operated. Some municipalities have offered free treatment to local industries, then not treated their wastes sufficiently to prevent pollution.

To ensure that the new funds are well invested, five major reforms are needed. One requires legislation: the other four will be achieved by administrative action.

—*I propose that the present, rigid allocation formula be revised, so that special emphasis can be given to areas where facilities are most needed and where the greatest improvements in water quality will result.*

Under existing authority, the Secretary of the Interior will institute four major reforms:

—*Federally assisted treatment plants will be required to meet prescribed design, operation and maintenance standards, and to be operated only by State-certified operators.*

—*Municipalities receiving Federal assistance in construction plants will be required to impose reasonable users' fees on industrial users sufficient to meet the costs of treating industrial wastes.*

—Development of comprehensive river basin plans will be required at an early date, to ensure that Federally assisted treatment plants will in fact contribute to effective clean-up of entire river basin systems. Collection of existing data on pollution sources and development of effluent inventories will permit systems approaches to pollution control.

—Wherever feasible, communities will be strongly encouraged to cooperate in the construction of large regional treatment facilities, which provide economies of scale and give more efficient and more thorough waste treatment.

INDUSTRIAL POLLUTION

Some industries discharge their wastes into municipal systems; others discharge them directly into lakes and rivers. Obviously, unless we curb industrial as well as municipal pollution our waters will never be clean.

Industry itself has recognized the problem, and many industrial firms are making vigorous efforts to control their water-borne wastes. But strict standards and strict enforcement are nevertheless necessary—not only to ensure compliance, but also in fairness to those who have voluntarily assumed the often costly burden while their competitors have not. Good neighbors should not be placed at a competitive disadvantage because of their good neighborliness.

Under existing law, standards for water pollution control often are established in only the most general and insufficient terms: for example, by requiring all affected industries to install secondary treatment facilities. This approach takes little account of such crucial variables as the volume and toxicity of the wastes actually being discharged, or the capacity of a particular body of water to absorb wastes without becoming polluted. Even more important, it provides a poor basis for enforcement: with no effluent standard by which to measure, it is difficult to prove in court that standards are being violated.

The present fragmenting of jurisdictions also has hindered comprehensive efforts. At present, Federal jurisdiction generally extends only to interstate waters. One result has been that as stricter State-Federal standards have been imposed, pollution has actually increased in some other waters—in underground aquifers and the oceans. As controls over interstate waters are tightened, polluting industries will be increasingly tempted to locate on intrastate lakes and rivers—with a consequently increased threat to those waterways—unless they too are brought under the same strictures.

I propose that we take an entirely new approach: one which concerts Federal, State and private efforts, which provides for effective nationwide enforcement, and which rests on a simple but profoundly significant principle: that the nation's waterways belong to us all, and that neither a municipality nor an industry should be allowed to discharge wastes into those waterways beyond their capacity to absorb the wastes without becoming polluted.

Specifically, I propose a seven-point program of measures we should adopt *now* to enforce control of water pollution from industrial and municipal wastes, and to give the States more effective backing in their own efforts.

—*I propose that State-Federal water quality standards be amended to impose precise effluent requirements on all industrial and municipal sources. These should be imposed on an expeditious timetable, with the limit for each based on a fair allocation of the total capacity of the waterway to absorb the user's particular kind of waste without becoming polluted.*

—*I propose that violation of established effluent requirements be considered sufficient cause for court action.*

—*I propose that the Secretary of the Interior be allowed to proceed more swiftly in his enforcement actions, and that he be given new legal weapons including subpoena and discovery power.*

—*I propose that failure to meet established water quality standards or implementation schedules be made subject to court-imposed fines of up to $10,000 per day.*

—*I propose that the Secretary of the Interior be authorized to seek immediate injunctive relief in emergency situations in which severe water pollution constitutes an imminent danger to health, or threatens irreversible damage to water quality.*

—*I propose that the Federal pollution-control program be extended to include all navigable waters, both inter- and intrastate, all interstate ground waters, the United States' portion of boundary waters, and waters of the Contiguous Zone.*

—*I propose that Federal operating grants to State pollution control enforcement agencies be tripled over the next five years—from $10 million now to $30 million in fiscal year 1975—to assist them in meeting the new responsibilities that stricter and expanded enforcement will place upon them.*

Air Pollution Control

Air is our most vital resource, and its pollution is our most serious environmental problem. Existing technology for the control of air pollution is less advanced than that for controlling water pollution, but there is a great deal we can do within the limits of existing technology—and more we can do to spur technological advance.

Most air pollution is produced by the burning of fuels. About half is produced by motor vehicles.

MOTOR VEHICLES

The Federal government began regulating automobile emissions of carbon monoxide and hydrocarbons with the 1968 model year. Standards for 1970 model cars have been made significantly tighter. This year, for the first time, emissions from new buses and heavy-duty trucks have also been brought under Federal regulation.

In future years, emission levels can and must be brought much lower.

The Secretary of Health, Education and Welfare is today publishing a notice of new, considerably more stringent motor vehicle emission standards he intends to issue for 1973 and 1975 models including control of nitrogen oxides by 1973 and of particulate emissions by 1975.

These new standards represent our best present estimate of the lowest emission levels attainable by those years.

Effective control requires new legislation to correct two key deficiencies in the present law:

(*a*) *Testing procedures.*—Under present law, only manufacturers' prototype vehicles are tested for compliance with emission standards, and even this is voluntary rather than mandatory.

I propose legislation requiring that representative samples of actual production vehicles be tested throughout the model year.

(*b*) *Fuel composition and additives.*—What goes into a car's fuel has a major effect on what comes out of its exhaust, and also on what kinds of pollution-control devices can effectively be employed. Federal standards for what comes out of a car's engine should be accompanied by standards for what goes into it.

I propose legislation authorizing the Secretary of Health, Education and Welfare to regulate fuel composition and additives.

With these changes, we can drastically reduce pollution from motor vehicles in the years just ahead. But in making and keeping our peace with nature, to plan only one year ahead or even five is hardly to plan at all. Our responsibility now is also to look beyond the Seventies, and the prospects then are uncertain. Based on present trends, it is quite possible that by 1980 the increase in the sheer number of cars in densely populated areas will begin outrunning the technological limits of our capacity to reduce pollution from the internal combustion engine. I hope this will not happen. I hope the automobile industry's presently determined effort to make the internal combustion engine sufficiently pollution-free succeeds. But if it does not, then unless motor vehicles with an alternative, low-pollution power source are available, vehicle-caused pollution will once again begin an inexorable increase.

Therefore, prudence dictates that we move now to ensure that such a vehicle will be available if needed.

I am inaugurating a program to marshal both government and private research with the goal of producing an unconventionally powered virtually pollution-free automobile within five years.

—*I have ordered the start of an extensive Federal research and development program in unconventional vehicles, to be conducted under the general direction of the Council on Environmental Quality.*

—*As an incentive to private developers, I have ordered that the Federal Government should undertake the purchase of privately produced unconventional vehicles for testing and evaluation.*

A proposal currently before the Congress would provide a further incentive to private developers by authorizing the Federal government to offer premium prices for purchasing low-pollution cars for its own use. This could be a highly productive program once such automobiles are approaching development, although current estimates are that, initially, prices offered would have to be up to 200% of the cost of equivalent conventional vehicles rather than the 125% contemplated in the proposed legislation. The immediate task, however, is to see that an intensified program of research and development begins at once.

One encouraging aspect of the effort to curb motor vehicle pollution is the extent to which industry itself is taking the initiative. For example, the nation's principal automobile manufacturers are not only developing devices now to meet present and future Federal emission standards, but are also, on their own initiative, preparing to put on the market by 1972 automobiles which will not require and, indeed, must not use leaded gasoline. Such cars will not only discharge no lead into the atmosphere, but will also be equipped with still more effective devices for controlling emissions—devices made possible by the use of lead-free gasoline.

This is a great forward step taken by the manufacturers before any Federal regulation of lead additives or emissions has been imposed. I am confident that the petroleum industry will see to it that suitable non-leaded gasoline is made widely available for these new cars when they come on the market.

STATIONARY-SOURCE POLLUTION

Industries, power plants, furnaces, incinerators—these and other so-called "stationary sources" add enormously to the pollution of the air. In highly industrialized areas, such pollution can quite literally make breathing hazardous to health, and can cause unforeseen atmospheric and meteorological problems as well.

Increasingly, industry itself has been adopting ambitious pollution-control programs, and state and local authorities have been setting and enforcing stricter anti-pollution standards. But they have not gone far enough or fast enough, nor, to be realistic about it, will they be able to without the strongest possible Federal backing. Without effective government standards, industrial firms that spend the necessary money for pollution control may find themselves at a serious economic disadvantage as against their less conscientious competitors. And without effective Federal standards, states and communities that require such controls find themselves at a similar disadvantage in attracting industry, against more permissive rivals. Air is no respecter of political boundaries: a community that sets and enforces strict standards may still find its air polluted from sources in another community or another state.

Under the Clean Air Act of 1967, the Federal government is establishing air quality control regions around the nation's major industrial and metropolitan areas. Within these regions, states are setting air quality standards—permissible levels of pollutants in the air—and developing plans for pollution abatement to achieve those air quality standards. All state air quality standards and implementation plans require Federal approval.

This program has been the first major Federal effort to control air pollution. It has been a useful beginning. But we have learned in the past two years that it has shortcomings. Federal designation of air quality control regions, while necessary in areas where emissions from one state are polluting the air in another, has been a time-consuming process. Adjoining states within the same region often have proposed inconsistent air quality standards, causing further delays for compromise and revision. There are no provisions for controlling pollution *outside* of established air quality control regions. This means that even with the designation of hundreds of such regions, some areas of the country with serious air pollution problems would remain outside of the program. This is unfair not only to the public but to many industries as well, since those within regions with strict requirements could be unfairly disadvantaged with respect to competitors that are not within regions. Finally, insufficient Federal enforcement powers have circumscribed the Federal government's ability to support the states in establishing and enforcing effective abatement programs.

It is time to build on what we have learned, and to begin a more ambitious national effort. I recommend that the Clean Air Act be revised to expand the scope of strict pollution abatement, to simplify the task of industry in pollution abatement through more nearly uniform standards, and to provide special controls against particularly dangerous pollutants.

—*I propose that the Federal government establish nationwide air quality standards, with the states to prepare within one year abatement plans for meeting those standards.*

This will provide a minimum standard for air quality for all areas of the nation, while permitting states to set more stringent standards for any or all sections within the state. National air quality standards will relieve the states of the lengthy process of standard-setting under Federal supervision, and allow them to concentrate on the immediate business of developing and implementing abatement plans.

These abatement plans would cover areas both inside and outside of Federally designated air quality control regions, and could be designed to achieve any higher levels of air quality which the states might choose to establish. They would include emission standards for stationary sources of air pollution.

—*I propose that designation of interstate air quality control regions continue at an accelerated rate, to provide a framework for establishing compatible abatement plans in interstate areas.*

—*I propose that the Federal government establish national emissions standards for facilities that emit pollutants extremely hazardous to health, and for selected classes of new facilities which could be major contributors to air pollution.*

In the first instance, national standards are needed to guarantee the earliest possible elimination of certain air pollutants which are clear health hazards even in minute quantities. In the second instance, national standards will ensure that advanced abatement technology is used in constructing the new facilities, and that levels of air quality are maintained in the face of industrial expansion. Before any emissions standards were established, public hearings would be required involving all interested parties. The States would be responsible for enforcing these standards in conjunction with their own programs.

—*I propose that Federal authority to seek court action be extended to include both inter- and intrastate air pollution situations in which, because of local non-enforcement, air quality is below national standards, or in which emissions standards or implementation timetables are being violated.*

—*I propose that failure to meet established air quality standards or implementation schedules be made subject to court-imposed fines of up to $10,000 per day.*

Solid Waste Management

"Solid wastes" are the discarded left-overs of our advanced consumer society. Increasing in volume, they litter the landscape and strain the facilities of municipal governments.

New packaging methods, using materials which do not degrade and cannot easily be burned, create difficult new disposal problems. Though many wastes are potentially re-usable, we often discard today what a generation ago we saved. Most bottles, for example, now are "non-returnable." We re-process used paper less than we used to, not only adding to the burden on municipal sanitation services but also making wasteful use of scarce timberlands. Often the least expensive way to dispose of an old automobile is to abandon it—and millions of people do precisely that, creating eyesores for millions of others.

One way to meet the problem of solid wastes is simply to surrender to it: to continue pouring more and more public money into collection and disposal of whatever happens to be privately produced and discarded. This is the old way; it amounts to a public subsidy of waste pollution. If we are ever truly to gain control of the problem, our goal must be broader: to reduce the volume of wastes and the difficulty of their disposal, and to encourage their constructive re-use instead.

To accomplish this, we need incentives, regulations and research directed especially at two major goals: a) making products more easily disposable—especially containers, which are designed for disposal; and b) re-using and recycling a far greater proportion of waste materials.

As we look toward the long-range future—to 1980, 2000 and beyond—recycling of materials will become increasingly necessary not only for waste disposal but also to conserve resources. While our population grows, each one of us keeps using more of the earth's resources. In the case of many common minerals, more than half those extracted from the earth since time began have been extracted since 1910.

A great deal of our space research has been directed toward creating self-sustaining environments, in which people can live for long periods of time by re-processing, re-cycling and re-using the same materials. We need to apply this kind of thinking more consciously and more broadly to our patterns of use and disposal of materials here on earth.

Many currently used techniques of solid waste disposal remain crudely deficient. Research and development programs under the Solid Waste Disposal

Act of 1965 have added significantly to our knowledge of more efficient techniques. The Act expires this year. I recommend its extension, and I have already moved to broaden its programs.

I have ordered a re-direction of research under the Solid Waste Disposal Act to place greater emphasis on techniques for re-cycling materials, and on development and use of packaging and other materials which will degrade after use—that is, which will become temporary rather than permanent wastes.

Few of America's eyesores are so unsightly as its millions of junk automobiles.

Ordinarily, when a car is retired from use it goes first to a wrecker, who strips it of its valuable parts, and then to a scrap processor, who reduces the remainder to scrap for sale to steel mills. The prices paid by wreckers for junk cars often are less than the cost of transporting them to the wrecking yard. In the case of a severely damaged or "cannibalized" car, instead of paying for it the wrecker may even charge towing costs. Thus the final owner's economic incentive to deliver his car for processing is slight, non-existent or even negative.

The rate of abandonment is increasing. In New York City, 2,500 cars were towed away as abandoned on the streets in 1960. In 1964, 25,000 were towed away as abandoned; in 1969, more than 50,000.

The way to provide the needed incentive is to apply to the automobile the principle that its price should include not only the cost of producing it, but also the cost of disposing of it.

I have asked the Council on Environmental Quality to take the lead in producing a recommendation for a bounty payment or other system to promote the prompt scrapping of all junk automobiles.

The particular disposal problems presented by the automobile are unique. However, wherever appropriate we should also seek to establish incentives and regulations to encourage the re-use, re-cycling or easier disposal of other commonly used goods.

I have asked the Chairman of the Council on Environmental Quality to work with the Cabinet Committee on the Environment, and with appropriate industry and consumer representatives, toward development of such incentives and regulations for submission to the Congress.

Parks and Public Recreation

Increasing population, increasing mobility, increasing incomes and increasing leisure will all combine in the years ahead to rank recreational facilities among the most vital of our public resources. Yet land suitable for such facilities, especially near heavily populated areas, is being rapidly swallowed up.

Plain common sense argues that we give greater priority to acquiring now the lands that will be so greatly needed in a few years. Good sense also argues that the Federal government itself, as the nation's largest landholder, should address itself more imaginatively to the question of making optimum use of its own holdings in a recreation-hungry era.

—*I propose full funding in fiscal 1971 of the $327 million available through the Land and Water Conservation Fund for additional park and recreational facilities, with increased emphasis on locations that can be easily reached by the people in crowded urban areas.*

—*I propose that we adopt a new philosophy for the use of Federally-owned lands, treating them as a precious resource—like money itself—which should be made to serve the highest possible public good.*

Acquiring needed recreation areas is a real estate transaction. One third of all the land in the United States—more than 750,000,000 acres—is owned by the Federal government. Thousands of acres in the heart of metropolitan areas are reserved for only minimal use by Federal installations. To supplement the regularly-appropriated funds available, nothing could be more appropriate than to meet new real estate needs through use of presently-owned real estate, whether by transfer, sale or conversion to a better use.

Until now, the uses to which Federally-owned properties were put has largely been determined by who got them first. As a result, countless properties with enormous potential as recreational areas linger on in the hands of agencies that could just as well—or better—locate elsewhere. Bureaucratic inertia is compounded by a quirk of present accounting procedures, which has the effect of imposing a budgetary penalty on an agency that gives up one piece of property and moves to another, even if the vacated property is sold for 10 times the cost of the new.

The time has come to make more rational use of our enormous wealth of real property, giving a new priority to our newly urgent concern with public recreation—and to make more imaginative use of properties now surplus to finance acquisition of properties now needed.

—*By Executive Order, I am directing the heads of all Federal agencies and the Administrator of General Services to institute a review of all Federally-owned real properties that should be considered for other uses. The test will be whether a particular property's continued present use or another would better serve the public interest, considering both the agency's needs and the property's location. Special emphasis will be placed on identifying properties that could appropriately be converted to parks and recreation areas, or sold, so that proceeds can be made available to provide additional park and recreation lands.*

—*I am establishing a Property Review Board to review the GSA reports and recommend to me what properties should be converted or sold. This Board will consist of the Director of the Bureau of the Budget, the Chairman of the Council of Economic Advisers, the Chairman of the Council on Environmental Quality and the Administrator of General Services, plus others that I may designate.*

—*I propose legislation to establish, for the first time, a program for relocating Federal installations that occupy locations that could better be used for other purposes.*

This would allow a part of the proceeds from the sales of surplus properties to be used for relocating such installations, thus making more land available.

—*I also propose accompanying legislation to protect the Land and Water Conservation Fund, ensuring that its sources of income would be maintained and possibly increased for purchasing additional parkland.*

The net effect would be to increase our capacity to add new park and recreational facilities, by enabling us for the first time to use surplus property sales in a coordinated three-way program: a) by direct conversion from other uses; b) through sale of presently-owned properties and purchase of others with the proceeds; and c) by sale of one Federal property, and use of the proceeds to finance the relocation and conversion costs of making another property available for recreational use.

—*I propose that the Department of the Interior be given authority to convey surplus real property to State and local governments for park and recreation purposes at a public benefit discount ranging up to 100 percent.*

—*I propose that Federal procedures be revised to encourage Federal agencies to make efficient use of real property. This revision should remove the budgetary penalty now imposed on agencies relinquishing one site and moving to another.*

As one example of what such a property review can make possible, a sizable stretch of one of California's finest beaches has long been closed to the public because it was part of Camp Pendleton. Last month the Defense Department arranged to make more than a mile of that beach available to the State of California for use as a State park. The remaining beach is sufficient for Camp Pendleton's needs; thus the released stretch represents a shift from low-priority to high-priority use. By carefully weighing alternative uses, a priceless recreational resource was returned to the people for recreational purposes.

Another vast source of potential parklands also lies untapped. We have come to realize that we have too much land available for growing crops and not enough land for parks, open space and recreation.

—*I propose that instead of simply paying each year to keep this land idle, we help local governments buy selected parcels of it to provide recreational facilities for use by the people of towns in rural areas. This program has been tried, but allowed to lapse; I propose that we revive and expand it.*

—*I propose that we also adopt a program of long-term contracts with private owners of idled farmland, providing for its reforestation and public use for such pursuits as hunting, fishing, hiking and picknicking.*

Organizing for Action

The environmental problems we face are deep-rooted and widespread. They can be solved only by a full national effort embracing not only sound, coordinated planning, but also an effective follow-through that reaches into every community in the land. Improving our surroundings is necessarily the business of us all.

At the Federal level, we have begun the process of organizing for this effort.

The Council on Environmental Quality has been established. This Council will be the keeper of our environmental conscience, and a goad to our ingenuity; beyond this, it will have responsibility for ensuring that all our programs and actions are undertaken with a careful respect for the needs of environmental quality. I have already assigned it major responsibilities for new program development, and I shall look to it increasingly for new initiatives.

The Cabinet Committee on the Environment, which I created last year, acts as a coordinating agency for various departmental activities affecting the environment.

To meet future needs, many organizational changes will still be needed. Federal institutions for dealing with the environment and natural resources have developed piecemeal over the years in response to specific needs, not all of which were originally perceived in the light of the concerns we recognize today. Many of their missions appear to overlap, and even to conflict. Last year I asked the President's Advisory Council on Executive Organization, headed by Mr. Roy Ash, to make an especially thorough study of the organization of Federal environmental natural resource and oceanographic programs, and to report its recommendations to me by April 15. After receiving their report, I shall recommend needed reforms, which will involve major reassignments of responsibilities among Departments.

For many of the same reasons, overlaps in environmental programs extend to the Legislative as well as the Executive branch, so that close consultation will be necessary before major steps are taken.

No matter how well organized government itself might be, however, in the final analysis the key to success lies with the people of America.

Private industry has an especially crucial role. Its resources, its technology, its demonstrated ingenuity in solving problems others only talk about—all these are needed, not only in helping curb the pollution industry itself creates but also in helping devise new and better ways of enhancing all aspects of our environment.

> *I have ordered that the United States Patent Office give special priority to the processing of applications for patents which could aid in curbing environmental abuses.*

Industry already has begun moving swiftly toward a fuller recognition of its own environmental responsibilities, and has made substantial progress in many areas. However, more must be done.

Mobilizing industry's resources requires organization. With a remarkable degree of unanimity, its leaders have indicated their readiness to help.

> *I will shortly ask a group of the nation's principal industrial leaders to join me in establishing a National Industrial Pollution Control Council.*

The Council will work closely with the Council on Environmental Quality, the Citizens' Advisory Committee on Environmental Quality, the Secretary of Commerce and others as appropriate in the development of effective policies for the curbing of air, water, noise and waste pollution from industrial sources. It will work to enlist increased support from business and industry in the drive to reduce pollution, in all its forms, to the minimum level possible. It will provide a mechanism through which, in many cases, government can work with key leaders in various industries to establish voluntary programs for accomplishing desired pollution-control goals.

Patterns of organization often turn out to be only as good as the example set by the organizer. For years, many Federal facilities have themselves been among the worst polluters. The Executive Order I issued last week not only accepts responsibility for putting a swift end to Federal pollution, but puts teeth into the commitment.

I hope this will be an example for others.

At the turn of the century, our chief environmental concern was to conserve what we had—and out of this concern grew the often embattled but always determined "conservation" movement. Today, "conservation" is as important as ever—but no longer is it enough to conserve what we have; we must also restore what we have lost. We have to go beyond conservation to embrace restoration.

The task of cleaning up our environment calls for a total mobilization by all of us. It involves governments at every level; it requires the help of every citizen. It cannot be a matter of simply sitting back and blaming someone else. Neither is it one to be left to a few hundred leaders. Rather, it presents us with one of those rare situations in which each individual everywhere has an opportunity to make a special contribution to his country as well as his community.

Through the Council on Environmental Quality, through the Citizens' Advisory Committee on Environmental Quality, and working with Governors and Mayors and county officials and with concerned private groups, we shall be reaching out in an effort to enlist millions of helping hands, millions of willing spirits—millions of volunteer citizens who will put to themselves the simple question: "What can *I* do?"

It is in this way—with vigorous Federal leadership, with active enlistment of governments at every level, with the aid of industry and private groups, and above all with the determined participation by individual citizens in every state and every community, that we at last will succeed in restoring the kind of environment we want for ourselves, and the kind of environment generations that come after deserve to inherit.

This task is ours together. It summons our energy, our ingenuity and our conscience in a cause as fundamental as life itself.

RICHARD NIXON

THE WHITE HOUSE

APPENDIX I

THE PRESIDENT

Executive Order 11472

ESTABLISHING THE ENVIRONMENTAL QUALITY COUNCIL AND THE CITIZENS' ADVISORY COMMITTEE ON ENVIRONMENTAL QUALITY

By virtue of the authority vested in me as President of the United States, it is ordered as follows:

Part I. Environmental Quality Council

Section 101. *Establishment of the Council.* (a) There is hereby established the Environmental Quality Council (hereinafter referred to as "the Council").

(b) The President of the United States shall preside over meetings of the Council. The Vice President shall preside in the absence of the President.

(c) The Council shall be composed of the following members:

The Vice President of the United States
Secretary of Agriculture
Secretary of Commerce
Secretary of Health, Education and Welfare
Secretary of Housing and Urban Development
Secretary of the Interior
Secretary of Transportation

and such other heads of departments and agencies and others as the President may from time to time direct.

(d) Each member of the Council may designate an alternate, who shall serve as a member of the Council whenever the regular member is unable to attend any meeting of the Council.

(e) When matters which affect the interest of Federal agencies the heads of which are not members of the Council are to be considered by the Council, the President or his representative may invite such agency heads or their alternates to participate in the deliberations of the Council.

(f) The Director of the Bureau of the Budget, the Chairman of the Council of Economic Advisers, and the Executive Secretary of the Council for Urban Affairs or their representatives may participate in the deliberations of the Environmental Quality Council as observers.

(g) The Science Adviser to the President shall be the Executive Secretary of the Council and shall assist the President in directing the affairs of the Council.

Sec. 102. *Functions of the Council.* (a) The Council shall advise and assist the President with respect to environmental quality matters and shall perform such other related duties as the President may from time to time prescribe. In addition thereto, the Council is directed to:

(1) Recommend measures to ensure that Federal policies and programs, including those for development and conservation of natural resources, take adequate account of environmental effects.

(2) Review the adequacy of existing systems for monitoring and predicting environmental changes so as to achieve effective coverage and efficient use of facilities and other resources.

(3) Foster cooperation between the Federal government, State and local governments, and private organizations in environmental programs.

(4) Seek advancement of scientific knowledge of changes in the environment and encourage the development of technology to prevent or minimize adverse effects that endanger man's health and well-being.

(5) Stimulate public and private participation in programs and activities to protect against pollution of the Nation's air, water, and land and its living resources.

(6) Encourage timely public disclosure by all levels of government and by private parties of plans that would affect the quality of environment.

(7) Assure assessment of new and changing technologies for their potential effects on the environment.

(8) Facilitate coordination among departments and agencies of the Federal government in protecting and improving the environment.

(b) The Council shall review plans and actions of Federal agencies affecting outdoor recreation and natural beauty. The Council may conduct studies and make recommendations to the President on matters of policy in the fields of outdoor recreation and natural beauty. In carrying out the foregoing provisions of this subsection, the Council shall, as far as may be practical, advise Federal agencies with respect to the effect of their respective plans and programs on recreation and natural beauty, and may suggest to such agencies ways to accomplish the purposes of this order. For the purposes of this order, plans and programs may include, but are not limited to, those for or affecting: (1) Development, restoration, and preservation of the beauty of the countryside, urban and suburban areas, water resources, wild rivers, scenic roads, parkways and highways, (2) the protection and appropriate management of scenic or primitive areas, natural wonders, historic sites, and recreation areas, (3) the management of Federal land and water resources, including fish and wildlife, to enhance natural beauty and recreational opportunities consistent with other essential uses, (4) cooperation with the States and their local subdivisions and private organizations and individuals in areas of mutual interest, (5) interstate arrangements, including Federal participation where authorized and necessary, and (6) leadership in a nationwide recreation and beautification effort.

(c) The Council shall assist the President in preparing periodic reports to the Congress on the subjects of this order.

SEC. 103. *Coordination.* The Secretary of the Interior may make available to the Council for coordination of outdoor recreation the authorities and resources available to him under the Act of May 28, 1963, 77 Stat. 49; to the extent permitted by law, he may make such authorities and resources available to the Council also for promoting such coordination of other matters assigned to the Council by this order.

SEC. 104. *Assistance for the Council.* In compliance with provisions of applicable law, and as necessary to serve the purposes of this order, (1) the Office of Science and Technology shall provide or arrange for necessary administrative and staff services, support, and facilities for the Council, and (2) each department and agency which has membership on the Council under Section 101 (c) hereof shall furnish the Council such information and other assistance as may be available.

PART II. CITIZENS' ADVISORY COMMITTEE ON ENVIRONMENTAL QUALITY

SEC. 201. *Establishment of the Committee.* There is hereby established the Citizens' Advisory Committee on Environmental Quality (hereinafter referred to as the "Committee"). The Committee shall be composed of a chairman and not more than 14 other members appointed by the President. Appointments to membership on the Committee shall be for staggered terms, except that the chairman of the Committee shall serve until his successor is appointed.

SEC. 202. *Functions of the Committee.* The Committee shall advise the President and the Council on matters assigned to the Council by the provisions of this order.

SEC. 203. *Expenses.* Members of the Committee shall receive no compensation from the United States by reason of their services under this order but shall be entitled to receive travel and expenses, including per diem in lieu of subsistence, as authorized by law (5 U.S.C. 5701–5708) for persons in the Government service employed intermittently.

SEC. 204. *Continuity.* Persons who on the date of this order are members of the Citizens' Advisory Committee on Recreation and Natural Beauty established by Executive Order No. 11278 of May 4, 1966, as amended, shall, until the expirations of their respective terms and without further action by the President, be members of the Committee established by the provisions of this Part in lieu of an equal number of the members provided for in section 201 of this order.

PART III. GENERAL PROVISIONS

SEC. 301. *Construction.* Nothing in this order shall be construed as subjecting any department, establishment, or other instrumentality of the executive branch of the Federal Government or the head thereof, or any function vested by law in or assigned pursuant to law to any such agency or head, to the authority of any other such agency or head or as abrogating, modifying, or restricting any such function in any manner.

SEC. 302. *Prior bodies and orders.* The President's Council on Recreation and Natural Beauty and the Citizens' Advisory Committee on Recreation and

Natural Beauty are hereby terminated and the following are revoked:

(1) Executive Order No. 11278 of May 4, 1966.

(2) Executive Order No. 11359A of June 29, 1967.

(3) Executive Order No. 11402 of March 29, 1968.

RICHARD NIXON

THE WHITE HOUSE,
May 29, 1969.

Glossary of Terms

Widening concern over the world's environment has opened up whole new areas of the vocabulary to popular usage. Following is a glossary for an ecological age.

ACCIPITER Any hawk of the genus *Accipiter,* of the family *Accipitridae,* that has short, rounded wings and a long tail, and that feeds chiefly on small mammals and birds.

ADDITIVE That which is added, as one substance to another, to alter or improve the general quality, or to counteract undesirable properties.

ALBEDO The ratio of the light reflected by a planet or satellite to that received by it. (Atmospheric dust increases albedo, causing some scientists to believe the earth is cooling.)

ALGAE Any of several motile or nonmotile, chlorophyll-containing plants of the phylum Thallophyta, ranging from unicellular, usually microscopic forms to multicellular forms sometimes 100 feet or more in length. Occurs in fresh or salt water, or in or on other organisms, or soil, rocks, trees, etc. Characterized by green color. Proliferates in polluted water.

AMBIENT AIR QUALITY CRITERIA A scientific relationship between particular concentrations and durations of specific air contaminants and the effects they produce on persons, animals, plants or materials.

AMORTIZATION For tax purposes, writing off against income a portion of the cost of capital assets in each of several years. Rapid amortization is a write-off in a fewer number of years than the capital equipment might be in use, such as five-year amortization for pollution-control equipment that might have a life longer than a five-year period.

ANADROMOUS FISH Salmon, shad, bass and others that migrate from the sea up a river to spawn.

ANSERINE Of or pertaining to the subfamily Anserinae, of the family Anatidae, comprising true geese.

AQUIFER Any geological formation containing water, especially one that supplies water for wells, springs, etc. The technical word for ground water.

AUTECOLOGY The branch of ecology dealing with the individual organism and its environment.

AVIFAUNA The birds of a given region, considered as a whole.

BASIC EQUILIBRIUM CONCEPT The theory that everything in the universe depends on everything else.

BIOCHEMISTRY The science dealing with the chemistry of living matter.

BIOCHORES Divisions of the biosphere.

BIOCLIMATIC Of or pertaining to the effects of climate on living organisms.

BIOCLIMATOLOGY The study of the effects of climate on the biological processes of plants and animals.

BIODEGRADABLE The property of a substance that permits it to be broken down by micro-organisms into simple, stable compounds such as carbon dioxide and water.

BIODYNAMICS The branch of biology dealing with energy or the activity of living organisms.

BIOECOLOGY The study of the interrelations between plants and animals and their environment.

BIOELECTRICITY Of or pertaining to electric phenomena occurring in plants and animals.

BIOGENESIS The production of living organisms from other living organisms.

BIOGEOCHEMISTRY The science dealing with the relationship between the geochemistry of a given region and its flora and fauna.

BIOGEOGRAPHY The study of the geographical distribution of living things.

BIOLUMINESCENCE The production of light by living organisms.

BIOLYSIS Dissolution of a living organism.

BIOMASS That part of a given habitat consisting of living matter, expressed either as the weight of organisms per unit area or as the volume of organisms per unit volume of habitat.

BIOME A complex of communities characterized by a distinctive type of vegetation and maintained under the climatic conditions of the region.

BIOMETRICS The application of mathematical-statistical theory to biology.

BIONICS The study of how man and animals perform certain tasks and solve certain problems, and of the application of the findings to the design of computers and other electronic equipment.

BIOSOCIAL Of or pertaining to social phenomena that are affected by biological factors.

BIOSPHERE The part of the earth's crust, waters and atmosphere where living organisms can subsist.

BIOSYNTHESIS The formation, by synthesis or degradation, of chemical compounds by a living organism.

BIOTA The animal and plant life of a region or period.

BIOTIC POTENTIAL The capacity of a population of animals or plants to increase in numbers under optimum environmental conditions.

BIOTYPE A group of organisms having the same hereditary characteristics.

BLACK LIQUOR OXIDATION The process which supplies oxygen to kraft black liquor, and through chemical oxidation of certain unstable or reduced sulphur compounds prevents them from escaping a recovery furnace system and thereby controls odor from this source.

BOD (Biochemical Oxygen Demand) A measure of the amount of oxygen used by micro-organisms to consume biodegradable organics in waste water. The BOD test is widely used to measure the organic strength of waste water in terms of dissolved oxygen that would be consumed if the waste water were discharged into a natural body of water.

CARBON DIOXIDE A colorless, odorless, poisonous gas present in the atmosphere and formed during respiration. Oil refineries contribute to the problem of this gas in the air.

CARBON MONOXIDE A colorless, odorless, poisonous gas discharged in automobile exhausts; also, by planes, industrial plants, furnaces and incinerators. Results from incomplete combustion.

CARCINOGENIC Cancer-producing.

CARNIVORE Any chiefly flesh-eating mammal of the ordor *Carnivora,* comprising dogs, cats, bears, seals, weasels, etc.

CATALYTIC CONVERTER A sealed container having no moving parts, inserted in the exhaust system of an internal combustion engine to convert the three chemical pollutants contained in automotive exhaust (unburned hydrocarbons, carbon monoxide and oxides of nitrogen) into water, carbon dioxide and nitrogen. Conversion is accomplished by passing exhaust gases through a catalyst, a benign substance whose presence accomplishes conversion.

CHAIN OF LIFE The system whereby little fish are consumed by larger fish, etc., until the offal or body of some higher life-form returns to dust or ooze.

CHLORINATED HYDROCARBONS Long-lived chemicals, such as DDT, which kill a particular object, such as insects, and which persist to damage other creatures in ground, sea and air.

CLIMATE The composite or generally prevailing weather conditions of a region, as temperature, air pressure, humidity, precipitation, sunshine, cloud cover, winds, etc.

CLIMATIC AMELIORATION The altering of a prevailing weather condition.

CLIMATOLOGY The science that deals with climates or climatic conditions.

CONSERVATION The act of preservation from loss, injury, decay or waste.

CONTINENTALITY The degree to which the climate of a region typifies that of the interior of a large land mass.

DECIBEL A unit of intensity of sound, equal to 20 times the common logarithm of the ratio of the pressure produced by the sound wave to a reference pressure. A measurement of 50 decibels is considered moderate sound; 80, loud; and 100, the level beyond which the sound becomes intolerable.

DEWATERING The removal of water from sludge by filtration, centrifugation, pressing, open-air drying or other methods which provide a material suitable for disposal by burning or landfilling.

ECOLOGY The branch of biology dealing with relations between organisms and their environment.

ECOSPECIES A taxon consisting of one or more interbreeding ecotypes.

ECOSPHERE The part of the atmosphere in which it is possible to breathe normally without aid, that portion of the troposphere from sea level to an altitude of 13,000 feet.

ECOSYSTEM A system formed by the interaction of a community of organisms with their environment.

ECOTYPE A subspecies that is especially adapted to a particular set of environmental conditions.

EDAPHIC Related to or caused by particular soil conditions, as of texture or drainage, rather than by physiographic or climatic factors.

EDAPHON The aggregate of organisms that live in the soil.

EFFLUENT The outflows, usually offensive, from sewage or industrial plants, etc.

EFFLUVIUM An invisible exhalation or vapor, especially one that is disagreeable or noxious.

ENVIRONMENT The aggregate of surrounding things, conditions or influences, especially as affecting the existence or development of people or of nature.

ENVIRONMENTAL RESISTANCE The limiting effect of environmental conditions on the numerical growth of a population.

ESTUARINE Something living in an inlet or river mouth, where tides flow through.

EUTROPHICATION The choking of waters, particularly lakes, rivers and streams, with algae; the depletion of waters of oxygen content.

EVEN-AGE STANDS Forest areas where the trees are all of the same age due to planting or harvesting the entire area at one time. Even-age stands are desirable for species whose young trees do not thrive in the shade of older trees.

FAULT A fracture in the earth's crust; a break in the continuity of a body of rock or of a vein, with dislocation along the plane of the fracture.

FISSION The act of cleaving or splitting into parts. In biology, the division of an organism into new organisms as a process of reproduction.

FLORA The plants of a particular region or period, listed by species and considered as a whole.

FLY ASH Fine particles of ash entrained in flue gases from the combustion of fuels.

FOSSIL FUELS Coal, petroleum and natural gas.

FOSSIL WATER Limited subterranean water deposits laid down in past ages but drawn on by modern man.

GENOTYPES The genetic constitution of an organism or group of organisms.

GEOMORPHOLOGY The study of the characteristics, origin and development of land forms.

GLACIER TABLE A stone slab supported over the surface of a mountain glacier by a column or columns of ice.

GREENHOUSE EFFECT The trapping of the sun's heat on earth by water vapor and carbon monoxide, thus accounting for the temperature of the earth.

HABITAT The native environment of an animal or plant, or the kind of place that is natural for an animal or plant.

HERBICIDE A substance or preparation for killing plants, and especially weeds.

HERTZ A unit of frequency, equal to 1 cycle per second. The highest frequency the human ear can hear is 20,000 hertz; the lowest, about 15 hertz.

HYDROCARBON Any of a class of compounds containing only hydrogen and carbon, such as in the emission from automobile exhausts.

HYDROSPHERE The water on or surrounding the surface of the globe, including the water of the oceans and the water of the atmosphere.

ICE SHEET A broad, thick sheet of ice covering an extensive area for a long period of time.

ICE SHELF An ice sheet projecting into coastal waters so that the end floats.

INTERNAL COMBUSTION ENGINE The basic gasoline and diesel engine in general use in automotive vehicles, and including fuel injection, turbine and Wankel types.

INVERSION A layer of cold air trapped beneath a layer of warm air, causing smog resulting in death, disease or discomfort.

ISOTHERM A line on a weather map or chart connecting points having equal temperature.

LANDFILL A method of disposing of refuse on land by utilizing the principles of engineering to confine the refuse to the smallest practical area and to reduce it to the smallest practical volume.

LEAD TETRAETHYL or TERTRAMETHYL A basic element which, when added to gasoline in the form of chemical compounds, provides the last few additional octane points to gasoline. Also known as lead alkyls.

LICHEN Any compound, thallophytic plant of the group Lichenes that is composed of a fungus in symbiotic union with an alga and has a greenish, gray, yellow, brown or blackish thallus growing in leaflike, crustlike or branching forms of rocks, trees, etc.

LIFE CYCLE The continuous sequence of changes undergone by an organism from one primary form to the development of the same form again.

LIGNIN The organic substance that holds together the individual fibers of wood. Lignin is responsible for the dark color in pulp mill effluents.

LITHOSPHERE The crust of the earth.

MACH or MACH NUMBER A number indicating the ratio of the speed of an object through a medium to the speed of sound in the medium. Speeds of airplanes are measured in mach numbers. Speeds of one, two or three times the speed of sound are termed Mach 1, Mach 2, Mach 3, etc.

METABIOSIS A mode of living in which one organism is dependent on another for preparation of an environment in which it can live.

MICROCLIMATOLOGY The study of local climatic conditions, especially the analysis of climatic profiles of the lowest stratum of the atmosphere.

NATURAL SELECTION A process in nature resulting in the survival and perpetuation of only those forms of plant and animal life having certain favorable characteristics that enable them to adapt best to a specific environment.

NITROGEN CYCLE The continuous sequence of changes by which atmospheric nitrogen and nitrogenous compounds in the soil are converted, as by nitrification and nitrogen fixation, into substances that can be utilized by green plants, the substances returning to their previous state after the plants decay, and by denitrification into substances that cannot be utilized by the plants.

NONRENEWABLE RESOURCES Substances such as oil, gas, coal, copper, gold, etc., which, once used, cannot be replaced, at least not in this geological age.

NUCLIDES An atomic species in which all atoms have the same atomic number and mass number; an individual atom in such a species.

OCTANE NUMBER An arbitrary figure which expresses the anti-knock properties of gasoline. The higher the octane number, the less knocking. The number is determined by comparing the knocking tendency of a gasoline sample in a specially built internal combustion engine to the performance of a standard sample in that engine under specified conditions.

ORGANIC MATTER Chemical compounds of carbon combined with other chemical elements, and generally manufactured in the life processes of plants and animals. Most organic compounds are a source of food for bacteria and are usually combustible.

ORGANISM A form of life composed of mutually dependent parts that maintain various vital processes.

PARTICULATES Small particles of liquid or solid matter.

PERMAFROST Perennially frozen subsoil.

PERMAFROST TABLE The variable surface constituting the upper limit of permafrost.

PESTICIDE A chemical preparation for destroying pests, such as flies, bugs, mosquitoes, etc.

PHYLOGENY The development or evolution of a kind or type of animal or plant.

POLLUTION Harmful substances deposited in the air or water or land, leading to a state of dirtiness, impurity or unhealthiness.

POPULATION PARAMETER A quantity or statistical measure which, for a given population, is fixed and which is used as the value of a variable in some general distribution or frequency function to make it descriptive of that population.

POPULATION PRESSURE The force exerted by a growing population upon its environment, resulting in dispersal or reduction of the population.

PREDATOR An organism or thing (e.g., animal) which habitually preys on something else.

PRESERVATION The protection and propagation of game, fish, forests, etc.

PRIMATE Any mammal of the order Primates, including man, the apes, monkeys, lemurs, tarsiers and marmosets.

QUALITY CONTROL A system for verifying and maintaining a desired level of quality in a product, process or species.

RADIOACTIVE WASTE The perilous end product of nuclear plants or processes.

RADIOCARBON DATING The determination of the age of objects or plant or animal origin by measurement of the radioactivity of their radiocarbon content.

RADIONUCLIDE A radioactive nuclide.

RECLAMATION The reclaiming of waste, desert, marshy or submerged land for cultivation, preservation, reuse, etc.

RECYCLE The salvage and reprocessing of used materials (paper, metals, glass, cloth, etc.).

REFORESTATION The replanting of trees in forests that have been affected by cutting, fire, disease, etc.

REM (roentgen equivalent man) The measurement for the amount of radiation absorbed in human tissues and also the quality of the type of radiation.

SANITARY FILL Used to describe the dumping process whereby the garbage or other refuse is covered with soil, thus controlling smell, rodent activity, etc., and speeding the decay of organic substances.

SECONDARY FIBER Fiber used as a raw material for making new products. The fibers have been reclaimed from waste paper or collected during the manufacture of paper and paperboard products.

SILVICULTURE The cultivation of forest trees; forestry.

SLUDGE The concentrated solid material which has been collected in treatment plants. Sludge must be treated and disposed of with minimum pollution of air, land or water.

SMOG Originally a combination of fog and smoke; now applied also to photochemical haze produced by the action of the sun and the atmosphere on automobile and industrial exhausts.

SOIL CONSERVATION Any of various methods to achieve the maximum utilization of the land and preservation of its resources and quality, through such controls as crop rotation, prevention of soil erosion, etc.

SOLID WASTE All items discarded after use in a solid state that must be collected and disposed of separately. Solid waste is collected by municipal collection systems. Solid waste does not include items discarded into sewage systems or those emitted with smoke or gas.

SONIC BOOM A loud noise caused by the shock wave generated by an aircraft moving at supersonic speed.

SPECIATION The process by which new species are formed.

SPECIES A class having some common characteristics or qualities. The major subdivision of a genus or subgenus, regarded as the basic category of biological classification, composed of related individuals that resemble one another, are able to breed among themselves but are not able to breed with members of another species.

SULPHUR DIOXIDE A colorless, nonflammable, water-soluble, suffocating gas. A pollutant emitted chiefly by industries and blamed for much lung trouble.

SYNECOLOGY The branch of ecology dealing with the relations between plant and animal communities and their environments.

THERMAL POLLUTION The influx of heated water, usually from a power plant, into stream, lake, bay or ocean, disturbing the temperature of the given body of water. Also has application to air, through waste heat emitted by industry, home appliances, machines, etc.

TOLERANCE LEVEL The capacity or point of endurance beyond which there is decline and possibly death.

VERMIN Pesty animals, especially those of small size, which appear commonly and are difficult to control.

WATER TABLE The depth below which the ground is saturated with water.

ZERO POPULATION GROWTH The maintenance or holding of population numbers at a fixed level so as to obviate increase.

INDEX